A History of the Ancient World

A HISTORY OF
THE ANCIENT WORLD

THIRD EDITION

CHESTER G. STARR

Bentley Professor of History
University of Michigan

New York   Oxford
OXFORD UNIVERSITY PRESS
1983

Library of Congress Cataloging in Publication Data
Starr, Chester G., 1914–
A history of the ancient world.
Bibliography: p.
Includes index.
1. History, Ancient.   I. Title.
D59.S75   1983   930   81-22408
ISBN 0-19-503143-1   AACR2
ISBN 0-19-503144-X (college cloth)

Printing (last digit): 9 8 7 6 5 4 3 2
Printed in the United States of America

To my wife
Gretchen
in loving token
of over
four decades

PREFACE

All the men discussed in this book have long been dead. Many of them have strange names, such as Hammurapi, Sophocles, and Cato the Censor; their customs and fundamental beliefs are often far different from ours. In their deeds and thoughts, in their hopes and fears, nonetheless, they fashioned a civilized base of life upon which the modern world directly rests. The history of the many peoples of antiquity is in itself enduringly fascinating; often it throws light upon the wide potentialities of mankind. For history, though closely bound to specific fact and date, is one of those liberating studies by which men come closer to understanding their own nature.

Those born and reared in the western world will quite properly be concerned mainly with the story of their Greco-Roman background, which occupies the largest place in this volume. Today at last, however, we are coming to realize that the civilization which streamed through the ancient Mediterranean was not the only advanced pattern which existed in early Eurasia; nor was it alone in having great effects on the modern world. Accordingly I have from time to time cast a glance at the parallel developments of the Eurasian nomads, of the historic Near East, and of the very important foundations of civilization in China and India.

To write a simple and direct account which would put in clear perspective the whole sweep of ancient times has been both an exhilarating and a sobering responsibility. The volume of modern scholarship concerned with ancient peoples is a great testimony to our abiding interest but at the same time presents an insurmountable hurdle for any one student. Insofar as it is humanly possible, the following pages rest upon the latest investigations, without forgetting the solid work of many scholars in past generations; the ever-swelling mass of physical evidence for ancient history requires us to recast our thoughts more frequently than is true in any other field of historical development.

Yet I would not have any reader take this story as the ultimate truth or accept uncritically the interpretations which I have advanced in order to give meaning to early human history. The issues, moreover, which faced ancient men were not always so straightforward as they must be pictured in a general survey. The present work, in sum, is also an invitation to its reader to correct and deepen, by further reading, his understanding of those aspects which most interest or concern him.

Seattle, Washington, June 1964   CHESTER G. STARR

PREFACE TO THE THIRD EDITION

One review of the first edition suggested that this work was written by a Whig historian, i.e., one who believed in progress. Nowadays it is unfashionable to adopt an optimistic point of view about human development, so this charge is a grave one. Yet I shall cheerfully admit that the early story of mankind, taken as a whole, does appear to me to have been a remarkable tale of the unfolding of the promise of human capabilities, even though disasters and temporary setbacks occurred repeatedly.

Certainly the study of ancient history is a subject which changes perhaps more rapidly than any other save that of the most recent decades. Archeological investigations are always producing new and unexpected evidence; material already on hand is reinterpreted by thoughtful scholars. In this edition I have altered very extensively the account of early man but have also recast a good many pages concerned with Greek and Roman history; the bibliographies have been revised throughout.

I am grateful to friends and colleagues for their counsel. My colleagues C. S. Chang and T. R. Trautmann have given kind assistance in bringing the bibliographies for early China and India up to date.

Ann Arbor, Michigan, August 1981   CHESTER G. STARR

CONTENTS

I THE ORIGINS OF CIVILIZATION

1. THE FIRST ACHIEVEMENTS OF MAN, 3
   The Paleolithic Age, 4   Transition to the Neolithic Age, 14
   The Neolithic Age, 17   Summation, 22

2. THE FIRST CIVILIZATION OF MESOPOTAMIA, 27
   The First Cities of Mesopotamia, 29   The Mesopotamian Outlook, 35
   The Results of Civilization, 41

3. EARLY EGYPT, 51
   Emergence of Egyptian Civilization, 53   The Old Kingdom, 56
   The Middle Kingdom, 63   The First Civilized Societies, 66

II THE FIRST EXPANSION OF CIVILIZATION

4. THE NEAR EAST IN THE SECOND MILLENNIUM, 75
   Invaders of the Early Second Millennium, 77   Mesopotamia and Syria, 82
   The New Kingdom in Egypt, 88   End of the Bronze Age, 94

5. NEW CIVILIZATIONS WEST AND EAST, 99
   Asia Minor and the Hittites, 100   The Minoan-Mycenaean World, 104
   Early India and China, 111   Eurasia in 1000 B.C., 116

III THE RISE OF NEW OUTLOOKS

6. THE UNIFICATION OF THE NEAR EAST, 123
   The Dark Ages, 124   Rise of the Assyrian Empire, 129
   Culture in the Assyrian Age, 134   The Successor States, 137

ix

7. HEBREW MONOTHEISM, 143
The Meaning of Hebrew Development, 144   Hebrew Political
History, 146   Early Religious Evolution, 152   The Testing of the
Faith, 156   Judaism in a Pagan World, 159

8. HISTORIC CIVILIZATIONS OF INDIA AND CHINA, 164
The Aryans and Early Hinduism, 165   Buddhism and the Expansion
of Historic India, 169   Chou China and Confucius, 172
The End of Chou China, 177   Conclusion, 178

IV   THE EARLY GREEK WORLD

9. THE BEGINNINGS OF GREEK CIVILIZATION, 185
Greece in the Dark Ages, 186   The First Signs of the Greek Outlook, 192
Myth and Epic, 196   The Greek World in 750 B.C., 202

10. RISE AND SPREAD OF THE GREEK CITY-STATE, 205
Nature of the *Polis,* 206   Greek Expansion Overseas, 213
Economic and Social Changes, 220   The New Greek World, 225

11. GREEK CIVILIZATION IN THE AGE OF REVOLUTION, 228
Progress of the Arts, 229   New Forms of Poetry, 234
Greek Religion, 238   The Greeks in 650 B.C., 244

12. THE SIXTH CENTURY, 247
Internal Evolution of Athens, 248   Spartan Imperialism, 256
Other Greek States, 260   Archaic Civilization, 263
The Greek World in 500 B.C., 268

V   THE CLASSIC AGE OF GREECE

13. THE GREEKS AGAINST THE PERSIANS, 275
Rise of the Persian Empire, 276   The Persian Attacks, 283
The Greek Offensive, 292   The Greek Victory, 294

14. ATHENIAN DEMOCRACY AND IMPERIALISM, 298
Athenian Democracy, 299   Athenian Imperialism, 307
Economic Expansion in the Fifth Century, 313   Greek World in the
Mid-Fifth Century, 317

15. FIFTH-CENTURY CIVILIZATION, 319
The Athenian Drama, 320   Letters, Philosophy, and Science, 327
Classic Art, 331   The Golden Age, 336

16. END OF THE GOLDEN AGE, 339
The Peloponnesian War, 340   The New Intellectual Outlook, 348
The Greek World in 404 B.C., 354

VI THE BROADENING OF GREECE

17. DECLINE OF THE CITY-STATE, 359
    Rivalries of Sparta, Thebes, and Athens, 360   Philip of Macedonia, 366
    Greece in the Fourth Century, 371

18. GREEK CIVILIZATION IN THE FOURTH CENTURY, 378
    Fourth-Century Philosophy, 379   New Literary Trends, 385
    Fourth-Century Art, 388   The Edge of a New World, 390

19. ALEXANDER AND THE HELLENISTIC WORLD, 394
    Alexander the Great, 395   The Hellenistic States, 403
    Social and Economic Aspects, 407

20. HELLENISTIC CIVILIZATION, 413
    Cities and Schools, 414   Literature and the Arts, 417
    Hellenistic Philosophies, 422   Hellenistic Science, 426
    Major Characteristics of Hellenistic Civilization, 430

VII THE RISE OF ROME

21. THE EARLY WESTERN MEDITERRANEAN, 437
    Prehistoric Development of Italy and the West, 438
    The Entry of Eastern Peoples, 446   The Western Mediterranean in the
    Sixth Century, 452

22. ROME IN ITALY, 456
    The Roman Kingdom, 457   Roman Conquest of Italy, 463
    Political Evolution of the Republic, 468   Rome in 264 B.C., 473

23. ROME IN THE MEDITERRANEAN, 477
    The Duel with Carthage, 478   Roman Conquest of the Hellenistic
    World, 488   Hellenistic Culture in Rome, 494

VIII THE CONSOLIDATION OF ROMAN RULE

24. DECLINE OF THE ROMAN REPUBLIC, 503
    The Roman World in 133 B.C., 504   The Gracchi Brothers, 512
    Marius and Sulla, 516

25. THE AGE OF CICERO AND CAESAR, 525
    The Ciceronian Age, 526   The Rise of Caesar, 533
    Civil Wars and Dictatorship, 538

26. THE AUGUSTAN AGE, 547
    The Rise of Augustus, 548   The Augustan Political System, 553
    The Augustan Age, 561

IX THE ERA OF EURASIAN STABILITY

27. THE ROMAN PEACE, 575
     The Unfolding of Absolutism, 576   The Economic Peak, 587
     Expansion of Culture, 591

28. THE SPREAD OF CHRISTIANITY, 603
     The Preparation for Christianity, 604   The Foundations of
     Christianity, 608   Christianity and the Pagan World, 613

29. THE FARTHER ORIENT, 626
     The Parthian Near East, 627   Mauryan and Kushan India, 631
     Han China, 636   End of the Era of Stability, 641

X DECLINE OF THE ANCIENT WORLD

30. THE FIRST SIGNS OF STRESS, 647
     Foreign and Internal Threats, 648   Political History of the Third
     Century, 655   Cultural and Religious Crosscurrents, 661

31. THE LATER ROMAN EMPIRE, 669
     Political Reorganization, 670   Victory of Christianity, 678
     Culture of the Late Empire, 685

32. THE END OF THE ANCIENT WORLD, 694
     Dissolution of the Roman Empire in the West, 695
     The Rest of Eurasia, 703   Old and New, 707

     General Bibliography, 715

     Index, 731

PLATES

I	Paleolithic hand-ax	*after page*
II	Crouching bison from Altamira	238
III	Sumerian gods and worshipers	
IV	King Menkaure and his wife	
V	Throne room at Cnossus	
VI	Gold face mask from Mycenae	
VII	Ashurbanipal killing a lion	
VIII	Early Greek pottery	
	A. Mycenaean *kylix*	
	B. Protogeometric amphora	
	C. Geometric amphora	
	D. Protocorinthian *oenochoe*	
IX	Dipylon amphora	
X	Griffin head from Olympia	
XI	Archaic *kouros* from Sunium	
XII	*Peplos kore* from the Acropolis	
XIII	Poseidon (or Zeus) of Cape Artemisium	
XIV	Heracles metope from Olympia	
XV	Athenian water carriers from the Parthenon	
XVI	Persian tribute-bringers from Persepolis	

XVII Athenian pottery
    A. Black-figure: Dionysus in his ship
    B. Red-figure: Leagros on horseback

after page 494

XVIII Greek coins
    A. "Turtle" of Aegina
    B. Attic "owl"
    C. Arethusa from Syracuse
    D. Antimachus of Bactria

XIX Hermes by Praxiteles

XX Dying Gaul and his wife

XXI Apollo of Veii

XXII Player on the double pipes from Tarquinia

XXIII "Brutus"

XXIV "Cato and Porcia"

XXV The emperor Augustus from Prima Porta

XXVI Pont du Gard

XXVII Interior of the Pantheon

XXVIII Philosopher sarcophagus

XXIX Buddha of Gandhara type

XXX Sassanian silver dish

XXXI The emperor Valentinian (?) in Barletta

XXXII The empress Theodora in Ravenna

MAPS

1 Origins of agriculture in the ancient Near East, 16
2 Early Mesopotamia, 29
3 Ancient Egypt, 52
4 Eastern Mediterranean about 1200 B.C., 84
5 Eurasian civilizations about 1600 B.C., 112
6 Assyrian empire, 126
7 Ancient Israel, 148
8 Expansion of Greek civilization 750–500 B.C., 214
9 Persian empire about 500 B.C., 278
10 Central Greece in the Persian wars, 284
11 Athenian empire about 440 B.C., 308
12 City of Athens, 332
13 Alexander and the Hellenistic world, 396
14 Ancient Italy, 442
15 City of Rome, 458
16 Roman world in 201 B.C., 480
17 Roman world in 133 B.C., 490
18 Roman Empire under Augustus, 562
19 Eurasian civilizations about A.D. 150, 628
20 Later Roman Empire, 658

TABLES

1 Early development of man, 6
2 The first civilizations, 34
3 Aegean and Near East in the second millennium, 78
4 Greece and the Near East 1100–500 B.C., 250
5 The Greek world 500–323 B.C., 300
6 Roman Republic 509–44 B.C., 506
7 Roman Empire 27 B.C.–A.D. 180, 578
8 Roman emperors A.D. 180–284, 649
9 Roman emperors A.D. 284–395, 671
10 Roman emperors A.D. 395–476, 695

I

THE ORIGINS OF CIVILIZATION

1

THE FIRST ACHIEVEMENTS OF MAN

Scientists now speculate that the age of the earth is 4½ billion years. History is concerned with only the last few moments, relatively speaking, of this immense span of time; for its province is the story of mankind. Students of history are attempting to account to themselves for the basic qualities of human culture and for the manner in which these have developed.

To frame answers on these important issues we need go back scarcely more than a few million years, to the origin of the immediate ancestors of modern man. Through almost all this period men lived virtually as animals. Physically their bodies underwent visible changes; but these alterations, which affected chiefly the shape of the head and the size of the brain, have been refinements of a biological structure already present in early times. Culturally men developed useful tools, knew a variety of food-gathering techniques, and accommodated themselves sufficiently to social requirements to safeguard the rearing of their children. Nonetheless they long remained at the mercy of nature. Not until about 7000 B.C. did the conscious practice of agriculture first appear in a few areas.

In this chapter we shall follow mankind across its food-gathering stage, called the Paleolithic age, and into the food-raising or Neolithic age. Although the historian can now hope to trace the main phases of this evolution, much of his account must be conjectural, and many aspects still remain obscure. Even so, the geographical and cultural expansion of mankind during the past million years remains a marvelous event.

Its Duration and Dating. Since the Paleolithic age is the earliest era of history, much of our evidence has been destroyed by natural decay. In any case, human culture in this period was not extensive enough to leave abundant remains. Physical anthropologists, the specialists who study the evolution of mankind, are inclined nowadays to set the date for the appearance of the earliest tool-makers at well before one million years B.C. This point, which is obviously approximate, rests upon correlations between human bones and tools and the strata of rock in which they have been found: geologically these strata belong to the Cenozoic period, which is divided into the earlier Pleistocene ("most recent") and later Holocene ("completely recent") epochs.

Man's evolution during especially the Pleistocene era is pegged down by means of the great climatic alterations of the period. In response to the almost unprecedented raising of mountain ranges and perhaps to subtle changes in the radiation of the sun, sheets of ice spread southward across Eurasia and North America a number of times, though not always in unison. In Europe the last four ice ages, which span human existence, are called, from sites in the Alps, the Günz, Mindel, Riss, and Würm. At their maximum, ice sheets and glaciers covered nearly one-third of the land surface. In the intervening interglacial eras and in minor moderate eras within each age the fauna and flora of warmer zones advanced northward. These great swings of the pendulum can generally be followed in the geologic evidence.

We can now use a variety of scientific means to obtain more precise dates. Fluorine analysis of bones helps to determine their relative ages; the decay of potassium-40 into calcium-40 and argon-40 can be measured as providing a scale for the earliest forms of mankind. For more recent eras very extensive employment has been made of analysis in organic deposits of carbon-14, that small part of carbon which is radioactive and has a half-life of about 5730 years. Careful determination of the decrease of this element in an organic substance like charcoal or wood permits location of the approximate age of the material up to about 50,000 years ago, though tree-ring calculation shows that dates measured by the radio-carbon method are about a thousand years too late by 5000 B.C. The Würm glaciation made its last retreat 10,000–8000 B.C., and man then began to pass out of the Paleolithic stage, first in the Near East and thereafter elsewhere. If we define this period, however, as one in which men gathered rather than raised their food, some people even today are still on the Paleolithic level in the Far North and in tropical forests.

Physical Development of Mankind. Although the Paleolithic age is by far the longest span of history, it need not be considered at equal length, for progress was infinitesimally slow. The main factors that require attention are the evolution of mankind as a physical type, the development of its material base for existence, and its intellectual progress.

The biological theory that animal species have arisen over long periods of time, largely by an accumulation of slow evolutionary adaptations in existing gene pools and to lesser degree by mutations, is now generally accepted. As applied to human development, it seems a sensible concept; but a tidy series of steps does not exist in the physical evidence to prove the theory in all its details. The historian can only take on faith the proposition that men emerged out of the Primate family of mammals.

Some of the great apes can also walk on two feet and use tools such as branches as clubs; but mankind has evolved its own special set of inter-related characteristics. Human eyes, like those of some apes, are located in such a position that they can focus in stereovision; for mankind sight largely replaces smell and sound as a mode of warning and of grasping the outside world. Instead of the large canine teeth of monkeys and apes, useful for tearing, men have smaller teeth and molars which can be employed in chewing. Man's hand has a thumb opposed to the other fingers which permits the manipulation, in precise details, of tools as specialized extensions of muscles; perhaps as a consequence human arms have become much shorter. From early times men had at their command, to assist their survival, a superior nervous and mental capacity, which was evident in a relatively large brain. Another physical characteristic of mankind, which he shares with very few other animals, is an ability to sit upright for long periods.

To explain the course of human change over most of the Paleolithic era, the historian can muster only a pitifully small quantity of human

TABLE 1

Early Development of Man

Approximate Date B.C.	Era	Type of Man	Typical Cultures
5,000,000 and before		australopithicenes	
1,500,000	LOWER PALEOLITHIC	*Homo erectus*	Abbevillian Acheulian
		Heidelberg	
		Choukoutien	
500,000		*Homo sapiens* (Swanscombe)	Clactonian
		(Fontéchevade)	Tayacian
110,000	MIDDLE PALEOLITHIC	*H. sapiens Neanderthalensis*	Mousterian (varied)
40–35,000	UPPER PALEOLITHIC	*H. sapiens sapiens*	Chatelperronian Aurignacian Gravettian Solutrean Magdalenian
10,000	MESOLITHIC in Near East Natufian and others Maglemosian in north-central Europe		
8000 6500	NEOLITHIC in Near East pottery		

bones, largely parts of skulls which have been fossilized, but these reveal the main line of physical evolution. Major developments include a steadily larger brain — though it is not easy to measure the equally important change of the brain structure and its increasing complexity — a decrease in the size of teeth and jawbone, a thinning of the bones of the head, and a more upright position of the head as a whole on the spine.

In southern and central Africa, reaching up to Ethiopia, hominids called australopithecines were present from about 5 million years ago.

They stood less than 5 feet high and weighed about 115 pounds; their cranial volume ranged up to 530 cc.; they had human teeth and strode or ran about the grasslands in an upright manner. By 3 million years ago they were making tools out of pebbles.

The last, most developed type of australopithecines is sometimes called *Homo habilis*, but the first "true man" was *Homo erectus*, who lived from about 1½ million to 500,000 years ago and spread with some rapidity from Africa to the rest of Eurasia, including Java, Europe (Heidelberg, Vértesszöllös), and a famous deposit near Peking, the Choukoutien caves or clefts. Men at this latter site, which was a late one, were over 5 feet high and had a cranial capacity averaging 1046 cc.; they definitely used chopping tools, scrapers, and flakes and had progressed into full-scale hunting.

Thereafter appeared types of man collectively called *Homo sapiens*, for whom both examples and firm dates are not as available as one might wish; but it appears clear that this type of man exploited his environment more systematically. Spears now were used; huts have been found at the French site of Nice; more refined methods of striking flakes from flints were developed.

By about 110,000 B.C. *Homo sapiens Neanderthalensis*, so named from the widely publicized discovery of his remains in a quarry in the Neander valley (*thal*) in Germany in 1856, was dominant. European specimens had a low forehead with heavy ridges over the eyes, large nose, teeth far forward, and heavy muscles. Males stood about 5 feet 4 inches high and had brains averaging 1438 cc., as large as those of modern men. A Neanderthal man, dressed in contemporary clothes, would not attract attention on a casual glance.

With relative suddenness modern *Homo sapiens sapiens* appeared about 40–35,000 years ago during a minor break in the bleak, cold era of the last (Würm) ice age. His origins remain one of the most fiercely debated problems in prehistory. Some argue that European Neanderthals became too specialized to survive and surmise that an independent line (Swanscombe, Fontéchevade skulls) replaced the Neanderthals; others posit a Near Eastern evolution from Neanderthal to modern man; others feel that *Homo sapiens sapiens* did largely evolve out of the previous Neanderthals of Europe, and note that its earliest specimens share earlier facial characteristics which have since been eliminated. It is at least unlikely that the Neanderthals were simply exterminated by an invading "superior" type of man; the important point is perhaps not so much where we came from as what we have done since we have arrived.

The Meaning of Race. All modern men belong essentially to the same type or biological species, inasmuch as they can interbreed; but we commonly talk of the "races" of mankind. Like many popular terms this concept is more easily used than analyzed; how does one define a race? Current theory tends to employ many factors for distinguishing human groups, such as color and shape of the hair on head and body, blood types, and so on; and since each student may choose different factors, there is no common agreement on the divisions. Many of the criteria, moreover, cannot be employed for early times, from which only skeletal parts survive. One popular mark, that of color of skin, seems to be an adaptive development which may have occurred rather late in human history in response to the quantity of ultraviolet rays and other factors.

Within the whitish-skinned part of mankind, which inhabits most of the area to be considered in this volume, various groups have been called "races." In Mediterranean lands the "Mediterranean" and allied types tend to be short of stature, relatively small-headed, sexually undifferentiated in hair, and often long-headed (though not always so). These types may have moved up out of Africa. To their north, the "Alpine" stock may early have pushed westward from Asia along the mountain ridges of central Europe. This variety tends likewise to be short, to have a short, broad face with dark eyes and hair, and to be round-headed; where it has merged with "Mediterranean" types, subvarieties called Dinaric and Armenoid appear (the latter often with a prominent nose). Northward again in Europe many people share "Nordic" characteristics; that is, they are tall, light of eyes and hair and long-headed.

Nowhere do such types seem ever to have existed in isolation. Nor is there any proof for the common prejudice that men marked by a certain color of skin or shape of head thereby share a common, distinguishing biological inheritance which extends to mental or artistic outlooks and capabilities. The so-called races of Eurasia are not in themselves important and will not be further considered in this work; what is truly important is the rise within the population of Europe, Asia, and Africa, of societies marked by distinct cultural attitudes and often falling into recognizable linguistic groups. Where a way of life and speech has become fixed and has resulted in a political unification, its members have often been led to assert an innate superiority. The ancient inhabitants of the Nile equated "Egyptian" and "man," while the Chinese considered all who lived beyond the confines of China as subhuman; this tendency is not yet dead among more modern peoples.

Early Material Culture. The ways into which men settled to make a living and to pass their existence are far more important than physical variations. Man is the oldest domesticated animal. His culture, a term which has been well defined as meaning "all those things which are *not* inherited biologically," has been a powerful force in determining his development. Throughout the Paleolithic period the outside physical world underwent great changes in temperature, elevation of mountains along with volcanic activity, and the spread or retreat of mammoth ice sheets; and mankind adapted its ways of life as best it could to suit this rugged environment.

Commonly men lived in the open. At least by the Gravettian era in Upper Paleolithic times they built lean-tos and other simple skin tents, but evidence of this type of habitat has rarely survived. In cool climates, in winter, or in dangerous terrain our primitive ancestors were at times driven to dwell in caves; this custom was particularly evident in Neanderthal times. Cave dwellers preferred sites with a southern exposure, a good source of water nearby, and a view of adequate hunting grounds. Here men might dwell for long periods and build up large deposits of garbage, into which their tools would fall and in which their own remains were interred casually or carefully. The Choukoutien clefts, for instance, attest that man early knew fire; the presence of skulls whose bases have been deliberately enlarged suggests either cannibalism or the preservation of trophies.

Paleolithic men made their living by gathering food. Adult males probably hunted; females and children sought out edible berries, plants, and fruits. Their basic needs could probably have been met, to judge from modern simple societies, by only a few hours of work each day. Across the long Paleolithic period only stone tools have survived in any quantity. These are enough to support very significant conclusions. First, early mankind did not everywhere use the same types of objects. Second, progress at first was extremely slow as men fought to survive, but speeded up toward the end; and, third, by this latter point new ideas as to how to make tools were certainly transmitted from one area to another.

The various assemblages of stone tools which were used in different regions or succeeded earlier patterns in the same district have been patiently analyzed by anthropologists. Generally men preferred stones that could be worked by fracture with some precision, for example, flint (which is harder than steel) or obsidian. In the manufacture of tools either flakes were struck off, or a suitable piece of stone was reduced to a core; both methods of producing tools were used concurrently.

The earliest men in Africa and Asia made crudely chipped pebbles of lava, quartz, or quartzite. By the early part of the second (Mindel) ice age the inhabitants of Africa, western Asia, and southern Europe had learned to process cores into a distinctive, all-purpose cutting and scraping tool. This is commonly but incorrectly called a hand-ax (see Plate I); beside it appear rude flake tools, stone balls, and other items. The culture of this era, named Abbevillian in its first phases and then Acheulian from French sites, was remarkably uniform from the Cape of Good Hope to England on the one extreme and to India on the other. Alongside it, however, were peoples (now called Clactonian, Tayacian, etc.) who did not use hand-axes proper and perhaps did not hunt but gathered food instead. For hundreds of thousands of years men everywhere lived in the same general ways with these types of tools. Then, by the third interglacial period (Riss-Würm), which ended about 70,000 B.C., the Eurasian cultures of the Lower or Early Paleolithic gave rise to assemblages of more specialized flake tools, which are collectively termed Mousterian. This is the culture of Neanderthal man, who dominated the Middle Paleolithic era and was a skillful hunter with wooden spears and stones.

Within the fourth (Würm) glacial period, human beings speeded up their progress remarkably in making tools and in other respects. This rise in tempo, which produced the Upper Paleolithic about 30,000 B.C., corresponds roughly with the arrival of modern man, though it is by no means certain that the two events were interconnected. What is visible is that improved social organization and technical equipment allowed man to exploit nature more methodically as in hunting reindeer, bison, and other animals not only with spears but also with spearthrowers and other missiles made in part from bone, antler, and ivory. As a result the numbers of men may well have increased. Whereas the Lower Paleolithic had known only a few types of tools, which were widely used over Eurasia, a large variety of Upper Paleolithic cultures can be distinguished in Europe alone, in addition to other well-defined cultures in Asia and Africa. As man progressed, it is more obvious that there was no *one* way by which he must live.

The European sequence in the last stage of the Paleolithic age can be approximately dated. First came the Chatelperronian, which mingled with earlier Mousterian forms, and then the more significant Aurignacian cultures (to about 22,000 B.C.): the discoveries at Cro-Magnon in France attest the presence of *Homo sapiens sapiens* in this era, and fishing surely appears. Then, after the Gravettian (22–18,000) and the Solutrean (18–15,000) eras, there arises the marvelous stage of Magdalenian culture. The latter covers about 15,000–8000 B.C. Throughout these successive stages changes can be observed in many aspects. Craftsmen worked their stone tools ever more skillfully; the symmetrical, finely chipped laurel-leaf points made in the Solutrean technique, in particular, are justly famous. At the end of the era the employment of microliths, small stones set in bone or attached to arrows, was borrowed from Africa. Other examples, too, attest the diffusion of techniques and materials; shells have been found, for instance, in burials in central France, which originated along the Mediterranean coast 200 miles away. Hafted tools appeared more commonly from the Aurignacian era onward; stone flakes were worked into gravers and scrapers, tools with which yet other tools could be made by sawing, grinding, and boring out of bone and antler. In Magdalenian times came needles and harpoons, which attest improvement both in clothing and in fishing.

Intellectual Progress (35–10,000 B.C.). Besides this material advance we can begin to see, though only dimly, swifter intellectual progress in the Upper Paleolithic period. To speak of progress over the course of human history may seem dangerous, if one is depressed today about the present situation of mankind; but there is no better corrective to undue pessimism than to see how many difficulties our ancestors surmounted. From the first the use of tools is an impressive testimony to the unique ability of man to reason out a solution to a problem of life and to fashion means of protecting himself from the brute forces of nature. While he perhaps came to many of his discoveries by accident, the role of deliberate curiosity and intent cannot be disregarded.

One of the most fascinating developments in the Upper Paleolithic era is the appearance of visible testimony that man lived to do more than simply hunt for food. Beads and other jewelry were made of animal teeth, shells, ivory, and so on; tattooing apparently was practiced. Bone flutes and other instruments now turn up to indicate the existence of music and probably of the dance. Some bone and ivory carvings seem to have been made purely for the joy of creation. Figurines of women with pronounced sexual characteristics but almost without facial features, the so-called Venuses in ivory, stone, and clay which appear from Gravettian times on may also have represented early man's ideal of womanhood or may have had religious significance as part of a cult of generative forces.

Even more tantalizing are the carvings on rocks in Europe and in parts of the Sahara now uninhabitable and also the paintings which have been found on cave walls in France and Spain. Beginning about 28,000 B.C., men ventured deep into hidden recesses, torch in hand, and painted animal after animal; at Lascaux some 400 oxen, deer, horses, bison and other figures survive. The artists' palette included brown, yellow, red, and black. In its superb, direct realism the drawing of animals was not to be matched for millennia (see Plate II). Men on the other hand are shown in distorted, shorthand form, and the symbols used in rock carvings were sometimes almost geometric and conventionalized.

The purpose of this work was surely not always artistic self-expression, and modern students initially assumed that it was basically magical. By drawing pictures of the animals they hunted men must have felt they would have a better chance of finding them in the real world. Sometimes the artist showed a spear or dart sticking out of the animal; at other times painting and sculpture reveal indentations as though they had been hit by a spear. While faith in the presence of spirits, which is called animism, recurs often in later societies, the objectives of cave painters may have included a variety of other purposes, such as the commemoration of social gatherings. Another branch of religious beliefs alongside those created by problems of subsistence and the generation of human life is attested by the deliberate burial of the dead, at times with objects to be used after death, which occurs from Neanderthal times. Sometimes the bones of the dead are covered by red ocher, perhaps to represent the life-giving qualities of blood; one Neanderthal burial has been proven to have been strewn with wild flowers, though no graves of this era have any beads.

On other important, nonmaterial aspects of early life we can only speculate. The development of speech did not leave visible marks, though it is most unlikely that culture could have progressed far until men used language. There is no evidence either that cave men secured their mates by force or that the mothers were the dominant element in primitive societies, to cite another modern theory. Women, true, must have been economically as important as were men, as gatherers of wild plants; but anthropologists feel that the monogamous, enduring family patterns of most later societies may have evolved only slowly. The long period of human dependence in childhood, as well as the risks of illness and injury, surely forced human beings to live together fairly permanently in packs rather than in single family cells. Yet from early time men had to learn to channel purely instinctive emotional and sexual urges if they were to emerge out of an animal state and form successful social groups. Since the packs lived by food-gathering, the total population was extremely small, perhaps not more than one person on the average per square mile even in good territories; but the presence of large masses of animal bones at the foot of cliffs shows that communal hunts took place by the Late Paleolithic stage.

A famous English philosopher, Thomas Hobbes, once defined the life of early man as "solitary, poor, nasty, brutish and short." Others have, with equally little justification, idealized our first ancestors in a cult of the Noble Savage, not yet beset by the cankers of advanced civilization. Two specific discoveries in recent years may perhaps suggest that the attitudes of men toward each other varied as much in the Paleolithic era as in more recent times. One is the skeleton of a Neanderthal male, arthritic and with only one arm from childhood, who apparently tended the communal fire in an Iraq cave for his fellows. The other is likewise a Neanderthal skeleton, from the Mt. Carmel caves of Palestine, which was clearly marked by the impress of a spearpoint. In any case life was indeed short; examples of early modern man show that 54 per cent died by 20 and 35 per cent between 21 and 40. If one considers just those people of the Neanderthal and early *Homo sapiens sapiens* periods who lived past 20, most women were dead by 30 while most men lived past that age.

TRANSITION TO THE NEOLITHIC AGE

End of the Paleolithic Era (10,000–7000 B.C.). Even as a food-gatherer, man had spread over the entire globe, especially from the Neanderthal era onward. Human beings had reached the continental United States by at least 12,000 years ago. In the Upper Paleolithic period men had devised a material and social structure capable of supporting them wherever they went in pursuit of game.

To us they may still look primitive, but certainly they had become exceedingly dangerous to all other forms of animal life. Over the hundreds of thousands of years we have already considered, the biological and cultural evolution of mankind had given it considerable physical and mental dexterity and also a useful complement of tools by which men could extend their powers. Many of our basic social attitudes and views of the surrounding world were surely formed in these distant ages.

As a result of the quickening tempo of development in the Upper Paleolithic stage, men achieved an intellectual and technical level far beyond anything in the past. They were, at least in some areas, ready to take a giant step forward. In doing so they may have been encouraged by the climatic changes after 8000 B.C. As the glaciers began that retreat which is still going on, the climate in Europe proper turned rainier, the forests grew, and the fauna moved northward. Northern Africa and western Asia had a damp climate; not until later did the Sahara and parts of the Near East begin to dry up as the rain-bearing winds shifted northward. Similar physical developments, however, had occurred frequently in earlier periods; only now was man sufficiently advanced to change his mode of life so as to fit the altered natural surroundings.

Different Responses of Mankind. The transitional phase at the end of the Paleolithic era is sometimes given the name of the Mesolithic period. In the Near East it may extend from about 10,000 to 8000 B.C.; but in central and northern Europe it reached on down to about 3000 B.C. Like all transitional epochs this period is marked by an uneven speed of advance, as different peoples gave up their old ways more or less reluctantly; and the rise of new ways of life is difficult to detect in the first stages. Archeological interest in the era is so very recent that we may be sure any preliminary conclusions today about the emergence of agriculture will have to be revised extensively in the next few years.

Over most of the earth it is clear that men simply continued to hunt their food. The brilliant Magdalenian stage in Europe collapsed as the climate changed and fauna moved accordingly. In the duller age that followed, the inhabitants of north-central Europe near the Baltic, called Maglemosian from a Danish site, improved further their food-collecting techniques and elaborated their physical equipment for life. Here men turned to exploit the resources not only of the land but also of the seacoast, which grew longer as the seas rose at the end of the ice age. Eventually they collected and ate oysters with such enthusiasm that they left kitchen middens or banks of oyster shells many feet thick. Maglemosian men also fished from canoes with nets and hooks, gathered nuts and fruits, and hunted with bow and arrow as well as with the spear. Thanks to their intensive exploitation of available food resources, such people could become more sedentary. Perhaps as a result they domesticated the dog and tended to polish stone tools so that they could work wood better with adzes, chisels, and gouges.

Cultures like that of the Maglemosian area represented a dead end, from which further progress would be limited and slow. To break out of the inherent limitations of the food-gathering society required a veritable revolution. This was the discovery of agriculture, which took place primarily in the area now known as the Near East (see Map 1).

In this district, stretching from the eastern end of the Mediterranean inland along the hills at the northern edge of Mesopotamia to Iran, men had lived since earliest times. A fairly large number of Neanderthal-type specimens have been found in the area; by shortly after 10,000 B.C. an almost sedentary population resided in the caves of the region, from Mt. Carmel in Palestine to the Caspian Sea.

The inhabitants of the Carmel rock-shelters and the nearby open settlements of Palestine, whom we may take as an example, are called Natufians. They lived in the same locality so continuously that they could adorn the terraces in front of their rock-shelters with low stone structures, the purpose of which has not yet been fathomed, and they re-

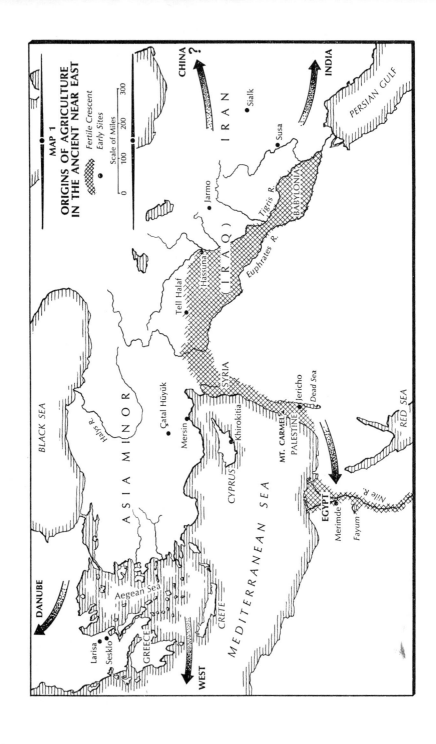

MAP 1
ORIGINS OF AGRICULTURE
IN THE ANCIENT NEAR EAST

Fertile Crescent
Early Sites

Scale of Miles
0   100   200   300

built their huts several times on the same spot. They also employed a fairly extensive equipment of physical objects, both useful and decorative. Their dead, for instance, were carefully buried with beads and headdresses. These people must have had an assured food supply. In large part they were hunters and fishers with the usual Mesolithic equipment of harpoons, fishhooks, spears, bows, and so on; but they seem to have been on the verge of discovering agriculture. Natufian man certainly reaped the wild grasses of the neighborhood with straight bone sickles set with small flint teeth, and then processed the kernels with milling and pounding stones; huts at times had built-in storage places and fireplaces.

In the hills of Iraq people in a similar state of development lived in pit houses which were grouped in regular villages. The ancestors of both wheat and barley grew wild in these upland districts, which enjoyed a regular, adequate rainfall; root vegetables, which may have been more useful before baking and brewing were discovered, were also available. Men of this area, as in Palestine, were sufficiently advanced in social and technical organization to settle down. The next step, to raise food deliberately, may seem inevitable, but it was nonetheless an amazing break with earlier customs.

THE NEOLITHIC AGE

Domestication of Food Supplies (8000 b.c. *on*). The decisive criterion for the arrival of the Neolithic age is the domestication of animals and plants. Mankind began the ever-continuing process of affecting its environment, even though this effort required more continuous attention than had the earlier food-gathering economy. Humanity has thus had to adapt further its own desires and drives to the resulting dictates of ever more complex social organization and increasingly intellectual approaches to the problems of life. These two factors — control over nature and control over instinctive impulses — have necessarily advanced at the same rate over the course of human history.

Agriculture seems to have developed independently in more than one area. In eastern Asia people began raising millet, yams, and rice. In the New World beans, squash, potatoes, and corn were cultivated in Central America and in Peru. The most important step by far was the domestication of wheat and barley by peoples in the Near East; from this region the idea of deliberately raising animals and plants spread outward to most of Eurasia and Africa.

The first step now appears to have been the taming of goats and sheep from about 9000 B.C. on. About 2000 years later came the deliberate cultivation of two kinds of wheat and barley with some vegetables, and the domestication of pigs and cattle. Not for another millennium, however, did cereals become a very important part of the diet. One remarkably early site was Jericho, an oasis by the Jordan river, which developed even before the true Neolithic stage; by 6000 it was a fortified town with ditch, stone wall, and even towers. Inside it were homes with walls of packed stone for as many as 2000 inhabitants. An even larger town, with some specialization of crafts, was Çatal Hüyük in southern Turkey. In both cases it has been suggested, on dubious grounds, that trade in items such as obsidian helped to support such unusually large populations. Normally the earliest Neolithic peoples dwelt in open villages. Their houses occasionally collapsed in violent storms and rains, but the inhabitants were so sedentary that they simply rebuilt their houses on top of the ruins. The excavators at Jarmo discovered 11 such levels in a mound 25 feet deep and 3 acres in area.

How herding and farming began in the Near East remains — and probably will remain — a matter of hypothesis. We may guess that food-gathering peoples had occasionally stored their surplus grain and that they came to speculate on the interesting fact that some reserves sprouted. If a statue were to be raised to the first farmer, it probably should be molded in the shape of a woman, for women did most of the collecting of grain. Whether the intentional shepherding of animals emerged from the keeping of pets, from the temporary retention of captured specimens to sacrifice before a hunt, or from some other process is equally unclear. Most early farmers raised both plants and animals and also continued to hunt, fish, and gather wild fruits, depending upon local circumstances. True nomads who lived off their domesticated animals were a relatively late specialization.

Elaboration of Neolithic Life. In the dimensions of its consequences the Neolithic revolution was an epochal step. Socially the activities of farming and shepherding required an intensification of group organization. Whereas Paleolithic packs numbered perhaps 20 to 50, Neolithic farmers either lived in family homesteads, in villages of 150 persons (as at Jarmo), or in even larger towns (as in Jericho). From the ways similar peoples lived in later times we may infer that authority lay in the elders of each village, who applied tribal tradition to the conduct of daily life, and that chieftains may have appeared afterward. Individual independence of action must still have been a virtually unknown concept, and people worked together within a close-knit society. One of the earliest villages in Egypt, in the Fayum area, had communal granaries, pits in the ground lined with coiled basketry.

A phenomenal increase in physical possessions resulted from the needs of more developed life, much greater population, and more sedentary routines. The first farmers were not always stable, and sometimes an area could try and then give up farming. Soils could be exhausted, and irrigation probably was used only in oases. In the climatic conditions of the Near East, however, cultivable areas were restricted, and farming practice soon learned to adapt itself to local conditions either by leaving lands periodically fallow or by manuring. Permanent or semipermanent capital resources accordingly could be built up in the settled clumps which elevated the hosts of Near Eastern mounds.

The earliest levels of the first villages had stone vessels but still lacked pottery, which is a relatively complicated product; clay must be carefully prepared, then molded, and finally fired either in the open or in kilns under expert supervision. By the late seventh millennium this valuable means of storing and cooking food appeared widely. Usually the first pottery was burnished or incised. Then came the application of painted design, a step which made pottery very useful to modern archeological research. Each local area had its own designs, which changed over the years; from these changes, more than any other source, it is possible to distinguish relative chronological stages. The spread of pottery shapes or motifs in decoration from one area to another gives a sure clue to the passage of ideas — and sometimes, though not so surely, of migrations of peoples. Pottery, moreover, while easily broken, is virtually indestructible as a substance, and its fragments survive admirably in most soil conditions.

A host of other steps also occurred. Basket-weaving had been known since Mesolithic days but now became more skilled. Through the presence of spindle whorls, of loom weights, and of actual textiles in the dry sands of Egypt it is evident that the weaving of wool and flax (into linen) soon appeared in the Near Eastern villages. Once ovens and pottery had been developed, grain could be prepared as porridge, as bread, and also as beer. Stone tools, which were generally polished, now included real adzes; the stone vases show that drilling techniques, which are basic in many technological processes, had been much advanced. The first use of metals began as people found and hammered in cold forms lumps of gold, silver, and copper, which lay here and there on the surface in the Near East. The heating and then working of native copper lumps came first; then by the fifth millennium smelting of ores and casting techniques were well developed. In the fourth millennium, the wheel was discovered, a step which the civilizations of Central and South America never achieved except for toys. In its early form — solid, without spokes — the wheel was used for wagons and for turning pottery more skillfully and swiftly.

Early farmers used only digging sticks and hoes in a garden-type cultivation; but by the fourth millennium the plow had been developed. This step represented the first considerable harnessing of nonhuman power of man's own ends. The concept nonetheless played a far less significant role in the ancient world than it has in modern times, for throughout antiquity men made virtually no use of water power and captured the winds only for the sails of ships. The monuments of those ages were primarily the product of human muscles; even animal power was neither extensively nor efficiently exploited.

Each early farming settlement was virtually self-sufficient, and localism is more prominent at·this stage than before or after. Still, the inhabitants of a village were linked to the physical and spiritual world which lay about them. The fact that the citizens of Jericho felt compelled to devote extensive energies toward walling themselves is significant; more peaceful connections are attested by the presence of foreign objects and materials, as in the discovery of obsidian, turquoise matrix, and cowrie shells at Jericho. The incipient professions of smiths and potters must have been in the hands of specialists, who perhaps traveled from village to village; but otherwise specialization awaited the next stage of development.

In Neolithic communities art tended to geometrical designs or highly formalized depictions. One of the most widespread products of the early farmers, found as far as Britain, was the manufacture of clay or stone figurines, at times of animals but very often of women, beginning in the seventh millennium. Modern students of religion commonly suggest that these figurines are linked to a worship of the fructifying power of Mother Earth, for the assurance of food supplies was everywhere an important aspect of agricultural religions. Yet we shall do well not to speculate too extensively upon early religious concepts until the rise of civilization begins to provide us with written evidence; in particular, not all religious concerns revolved about food supply. It may be noted that Jericho early had a real temple, with cult figures.

Spread of Agriculture. Once the domestication of plants and animals had begun, men seem to have needed time to digest their great achievement. The Neolithic villages of the Near East changed very slowly over the millennia down to and past 4000 B.C. The concept of agriculture, however, was easily transmitted and was avidly seized by other peoples. In part the spread of agriculture from its home in the Near East may have reflected the expansion of its population, based on the greater food resources, but more often other food-gathering peoples probably picked up the idea via the thin lines of prehistoric trade.

As a result historians cannot altogether determine the dates or routes of agricultural expansion, unless the styles of pottery or the use of figurines gives clues. Eastward, farming turns up in northern China, along the Yellow river, by the fifth millennium, but this development may well have been independent. Westward, Greece had farming villages at least by the seventh millennium. Europe itself was held back by the widespread forests and by the presence of a much different, continental climate. Whereas its Paleolithic inhabitants at times seem to have been well in the forefront, as in cave painting, after 10,000 B.C. the population of the area north of the Alps remained in a backwater until the time of Christ. In and after the sixth millennium peasant cultivators made their way up the Danube in a technique of slash-and-burn, moving on when the roughly cleared soil was exhausted. Probably agriculture also spread westward by sea to other districts of Europe; there were farmers in Britain by 3500 B.C. South of the Sahara, where Neolithic peoples made marvelous rock-paintings until desiccation set in, agriculture did not become common until the first millennium B.C.

SUMMATION

Now that we have brought the history of mankind past 4000 B.C., almost the whole course of human existence on this planet has been described. Yet the truly historic era, the period of civilization, is yet to begin. At this date men over most of the earth's surface were probably still in the food-gathering stage.

In the central latitudes of Eurasia, however, the more favored tribes had commenced to liberate themselves from complete, direct dependence on the vagaries of natural food supplies. No subsequent calamity of war or social and political disintegration has lastingly depressed mankind again below the Neolithic level. From the point of view of technological change and expansion of population only two later events — the rise of civilization and the Industrial Revolution — can be compared to this advance.

If one surveys the agricultural world in its developed stages, an obvious characteristic is its still-primitive simplicity. Men dragged their crops from the soil by hard, back-breaking work; in both the prehistoric and the historic eras of antiquity the average human being had a life-expectancy at birth of less than 30 years. Plague or famine could wipe out an entire countryside, and in the last months before a new crop the villagers lived on very thin rations, still often supplemented by products of the hunt. Much remained to be achieved toward giving men physical and intellectual security.

By this time local ways of life had come to differ widely and sharply. In the region of modern Switzerland men were soon to drive piles and create villages along the shores of the lakes. On the Danube whole clans and their animals lived in communal, wooden "long houses," 20 or so of which would form a village. Elsewhere families heaped up stones in huts or created lean-tos of bundles of reeds; over much of the Near East houses of sun-dried brick were customary. As the methods of housing varied, so too did the tools employed by their inhabitants; and, above all, the ideas inside men's heads crystallized into many different patterns. To give only one example, such broad groups of languages as the Indo-European and Semitic had already evolved far before writing appeared.

The course of man's history to this point may suggest to the careful observer some more generalized conclusions. Human society, for instance, commonly favors stability and the ways of its ancestors; continuity is a very evident factor in history. Yet the change that occurred, however slowly, across the Paleolithic and Neolithic eras always forced men into new paths. To be sure, this development did not occur at an even tempo; especially from the beginning of the Neolithic age onward change can be shown to have come in spurts, which were separated by long periods of relative stagnation. It is worth noting too that neither then nor in more recent times did all parts of the world progress at the same speed. By the fourth millennium history had begun to have a main thread, the eventual source of which was the Near East; here too was the site of the next major step, which will be examined in the following chapter.

In history, that is to say, change in any one area has largely been a matter of the borrowing of ideas from an alien source. But the subsequent development of man illustrates the point that each region, while borrowing from other peoples, could vary and reinterpret these ideas and practices into virtually new forms. What has occurred on the broad level of history takes place, of course, on the individual level; each one of us has derived most of his ideas and principles from outside sources but has combined them into a personal blend.

BIBLIOGRAPHY

Sources. How do we know what happened in history? This problem may not deeply concern a beginner in history, who perhaps tends to take every statement in a book as true — until he reads another book on the same subject and finds that opinions differ amazingly. Too often the result of this process is the other extreme, skepticism as to whether anything in history is true.

The story of any era rests in the end not upon secondary accounts, written by modern scholars, but on contemporary materials. These, and these alone, may be called the sources for the period; they rise directly out of the life and events of the times and must be used by the historian to re-create its story. A general survey is only an introduction to history, which must reflect in part the prejudices and interests of its author; but in reading it a student may become deeply interested in some aspect of the past development of mankind. Then he should exercise his imagination by turning to the sources themselves.

For the period covered in this chapter there were no written sources, and so we must rely upon material remains left by its peoples. Anything that has been tangibly touched by human hands or is a product of human activity — even the hole left in the ground by a support for a lean-to — aids the historian in reconstructing the first stages of man's existence. It is the function of the archeologist to discover these remains by observation and excavation. To understand their meaning and date he in turn calls upon many auxiliary sciences, including soil chemistry, geology, metallurgy, and various techniques of chemistry and physics. Although the archeologists have become ever more skillful, it must be pointed out that many products, made of wood, fur, and so on, are perishable. More important yet, not all of man's thoughts, social, political, and religious, give rise to physical testimony.

Often scholars have tried to overcome this latter deficiency by seeking light from comparative anthropology, the study of primitive peoples in more recent times. This is a very dangerous procedure, though sometimes it is suggestive. Modern backward tribes have had millennia in which to be backward, that is, to fix their patterns. Even more severe distortion has often resulted from reading back modern theories about the nature and drives of humanity. Marxists have found that early men were primitive communists, unspoiled by class exploitation; idealists have created a halcyon portrait of men who did not smoke, drink, or wage war; ethnologists of the Victorian age, affected by theories of "survival of the fittest," built up on the other hand a picture of semihuman cave men, who lived by force in utter barbarism.

Much undoubtedly will be discovered to change even sober portrayals of man's first steps, as they are written today. The serious study of prehistoric man and general willingness to accept the view that mankind existed before 4004 B.C. (the date assigned by Archbishop Ussher to the Creation) commenced only in and after the 1850s, when students began to comprehend the meaning of the early skulls and tools which had been turning up; the terms Paleolithic and Neolithic were coined by Sir John Lubbock in 1863. This realization is directly connected with the spread of Darwin's theories about the slow evolution of animal species, which made the antiquity of man himself a philosophical necessity, but the bio-logical theories themselves were in large part a result of historical and philosophical meditation earlier in the century on the processes of devel-opment and change in history. As modern mankind has come to desire ever more deeply to understand the stages of its cultural evolution, ar-cheology has become a widely fascinating subject and has produced the evidence on which the present account rests.

Further Reading. Any study of early man will be partially or com-pletely out of date on the factual side in 10 years, though most scholars are deeply in debt to V. Gordon Childe, whose *What Happened in His-tory* was first published in 1942 and often reprinted. Among recent read-able accounts of our origins, see Grahame Clark, *World Prehistory in New Perspective* (3d ed.; Cambridge: Cambridge University Press, 1977); M. H. Wolpoff, *Paleoanthropology* (New York: Knopf, 1980); and more succinctly Robert Stigler et al., *The Old World* (New York: St. Martin's, 1974). Myra Shackley, *Neanderthal Man* (Hamden, Conn.: Archon Books, 1980), takes up one famous type in detail. Discoveries of earliest man are discussed by Ruth Moore, *Man, Time, and Fossils* (2d ed.; New York: Knopf, 1961); H. L. Shapiro, *Peking Man* (New York: Simon & Schuster, 1974), who explores the mysterious disappearance of the Choukoutien material in World War II; G. H. R. von Koenigswald, *Meeting Prehistoric Man* (New York: Harper, 1956). The physical background may be found in K. W. Butzer, *Environment and Archaeol-ogy* (rev. ed.; Chicago: Aldine, 1971).

W. F. Libby, *Radiocarbon Dating* (2d ed.; Chicago: University of Chicago Press, 1955), describes the method for which he received a No-bel Prize; Colin Renfrew, *Before Civilization* (Cambridge: Cambridge University Press, 1979), discusses difficulties in radiocarbon dating, partly to counter the theory accepted in the present work that agriculture dif-fused from the Near East. The extent to which cultural characteristics, including much more than technical invasions, are independent in origin or are diffused from one center is a serious general problem throughout history; Thor Heyerdahl (*Kon Tiki, Ra,* etc.) is a famous example of a diffusionist.

F. Bordes, *The Old Stone Age* (New York: McGraw-Hill, 1968), re-mains an excellent account; J. M. Coles and E. S. Higgs, *The Archaeol-ogy of Early Man* (London: Faber and Faber, 1969), is a survey of the

Paleolithic period area by area. More detailed essays are collected in S. L. Washburn, *Social Life of Early Man* (Chicago: Aldine, 1961), which suggest the anthropological views. See also, on art, G. Bataille, *Lascaux* (New York: Skira, 1955); Ann Sieveking, *The Cave Artists* (London: Thames and Hudson, 1979); P. J. Ucko and A. Rosenfeld, *Paleolithic Cave Art* (New York: McGraw-Hill, 1967), sensible in its interpretation. K. P. Oakley, *Man the Tool-Maker* (6th ed.; Chicago: University of Chicago Press, 1976), is good; a balanced exploration of a much-argued subject is R. A. Goldsby, *Race and Races* (2d ed.; New York: Macmillan, 1977). See also Gega Révész, *The Origins and Pre-history of Language* (Westport, Conn.: Greenwood, 1978).

The rise of the Neolithic period is now seen as much more compli-cated than as sketched by V. Gordon Childe; but his ideas remain semi-nal. See S. Cole, *The Neolithic Revolution* (5th ed.; London: British Museum, 1970); Jane Renfrew, *Paleoethnobotany* (New York: Co-lumbia University Press, 1973); P. J. Ucko and G. W. Dimbleby, *Domestication of Plants and Animals* (Chicago: Aldine, 1969); J. B. Hutchinson et al., *The Early History of Agriculture* (London: British Academy, 1977). R. Oliver and B. M. Fagan, *Africa in the Iron Age c. 500 B.C. to A.D. 1400* (London: Cambridge University Press, 1975), is a good summary. See also the works listed in Bibliography, Chapters 2, 3, and 21.

2

THE FIRST CIVILIZATION
OF MESOPOTAMIA

To understand any era of the past one must be able to penetrate into the minds of its inhabitants. This is an ever-challenging, yet extremely difficult task, to which the historian should bring sympathetic imagination and a wide knowledge of the passions of man; if he is to have any success, there must also be adequate written records as well as physical objects. Such records are available only for the past five millennia of human existence and then only for certain areas. This period is the historic age proper, the era of civilization.

The term "civilization" may have many meanings. At the present point we are seeking to detect its first appearance and early growth; and for this end certain fundamental characteristics of civilized society distinguish it from the "cultures" of earlier eras. Among these characteristics are the following: the presence of firmly organized states which had definite boundaries and systematic political institutions, under political and religious leaders who directed and also maintained society; the distinction of social classes; the economic specialization of men as farmer, trader, or artisan, each dependent upon his fellows; and the conscious development of the arts and intellectual attitudes. In the last point are included the rise of monumental architecture and sculpture, the use of writing to keep accounts or to commemorate deeds, and the elaboration of religious views about the nature of the gods, their relations to men, and the origin of the world. Usually civilization is connected with cities, but there had been large agglomerations at Neolithic Jericho; and Egypt became civilized without developing true urban centers. Still, the cities of Mesopotamia were vital to the appearance of civilization there.

Once mankind had developed the practice of agriculture, it might be assumed that the step to a civilized level would be simple and automatic. Actually, however, many peoples of the world remained in the purely food-raising stage down to modern times; most areas that became civilized did so in imitation of peoples already more advanced. Only in three corners of the globe does it appear that men independently created civilization.

One of these was northern China, which we shall examine later; a second was Central America-Peru where the Mayans and Peruvians developed civilizations in the first millennium after Christ. Whether they were affected by forces moving across the Pacific from Asia remains hotly debated, but as far as we can now see they were of native origin. In any case the American forms of civilization were seriously limited by their failure to make practical use of the wheel, by the limited use of copper, and by the absence of good draft animals; in Peru even writing was lacking. The historian must doubt if these civilizations had any promise of a brilliant future. The Mayans declined by themselves shortly before A.D. 1000. The Peruvian and Mexican cultures, while still alive and thriving at the time of the Spanish explorations, were not able to withstand the attack from Europe.

The ultimate source of the civilized strengths which carried western Europe overseas in the modern period lay far back in the other great center where man had independently created the patterns of civilization. This was the Near East. More specifically, the original habitat of civilization in this district was those valleys of Mesopotamia and Egypt in which rivers cut across almost desert wastes and gave never-ceasing sources of water. Thence the impetus to develop civilized structures radiated out to India and the Mediterranean basin. This chapter will consider the progress of Mesopotamia from the fourth millennium B.C. down to about 1700 B.C.; Chapter 3 will take up the parallel story of Egypt, which is markedly similar and yet offers interesting differences.

THE FIRST CITIES OF MESOPOTAMIA

Geographical Framework of the Area. Mesopotamia is a Greek word meaning "between the rivers." The rivers in question are the Tigris to the east and the Euphrates to the west, both of which rise in the Armenian highlands and flow generally southeastward to the Persian Gulf. In their upper reaches the rivers lie far apart. Between them is a hilly, rolling country; this region is watered by a number of major tributaries of the great streams as well as by winter rains. The southern part, where the Tigris and Euphrates diverge again to a distance of up to 100 miles, was the home of the first civilization. This area, which is about 200 miles long, was in early times the land of Sumer and Akkad; after the rise of Babylon it is called Babylonia (see Map 2).

Here rain falls rarely but in sudden storms. Throughout the day the sun beats down fiercely from the great bowl of Heaven, and violent winds at times lash the dull brown countryside with dust. In its natural

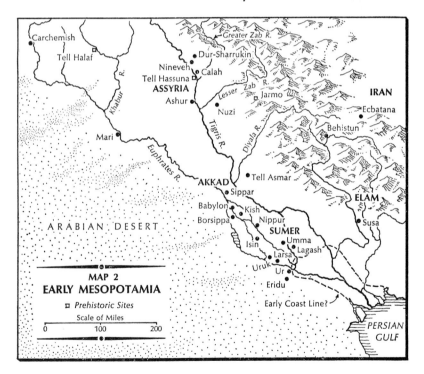

MAP 2
EARLY MESOPOTAMIA
□ Prehistoric Sites
Scale of Miles
0   100   200

state the district is a wild waste of dried mud flats, stagnant pools, and reed swamps; apart from clay there are no building materials, no sources of metals. Sumer and Akkad offered little to men save the soil, which in most areas was light and easily worked, and a constant source of water in the great rivers. Upon this potentially fertile land, however, farmers could expand their numbers greatly and could throw up nonagricultural elements to create the complex structure of civilization once they had learned to draw off water from the high bed of the Euphrates river to irrigate their fields and then drain away this water lest the salts which it brought ruin the land even for barley. The floods of the rivers, which came irregularly in the late spring as crops were maturing, were useless and had to be warded off by further extensive labors of diking and walling.

Another significant geographical aspect of Mesopotamia is its openness. To the south and west lie the vast expanses of the Arabian desert, the oases of which nourished a seminomadic population of Semitic-speaking peoples. These tribes ever tended to seep or pour into the river plains; eventually they became dominant there. To the east and north are first foothills and then the mountains of Iran and Armenia, from which other peoples recurrently rushed down into Mesopotamia. The leaders in the first evolution of Mesopotamian civilization, the Sumerians, seem to have come from this direction.

From the mouths of the great rivers, which in early days probably emptied independently into the Persian Gulf, traders could make their way down the sea and the coasts to Bahrein island and on the Indus river in India. Others moved up into the mountains to gain usable wood, metals, stone, and other resources; daring men thus crossed into Asia Minor or to Syria and the Mediterranean. A great sweep of cultivable land, which has been aptly called the Fertile Crescent, reaches from lower Mesopotamia around through Syria and down by Palestine to Egypt. Mesopotamian civilization, as a result, was far more receptive of external influences and spread its own achievements more widely over the Near East than did the secluded civilization of early Egypt.

Neolithic Background (5000–3500 B.C). As we saw in the preceding chapter, agriculture was discovered in the grassy uplands of the Near East. The first farmers avoided the difficult river plain. Settled communities of the late Neolithic stretched all across the upper Fertile

Crescent as far as southern Turkey and Syria; prominent in this area was the painted Halafian pottery, which derived its designs in part from textiles. Then suddenly the archeological record suggests disruption and decline, which was followed by the widespread appearance of pottery of Ubaid type (so named from a site near Ur). Thenceforth Mesopotamia was the major motive force in development, for exploitation of the agricultural riches of the river valley had begun. Inhabitation here had to be a virtually conscious action by fairly large groups, prepared to dam and dike and to dig short canals so as to make efficient use of the water supplied by the Euphrates river. Extensive irrigation schemes came only after the rise of civilized states, but barley and dates provided steady crops. By the beginning of the fifth millennium villagers began to appear in southern Mesopotamia.

Two major forms of Neolithic culture cover the domestication of the river plain in the fifth and fourth millennia. The first is the Ubaid; the second, the Uruk phase during which Uruk pottery spread northward as far as Turkey and eastward into Elam. New techniques and devices slowly evolved, such as the wheel, plow, new methods of casting copper, and sailing craft; Ubaid men made their way down the Persian Gulf as far as Bahrain. They also improved their political, social, and intellectual organization — and in this area lay the main prerequisites for the rise of civilization, which is primarily a social and rational step. One mark of change in these respects was the expanding use of seals to attest ownership and to identify individuals or temples; seals were carved as cylinders decorated with divine and human figures which could be rolled across clay lumps. Temples succeeded each other on the same site and were erected in ever more majestic, more consciously calculated patterns. The first temple of sun-dried bricks at Eridu was a square about 10 feet on a side; but by the dawn of civilization the White Temple at Uruk was a rectangular edifice of the later customary form. It stood on a terrace 40 feet high which must have taken 1500 workers 5 years of continuous labor. Such structures, totally unknown in all earlier history, suggest the growth in resources and veritable explosion of population that had occurred as people exploited the fertility of the plain. Whereas the village at Jarmo encompassed only 3 acres and had perhaps 150 settlers in all, an early Mesopotamian city like Ur covered 150 acres and numbered its citizens at about 24,000.

Appearance of Civilization (3500–3000 B.C.). Across the small plain of lower Mesopotamia a limited number of distinct settlements had emerged by the last centuries of the fourth millennium. These were the kernels of its historic city-states, such as Ur, Uruk, Lagash, Umma, and so on. These sites were not only larger than earlier villages; they also soon displayed evidence of economic specialization and firm political organization. The term "city" is used by ancient historians only for such units, as distinguished from purely agricultural, tribal "villages." A city includes an advanced nucleus of settlement together with its surrounding farmland, like a modern American county and its county seat combined. In early Mesopotamia as in later Greece and Rome each city was also an independent political system and so may be called a "city-state," which tended to endure as a stable unit.

After the steady development of the Ubaid and Uruk periods had produced these crystallized centers, men were ready to jump into civilization. The era in which they took the plunge is called the Protoliterate stage and occupied a brief span of time just before 3000. In human history there are revolutions as well as slow eons of evolution; one of the greatest explosions now took place and affected virtually all phases of life in an amazing, interconnected forward surge.

By 3000 the physical appearance of the landscape shows at a glance that man had stamped the impress of order upon nature. The great rivers still set the stage, but their precious gift of water was tapped and managed by a system of major canals and subsidiary channels carefully planned to cover all the city's farmlands. By canals and by roads the countryside was divided into relatively regular plots which were defined by geometrical means. Farmers employed wooden plows, seed-drills, and stone hoes to reap 40-fold returns of barley; shepherds and dogs watched flocks of sheep and goats; other areas were gardens with mudbrick walls, set about with fruit trees and overshadowed by date palms. Asses on the paths and boats on the canals carried the rich products of the fields to the vital hubs, the cities.

Each city proper was girdled by a moat and wall of sun-dried brick; that of Uruk eventually stretched almost 6 miles, with over 900 towers, and was deemed the work of the great legendary hero Gilgamesh. Within the gates, where a regular guard of soldiers watched traffic, streets wide enough for chariots and wagons ran between blocks of the houses of the well-to-do; behind these were alleys and great masses of small, flat-roofed huts. Here lived mostly the farmers, who trudged out every day to the fields (though some lived in subsidiary mudbrick villages); but there were also smiths, potters, and the like.

Looming over the homes of men were the temples, very literally conceived as the "houses of the gods." The special god of the city had his own walled precinct, and his temple was often elevated on an artificial mound. The stepped mounds or *ziggurats,* such as the Biblical Tower of Babel, were imitation mountains; according to early Mesopotamian thought the mountains were the focus of the powers of earth.

Political and Social Bonds. Man had also impressed order upon himself as well as upon nature, for a Sumerian city was a tightly interlocked political and economic structure resting upon a common cultural and religious outlook. The changes in these respects in the late fourth millennium were equally impressive.

Economically, agriculture remained the basic mode of life for 80 to 90 per cent of the population and was carried on in ways not greatly dissimilar from advanced Neolithic practices. But farmers could no longer live by themselves. Some part of their product was yielded to the smiths, potters, and merchants, who assembled at the quays and gates, in exchange for their manufactured wares. The farmers also had to dedicate a portion of their crops and of their own labor to communal activities. The canals must be maintained and extended; walls were ever more necessary, and able-bodied men must fight in the army of the state; temples were built and adorned in lavish fashion. Private enterprise was minimal in such a planned economy, the managers of which were the priests.

The first cities to emerge out of tribal life were at the outset apparently governed by the citizens as a whole, who met in assembly. Yet we hear also of a chief man or "governor" (*ensi*) for the gods, and soon a king (*lugal*) appears. Even though hereditary rule does not yet seem to have existed and the leader's will was checked by the will of the gods as manifested in striking phenomena of nature, in dreams, and in processes of divination, the power and functions of the monarchical element were to grow greatly.

Much of the political and social structure in these early cities lasted across the following stages of Mesopotamian history, but much altered in the next 1500 years. At the present time scholars divide this period into the Early Dynastic era, (*c.* 3000–2300), the Sargonid epoch of Semitic domination (*c.* 2300–2150), the Sumerian revival under the Third Dynasty of Ur (*c.* 2150–1950), and the Old Babylonian era culminating in the reign of Hammurapi *c.* 1700). Before going on, however, to the course of Mesopotamian political history, one needs to be clear as to the

TABLE 2

The First Civilizations

B.C.	Mesopotamia	Egypt
5000	HALAFIAN	FAYUM, TASIAN
4000	UBAID	BADARIAN
		AMRATIAN
3500	URUK	GERZEAN
	rise of cities	
3100	PROLITERATE	PROTODYNASTIC (Dyn. I-II)
		Dyn. I: *Menes (Narmer?)*
3000	EARLY DYNASTIC	
2700	royal tombs of Ur	OLD KINGDOM (Dyn. III-VI)
		Dyn. III: *Zoser*
		Dyn. IV: *Khufu*
		Khafre
		Menkaure
2300	SARGONID ERA	
	Urukagina, Lugalzaggisi	
	Sargon I	
2200	*Naramsin*	FIRST INTERMEDIATE PERIOD
	THIRD DYNASTY OF UR	(Dyn. VII-X)
	Gudea	
2050		MIDDLE KINGDOM (Dyn. XI-XII)
1950	OLD BABYLONIAN ERA	
		SECOND INTERMEDIATE PERIOD
1700	*Hammurapi*	(Dyn. XIII-XVII)
		Hyksos
1600	KASSITES	
		NEW KINGDOM (Dyn. XVIII-XX)

main lines of its intellectual and religious outlook. This emerged very early and remained an enduring quality of Mesopotamian civilization.

THE MESOPOTAMIAN OUTLOOK

Sumerian Civilization. The Sumerians, who were in the forefront of early Mesopotamian progress, are linguistically a puzzle, for their agglutinative, largely monosyllabic speech cannot be connected with any of the major groups of languages. By about 3500 B.C. they had begun to draw conventionalized pictograms (representations of physical objects) on clay tablets, found at Kish and Uruk, and perhaps on other, less enduring materials. Three hundred years later, about 3200, tablets show that the scribes of Sumer took a tremendous step, which we do not know ever to have occurred independently elsewhere; that is, they advanced to a mixture of ideograms (marks representing concepts such as "day") and phonograms (symbols expressing syllabic phonetic values, as we might draw a bee for the sound be). Since some symbols expressed more than one phonetic value and, on the other hand, one single sound could be expressed by up to 14 different marks, sometimes "determinatives" were prefixed to indicate the class to which the word in question belonged, as deity, bird, and so on. These elements came to be wedge-shaped marks impressed in the clay by a stylus; from the Latin word *cuneus* for wedge the Mesopotamian script is called "cuneiform."

From this stage onward cuneiform script could be employed to set down languages of any type; both Semitic dialects like Akkadian and Indo-European tongues like Hittite and Old Persian were so written. Due to the mixture of ideograms, syllabic phonograms, determinatives, and other complications the number of individual signs was much larger than in an alphabetic form of writing. The earliest Sumerian script had perhaps 2000 symbols, but eventually 500 basic signs sufficed. Each of these, though considerably simplified over the years, remained so complicated that only professional scribes commonly wrote in the ancient Near East. Writing was an arcane mystery down to Greek times.

The earliest Sumerian tablets are very difficult to comprehend. Largely, though not entirely, they are temple accounts: "so many sheep, so many goats"; or "to so-and-so, beer and bread for one day." If we place them against the much larger bulk of written documents which had appeared by the end of the third millennium, it is nonetheless possible to gain precious light upon early Sumerian thought. The main characteristics of this outlook appeared very swiftly and were essentially fixed as the main lines of Mesopotamian civilization over the next 2500 years. Yet we can also observe that the structure of this outlook became ever more complicated and advanced. The "black-headed people," as the Sumerians called themselves, affected greatly their Semitic neighbors and followers, reaching on up through the Fertile Crescent, and were in turn influenced from the outside.

To a modern observer the pattern of thought which developed in third-millennium Mesopotamia is marked by its formal, outwardly static, and religious qualities. In the Sumerian view their arts and crafts had been "revealed" to them by the gods above and were unchanging. Everything must have its name to assure its place in the universe, and one who knew the true name of something had a power over it. Among the earliest Sumerian documents are lists of stones, animals, plants, and the like, classified on their outward characteristics. Yet these lists, which students probably learned by heart, reflect the fact that men were deliberately analyzing and imposing abstract order upon the materials of nature. We must not make the mistake of underestimating the tremendous achievements of these first civilized thinkers merely because their approach was so different from our own; indeed, they created many of the basic tools of thought and concepts we take for granted.

It was now, for instance, necessary to count and to write down numbers; Mesopotamian arithmetic was based sometimes on units of 10, sometimes on units of 60. The latter style, which through its fractions gives us our division of the hour and of the circle, was eventually used especially in astronomy, where men charted the major constellations still marked on modern sky-charts. By the first millennium Mesopotamian scholars began a tradition of ever more refined, precise, and abstract thinking and evolved a concept of place-value notation which was the root of our number system. Civilization also required the measurement and weighing of quantities of grain and metals; the chief weight, a talent of 60 minas, remained the standard quantity on down through the Greek era. Geometry began in the measurement of fields and the requirements of building. The year was solar but was defined in 12 lunar months, with an intercalary month inserted about every 3 years, to fix the great religious festivals and so to regulate agricultural activity.

The arts also progressed. The use of mudbrick and baked brick produced heavy, massive architecture, in which true arches and vaults were developed. To cover the ugly brick walls the Sumerians decorated their temples with bands of colored clay cones rammed into the walls and semicolumns; painted frescoes appeared later.

The gods were now visualized in human shape and were represented in statues which are, as it were, the gods themselves; for any transcendental quality was lacking. In some temples there were placed before the gods statues of the rulers, commemorating their devout piety in an equally straightforward, factual, yet reverent manner.[1] The technical problem that stone was hard to come by forced sculptors often to create seated figures and almost always to exaggerate the size of the head. Although some pieces are sharply conceived, they do not exhibit in general an intense interest in nature or a sense of human individuality. Equally significant are the many cylinder seals of men of property, carved with a representation of gods, imaginary animals, or myths. The demonic or bestial motifs that developed in this field were a rich repertoire of great influence on other Near Eastern and Greek art forms, but a modern rationalist will often feel disturbed by their suggestion that man did not yet recognize the distinctiveness of his own nature.

Early Mesopotamian Religion. Man's failure fully to recognize himself is reflected in the religious aspect of the early Mesopotamian outlook. Sumerian civilization had a very strong religious imprint. Only in the confidence born of their common belief in divine support could these men have endured the hardships and unremitting toils necessary to assure a firm foothold in the valley. Their greatest buildings, the temples, are a mighty testimonial to a human ideal; the priests who clustered

---

[1] From Early Dynastic times comes the group of 10 veined gypsum figures illustrated on Plate III, which were deliberately buried under the floor of the Abu temple at Tell Asmar. The god Abu, lord of vegetation, is the largest figure, 30 inches high, and conveys a sense of dominating power from his huge, staring eyes (of shell, with pupils of black limestone). Beside him is a mother goddess; the other figures are earthly worshipers. The artistic creation of order by abstract thinking is visible in the truncated cone of the kilts and the squareness of the bare upper bodies.

about these temples were so important that one may almost call an early Sumerian city-state a theocracy.

The character of this religious system becomes more apparent once there are written copies of Mesopotamian myths and artistic representations of the gods and heroes. To the inhabitants of Mesopotamia the gods were many, for they represented the forces which drove mankind; and in primitive thought these forces were many, distinct in origin. Yet the gods were grouped in a regular pantheon.

Highest was An, the divine force, which could be visualized in the over-arching bowl of Heaven; his name meant "sky" or "shining." Then came Enlil, the active force of nature, who at times manifested himself in the raging storms of the plains, and at other times aided men. The goddess of earth was worshiped as Nin-khursag and under other names. Last of the four creator gods came Enki, the god of waters who fertilized the ground, and by extension became the patron of the skills of wisdom. To these were added 50 "great gods" who met in the assembly of the gods, the Annunaki; a host of other deities, demons, and the like also floated in the Mesopotamian spiritual world.

To the Sumerians their physical environment had come into being from a primordial chaos of water, whence the forces Tiamat and Abzu arose and, by processes of procreation, created the gods. Thereafter came the sky, the earth, and finally mankind. In the spring of each year occurred the greatest religious festival of the land, known as the Akitu in later Babylonia. This was the New Year's feast, an 11-day ceremony of gloom and purification and then of joy, which ended as the gods set the lots for mortal men during the coming year. On the fourth day of the festival the priests recited a myth of the creation, called from its opening words *enuma elish:*

> When on high the heaven had not been named,
> Firm ground below had not been called by name . . .
> No reed hut had been matted, no marsh land had appeared.[2]

Beside this ritual myth many other tales evolved to explain the nature of life. The underlying scheme of thought expressed therein postulated that the world was the product of conscious divine action for divine

[2] Tr. E. A. Speiser, in *Ancient Near Eastern Texts Relating to the Old Testament,* ed. J. B. Pritchard (Princeton: Princeton University Press, 1950), pp. 60–61.

purposes; obvious, too, is the feeling that the world was all animate. Throughout ancient times, down to and past the rise of Christianity, mankind could not quite divest itself of the idea that trees, springs, and the like were endowed with human characteristics or were directed by manlike immortals. In Mesopotamia, as elsewhere, religion not only bound together society but also assured to man the fertility of his fields, his flocks, and himself. One of the greatest figures in Mesopotamian myth was the goddess of human fertility, Inanna (later Ishtar), who may in root have gone back to the Neolithic female figurines found in Halafian levels. Her descent to the underworld and then her return symbolized the renewal of agricultural life; her husband Dumuzi (later Tammuz) went permanently to the nether regions as a substitute for her. Each year he was mourned, and his marriage with Inanna was celebrated at the New Year's feast.

To modern men, who approach these early myths from a scientific point of view, the tales of the gods are neither sensible nor logical, and the view of life which they express in their repetitious verse is basically a primitive one of gross action and elemental passions. In explaining the nature of the universe men translated into divine terms their own earthly concepts of personal clash and procreation. Yet in early civilized societies these tales were so satisfying that people all over the Near East accepted them. Mesopotamian stories thus passed into the early chapters of the Book of Genesis, where they continued to answer men's curiosity about the Creation down to the past century.

Place of Man. The gods, though human in appearance, paid little attention to mortal men as they drank and made merry, and also wrangled and abused each other in the divine assemblies. Men feared and honored the gods; each city-state was but the earthly domain of certain divine forces on high, for whose ease men toiled throughout their lives. Once dead, men and women could expect only to go to a shadowy, gray land of departed spirits. Such views befitted a land that had recently raised itself to the level of civilization by hard labor, where the climate was severe, where the dangers of flood and sudden disease were ever present, inexplicable, and incurable by human means.

Yet two further reflections may be made. In the first place, the spiritual world of early Mesopotamia was an orderly structure, within which men could operate in a rational fashion; the gods could be propitiated by their human servants through the creation of divine ceremonies. Again, mankind could not quite forget that *it* was the agent that built and tilled, even though human society was far from perfect. In part this hidden realization led to a nagging fear that men might be upsetting an order laid down by the gods. One myth thus depicted the gods, angered by the clamor of men, sending down the Flood; other myths seem akin to the Hebrew story of the Fall of Man from a primitive grace and leisure through his own unwillingness to be passive. In part, however, men were proud of their achievements. A prime reflection of this point of view is the myth of Gilgamesh.

The Gilgamesh Epic. The tale of the hero Gilgamesh, two-thirds god in origin, had Sumerian roots but was more fully formulated into a continuous epic about 2000 B.C. Then it spread all over the Near East and long exercised men's imagination; one artistic symbol drawn from it, that of Gilgamesh strangling a lion, was handed down age after age until it appeared on medieval cathedrals in Western Europe.

Unlike the other myths, which were largely theological creations associated with certain rituals, this epic was centered on human figures. Essentially it was a mighty reflection on the nature of man, who strives and creates but in the end must die. Gilgamesh himself was a legendary king of Uruk, who built its great wall but treated his subjects so harshly that the gods created a wild man, Enkidu, to subdue him. Gilgamesh, wily as well as harsh, did not meet Enkidu head-on, but sent out a harlot, who by her arts tamed Enkidu — this taming we may perhaps take as an exemplification of the passage of mankind to civilization. "Become like a man," Enkidu put on clothing and went forth to protect the cattle against lions and wolves. The bulk of the epic then recounts the heroic adventures of Gilgamesh and Enkidu against various inhuman monsters:

> Who, my friends, [says Gilgamesh] is superior to death?
> Only the gods live forever under the sun.
> As for mankind, numbered are their days;
> Whatever they achieve is but the wind![3]

So, while they lived, let them at least make a name for themselves.

During the course of these exploits Enkidu offended the gods (espe-

---

[3] Tr. E. A. Speiser, in *Ancient Near Eastern Texts,* p. 79.

cially Ishtar), and died after a long death-bed scene of recrimination against divine decrees. Gilgamesh first lamented, then set out to seek the plant of eternal life so that he might bring his friend back to life. Eventually Gilgamesh made his way to Ut-napishtim, the original Noah, who told him the story of the Flood and advised him how to get the miraculous plant under the sea. Although Gilgamesh succeeded in his quest, on his return journey he lost the plant to a snake. The dead, in sum, cannot be brought back to life.

When later we come to Greek civilization we shall meet another half-divine hero, Achilles, who fought in the war against Troy and there lost his friend Patroclus; and at that point we shall be able to compare the essential qualities of two different civilizations, the Greek and the Mesopotamian, as reflected in their great epics, the tale of Gilgamesh and the *Iliad*. Here it may be observed that in the earlier tale the story is balder and has less artistic unity; it is more naive, far earthier (especially in the harlot scenes). Monsters are prominent in the plot of Gilgamesh's adventures, and the appeal is rather to emotion and passion than to reason, as is that of the *Iliad*.

In both epics the divine plane determines earthly events, though men have freedom to oppose the gods; but the heroes of the *Iliad* are more strongly characterized and are far more optimistic. Mesopotamian pride in human achievements went hand in hand with fear for human audacity. Men must cling closely to their fellow men on earth and must appease the jealous gods carefully. The individualism of Homer's heroes, their ability to accept human fate while yet enjoying life, their passionate curiosity and delight in the physical world — these were qualities which did not exist in early, god-fearing Mesopotamia. Yet in saying so much, in an effort to relate the alien world of Gilgamesh to a world that most of us know far better, we must not depreciate the earlier epic too much. Poetically it was a magnificent creation, and psychologically it reflects a truly civilized meditation upon the qualities of mankind.

THE RESULTS OF CIVILIZATION

Rise of Classes (3000–2000 B.C.). That the early Mesopotamian outlook had at times a gloomy cast the modern historian can well understand. Not only did the fabrication of civilization itself impose terrific social burdens upon its human creators, but also the subsequent developments during the third millennium resulted in disturbing changes.

This evolution must be considered, if only briefly, in any sketch of early Mesopotamian civilization, for the structure of society had been greatly elaborated by the time of Hammurapi (1700); therewith, inevitably, the outlook of the Mesopotamian world was modified in important particulars. Although the documents available at the present time are not yet adequate to trace the political history of the third millennium in detail, it is amazing — and instructive — to see even dimly the rise of many critical problems which have been enduring issues in all subsequent civilized societies. Social classes, for example, became differentiated. Economic exploitation and social unrest inevitably followed hard upon this differentiation; law developed both to regulate social and economic relationships and to prevent undue oppression. Interstate warfare appeared and led to imperialism, which in turn produced military classes and bureaucratic systems to run the larger states born of conquest.

The first cities seem to have been masses of relatively undifferentiated fellow workers who were tightly grouped in an economic and spiritual unity. Separate classes, however, evolved rather quickly. Toward the top were the priests, who also worked in the early days but tended to become managers on behalf of the gods; the temples grew into powerful economic centers, which owned much of the land and absorbed a large part of the product in rents and temple dues. The records of Baba, divine consort of the main god of Lagash, show that her priests directed about one-sixth of the farm land of the city-state in the Early Dynastic period. Half of this domain was rented out to peasants, who paid their dues at the rate of one-third to one-sixth of the yield and also owed sums in silver, which they obtained by selling other parts of their produce in the city. The second half of her domain was cultivated by the labor of the peasants, organized in guilds under foremen. The goddess also controlled large flocks, shipping craft, fishermen, brewers, bakers, and spinners of wool; the growth in industrial production in Early Dynastic times, which was remarkable, was largely for purposes of cult as well as for military use and for the kings and their henchmen. The raw materials needed from outside Mesopotamia were obtained by merchants, who trafficked by sea, by river, and by land for stone, metals, wood, incenses, and jewels.

Beside and above the priests rose the king or *lugal*. In later views kingship "was lowered from heaven by the gods" as a guarantee of earthly order. Palaces began to appear; the tomb of one queen of Ur, about 2500 B.C., astounded the modern world with its wealth of delicate jewelry, its harps, and the masses of sacrificed servants. To conclude that the kings and priests were simply parasites would be unjust, for these upper elements held together the state, harbored its reserves, and expanded its strength. Yet they did draw profit from their superior position, and the rest of society now fell into a dependent status.

One mark of this situation is the appearance of slavery. Some men were forced to sell themselves or their children into bondage through the workings of debt; others were captives, especially from the hilly country to the east. While the reduction of human beings to the legal level of chattels always has a distorting influence upon social relationships, morals, and general views of human nature, its effects must be assessed soberly. In the present case, the institution of slavery was but the extreme edge of the fact that the leisure of the upper classes and the great monuments of early times rested upon the forced labor of the multitude and otherwise would have been impossible. In other words, civilization was not lightly bought and did not directly benefit all men alike. Most of the labor force, however, in Mesopotamia as in other slave-holding societies of the ancient world consisted of technically free men. Slaves were rarely used in agriculture, the main occupation of mankind throughout the ancient world; rather, slaves lived in cities, where they were domestic servants, concubines, and artisans. As valuable pieces of capital, slaves were usually accorded a minimum standard of human needs, and at times were able to rise again into freedom through hard work.

More significant, socially and politically, than the appearance of slavery was the depression of the tribal farmers into the position of peasants, from whom the machinery of state and religion extorted a large part of their product. Whether they lived in village or city, the peasants bought, sold, and borrowed in markets that were dominated by other elements. Patterns of civilization tended to bifurcate into upper and lower levels. The unlettered lower classes remained more conservative and sank into distrust of the "city ways" of their betters; the upper classes began to crystallize modes of exploitation and to accompany these with an assumption of cultural superiority. In yet another aspect differentiation became evident socially, in the relation of the sexes. Although the position of women was still so high in Sumerian days that they could buy and sell property, their independence tended to wane rather than to rise as civilization progressed.

Codes of Law. Society cannot endure if exploitation becomes too widespread. Out of the murky distance of 4000 years ago rise outcries against oppression and injustice which sound like those of yesterday and of today; the result was the first great effort to bring justice through law and thus to protect the rights of man. Already by about 2275 the first reformer in history had appeared, the *ensi* Urukagina of Lagash, who boasted that he took away the prerogatives of the foreman and officials and contracted with the city gods not to deliver up orphans and widows to men of power. Urukagina, alas, could not reverse the current of social differentiation and fell before a neighboring king, Lugalzaggisi of Umma. Further efforts at reform and regularization of men's relations with each other produced in succeeding centuries one law code after another; the most famous of these, the laws established by Hammurapi, we shall inspect shortly.

War and Imperialism. Throughout the land of Sumer and Akkad the "black-headed men" shared an essentially common way of life. Politically, however, they were divided into independent city-states, which easily fell to war with each other. Some causes of war were economic, in the form of searches for raw materials and quarrels over canals and small bits of arable land. Historical records show over five or six generations such a debate concerning territory on the frontiers of Umma and Lagash, which lay on the same branch of the Euphrates. Struggles of this type gave rise to the cynical proverb, "You go and carry off the enemy's land; the enemy comes and carries off your land."[4]

Battles were also visualized as struggles between the gods of the respective cities, who gained or lost glory as the heavy chariots and serried infantry of their earthly servants won or fled. One of the earliest artistic monuments of Mesopotamia depicts on one side of a stone the victorious troops of Eannatum of Lagash marching over the prostrate bodies of the army of Umma, while vultures and lions devour the corpses; and on the other side the god of Lagash nets the men of Umma. Here spiritual,

---

[4] Quoted by Samuel N. Kramer, *History Begins at Sumer* (New York: Anchor A175, 1959), p. 183.

perhaps even patriotic, motives can be sensed. And a third source of the military spirit, the pride and profit gained by the military class, can be detected in a standard of victory from Ur, where the king and his warriors feast amid the booty of their conquest.

In the Early Dynastic era wars generally were waged for limited purposes and left the individual cities in a state of rough equilibrium, though some Sumerian kings spread their rule far to the north. The first great imperialist in history was the Semitic Sargon I (*c.* 2276–21), who marched into Syria; here he or a successor destroyed the native state of Ebla, recently uncovered with its huge archives. Legend told that Sargon was originally a waif left by the water's edge, became a gardener, and then rose to be king. A later, exaggerated account of his deeds asserts that "he spread his terror-inspiring glamor over all the countries. He crossed the Sea in the East and he, himself, conquered the country of the West. . . . He marched against the country of Kazalla and turned Kazalla into ruin-hills and heaps of rubble. He even destroyed there every possible perching place for a bird." [5] So began a long tradition of Near Eastern imperialism. Sargon's grandson Naramsin (*c.* 2196–60) called himself King of the Four Quarters of the World, a title which was to be held by subsequent rulers on down to Persian days. Both rulers placed before their names a star to signify their divine character.

Even this early, vengeance followed imperialism. According to legend, Akkad fell in retribution for Naramsin's sack of the great sanctuary of Enlil at Nippur. In more prosaic terms, we can detect the incursions of a wild people from the hills of Elam, the Guti, who ended the first Mesopotamian empire. For a brief time the Sumerians again gained the upper hand in the period of the Third Dynasty of Ur (*c.* 2150–1950). The economic aspects of this era are lit by a tremendous mass of contracts, records of work, and other documents. The rulers of the time, such as the *ensi* Gudea of Lagash, never tired of celebrating their piety toward the divine masters and mistresses of earthly life. The priesthoods had, to judge from our evidence, wide powers over the economic activity of the countryside; but it appears occasionally as if the kings were whittling down their holdings of land.

Age of Hammurapi (1700 B.C.). By the end of the third millennium

---

[5] Tr. A. Leo Oppenheim, in *Ancient Near Eastern Texts*, p. 266.

the Sumerian political and cultural system had lost its vigor, and a new wave of Semitic invaders from the desert, the Amorites, brought the end of its dominance. Thereafter the Sumerian language became a sacred tongue, which priests learned and preserved much as Latin has been handed on in the Catholic Church; a great Assyrian king, Ashurbanipal, paraded his ability to read "obscure Sumerian." The old city-states yielded to Babylon, a relatively new state which stood at the junction of major routes of trade at the north end of the Mesopotamian plain. Its greatest king, Hammurapi (c. 1728–1686), concentrated on providing internal justice during his first 29 years but then seized an opportunity to conquer all Mesopotamia.

The reign of Hammurapi forms in many ways the climax, and the end, of early Mesopotamian civilization. Although a Semitic tongue was now the language of the land, the learning, the arts, and the myths of the preceding Sumerian millennium formed the base of culture. The epic of Gilgamesh had been consolidated in a lasting form; the Creation Epic was now recited at the New Year's festival of Marduk and celebrated the beneficent force of this deity, who eventually became the greatest god of Babylonia. Mathematics had advanced to the drawing up of extensive multiplication tables, tables of square and cube roots, and the use of virtually algebraic equations. The Pythagorean theorem was known; astronomers recorded for several years the appearances and disappearances of Venus to provide raw materials for state omens. Men's questioning of the nature of the world had proceeded to such a point that they could brood on the fact the just did not always prosper. An epic of the Righteous Sufferer strikes much the same note as does the Book of Job in Hebrew literature.

While it is still far too early to speak of individualism, the concept had evolved that each man could have a little god as personal protector, to whom he could pray as intercessor in his individual problems; and in other respects the tight communal patterns of the past had yielded greatly. The merchant by the time of Hammurapi was largely an independent agent, trading with his fellows in guilds far and wide under the protection of his state. Land was often held in personal ownership, especially by the military class which formed a main support for the monarchy; by this time the priesthoods had certainly lost some of their economic power and control of the judicial machinery. The society of the early second millennium was far more complicated in organization and in motive forces than that of the first cities.

Over all stood the righteous king Hammurapi. A great mass of his correspondence has survived and shows his unremitting supervision of the bureaucracy which had risen to direct the larger unit of government now customary. The ruler boasted his maintenance of the canals, defense of the land, and protection of justice in proud terms,

> I rooted out the enemy above and below;
> I made an end of war;
> I promoted the welfare of the land;
> I made the peoples rest in friendly habitations;
> I did not let them have anyone to terrorize them . . .
> I have governed them in peace;
> I have sheltered them in my strength.[6]

Most famous of all is his lengthy code of laws, carved on a great basalt slab; this was carted off by later Elamite conquerors to Susa, where it was excavated in 1901. Its 282 sections do not form a full set of laws, but may represent the king's innovations. Punishments for crimes were distinguished by three classes; to give one example,

> If a noble has broken another noble's bone, they shall break his bone. If he has destroyed the eye of a commoner (*mush-kenum,* whence the French word *mesquin* derives through the Arabic) or has broken the bone of a commoner, he shall pay one mina of silver. If he has destroyed the eye of a noble's slave or broken the bone of a noble's slave, he shall pay one-half his value.[7]

Vengeance thus was now on the principle of an eye for an eye unlike in earlier Sumerian codes, which calculated punishments in money payments. Women, though still relatively independent, were viewed essentially as pieces of property, especially in regard to marriage rights; but masculine arrogance had not yet reached the level of the Assyrian laws of the twelfth century B.C., which ordained that "when she deserves it, a man may pull out the hair of his wife, mutilate or twist her ears, with

---

[6] Tr. Theophile J. Meek, in *Ancient Near Eastern Texts,* p. 178.
[7] Ibid. para. 197–9, p. 175.

no liability attaching to him."[8] Many of Hammurapi's rules related directly to economic life and regulated contracts, irrigation procedures, debts (set at 33⅓ per cent interest for loans in grain, 20 per cent in silver), maximum wages, and the like. While some provisions can be traced back to earlier Sumerian codes, it is clear that the king was trying to reform economic abuses; yet court records of his day almost never cite the code itself, only briefer enactments on specific problems.

After the long reign of this powerful monarch Babylonia again fell to pieces, and thus opened itself once more to external invasion. The earlier particularistic tendencies of the Mesopotamian city-states were not easily to be overcome; and Babylonia itself rarely had any major political significance thenceforth. To go further at this point, however, would lead us into the main stream of the second millennium b.c., which must be considered in Chapter 4.

Conclusion. If we look back, rather than forward, the story of man's advance in Mesopotamia from the first Neolithic villages of the valley down to the age of Hammurapi must strike us as one of the most amazing achievements of mankind. Despite the difficulties of climate and terrain the settlers had harnessed their energies toward a remarkable physical progress, and the compact masses of population which now dotted lower Mesopotamia were far larger than had ever before been possible.

Within these units the progress in political, religious, and intellectual aspects had been equally swift. Civilization brought with it serious problems, but the advances are even more significant. When we turn to the other great civilization of the early Near East, that of Egypt, we shall see that the land of the Nile in part pursued the same path but in other respects reached quite different solutions to the social and political needs of civilized man.

BIBLIOGRAPHY

Sources. In early Mesopotamian history the physical evidence remains of primary importance, and grows greatly in quantity and diversity as civilization emerges. Archeological research in the area began at Assyrian sites, from 1842 on, and slowly moved into the earlier stages of

[8] Ibid. para. 59, p. 185.

development. The Sumerians have come into the light mainly in the last half-century; only since World War II have the very earliest levels been analyzed. While cities long forgotten have been resurrected from the mounds of Mesopotamia, no single site has been completely excavated; and many remain to be explored. C. L. Woolley describes one famous site in *Ur of the Chaldees* (rev. ed.; Harmondsworth: Penguin A27, 1950); Seton Lloyd, *The Archeology of Mesopotamia from the Old Stone Age to the Persian Conquest* (London: Thames and Hudson, 1978), discusses the most famous excavations.

Written documents are few for the Protoliterate and Early Dynastic eras, then become more common. Some 250,000 Sumerian texts have been found thus far, though most are not yet published; over 95 per cent of these arise out of the economic side of life. Such contracts, bills of sale, and the like, are fairly easy to read, but myths are more difficult; the most famous may be found in N. K. Sanders, *The Epic of Gilgamesh* (Harmondsworth: Penguin L100, 1960), and in greater detail in J. H. Tigay, *Evolution of the Gilgamesh Epic* (Philadelphia: University of Pennsylvania Press, 1982). Other myths and the laws are available in James B. Pritchard, ed., *Ancient Near Eastern Texts Relating to the Old Testament* (3d ed.; Princeton: Princeton University Press, 1969); A. Leo Oppenheim, *Letters from Mesopotamia* (Chicago: University of Chicago Press, 1967), gives mostly later material.

Translation of cuneiform scripts was initially made possible by the study of Persian inscriptions which were carved on cliffs in Old Persian, Elamite, and Babylonian parallel versions. By 1802 George F. Grotefend (1775–1853) had broken down Persian royal names written in cuneiform. Henry Rawlinson (1810–95) copied the most famous Persian inscription, that of Behistun, in 1835–37 and 1847 and proceeded further in the decipherment first of the Persian, then of the Babylonian versions. Great public interest in Mesopotamian myths followed the publication by George Smith in 1872 of an Assyrian version of the Flood story (in the epic of Gilgamesh).

Mesopotamian chronology must be determined by dating events backward from the first millennium B.C. through the use of ancient lists of kings and other careful calculations. The date of Hammurapi, which has recently been lowered two centuries, is now approximately fixed. From that point can be estimated the period of Sargon I, but earlier history is dated very approximately. Scholars still vary between a little before 3000 or about 2850 for the origins of political history in Egypt and Mesopotamia; I have here followed the earlier chronology.

Further Reading. The passage to civilization is thoughtfully but briefly described by Henri Frankfort, *Birth of Civilization in the Near East* (New York: Barnes and Noble, 1968); in greater detail by James Mellaart, *The Neolithic of the Near East* (New York: Scribner's, 1976) and *Earliest Civilizations of the Near East* (New York: McGraw-Hill, 1966). Rushton Coulborn, *Origin of Civilized Societies* (Princeton: Princeton University Press, 1969), and R. M. Adam, *The Evolution of Urban Society* (Chicago: Aldine, 1966), are comparative studies; E. R. Service, *Origins of the State and Civilization* (New York: Norton, 1975), is a widely accepted anthropological model.

S. N. Kramer has written a number of general studies on the Sumerians, including *Sumerian Mythology* (Philadelphia: University of Pennsylvania Press, 1972), *History Begins at Sumer* (Philadelphia: University of Pennsylvania Press, 1981), and *The Sumerians: Their History, Culture, and Character* (Chicago: University of Chicago Press, 1971). Extremely valuable is H. Frankfort and others, *The Intellectual Adventure of Ancient Man* (Chicago: University of Chicago Press, 1977). A. Parrot, *Sumer: The Dawn of Art* (New York: Golden Press, 1961), and A. Moortgat, *The Art of Ancient Mesopotamia* (London: Phaidon, 1969), are handsomely illustrated.

T. Jacobsen, *The Treasures of Darkness* (New Haven: Yale University Press, 1976), is a thoughtful study of Mesopotamian religion; for other works on art and religion see General Bibliography (Ancient Near East). The fascinating discovery of Ebla is described by P. Matthiae, *Ebla* (Garden City, N.Y.: Doubleday, 1981).

3

EARLY EGYPT

In recent decades archeologists have generally agreed that lower Mesopotamia was the first area of the world to advance into civilization. The emergence of Egypt onto the same level, however, took place very little later and in its roots was probably an independent step.

It is fascinating and instructive to compare these neighboring civilizations. Both proceeded from roughly the same type of Neolithic base. In both the fundamental geographic factors were very similar. Although Egypt lies in Africa, it was connected far more to the Fertile Crescent than to its adjacent continent. As a result the civilized outlooks of early Mesopotamia and early Egypt shared major common characteristics, which continued to persist in later ages. Yet as we look at the main stages of Egyptian progress down to about 1700 B.C., we shall also find marked differences from Mesopotamia in many respects of political organization, religious views, and esthetic spirit. Some of these divergencies may be attributed to minor variations in geography and climate; but others cannot be so simply explained. Wherever men have risen to civilization, their outlook has taken on a distinctive flavor.

Since Egypt abuts on the Mediterranean Sea, its ancient wonders have always been known and marveled at by the other civilized societies which have fronted on this sea. From the days of Greece and Rome on down to modern times the civilization of the land of the Nile has exercised an influence directly upon western civilization; for most of us

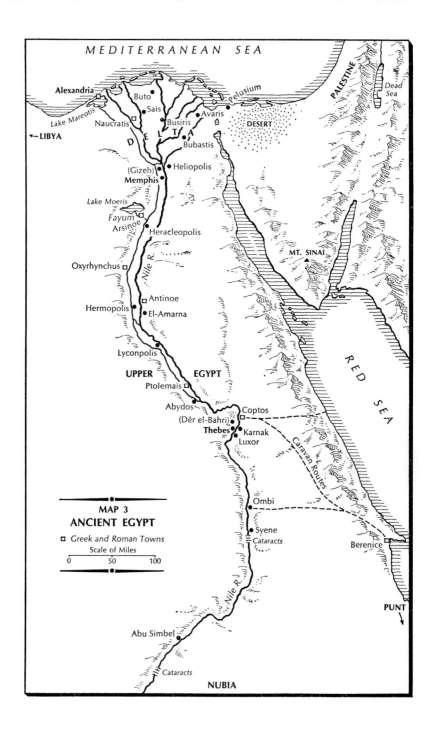

MEDITERRANEAN SEA

PALESTINE

Dead Sea

Alexandria

Buto

Sais

Busiris

Avaris

Pelusium

Lake Mareotis

Naucratis

DESERT

← LIBYA

D E L T A

Bubastis

(Gizeh)

Heliopolis

Memphis

Lake Moeris

Fayum

Arsinoe

Heracleopolis

MT. SINAI

Oxyrhynchus

Nile R.

Antinoe

Hermopolis

El-Amarna

Lyconpolis

RED SEA

UPPER EGYPT

Ptolemais

Abydos

Coptos

(Dêr el-Bahri)

Thebes

Karnak

Luxor

Caravan Routes

MAP 3
ANCIENT EGYPT

□ Greek and Roman Towns

Scale of Miles

0   50   100

Ombi

Syene

Cataracts

Berenice

Nile R.

PUNT

Abu Simbel

Cataracts

NUBIA

the pyramids and pharaohs of Egypt seem more understandable than the *ziggurats* and *lugals* of Mesopotamia. Nonetheless this fact does not mean that later ages necessarily drew more on Egypt than on Mesopotamia. Each contributed much to the history of the ancient Near East and so to the subsequent civilized societies of Greece and Rome; but of the two the lasting influence of Mesopotamia was almost surely the greater.

EMERGENCE OF EGYPTIAN CIVILIZATION

Geographical Framework of the Nile Valley. When the first great Greek historian Herodotus sailed down from his simple, poverty-stricken homeland to visit Egypt, he was fascinated by its pyramids and other great monuments and felt as much awe before its age-old civilization as did the later Greek philosopher, Plato. In Herodotus' geographical description of Egypt occurs a famous phrase, "the gift of the Nile," which well sums up the great geographical fact about Egypt.

The Nile river rises in the lakes of equatorial Africa and the highlands of Ethiopia and flows generally northward down a great earth-fault. Seven hundred and fifty miles from the sea it breaks over the last of six rocky ledges or cataracts; from that point the muddy, yellow stream slips slowly, without interruption, through a narrow valley almost 600 miles to the Delta, where it branches out in several mouths (see Map 3). The valley (called Upper Egypt) and the delta (Lower Egypt) have about 12,500 square miles of cultivable land which can be watered. The annual floods in later summer and fall (the occurrence of which baffled the Greeks) are far more useful than those in Mesopotamia; the Nile brings water but also leaches out the salt from the fields. A heavy population could be supported once men had learned to extend the watered area by short canals and basins. Rain falls only in the Delta, but even here is insignificant.

The Nile furnished not only water but also a fine artery of communication which encouraged an early and lasting political unification. Egypt was relatively isolated by the cataracts to the south and the Mediterranean to the north. On either side are deserts, which come down red and bleak to the very edge of the black, irrigated land; almost all the area which is marked Egypt on a map is completely uninhabitable. The cultivated strip throughout most of Egypt can be only 4 to 13 miles wide, but in it the population tends to be virtually continuous. Accordingly men dwelt in villages rather than in cities of the Mesopotamian type; their mudbrick hovels were almost always located just off the cultivated fields so as not to lose any useful land.

While the lot of the Egyptian farmer was one of hard work, his life was considerably more secure than was that of a Mesopotamian peasant; and the Egyptian outlook had a tone of confidence and even enjoyment in life which was quite unknown in the land of Sumer and Akkad. Each day ancient Egyptians celebrated the rebirth of the sun in the east, God's land, and watched with sorrow its disappearance in the land of the dead to the west; each year came a great festival, the rebirth of life, as the Nile flooded and gave water and new fertility to their fields. Egypt knew three seasons: Inundation; Going Down of the Inundation, in which crops were planted; and Drought, in which the barley and wheat were harvested in March-April.

Neolithic Development in Egypt (5000–3100 B.C.). The population of ancient Egypt seems to have been a mixture of peoples who pressed in from Nubia to the south, Palestine and Syria to the north, and Libya to the west. Its language belonged basically to a linguistic group often called Hamitic, which was spoken along the north coast of Africa; but in Egyptian at least there were very strong Semitic affinities from earliest times. The first farming villages are peculiarly late, beginning in the fifth millennium along the Fayum lake and then by the edge of the upper Nile valley; closer to the river was a land of marshes and sand banks where papyrus reeds flourished and fierce animals like the crocodile and hippopotamus held sway. The steady process of desiccation along the north African coast made the highlands ever more arid even after historic times had begun and thus drove people toward the sure source of water represented by the Nile. Yet only after 4000 were the farmers confident enough of their techniques and social organization to start taming the fertile fields by the river.

Then came the same onrush which occurred in Mesopotamia. The swift rise of Egypt across the fourth millennium is marked by successive cultures which are called the Badarian, the Amratian, and especially the Gerzean. Systematic draining of swamps, the regular use of copper, the construction of boats from papyrus bundles, the very fine working of even such hard stones as basalt and porphyry into vases — all betoken a great growth of skills and increase in population.

While most of this development stemmed from purely native roots, there is strong testimony that styles in pottery and tool-making were interconnected between Palestine and Egypt and that in the Gerzean period Semitic-speaking invaders from Asia entered the land. In the later stages of this era (c. 3250 B.C.) an even more intriguing event occurred, for a brief flurry of Mesopotamian influence, of Uruk type, made itself felt. Among the tokens of this influence are the presence of cylinder seals, construction in brick, and ships shaped in Mesopotamian form. The Egyptians may even have gained the idea of writing from the east, but the actual symbols they used were certainly of native origin. We cannot determine the route of contacts, though the spread of Uruk pottery through Syria suggests a Mediterranean route. On the even more critical problem, the extent to which the appearance of civilization in Egypt was stimulated by contact with another advanced area, our evidence thus far scarcely permits a dogmatic answer.

Union of Egypt (*about* 3100 B.C.). On the whole the men who dwelt by the Nile probably needed very little encouragement from the outside to break across the subtle barrier which separated civilization from their advanced Neolithic ways. Legends which survived into later times suggest that the valley and the Delta first came together into small principalities called nomes; in historic times there were 22 nomes in Upper Egypt and 20 in Lower Egypt. Then, apparently, the two areas united under separate kings. The last step, which came at the beginning of the civilized era, was the creation of a unified kingdom by Menes. This event is usually assigned to about 3100, though some scholars wish to lower it to about 2850.

The long centuries of Egyptian history that followed are conventionally divided into the Protodynastic stage, to 2700; the Old Kingdom, 2700–2200; the First Intermediate period, 2200–2052; the Middle Kingdom, 2052–1786; the Second Intermediate period, 1786–1575; the New Kingdom, 1575–1087; and the Post-Empire era (see Table 2 in Chapter 2). In Egyptian memory the history of the land was organized by dynasties of kings, which might or might not be related. These dynasties extended from Menes of the First Dynasty down to the Thirty-first Dynasty in 332, when Alexander the Great conquered the land.

THE OLD KINGDOM

Protodynastic Stage (3100-2700 B.C.). In the Protodynastic era civilization became firmly established in Egypt as the political structure of the land was unified in the hands of the king. The population and physical resources at his disposal rose greatly as life became more secure; probably irrigation was also expanded widely. A well-defined, rounded outlook on life emerged with remarkable speed and stamped all aspects of culture, religion, and politics. The height of this unified system is called the Old Kingdom proper (Third through Sixth Dynasties).

To a modern observer the most appealing aspect of early Egyptian civilization is its art, and here we can sense most easily the particular qualities of the outlook shared by the inhabitants of the Nile valley. Further light can be gained from looking at Egyptian views on afterlife, the royal despotism, and the religious pattern.

Arts of the Old Kingdom (2700–2200 B.C.). A modern visitor to Egypt often feels that the most widely spread and the most satisfying form of early Egyptian art is its style of writing. Hieroglyphic script, as this style is called from Greek words meaning "sacred carving," covered the walls of tombs and temples alike in stately rows of stylized, repetitious symbols. From the artistic point of view these inscriptions are a truly elegant decoration, as well as serving as a means of conveying religious texts and praises of the rulers and their aides. Egyptian scribes used a complex combination of ideograms and phonetic signs (phonograms) with determinatives required to indicate to what class of objects a word belonged; even signs for single consonants appear. Frequently words were expressed both pictorially and phonetically, and the direction of writing varied according to the requirements of space and symmetry. Partly because the scribes along the Nile wrote on paper made from papyrus as well as carved on stone, their writing remained more pictorial than did cuneiform script, though a more cursive style (called hieratic) also developed. But the conservatism of ancient Egypt and the esthetic sense of its inhabitants combined to preserve the use of the formal hieroglyphic symbols in state documents.

The depth of artistic feeling in any civilization is reflected in the way its utilitarian objects are designed. The same spirit which one may find in Egyptian writing is visible also in its furniture, vases, game-boards, jewelry, and a host of luxurious items buried in the tombs. These were made from the hardest of stone, from ivory, from glass, and from many other substances by patient workmen who knew a host of skillful techniques; the patterns are graceful, delicate, and also static over many centuries. Beside these minor arts, however, there occurs also developed work in painting, sculpture, and architecture.

The inscriptions which march across the limestone walls of Old Kingdom tombs often explain — or are in turn illuminated by — several rows of pictures in lightly raised relief, accentuated by color. The subjects of these scenes are often, especially in tombs, drawn from life. Peasants till the fields and harvest their ample crops; nobles hunt and fish; flocks of animals and vases loaded with food abound; feasts are depicted in graphic detail. To a modern spectator the fascinating panorama of activities and the artistic spirit of the pictures furnish a vivid introduction to Egyptian culture about 5000 years ago. Comical scenes, even jokes, appear. But the purpose of this work was a mixture of magic and religion; the pictures were to provide the dead with a view of human life and with earthly luxuries in the next world.

True sculpture appears in the statues of the dead. Since these figures were believed to contain some part of the soul of the departed and were so placed as to "receive" the food and drink offered to the dead, sculptors often worked in very hard, lasting types of stone as well as in more easily carved wood. The face of the subject was depicted in a realistic fashion, but the general intent was to incarnate the dead man in a static pose which would reflect a quality of eternal security. Some of the greatest Egyptian sculpture came very early, before society had set that pattern of rigid conventions which dominated all later Egyptian arts. The sculptors were, on the whole, far more interested in the physical world and in reality than Sumerian artists ever dreamed of being.[1]

The requirements of conventionality, however, limited their experiments. Even in the best work very primitive conceptual views still reflect

[1] The slate statue of Menkaure and his queen illustrated on Plate IV was found in the king's valley temple. Menkaure (Mycerinus in Greek tradition) built the last and smallest of the three great pyramids (Fourth Dynasty). This work, which lacks its final polishing, suggests the amazing achievements of the first Egyptian sculptors in its tranquil firmness; interesting, too, is the appearance of true affection.

the limited intellectual analysis possible in Egyptian civilization. Bodies are stiffly posed in standing or seated posture and have a cubical form. In reliefs the sense of composition is very limited; and here human bodies are normally contorted: the lower body is shown is side view, the torso is turned frontally, and the head is in profile. The imagination of Egyptian artists was of a very matter-of-fact type.

Our knowledge of the houses and palaces of the Old Kingdom is extremely limited, for they were built of mudbrick. The abodes of the dead are another matter, particularly after they came to be made of stone, and provide a wealth of information on architecture as well as other arts. In the Neolithic period the dead had been buried in holes lined with mats and were accompanied by their most valued possessions. Then came brick-lined burial chambers, crowned by *mastabas* or bench-like superstructures designed to protect the supplies for the dead ruler and to serve as a temple for his cult. From these, apparently, developed the more impressive works in stone, a substance reserved for tombs and temples. The preservation of the actual corpse was a serious matter for the king especially, and royal graves became amazingly complicated in the Old Kingdom. Already by the Third Dynasty the ruler Zoser (*c.* 2700) had his famous architect Imhotep build a step pyramid 204 feet high, made of small squared stones and located at the edge of the desert near the capital, Memphis. This great mound was accompanied by a majestic courtyard, which was adorned with engaged stone columns in the shape of reed bundles and also with subsidiary buildings, including a mortuary temple for the continuing worship of the dead ruler.

Within 75 years the kings of the Fourth Dynasty had progressed to the construction of the famous pyramids of Gizeh a few miles north of the step pyramid of Zoser; these were built of huge stone blocks encased by a smooth limestone exterior. The most mammoth of these monuments, the pyramid of Khufu (*c.* 2600), contained almost 6,000,000 tons of stone in a structure 481 feet high. The rock base of this pyramid did not vary in elevation more than half an inch; its orientation is almost precisely aligned with the points of the compass; the stones were very skillfully dressed for perfect fits. Construction of this pyramid with its valley chapel, causeway, and funerary temple proper — all forming a unified complex — must have taken thousands of men years of work with barges, sledges, levers, and rollers. By and large Egyptian architecture always remained most impressive for its size; the qualities of architectural synthesis, finely detailed work, and even honest workmanship, as in making a solid foundation, are rarely present.

The First Absolutism. The pyramids reflect two important aspects of the Old Kingdom: the ability of its rulers to marshal the agricultural wealth of the land; and the development of very interesting religious concepts about afterlife. To take up first the political aspect of these conjoined forces, the king rose to become the overpowering focus of earthly life in reality as well as in the arts; as a later inscription put it, "The king of Upper and Lower Egypt is a god by whose dealings one lives, the father and mother of all men, alone by himself, without equal." [2] On an early macehead he is shown opening a canal; on the famous Narmer palette he is overwhelming in size as he strikes down his enemies; writing was largely used to celebrate his deeds. By the Fourth Dynasty inscriptions show in some detail the pattern of government, which has been well called undifferentiated royal absolutism. The king, that is, governed all aspects of life with the aid of a simple central administration, directed by a vizier and largely composed of his sons and other relatives. Below him, nomarchs moved from nome to nome to conduct the local administration.

The peasants were virtually serfs, registered in careful censuses and yielding their surplus in a variety of taxes and dues. Genesis 47:24 asserts that one-fifth of all the produce was owed to the government; this is probably not far from the mark. From the First Dynasty on, royal expeditions worked the turquoise and copper mines of Sinai, a main source of Egyptian metals. Other expeditions, especially in the Fifth and Sixth Dynasties, explored up the river to Nubia and along the Red Sea to Somaliland, seeking ivory, incenses, rare animals, and dwarfs; northeastward the Egyptians made their way by sea to Phoenicia for the cedars of Lebanon. Slaves were very uncommon at this time; but the free artisans worked almost solely for the king and greater nobles.

The monarch, who dwelt in a Per-ao (Pharaoh in Hebrew) or Great House, lived and died in great pomp and luxury. About his tomb stretched hundreds and thousands of graves of his attendants and officials, some of whom were slain in the First Dynasty to accompany their master; over 10,000 stone vases were found in the step pyramid of Zoser.

[2] Quoted by E. O. James, *The Ancient Gods* (New York: Putnam, 1960), p. 108.

But the ruler also had great responsibilities, which explains the willingness of his people to heap up the pyramids. He was a god on earth, who assured the rise of the Nile, the prosperity of the land, and its peace and order. The pharaoh's will was thought to become reality as soon as he had spoken. Partly for this reason Egypt never developed the written law codes of Mesopotamia; but the royal fiat was one which incarnated *ma'at* or justice. To unify itself, in sum, early Egypt took the intellectually simple approach of raising its ruler to the position of a superhuman symbol incarnated in human form. The pharaoh of the Old Kingdom was a lonely creature elevated on a great pedestal and enveloped in a maze of ceremony; about this figure revolved much of the development of religion and mythology.

Egyptian Religion. The religion of Egypt remained always a medley of so many concepts, which themselves changed over the centuries, that it is not easily defined. Each nome had a sacred totem, often in the form of an animal, and in times of unrest the nomes fought each other as bitterly in the name of these patron deities as did the Sumerian city-states. Higher yet stood a range of greater gods, who were conceived in animal as well as human shapes. The visible world had been created out of a watery waste by divine forces, who had also brought the gods into existence; and the gods governed all aspects of human life no less than did the similar deities of Mesopotamia. One of these great gods was Ptah of Memphis, whose priests fashioned a story that he had created the world. The sky was worshiped as Horus, who was a soaring falcon at times, and in yet different concepts was the son of Osiris; yet the sky could also be visualized mythologically as a cow, an ocean, a woman, and in other ways. The sun-disk came to be known principally as Re, apparently a Semitic importation whose cult centered at Heliopolis near the modern Cairo; Re became steadily more powerful from the Fourth Dynasty onward, as a combination of the forces of nature. But a host of other deities populated the Egyptian mind.

Within the common polytheistic framework there were marked differences between Egypt and Mesopotamia. The gods who watched over the land of the Nile were visualized in a far more cheerful light, partly perhaps because men worked directly for the king rather than for the gods. Their natures were less distinct and flowed into each other. Above all, the kings of the Old Kingdom held a firm control over the religious system, the priests of which were essentially his deputies for the detailed conduct of sacrifices and other ceremonies. Pharaoh was a god on earth and was related to many of the other gods. His royal title bore a "Horus name," he was visualized very literally as the son of Re, he incarnated Ptah, and on death he came to be unified with Osiris. His unfettered strength was reflected in his identification now with the wild bull, now with the swift hunting falcon. Only in the period of the New Kingdom were the priests to assert their independence, and the strength of Egypt irretrievably waned when eventually they became virtual masters of the land themselves.

Another fascinating difference between Egyptian and Mesopotamian religious views lay in the relative concepts of afterlife. In Mesopotamia, men served the gods in this life but, once dead, had only a shadowy existence. The Egyptian, on the other hand, had a very complex concept of the human soul. Accordingly he buried his dead carefully along the edge of the western desert and gradually developed detailed, graphic views of afterlife revolving about the *akh*, that part of a man which became an "excellent spirit"; the *ka*, to which funerary offerings were made; and the *ba*, a manifestation of the soul which could enter or leave the dead body. Such an emphasis does not mean that the inhabitants of the Nile valley were morbid, though religious fears did exist and became more pronounced by the time of the New Kingdom; the upper classes at least enjoyed life so much that they wished to cling to its delights, even after death. The inscriptions and pictures on the walls and the rich physical equipment buried in their tombs were designed in large part to achieve this aim.

At the beginning of history the god who conducted the dead to the world of afterlife was Anubis, who was visualized as a jackal-headed god. During the Old Kingdom the cult of Osiris rose greatly. Osiris was a legendary king, who seems to have been an embodiment of the forces of agriculture; as often happened elsewhere in the ancient Near East the fertility cults connected with farming led men on to interlinked concepts of afterlife for themselves. In the early form of his myth, Osiris was killed by his wicked brother Seth — who at times symbolized the desert — and his corpse was thrown in the Nile. His wife Isis rescued and temporarily resuscitated him so that he might sire a child by her; this was Horus, who eventually secured a trial of Seth and became king in

Egypt. Osiris passed to the underworld where he was ruler and admitted the dead to his realm after testing their conduct during life on earth; in the New Kingdom he is depicted at times as weighing the soul of a dead man against a feather to see if it were light enough of earthly misdeeds.

In addition to ritual celebrations every year of the deeds of Osiris an enormous mass of burial practices and religious customs grew up to protect the dead on their trip to the next world. While the nobles who were buried about the pyramids of the Old Kingdom rulers might thus hope to secure afterlife, only the king himself at that time could become unified with Osiris. To secure this end the Pyramid Texts of the Fifth and Sixth Dynasties gave extensive magical spells and advice on entry into the world to come.

Literature and the Sciences. To round out a picture of Egyptian civilization in the Old Kingdom one must place beside its artistic, political, and religious aspects the literary and scientific attainments of the age. In these latter fields, however, Egyptian progress was very limited.

The arts, as we have seen, were stimulated by the rise of royal absolutism and the evolution of views on afterlife and were to have considerable effects across the ancient Near East in the second and first millennia B.C. These motive forces played much less directly on other fields. Having evolved the figure of the pharaoh, the practical Egyptians did not feel so keenly as did the Sumerians the need to brood on the nature of the gods and the meaning of life or to fashion heroes as mediators between the divine and human planes. The tragic figure of Gilgamesh could never have arisen in the land of the Nile, which did not create any significant myths or epics to illuminate the place of man. Beyond magical incantations and praises of the ruler, which were only semihistorical, Egyptian literature consisted of travelers' tales, little stories, and manuals of advice on getting ahead in the world. Egyptian sciences, too, remained on a practical, comparatively low level. To Egypt we owe a solar calendar of 365 days, which perhaps crystallized about the beginning of the Old Kingdom proper; to 12 months of 30 days each were added 5 days at the end of each year, and the day was divided into 24 hours — the further subdivision of an hour into 60 minutes came in Greek times on the basis of Mesopotamian sexagesimal reckoning. Some very early papyri show considerable skill in surgery (as well as containing magical spells to cure the ill). In mathematics and other areas, on the other hand, Mesopotamia was far more advanced; and such a practical invention as wheeled vehicles was not used in Egypt until the New Kingdom.

THE MIDDLE KINGDOM

End of the Old Kingdom (*about* 2200 B.C.). As the Mesopotamian epic of Gilgamesh reflects some of the basic views of that land, so the vast pyramids of Gizeh are a symbol of the Old Kingdom in Egypt. In their stark outline and great bulk they suggest the simplicity, the concentration, and the earthly riches of the civilized society that erected them. The directors of Egypt had a naive confidence in human powers which also shines through the reliefs and statues of the era; the height of the Old Kingdom was an optimistic age in which men were enthusiastic about sheer materialistic achievements. Yet the pyramids can also justly be called "acts of faith," for they arose in an effort to safeguard the body of the dead pharaoh, who was thought to watch over the safety of his people so long as his body survived and his spirit was nourished by sacrifices at his mortuary temple. And finally, in the facts that even such masses of stone could not protect the dead rulers from grave-robbers and that the pyramids after that of Khufu dwindled rapidly in size, one can sense the incipient decline of the Old Kingdom.

By the Fifth Dynasty this decline was well under way. Strife broke out in the royal family; the nomarchs tended to become hereditary local lords; tribes trickled into Egypt from Palestine and Syria. The consumption of Egypt's resources in mortuary endowments for the dead rulers became heavy; and the peasants who tilled the lands along the Nile seem to have grown weary of their burdens.

Thus came the end of the Old Kingdom, toward 2200 B.C. To illuminate the troubled two centuries that followed, the First Intermediate Period, there are several papyri which reflect the pessimism produced when a rather materialistic outlook could no longer count on prosperity. Equally interesting are the portrayals of the lawlessness and usurpations of property rights. Even in men's views of afterlife a disregard for the old restrictions spread widely, for the nobles at least — and perhaps others — now claimed for themselves that right of unification with Osiris after death which previously had been reserved for the king.

The Middle Kingdom. The local rule of nomarchs lasted only until shortly before 2000 B.C. Then the kings of the Eleventh Dynasty, who ruled from Thebes, far inland in Upper Egypt, once more pulled together the valley and the delta into one state. Under their successors, the Twelfth Dynasty, the Middle Kingdom of Egyptian history (2052–1786 B.C.) reached its height.

In the most general terms Egyptian civilization continued along the lines already well set, for Egypt always retained its initial patterns far more than Mesopotamia could. Yet the ways of the Middle Kingdom were noticeably different from those of the Old Kingdom artistically, politically, and religiously.

Since the arts and crafts depended heavily on royal patronage, which secured the necessary raw materials and supported the artisans by commissioning their products, there was a natural reinvigoration of artistic output as political unity reappeared. The scale, however, of building was smaller; the cautious rulers of this age erected no pyramids to advertise their graves. Sculpture, painted reliefs, and the household luxuries produced by the minor arts have survived in considerable volume. In this work the naive yet powerful inventiveness which had resulted in the masterpieces of the Old Kingdom now yielded to a more sophisticated complexity.

Politically the pharaohs of the Twelfth Dynasty were once again the focus of the land, and their military power is a more obvious phenomenon than in earlier centuries. External trade was resumed under their protection and became more extensive than it had been earlier. At times rulers of Egypt seem to have held parts of the Syrian coast, like the port of Byblos; the mines of Sinai were exploited intensively. Egyptian objects even turn up on the island of Crete, and Egyptian models helped to spark the remarkable surge of civilization on that island which is called Minoan (see below, Chapter 5). Nonetheless the pharaohs were not entirely masters at home as the rulers of the Fourth Dynasty had been. Both in this world and in the next the nobles held a relatively independent place. They continued to dominate the local countrysides and buried their dead in provincial centers, rather than about the graves of the kings. To secure afterlife they appropriated royal symbols of the earlier age and invoked magical spells from the Pyramid Texts to persuade Osiris that they were "justified" for entry into his realm. These literary and artistic elaborations are called the Coffin Texts and were the source of the Book of the Dead in the New Kingdom.

Whereas the kings of the Old Kingdom had relied largely upon their own relatives for advice and aid in running Egypt, the governmental bureaucracy of the Middle Kingdom seems to have been open with relative ease to anyone who had learned the difficult art of the scribe. One ruler, while advising his son to "respect the nobles and make thy people to prosper," also laid down the dictum,"do not distinguish the son of man of birth from a poor man." [3] Further, and grimmer, advice comes in the apocryphal advice of king Amen-em-het I, just after 2000, to his son, "hold thyself apart from those subordinate to thee . . . Even when thou sleepest, guard thy heart thyself," for this essay on practical government goes on to recount the assassination of the king by his own courtiers.[4]

Ethical Interests. The political and religious temper of the Middle Kingdom has ethical notes which must interest any student of Egyptian development. Throughout their history the Egyptians conceived the cosmic order as one of justice (*ma'at*), and the gods generally favored the right. Yet the earthly guardians of this justice, the pharaohs, were now depicted in sculpture and described in literature in a manner which markedly differed from that of the Old Kingdom. While the statues of the kings were still awe-inspiring figures tinged with superhuman majesty, their portrait heads at times were lined with care, a testimony to their concern to secure justice and good government for their subjects. Literature, now far more mature in style, contains a number of folk tales which emphasized this side of royal rule. One such tale, the story of the Eloquent Peasant, recounts how a peasant was mistreated by a bureaucrat but insistently and successfully sought redress for his wrongs. In the first essay of royal advice quoted in the previous paragraph occurs the impressive statement, "more acceptable is the character of one upright of heart than the ox of the evildoer." Similar ethical notes may be found in the boast of a king's steward that he fed the poor, protected the widows and orphans, refrained from maligning others for his own profit, and refused bribes in the conduct of justice.

[3] Instruction for King Meri-ka-re, tr. John A. Wilson, in *Ancient Near Eastern Texts,* p. 415.
[4] Instruction of King Amen-em-het, ibid. p. 418.

Whereas the outlook of the Old Kingdom had been one of pride in its achievements, the unrest that terminated that era seems to have administered a rude shock to Egyptian society. For at least a moment the inhabitants of the Nile valley were driven, like their brothers in third-millennium Mesopotamia, to reflect upon some of the problems inherent in the rise to civilization. This reflection was not as continuous as that which later produced the Hebrew views of divine justice or the Greek philosophical outlook; Egyptian thought was too practical and on too simple a plane. Again, in Egypt the problems were conceived in earthly fashion, for life in Egypt was directly administered by the god-king and his aides. Deep class divisions, which were prominent in Mesopotamia, accordingly were less pressing problems in Egypt.

And so the ethical tinge to views of life which we find in the Middle Kingdom represents scarcely more than a temporary flash of illumination. A truly conscious crystallization of ethical requirements for civilized life and their union with religious views was not to be easily attained, and was not reached in Egypt; nor did the men of the Middle Kingdom come to conceive the next world in nonmaterial terms. In their tombs there is, if anything, an even greater emphasis than previously upon providing a host of material supplies for the hereafter. The museums of the modern world contain from these tombs hosts of models, as of gardens, breweries, boats, concubines, servants (called *ushabti* or "answerer" figurines), which were intended to serve the rich men buried therewith or to take their places in working for the gods.

Decline of the Middle Kingdom. As the Middle Kingdom proceeded, the forces of local independence rose once more. General unrest again brought a disruption of political unity by the eighteenth century b.c. and even a foreign rule, at least of the Delta. After the Second Intermediate Period (1786–1575) Egypt was to be drawn far more directly into the main course of ancient Near Eastern history; but this, like events in Babylonia after Hammurabi, must be reserved for the next chapter.

THE FIRST CIVILIZED SOCIETIES

Qualities of Near Eastern Civilization. Even brief surveys of the developments in Mesopotamia and Egypt down to 1700 b.c. will provide the thoughtful student of history with ample food for reflection. In the entire sweep of ancient history, the appearance of agriculture in the Neolithic era and the rise of civilization just before 3000 B.C. are the two most revolutionary steps in man's progress, if one measures events solely in terms of the physical basis of life. To consider only the latter step, the appearance of civilization was marked by a tremendous explosion of population in the river valleys, where settlement became denser than had ever before been possible in human history. Buildings, both secular and religious, were erected on a mammoth scale; industrial and agricultural techniques were much refined; the leaders, at least, in this new world lived and died in pomp and luxury hitherto unknown.

If the historian is to measure correctly the meaning of the rise of civilization, he must not fix his eyes solely upon this material progress. The qualities of civilization, as the term was defined at the beginning of Chapter 2 are basically intellectual and social. A civilized structure of life requires much of mankind in mutual adaptation and acceptance of a necessary interdependence. Nor was all achieved, once the Sumerians and Egyptians had risen to this level. We have already surveyed some 1500 years of the historic period in Egypt and Mesopotamia and have seen that society in both areas found itself confronted by great problems inherent in the new intellectual and social patterns. Spiritually, intellectually, and politically remarkable changes were to occur in the subsequent spread and intensification of civilized systems.

In comparison with these later developments, the ways of life in early Egypt and Mesopotamia have certain obvious characteristics. One of the most evident is their strongly religious flavor. Religion, indeed, has always been a prominent force in human culture, for here mankind explains to itself the meaning of existence and visualizes the unseen powers which at once limit and impel men's actions. But in the early Near East all aspects of life were conjoined under the guidance of religion to a degree which rarely recurred thereafter in ancient times. The gods were simply conceived as forces directing nature; their ethical qualities were not quite, but almost, incidental; and the physical needs of an agricultural population were evident in the prominent place of fertility cults. Magic and ritual observance of ceremonies bulked large both in daily life and in the activities of the states.

In the realm of knowledge the practical, conventional cast of thought at this time is also apparent. Scientific interests were directed largely toward the end of classifying and naming objects. Between the artists and the visible world stood a host of almost unchanging conventions, often ironclad, as well as the requirements laid down by priestly and royal patrons. Literary thought was often cast in the form of myth. Fields of knowledge were not yet specialized and distinct, nor were they explored by tools of abstract thought. Behind all these qualities stands the fact that the earliest civilized men had as yet only begun that long process of conscious self-analysis which still occupies thinkers today. In rising to the level of civilization men had necessarily grouped themselves in tight social and political units under gods and pharaohs, and the conventions and social stratification which early resulted from that grouping were not easily to be modified or enlarged.

If we thus note the limitations and primitive characteristics of early civilization in the Near East this must not lead one to underestimate its remarkable achievements. Beside such imperialists as Sargon I stood reformers like Urukagina. Most of the artists turned out conventional work; but those who designed the pyramids and carved the statue of Menkaure and his queen were true masters, sure in touch and esthetically creative. In applied metallurgy, agricultural techniques, astronomy, mathematics, and many other fields firm bases had been created for later advances. So too the social, political, and economic structure of life had become far more complex and differentiated and stood as a foundation for later evolution and expansion.

Differences between Egypt and Mesopotamia. The interlocked set of qualities which we sum up in the term "civilization" appeared first in the cities of lower Mesopotamia. Throughout history the rise and fall of civilization has been closely connected with the waxing and waning of cities; the word itself is derived from the Latin term for city-state (*civitas*). Although the basic natural resources upon which the cities build have usually been the product of the countryside, the conscious, ordered qualities of this advanced form of life are very directly linked to the social and political characteristics of urban organization.

Yet the historian must always guard against simple generalizations; for the history of Egypt serves as a partial exception to the equation which has just been made. By the end of the Middle Kingdom even Thebes was no more than an administrative capital. The differences between Egypt and Mesopotamia were deep in other respects. The land of the Nile commonly accepted political unity rather than division into small, particularistic units. Its inhabitants appear to have had a more cheerful outlook and to have brooded less darkly (and penetratingly) about the place of man before the gods. While weaker in the sciences, Egypt nourished an art which was far more diverse than that of Sumer and much more appealing to later ages.

Each civilization which has appeared in the history of the world must fascinate the historian as a manifestation of mankind's varied capabilities, and each has contributed material to the general outlook of those which have come afterward. There is no need to draw up a detailed list of the wide debts which subsequent civilizations owe to Sumerians and Egyptians, for after all the very concept of civilization itself was first born in the Near East. Inevitably, as a result, the "first" in many fields of learning, technology, political organization, and so on must be located here, and more particularly in Mesopotamia than in Egypt. Not until we come to the Greeks will we find a people who influenced the course of civilization in so many respects as did the "black-headed people" of Sumer. Although life in Mesopotamia was not so sure and relatively tranquil as that in the Old Kingdom of Egypt, its influences were perhaps the more significant as a result.

BIBLIOGRAPHY

Sources. The modern historian can speak of some aspects of Egyptian life 4000 years ago with greater sureness, and in more detail, than for virtually any other part of ancient (or even medieval) history. In the dry air of the land amazingly detailed reflections of life have survived, especially in the tombs; sites in the Delta are overlaid by later deposits and have not endured as well as those on the desert edge of the valley proper. Although the bulk of this evidence comes from the tombs of the dead rather than from the villages of the living, the distortion is limited by the fact that the aim of burial practices was largely an effort to give the dead man an afterlife of material pleasure.

Some evidence on Egyptian history has always been available in the writings of Greek and later authors, especially the histories of Herodotus and Diodorus and some Hebrew records. A native priest, Manetho, set down about 280 B.C. an account in Greek which was in part a useful survey of ancient traditions; this in turn was used by Jewish and Christian writers to help in determining Hebrew chronology. Serious modern interest in the physical remains of Egyptian culture began with the French expedition to Egypt under Napoleon (1798–1801); the famous Rosetta stone was found at this time and was captured by the English when the French army surrendered. Archeologists have labored fruitfully in Egyptian sands for over a century. Among the greatest in the field have been the American James Henry Breasted (1865–1935), who founded the Oriental Institute, and the Englishman Sir W. M. Flinders Petrie (1853–1942), who helped to make archeology a more scientific discipline.

We have more descriptions of the deeds of the pharaohs than of Mesopotamian rulers, as emblazoned on the walls of temples and stones for the glory of the Egyptian kings. The credit for deciphering the hieroglyphic script of these accounts goes chiefly to Jean François Champollion (1790–1832), who dedicated his life to Egyptology; his main key was the Rosetta stone, carved in 196 B.C. with parallel texts in formal hieroglyphic, demotic (cursive script), and Greek. The standard modern grammar is Alan Gardiner, *Egyptian Grammar* (3d ed.; Oxford: Oxford University Press, 1957). Translations of the written evidence may be found in J. H. Breasted, *Ancient Records of Egypt,* 5 vols. (New York: Russell, 1962); A. Erman, *Ancient Egyptians* (New York: Harper TB 1233); and *Ancient Near Eastern Texts.*

Further Reading. The most illuminating work on Egyptian civilization is that of John A. Wilson, *Culture of Ancient Egypt* (Chicago: University of Chicago Phoenix P11, 1956). Expert essays may be found in J. R. Harris, ed., *Legacy of Egypt* (2d ed.; Oxford: Oxford University Press, 1971); a brief appreciation is Cyril Aldred, *Egypt to the End of the Old Kingdom* (New York: McGraw-Hill, 1966). Alan Gardiner, *Egypt of the Pharaohs* (Oxford: Oxford University Press, 1964), gives a political and chronological survey, from which I have drawn the dates in Chapters 3 and 4. In the New Kingdom rulers can be placed within 10 to 15 years; in the Middle Kingdom, within 75 years. The First Dynasty is here put at 3100, but others lower it to 2850. Specialized studies are M. A. Hoffman, *Egypt before the Pharaohs* (New York: Knopf, 1979), graphic on the excavations; W. B. Emery, *Archaic Egypt* (Harmondsworth: Penguin A462, 1961); and H. E. Winlock, *Rise and Fall of the Middle Kingdom in Thebes* (New York: Macmillan, 1947).

Kurt Lange and Max Hirmer, *Egypt* (London: Phaidon, 1956), has excellent photographs. See also W. Stevenson Smith, *Art and Architecture in Ancient Egypt* (Harmondsworth: Penguin, 1958), and his more detailed study, *History of Egyptian Sculpture and Painting in the Old Kingdom* (2d ed.; London: Oxford University Press, 1978); A. Mekhitarian, *Egyptian Painting* (New York: Rizzoli, 1978); W. C. Hayes, *Scepter of Egypt,* Vol. I (Cambridge, Mass.: Harvard University Press, 1953), based on the collection in the Brooklyn Museum. A. Lucas, *Ancient Egyptian Materials and Industries* (4th ed.; London: Arnold, 1962), is detailed.

The physical background appears in Hermann Kees, *Ancient Egypt: A Cultural Topography* (Chicago: University of Chicago Press, 1977); the hallmarks of Egypt are well described in I. E. S. Edwards, *Pyramids of Egypt* (New York: Penguin, 1975). On Egyptian religion see Henri Frankfort, *Ancient Egyptian Religion* (New York: Peter Smith); or J. Cerny, *Ancient Egyptian Religion* (New York: Greenwood, 1979).

II

THE FIRST EXPANSION
OF CIVILIZATION

4

THE NEAR EAST IN THE
SECOND MILLENNIUM

All about the tiny kernels of civilization that had appeared in Egypt and Mesopotamia by 3000 B.C. there lived nearby peoples who were on a lower plane of organization. It is rather unlikely that many of these could have developed the complicated patterns of civilized society independently; but once civilization had been achieved, its basic concept became an exportable item. To many of the neighbors of the river valleys, indeed, the new achievements were highly attractive, for when these people looked at the first civilizations they probably saw, not the problems which were there appearing, but rather the remarkable physical progress.

The subsequent expansion of the new ideas within the Near East was not a process of even diffusion outward from the first centers. Some peoples adjacent to the Fertile Crescent took a short cut toward attaining a similar level by infiltrating or conquering the river valleys. Others remained at home and sought to imitate the models offered by Egypt and Mesopotamia. In general any area which had a secure Neolithic foundation could become civilized if it were willing to consolidate its political and social system; but in point of historical fact civilization jumped at points very far afield while nearer peoples remained wedded to their simpler ways. Not everyone considered change and complexity more desirable than following the customs of his ancestors.

The development of trade seems to have been the most important single factor in promoting foreign awareness of the amazing advances of Egypt and Mesopotamia, and the lines along which the new outlooks radiated outward are essentially those of the major Near Eastern routes of trade. Lower Mesopotamia, in particular, needed many resources which its alluvial plain could not furnish; but Egyptian rulers too, beginning with the first pharaohs of the Old Kingdom, sent expeditions abroad. As economic connections between the river valleys and the outside world grew in intensity, so too did cultural and political ties. To some extent the traders in question came from the civilized lands; but very often the surrounding peoples, especially those of mobile nature, themselves provided the metals, slaves, and other items desired by civilized societies.

The effects were pronounced, both abroad and at home. The initial seats of civilization were exposed to outside envy, which brought invasion; both to defend themselves and also to counter internal social unrest the political structures of Egypt and Mesopotamia tended to become more unified, to throw up military classes, and even to engage in imperialism. Especially in Mesopotamia the early city-states were grouped from time to time under monarchs, beginning with Sargon I, and the resulting empires expanded into upper Mesopotamia. The Middle Kingdom of Egypt exercised some hegemony over parts of the Syrian coast.

By the second millennium B.C. this expansion, together with the rise of local centers of civilization, had spread a civilized tissue over most of the Fertile Crescent. In arts and letters, in religion, and in many other aspects there now occurred a remarkable refinement and intensification of ideas and concepts. These were inherited mainly from the original outbursts which had created the first civilizations, for few truly independent and significant discoveries took place in this period. One mark of the era was a very much more widespread and skillful use of bronze, a deliberate mixture of copper and tin, which was especially employed in the manufacture of swords and other weapons. Bronze had been known since the third millennium, but the height of the Bronze age came in the centuries 1700–1200 B.C.

This chapter will consider the achievements of the era in the Fertile Crescent proper. In Chapter 5 we shall see the contemporary expansion of civilization outside the Near East proper; but some of the peoples who will occur there, such as the Hittites of Asia Minor, must also turn up from time to time in the present story.

General Patterns of the Second Millennium. The chronological boundaries that have just been set for the culmination of the Bronze age are determined by two great waves of invasion across the Near East, an earlier one running down to about 1700 and a later one coming about 1200. Throughout the third millennium the early states of Mesopotamia and Egypt had been subjected to sporadic attacks and infiltrations, but an especially powerful assault came in the first centuries after 2000. Among its eventual effects were the end of the Middle Kingdom and the fall of the Babylonian realm of Hammurapi's line.

Even at this time, however, cultural and economic connections throughout the Near East were expanding; through the following five centuries the Fertile Crescent blossomed in relative tranquillity. The governing layer, in particular, which was an amalgam of invading and local warlords and priests, enjoyed greater luxury than had ever been known before. Then the civilized societies declined, and a terrific mass of invaders drove in about 1200 B.C. to set the Near East on a radically new course.

The Semites. The earlier wave, which forms the background for the golden era after 1700, came from two sources. Some peoples moved down from the mountains which lay to the north and east; others infiltrated from the desert fringe to the south. The latter, who were more important, spoke Semitic languages and shared a generally similar pattern of life in other respects.

Whether the Semites originated in the Arabian peninsula cannot yet be established, but certainly this area was in historic times a constant reservoir from which Semitic-speaking peoples poured out periodically. Even before civilization had emerged, men of this stock had settled in Mesopotamia and elsewhere in the Fertile Crescent; from the days of Sargon I the Semites of Akkad rose in dominance over the Sumerians. Further invasions, especially by the Amorites, consolidated this mastery, which was definitive by the days of Hammurapi. Thereafter most inhab-

TABLE 3
Aegean and Near East—Second Millennium

B.C.	Greece	Crete	Asia Minor	Syria–Palestine	Mesopotamia	Egypt
2700	EARLY HELLADIC	EARLY MINOAN		Egyptian trade to Byblos	EARLY DYNASTIC	OLD KINGDOM
2300			tombs Alaca Hüyük entry of Hittites	expedition of Sargon I entry of Amorites— Canaanites	SARGONID ERA Hurrian infiltration	FIRST INTER-MEDIATE PERIOD
2000	MIDDLE HELLADIC Greek-speaking invasions	MIDDLE MINOAN rise of cities— palaces	Assyrian traders	Egyptian trade	OLD BABYLONIAN ERA	MIDDLE KINGDOM SECOND INTER-MEDIATE PERIOD
1700			kingdom of Hatti Hattusilis I Mursilis I		Hammurapi Hittite sack of Babylon	Hyksos

	MYCENAEAN ERA	LATE MINOAN	HITTITE EMPIRE		KASSITE ERA MITANNI	NEW KINGDOM
1575	shaft-graves					Dyn. XVIII: *Ahmose* *Thutmose I* *Hatshepsut* *Thutmose III* *Amenhotep III*
1400	*tholos* tombs palaces overseas expansion (Troy?, Cyprus, Ugarit)	burning of Cnossus	*Suppilu-liumas*	Egyptian domination bloom of Ugarit alphabets Hittite domination	Disappearance of Mitanni Rise of Assyria	*Akhenaten* (Amarna age) *Haremhab* Dyn. XIX *Seti I* *Ramesses II*
1200	Dorian invasion fall of Pylos fall of Mycenae		fall of Hittites Phrygian invasion	entry of Arameans—Hebrews Assyrian expeditions	*Shalmaneser I* *Tukulti-Ninurta I* *Tiglath-Pileser I*	Dyn. XX *Ramesses III* invaders by land-sea internal decay
1100	DARK AGES Protogeometric pottery (Chap. 9)			local states— Phoenician, Hittite, Aramean, Hebrews *David* *Solomon* *Hiram*		
1000						Dyn. XXII (Libyan)

itants of the Near East spoke closely allied Semitic languages; the major representatives of this class are Akkadian (including Assyrian), Canaanite (the source of Hebrew), and Aramaic together with the later Arabic and Ethiopian.

This group of languages is weak in vowel structure and has only two temporal tenses for its verbs, unlike the more complex Indo-European verbs. In sentence structure, Semitic languages are less inclined to use subordinate clauses, that is, to synthesize and organize thought sharply. From the point of view of European thought Near Eastern literature seems poetic and symbolic in cast.

Culturally the ways of thought shared by the dwellers in the desert diverged significantly from those evolved in the agricultural lands. Most desert peoples were seminomadic, on the basis of using asses and camels as beasts of burden. They were organized in tribal groups under elected chiefs and were impatient of tight social and political structure; repeatedly their irruptions wiped out the kingdoms which even their own kinfolk had erected in the settled lands. The unit of life for these peoples was the patriarchal family, living largely off its flocks and feuding with its neighbors. Kinship, not territorial connection, determined one's position, and concepts of private property and the measurement of life in material terms were often lacking or suspect.

On the other hand the mobility of the Semites made them traders all over the Fertile Crescent, and on occasion their leaders, who thought in broader terms than the lords of small, settled states, could erect vast empires. As one would expect, the developed fertility rites of the farming areas were absent among the nomads, who conceived their gods or *baals* of the tribes in less human, more abstract form. Nonetheless these forces were worshiped as protective parents in close contact with their earthly followers or children. Here, as in other respects, the ever-renewed infiltration of men with such different patterns had powerful effects on the more static outlook of peasant societies.

The Indo-Europeans. The Semites, however, were not unchallenged in their movements. From the other side of the Fertile Crescent mountaineers also trickled down to the plains; behind and with them came in the early second millennium members of a great group of peoples who spoke Indo-European languages. Inasmuch as English and almost all other languages of modern Europe (apart from Basque, Hungarian, and

Finnish) are of Indo-European origin, historians tend to be very interested in this group of peoples and its migrations.

The discovery that some elements of the group had moved in early times all the way across the Near East to India was one of the greatest achievements of the modern study of comparative philology. As British officials and traders in India became acquainted in the eighteenth century with Sanskrit, the early sacred tongue of that vast peninsula, they found that it had clear ties with the languages of western Europe. Throughout the nineteenth century philologists explored the fascinating ramifications of this fact and fitted into it other linguistic findings so as to create an impressive panorama of prehistoric movements of Indo-European peoples across the northern and central stretches of Eurasia.

While this evidence has been of great value to the historian, its side effects have not all been equally beneficial. The racial theories of some scholars and the strong nationalistic pride of recent generations in Europe have misled far too many people into considering this linguistic group a real race and so to speak of "Aryan" blood and the like. Any man who speaks an Indo-European tongue is, after all, an Indo-European, regardless of his body type or color of skin; one extinct branch, the Tocharic of central Asia, was spoken by men of Mongoloid appearance. Another serious mistake committed by historians who were born in the comfortable sense of European superiority over backward Asiatics has been to assert that the Indo-Europeans had remarkable capacities for civilization and, wherever they went, impelled a great advance. The truth of the matter is that, wherever we first meet Indo-European peoples in history, they were barbarians; and their invasions often produced a serious decline in the civilizations they encountered.

Since they were so backward, it is very difficult to use archeological evidence to help to pin down the original home of the Indo-European tongues. No specific patterns of physical culture can be attached to the languages; and they were written only after their speakers came into contact with civilized peoples. Presumably they came from somewhere on the great plains stretching across central Europe eastward into Siberia, inlanders who had no common word for "sea." The various dialects, however, did have very similar words for cattle, horses, wheeled vehicles, and the like; philologists thus assume that the earliest Indo-Europeans were a group of related tribes essentially nomadic and patriarchal, but acquainted with the raising of cereals. Even these assumptions are dangerous, for the Indo-European peoples may have picked up and passed to each other skills as they went. In their nomadic life sky-gods were more important than fertility deities, and at least while they were on the move a warlike aristocracy was often prominent.

The best clues to the character of these peoples and to their movements are literary references by civilized communities and also the distribution of the Indo-European languages themselves. From such evidence one may conclude that, for unknown reasons, the group went into a ferment shortly before 2000 B.C. and started spilling out all over Europe and western Asia. Some, who spoke the ancestors of Latin and kindred dialects, eventually drove into Italy. Others, who spoke Greek, came into Greece. The Hittites entered Asia Minor, and, as we shall see in the next chapter, became the first Indo-Europeans to write down their language. In the Fertile Crescent the mountaineer Hurrians and Kassites, who will be considered shortly, had Indo-European connections, though they were not themselves Indo-European in speech. Others went into Persia and on into India.

Taken as a whole, the Indo-European language group is often subdivided into two major sections, called *centum* and *satem* from their respective words for "hundred." The *centum* group, the ancestors of the Romance, Teutonic, Celtic, and Greek tongues, generally came to lie in the west; and the *satem* languages, such as Slavic, Armenian, Iranian, and Indian, are mostly eastern. Some varieties, such as Hittite, do not really fall into either division. As examples of the basically common ancestry of these many tongues the words for the parents of a family are illuminating. "Father" appears as *pitar* (Sanskrit), *pacar* (Tocharic), *hair* (Armenian), *pater* (Latin), *tad* (Welsh), *otec* (Russian); the last two come from some nursery diminutive for "papa." The "mother" was perhaps less frightening and so needed less irregular forms: *matar* (Sanskrit), *macar* (Tocharic), *mair* (Armenian), *mater* (Latin), *mam* (Welsh), *mat'* (Russian).

MESOPOTAMIA AND SYRIA

Results of the Invasions (1700–1200 B.C.). The invasions of Semitic, Indo-European, and other barbarian tribes were attended by murder, by looting, occasionally even by the destruction of cities. The Middle Kingdom in Egypt and Hammurapi's descendants were swept away. The general effects, however, were not catastrophic. By shortly after 1700 B.C. an extensive and complicated pattern of states was arising across the Fertile Crescent, and civilization was more widely spread than ever before. Some of the units were small city-states; more commonly kingdoms of some size appeared, within which the military and bureaucratic classes were more prominent than in the third millennium.

Thanks to the great development international trade, once relative peace had been restored, the political and cultural contacts of these states were fairly consecutive; and one can begin to speak of Near Eastern history as a whole, unlike the widely separated, unconnected flow of Egyptian and Mesopotamian history in the preceding 1500 years. In the international politics of the high Bronze age, the New Kingdom of Egypt was a leader; culturally, most areas drew chiefly from Mesopotamia.

Mesopotamia. In surveying these developments we may move from east to west along the Fertile Crescent, but need not spend long upon the oldest seat of civilization, lower Mesopotamia. Here a people called Kassites, which had an Indo-European sun-god but did not speak an Indo-European tongue, had come down from the eastern mountains to end the rule of Hammurapi's successors. They did not further expand their rule after consolidating their Babylonian position in the sixteenth century. Throughout the height of the Bronze age Babylonia accordingly lay in a backwater (see Map 4).

The open country immediately north of Babylonia could not easily be irrigated and so always remained virtually desert. Beyond this stretch lay upper Mesopotamia, which began in the second millennium to assume new importance as a central part of the Fertile Crescent. In the eastern reaches of upper Mesopotamia the Tigris and its tributaries watered a rolling land where rain also fell in sufficient quantity to support winter crops. Local conditions in this area would not in themselves have promoted the rise of civilization; though farming and herding had long been practiced in the region, soil conditions and the general availability of water did not favor the swift concentration of life in cities. Yet the adoption of civilized ways was a fairly easy step once the natives had observed the developments to their south, for the main trade route from Babylonia ran up the Tigris, which was safer from nomad attacks.

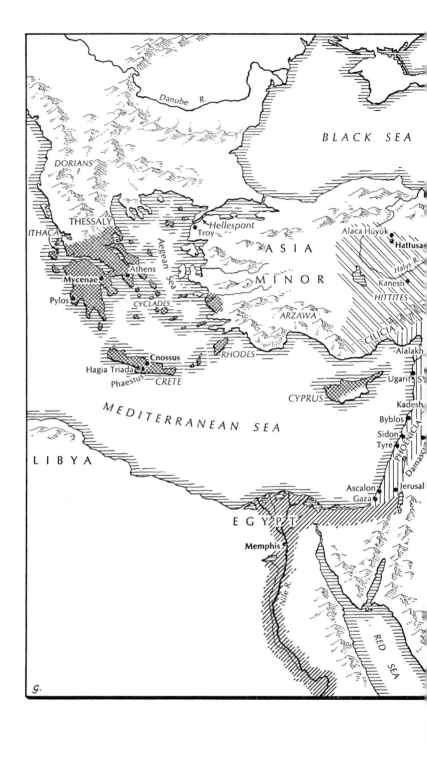

DORIANS
?

THESSALY
ITHACA
Hellespont
Troy
Athens
Mycenae
Pylos
CYCLADES
ARZAWA
Aegean Sea

ASIA
MINOR
Alaca Hüyük
Hatfusas
Halys R.
Kanesh
HITTITES
CILICIA
Alalakh

RHODES
Cnossus
Hagia Triada
Phaestus
CRETE
CYPRUS
Ugarit S.
Kadesh
Byblos
Sidon
Tyre
PHOENICIA
Damascus

MEDITERRANEAN SEA

LIBYA
Ascalon
Gaza
Jerusal

EGYPT
Memphis
Nile R.
RED SEA

BLACK SEA

Danube R.

G.

MAP 4

EASTERN MEDITERRANEAN
ABOUT 1200 B.C.

CIVILIZATIONS:
Mycenaean   Hittite
Egyptian   Mesopotamian

Scale of Miles
0   100   200   300

CASPIAN
SEA

Malatia

Harran
Carchemish
MITANNI
ASSYRIA
Ashur   Nuzi

Mari   ELAM

Euphrates R.   Tigris R.

Babylon   Nippur   Susa
BABYLONIA
Ur

Early Coast Line?

ARABIA

PERSIAN
GULF

Along this route urban centers appeared spottily in the third millennium. Of particular importance in the long run was the rise of the city of Ashur, called after its patron sun-god of the same name. On this nucleus there developed a Semitic-speaking kingdom of Assyria, which served in its turn as a focus for the spread of civilization even further. Assyrian merchants who traded into eastern Asia Minor before 1900 B.C. have left a host of interesting economic documents at one site, Kanesh, where they formed a well-organized trading quarter outside the local fortress; another similar quarter lay below the native citadel at Hattusas in the Hittite lands. At home the Assyrian kings tried to maintain and expand their power against Babylonia to the south and the Hurrian mountaineers to the north. Late in the Bronze age they were to have some temporary success, but the great days of Assyria came only in the first millennium B.C. Although Assyrian culture always remained a country cousin of Babylonian ways, its military tone and its partial adaptation of Hurrian artistic and other influences gave it a distinctive flavor.

Far up along the great westward bend of the Euphrates other civilized states appeared in the third millennium. By the period considered in this chapter the area was already largely under the control of Hurrians. The Hurrians, perhaps from Armenia, had come early; in the days of Hammurapi their names were prominent in one major Amorite state of the district, Mari. Thereafter Hurrian influence was consolidated in the large kingdom of Mitanni. The culture of this state was a fascinating medley from many sources. The Hurrian speech, like several other tongues of the mountain belt in the Near East, does not fit into any major linguistic group; but the rulers of Mitanni had names akin to those of the Indo-European invaders of India, as did such of their major gods as Indra and Varuna. In their religious and legal concepts and in their myths the Hurrians spread Babylonian ideas on to the Hittites of Asia Minor and to the early Hebrews of Palestine. Their art, which likewise drew from Babylonian models, nonetheless had a distinctive stamp which much influenced the art of more distant regions, as in its emphasis on fabulous creatures; the motif of the winged sundisk, which the Hurrians adapted from Egyptian roots, continued to be a major religious symbol on into Assyrian and Persian reliefs. Mitanni in one sense was fortunate in holding a central position in the Fertile Crescent, but this very location exposed it to attacks from all sides. As a state, it was to be under such pressure from Assyria, the Hittites, and Egypt that it vanished well before the end of the Bronze age.

Cities and Ports of Syria. By the second millennium the first centers of civilization in Syria, which had appeared in the third millennium, had expanded their influence wherever the terrain permitted. The principal geographical feature of the land consisted of two parallel mountain ranges, the Lebanon close to the Mediterranean coast and the Anti-Lebanon inland. Between these the fertile valley of the Orontes river supported Damascus and other cities; along the coast small plains gave rise to such cities as Sidon, Byblos, and Ugarit. Further south stretched the less fertile land of Palestine, up which ran the main land route from Egypt to the plain of Esdraelon, below Megiddo, and then inland to Damascus. Syria itself was an admirable center for trade inland to the Euphrates districts, northward through the plain of Cilicia and across the Taurus range into Asia Minor, and westward by sea out into the Mediterranean basin and also to Egypt. The great power of Mesopotamian culture displayed itself in the fact that all this area, including Palestine, drew inspiration from the east even more than from the relatively isolated land of Egypt.

Among the small kingdoms and trading cities of the area one of the best illuminated is Ugarit (modern Ras Shamra), which has been excavated in the past 30 years. In the city, which lay a mile inland, and in its port artistic objects have been found which originated in Mesopotamia, in Egypt, and also in the Minoan-Mycenaean world of the Aegean Sea; Ugarit in turn manufactured and exported cosmetics, wooden objects, textiles tinted in a famous purple dye derived from the shellfish of the coast, and bronze work based on the copper of Cyprus. Among the languages used for documents in the city there occur Egyptian, Akkadian, Hittite, Hurrian, and the native Canaanite dialect (of Semitic type); the latter was set down in a cuneiform script which used 30 signs for single consonants (and 3 vowels) — a true alphabet. In the neighborhood of Ugarit other Semitic-speaking peoples were at the same time experimenting with other alphabets of a more cursive style, some of the letters of which were derived from hieroglyphic symbols. One of these alphabets was in the end to carry the field and become the ancestor of the Greek and Latin scripts (see below, Chapter 6).

The myths and religious concepts of Ugarit have thrown a fascinating light upon Canaanite beliefs at the time when the Hebrews entered Palestine. The highest divinities were the couple El, "creator of creatures," and his wife Asherah, who shared many of the qualities of the Babylonian Ishtar. More prominent in popular cult, however, were their son Baal, a solar deity, and his wife Anath; much myth and ritual revolved about the ever renewed fight of Baal (and in turn his son Aliyan, lord of springs and wells), with Mot, lord of the hot summer. Only if Baal won could men be sure of the regular recurrence of winter rains. Besides the myths of this fertility cult, the inhabitants of Ugarit had also myths connected with human beings, especially Aqhat and king Keret, which reflected their meditation on the mortality of mankind and its desire to perpetuate itself through sons. From this religious pattern the Hebrews were to learn much; but they were also to react strongly against the sacred prostitution, human sacrifice, and primitive polytheism of Canaan.

Ugarit and its neighbors lay in the cockpit of the second millennium, where the great powers around exerted their swaying power. The history of Syria can be understood only when placed against the major currents of the age, but the growing attempts of outsiders to exert formal control over it reflects the increasing commercial wealth of the area.

THE NEW KINGDOM IN EGYPT

The Hyksos and the Revival of Unity. The pharaohs of the Middle Kingdom had never been able to concentrate in their hands that tight control which had been exercised by the Fourth Dynasty of the Old Kingdom. In the eighteenth century B.C. the power of the Thirteenth Dynasty had dwindled, and this led to internal disintegration in the Second Intermediate Period (1786–1575). Culturally the collapse was not so severe as that at the end of the Old Kingdom; but politically its effects were compounded by an infiltration of peoples from Palestine. These produced a ruling class called by the Egyptians the Hyksos, a term which probably meant "rulers of foreign countries." Although their origin is still much debated, opinion is swinging toward the view that the Hyksos were mainly Semitic-speaking. In Egypt they gained strength enough to control for about a century the Delta from a strongpoint at

Avaris. Objects marked by the name of the same Hyksos king (Khayan) have been found as far apart as southern Egypt, Palestine, Babylonia, and Crete. The Hyksos spread the use of the light, horse-drawn chariot with spoked wheels, manned by archers with bows, lances, and new types of bronze swords — a technique which spread rapidly in an era of much war and prominent military circles; Hyksos fortifications are marked by a great glacis intended to keep off rams. The native masters of Upper Egypt yielded only grudging obedience to the overlordship of the Hyksos, and after long-protracted struggles the founder of the Eighteenth Dynasty, Ahmose (1575-50), expelled them from the Delta. Not content with this victory he and his successors pursued the Hyksos into Palestine; for the first time in its history Egypt entered upon a path of continuing imperialism.

The boastful records of the pharaohs and their generals reveal that this imperialism rested upon an intriguing medley of interlocked motives. The booty of victory furnished a handsome profit; the kings and the military nobility who had risen about them gained glory from their valorous deeds; divine support was eagerly vouchsafed by the priesthood of the ever more powerful god of Thebes, Amen, the "Hidden One" or all-pervasive force who was grafted onto the older sun-god, Re. The Egyptian expansion abroad appears at times in contemporary records almost as a crusade to prove the power of Egyptian civilization; in modern psychological terms it has been called a compensation for the serious blow to native pride which had come in the Hyksos conquest.

The Egyptian Empire. The empire which the pharaohs swiftly built up in Africa lasted for a considerable period. Southward its boundary was the fourth cataract of the Nile, where frontier garrisons and forts under a viceroy solidified Egyptian control over Nubia. Eastward the Egyptian rulers opened up old caravan routes to the Red Sea, down which they sent expeditions to Punt (Somaliland).

The main arena for Egyptian battles, however, was the coastal route through Palestine and Syria; and here the serried armies of chariots and infantry led by the pharaoh under the divine protection of Amen plunged as far as the upper Euphrates. The first great conqueror in this district, Thutmose I (1528-10), set up a tablet of victory on the banks of the Euphrates and proclaimed in the Osiris temple at Abydos, "I have increased the work of others, the kings who have been before my time; the gods had joy in my time, their temples were in festivity. I made the boundaries of Egypt as far as that which the sun encircles . . . I made Egypt the superior of every land." [1]

Historians soon learn to distrust war communiques and the boasts of kings; in actual fact, this and similar Egyptian attacks into Asia seem mainly to have been looting, punitive expeditions. Nor does it appear that all elements in Egyptian society favored overseas expansion. An intriguing interlude of peaceful trade and concentration upon internal luxury occurred in the reign of queen Hatshepsut (1490–68), daughter of Thutmose I. This vigorous woman, one of the most interesting of ancient times, was half-sister to and also wife of Thutmose II; brother-sister marriage, it should be observed, was occasionally practiced in the Egyptian royal house. On his death she seized the reins of power and kept the actual heir, her stepson Thutmose III, firmly under control. For 22 years Hatshepsut ruled in her own name and maintained peace abroad, despite the difficulties that were caused to court etiquette by a female ruler; on monuments, for instance, she had to be depicted with the ancestral beard of royalty.

Whether her death in 1468 was due to natural causes or not, we do not know; but certainly Thutmose III was chafing to be master. Once rid of his stepmother, he savagely obliterated her name from her great monuments and quickly showed himself to be one of the most forceful men ever to rule Egypt. By his death in 1436 he had led 16 or 17 expeditions into Palestine and Syria. Persistent and skillful, he broke the recurrent revolts and forced even Mitanni under his suzerainty.

Egyptian supremacy in Palestine and Syria continued for the next century, which was a temporary era of balance among the many contending states and pressures of the Fertile Crescent. By a stroke of historical fortune the state archives for part of this period were discovered in 1887 by a peasant digging for fertilizing mud at an Egyptian site called El-Amarna. Written in cuneiform, the clay tablets contain letters from dependent princelings and also from Kassite, Assyrian, and Hittite monarchs, who call the Egyptian pharaoh their brother, seek wives from his family or dispatch their own women to his harem, and urge that he

[1] J. H. Breasted, *Ancient Records of Egypt,* II (Chicago: University of Chicago Press, 1906), p. 40.

"send gold in very great quantity which cannot be counted . . . For in my brother's land gold is common as dust." [2]

If we call Egyptian rule in Syria an "empire," we are likely to visualize it as a more powerful, coherent system than it actually was. In modern terms it was rather a sphere of influence along the main road from Egypt to Syria and in the Syrian ports, the chief of which was Byblos, nearest the forests of Lebanon. A "governor of the north countries" mainly oversaw the collection of tribute; occasional "residents" watched the courts of the dependent local rulers, whose sons were reared as hostages at Thebes. Here and there were a few forts, manned by mercenaries who were often of local origin. Ultimately Egyptian power rested upon the willingness of the subjects to pay their tribute, and this in turn depended upon their fear of Egyptian arms. Under Amenhotep III (1405–1367) and his son, Amenhotep IV or Akhenaten (1367–50), royal attention waned, and the subjects were tempted by Hittite blandishments to cast off their Egyptian attachments. Ribaddi of Byblos wrote repeatedly for help, but finally no more letters came from him to report that bad news which the pharaoh disliked hearing; instead, another tablet briefly reports his capture by rebels and his death. A faithful supporter at Jerusalem sought to break through the disinterest of the king's court by urging his secretary to tell the king that "all the lands of the king, my lord, are lost." [3] Thus the rule of Egypt in Asia dissolved, without any real battles, about a century after its inception.

The Imperial Age. During the height of its overseas rule Egypt shone resplendent. Internally there was peace, which permitted once more a full utilization of the land's resources; foreign mastery produced quantities of slaves and tribute. Upon the basis of these revenues the kings and nobles led a luxurious life, which they passed in gay, rambling houses and palaces, while the artisans and peasants dwelt in close-packed quarters. But the gods who safeguarded the empire were not forgotten. The main temple of Amen, patron of victory, was at Karnak, across the Nile from Thebes. Here the Eighteenth Dynasty erected a huge hall, one of

[2] J. A. Knudtzon, *Die El-Amarna-Tafeln* (Leipzig: Vorderasiatische Bibliothek, 1907–15), No. 19 from Tushratta of Mitanni; tr. J. H. Breasted, *Cambridge Ancient History,* II (Cambridge University Press, 1926), p. 95.
[3] Knudtzon, No. 286.

the most impressive architectural remains of ancient Egypt, and went on to pile up one structure after another. The religious complex of Karnak is perhaps the most extensive ever created in the western world, and additions were still made to it in the days of Greek rule after Alexander.

After their death the pharaohs remained powerful figures, as had been true in earlier Egypt. At Dêr el-Bahri, Hatshepsut carved out of the western cliffs of the Nile valley a mortuary temple for herself and Thutmose I. Her architect Senenmut showed notable esthetic sense in the arrangement of the three stepped terraces and the details of their decorative colonnades; the reliefs, which among other matters show in graphic detail a great expedition to Punt, are among the most attractive of all Egyptian art. In a grim valley of the desert behind this temple, now called the Valley of the Kings, the rulers of the New Kingdom were hidden in tombs where they hoped to escape grave-robbers. Only one, Tutankhamun, was successful; but the wealth of gold, inlaid furniture, and other luxuries packed into the small tomb chamber of this minor pharaoh is amazing in quantity, even though its workmanship shows signs of the decline which was then beginning to affect Egyptian art.

An imperial power affects other peoples by its expansion and in turn must yield some of its ancestral ways. Foreign wares were now more common in Egypt; hostages and slaves of alien customs trod the streets of the capital; women of foreign royal houses sat beside the pharaohs as queens. The ambassadors who came before the pharaoh "to make supplication to the good god and to beg breath for their nostrils" are lovingly depicted in their variegated costumes on the walls of the tombs of viziers and other bureaucrats at Thebes.[4] Egyptian culture broadened its view to some degree, though the fundamental lines of the past still controlled its restless, sophisticated forms of expression. The influence of the militaristic, imperial tendencies was even greater in Egyptian attitudes and institutions. The zest of the military elements is evident in the tombs of royal generals as well as in the huge reliefs of victorious Egyptian armies which were splashed across the walls of the ever larger temples. Beside the generals stood the priests, who had begun to gain an independent role in the Middle Kingdom and now exerted an ever more powerful influence both openly and in the intrigues of the royal court.

Reforms of Akhenaten (*Amenhotep IV*, 1367–50 B.C.). This latter de-

[4] Tr. J. A. Wilson, in *Ancient Near Eastern Texts*, p. 249.

velopment threatened to lower the pharaoh from his earlier role as god on earth to that of a mere agent for Amen, a trend which the young ruler Amenhotep IV resisted on coming to the throne. Abetted by relatives and advisers, he opened the way to an amazing wave of reform, which spilled over from the political and religious fields into artistic and cultural revolution. Amenhotep IV is the first reformer in history whose activities we can see with some clarity.

Much of the new king's activity was intended to regain full authority from the priesthoods. As he proceeded, Amenhotep IV made the usual discovery of reformers that any attempt to reduce the power of vested interests must lead one to ever more extreme measures. Eventually, thus, he decided to make a clean break with Amen, who had become almost *the* god of Egypt. In Amen's place he set up the sundisk, Aten; the hymns in Aten's honor that have survived emphasized the universal power of the god as a kindly, nurturing force. All over Egypt the temples of the local gods were closed, and the name of Amen was chiseled out of inscriptions. In assessing this religious reform, however, we must always remember that Aten was to be worshiped by the pharaoh and his family, and that all others were to worship Akhenaten. Even this was not enough. Since Thebes was committed to Amen, whose priest-hood bitterly opposed the new cult, Amenhotep in his sixth year moved the capital 300 miles north to an entirely new site called Akhetaten (the modern Amarna), isolated and well guarded. He also changed his own name to that of Akhenaten, "It pleases Aten," by which he is commonly known. The advisers and officials of the king were no longer priests but new men, soldiers and even foreigners.

In art the old conventions of internal tranquillity and static pose had been losing their mastery and their ability to inspire artists. The dissolv-ent effects of the new imperialism now gained fresh force in the political and religious upheaval of Akhenaten's reign, and the ruler himself seems deliberately to have encouraged artists to depict his thin face and shoul-ders, swollen stomach, and large thighs in more realistic fashion. The art of the Amarna age, as this period is called, was fluid, naturalistic, and inclined to curved lines; color was employed with delicate brushwork and with pictorial sensitivity.

While Amarna art struck a fresh note in Egyptian culture, a modern observer of its products is likely to feel uneasy. The old standards had been confining, but they had also given a solid base for centuries of artistic attainment; now there came an extravagant, anemic flavor, which suggests all too clearly a quality of desperation and a decline in inspiration. The same loss of earlier patterns is apparent to a lesser degree in the literature of the era. Although some of the Aten hymns struck a noble note, the style of writing became more colloquial; love poems emerged as a popular form; and irreverent humor toward the ruler and the gods appeared more commonly.

END OF THE BRONZE AGE

Decline of Egypt (1300 *on*). Despite the opinion of many modern historians that the only true subjects for historical study are political and economic developments, one can often learn a great deal from examining the artistic, literary, and philosophical evidence for an age. The declining strength of Egypt is visible in the reign of Akhenaten not only in the fact that its Asiatic sphere of influence dissolved but also in the cultural evolution at home.

Before the end of Akhenaten's reign the conservative reaction against his reforms was mounting, and after his death the new city of Akhenaten was quickly abandoned. Tutankhamun (1347–39) reverted to the worship of Amen, as his name indicates, but ruled only briefly. Then the general Haremhab (1335–08?) seized the throne. Under his successors, who formed the Nineteenth Dynasty, Egypt still exercised intermittent sway in Asia; but the course of the New Kingdom was turning downward. The very harshness of royal edicts suggests that the control of the pharaohs was becoming shaky; the priests steadily expanded their sway. The Great Papyrus Harris, which surveys religious holdings, indicates that the temples controlled at least one-tenth of the population and one-eighth of the farmlands in the Nile valley.

That this decline was due to internal factors rather than to external pressure is obvious. In cultural respects, too, the old Egyptian outlook was yielding, and creativity departed. Skepticism, gloom, and passivity replaced optimism and joy in the inscriptions, and men's care for their afterlife became steadily more a matter of desperate ritual and magic. A famous product was the Book of the Dead, a collection of miscellaneous spells numbering in all nearly 200, which would guarantee the dead man safe passage in the next world and his acceptance there by Osiris, rather than his destruction by a monster, part hippopotamus, part crocodile, and part lion. Drawn from the Coffin Texts of the Middle Kingdom, this work was copied and used until Christian times. While the fluid naturalism of the Amarna spirit continued to play a part in art, the vitality of artistic products sank rapidly. The Egyptians were not able to derive fresh impetus from their long-established conventions, yet were unable to develop a new, coherent outlook on life.

Decline of Syria and Palestine. What was happening in Egypt was, in many respects, typical of developments elsewhere across the Fertile Crescent; but here international politics and war also played a more evident part. After Egyptian rule in Asia had quietly dissolved under Akhenaten, almost two centuries passed before the next great wave of invasions. During this era Syria and Palestine become the objects of international rivalries which strongly resemble the politics of Europe in the seventeenth and eighteenth centuries after Christ. The major states engaged in dynastic marriages, sent ambassadors back and forth to make treaties of alliance, and sought to maintain balances of power; and yet wars broke out repeatedly to exercise the military circles that dominated most states.

Here the Hittites, whom we shall observe more closely in the next chapter, played a major role. A contemporary of Akhenaten and one of the greatest of the Hittite kings, Suppiluliumas (c. 1375-35), asserted general control over the upper Fertile Crescent and made Mitanni a buffer against Assyria, which now began to rise in power. Thereafter the Hittite kings had to face a temporary resurgence of Egypt under Seti I (1309-1291) and the long-lived, boastful Ramesses II (1290-24). Ramesses repeatedly invaded Syria. According to his own account he secured a great victory against the Hittites at Kadesh, though his troops were ambushed by the enemy; but the upshot was a treaty of nonaggression and alliance about 1280 between Egypt and the Hittites. Copies of this document, surprisingly enough, have been found both in Egypt and in the Hittite capital of Hattusas; by it Egypt virtually accepted Hittite mastery of north Syria. Assyria, for its part, gained full mastery over the land of Mitanni under Shalmaneser I (1272-43) but was continually plagued by contentions with the Kassites of Babylonia.

No power was able to gain complete control and to break the strong tendencies toward local independence which still marked the several parts of the world of the Bronze age. Neither in art, in commerce, nor in cultural outlook was there yet a general unity of the Fertile Crescent on which a lasting empire could be created.

New Invasions (1200 *on*). While the greater powers thus contended in inconclusive fashion, their internal strength was weakening. The noble classes supported the kings less wholeheartedly; in art a sense of decline is widely visible. Worst yet, the monarchs failed until too late to notice that new waves of invasion were mounting. From the desert Semitic tribes lapped about the strongpoints of the cities; from the north a terrific assault broke forth in the late thirteenth century. Ugarit was burned and destroyed forever, as were many other Syrian centers; the Hittite realm vanished from the map shortly after 1200, as did also the Mycenaean kingdoms in Greece. Egypt, attacked by land and sea under Ramesses III (1182–51), barely rode out the storm. So too Assyria survived, but lost any capabilities of expansion for the next few centuries.

Before we turn to investigate the precise course of these attacks, we must first consider the widening out of civilization beyond the Near East proper which had occurred by 1200 B.C.; for much of the civilized belt of Eurasia was to be affected by these invasions. No later assault by the barbarians of northern Europe, indeed, was to be as influential until the outpourings of the German and Hunnish tribes ended ancient history. To sum up, however, what took place about 1200 in metaphorical terms one might say that an age which had shimmered in golden luxury fell prostrate before the sharp edge of iron weapons. Thereafter the course of history in the Fertile Crescent entered upon a virtually new phase.

BIBLIOGRAPHY

Sources. During the height of the Bronze age historical evidence is more abundant and varied than in any previous era. This fact is reflected in the preceding pages, where dates and names appear with greater frequency than in the first three chapters; the backbone of second-millennium chronology is the sequence of Egyptian kings, which can be pinned down to within 10 to 15 years.

Our sources for this period are of three types. First, the luxury of the ruling classes resulted in the creation of buildings and other physical objects on a wide scale. Luxor and Karnak, El-Amarna, and other sites in Egypt are famous; over the past few decades excavation has broadened our knowledge greatly in Palestine, Syria, and upper Mesopotamia. Second, written documents appear in numbers on the walls of the temples and tombs of Egypt (see Breasted's *Ancient Records of Egypt*) and also in the form of papyri and cuneiform tablets; a good selection of documents from Assyria, Syria, and Egypt is given in *Ancient Near Eastern Texts*. See also E. A. T. W. Budge, *Book of the Dead* (New York: Barnes and Noble, reprint of 1909 ed.), and G. R. Driver, *Canaanite Myths and Legends* (Edinburgh: Society for Old Testament Study, 1956). Third, the contributions of comparative philology have been noticed in the text. The first to suggest that Sanskrit was linked to western tongues was Sir William Jones in the eighteenth century (see the sketch in A. J. Arberry, *Oriental Essays* [London: Allen and Unwin, 1960]); but solid grammatical comparison began with studies of the Indo-European verb by Franz Bopp (1816).

At this point the increasing abundance of facts may justify a comment about the procedures of the historian. Whether in studying the careers of Akhenaten or of Franklin D. Roosevelt, one always finds that important pieces of the story are absent or are confused — the motives which impelled a man, the relative weight of various factors, and so on. In the ancient history of the Near East down to this point, moreover, we lack true history in the sense of formal written documents which seek to preserve the course of past events. In an account like the present one the story may seem straightforward and clear; but much that appears here is the product of inference — however carefully made — and even of suppositions.

While history must rest upon the actual facts insofar as these are preserved to us, the *meaning* of the story which is presented in any historical volume is the fruit of the author's meditation. It does not rise automatically from the facts. As a result, each historian will emphasize different facts and may even differ from his colleagues as to which statements in the sources are really true; and his views of the past will depend quite largely upon what he thinks about the present and expects for the future.

Further Reading. V. Gordon Childe, *The Aryans: A Study of Indo-*

European Origins (New York: Knopf, 1926), remains one of the few surveys of the invaders in English; see also Hugh Hencken, *Indo-European Languages and Archeology* (American Anthropologist, Memoir No. 84, 1955); and S. Moscati, *Ancient Semitic Civilizations* (New York: Putnam Capricorn 202, 1960). Aspects of Syrian development appear in the latter work and also in C. L. Woolley, *A Forgotten Kingdom* (New York: Norton, 1968) and T. H. Gaster, *Thespis* (New York: Norton, 1977). L. L. Orlin, *Assyrian Colonies in Cappadocia* (The Hague: Mouton, 1970), describes their commercial activity.

Most of the works noted in the Bibliography, Chapter 3, include also the New Kingdom. More specific accounts may be found in G. Steindorff and K. C. Steele, *When Egypt Ruled the East* (4th ed.; Chicago: University of Chicago Phoenix 125, 1965), and the popular works by Geoffrey Bibby, *Four Thousand Years Ago* (New York: Knopf, 1961), and P. H. Newby, *Warrior Pharaohs* (Boston: Faber and Faber, 1980). The expansion of civilization up the Nile is noted in Walter A. Fairservis, Jr., *Ancient Kingdoms of the Nile* (New York: Mentor MT460, 1962). J. H. Breasted, *Dawn of Conscience* (New York: Scribner, 1934), gave a famous, exaggerated picture of Akhenaten; see also J. D. S. Pendlebury, *Tell el-Amarna* (London: Dickson and Thompson, 1935). W. C. Hayes, *Scepter of Egypt,* Vol. II (Cambridge, Mass.: Harvard University Press, 1959), concentrates on the art of the New Kingdom; pictures of the rich tomb of Tutankhamum are given by Christiane Desroches-Noblecourt, *Tutankhamen* (New York: New York Graphic Society, 1976), and Cyril Aldred, *Tutankhamun's Egypt* (New York: Scribner's, 1978). The latter's *Akhenaten: Pharaoh of Egypt* (London: Thames and Hudson, 1968), is also well illustrated. Pierre Montet, *Everyday Life in Egypt* (Philadelphia: University of Pennsylvania Press, 1981), is laid in the Nineteenth Dynasty. A lighter side of Egyptian character is well presented in J. L. Foster, *Love Songs of the New Kingdom* (New York: Scribner's, 1974).

5

NEW CIVILIZATIONS
WEST AND EAST

The concepts and forms of civilization which had originated in the river valleys of the Near East spread widely in the third and second millennia B.C. One area of expansion was the Fertile Crescent itself; developments down to 1200 B.C. in this region were sketched in the previous chapter. Much more remote districts, which lay further to the west and to the east, also made great advances during the period.

In the relative speed or slowness with which the more distant reaches of Eurasia progressed, one can see the potent effects of geographical conditions on human history. Some peoples were handicapped by a physical environment which did not easily permit the concentration of population and the creation of social and political superstructures as required by civilization; among these may be reckoned the tribes who lived in the far north, in the desert regions, and in the mountains. Most inhabitants of the temperate belt which stretches across Eurasia from the Atlantic to the Pacific were not so severely restricted and could shape their institutions and ways of life with considerable latitude. Historical change in this belt has largely depended, from age to age, upon the local qualities of each population as affected by two conjoined geographical factors: the location of the main centers of culture, and the main lines along which their inspiration was likely to radiate.

The new ideas of Mesopotamia and Egypt, in sum, were not likely to be taken up quickly either by the inhabitants of the Eurasian steppes or

by the tribes which lived in the Arabian desert. The Near East, nonetheless, was far from isolated, for important avenues of contact led east and
west, both by land and by sea. One land route stretched northwestward
into Asia Minor, where Hittite civilization emerged. Another path, the
famous Silk Route of later days, reached far across central Asia to
China; civilization in the valley of the Yellow river had emerged by the
second millennium B.C.

Throughout history, however, sea routes have commonly been more
influential than trade and travel by land. Waterborne transport is
cheaper and more efficient — in ancient times land portage by men and
animals was practicable as a rule only for luxuries — and the perils of
shipwreck have in most eras been matched by the dangers of brigandage
on land. Mesopotamia was early in seaborne contact with the valley of
the Indus river, where civilization had made great strides before 2500
B.C.; and the coasts of Syria and Egypt had important links with the
Aegean basin.

The remarkable outburst that occurred in the latter district is one of
the most interesting developments from the point of view of western
history. The bulk of the European continent was so remote, so set off by
mountains, and so different in climate that its inhabitants remained
virtually Neolithic down to the first millennium B.C. The southeastern-
most extension of Europe, however, which ran down into the narrow
valleys of Greece and the islands of the Aegean, could, and did, respond
to the new waves pulsating in the Near East. By 2000 B.C. the inhabitants
of the island of Crete had risen into Minoan civilization, from which
the Greek mainland evolved an offshoot called Mycenaean civilization.
This advance lay immediately in the background of Greek history and
so will concern us again later; but at this point it must be considered
along with Hittite, Indian, and Chinese development so as to round out
our view of the general progress of Eurasia down to 1200 B.C.

ASIA MINOR AND THE HITTITES

Discovery of the Hittites. In the Bible, in the Amarna tablets, and in
other Near Eastern sources there are a few references to a people called
Hittites, who otherwise remained virtually unknown until very recently.
From 1906 on down to the present day excavation on a ridge of north-

central Asia Minor, called in Turkish, Boghazköy, has revealed a city with majestic walls, temples, palace, and state archives of more than 10,000 cuneiform tablets. Some of these records are in Akkadian, Hurrian, and similar tongues which could be read from their first discovery. Others were in unknown languages; but these soon yielded their secrets to scholars, led by the Czech, Bedrich Hrozny. It thus appeared that the rulers of Hattusas, as the city was called in antiquity, spoke an Indo-European tongue; besides the Hittite of the governing class two other Indo-European languages, Luvian and Palaic, were also used, as well as an apparently earlier, non-Indo-European speech. The Hittites have now taken their place as one of the major peoples of the second millennium B.C. They have particularly interested modern historians inasmuch as they are the first Indo-European group to rise to the level of civilization and so to appear before our eyes with some clarity.

Since the Hittites did not learn how to write until after they had begun to borrow Mesopotamian civilization, their earlier history can be reconstructed only on the basis of archeological hints and linguistic distributions. It is generally agreed that they came into Asia Minor from the outside, either from Europe or across the Caucasus mountains. The movement seems to have been part of the great outpouring of Indo-Europeans at the turn from the third to the second millennium B.C., though the Hittites themselves were in Asia Minor before 2000 B.C. (see Map 4).

This area is essentially a great tableland, hot in summer and cold in winter and ringed with mountains which impede but do not entirely cut off communications with the enfolding seas and the Fertile Crescent. While the coastal regions are in part well watered, the interior, or Anatolia proper, is at points virtually desert. The main river, the Halys, makes a great loop about the kernel district of the main Hittite state and flows into the Black Sea.

Political History of the Hittites (*to* 1200 B.C.). Although agricultural villages of early date have recently been discovered at various spots in Anatolia, the region seems to have been slow in development. The plain of Cilicia in the southeast, which is virtually an adjunct of Syria, progressed more rapidly; and at the other extremity of Asia Minor, in the northwest coastal district facing Europe, settlements of some size have also been found. The most famous of these is the fortress of Troy, which began about 3000 B.C. and underwent many changes thereafter in reaction to influences both from Europe and from the hinterland of Asia Minor.

In the interior one of the most notable signs of advance in the third millennium consists of the remarkable set of royal tombs at Alaca Hüyük, where skilled work in gold and copper was abundant and even iron appeared. A truly great landmark, however, occurred when the Hittites rather suddenly became civilized. Apparently a number of kingdoms evolved early in the second millennium, including Arzawa in the southwest and Kizzuwatna in Cilicia; the major state appeared in the great Halys bend, the land of Hatti proper. Its vigorous king, Hattusilis I, harnessed the strength of his warrior nobles in the middle of the seventeenth century B.C. and gained general lordship over his neighbors, including Arzawa. Hattusas became the capital at this time. His immediate successors struck across the Taurus mountains into Kizzuwatna, and one ruler, Mursilis I (d. 1590), even sacked Babylon. This crippling raid paved the way for the Kassite domination of Babylonia (see Table 3 in Chapter 4).

For a century thereafter the land of Hatti sank back into relative obscurity. Palace feuds broke out over the succession to the throne, barbarians from the north coast of the peninsula raided southward, and the warrior chiefs ruled their own domains, almost indifferent to the weak central authority of the kings. Not until firm rules on succession to the throne were laid down and the kings began to enforce more developed principles of administration derived from Near Eastern practice did the Hittite state revive.

From about 1460 on came the period which is called the Hittite Empire. At home the rulers governed through officials, rather than using their own kinsmen or vassals; an earlier *pankus* or "whole body of citizens," which had acted as an assembly, seems no longer to have met. Abroad the monarchs were strong enough to interfere in north Syria against Egypt, Mitanni, and Assyria. The general course of internal relations has already been sketched in Chapter 4, where we saw that Suppiluliumas (*c.* 1375–35) gained definitive control in the area; at this time the palace and city of Hattusas were enlarged. His successors maintained the lordship over north Syria against the efforts of Ramesses II.

Politically as well as culturally the Hittite state was a fragile system which lacked the deep roots of the older societies in the Fertile Crescent. By the latter part of the thirteenth century the Hittite kings were facing trouble in the southern and western reaches of Asia Minor, which they had never ruled directly; internal difficulties emerged; and by shortly after 1200 their realm dissolved forever as a fresh wave of Indo-European invaders poured across the Hellespont from Europe. Under these peoples, the chief of whom seem to have been the Phrygians, Asia Minor abruptly sank back to a primitive level and remained on an uncivilized plane until about 800 B.C.

Hittite Civilization. Hittite civilization, which covers the era 1600–1200 B.C., was heavily dependent upon Mesopotamian models. Especially in the period of the Empire these were in large part filtered through the Hurrians to Asia Minor. Around the capital the main form of writing was cuneiform, and well over half of the Hittite vocabulary had non-Indo-European roots. Alongside cuneiform script there existed for the Luvian dialect a "hieroglyphic Hittite," which endured in north Syria down into the first millennium B.C.; this has been translated only in the past 10 years.

Writing was used for both secular and religious purposes. A new quality of Hittite literature which is not easily to be paralleled elsewhere in the contemporary Near East is the forthright tone of the kings' speeches and the extensive historical preambles to their decrees and treaties. Such historical accounts eventually came to stand by themselves; whereas royal inscriptions in Mesopotamia were pious accountings by the kings to their gods, the Hittite records basically told the reader what had happened. The cuneiform script may even have been introduced for the purpose of reciting royal words and deeds.

Besides letters and reports, law codes have also been found, which in general pattern were adapted from Mesopotamian principles. Punishments differed according to the culprit's class, though pure retribution and bodily mutilation were not so common as in Hammurabi's code. Merchants were very stringently protected, and craftsmen were a well-defined group; among the latter were the first ironsmiths.

Other tablets contain religious material. Royal religious ceremonies involved great masses of ritual; the Hittites also took over many Mesopotamian beliefs in demons, magic, and omens. Myths are also to be found. Some are Mesopotamian, as the epic of Gilgamesh, which occurs both in Hittite and Hurrian dialect. Others have Hurrian roots, as the legend of Kumarbi, father of the gods, who was overthrown and castrated by his son; later this tale made its way to Greece via Phoenicia and was used to explain the overthrow of Kronos by Zeus.

In myth and art alike it is apparent that Hittite religion was much affected by Hurrian influence; no Indo-European deities appear, as among the Mitanni and the Kassites. One of the great monuments, the rocky cleft two miles from Hattusas now called Yazilikaya, "Inscribed Rock," is entirely Hurrian. On its walls great processions of gods and goddesses were carved. One procession was led by the Hurrian sun-goddess Hebat, whom the Hittites equated with their local sun-goddess of the holy city Arinna; the other was led by her husband, the Hurrian weather-god Teshub — a fit deity for a land of storms.

Some figures of art and myth, however, were of local origin and generally stood on a simpler level. Telipinu, a god of agriculture, vanished every year, fell to sleep, but was reawakened by the sting of a bee. The coming of the New Year was celebrated by great festivities, in which priests recited a primitive myth about the slaying of the dragon by the weather-god.

In the technique and subjects of Hittite art we can see most clearly the heavy indebtedness of the Hittites to earlier patterns of civilization. Some of the rock-carvings, which often show the king worshiping his divine protector, and the figures of animals or divine protectors at city-gates betray a rugged spirit, but this art never had a chance to rise past a rude, provincial level. The Hittites, that is to say, were not able to evolve a truly independent, advanced culture of their own. For the historian the most suggestive aspect of their history lies in its revelation of how difficult a task faced the invading elements in the Near East merely in absorbing what they found, let alone striking out on new paths.

THE MINOAN–MYCENAEAN WORLD

The Early Aegean (6000–1600 B.C.). The second civilization which arose to the west of the Fertile Crescent is the more amazing in its true originality when we compare it to the Hittite experience. On the island of Crete, Minoan culture had reached a high level by the early second millennium and inspired a derivative system on the mainland of Greece, which is called Mycenaean. Whereas the Hittite world lived and died without any major effects on subsequent ages, the long-range influence of the Minoan and Mycenaean outlooks was of great importance in the origins of Greek civilization, the foundation of western culture.

Crete and Greece face on the Aegean Sea. This is an almost land-locked body of water, which at once divides Europe and Asia and also links the peninsula of Greece with the islands and the coast of Asia Minor. Such a geographical position has had an enduring effect upon the history of the Aegean basin. Peoples driving down out of Europe by land have commonly come thus far and no farther. On the other side, Near Eastern ideas brought by traders sailing over the Mediterranean have made their way — though with difficulty — to the Aegean but have not easily penetrated on into continental Europe. From Paleolithic times the area was inhabited, but extensive settlement becomes visible only in the sixth millennium B.C., when agricultural villages appear. In the development of pottery, the modeling of figurines, and the use of seals these early villages betray eastern cultural affinities, but they lay sufficiently removed to develop a distinct, though simple pattern of life.

By the third millennium B.C. most of the later Greek sites had been settled. Metals were being used, and local chieftains had become powerful enough to build up really remarkable hoards of gold and silver jewelry, examples of which have turned up at Troy on the Asiatic coast, and elsewhere. At the seacoast village of Lerna, near the historic Greek town of Argos, the mansion of such a chieftain has been found; two stories high, it was made of yellow, stuccoed mudbrick on stone foundations with a flat roof of terra-cotta tiles. The stores in this House of the Tiles were marked by their master's seal, and an abundance of imported items shows trade out into the Aegean islands (the Cyclades) and to Crete. In Greece this era is called Early Helladic; in Crete, which was generally similar, Early Minoan (see Map 4).

About 2000 B.C. the House of the Tiles was destroyed, and many other sites on the Greek mainland attest a fierce onslaught. In view of what was happening in the Near East it seems probable that Indo-Europeans were the cause of this destruction, and since writing appeared in the course of the next centuries in Greece we can be sure the invading people spoke Greek. They took over the simple agricultural sites they found — such great later Greek sites as Athens, Thebes, and Corinth have non-Greek names — but tended to withdraw somewhat from the seacoast. The ensuing Middle Helladic period (2000–1600 B.C.) was an undistinguished era, in which conquerors and conquered learned to live together. Crete, however, was not affected by this disruption; life there proceeded on a more continuous course.

The Minoan Glory (2000–1400 B.C.). Although there is no sure evidence that Crete was invaded in the Early Minoan era, it lay open to influences from many regions; objects or ideas from Asia Minor, Syria, Egypt, and the Cyclades can be detected in the archeological records of the island. In the Middle Minoan stage (*c.* 2000–1570 B.C.) the eastern and central parts of Crete skyrocketed into a type of civilization so urbane and polished, so novel in flavor that it has been almost overidealized since its discovery 60 years ago.

Even more than in the discovery of the Hittites our view of Minoan Crete and kindred developments rests upon archeological exploration at Cnossus, Mycenae, and many other sites; for the legends which the Greeks later told of their own origins and of a king Minos of Crete are without any deep historical value. Writing, to be sure, now came into use. This script, first pictorial and then linear (called Linear A), was of a syllabic type and was written on clay tablets, probably from Mesopotamian influence, and perhaps on more perishable substances; but the materials so far at hand are both scanty and indecipherable.

The picture of Minoan civilization which we can draw from our evidence is at once fascinating and puzzling. At Cnossus and elsewhere real cities existed, the only ones known in Europe down to the first millennium B.C. Here citizens dwelt in several-storied houses, which had windows and internal courts; they surrounded themselves with artistic products. Over them stood kings, who introduced some Near Eastern principles of government, including the written accounts just noted. Yet in the lack of records of historical type, in the absence of military braggadocio and a warlike class, in the failure of the kings to swallow up all disposable resources of their realms, the states of Crete stand virtually unique in the second millennium.

Equally unusual is the absence of great temples, though large areas of the palaces were used for religious ceremonies probably under the direction of the priest-kings. While it appears from the representations on the seals that the Cretans worshiped especially goddesses, their statues have thus far turned up only on an Aegean island, not in Crete. The dove, tree, snake, and double-headed ax seem to have been sacred symbols. Religious ceremonies were conducted on the tops of mountains, in sacred caves, and at small altars in the houses. The strange practice of bull-leaping, where young men and maidens seized the horns of trained bulls and vaulted over their backs, was probably one of these ceremonies. Since we lack written records of Cretan religion, it is dangerous to generalize about the basic beliefs of the era; modern scholars, however, tend to see in the physical evidence, and in the later Greek myth that Zeus died every year in Crete and was reborn, signs of fertility cults and of an unusually direct, naive worship of the forces of nature.

Palaces of the period have been found at Cnossus, Hagia Triada, Phaestus, and elsewhere. Architecturally the palaces consist of mazes of rooms and living quarters organized around central courtyards and well equipped with drains and baths. In their sprawling nature they may well have been remembered in the later Greek myth of the "labyrinth," a term which means House of the Double Ax. This symbol was carved on the walls and was represented in gold and silver models. The staircases and other architectural details of these buildings display on a small, intimate scale an esthetic sense which one may look for in vain in most Egyptian architecture. The major rooms were decorated with delightfully colored frescoes which depict plants and animals, real or imaginary, on a gay scale.[1]

In the painting, as well as in other arts, a modern observer senses a different artistic spirit than is to be found anywhere in the older seats of civilization. The best of the pottery, which is termed Kamares ware, is almost eggshell thin, flowing in shape, and adorned with polychrome designs drawn from plant and animal life and based commonly on a whirligig principle. Human beings do not bulk large in this art. Sculpture was all small in scale; among its products are lithe ivory figurines of acrobats, the very essence of fugitive motion.

Politically, religiously, and culturally the Minoan world thus stands far removed from any civilization which we have thus far seen. In many

---

[1] The throne room at Cnossus (Plate V) was restored by its excavator, Sir Arthur Evans; between wingless griffins in a field of flowers, on a wine-red background, stands the simple gypsum throne. This was one of the latest rooms of the palace.

respects of organization and techniques it was indebted to the Near East, and new similarities have become ever more visible as archeologists have explored such coastal cities of Syria as Ugarit. Minoan products have turned up here as well as in Egypt, where tomb reliefs of the Middle and New Kingdom seem to represent Cretan traders. The basic character of Cretan life, however, was of quite different type from these sources.

On the other hand the art historian looks to Cretan products in vain for "the innate love of balanced order, the feeling of structural symmetry which are the most essential qualities of Greek art." [2] The historic civilization of Greece owed much to early Crete, but neither in its political values nor in its cultural outlook did later Greece descend in a straight line from the palaces of the island or from the almost childish, direct joy of the Cretans in representing motion and nature.

Mycenaean Kings and Traders (1600–1100 B.C.). To follow the main course of Aegean development we must turn back to the Greek mainland. Minoan traders do not seem to have been much interested in this backward area, but its own inhabitants grew to learn of the advanced life in the island to their south. During the Middle Helladic era the use of bronze, of the potter's wheel, and of other skills spread over the mainland; in the graves which the lords of the fortress at Mycenae dug in deep shafts, luxuries such as crystal ducks, ivory gaming boards, and an amazing host of golden jewelry and face masks were buried from 1600 onward.[3] Behind the watery barrier of the Aegean the cities and palaces of Crete lay virtually defenseless, a tempting prey for the warlike, semibarbarous lords of such fortresses, who swooped down in the fifteenth century and took the central Cretan site of Cnossus.

During the following two centuries, 1400–1200, the focus of Aegean political strength and culture lay on the mainland; to mark this shift the culture of the mainland is called Mycenaean. Over southern and central Greece elegant palaces, decorated with frescoes and colonnaded halls, appeared at Mycenae and Tiryns, at Pylos on the west coast, on the

[2] Georg Karo, *Greek Personality in Archaic Sculpture* (Cambridge, Mass.: Harvard University Press, 1948), p. 5.
[3] When Heinrich Schliemann excavated in 1876 the gold face mask illustrated on Plate VI, he excitedly telegraphed, "I have looked upon the face of Agamemnon." Actually it represents in its small, tight mouth, Grecian nose, and tuft of beard a much earlier warlord of Mycenae; four other masks were also found in the shaft graves.

Acropolis at Athens, and as far north as Thessaly. In death the powerful kings of these palaces were often buried in great, rock-lined tombs with false domes, called *tholos* tombs, which required great amounts of man-power. Neither palaces nor tombs on such a scale were ever again to appear in Greece; and the Treasury of Atreus, a *tholos* tomb with a lintel weighing over 100 tons, was the most impressive work thus far erected on the continent of Europe.

A syllabic form of writing with 89 characters, called Linear B, which was adapted from the Cretan script, was employed by palace adminis-trators and tax collectors. Tablets in this writing have turned up at Cnossus, Pylos, and Mycenae; when they were deciphered recently, they turned out to be an early form of Greek. The lords of the Mycenaean palaces thus attempted to imitate the advanced political and economic systems of the Near East, but it should be noted that they were not able to develop true cities about their fortresses. Most of the population con-tinued to live in purely agricultural villages, and much of it took no direct share in the advanced culture known in the palaces.

The riches of the Mycenaean age rested partly upon exploitation of this native peasantry, partly upon masses of slaves gathered in piratical raids and war, partly upon far-flung trade. The warlords of Greece not only took and ruled Crete; they also seem to have attacked Troy, an event which eventually gave rise to the great epics of the *Iliad* and the *Odyssey*. To judge from unclear references in Hittite records they also ravaged eastward along the coast of Asia Minor. Elsewhere they traded. Mycenaean objects have turned up in some quantity in Sicily and south-ern Italy, to which men of Aegean origin had long been sailing to secure raw metals; scattered items made their way even as far as Britain. To the east Greek-speaking peoples settled down at this time in Cyprus, and a large deposit of Mycenaean pottery has been discovered on the Syrian coast at Ugarit. Mycenaean traders served as intermediaries between Asia and Europe; the development of the farther reaches of Europe, such as Italy and the central Danube, began to speed up at this time as a reaction to the demand of the eastern Mediterranean for copper, tin, and amber.

Mycenaean culture in itself was a rather dull, mechanical effort to absorb the influences of Minoan Crete and, to a much lesser degree, of the Near East. Its pottery, for instance, occurs over a far wider area than had that of Crete but consists of great masses of very similar ware, in which old motifs were copied and adulterated into meaningless squiggles.[4] From the tablets written in Linear B we can see that the Greek-speaking inhabitants of the mainland took over Semitic words for spices and other objects; in historic times half of the Greek vocabulary had non-Indo-European roots. On the whole Mycenaean civilization did not advance even so far as the Hittites had done, yet on the other hand it remained essentially more independent of Near Eastern models. The culture which flourished in the Mycenaean palaces was, after all, the farthest edge of the civilization of the high Bronze age in the second millennium B.C.; and of all the European continent this was the only area which progressed even so far.

If we may judge from its pottery, Mycenaean civilization was declining throughout the thirteenth century; but its end was not to be one of gradual disintegration. Shortly after 1200 B.C. the great citadel of Mycenae went up in flames. Off on the west coast the palace of Pylos had already been sacked. Virtually everywhere in Greece, save on the Acropolis at Athens, there is parallel testimony to a terrific storm of invasion, which swept away the fragile superstructure of royal centralization. The palaces thenceforth lay roofless, moldering in sun and rain, with fragments of gold leaf on their floors and useless archives abandoned in their record rooms. The invaders were barbarians from the fringe of the Greek world, whom legends remembered as the Dorians. The skills of civilization were of no interest to these people; writing disappeared and was not to recur in Greece for centuries.

Well before 1000 B.C. Greece thus had sunk back into as primitive and as poverty-stricken a stage as did Asia Minor after the Hittite collapse. Yet the remarkable Minoan and Mycenaean variations on Near Eastern themes were not entirely in vain. The full meaning of this first phase of Aegean history and also of the fact that the new invasions cut the Aegean lands off from the Near East for the next five centuries will

---

[4] Plate VIII.A shows a high-stemmed Mycenaean goblet or *kylix* of a very popular type. The contrast between Mycenaean and early Greek artistic principles is manifest both in the seminaturalistic, weak decoration of the *kylix* and in its top-heavy shape. The same contrast appears in Mycenaean (and Minoan) columns, which are larger on top than bottom, whereas Greek columns taper upward and so appear solidly based (see Plate V).

become apparent when we turn later to the emergence of the historic Greek outlook.

The Farther East. The connections of Hittite and Minoan-Mycenaean civilization with the Fertile Crescent are clearly demonstrable in many particulars; and the course of development in these western outliers can be seen in its major respects. For the two civilizations which arose to the east in India and China the situation is far less clear.

The vast Indian peninsula, though largely isolated, was not quite cut off by land or by sea from the Near East. From the first days of human existence Indian cultures had been in contact with the lands to their northwest; in the third millennium B.C. civilized patterns appeared in the valley of the Indus river. The relations of China to the west are much more problematical, for the early history of China is still largely to be ferreted out. What can be seen is the absorbing fact that progress in both India and China moved somewhat more slowly but nonetheless in much the same fashion as did the Near East. Yet the first dim hints of the historic Chinese and Indian outlooks appear in the era before 1000 B.C., just as early foreshadowings of the Greek spirit had marked Minoan-Mycenaean times (see Map 5).

The Indus Civilization (2500–1500 B.C.). From 1920 onward excavators in northwest India turned up along the Indus river and its tributaries some of the largest early cities which have ever been found. Mohenjo-daro and Harappa, two of the major sites, each cover a square mile. They lie, moreover, 350 miles apart, and other settlements reproduce exactly the same patterns of civilization over a district 1000 miles long; for recent evidence shows that cities of the Harappan type extended south along the seacoast and eastward inland to the vicinity of modern Delhi. The civilization which was centered on the Indus river in the third and early second millennia B.C. was the most extensive down to that time in terms of geographical extent and quantity of affected population.

In prehistoric times the Indus valley had been a wild jungle, teeming with such savage animals as the water buffalo, rhinoceros, elephant, and crocodile. Human settlement lay largely in the Baluchi hills to its north-

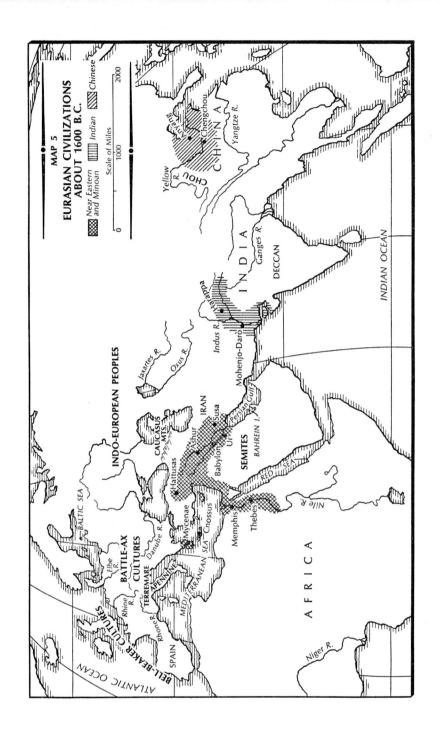

MAP 5
EURASIAN CIVILIZATIONS
ABOUT 1600 B.C.

Near Eastern
and Minoan   Indian   Chinese

Scale of Miles

0   1000   2000

west, better watered then than now; the villages of the area had existed on a simple Neolithic level. Then, quite suddenly, there occurred an explosion as men moved down into the valley and harnessed its resources. Whereas Mesopotamian cities like Ur developed slowly and long had primitive marks in their twisting streets, Mohenjo-daro was laid out on a rectangular pattern from the outset.

Historians are inclined to suspect that the inhabitants of the area had gained inspiration from the earlier rise of Mesopotamian civilization. To support this conclusion Mesopotamian records have clear references to trade down the Persian Gulf via the island of Telmun (modern Bahrein); Indian stamp seals and Mesopotamian cylinder seals have turned up in sites of the other area. This trade endured from about 2500 into the second millennium.

Yet the Indus civilization was quite distinct. Its walls and buildings were erected in baked bricks, not the sun-dried bricks of Mesopotamia; drainage systems excelled those found anywhere else at this period. Thus far no palaces or temples have been uncovered, though a strong government is suggested by the regular layout of the cities, their capacious granaries, and the existence of citadels beside the cities proper which were perhaps the homes of the priests. The style of writing was so different that it cannot yet be read; cotton, elephants, and water buffalos were domesticated. Interesting suggestions of later Indian concepts and physical ways of life also occur in the clay and bronze models of ox carts, bracelets and ear ornaments, the shapes of ivory combs, ubiquitous baths, and the emphasis on horned bulls. A male god, three-faced, flanked by animals, and seated in a yoga-like posture reminds one of the later god Siva; the female figurines, mostly nude, seem to have been household idols, set in niches in the walls, like the guardian mother goddess today in India.

Thus far, signs of evolution and change in the Indus valley are almost absent, unlike Mesopotamian or Egyptian progress. The residents of Mohenjo-daro and Harappa seem to have lived for centuries in a monotonous, complacent stage, repeating the ways of their ancestors; their life was punctuated only by river floods which forced a rebuilding from time to time of their standardized patterns of houses. After 2000 signs of decline can perhaps be detected in poorer building methods and in the subdivision of rooms. Then came destruction, and civilization ended in the Indus valley itself; some of the outlying settlements lasted longer.

While the date of this catastrophe cannot be set more closely than at the middle of the second millennium b.c., it is commonly linked with the invasions which brought the peoples later called Aryans or "nobles," who spoke the Indo-European language Sanskrit. Both the social and the religious patterns of later India rest upon a merging of the ideas introduced by the Aryans and the customs which survived the fall of the Indus civilization. To these developments, from *c.* 1500 on, we shall return in Chapter 8.

Men of the Yellow River (to *c.* 1122 b.c.). Whereas even the Paleolithic remains of India have an affinity to the hand-ax cultures of western Eurasia, China had followed a quite different road from the days of the Choukoutien caves. Toward the end of the Paleolithic era a widespread cultural pattern covered not only China but also southeast Asia and Japan; the Neolithic stage in northern China, however, evolved a quite distinct way of life. Its beginnings have not yet been clearly identified, but scholars now judge that it was the product of purely native developments. Wheat may have made its way across Asia from the west; the Neolithic villages of north China from at least the fifth millennium b.c. relied mainly on millet and later also on rice (domesticated in southeast Asia) as well as dogs and pigs. Other Neolithic cultures appeared along the coast and in the Yangtze valley; all seem to have lived in local independence.

Chinese traditions remembered three dynasties at the dawn of civilization: Hsia, Shang, and Chou. The first of these, Hsia (*c.* 2205–*c.* 1766 b.c.), is still very dim but is increasingly believed to have existed; the earliest, however, which can be described in any detail is the Shang dynasty (*c.* 1766–*c.* 1122 b.c.), an era of sudden advance in many aspects of Chinese culture. The Shang state was localized in the basin of the Yellow river, a violent stream which frequently shifts its beds across the plains of north China. Of the many sites that have been found, the most illustrative are those of Chengchou and thereafter Anyang. The latter, in a bend of a river, was the capital for almost three centuries. Major houses and temples, which were not monumental in style, were built of wooden pillars supporting wattle-and-daub and thatched roofs on foundations of packed earth; this style was traditional in later China, though the pattern of the coutyard house came only in Han times. Shang cities were primarily religious and ceremonial centers covering wide areas, much like Mayan cities, but they also had extensive industrial sectors for the skillful working of bronze, bones, clay, jade, and other materials.

Shang oracle bones carry some 2500–3000 syllabic characters which were the ancestors of the standard Chinese scripts. These tortoise shells (which were imported in numbers) and ox shoulder bones were polished and inscribed with questions, then heated by a bronze point applied to a shallow pit until they cracked; the form of the crack gave the answer of Yes or No, Lucky or Unlucky. The questions on the thousands of bones that have been excavated at Anyang and elsewhere concern wars, hunting trips, crops, illness, sacrifices, the latter of which might involve the slaughter of captives by the hundreds. Verification of the oracle was often added; on one bone there is the query, "Will it rain tonight?" and the later, disgusted notation, "It really didn't rain." The greatest deity shown on these bones was Shang Ti, "ruler above," but other gods of earth and sky were worshiped as well as the royal ancestors.

Beside the sites of Shang towns, some of which were fortified, a major source of evidence has been the graves of the rulers and their nobles. These were great pits with access ramps on all four sides (or at times only north and south); the ruler was buried in a coffin within a grave chamber in the center of the pit and was surrounded by hosts of ornaments, weapons, vessels, dogs, and sacrificed slaves and servants. Horses, chariots, and charioteers were also buried, either in the pit or in a separate entombment. From such magnificent graves as that of a Shang queen (Fu Hao), who led military expeditions, have come lovely jade ornaments and bronze ritual vessels decorated with a limited number of motifs which were combined into remarkably complex patterns. Some of these motifs, largely of bizarre animals, became a lasting part of Chinese art; nowhere else in Eurasia was bronze-casting so advanced at the time as here. Pottery was no longer painted but was well glazed; some vases were pure white, but this forerunner of the later famous Chinese porcelain died out temporarily at the end of the Shang era.

With their bows, bronze halberds, and chariots the armies of the Shang rulers gave a strongly military cast to the earliest Chinese civilization. The kings, the focus of society and of religious ritual, exploited the native peasants and waged war to gain tribute and captives for sacrifices and funerals. Possibly, too, irrigation was being employed on a scale which encouraged political unification of the plains and the development of an administrative hierarchy. Looming above the low country, however, stood the highlands just to the southwest, from which less-civilized but more-vigorous peoples were to pour down several times in early Chinese history. In tradition, thus, the Shang dynasty was eventually overthrown from this direction by the Chou dynasty (*c.* 1122–256 B.C.).

The new dynasty continued the earlier structure of life to a far greater degree than was true in the Aegean world or in India, which were more open to outside influence; but only in the Chou era did the historic characteristics of Chinese civilization come closely into focus. Here again we shall pick up the later threads of the story in Chapter 8.

EURASIA IN 1000 B.C.

Its Civilizations. We have now swept across Eurasia from Greece to China and have surveyed the major developments down to about the end of the second millennium B.C. Most of this great area still lay in black darkness as its tribes gathered their food or farmed in a traditional manner, living and dying generation after generation without leaving any marked physical impress on their world. Only a few scattered districts had attained the complicated, conscious ways of civilized societies.

These latter districts were, for the most part, major river valleys. Here agricultural resources could be exploited to support relatively large concentrations of population, provided only that the men of those valleys were willing to harness themselves into firmly organized systems. In China the inhabitants of the Yellow river basin had done so; in India, those of the Indus valley; in Mesopotamia, the Sumerians and Semites; and in Africa, the subjects of the pharaohs dwelling in the narrow cleft of the Nile.

Civilization, however, had become a set of qualities sufficiently generalized and pliable that it could be attained by peoples who did not share the physical resources of the great river plains. In Syria, in Asia Minor, and in the Aegean basin men had learned how to unite their strength in common endeavors, usually under the direction of kings and bureaucracies centralized in great palaces.

As men raised themselves to this level, they did so largely in imitation of peoples who had already made the great step. The archeological evidence alone is enough to prove that the complicated skills required in the working of metals, manufacture of pottery, and other industrial techniques were diffused from the first centers of civilization; and through written and artistic materials the transmission of religious concepts and myths can be shown. Yet the expansion of new ways that we have followed in the past two chapters was not simply a matter of borrowing. While imitating alien advances, men could adapt and modify their loans into such a novel structure as that of Minoan Crete.

As a concept, civilization may be unitary, but the historian finds that in practice it is encased in distinct forms, each of which forms a civilization in its own right. The use of writing, which is one major mark of the civilized level, shows this important fact clearly. No one could confuse the signs scratched on Shang oracle bones with the marks drawn on the tablets of Mycenaean bookkeepers, or these in turn with the serried rows of hieroglyphs which convey the boasts of Ramesses II on an Egyptian temple. While a member of a modern western society will feel a certain dim affinity in the artistic products of Minoan Crete or even of ancient Egypt, the physical remains of early Mesopotamia, India, and China must seem alien indeed. Not all civilizations, in truth, can be measured by the same standards; and a candid observer must infer that civilized men do not always and everywhere fasten on the same objectives in life.

The End of an Epoch. Repeatedly in the preceding pages our surveys of the earliest civilizations in Eurasia have brought out the fact that each underwent a great shock just before 1000 B.C. Some areas, such as the Aegean world, Asia Minor, and India, slipped back to uncivilized levels. Others, however, rode out the storms with resilient tenacity. Civilization may appear at first sight to be a fragile structure, a system which demands too much from its participants in the way of restriction of individual license for the communal good. Yet the cities of the Near East for the most part survived the threats of internal unrest, external imperialism, and barbarian invasion in the late second millennium, just as the great modern centers of London, Tokyo, and Hamburg stood up defiantly under the bombing assaults of World War II. Advanced society has its strengths as well as its weaknesses; not every area was yet civilized, but the roots, where they had plunged deep, were not easily cut off.

The end of the second millennium B.C., nonetheless, was one of the great turning points in ancient history. Thereafter the major districts of Eurasia evolved far more clearly and consciously those patterns of life and thought which have stamped their subsequent history down to modern times. In observing this development, however, one must always keep in mind the preliminary steps which had been taken in earlier eras; continuity and change are intricately interwoven in human progress.

BIBLIOGRAPHY

Sources. While writing was used in all the areas surveyed in this chapter, the written records are rarely so useful as for Egypt and Mesopotamia proper. The Hittites, who lived closest to the Fertile Crescent, had the most extensive and illuminating records (see the selection in *Ancient Near Eastern Texts*); we cannot yet read the writing of Crete and of the Indus civilization; the materials from Shang China and Mycenaean Greece are quite limited and not easy to interpret. For the latter area, see Michael Ventris and John Chadwick, *Documents in Mycenaean Greek* (2d ed.; Cambridge: Cambridge University Press, 1973). In all these areas except China writing disappeared before 1000 B.C.

Later civilizations were to preserve myths and legends which may go back to the earlier eras. Historians have often been tempted into using such oral materials extensively inasmuch as other evidence is lacking, but no careful scholar will go far on this path (how far back do oral memories go in modern families?); at most, one can hope to make very general inferences of migration or catastrophes from this material.

Physical evidence, accordingly, is even more basic for these civilizations than for those of the Near East in the second millennium B.C. Commonly it is less extensive and less detailed, in keeping with the thinner roots of civilization in the more recently advanced areas; consecutive patterns of development are not so easily seen. We have come to know Hattusas, Cnossus, Mohenjo-daro, and Anyang only recently; on the excavation of the latter see Li Chi, *Anyang* (Seattle: University of Washington Press, 1977). While surface exploration of most of Asia has now been conducted in at least a sampling fashion, a fortunate excavator may yet turn up another hitherto unknown civilization.

Further Reading. The best work on the Hittites is O. R. Gurney, *The Hittites* (rev. ed.; Penguin, 1975); see also J. G. MacQueen, *The Hittites and Their Contemporaries in Asia Minor* (Boulder: Westview Press, 1976). Hittite art is well illustrated in Ekrem Akurgal and Max Hirmer, *Art of the Hittites* (New York: Abrams, 1962).

Among the many studies of the early Aegean see Emily Vermeule, *Greece in the Bronze Age* (Chicago: University of Chicago Press, 1972); M. I. Finley, *Early Greece* (New York: Norton, 1970); S. Hood, *The Minoans* (New York: Praeger, 1974); J. T. Hooker, *Mycenaean Greece* (Boston: Routledge & Kegan Paul, 1976); J. W. Graham, *Palaces of Crete* (Princeton: Princeton University Press, 1969); and for Aegean art S. Hood, *The Arts in Prehistoric Greece* (Penguin, 1978). Accounts by the major excavators may be found in Arthur Evans, *Palace of Minos at Knossos,* 5 vols. (London: Macmillan, 1921–35); Carl W. Blegen, *Troy and the Trojans* (New York: Praeger, 1963); and A. J. B. Wace, *Mycenae* (Princeton: Princeton University Press, 1949). The famous code-cracking of Linear B is described by John Chadwick, *Decipherment of Linear B* (2d ed.; New York: Vintage, 1968). The invaders at the end are discussed in N. K. Sandars, *The Sea Peoples* (New York: Thames and Hudson, 1978).

The earliest stage of civilization in India is described by W. A. Fairservis, Jr., *The Roots of Ancient India* (2d ed.; Chicago: University of Chicago Press, 1975), and the essays in G. L. Possehl, *Ancient Cities of the Indus* (Durham: Carolina Academic Press, 1979). For China, see George B. Cressey, *China's Geographic Foundations* (New York: McGraw-Hill, 1933); K. C. Chang, *Shang Civilization* (New Haven: Yale University Press, 1980); P. Wheatley, *The Pivot of the Four Quarters* (Chicago: Aldine, 1971), on cities; Phyllis Ackerman, *Ritual Bronzes of Ancient China* (New York: Dryden, 1945). The archeological evidence proper may be found in K. C. Chang, *Archaeology of Ancient China* (3d ed.; Yale University Press, 1977); D. N. Keightley, *Sources of Shang History* (Berkeley: University of California Press, 1978).

III

THE RISE OF NEW OUTLOOKS

6

THE UNIFICATION OF
THE NEAR EAST

During the middle centuries of the second millennium B.C. the Fertile Crescent had attained a peak both in the extent of civilization and in its outward magnificence. Then, rather abruptly, came a decline about 1200 B.C. The deterioration affected particularly the superstructure of civilization, where kings, warrior nobles, and priests abode; in the Aegean, in Asia Minor, and in some parts of Syria and Palestine this layer was virtually swept away completely. Elsewhere it was more toughly rooted, but even there peasants and artisans suffered as well as the upper classes. When societies became civilized, all elements were so interlinked that changes on any level necessarily affected other parts as well.

This decline was foreshadowed by, and in part caused by, internal developments in the Near Eastern states. In the New Kingdom of Egypt, for instance, generals and the priests of Amen and other gods exerted ever greater influence on the throne. In many areas local landlords, who also controlled the political and military resources of the countryside, asserted their independence while the kings themselves exhausted their strength in profitless wars against each other. The most significant token of deterioration was the fact that artists and craftsmen showed an inability to think new ideas and sank into sterile repetition of old motifs. Whether the societies of the Fertile Crescent could have stood up to foreign assaults if they had still been vigorous, we do not know; but weary as they were they collapsed before the great wave of invasions at the end of the Bronze age.

The ensuing period from 1200 to 900 is a dim and dreary one. The kings, warlords, and priests could no longer heap up great buildings and patronize the arts. Earlier there had been preliminary tendencies to link together the main parts of the Near East economically and culturally; now life was concentrated in tiny, local units. Nonetheless very basic technical developments occurred in this era; and in wider, less specific ways the poverty-stricken, localized systems of the centuries just on either side of 1000 B.C. paved the way for a spectacular advance. Every so often civilization seems to work itself into a corner from which further progress is virtually impossible along the lines then apparent; yet if new ideas are to have a chance the old systems must be so severely shaken that they lose their dominance. Two such major collapses occurred in ancient times, one at the end of the Roman Empire in the west, the other at the end of the second millennium B.C.

The eventual products of the latter collapse, which we are examining here, were a wider, more consolidated web of civilization and a tighter unification than the Near East had ever known before. From 900 to 600 the ancestral centers of civilization came together politically in the Assyrian empire, culturally in a cosmopolitan art which was attractive as far as India and the western Mediterranean, and economically in a remarkable growth and intensification of trade. Although the Assyrian empire fell in 612 B.C., the ensuing political split was only temporary. By 550 the kings of Persia were reassembling the pieces, but for the purposes of the present chapter we shall stop at this point.

THE DARK AGES

The Invaders. The uncivilized peoples who helped to deliver a death blow to the declining cultures of the second millennium came from the same areas and followed much the same avenues as had the influential invasions early in the millennium. From the northern fringe poured out barbarous speakers of Indo-European tongues. In the Aegean and in Asia Minor these tribes overwhelmed those kindred peoples, Mycenaeans and Hittites, who had managed to raise themselves to the level of civilization; others seem to have pushed into Italy and western Europe, into Persia, and on to the confines of China. Within the Fertile Crescent proper they picked up other wanderers and ravaged Syria, where

Ugarit and other cities fell forever. Egyptian records depict in word and picture the desperate battles of Ramesses III against the invaders by land and sea, who were barely beaten off in the early twelfth century.

In the Near East proper, Indo-European groups did not settle down and leave a lasting imprint. It was probably at this time that Europe as a whole, and perhaps Persia too, became definitely Indo-European in speech; and shortly thereafter the nomadic way of life of peoples mounted on horseback, driving their flocks across the steppelands, developed in the great plains of Eurasia. But in the Fertile Crescent the Semitic invaders from the desert fringe were more lastingly important; these waves bore the names of Arameans, Hapiru, and the like, which turn up in written records from the middle centuries of the second millennium. The new Semitic peoples, organized in patriarchal tribes, each of which worshiped its particular divine spirit, trickled in and lapped about the previously consolidated centers of civilized life. Eventually they amalgamated with the earlier inhabitants and drowned out the isolated remnants of non-Semitic tongues. From the time when civilization revived once more in the Near East on down to the present day, the basic speech here has been Semitic.

Palestine and Phoenicia (1200–800 B.C.). In the centuries from 1200 on Egypt lay in somnolence, divided into small states until a Libyan dynasty (the Twenty-second) reunited it about 945. Assyria and Babylonia were quiescent. The intervening stretches of the Fertile Crescent thus had an unusual opportunity to assert their local political and cultural independence; and so the interesting developments of the period largely occurred in Palestine, Phoenicia, and Syria (see Map 6).

The state which the Hebrews erected in Palestine about the city of Jerusalem was the most important, not so much for its political history — which was one of temporary glory and then of bitter division and deterioration — as for its religious achievements. These have had such powerful influence on later times through the avenues of Judaism, Christianity, and Islam that they deserve very close inspection. The history of Palestine accordingly will be taken up by itself in the next chapter.

To the north of Israel lay other states in Phoenicia and Syria. The land of Phoenicia, which had connections with almost all parts of the Fertile Crescent, is a narrow strip between mountains and sea, about 200

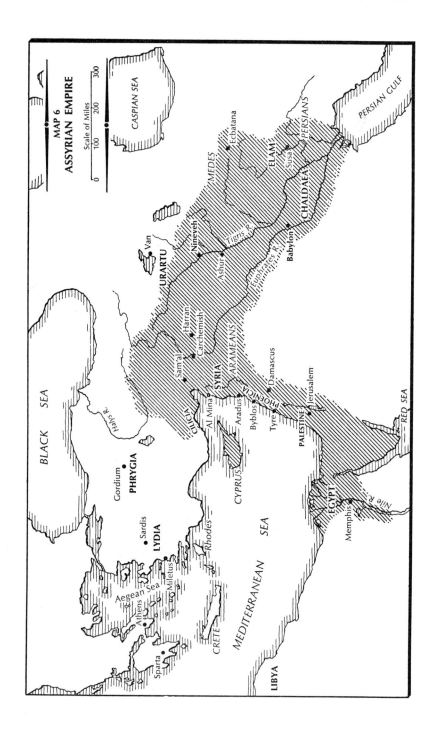

MAP 6
ASSYRIAN EMPIRE

Scale of Miles
0   100   200   300

CASPIAN SEA

PERSIAN GULF

Ecbatana

MEDES

ELAM

PERSIANS

Susa

CHALDAEA

Van

URARTU

Nineveh

Tigris R.

Ashur

Babylon

Euphrates R.

Harran

Carchemish

Sam'al

ARAMEANS

SYRIA

Damascus

CILICIA

Al Mina

PHOENICIA

Jerusalem

Aradus

Byblos

Tyre

PALESTINE

Halys R.

Gordium

PHRYGIA

CYPRUS

RED SEA

BLACK   SEA

Sardis

LYDIA

Rhodes

EGYPT

Nile R.

Memphis

Aegean Sea

Miletus

MEDITERRANEAN   SEA

Athens

CRETE

Sparta

LIBYA

miles in length and rarely over 20 miles in width. Here small plains which rose into terraced hills supported seacoast towns, the houses of which were close-packed buildings of several stories. The chief towns from south to north were Tyre, Sidon, Berytus, Byblos, and Aradus. Byblos at least went back to the third millennium B.C.; all had been ruled by the pharaohs of the New Kingdom; and several centers had been destroyed by the great invasion of 1200. The Semitic stock of the area survived this blow, and the cities began to revive from about 1000 on. An Egyptian envoy, Wenamon, who traveled to Byblos in search of cedars from Lebanon about 1060, has left a grimly fascinating tale of his robbery and other misadventures, which incidentally portrays active shipping along the coast. Tyre, located on an island just offshore, became the major state of Phoenicia, partly because a great king, Hiram (c. 970–40), the friend of Solomon, developed its trade and improved the harbor.

The culture of this area was derived from the earlier Canaanite patterns. The natives, whom we term Phoenicians (after the Greek custom), called their land Canaan; they represented, indeed, the major surviving fragment of a once much larger grouping. Their civilization was not in itself particularly original or distinguished except in the creation and spread of an alphabet. In its origins the alphabet went back to experiments of the eighteenth century and later, which drew many symbols from Egyptian script. Before 1000 there had appeared north Semitic and south Semitic alphabets. The latter, known from Arabian examples, eventually produced the Ethiopian alphabet; the former gave rise to the Phoenician and very similar Aramaic alphabets. These used only 22 signs, each of which stood for a consonantal sound, and were written from right to left. Admirably suited for the setting down of all kinds of information, both economic and literary, the script could easily be learned; peoples who accepted it did not need to create the learned type of scribe which had been common in the earlier Near East. The new style spread only as trade revived in the Near East, and throughout the Mediterranean drew from the Phoenician form; the Greek adaptation, which we shall consider later, probably came just after 800 B.C.

During the dark ages Phoenician craftsmen developed an amalgam of earlier artistic ideas, especially of Egyptian origin, which they executed in bronze, ivory, wood, textiles (often dyed a Tyrian purple), and other media. These wares became popular and were mass-produced in repetitious patterns; a growing Phoenician trade peddled local and foreign products widely, especially by sea. Before 800 the Phoenicians were trading in Cyprus, and not long after that date they plunged all the way : west to northwestern Africa, where they established posts at Utica, Carthage, and westward as far as Spain. The full meaning of this step will become apparent later when we turn to the development of the western Mediterranean, but at this point it will suffice to note that by the eighth century B.C. the Mediterranean was beginning to assume the great role which it exercised in Greek and Roman times, that is, a unifying rather than a dividing factor for the coastal areas of Europe, Africa, and Asia. This process, however, was still in its first stages. Down through Assyrian times the history of the Near East was played within the boundaries of the Fertile Crescent.

States of Syria (1200–800 B.C.). During the dark ages Syria was also fragmented into a host of tiny states. Elements which called themselves Hittite held local domination at cities like Carchemish on the Euphrates; these lords used hieroglyphic Hittite script for a language which was essentially the earlier Luvian, and maintained a mixture of ancestral Hurrian and Hittite artistic styles. These alien ingredients were destined to die out; most states had already fallen to the Arameans, who ruled Damascus, Sam'al, and other major cities. Their traders, who were as dominant by land as were the Phoenicians by sea, spread the Aramaic variety of the alphabet and with it their speech; they also sold artistic products which had more of a Mesopotamian flavor than did the Phoenician wares. By 800 the Hittite and Aramaic kings of the small Syrian principalities were gaining enough revenues to build palaces of some size, which they decorated with coarsely carved orthostats or alternating black and white stone slabs about a yard high which covered the bottom of important walls.

In the revival of economic activity two developments were significant alongside the use of the alphabet. One was the wider use of the camel as a beast of burden. Although camels were mean, quarrelsome beasts, they could carry far more than could donkeys or asses; the tariff of a later trading city, Palmyra, assessed their loads at five times that of a donkey. Another change was the common use of iron. While iron ores can be melted and refined at a lower temperature than that required for copper, the process takes a longer time, and truly useful weapons and tools of iron involved a complicated technique of repeated heating, quenching, and hammering. Iron objects have turned up even in fifth-millennium levels (sometimes of meteoric source); Hittite smiths in Asia Minor went further in working the metal; but adequate methods of hardening iron products became commonly known only after 1000. Iron accordingly came to be used on a large scale only from 800 onward.

Whereas the manufacture of bronze had been limited by periodic shortages of tin, which is a rare metal, and had been restricted largely to weapons and objects for the upper classes, iron ores occurred widely over ancient Eurasia and could be turned into tools of common use as well; in one Assyrian warehouse over 150 tons of iron ingots were discovered. Ancient techniques, which introduced a good deal of carbon, generally produced a mild steel or at times wrought iron; cast iron was uncommon. On the basis of these and other specific changes trade and industry across the Fertile Crescent had reached unprecedented heights by 800 B.C.

RISE OF THE ASSYRIAN EMPIRE

The Assyrian Kingdom. The fruit of renewed order was first the rise of petty kingdoms, which guaranteed local stability but also exploited the subject peasantry. Then came the consolidation of these units into one great territorial state, a step which perhaps pleased industrial and commercial elements but was bitterly opposed by the local rulers. The people who transmuted the growing economic and cultural unification of the Near East into political unity were the Assyrian folk.

If we are to explain why this particular kingdom rose into dominance over the others, we must look both to the earlier tradition of Assyria and to its location. Assyria, as a state grouped about the heavily fortified city of Ashur on the middle Tigris, had become civilized in the third millennium B.C. under the impetus of Mesopotamian development. In the second millennium it had maintained itself against Hurrian pressure, though for a time it was subject to Mitanni. Toward the close of the Bronze age, Assyria had expanded westward into the middle Euphrates district, especially under Tukulti-Ninurta I (1242–06), who also held Babylon temporarily. A successor, Tiglath-Pileser I (1114–1076), was even able to exploit the collapse elsewhere by extending Assyrian rule briefly to the Mediterranean where, he boasted, he had killed in the sea a narwhal. But though Assyria was not directly hit by the great invasions it could not maintain so widely ranging a rule in an era of localism; for the next two centuries its kings sank back into obscurity.

When Assyria began to revive about 900, it was a small kingdom scarcely more than 75 miles on a side, a region in which culture and commerce were secondary to farming, herding, and military activity. The relation of Assyria to Babylonia has often been compared, with justice, to the later relation of Rome to Greece. Both Assyria and Rome were deeply indebted to their more civilized neighbors, though neither Assyrian nor Roman culture was simply a blind copy of its model; the Assyrian outlook, thus, owed much to Hurrian and native influences. Both Assyria and Rome, again, had a military structure to life, born of the necessity for constant warfare against nearby hillsmen; and both had a somewhat primitive yet intense sense of divine protection by their native gods. The main deity of Assyria was the sun-god Ashur, who was conceived as far more abstract, less mythical, than the Babylonian Marduk; for his glory the Assyrian monarchs fought stubbornly and successfully on earth.

Expansion of Assyria (911–612 B.C.). By the early ninth century the kings of Assyria were once more leading their warlike nobles and peasants in external raids. Adadnirari II (911–891) may be called the father of Assyrian imperial adminstration; even more successful was his grandson, Ashurnasirpal II (883–59), who improved the army, made Calah the capital, and built there a great palace. These kings, as well as their successors, faced serious opponents in almost every direction. To the south lay Babylonia, too weak to expand its own sway, yet so reluctant to accept alien rule that it was repeatedly to rebel against Assyrian rule. The mountains to the north stretched on so far that Assyria was never able to hold permanently more than the first foothills; under Assyrian pressure a native state called Urartu, based on Hurrian stock, rose in Armenia and barred Assyrian expansion in that direction.

Only westward, toward the valuable forests and trade centers of Syria, was the path of Assyrian aggression relatively simple, yet even in this district the Aramaic and Hittite kings were reluctant to submit. A combination of Phoenician and Syrian states, joined by king Ahab of Israel, held the Assyrians at the great battle of Qarqar (853). Throughout the ninth century the wars of Assyria, however magniloquently described in royal records, were really raids which did not produce a lasting empire.

After a temporary quiescence early in the next century one of the greatest Assyrian warlords, Tiglath-Pileser III (744–27), seized the throne and fought relentlessly to break the resistance of his foes. In Babylonia he was crowned king; Urartu lost its temporary control over north Syria; Assyrian armies took Damascus and moved as far as the Mediterranean. Annexations followed and were extended by his successors. Sargon II (721–05), a usurper who took his name from the famous early Akkadian imperialist, beat down the Chaldaeans, an Aramaic dynasty in Babylonia; to the west he exiled the leaders of the northern kingdom of the Hebrews, Israel, and the royal annals boast that seven Greek kings of the island of Cyprus yielded fealty and tribute.

Each new ruler, however, faced renewed rebellion in the subject territories. Sennacherib (704–681) ruthlessly punished Babylonia after it had betrayed its governor, his eldest son, to the foreign power of Elam. He also added Cilicia, where kings of Greek ancestry bowed before Assyrian might, and drove Egyptian influence out of Palestine. It was at this time that Nineveh, across the Tigris from the modern Mosul, became the capital city. Some 10,000 captives must have worked 12 years to raise a platform for its great buildings; double walls and moats encircled the city over a course of 8 miles; and a special canal provided fresh water. The successor of Sennacherib, Esarhaddon (680–69), finally secured temporary control over Egypt and restored the position of Babylon as a city; under his son Ashurbanipal (668–after 633) the Assyrian empire was outwardly at its apogee, the largest state the world had yet seen.

The Assyrian Empire. This was the first empire in history, in the sense that it had the first imperial administration. Yet the Assyrian empire must not be visualized as a tidy, permanent system. Its duration was brief, from Tiglath-Pileser III down to the fall of Nineveh in 612; always Assyrian mastery was subject to severe internal strains and external threats. Basically the empire consisted of the home kingdom of Assyria with a number of subject territories, the obedience of which was marked pre-eminently by their payment of tribute to avoid Assyrian raids.

The homeland was a complex mixture of cities and rural districts. The latter were dominated by local lords, who ruled the peasants almost as

serfs; but the cities of Assyria often had regular charters and a considerable amount of self-rule under their councils of elders. Their taxes were
limited, and they were free of military service; troops were provided
largely by the landlords who held rural land virtually in military tenure.
Around the homeland lay the dependent regions, which for the first time
were organized into provinces, each with an Assyrian governor. Although powerful, the governors were closely checked by subordinates or
by agents and spies from the central court. In the provinces some cities
were ruled directly by Assyrian deputies; Assyrian garrisons lay in a few
major fortresses. Other local kings and princelings had Assyrian "residents" to watch their behavior, and relatively safe areas were left free of
such direct or indirect control.

The heart of the system was the Assyrian king, "the great king, the
legitimate king, the king of the world, king of Assyria, king of all the
four rims of the earth, king of kings, prince without rival, who rules
from the Upper Sea to the Lower Sea." [1] Most of the rulers were forceful men, who spent the campaigning season in the field; weaklings had
little chance to keep their throne against ambitious relatives or outsiders.
Sargon II informs us that he was always guarded, and with good reason;
for a number of the monarchs fell victim to internal plots. To support
their position the kings built up an extensive court and central bureaucracy, including a *turtanu* or vizier, chief cupbearer, chamberlain, eu-
nuchs, and the like. Some parts of the royal archives have survived. In
the petitions, diplomatic correspondence, intelligence reports, letters, and
the like one can see the careful royal supervision of the imperial administration and can sense the unending struggle to keep the subject peoples
under control.

The army upon which this royal power rested was drawn initially
from the Assyrian nobles and peasantry, but as this source became exhausted in continual war the kings also had to employ subjects and
mercenaries. It was the first great army to use iron weapons, and it was
well organized. The shock mobile force was the chariotry, equipped
chiefly with the bow, alongside which skirmished light cavalry; the basic
infantry block consisted of men with helmet, shield, spear, and dagger —
the ancestor of the later Greek infantry phalanx — but light-armed infantry were also useful. The quality of any army can often be measured

[1] Tr. A. Leo Oppenheim, in *Ancient Near Eastern Texts,* p. 297 (Ashurbanipal)

by its ability to traverse mountains, which are a fertile field for ambushes and impose severe stress on supply systems, and also by its willingness to stick to the monotonous, protracted operations of a siege with mines, rams, and towers. In both respects the Assyrian army had no equal down to its time. The governors and "residents" provided good information to the kings, who were often able to forestall a revolt or nip insurrection in the bud.

Neither at the time nor in later memory did the Assyrian empire enjoy a favorable reputation. Peace and order were purchased by the subjects at a heavy price in cash and lives, a price which is frightfully evident in the frank Assyrian records. The annals of the kings itemize jubilantly the booty of conquest — the silver, gold, copper, iron, furniture, cattle, female slaves, and hosts of other trophies — and recount directly the brutalities inflicted on the defeated. Ashurnasirpal II, for instance, boasts, "I destroyed them, tore down the walls and burned the towns with fire; I caught the survivors and impaled them on stakes in front of their towns." [2] Even more disturbing is the open parade of brutality and violence in the great palace reliefs, which depict the heads of conquered kings hung in the trees of the royal gardens and the human debris of battlefield and siege. Often the leaders in an area which rebelled were transplanted to areas far from their homeland; at other times they were slain by the hundreds and their grinning skulls piled neatly by the roadsides, there to give food for thought to travelers.

This ruthless spirit perhaps proves not so much that the Assyrians were inhuman monsters as it shows the sternness required to break and harness the Near East. The Assyrian period was in reality one of the greatest turning points in the civilized history of the area, and in this fact must be sought the justification for the booty and tribute of empire — if empire needs justification. Politically, such kings as Tiglath-Pileser III took decisive steps toward uniting the Fertile Crescent; the next great empire, the Persian, reaped the benefit and so could afford to exercise its sway in a more lenient style.

The conscious source of the Assyrian empire was the ambition of its rulers and upper classes for the glory and profit of war and also perhaps their zeal to spread the sway of the sun-god Ashur; but it had also an unconscious base in economic and cultural benefits. The Assyrians pro-

[2] Tr. A. Leo Oppenheim, in *Ancient Near Eastern Texts*, p. 276.

vided peace and order, built roads, and spurred the urbanization of much of upper Mesopotamia. Sargon II specifically boasts that he forced Egypt to unbar its frontier to external trade; Esarhaddon, in restoring the position of Babylon, formally opened its trade routes "to the four winds." Much of the burgeoning trade and industry of the era was carried on by slaves of great nobles, who ran their own businesses and could receive the reward of freedom for good service. Lending, buying, and other economic activity was largely in terms of silver bars and units of weight like the shekel — virtually a money economy, though true coins were not yet used.

Culturally the kings cherished the cosmopolitan Mesopotamian civilization which formed a large part of their inheritance. Like the rulers of the Roman Empire in later days they fostered the spread of a consolidated pattern of artistic and intellectual life widely throughout their domains. From the days of the Assyrians down to the invasions of the Mongols in the fourteenth century after Christ the Near East remained a unified cultural sphere as it passed through Persian, Hellenistic, Sassanian-Byzantine, and Arab hands.

CULTURE IN THE ASSYRIAN AGE

The Arts. To detect the flavor of culture in the Assyrian period one must turn first to the palaces of the kings. Among the greatest of these were the mammoth structures of Ashurnasirpal at Calah, of Sargon at the ephemeral city of Dur-Sharrukin, of Sennacherib and Ashurbanipal at Nineveh. The rulers also built temples to Ashur, Ishtar, and the other gods and goddesses who protected their lands and peoples, but these were often virtually adjuncts to the palaces.

In their artistic aspects and building techniques the palaces reflect an inheritance from Babylonian, Hurrian, Hittite, and other sources. At each corner an inscription in clay or precious metal was buried to ensure divine protection. The exterior was heavily walled; inside was a maze of servants' quarters, harem area, treasuries and state apartments. Great audience halls, which were a focus for public activities, were built in the *liwan* style, rectangular with a throne platform against one long side and sometimes with an arched roof.

In the minor palaces the corridors and major rooms were adorned with painted frescoes, as had been the custom in the second millennium, but for the great palaces veritable miles of stone relief were carved on gypsum orthostats about seven feet high. These surfaces, which gave room either for one large band or more often two smaller bands of relief, admit us to the fascinating world of Assyrian monarchy. Everywhere the king stands as the center of attention; the divine realm is suggested at times by winged and other gods or by the winged sun-disk in which Ashur rode above the head of his earthly representative. Sometimes the king dines in lovely gardens planted with trees and fruits; elsewhere tribute bearers bring him the riches of the realm; in the hunt scenes he unerringly draws his bow from his great chariot; often he leads his troops in war. While the slow-moving chronicle of inevitable victory is monotonous, it is also impressive.

From the artistic point of view Assyrian relief was the highest point thus far reached in Near Eastern art. Sieges and battles at times had almost a sense of space, and in the scenes of hunting animals were shown with more realism than had ever before been achieved.[3] Here the artists gave a vivid sense of motion, even at times of pity for the dying lions or wild asses; in other scenes the king, with fringed robe, long, curled beard, and heavy shoulders and legs, was a static but powerful figure. Not until we come to Roman imperial art shall we find again artists who concentrated upon seizing the specific quality of individual historical events.

Besides this great relief work in stone the Assyrian palaces at times were decorated with colorful scenes in baked tiles, and the gates were guarded by huge human-headed bulls or lions. Free-standing sculpture was scanty, but the rooms of the palaces must have blazed in their prime with products of the minor arts. Modern excavators have found scraps of glass and of the ivory work, in Phoenician, Syrian, and other styles, which adorned the beds and chairs; the gold and silver vessels, looted or made at royal command, have long since been melted down. In this work the artistic traditions of the Near East were drawn together into an imperial style which continued on into Persian days; the counterpart,

[3] On Plate VII, from Nineveh, Ashurbanipal kills a lion with unerring sword thrust (the sculptor has omitted the guard of goat yarn on the king's left arm which would protect it from the lion's jaws). The observing eye of the artist has caught the lion in the very moment when his force is broken and his body stiffens before collapsing.

to be sure, of this coalescence and of Assyrian rapine was the decline of many previously vigorous local artistic traditions.

Letters, Sciences, and Religion. The palaces give us evidence not only of the artistic achievements of the age but also of its literary activities. Ashurbanipal, the last major king, was an extremely learned man, who studied mathematics, astronomy, and divination, as well as the arts of war; he boasted of his ability to write ancient Sumerian and spent almost more time over his books than on his imperial duties. In his palace at Nineveh were discovered about 20,000 tablets, a great part of his library, which contained the Akkadian version of the epic of Gilgamesh and many other old Mesopotamian tales; letters reveal his efforts to secure copies especially of incantations and other religious texts of the past.

On stone and clay prisms the annals of the kings were inscribed to invoke the gods, to list building operations, and to recount year by year the sweep of the ever victorious expeditions. These were the most extensive historical works yet composed in ancient times, but it should be noted that their scribes had to magnify the deeds of the monarchs, even to the extent of incredible inflation of the numbers of captives and killed. These annals, moreover, were designed largely to prove the benign support of the god Ashur, whose majesty revealed itself in the success of his earthly representative, the king. Truly secular history was to begin only in Greek times; and apart from the annals the Assyrians composed very little original literature of their own. Like the Romans of later times, their major role was one of conserving and transmitting to subsequent eras the more creative achievements of earlier peoples.

Eclipse records available to Greek astronomers later went back to 747 B.C., and other astronomical material about the fixed stars and planets was built up in Assyrian times as a background for an amazing theoretical systematization of Babylonian astronomy which occurred after 500 B.C.; the mathematical knowledge required for this seems already to have been developed in the second millennium. The practical arts and crafts had also developed an extensive, if traditional, technology, by the Assyrian age. On this body of knowledge the Greeks and other Mediterranean peoples were to draw heavily over the next centuries; for technological improvement in the ancient world was thenceforth of very limited degree.

The astronomical observations, however, were not made for purely scientific ends but to give astrological guidance for the actions of the king. The pride of the Assyrian monarchs and nobles in their earthly achievements and the secular tone of their art must not lead one to forget that religious rites and superstition continued to have a great place. Much of the daily routine of the king, "the holy high priest and tireless caretaker of the temple . . . who acts only upon the trust-inspiring oracles given by Ashur, his lord," [4] was concerned with religious ceremonies. The cycle of the agricultural year was marked by fertility rites, the greatest of which remained the New Year's festival. Divination took place not only through observation of the stars and planets but also by the inspection of sheep livers, conceived as the seat of emotions and yielding sure signs by their configuration and color. Magical practices had had millennia in which to become set and constituted the backbone of medical efforts to cure the sick.

The priests, though now generally subordinated to secular power, still remained influential, and much of man's surplus resources was dedicated to the gods who safeguarded his passage through life. The Assyrian kings attempted with some success to promote the general worship of their own god Ashur throughout the conquered areas, but this missionary activity simply added yet another deity to the many local divine forces who were worshiped by all peoples, except among the Hebrews.

THE SUCCESSOR STATES

Fall of Nineveh (612 B.C.). Both politically and culturally the conquests of the Assyrian kings reflect the unification and strength of the Near East, once it had revived. To the growing economic integration of the area, as measured on the upper levels of trade and industry, the Assyrians added a political superstructure which brought some peace and order. In the seventh century Assyria had to face a wild onslaught of nomadic invaders from the north, the Cimmerians, who ravaged Urartu and Asia Minor as far as the Greek cities along the Aegean and broke into Syria and Palestine. Finally, however, the skilled armies of the Assyrian kings repelled this threat; thereafter, for over a thousand years,

[4] Tr. A. Leo Oppenheim, in *Ancient Near Eastern Texts,* p. 281 (Adadnirari III, 810–783 B.C.).

the civilized belt of the Near East remained strong enough to keep out northern invaders.

Yet one can understand why the conquered peoples disliked their enforced unification. In the end, empires must rest upon the consent of the governed, and this consent the Assyrians could not gain. Throughout the last 50 years of their hegemony they were on the defensive. Internally the backbone of empire, the Assyrians themselves, was exhausted by the drafts of the wars. Externally their kings had trouble in three major areas.

They were, thus, never able to create a satisfactory mode for ruling the more advanced, highly urbanized area of Babylonia. Sennacherib took the desperate recourse of destroying Babylon, but his son Esarhaddon had to rebuild this vital economic center and had himself crowned as king of Babylon. He in turn divided his realm between his sons Ashurbanipal in Assyria and Shamash-shum-ukin in Babylon; yet, despite the oaths of allegiance to Ashurbanipal, which still survive, the separatist tendencies of Babylonia led his brother eventually to rebel. When Babylon was retaken, it remained a distinct unit under an Aramaic viceroy.

Egypt was another major area of the Near East which absorbed far too much Assyrian energy in the seventh century. As imperialists the Assyrians could not overlook this rich segment of the known world, yet it was too isolated and remote to be easily conquered and held. Taken by Esarhaddon, the Delta was again freed by the able pharaoh Psammetichus I (664–10), founder of the Twenty-sixth Dynasty. And, finally, a powerful state had begun to rise in the hills to the east of Assyria, where the Indo-European natives of Iran grouped themselves against Assyrian pressure around the Median dynasty, centered at Ecbatana.

After the death of the learned but sluggish Ashurbanipal Babylon again became independent in 626 under Nabopolassar, of Aramean stock. He joined with king Cyaxares of Media to lead a general insurrection. Egypt took little part, but the other two were able to pull down the rotten shell of Assyrian might. Nineveh, the cosmopolitan capital, was destroyed in 612. Some of the Assyrian subject territories, interestingly enough, supported the last Assyrian kings, but in vain; far off in Judah the Hebrew prophet Nahum exulted at the news, "Woe to the bloody city! It is all full of lies and robbery . . . Nineveh is laid waste: Who will bemoan her!" Assyria had collapsed forever; within a century Nineveh had dissolved into huge mounds of ruins.

The Early Sixth Century. For the next half-century the Near East experienced a temporary stage of political division. Median kings ruled Iran, upper Mesopotamia, and Syria, where their confines marched with those of a new power in Asia Minor, the kingdom of Lydia. Lower Mesopotamia was held by Babylon, which was dominated by people of Aramean stock sometimes called Chaldaeans. Chaldaean power reached across the desert trade routes to Palestine, where the small Israelite kingdom of Judah, centered in Jerusalem, lingered on to 597; then king Nebuchadrezzar ended its independence and in 586, after a revolt, razed its temple. The last of the great powers, Egypt, was called upon in vain by the desperate Hebrews but proved as much a "shattered reed" as it had in the days of Sennacherib.

The Median and Chaldaean realms were each larger and more complex than true kingdoms and are therefore often called "empires." Yet neither formed a rounded whole, geographically and politically considered. Culturally, too, this interregnum between Assyrian and Persian periods has an air of suspense, which is most evident in the tendency of men to look back to earlier tradition and attempt to revivify old ideas. In Egypt archaism is marked in efforts to reproduce the spirit of the Old Kingdom; this affected the art of the Saite period (664–525 B.C.). In Babylonia the kings devoted great resources to restoring old religious monuments and customs as well as to improving canals. Nebuchadrezzar (605–562), who was famous in this regard, also built the fabulous Hanging Gardens (a roof garden supported on brick arches) and surrounded his capital by a double wall 10 miles long. The great entry, the Ishtar Gate, was decorated with beautiful tile depictions of bulls and monsters; a processional street crossed the city. The religiosity of the age can be seen in the assertion of a contemporary tablet that "there are altogether in Babylon 53 temples of the great gods, 55 shrines for celestial divinities, 180 altars to the goddess Ishtar, 180 to the gods Nergal and Addad, and 12 other altars to various deities." [5]

The successor of Nebuchadrezzar was a puzzling figure, Nabonidus (555–39), who fell into sharp disagreement with the powerful priesthood of Marduk and spent long periods in residences at oases. At Harran he built a temple to the moon god Sin while his son, Belshazzar, served as regent at home; in the end the people of Babylon opened their gates in

[5] Georges Contenau, *Everyday Life in Babylon and Assyria* (London: Arnold, 1954), p. 279.

539 to a new conqueror, Cyrus the Persian, who once more united the Near East.

Beginnings of the Persian Empire (550–30 B.C.). The Persians were one of the minor Indo-European tribes of Iran, located in the mountains southeast of Susa in a district called Anshan. Their royal dynasty traced its ancestry from a man named Achaemenes (in his Greek form) and occasionally intermarried with the more powerful Median line to the north; but the Achaemenids were utterly unimportant until a brilliant youth, Cyrus, ascended the throne in 557. First Cyrus gained the support of the Iranian nobility to oust the Median dynasty in 550, then he struck far west and overthrew Croesus of Lydia in 547, thereafter he turned back on Babylon, where Marduk, according to Cyrus' story, was "searching for a righteous ruler." This he found in Cyrus, whom he called "to become ruler of all the world." [6] Babylon fell without a struggle in 539 as the priests and people refused to support their own dynasty. Cyrus sent back to their homes all the images of Mesopotamian gods which Nabonidus had stripped from their shrines, and also boasted of returning the native peoples whom the Chaldaeans had transplanted. Among these, as we shall see in the next chapter, were the Israelite leaders of Jerusalem.

When Cyrus died in battle against Eurasian nomads on the river Jaxartes in 530, his empire was well established, and Persian kings were to hold in fief the Near East for the next two centuries, down to the dazzling conquest of Alexander the Great. The Greeks, however, were already in close touch with the Fertile Crescent by the time of Cyrus. Economic and cultural connections between the Aegean and the Near East had been resumed in the eighth century; by 600 Greek mercenaries and traders entered Saite Egypt in some numbers; and a brother of the Greek poet Alcaeus served Nebuchadrezzar. When the generals of Cyrus conquered the Asiatic seaboard of the Aegean, Greek and Persian stood face to face.[7]

The subsequent course of history interlinks the two so closely that we must postpone full consideration of the Persian empire until after Greek development has been considered. In general it may be said that by 550

[6] Tr. A. Leo Oppenheim, in *Ancient Near Eastern Texts,* p. 315.
[7] For a comparative chronology of the Near East and Greece, see Table 4 in Chapter 12.

the Mediterranean world was advancing swiftly and had already created a dynamic political and cultural pattern. The Near East, on the other hand, had drawn itself together in a political and cultural unification which was perhaps more mature, if also more static. The strengths of this latter world are symbolized in the great Assyrian palaces, the embellishment of Babylon by Nebuchadrezzar, or in the later Persian palaces — tremendous structures based on great material wealth and political power, tastefully decorated and furnished in cosmopolitan styles. The companion weaknesses of inherited religious conservatism and an underlying cultural weariness are perhaps best suggested in Saite Egypt and Chaldaean Babylonia.

BIBLIOGRAPHY

Sources. For the dark ages 1200–900 our literary evidence is naturally weak, except for the events discussed in the Old Testament (see below, Chapter 7). Apart from the tale of Wenamon (Ancient Near Eastern Texts, pp. 25–9) we lack, in particular, the sources we should like to have on the history of Phoenicia. The best evidence for Syria is the physical material uncovered in various excavations, especially at Carchemish and Tell Halaf.

As economic activity resumed and Assyrian might mounted, information becomes much more abundant. Serious attention to Mesopotamian archeology began with the excavation of Assyrian sites, as by Paul Emile Botta at Nineveh and Dur-Sharrukin in 1842–44 and by Austen Henry Layard at Calah in 1845 on. Much of the early digging was intended primarily to acquire works of art and inscriptions; scientific exploration commenced with the careful uncovering of Ashur (1902–14) and of Babylon (1899–1917), both by the Germans, who were the first to use light railways to remove the dirt. The Assyrian palaces themselves were so tremendous in size that they have never been fully cleared. On Assyrian archeology see Seton Lloyd, Foundations in the Dust (New York: Thames & Hudson, 1981).

The reliefs of the palaces have been noted in the text, as have also the royal archives. At Nineveh alone some 24,000 whole and fragmentary tablets were discovered; most significant among these are the copies of earlier myths and the royal annals. The latter sometimes exist in several redactions, in which the numbers of cattle captured and other details are increased amazingly from the earlier to the later version. Frequently the accounts of campaigns are quite detailed, but royal egotism sometimes muffles disagreeable events and the geography is not always identifiable. Nor can we see clearly all aspects of the nobles or of the cities from this material, which is translated by A. K. Grayson, *Assyrian Royal Inscriptions*, 2 vols. (Wiesbaden, 1972–76), *Assyrian and Babylonian Chronicles* (New York: J. Augustin, 1975), *Babylonian Historical-Literary Texts* (Toronto: University of Toronto Press, 1975); L. Waterman, *Royal Correspondence of the Assyrian Empire*, 4 vols. (Ann Arbor: University of Michigan Press, 1930–36). *Ancient Near Eastern Texts* contains a good selection from both Mesopotamia and Syria.

Further Reading. Despite their importance the Assyrians have not attracted modern biographers or writers of general studies. The most extensive survey in English, A. T. Olmstead, *History of Assyria* (Chicago: University of Chicago Press, 1975), is not lively; beside it may be placed the relevant chapters in *Cambridge Ancient History*, Vol. III (3d ed.; Cambridge: Cambridge University Press, forthcoming). Assyrian art is lavishly illustrated by André Parrot, *Arts of Assyria* (New York: Golden Press, 1961); this and other Near Eastern arts are well discussed by Henri Frankfort, *Art and Architecture of the Ancient Orient* (rev. ed.; Harmondsworth: Penguin, 1971). Other aspects are treated in H. W. F. Saggs, *Everyday Life in Babylonia and Assyria* (New York: Putnam, 1965); see also S. H. Hooke, *Babylonian and Assyrian Religion* (Norman: University of Oklahoma Press, 1963).

R. W. Bulliet, *The Camel and the Wheel* (Cambridge, Mass.: Harvard University Press, 1975), is thoughtful on the effects of domesticating the camel; T. A. Wertime and J. D. Muhly, *Coming of the Age of Iron* (New Haven: Yale University Press, 1980), has useful essays, though some are technical.

Syrian developments are sketched in S. Moscati, *Ancient Semitic Civilizations* (New York: Putnam Capricorn 202, 1960). Donald Harden, *The Phoenicians* (New York: Praeger P128, 1963), and S. Moscati, *The World of the Phoenicians* (London: Weidenfeld and Nicolson, 1968), discuss the little we know about the Phoenicians; David Diringer, *The Alphabet: A Key to the History of Mankind* (3d ed.; Topsfield, Mass.: Newbury, 1977), is good. Works on the Persian empire are given in Chapter 13.

7

HEBREW MONOTHEISM

In the creation and the crystallization of new outlooks the middle centuries of the first millennium B.C. were among the most fruitful which the world has ever seen. Politically, for instance, the Near East had progressed to the unity of empire; but this was not the only way to organize men. In Greece at the same time very primitive social and political concepts were consciously refined into the ideal of the city-state, in which the individual citizen enjoyed a sense of independent political worth. To the west Rome was beginning to rise; far in the east China was settling upon a lasting framework of political and social values.

Intellectually, too, this was an age in which men were ready throughout Eurasia to break fresh ground. Artists manipulated their ancestral inheritance in new ways to create esthetic patterns which have underlain all subsequent western as well as Chinese art. New literary styles were created in Greece and China, and the Hebrews wrote one of the most enduringly influential works of all time, the Old Testament. As these examples may suggest, men were now consciously formulating — at times out of old materials — new explanations of human nature and of the problems of human existence.

Historians have often noted in amazement that the Buddha, Confucius, some of the major Hebrew prophets, and the first Greek philosophers all lived within a century of each other. While the Greek and Chinese answers to men's most basic concerns were essentially secular, those of the Indians and Hebrews were to be more religious; these four outlooks are among the greatest forces which have molded subsequent civilization. In this chapter we shall concentrate upon the Hebrews, whose history took place against that background of Near Eastern development which has been considered in previous pages.

THE MEANING OF HEBREW DEVELOPMENT

Uniqueness of Judaism. Although the Hebrews lived in the Near East, they certainly did not fit into its conventional political and religious systems. Fitfully they too tried to create the usual type of bureaucratic kingdom and to throw up a militaristic upper class, but apart from a brief blaze of glory under David and Solomon the Hebrews were not willing to sacrifice their own rights in favor of royal absolutism. In the end their feeble political system was to be ground down by the great empires of the first millennium.

The Hebrews, too, occasionally made efforts to adapt themselves to the usual religious patterns of the Fertile Crescent, which included fertility cults, all-powerful priesthoods, and the conception of many gods in very human terms. But here again they could not sacrifice their ancestral bond to one jealous God, who lived in the storm and spoke directly to man.

More decisively than any other thinkers of the ancient world the Hebrews broke with the older polytheisms; the product was Judaism. This is a peremptory code which regulates for its followers the most intimate details of daily life and ethics. Few faiths have made as stern demands upon the individual; but in doing so Judaism recognized man to be an entity of worth and concern in God's eyes. The Hebrew prophets expressed a soaring faith in God as unique and as ethical; His concern was with man's righteousness far more than with man's crops or earthly prosperity. Yet Judaism was a practical, clear, dynamic outlook, into which mysticism entered only to a limited degree. Both through Judaism and through its close relatives, Christianity and Islam, these views entered into the main stream of history.

The Old Testament. The development of Judaism is a long process, which began by at least 1200 B.C. and has continued on to the present day; it is the oldest *formed* religious outlook still active in the modern world. The first period in the development, on which we must concentrate here, is called the Biblical era, 1200–400 B.C. Our information for this stage consists chiefly of the books of the Old Testament, which include legal codes, moral ordinances, commentary and exposition by great teachers and prophets, traditional poetry of the Hebrew people, mythological explanations, and much else.

The Old Testament also contains a great deal of formal history. To the Hebrews, God operated through history to enlighten and mold His chosen people and, through them, the rest of mankind. The account of history, thus, was not chaos nor an endless cycle but a continuous development; the backslidings and advances of foolish, stubborn man were of truly great importance. From the religious point of view the historical parts of the Old Testament, from Genesis-Exodus-Leviticus-Numbers-Deuteronomy (the Pentateuch) on through the parallel accounts of later times in Chronicles and Kings, are at once an inspiring testimony to God's justice and an awful warning of His punishments. But they are also of great historical value; for the detailed development of Hebrew history we have more light than for that of any other ancient Near Eastern people.

The historical student, nonetheless, runs quickly into serious trouble when he turns to the Old Testament. Since the record was written for religious purposes, it omits much of secular importance and magnifies events which had a purely religious significance. The accounts which we now possess are clearly a combination of several chronicles written at different times and from different points of view (see Bibliography), and in the process of combination later concepts have crept into earlier materials. To add another element to this confusion, the modern reader brings to the Biblical story his own religious and intellectual preconceptions — whereas few of us feel emotionally involved in the progress of the Sumerians or Assyrians.

It is also unfortunate that the literature of neighboring peoples, such as the Egyptians and Assyrians, gives only occasional direct references to the Hebrews, and that in so poverty-stricken a land as Palestine the archeological record is scanty. From these subsidiary sources, however, we can gain a view of the backdrop against which Hebrew history moved in response to the will of God as exerted on an often erring people.

Days of Abraham and Moses (2000–1200 B.C.). The religious development of Judaism is closely connected with the social and economic
evolution of the Hebrews and with the political rise and fall of Israel.
The story begins early in the second millennium among wandering
bands of Semitic-speaking, patriarchally organized tribes like those
which infiltrated the Fertile Crescent from the days of the Amorites.
Genesis concentrates on one such group, the seed of Abraham, who
migrated from Mesopotamia to Palestine and there lived a pastoral life.
The religious and legal customs which appear at this stage in the Bible
are best illuminated from Hurrian documents of upper Mesopotamia,
especially those of the site called Nuzi. The Biblical story of the Flood
localized the Ark on Mt. Ararat in Armenia because the Hurrian version
of the Mesopotamian myth did so; the practice that a man married the
childless widow of his deceased brother (levirate marriage) is known in
Hurrian law; and the story of Rachel's stealing the gods of her father
(Genesis 31:19–35) becomes intelligible against the fact that in Hurrian
custom the property of a family group went with its gods. General
Semitic religious views explain the appearance of sacred trees in the Old
Testament along with worship on high places and especially the significance of sacred stones (as in the dream of Jacob at Bethel in Genesis
28:11–22).

According to the Bible some of Abraham's stock descended into Egypt
during a famine and remained there for several generations, serving
Egyptian masters, until they made their famous Exodus under Moses
about the end of the thirteenth century B.C. This Exodus has never been
discovered in Egyptian records and probably never will, for the Hebrews
were quite unimportant in the eyes of the magnificent Egyptian lords of
the New Kingdom. Only if the slaves and captives called Hapiru, who
turn up in the Amarna tablets, are to be equated with the Hebrews is
there any reference at all in New Kingdom sources; but this equation is
now generally doubted.

Whatever faith one wishes to place in the details of the story of the
Exodus, it does appear that a truly crucial step occurred among the
tribes wandering on the desert fringe of Palestine, and that this step is to

be connected with the figure of a great leader, Moses, semilegendary though he may be. The descendants of Abraham had worshiped his God, a tribal spirit conceived in the common nomadic style as impersonal and all-pervasive. Moses, however, made a new covenant with God, which embraced all of his followers. Thenceforth a far more definite and conscious set of rules and beliefs bound God and His worshipers in their voluntary union. This step is also marked in nomenclature. During Moses' stay with Jethro of the Midianites he learned to know the Lord as YHWH. Since vowels were not written in early Semitic scripts, we can only guess that this term was pronounced Yahweh (= Jehovah); thenceforth God was commonly so called. The term Hebrew, as meaning a member of an ethnic group, gave way to Israel, as meaning a nation the members of which were united with each other and with the one God who protected them; the first mention of the term is in a victory stele of the pharaoh Merenptah (1224-14).

The Entry into Canaan. From this time on the Israelites pushed into the hills of Palestine or Canaan. The book of Joshua presents the entry as a specific event or campaign, which ruthlessly exterminated the previous population, but the book of Judges suggests a more credible process of infiltration and fusion. Once in the hills of Palestine, the pastoral tribal people of the desert fringe began a long, often painful process of adaptation to the ways of civilization. Canaanite culture, fortunately for the Israelites, was not a powerful, independent civilization. As we saw above in Chapter 4, the ways of life and thought in Ugarit and similar cities were in the main a Semitic adaptation of Mesopotamian concepts. In earlier days the stock of Abraham had drawn from this source via the Hurrians; now the force of Mesopotamian models was intensified. Despite their sojourn in Egypt, the Israelites were never to borrow extensively from Egyptian culture.

Nonetheless the dangerous temptations of Canaanite culture seriously threatened to turn the Israelites into another commonplace folk of the Fertile Crescent. The tongue now known as Hebrew was taken over at this time from the Canaanites; the poetic style which appears in the very early parts of the Bible, such as the song of Deborah (Judges 5), is like that of Ugaritic verse; and some of the aphorisms in Proverbs can be matched in Phoenician wisdom. Men turned to farming, intermarried with the natives, and accepted many of the more advanced social and

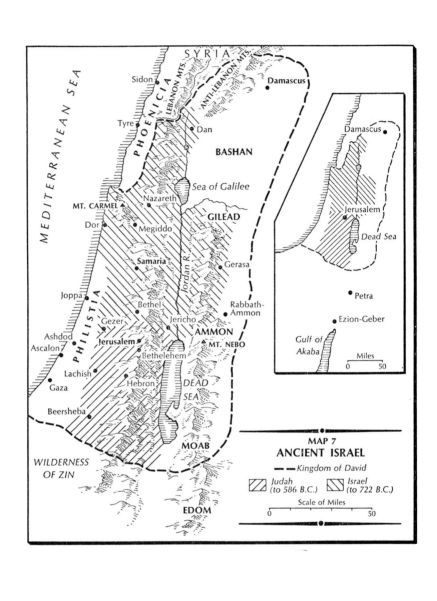

MEDITERRANEAN SEA

S Y R I A

Sidon
Damascus

PHOENICIA
LEBANON MTS.
ANTI-LEBANON MTS.

Tyre
Dan

BASHAN

Sea of Galilee

Nazareth
MT. CARMEL

GILEAD

Dor
Megiddo

Jordan R.

Samaria
Gerasa

Joppa
Bethel
Rabbath-
Ammon

PHILISTIA
Gezer
Jericho

Ashdod
Jerusalem
AMMON
MT. NEBO

Ascalon
Bethelehem

Lachish
Hebron
DEAD
SEA

Gaza

Beersheba

MOAB

WILDERNESS
OF ZIN

EDOM

Damascus

Jerusalem

Dead Sea

Petra

Ezion-Geber

Gulf of
Akaba

Miles
0   50

MAP 7
ANCIENT ISRAEL

━ ━ Kingdom of David

Judah
(to 586 B.C.)

Israel
(to 722 B.C.)

Scale of Miles
0   50

economic conventions of Canaan. In particular they were sorely tempted to embrace the worship of the local *baals* or deities who appear in the Ugaritic literature, such as the agricultural Dagan, "the lord of grain and tillage, the inventor of wheat and the plow," and the fertility couple Baal-Anath. If the natives believed that the crops depended upon propitiation of these deities, how could the newcomers do otherwise?

Yet the Hebrew inheritance did not entirely disappear in the culturally mixed stock which began to emerge in the hills of Palestine. The Israelites took over the principle of private property; but the spirit of the patriarchal family, in which all goods were owned in common and each man was bound closely to his clansmen, continued to influence their social and economic attitudes. The dislike of authority and the nomadic spirit of individual rights hampered the full adaptation of the Israelites to local political institutions. Throughout their history they were to remain a people apart from the conventional systems of the Near East.

Kingdom of David and Solomon (1050–925 B.C.). When the Israelites crossed the Jordan, they entered an area which was at a low ebb in political and social vigor after the great invasions of the late second millennium. Accordingly they were able to establish themselves alongside the local agricultural population, but they did face one serious threat in the form of another group of invaders, the Philistines. This people had come in from the sea, probably from somewhere in the Aegean, late in the second millennium and had settled down in cities along the coast (see Map 7).

Equipped with iron weapons and better organized, the Philistines raided inland and tended to push together Canaanites and Israelites in opposition. The Israelites were seriously weakened by their loose grouping under local priests and "judges," or military chieftains; as the Book of Judges (21:25) puts it, "In those days there was no king in Israel: every man did that which was right in his own eyes."

Gradually the need for unity became more apparent, and late in the eleventh century B.C. one of the better warriors, Saul, was anointed king by the priestly seer Samuel. Saul failed partly because his fellow tribesmen refused full obedience; in his place rose the shrewd leader David, who had learned the art of war as a brigand and also as a mercenary captain for the Philistines. David built up a state reaching as far as Damascus, which was the most important along the Mediterranean seacoast of the Fertile Crescent. Its capital was the hill city of Jerusalem, which David had captured and kept under his own control as a fortress outside the tribal districts of Israel. For some part of his career we have one of the frankest accounts of the Bible in II Samuel 9–20, an almost contemporary record.

The son of David was the glorious Solomon (c. 965–25), who aped the styles of Near Eastern monarchy as far as his resources permitted. For seven years his subjects labored at Jerusalem to build a temple to Yahweh, which was partly calculated to put the ancestral faith under royal domination; but other temples were erected to the gods of his many wives. These gods continued to be worshiped at Jerusalem for the next three centuries. Solomon's own palace took 13 years to build and was adorned by the resources of Phoenician craftsmen, for Solomon and king Hiram of Tyre were closely allied.

Execution of the ambitious works at Jerusalem and other centers, such as Gezer and Megiddo, called for considerable resources and organization. The land of Israel was divided into new districts for the collection of taxes, forced labor, and administration, so that local independence was destroyed; a professional bureaucracy was developed. Royal trading expeditions also were sent down the Red Sea in conjunction with the Phoenicians; mining of copper and other metals was prosecuted in the southern desert.

While later generations magnified the greatness and the wisdom of Solomon, they could not entirely forget that the greatness had been purchased at the price of royal autocracy. Even in his lifetime there was grumbling over the requirement that men work four months of every year upon the king's buildings, and parts of his state broke away. On his death the Israelites refused to endure the perpetuation of this conventional Near Eastern absolutism and split apart. The northern kingdom, which was still called Israel, created a new capital at Samaria; the smaller southern state, Judah, was centered about Jerusalem.

Centuries of Decline (925–539 B.C.). The political vicissitudes of Israel and Judah are retailed at great length in the Old Testament so as to show God's hand at work. This history, interestingly enough, is couched in terms of the people as a whole, not of the kings alone. At the time the kings were a powerful element in the worship of Yahweh, but as later tradition looked back it witheringly condemned almost all the monarchs for slipping off into the worship of foreign gods and for mistreating their subjects, who are nonetheless presented as far from perfect. Politically, indeed, the small kingdoms of Palestine had an ever more hopeless position, for the course of development across the Near East was toward empire.

The kingdom of Israel lay closer to Phoenicia and Syria and so played a larger role than did Judah. In the ninth century the rule of Israel was seized by an able leader, Omri, whose son Ahab (869–50) married a Phoenician princess, Jezebel, and helped to check the Assyrians at the battle of Qarqar (853). Then the line of Omri was overthrown by an internal revolt under Jehu, the main effect of which was to weaken the power of the kings of Israel. In the eighth century the nobles of the kingdom profited greatly from the steady rise of economic activity, but the monarchs could only bow hopelessly before Assyria. In the end, after an ill-judged revolt, Samaria was destroyed by Sargon II in 722, and the leaders of the northern kingdom were transplanted to Mesopotamia. These were the famous Lost Ten Tribes, for the deported elements never returned from their new homes in Mesopotamia; but the lower classes about Samaria continued to worship Yahweh.

Judah, off in the hills, lingered longer as a client kingdom. Early in the seventh century one king, Manasseh, went so far as to introduce the worship of Ashur in the temple at Jerusalem; and the fertility cults centered on Anath (Queen of Heaven) and Astarte were widely practiced. Then a young ruler, Josiah (640–09), threw off Assyrian religious and political domination in the days when Assyria was plunging to its fall; but he and his successors made the serious mistake of opposing the new Chaldaean empire. In 597 Nebuchadrezzar eliminated the kingdom of Judah; then, after a further revolt, he wiped out the temple and the religious authorities at Jerusalem in 586. The leaders of Judah, removed to Babylonia, wore out their hearts in exile until Cyrus conquered Mesopotamia and permitted those who wished to do so to return home about 539. Thereafter Palestine became a small subject state of the Persian realm, administered politically by a governor usually of Jewish origin and subject religiously to the high priest at Jerusalem.

Politically the tale of the Israelites is a somber one. Only while the rest of the Near East was weak could they hope to be independent; but their very reluctance to permit autocracy may have made the collapse of their kingdoms more inevitable. Yet the trials which afflicted the worshipers of Yahweh are intrinsically connected with the purification of their belief in God as unique and as ethical.

The God of Early Israel. Once Moses had made his covenant with God, the Israelites and Yahweh were closely, indissolubly bound together. Always the men of Israel faced the temptation to drift into the worship of alien gods of more developed character and cult, first the agricultural deities of Canaan, then the imperial divinities of the Assyrian overlords. Time after time the chosen people of Yahweh slid away into foreign abomination; such figures as the night-hag Lilith lay always in the back of their minds as real forces. Yet the basic spirit of reverence for Yahweh as the god of Israel never quite yielded.

While the covenant was thus a static, enduring force in Hebrew history, one may doubt if the Israelites would have continued their allegiance had they not steadily developed their concept of Yahweh. The unfolding of Hebrew religious thought is the principal underlying thread of the Old Testament; and certainly the Israelites had a long road to traverse in shaping their conception of God.

At the outset the existence of other gods was admitted. "Who," says Exodus 15:11, "is like unto Thee, O Lord, among the gods?" But Yahweh was a "jealous" god whom His chosen people must alone worship; from this root came slowly the claim of monotheism. Nor was Yahweh initially described or defined in primarily ethical terms. He was a god of storms who appeared now in the cloud, now in a burning bush; His voice was the thunder, His arrow the lightning, and He was above all "a man of war." It may even have been believed that He usually lived in a box borne along with the Israelites upon a wagon, the Ark of the Covenant, but He was not incarnated in a physical statue. His worship revolved about the bloody sacrifice of beasts, parts of whose carcasses were burned while the rest was cooked and eaten by the celebrants. With the feast inevitably went the consumption of much wine, and a veritable din must have risen on high beside the spiraling smoke of the altar. If we suddenly could see David "leaping and dancing before the Lord" (II Samuel 6:16) we might feel we had stumbled on some aboriginal rite. The "righteous" conduct which Yahweh demanded from His adherents thus far meant little more than due celebration of such ritual.

In the maintenance of ancestral beliefs and in the evolution of new concepts a large part was played by the priests of the temples of Yahweh. On the side they elaborated the worship of their God as an agricultural divinity — many of the enduring festivals of Judaism (Passover in the spring, Rosh Hashana in the fall) have close connections with the farming year—and borrowed many aspects of the developed worship of the Canaanite *baals*. Yet on the other hand they maintained the uniqueness of Yahweh and fought against the tendency of the kings to seize control of the religious machinery. Another potent force was the remarkable surge of lay leaders from the people itself, the famous prophets.

Voice of the Prophets. The ancient Near East had long known foretellers of the future, who interpreted dreams, examined the livers of sheep, watched the flight of birds, or observed the stars. Generally such men were professionals and were organized in guilds, which handed down the secrets from father to son; commonly they worked primarily for the kings. The prophets of Israel were of quite a different sort. They were called out of the laity by an imperious inner drive to speak the words of God; they addressed the people as well as the monarchs; and their prophecies were far more criticisms of the present than predictions of forthcoming events.

Sometimes these prophets spoke almost from frenzy in an ecstatic, involved style full of veiled meanings; both the balanced verse form of their utterances, which required reiteration of thought, and the wealth of imagery often cause confusion to a modern reader. At times, too, the prophets engaged in symbolic acts, as when Jeremiah broke a pot at the gate of Jerusalem to suggest its coming doom. But other figures, like Isaiah and Amos, were relatively straightforward in their sober, calculating, yet fiery judgment. Whatever their approach, the theme of virtually all the prophets was the same. The covenant linked for all time God and His chosen people, who would be protected if they freely rendered Him the proper service. The corollary, which was expressed at times in prediction of the future, was grim: if the Israelites went astray in the worship of foreign gods or in unrighteous behavior, Yahweh would punish them the more severely.

The prophets stood beside the priests in making religion the dominant thread of life, in attacking the wiles of polytheism, and in calling for a return to earlier ways. Far more than the priests, however, the prophets construed a righteous life in ethical terms. When the prophets saw the king or the rich oppressing the poor, reveling in luxury while the humble were sold into slavery, marrying foreign wives who brought alien social and religious customs, they cried out in rebuke, whatever the cost to themselves in scorn or even physical punishment. As the priesthood slowly codified ancestral customs in the law of Moses, its activity was strongly tinged by the prophetic insistence that purity lay more in the attitude of the heart than in ritual observance. The burden of living by God's law was ever more clearly placed on the conscience of each individual follower of Yahweh.

In their message the prophets were rarely pleasant to hear and not always easy to fathom; yet in the course of Hebrew history their voice was both commanding and consoling. Perhaps such minor peoples as the Israelites were bound to suffer at the hands of the Assyrians and the Chaldaeans, but the prophets helped their people to understand this oppression as the result of God's will. Always in the background lay the prophetic promise that if Israel purged itself it would be forgiven. In ethical matters the prophets were radical, but in terms of social and economic organization they were conservative and did not insist on sweeping reforms.

From the eighth century on their words were written down. Although edited and adulterated in later days, the prophetic view was incorporated into the main body of Biblical thinking. Across subsequent ages the Hebrew prophets have appealed to many generations as a tremendous outcry against man's injustice to man and as a chant of God's mercy.

Critics of the Ninth and Eighth Centuries. To deal with all the major and minor prophets would be a repetitious task, for spokesmen of the Lord rose repeatedly through the centuries from shortly before 800 B.C. down past 500 B.C. The first men of this stamp seem to have appeared in the northern kingdom of Israel in the ninth century in reaction to its close ties with Phoenicia. Ahab, thus, permitted his wife Jezebel to bring in the Phoenician cults of Baal (Melkart) and Astarte and in other ways "did evil in the sight of the Lord above all that were before him" (II Kings 16:30). To challenge him, there arose the harsh figure of the rainmaker Elijah, who demonstrated the superiority of Yahweh over Baal in a famous contest to bring down fire on a pyre.

The case of Naboth threw Elijah in even more opposition to his king and queen. When Naboth, a simple peasant, refused to sell his garden, the inheritance of his fathers, to Ahab, the king was stopped; for unlike most rulers of the Fertile Crescent Israelite monarchs had to recognize the rights of their subjects. Jezebel, who had been trained in the tradition of royal omnipotence, pushed on to secure the judicial murder of Naboth. Elijah sternly indicted this infringement of popular rights and predicted that the author of the injustice would be thrown from the palace as food for the dogs, a prediction which came true in the revolution of Jehu.

In the eighth century the power of the kings weakened, and the nobles of Israel became increasingly free to reduce the peasants to serfdom by exploiting their control of the courts, by lending grain at high rates of interest, and by other means. Socially and religiously as well they turned from the simple ways of the past, only to meet a great wave of popular protest through the mouths of such prophets as Amos, Hosea, Isaiah, and Micah.

Of all these, the most uncompromising assailant was the sheepmaster of Judah, Amos, who burst down upon Israel briefly about 750 B.C. Indignantly he promised God's punishment to those who "sold the righteous for silver, and the poor for a pair of shoes; that pant after the dust of the earth on the head of the poor" (2:6-7). In short, swift strokes Amos displayed the anger of Yahweh at his chosen people: "You only have I known of all the families of the earth: therefore I will punish you for all your iniquities" (3:2). Here, first of all the prophets, appear the implicit concepts that there is only one God in the universe, and that He is omnipotent and impartial. Far more conscious is the feeling that His service requires ethical purity. In Amos (5:21-24) God indignantly rejected burnt offerings and the noise of songs; "but let judgment run down as waters, and righteousness as a mighty stream."

So violent an attack neither the priests nor the king of Israel could abide, and Amos was driven out of the kingdom. But the rotten shell of Israel fell within three decades to Assyrian might; and the words of Amos, the first direct account of a prophet which survive in the Old Testament, continued to inspire Israelite thought.

THE TESTING OF THE FAITH

Triumph and Fall of the Temple (722–586 B.C.). Although Isaiah of Judah, one of the most worldly-wise of the prophets, continued to voice warnings for several decades and to stress the holiness of God as demanding morality among His worshipers, the prophetic strain tended to die down in the early seventh century. This was a period when Assyrian arms rolled resistlessly across the Fertile Crescent, when the tiny kingdom of Judah cowered in its hills. The degree to which Assyrian religious customs penetrated Jerusalem in the days of Manasseh has already been noted. Other alien gods, as well, had long been worshiped in Jerusalem; one of the grimmest pagan rites was the fearful Moloch in the valley of Tophet, where first-born children were sacrificed in times of stress.

The priestly and prophetic reinterpretation of the worship of Yahweh, nonetheless, had proceeded far and wanted only an opportunity to burst forth. The chance came in the reign of king Josiah, who swept out all foreign cults from Jerusalem and killed their priests; condemned magic and the calling up of spirits; abolished all the local shrines built around sacred stones and trees; and concentrated the worship of Yahweh solely at the temple of Jerusalem. Then, according to II Kings 22:8ff., "the book of the law" was discovered in 621 in the temple. After it had been brought forth and publicly read, the king and his people "made a covenant before the Lord, to walk after the Lord, and to keep his commandments, and his testimonies, and his statutes, with all their heart, and all their soul, to perform the words of this covenant that were written in this book." The volume apparently contained part of the present book of Deuteronomy, which may have been hidden away during the Assyrianizing epoch; its prescriptions consolidated the priestly elaboration of the law of Moses, but within the framework of the prophetic revelation that Israel and God were bound in an unique, ethical relationship.

The triumph of the central temple was all too brief. Judah was close to its fall, and one sorrowful inhabitant of the capital, Jeremiah, could foresee the rise of Chaldaean power. Worse yet, Jeremiah knew that his fellow citizens must be punished for their sins and that Babylonia was only God's agent to this end. Although he spoke out desperately, even in the temple, men failed to hearken. When he continued to voice his gloomy, defeatist views during the great siege of 597, an irate mob tossed him in a cistern. This indignity he survived, as well as the fall of the city; eventually he was dragged off into Egypt by a group of refugees, who turned aside from Yahweh to worship Anath, queen of Heaven. The greatness of the disaster was marked by the greatness of the views of this prophet, who was perhaps the favorite of Jesus. Jeremiah stands out for his constant reiteration of the points that men must individually worship God and that this worship was not bound to the ceremonies conducted at the temple. To the faithful who saw the temple destroyed in 586 this line of thought was a vital comfort.

Babylonian Exile (597–39 B.C.). While many of those exiled in 597 and 586 settled down in Babylonia and even prospered, a stubborn nucleus continued to hope that it might return to its native land. By the waters of Babylon, this group clung to the worship of Yahweh and felt in its loneliness ever more its difference from the pagan world. The Exile was the supreme test of Israel's faith in God, the point at which the reformed outlook of the late seventh century became definitely set. Two of the greatest prophets, the Second Isaiah and Ezekiel, rose at this juncture to support the faith.

The Second Isaiah was an anonymous prophet whose message was incorporated in the book of Isaiah, where it includes chapters 40 through 55. His rhapsodic poetry, charged with symbolism, begins, " 'Comfort ye, comfort ye my people,' saith your god . . . 'Her iniquity is pardoned; for she hath received of the Lord's hand double for all her sins.' " Then follow chants in praise of the power of God as the inscrutable Creator and master of all the world; the graven images of the heathen are mere idols. When one compares the terse, bitter sermons of Amos and the ecstatic, optimistic outpourings of the Second Isaiah, the continuous clarification of the prophetic tradition over two vital centuries becomes apparent. To the Second Isaiah there was only one God, loving and merciful, Whose light must be spread to the ends of the world; but the covenant of old bound Him particularly to His chosen people, whom He would send back to Israel through Cyrus the Persian.

While the Second Isaiah addressed his fellow believers as individuals and emphasized the need that they be just, Ezekiel first among the prophets fully expressed the doctrine of individual responsibility and punishment for one's misdeeds. God is unutterably great and majestic, and in His power will regenerate Israel; Ezekiel's vision of the valley of dry bones which regained life, a parable of the sin and restoration of Israel, is one of the most famous allegories of all the prophetic writings. Both these prophets, however, sensed that the people could not live by faith alone but needed a scheme of daily rites, conducted by a priesthood, and a physical focus for the worship of Yahweh. To Ezekiel, in particular, the restoration of the temple was a basic necessity.

Codification of Judaism (539 B.C. *on*). After the Persian conquest the peoples who had been transplanted in Chaldaean days were free to return home. A determined band of the Babylonian exiles did so. They found their kinsmen at home not altogether willing to accept their leadership, and the tiny district around Jerusalem was too poor to permit a magnificent rebuilding of the temple. Despite all the difficulties chronicled in the books of Ezra and Nehemiah a solid kernel of fellow worshipers was yet established as a Persian vassal state. The basic books of the Law — the first five books of the Old Testament (the Pentateuch) — were published by Ezra as a guide to the conduct of life; those who accepted this Law and worshiped at Jerusalem may thenceforth be called Jews and their faith Judaism, a blend of ritual and ethical purity welded out of seven centuries of priestly and prophetic contributions.

Not all of those who worshiped Yahweh at the second temple revered Him alone, for female figurines (Anath-Ishtar) continue to turn up now, as earlier, in the archeological evidence. Nor did all Jews live close to Jerusalem; we have specific evidence of Jewish colonies all the way from Elephantine in southern Egypt to Babylonia. These are the Jews of the Diaspora, the "dispersion," who were a potent force in preserving Judaism from too narrow a point of view. As practiced by the priests of the homeland the ethical requirements of the faith were often obscured or forgotten in ritual observances, and were to require later reinterpretation and emphasis anew in apocryphal books of the Old Testament and in Talmudic commentary. Nonetheless one major chapter in the history of Judaism was essentially closed by 400 B.C. The canonical books of the Old Testament fail to discuss openly any historical events after this date.

JUDAISM IN A PAGAN WORLD

In the general history of the ancient Near East the people whom we call successively Hebrew (down to 1200), Israelites, and then from 500, Jews were an utterly insignificant group politically or artistically. Only in the field of religion and in the great literary monument which resulted therefrom, the Old Testament, did they excel. The stream of religious ideas which bubbled from the priests and prophets of Palestine was an amazing, unique phenomenon. Repeatedly their followers were tempted away by alien cults and economic gain, but always there emerged from the mass of the people great leaders, who spoke the word of Yahweh now in blazing anger, now in comforting hope.

The end product was a clearly defined sect which was set off sharply in many aspects from its neighbors. Socially, thus, the Sabbath became a firm holiday; the prescriptions of the law of Moses on diet and on many other details of life distinguished Jew from non-Jew. Mixed marriages, accordingly, with gentiles were banned despite the protest of the book of Ruth; but at least in the Diaspora the followers of Yahweh were to face the need for sundry accommodations with a pagan world.

Religiously the Jews had rejected the dross of paganism, including polytheism, the worship of gods in human form who were represented in statues and symbols, magic, and that mumbo-jumbo of fertility cults which often led to ritual murder and prostitution. Judaism stood alone in its emphasis on the uniqueness of God, to be worshiped by righteous men.

> It has been shown to you, O man, what is good
> and what the Lord requires of you:
> Only to do justice
> and to love loyally
> and to walk humbly with your God.[1]

This was not an easy faith. It appealed to the individual and gave him a new freedom; yet it thereby placed upon him a new responsibility and fenced him in with many rigid prescriptions. Judaism was not mystical.

[1] Micah 6:8, tr. Harry M. Orlinsky, *Ancient Israel* (Ithaca: Cornell University Press, 1954), p. 151.

It was a religion for men who lived in this world, but those who accepted it realized that physical temptations and material requirements were secondary. In the trials of life, however, they might pray to a just God, one of Whose greatest marks was divine forgiveness. Not the least among the achievements of this faith, when one considers the character of western civilization, was the insistence of the prophets that God dealt with each man by himself and their rejection of political autocracy when God called one to stand for justice. Nowhere in the ancient Near East does there occur such a magnificent gallery of individual human figures as in the pages of the Old Testament.

In its account of the origin of the world and in many other respects this great book of Judaism passed on to the western world important strands of ancient Near Eastern thought. Judaism did not rise as a phenomenon entirely apart from the traditions of the Fertile Crescent, and at times its followers were tempted back into magic and other older ideas; yet it was far enough off the main stream not to be greatly popular within its world. The higher ethical and spiritual beliefs incorporated in Judaism and its proffer of a close relationship between the individual human being and the divine were not to be widely known in the Mediterranean world until the last century b.c. and later, when that world was ready to receive and elaborate such views. The words of the prophets then were to be a powerful seed in Christianity and Islam alike, as well as in their own right in the continuing existence of Judaism.

BIBLIOGRAPHY

Sources. The Old Testament, which was codified in the last centuries b.c., is a collection of 24 historical, legal, prophetic, and poetic books grouped into the Law, the Prophets, and the Writings. Already in ancient times this material was subject to commentary, which eventually gave rise, for example, to the Babylonian Talmud (basically complete by the sixth century after Christ); Christian fathers also wrote prolifically to explain its meaning in terms of the Christian revelation and to show that it foreshadowed their own faith. Thus, for instance, the words of Isaiah 7:14, as given in the King James version, that "a virgin shall conceive, and bear a son" were already taken in Matthew 1:23 as a prophecy of the coming of Christ — though the original Hebrew perhaps meant solely "young woman." Interpretation of the Old Testament is a venerable study which for long was pursued to seek allegorical truths; more recently it has been commonly conducted in a more sober and restricted fashion to place the development of Hebrew religious thinking in its historical framework. Useful surveys on this aspect are R. H. Pfeiffer, *Introduction to the Old Testament* (2d ed.; London: Black, 1952); more briefly, Stanley Cook, *Introduction to the Bible* (Harmondsworth: Penguin A144, 1945); see also H. H. Rowley, ed., *Old Testament and Modern Study* (Oxford: Oxford University Press, 1951), or W. O. E. Oesterley and T. H. Robinson, *Introduction to the Books of the Old Testament* (New York: Meridian LA23, 1958), on the prophetic books especially.

Textual criticism, that is, the effort to establish precisely the wording of the Old Testament, is also a discipline of long standing. By the third century after Christ the Christian scholar Origen found it necessary to set down and compare several texts (the *Hexapla*): the Hebrew, the Hebrew in Greek letters, the Septuagint translation into Greek which was made by Jews at Alexandria in the third century B.C., and three other Greek versions. From these sources Latin translations were made, the most famous of which is the Vulgate version by Jerome in the late fourth century after Christ. Modern English versions of the Old Testament rest upon all this material, which was copied by hand for century after century; the oldest manuscripts which we have at present are parts of Isaiah and other books found in 1947 and subsequently in Palestine (the Dead Sea scrolls), dating from the first century B.C. See Sir Frederic Kenyon, *Our Bible and the Ancient Manuscripts* (rev. ed., London: Eyre and Spottiswood, 1958).

In the nineteenth century after Christ Biblical criticism entered upon a new, more rigorous stage. Some of the results were farcical, as the sweeping conclusion that Moses was an utter figment of later imagination; but much was of great value. It is now generally accepted that the material incorporated in the Old Testament in part goes back to the days of the first settlement in Canaan, if not before, while other parts were composed in the second century B.C.; and that almost all books were subject to later additions and revisions.

In particular Biblical scholars generally agree in distinguishing in the Law (Pentateuch) several layers. The J tradition, which speaks of Yahweh (Jehovah), was the product of a powerful thinker (perhaps ninth-century B.C.) who stressed the meaning of the covenant; interwoven with this are pieces from a similar point of view which is called the E tradition, because it avoids the use of the term Yahweh until the era of Moses and speaks instead of Elohim, a plural word for God used especially in nomadic circles. Then comes D, the source of Deuteronomy; later, after the Exile, P, or the priestly code, served as the base into which material and views from JED were fitted. Even later reworkings took place to sharpen the manifestation of God's will under prophetic teachings. Beside this stream stood a far duller account of I–II Chronicles, Ezra, and Nehemiah, composed considerably after the return from the Exile to uphold the temple at Jerusalem and to point out more sharply divine intervention.

From Palestine we have almost no royal inscriptions and only a few scattered documents, as brief notes written on clay at Samaria (eighth century) and at Lachish just before its siege in 589 or 588, and a calendar of festivals from Gezer (tenth or ninth century). The Assyrian royal annals have a few references to Israel and Judah; and a famous inscription of king Mesha of Moab (c. 830) shows how powerful Omri had been (see *Ancient Near Eastern Texts*). The soil in Palestine has been subject to more intensive archeological investigation than has any other part of the Near East, and significant finds are still being made today by Christian and Israeli scholars. One result has been the demonstration of the relative poverty of this area; another, the revelation that non-Yahwistic cults long had considerable adherence. Only sporadically, however, does archeological material bear specifically upon passages in the Old Testament itself.

Further Reading. Kathleen M. Kenyon, *Archaeology in the Holy Land* (4th ed.; New York: Praeger, 1979), cautiously interrelates archeological and literary evidence. See also G. Ernest Wright, *Biblical Archaeology* (rev. ed.; Philadelphia: Westminster Press, 1963; H. H. Rowley, *From Joseph to Joshua* (London: Oxford University Press, 1950), which connects Biblical and outside evidence; and for earlier developments in Palestine Emmanuel Anati, *Palestine before the Hebrews* (New York: Knopf, 1963). James B. Pritchard, *Gibeon Where the Sun Stood Still* (Princeton: Princeton University Press, 1962), gives a fine description of the model excavation of one Palestinian site.

Political history is treated at length in T. H. Robinson and W. O. E. Oesterley, *History of Israel,* 2 vols. (Oxford: Oxford University Press, 1932) and T. H. Robinson, *Decline and Fall of the Hebrew Kingdoms* (New York: AMS Press, 1971); more briefly but well in Harry M. Orlinsky, *Ancient Israel* (2d ed.; Ithaca: Cornell University Press, 1960). Social institutions are well described in Roland de Vaux, *Ancient Israel: Its Life and Institutions* (New York: McGraw-Hill, 1961).

W. Robertson Smith, *Religion of the Semites* (New York: Schocken, 1972), is a classic; a more recent study of primitive survivals in Hebrew religion and of its development is W. O. E. Oesterley and T. H. Robinson, *Hebrew Religion: Its Origin and Development* (Geneva, Ala.: Allenson). The prophets are well treated by J. M. Powis Smith, *The Prophets and Their Times* (2d ed.; Chicago: University of Chicago Press, 1941), and R. B. Y. Scott, *Relevance of the Prophets* (New York: Macmillan, 1965). On the Hebrew achievement as a whole Mary Ellen Chase, *Life and Language in the Old Testament* (New York: Norton: N109, 1962), is thoughtful; there is a good collection of essays in E. R. Bevan and C. Singer, ed., *Legacy of Israel* (Oxford: Oxford University Press, 1927).

8

HISTORIC CIVILIZATIONS OF
INDIA AND CHINA

The very remarkable developments in China and India during the early
and middle centuries of the first millennium B.C. led to ways of life
which were even more divergent from the main stream of Near Eastern
civilization than was Judaism. Directly, these Indian and Chinese advances had little effect either on the Near East or on the civilization of
Greece and Rome, which must be the main concern of a western observer of ancient times; yet it is worth keeping an eye upon man's
progress in the farther reaches of Asia. Not only can one gain light upon
forces which are obviously important in their modern forms, but also a
study of these different forms of culture leads to a keener appreciation of
the unique qualities of Judaism and of Greek civilization.

The emergence of civilized societies in India and China was
considered briefly in Chapter 5. In many physical and cultural aspects
these early stages underlay the historic institutions of the two areas, but
well-defined patterns of thought and social organization became visible
only in the first millennium. More specifically, our concern in this chapter will be with events from the end of the second millennium down to
the coming of Alexander into India (327 B.C.) and the fall of the Chou
dynasty in China (256 B.C.). This period embraces, in India, the
elaboration of Hinduism and the life of the Buddha; and, in China, the
consolidation of civilization which produced a great host of vigorous
philosophers, including Confucius.

164

THE ARYANS AND EARLY HINDUISM

The Land of India. India is a vast land, two-fifths the size of Europe. Politically it has never been unified into one state; its cultural and geographical foundations vary greatly. Today some 150 languages are spoken within the subcontinent, mostly of Indo-European stock in the north but often of an earlier root (Dravidian and others) in the south. By north we mean chiefly the great river plains of the Indus to the west and the Jumna-Ganges to the east; a narrow corridor of jungle near the modern Delhi connects these plains, which otherwise are sundered by the Thar desert. Below them lies the Vindhya range, with extensions, which separates northern India from Gujurat, the Deccan, and other districts of southern India (see Map 5).

In many respects India shares important common characteristics. Most of it lies within the tropics and subtropics and, especially in the important Ganges basin, experiences the regular alternation of the monsoon winds, bringing heavy rains from the ocean in summer, and the anti-monsoon winds. Some students have emphasized the lush fertility and rapid death, the enervating effects upon human drives, and other aspects of Indian climate as bases of its thought. Everywhere, again, the agricultural village eventually became the social and economic unit of life, a conservative structure which very rarely progressed into a true city. Perhaps even more significant as a generally unifying factor was the rise, out of an Aryan background, of the all-encompassing system of life and religion known as Hinduism. This eventually spread over most of India.

Coming of the Aryans (c. 1500–1000 B.C.). The history of India is very little known down to the sixth century B.C. When archeological and literary evidence then begins to become more abundant in the northern plains, it shows a basically Hindu world both in social and in religious aspects. In the dim backgrounds are legends of invasions by peoples who called themselves Aryans or "nobles."

These people were not a racial type; their most notable characteristic was the fact that they spoke an Indo-European language, the root of historic Sanskrit. Modern scholars consider them a part of the great migrations of the second millennium, which drove into India from the northwest by the main land routes connecting India to the rest of Asia.

The date of the invasion is commonly put about 1500 B.C., and the barbarian, pastoral invaders seem to have given the final push to the already tottering Indus civilization. Such advanced developments as the use of writing, organized states, and conscious art vanished. In remote corners, to be sure, remnants of the Indus civilization survived until much later, and the Aryans took over a good many basic physical and cultural achievements from their predecessors; but, judging from the pottery, northern India did not re-establish a solid base for cultural development until about 1000 B.C. Southern India, incidentally, remained on a virtually Neolithic level and was not invaded by the Aryans.

The evidence for the Aryans comes mainly from four collections or *Vedas* of their hymns, chants, and ritual formulas. The most famous of these is the *Rig-Veda* or Royal Veda, a group of 1028 hymns to accompany sacrifices for various deities, such as the sky-god, Varuna; Indra, the mighty god of rain and patron of war; and the all-consuming Agni ("fire," cf. Latin *ignis*). These poems show the gods fighting the devils (*asuras*) and drinking the sacred *soma* (perhaps rhubarb juice); but they also throw scattered light upon the earthly worshipers of the gods. The fair-skinned Aryans war with the darker, non-Aryan natives (Dasyus, and the like, who were the source of the later Dravidians), dwell in villages where they farm with plows and raise cattle, and delight in swift horses harnessed to war chariots.

The Vedic material also indicates that the Aryans were divided into classes, the kernel of the historic Hindu castes. As described in a later source, "Brahmans, Kshatriyas, Vaisyas, and Sudras are the four castes. The first three of these are called twice-born . . . Their duties are: for a Brahman, to teach the Veda; for a Kshatriya, constant practice in arms; for a Vaisya, the tending of cattle; for a Sudra, to serve the twice-born." [1] The last of these, the Sudra, represents the earlier population; the first three, the priests, warriors, and herders, are the Aryan masters.

The social distinctions implicit in this grouping were relatively simple though firm from the outset, and the economic predominance of the leading classes remained a fundamental characteristic. Yet only in the later first millennium B.C. and in the centuries thereafter did the Indian

---

[1] Vishnu-Sutra, quoted by Jack Finegan, *The Archeology of World Religions* (Princeton: Princeton University Press, 1952), p. 160.

population divide itself rigidly into up to 3000 castes, partly as a response to the threat first of Buddhism and Jainism, then of Islam. Eventually each caste developed its own peculiar rituals of diet and marriage and became a fixed ingredient of Indian life. On the one side this division tended to perpetuate early linguistic and cultural divergences; but on the other it gave an enduring stability to Indian society despite repeated invasions. To understand Hinduism one must always remember that it is not only a pattern of religious thought but also a social structure.

Elaboration of Hinduism (*c.* 1000–500 B.C.). The development of Vedic religious views into the historic Hindu outlook is obscure, as is the social and cultural evolution of India in the early first millennium. Like the caste system it was far from complete by the time of the Buddha. While the great, but ill-defined deities of Aryan worship continued to be powerful, popular reverence seems to have elevated other forces, who were an amalgam of Aryan and pre-Aryan origins. One of these was Vishnu, the sun in some aspects, who was an ideal for the Kshatriya warrior class. The mythical tales told about his earthly incarnations which gave rise eventually to the *Ramayana* and the *Mahabharata* will concern us later in Chapter 29. Another great god was Siva; asceticism and hypnotic withdrawal via the yoga meditation were closely connected with his cult.

For the common man Hinduism tended to develop into a conglomerate of fertility cults, caste deities, and local faiths, all piled pell-mell into a great jumble which appealed to every taste. It thus came to mirror the diversity of India.

Ideas, however, which were held in a fairly crude form on this level were also explored by far more profound thinkers among the main body of priests, the Brahmans, and among the many ascetics. As they considered the meaning of life and the nature of the world, their teachings became ever more mystical and refined; the product was one of the most abstract forms of religious thought which has ever been evolved. This search revolved about the great spirit of the world, called Brahma, all-encompasssing and so impersonal Brahma could be described only by saying what it was not.

The literature produced by this search formed two main collections. On the one side were the *Brahmanas,* which were prose commentaries on rites connected with the *Vedas;* these were produced by the priests. On the other side was the vast collection of the *Upanishads,* a word meaning "sessions" of seekers after wisdom. The *Upanishads,* which included formulas and aphorisms as well as philosophical treatises, were in large part the work of the ascetics; the most important essays in this group date from the eighth to the sixth centuries B.C.

As Hindu thought developed and became crystallized in this litera-ture, man was pictured as having a spirit (Atman) which was identical with the great spirit of the world (Brahma). A famous shibboleth of Hinduism thenceforth ran, "That art Thou," that is, man and God are the same. "The supreme Brahma, the self of all, the chief foundation of this world . . . that thou art; Thou art that." [2]

To accomplish this realization was the duty of man, and the best method to that end was meditation. Failure to reach the goal produced rebirth in another form in the next life. Transmigration, which was unknown in the *Vedas,* thus became a cardinal principle of existence, and the results of one's acts in all previous lives (called *karma*) deter-mined whether one was reincarnated as a member of a higher or lower caste or as animal, plant, and the like. In Upanishadic thought the world became *maya,* pure illusion, a shadow play without purpose; but not all Hindu belief led to such nihilism about the world into which one, after all, was born and reborn. Yet the fact that the ultimate goal was to release oneself from the endless cycle of rebirth may help to explain many basic qualities of Hindu life and thought. If India failed to throw up lasting political structures on a large scale, the cause was perhaps more than geographical; the earthly relations of man to his fellow men were in some respects of quite minor importance and might be left to the governance of the caste and village structure.

Both socially and religiously Hinduism was intertwined ever more closely with all aspects of Indian life. In its homeland it had still to meet the challenge of some important religious reformers and then of closer contacts with Near Eastern culture in the days of the Persian empire and thereafter. Hindu art, for instance, had scarcely begun to appear in the period we are here considering.

[2] Kaivalya Upanishad 16, in S. Radhakrishnan, *The Principal Upanishads* (New York: Harper, 1953), p. 930.

BUDDHISM AND THE EXPANSION OF HISTORIC INDIA

The Sixth Century. Now that archeological exploration in India is rising rapidly, it may eventually be possible to illuminate a continuous course of development in the dim early part of the first millennium. At the present time, however, the sixth century B.C. seems to have been the era in which civilization reappeared in the subcontinent. The use of iron, though the metal was known earlier, became widespread only about 500 B.C. and helped to produce the superiority of regular infantry and cavalry over the individualistic noble charioteers chanted in the Sanskrit epic tradition. Coinage began, on the Persian standard; the Aramaic alphabet was taken over and adapted in the form of the Kharoshthi script, beside which stood a somewhat earlier form called Brahmi, probably Aramaic in origin also. Behind these events lay the rise of commerce with Babylonia, the appearance of true cities in India, the growth of irrigation along the Ganges, and the companion consolidation of kingdoms in the Ganges basin, which became the center of Indian culture.

Much of the specific line of development was due to the great unification of the Near East from Assyrian times onward, but the basic wellsprings were Indian. Men were ready to change over most of the peninsula, for the progress visible in the river plains spilled out into southern India, which began to emerge onto a historic plane. The Dravidian dialects of this area eventually produced Tamil and other modern tongues, but some districts of the south became Aryan in speech.

The winds of change blew in more than political and economic fields. The elaborate rituals and ancient sacrifices of the Vedic cult no longer could satisfy all thinkers; the increasingly wealthy and self-assertive elements of the cities and kingdoms grew restless under the claims which the Brahmans advanced to superiority. The result was an outburst of religious reform, partly within Hinduism itself but partly on such extensive lines that it led to virtually new religions. The greatest of these was Buddhism, which became India's main gift to the rest of Asia; an interesting companion in India itself was Jainism.

Life of the Buddha. Gautama Siddharta (d. *c.* 485) called by his followers the "Buddha" or Enlightened One, was born in the kingdom of Magadha, now part of Nepal. Mahavira or Vardhamana, the contemporary founder of Jainism, also came from northeast India, which lay on the rapidly expanding fringe of the Aryan area and was perhaps less inclined to accept Brahman pretensions. Both reformers, interestingly enough, stemmed from the Kshatriya class and used local tongues rather than the sacred Sanskrit in their preaching.

The birth of Gautama and his early years, like those of Mahavira, were attended by a succession of miracles which were much elaborated by later pious legend. The Chinese Buddhist canon eventually comprised more than 1600 works in over 5000 volumes, but virtually all of this took shape in and after the time of Christ. We have no contemporary documents and can make out only hazily the main events in the life of the Buddha, who delivered his teaching in oral form.

In the tradition, Gautama pursued a shielded life as a well-to-do aristocrat until he was 29, when be became discontented with his life of pleasure. One motive of his unrest was said to have been the sight of death and old age; another was the birth of a son. "Rahula is born, a chain is born," said Gautama; and that night he left his wife and babe so that he might follow the ascetic way, the common means in India to secure illumination. For six years he mortified his flesh in the conventional manner of the yoga doctrine. When he failed to gain any revelation of his union with Brahma, he abandoned his semistarvation diet and life in the wild, came to the nearest village, and ate. While sitting under a *pipal* (sacred fig) tree, he suddenly received his long-sought revelation of the true way.

Buddhism (and Jainism). Thereafter the Buddha preached serenely for 45 years along lines which are best summed up in his first sermon, delivered at the holy city of Benares:

> There are two extremes, O disciples, which the man who has given up the world ought not to follow — the habitual practice, on the one hand, of those things whose attraction depends upon the passions, and especially of sensuality — a low and pagan way unworthy, unprofitable, and fit only for the worldly-minded — and the habitual practice, on the other hand, of asceticism, which is painful, unworthy, and unprofitable.

There is a middle path, O disciples, avoiding these two extremes . . . a path which opens the eyes, and bestows understanding, which leads to peace of mind, to the higher wisdom, to full enlightenment, to Nirvana! [3]

This proper road was "the noble eight-fold path" of right views, right aspirations, right speech, right conduct, right livelihood, right effort, right mindfulness, and right contemplation. Translated, this definition essentially called for a practical conduct of life. The aim was still a mystical identification with the great spirit of the world, but the passions were to be removed by a moderate rather than an ascetic conduct. In this system, ethical relations to one's fellow men definitely mattered; Buddhists must lead a kindly life in which they must not injure living creatures (*ahimsa*), a doctrine even more emphasized by Jainism.

At the end of the Buddhist path lay passionless Nirvana, where men were freed from the sufferings of constant reincarnation. On the whole, however, the Buddha refused to lay down views on metaphysical problems. He was little concerned with the nature of afterlife and did not even show a clear belief in a god at all. His teachings cannot be understood apart from their Upanishadic background but were directed as a practical guide to life in this world. Their originality was scant; what counted was their simplicity, moderation, and directness and also the model of the Buddha himself, who inspired generations of followers. Slowly Buddhism drew apart from the more local characteristics of Hinduism, and by the third century B.C. it was ready to become a missionary religion in its own right.

Jainism, on the other hand, remained more purely Indian. As taught by Mahavira, it was said to be a reformation of earlier doctrines, in which the universe was an endless series of cycles. During each cycle 24 saviors (or *tirthankaras*) appeared at various points to aid suffering mankind. Mahavira, one of these *tirthankaras,* had gained his omniscience in the thirteenth year of his search, through the means of asceticism. Far more than the Buddhists the followers of Jainism emphasized an ascetic life and the doctrine of *ahimsa.*

Expansion of Historic India. Through the fifth and fourth centuries

[3] Tr. T. W. Rhys David, in *Sacred Books of the East,* XI (Oxford: Oxford University Press, 1881), pp. 146–7.

civilized patterns of life progressed southward in India. The kingdoms
of the river plains grew ever larger and more advanced with royal
bureaucracies; some states were republics. Rice, sugar cane, and cotton
became common crops, and both industrial and commerical life expanded.

On the northwest fringe the Persian empire rose in majesty and
pushed its rule down through Afghanistan to the edge of the Indus
valley. Recent study has begun to suggest some of the ramifications of
economic and intellectual contacts between the Mesopotamian hub of
the civilized world and India. Indian ideas such as transmigration may
have made their way across the Persian empire to Greece, where the
famous philosopher Pythagoras believed in reincarnation. The famous
Hindu numerals from which Arabic and our own numbers were derived came down to India from Mesopotamia, though probably only
after the era of Alexander.

As we shall see later, the ever closer contacts between the Near East
and the outlying corner of Greece led to the great invasion and conquest
of the Near East by Alexander during 334–23 B.C. Alexander came to
India in 327 and conquered most of the Indus valley; though his conquest did not last, it had serious effects in shaking up Indian political
institutions and opened India more widely to external influences. Under
these diverse pressures Hindu civilization inevitably developed and altered, and Buddhism began to expand into central Asia. Nonetheless
Indian development clung to the lines which had been established in the
earlier centuries of the first millennium B.C. Down to the present day
many of the forces which lie deepest in Indian thought and action are
the enduring reflection of the basically stable outlook already attained at
that time.

CHOU CHINA AND CONFUCIUS

The Isolation of China. Throughout Chinese history the observer
must always come back to the relative isolation of this land. Far more
than any other civilization of Eurasia the Chinese culture has developed
on an essentially uninterrupted path with little spur or check from
outside, and its calm assumption of superiority over its mostly barbarian
neighbors is understandable. Between China and India lie the forbidding

plateau of Tibet and the highest mountain peaks on earth. Traffic by sea between the two lands must cope with the long southward prong of the Malay peninsula. Traders by land across central Asia had to traverse 3000 miles of steppe and semidesert between the westernmost outposts of China Proper and the easternmost outliers of Mesopotamian civilization. Contact by land was possible and occasionally was significant; but in ancient times it was far more restricted even at its peak in the early Christian era than was true in the case of Indian relations with the Near East.

China itself is a vast area, larger than the United States if one counts such outlying dependencies as Manchuria, Mongolia, Chinese Turkestan, and Tibet. Of its two main rivers the southernmost, the Yangtze, flows 3000 miles and is navigable from the sea for over half its course; the northern, the Yellow, pours down in vicious floods for 2500 miles. Along the lower reaches of the latter was the seat of the earliest civilization in China, the Shang dynasty which was discussed in Chapter 5. Here millet was the staple food, and the climate was much like that of western Europe. Farther south lay many independent political, ethnic, and economic enclaves stretching on to subtropical rice-growing areas. Many of the inland districts in the south seem to have been heavily forested throughout early times. The physical type of the southern population also differed from that of the north in being shorter, browner, and less Mongolian in slant of eyes or prominence of cheekbones.

The remarkable fact is that all the vast region of China Proper became the home of an essentially unified civilization in the first millennium B.C. Despite serious problems in communication — far more difficult than on the sea-swept shores of the Mediterranean — China had also evolved a political unity by 221 B.C. From this kernel Chinese culture spread its influence over most of the rest of the Far East.

Chou China (*c.* 1122–256 B.C.). When the Shang dynasty fell *c.* 1122 B.C., the heartland of this culture was a fairly small district in the north China plain, and the main qualities of historic Chinese civilization were not yet fixed. Traditionally the new line, the Chou dynasty, was a less civilized people living in the hills to the southwest, but it took over the earlier patterns of the plain much more than had the Aryans in India.

For a time the Chou kings were capable and held their nobles in check by insisting that eldest sons be educated at the capital. In this

Western Chou period (*c.* 1027–771) their realm and culture expanded southward as far as the Yangtze valley. In 771 the Chou were defeated by barbarians on their western frontier and moved to an eastern capital, Chengchou near the modern Loyang. Already they had granted large parts of the kingdom to subordinate lords virtually in fief; the result of this decentralizing tendency was the line of weak monarchs known as the Eastern Chou (771–256 B.C.). From the eighth century on a host of virtually independent states vied with each other for pre-eminence.

To their titular and ritual master, the lord of Heaven, the local lords paid formal respect in periodic assemblies at Loyang, but each sought his profit in ruthless manner. The principalities in the old heartland of north China were generally more cultured but less powerful, so the main contenders came to be two: Ch'u, which became master of all the south; and Ch'in, which was warden of the western marches in the hills. At first an elaborate code limited the destructiveness of the chronic warfare, but hositilities grew more savage in the last centuries of the Chou period. As one poet groaned,

> Great pitiless God!
> Will disorders never cease?
> Every month they grow
> And people have no peace.

Inside each little state individual self-assertion was equally vindictive. The nobles ground down the peasants, who were virtually serfs; assassination and bribery were rife; the retainers and aides of the warlords cynically vied for power. "If you are successful in your job," said one, "you become a high official; if you fail you are boiled alive. That is the kind of business it is." [4]

Yet neither foreign war nor internal dissension seriously hampered the spread and intensification of Chinese civilization. The population seems to have risen steadily, for it threw out a constant stream of emigration to the south as well as engaging in large-scale irrigation and drainage projects on the loess soil of the north; to manage these projects the warlords needed, ever more, a literate bureaucracy. Commerce grew. The buffalo-drawn plow, metal coinage, silk, and other innovations ap-

[4] Burton Watson, *Ssu-ma Ch'ien: Grand Historian of China* (New York: Columbia University Press, 1958), p. 24.

peared. Formal taxation of agricultural land began early in the sixth century, and cities became compact masses of houses, unlike the sprawling Shang centers. Cast iron and steel were employed ever more widely. While the cult of the ancestors and other spirits remained powerful, the great Shang divinity, Shang Ti or T'ien, now equated with Heaven, gained a chief place, and the ritual of worship was developed in detail.

Chinese Culture. Culturally there was great progress. In art the complicated patterns of Shang bronzes were in part continued, but new forms also appeared. Closely connected with the formalization of worship were the Book of Changes, on foretelling the future, and the Book of Rituals. Beside these emerged the Classic of Poetry, containing lyrics on courtship, marriage, agriculture, and sacrifice. The Classic of History or Spring and Autumn Annals detailed dryly the chronicles of one Chinese state (Lu, the homeland of Confucius), for 722–481 B.C.; in the period it was invaded 21 times.

Although these, with some later works, have been the backbone of Chinese thought ever since, they were perhaps a less important achievement than was the emergence of a scholarly class, which taught the young and served the princes of the land in their religious and political activity. Many of this group were led by the disturbed life about them to refine the conduct of society itself and the life of man in a rational, skeptical fashion. These were the first Chinese philosophers, who emerged about the same time as the Greek philosophers.

The prime problem for the Chinese thinkers was the salvation of civilized order and the definition of its basic values. In seeking their answers they traveled widely, and thanks in part to the divided political rule of the land they debated in as free and profound a discussion as China ever experienced. To ascertain the ideal human society thinkers had to assess the nature of man, whether good, bad, or neutral — and also the nature of the universe. Yet their practical aim always brought them back to earth. Chou thought did not lose itself in mysticism or in overly great concern for the meaning of the individual by himself; these aspects received attention only in the later rise of Taoism and Buddhism.

Confucius. The greatest single philosopher who ever influenced China lived at this time, though at the close of his long life he groaned in dejection at his outward failure. This was Kung Fu-tze, Master Kung, or in Latinized form Confucius (551–479 B.C.).

Much of the life of Confucius is traditional legend. He was, thus, said to have been the son of an aged father who had had nine daughters previously, took a new wife, and died promptly after producing Confucius. Physically the sage is described in most unflattering terms, over six feet in height, with huge ears, flat nose, and two buck teeth. What is clear from the accounts is chiefly the fact that he displayed from early childhood a remarkable absorption in the old rites and the learning of his day and so became a member of the scholar class.

As such he gathered about him a band of disciples who heard his discourses on ethics, music, poetry, and the traditional rituals (*li*), knowledge of which produced the true gentleman. Always his prime objective was not to impart facts, but to implant a mental discipline which might shape the character of those who resorted to him for guidance; his students were then expected to go out and serve the princes of north China. Since public employment seemed to be the only way to put his ideas into practice, Confucius ever hoped to be called by some lord to high office, but he hoped in vain. Once he had a brief, unsuccessful chance in his homeland of Lu; in his 50s he made a long pilgrimage from state to state, seeking a post.

Confucius wrote little, apart from perhaps editing the Book of Poetry; but his friends set down his conversations or *Analects* after his death. The *Analects,* one of the Chinese classics, are a mass of dry, sketchy remarks without organization, which at first sight are far from impressive. Yet through them shines the character of Confucius himself, transparently sincere, concentrated on fundamental principles; his own high-minded, conscientious, noble example kindled a group of devoted followers. Remarkable in his teaching were his humorous outlook and his lack of dogmatism: "There were four things that the Master wholly eschewed: he took nothing for granted, he was never over-positive, never obstinate, never egotistic." [5]

Another great quality of the *Analects* was his concept of man and society, which became one of the greatest strands in Chinese civilization — though often corrupted in later days. In itself the thought of Confucius was not outstanding either in originality or in sheer intellectual

[5] *Analects,* tr. Arthur Waley (London: Macmillan, 1938), 9.4.

power; as he himself put it, "I for my part am not one of those who have innate knowledge. I am simply one who loves the past and who is diligent in investigating it." [6] Although his attention was thus centered on purifying and enhancing the formal rituals of the past, he paid little attention to problems of religion and afterlife. Man must live an ethical life within the basic units of the state and the family. What Confucius could do was to try to educate the political leaders as an example of righteousness for the ruled, who would then bend toward the good just as the grass bends before the wind.

With Confucius, in sum, there was incarnated in Chinese thought a force toward flexible, earthly, rational analysis. This must remind a member of western civilization of the contribution of the Greeks to our own mental outlook, but even more than in Greek philosophy Confucianism had a secular flavor. Political and intellectual dictation was to recur repeatedly in later China, but always the fundamental outlook of the tolerant Master Kung lay beneath the surface. As a famous Chinese historian said four centuries later, "There have been many kings, emperors, and great men in history, who enjoyed fame and honor while they lived and came to nothing at their death, while Confucius, who was but a common scholar clad in a cotton gown, became the acknowledged Master of scholars for over ten generations." [7]

Later Confucians. In the chaos of the Late Chou period, called the era of the Warring States (481–221 B.C.), there was room for many schools of thought. The ideas of Confucius expressed so well some of the deepest and most conservative bases of Chinese beliefs that they attracted several powerful thinkers, especially Mencius (372–288) and Hsün Tzŭ (*c.* 320–235).

To Mencius the welfare of the people was the highest aim of the state, which should be put in the hands of scholars like himself (and on occasion he succeeded in gaining public office). He held dogmatically that men were good by nature and could be judged by simple formulas.

[6] *Analects* 7.19.
[7] Ssu-ma Ch'ien, quoted by Lin Yutang, *The Wisdom of Confucius* (New York: Modern Library, 1938), p. 100.

Hsün Tzŭ on the other hand believed man to be evil. Goodness, therefore, could be acquired only by laws enforced by wise rulers; and *li,* the proper conduct of a gentleman, must be carefully defined and studied. Whereas Confucius had firmly believed that T'ien or Heaven was an impersonal righteous force, Hsün Tzŭ denied the existence of spirits. "Prosperity and calamity," he pronounced, "do not come from Heaven." [8] The last of the great early Confucians, Hsün Tzŭ systematized and clarified this line of thought into an authoritarian system. Confucianism was now ready to be taken up by a centralized state as a main ingredient in its philosophy of life and government.

Other Schools. The construction of a unified Chinese political system by 221, which we shall examine more fully in Chapter 29, did not draw all its ideas from the Confucian tradition. On the one extreme lay the sharply logical doctrine of the thinker Mo Ti (fifth century) that all life must be based on love. Far in the other direction pointed a loose group of thinkers summed up in Chinese history as the Legalist school. Members of this wing, while disagreeing in detail with each other, could not accept the freedom of the individual implicit in Confucius' views, and concentrated more baldly upon the problems of the present than upon refinement of codes handed down from the past. To gain civil order and political unity the state must be dominant and lay down prescriptions for communal life. The great, though ruthless, emperor Shih Huang Ti (221–10), who welded together the Chinese empire, was to draw heavily upon Legalist endorsements of autocracy and other ideas which had emerged by his day.

CONCLUSION

Eurasia in 500 B.C. Historians have often been impressed by the roughly coincidental appearance of such Hebrew prophets as the Second Isaiah and Ezekiel, the Buddha in India, Confucius in China, and the first Greek philosophers. Artistically and politically, as well, much of the civilized belt of Eurasia was making great strides in the middle centuries of the first millennium B.C. To seek an explanation of this amazing phenomenon we can make little use of principles of cross-fertilization. The development of India and of Greece owed something to their con-

[8] H. H. Dubs, *The Works of Hsüntze* (London: Probsthain, 1927), p. 177.

tacts with the hub of the ancient world, that is, the Fertile Crescent; but the course of progress in each area was far too diverse and the visible links were far too tenuous to support any assumptions that one district simply borrowed from another. China, moreover, lay far on a distant horizon with no evident connections to the other regions.

We must, rather, look to the earlier developments in each area to explain its progress. The preceding three chapters have taken up in turn the Fertile Crescent, Palestine, India, and China so as to show how the residents of each had moved beyond their inheritance from the second millennium to throw up new patterns of thought and political organization. The men of the early first millennium were, to be sure, indebted to the past, but their views were essentially of a new order. In this process, it is interesting to observe, the first seats of civilization had commonly lagged behind. Egypt and Babylonia were too attached to deeply rooted systems of life to be able to enter fully into the new streams. So it had been first the Assyrians and then the Persians who united the Near East; the Hebrews, off in the obscure corner of Palestine, had advanced to an ethical monotheism; the Buddha and Mahavira came from the fringe of the Aryan world; and even Confucius was the native of a minor north China state.

Two more peoples who were still backward remain to be considered, for they were actually to set the main frame of western civilization. The Greeks were only now beginning to advance with giant strides; and the Romans, in an even more remote district, were preparing for a mighty course of expansion.

The Variety of Civilizations. A true student of history soon becomes wary of setting forth "laws" of human progress. The basic needs of men may everywhere be of the same types, but the manner in which they associate themselves to satisfy those needs differs greatly. Inhabitants of the western world, both in Europe and in the Americas, draw from one great cultural tradition, yet even so the outlooks of Germans, French, Russians, and Americans vary sharply in matters which are far from minor. We have now seen enough of early developments in Asia to realize that there has never been a common Oriental civilization which may be placed over against the Occident. Politically as well as culturally India has always differed fundamentally from China, and the schemes of thought which are called Hinduism, Buddhism, and Confucianism — to

name only a few of the greater systems — give quite different answers to
the problems of man's life.

In the future it may come to pass that either China or India may mean
more to the world than will western Europe. Down to this date, however, the most dynamic system in history has been that which traces its
roots to the ancient Near East but which owes its basic qualities to the
addition of vital concepts from Israel, Greece, and Rome. It is accordingly time we turn to consider the emergence of Greek thought and the
political unification of the Mediterranean world, which permitted the
expansion of ancient civilization under the control of Rome.

BIBLIOGRAPHY

Sources. For many of the aspects of Indian and Chinese development
in the first millennium the only sure guide is that provided by archeological evidence. Excavation in India began in the nineteenth century under
British guidance; but only in recent decades has it begun to throw much
light upon the period covered in this chapter. Far more remains to be
done in India than in the Near East. The disturbed conditions of modern China have hampered archeologists so severely that only scattered
digs have been possible. Under Communist rule archeological investigation in China has stepped up its pace considerably; see Chêng Te-k'un,
Chou China (Cambridge: Heffer, 1963).

Down into the Christian era India lacked an independent historical
tradition, and solid dates and facts are available usually only when
Greek literature has preserved references to Indian events. This lack may
in part be the result of learned Hindu disinterest in matters of this
world; it also stems from the slow, weak development of large political
units. All the more valuable, as a result, are the Vedic hymns and
religious myths and speculations noted in the text, though these are
often undatable and obscure in reference; the text of the *Vedas* was
probably not set until after 600 B.C. These may be found in translation in
part in A. A. Macdonell, *Hymns from the Rigveda* (London: Oxford
University Press, 1923); for the *Upanishads,* see Swami Nikhilananda,
The Upanishads, 4 vols. (New York: Harpers, 1949–59), or the excerpts
in R. A. Hume, *Thirteen Principal Upanishads* (Oxford: Oxford University Press, 1921). Edwin A. Burtt, *Teachings of the Compassionate
Buddha* (New York: Mentor MP380, 1955), is a brief introduction to a

great mass of material. But when the historical student of western origin surveys the selection contained, for instance, in *Sources of Indian Tradition,* ed. W. T. de Bary (New York: Columbia University Press, 1958), he feels ever more keenly that an alien world lies before him.

China, on the other hand, eventually developed a very extensive historical tradition, and was the only nonwestern area to do so. The first great historian of China, Ssu-ma Ch'ien, will be discussed in Chapter 29; to what extent the tradition of the Chou period contained in Han and later writers is valid remains debatable. A good translation of Confucius' *Analects* is by Arthur Waley (New York: Random House, 1966), who has also translated Lao Tzu, *The Way and Its Power* (New York: Grove E84, 1958), and the *Classic of Poetry* (Shih Ching) in *Book of Songs* (New York: Grove, 1960).

Further Reading. A comprehensive, well-written survey of Indian history is A. L. Basham, *The Wonder That Was India* (3d ed.; London: Sidgwick & Jackson, 1967). The archeological evidence is described by Sir Mortimer Wheeler, *Early India and Pakistan to Ashoka* (New York: Praeger, 1959). Studies of Hinduism, not all of which bear solely on its earliest days, are E. Senart, *Caste in India* (Mystic, Conn.: Verry, 1976); T. J. Hopkins, *The Hindu Religious Tradition* (Encino, Cal.: Dickenson, 1971); H. Zimmer, *Philosophies of India* (Princeton: Princeton University Press, 1969), with others; Sir Charles Eliot, *Hinduism and Buddhism,* 3 vols. (Boston: Routledge & Kegan Paul, 1968). E. J. Thomas discusses *The Life of Buddha as Legend and History* (Boston: Routledge & Kegan Paul, 1969), and also *History of Buddhist Thought* (Boston: Routledge & Kegan Paul, 1963). A. K. Warder, *Indian Buddhism* (Delhi: Motilal Banarsidass, 1970), is technical but good.

H. Maspero, *China in Antiquity* (Amherst: University of Massachusetts Press, 1978), comes down to Han times; Hsu Cho-yun, *Ancient China in Transition* (Stanford: Stanford University Press, 1968); H. G. Creel, *The Western Chou Empire* (Chicago: University of Chicago Press, 1970). The latter's *Confucius and the Chinese Way* (Magnolia, Mass.: Peter Smith), is controversial; see also F. W. Mote, *Intellectual Foundations of China* (New York: Knopf, 1971); D. J. Munro, *The Concept of Man in Early China* (Stanford: Stanford University Press, 1969). Fung Yu-lan, *Short History of Chinese Philosophy* (New York: Free Press, 1966), is excellent.

IV

THE EARLY GREEK WORLD

9

THE BEGINNINGS OF GREEK
CIVILIZATION

At first sight much of Greek civilization must appear as alien to our experience as does the ancient culture of the Near East. In Homer's *Iliad,* for example, the human characters are childishly boastful heroes, who have strange names and customs, and the gods who move the heroes almost like puppets are both many in number and almost amoral in spirit; the epic style itself is far removed from that of modern fiction. The most perfect building erected in ancient times, the Parthenon, differs sharply in its restricted sense of space from modern architectural principles. Or, to give a third instance, Aristotle's great analysis of man's political relationships, the *Politics,* is laid in a world of tiny states, and its author completely rejects the idea that all men should be politically equal.

Yet the *Iliad* is rightly called the first masterpiece of European literature; and the Parthenon, *Politics,* and other products of Greek genius are basic foundations of the western outlook. When modern men talk or think of the beautiful, their ideas are essentially those formed by Greek artists. Many of our political terms are Greek in origin; more important, the concept that every citizen of a state has rights and duties, under law, is Greek. Our literary forms and standards derive directly from Greek literature, and Greek mythology has been a storehouse for modern poets, psychologists, and other thinkers. The logical, analytical approach shared alike by modern philosophers and by modern scientists was born in ancient Greece. To sum up, Hellenic civilization was the first great phase of western civilization.

This marvelously interlocked body of esthetic, literary, and political values emerged in the southeastern districts of Greece proper during the dark ages between 1100 and 750 b.c. After this initial stage came four other major divisions: a great age of expansion just on either side of 700 b.c.; the archaic era down to 500 b.c.; the golden or classic period, which ended with the reign of Alexander the Great (336–23 b.c.); and the Hellenistic age to the time of Christ. Even during the merger of Greek and Roman culture in the Roman Empire and during the Christian Byzantine Empire in the Middle Ages many important aspects of Greek civilization continued to be active.

In this part we shall consider developments to 500 b.c. The present chapter will be limited to the first stage, the dark ages (1100–750 b.c.).

GREECE IN THE DARK AGES

Geography of Greece. The fascinating course of Greek history occurred principally in a small district about 300 miles on a side. The center of this district was a body of water, the blue, almost landlocked Aegean Sea. Ancient Greece consisted thus of three parts: the western coast of Asia Minor, the Aegean islands, and Greece proper.

The western coast of Asia Minor, which became Greek in culture during the dark ages, has fairly extensive plains. These are cut by rivers such as the Hermus and Maeander, which plunge down from the central plateau through rocky ridges. Not until the hinterland was unified into a powerful kingdom were the Greeks along the coast likely to trade or turn their attention inland. The islands of the Aegean, which are almost innumerable, serve as stepping stones across the sea. In early days the central Cyclades islands were important trading centers, and one of them, Delos, became a great religious shrine. By archaic and classic times, however, the larger islands along the coast of Asia Minor (Lesbos, Chios, Samos, and Rhodes) were more significant. Crete, which lies like a bulwark all across the southern end of the Aegean, had had its greatest days in Minoan times, long before Greek civilization emerged.

The third part of the ancient Greek homeland was the most important. The western border of the Aegean, or Greece proper, is a region mainly of limestone mountains which have sunk at their southern end in recent geologic times. Where they meet the main bulk of the Balkans, the mountains still stand tall and are bordered by the major plains of Macedonia and Thessaly. In the south the sea sends long fingers up between the mountain ridges; and the plains, which are small, are sometimes landlocked valleys, sometimes narrow coastal strips.

Although the mountains appear everywhere, a belt of north-south ridges separates the east and west coasts of Greece, while another ridge from Olympus south to Euboea cuts off Thessaly from the coast; other ridges run roughly east and west to mark the northern and southern limits of Thessaly and Boeotia. An even sharper division is that of the Saronic gulf and the gulf of Corinth, the latter of which almost sunders the Peloponnesus from central Greece. Greece was thus fragmented into a host of tiny districts, many of which we shall meet later as independent states.

Greek history was not simply an expression of its geographic framework, but the influences of topography and climate were important. Diversity was encouraged, and yet seaborne forces tended to link all parts of this world. The Greeks accordingly developed a common pattern of civilization which nonetheless had many local variations.

Trade and industry were facilitated by the abundance of harbors, by the normally calm waters of the Aegean in the summer, and by the fact that no part of Greece was more than a day or two on foot from the sea. One should not, however, make the mistake of assuming that at any stage in Hellenic history most men were sailors; on the contrary only a small proportion ever made its living from the sea either by fishing or by sailing. The primitive agricultural processes of antiquity rarely produced large food surpluses save in the great river valleys; especially in Greece most inhabitants had to raise their own food and so were home-abiding farmers living off bread, cheese, wine, and a few other staples. In Greece too population could be only relatively thin, though it was clustered in groups about the small agricultural plains where never-failing springs were available. Farming practices had to be adjusted to the Mediterranean-type climate, in which the rains fall mainly in the winter; the relatively sunny, temperate weather permitted outdoor life most of the time in the lowlands. While true pastures and irrigable lands were few, the usual Mediterranean scrub growth of the mountains supported flocks of sheep and goats, and swarms of honey-producing bees buzzed among the thyme and other flowers of the hillsides. Good timber for ships and for building was rarely abundant, but olive trees and vines could be grown widely. Crystalline layers along the western shores of the Aegean provided veins of silver, copper, and other metals, though Greece had usually to import large parts of its needs in metals. Here and in the islands the rock was often marble of good quality.

On the one hand life in Greece had necessarily to be simple and could not support the great kingdoms and lavish luxuries of the Near East. In the spring, as an early poet tells us, "when things grow but a man cannot eat his fill," [1] the June harvest was eagerly awaited. On the other hand men's needs of food, fuel, and habitation were relatively simple in the semitropical climate and could be provided with relative security.

An enduringly important influence on Greek history was its position relative to other principal centers of population and culture. As we saw in Chapter 5, migrations from the land mass of Europe could sweep down into Greece, though only after traversing the broken, mountainous Balkans. Traders with wares, ideas, and techniques from the Near East could make their way to the Aegean, though only after skirting the dangerous southern coast of Asia Minor. Owing to this factor the major political and cultural centers of historic Greece were located along the eastern coast, where their inhabitants could reach the Aegean and tap the influences from the Near East, even if the more favored lands, from the point of view of rainfall and agricultural potential, stretched along the western coast of Greece proper.

Greece, then, lay on the frontiers of Europe and Asia, but was not necessarily subject to direct, continuous influences from either direction. While the rise and development of Greek civilization were directly connected to the earlier and contemporary history of the Near East, the Greeks were far enough removed that they might mold borrowed concepts into a virtually new form of culture. During the dark ages the Aegean was almost completely isolated from outside contacts, a point of great importance in facilitating the emergence of the historic Greek outlook.

Mycenaean Collapse and Aegean Reorganization (1200–750 B.C.). During the Minoan and Mycenaean periods of the second millennium B.C.

[1] Alcman, fragment 56 (ed. Diehl).

the powerful lords of the palaces had had wide contacts with the Near East and had borrowed much from its Bronze age cultures. At least on the mainland the dominant element had spoken Greek since the invasions early in the second millennium, but politically and culturally Mycenaean civilization differed sharply from that which was to flourish later in historic Greece. The Mycenaean world seems to have been declining by the thirteenth century B.C., but a violent invasion, remembered as the coming of the Dorians, brought it to an end just after 1200 B.C.

In the Near East similar waves of invasion had had serious results; in Greece the effects were catastrophic. The use of writing vanished once the palaces had been sacked and their royal bureaucracies were dispersed; artists and architects no longer had patrons, let alone security; overseas trade virtually ended. Settled agricultural life itself may have become impossible in the more exposed districts, for archeological evidence for villages in the dark ages is only spottily available. By 1000 life in Greece had sunk to a bare level of subsistence, either by farming or by nomadism, and remained on this level for two centuries. The world outside Greece became an area of fable, populated by monsters and strange races.

Although the picture is black and dark, very important developments for the future history of Greece were occurring. The local collapse, together with the general decline of trade in the eastern Mediterranean, meant that the Aegean basin was isolated and was thrown back on its own resources. On the other hand the area now came to possess basically a common cultural pattern.

During the chaos attending the Dorian invasions some of the earlier inhabitants of Greece seem to have escaped across the central islands of the Aegean to the coast of Asia Minor, where very scattered Mycenaean colonization had occurred. The Dorians themselves swept across the southern islands through Crete and Rhodes to the opposite coast. These nuclei of Greek-speaking peoples remained in contact with each other, and as the mainland of Greece proper began to evolve new cultural patterns in the eleventh and tenth centuries B.C. they picked up its developments. Through imitation by the other inhabitants of the Aegean, intermarriage, and at times conquest, the major districts of the Aegean basin had come to possess a basically uniform culture well before 800 B.C.; and the many local cultures which had existed in the second millennium vanished. This development was important in itself as showing that Greek civilization had very attractive qualities from early days; but it was also significant in giving the Greeks a broad geographical base from which they could expand greatly after 750 B.C.

The Greek Dialects. The evidence for this consolidation of the Aegean population lies both in archeological testimony, particularly that of the pottery, and also in the fact that both shores of the sea had common political, social, religious, and poetic characteristics when they again came into the light of written records from 700 B.C. onward. Another mark of the unification is the victory of the Greek language, for only in a few outlying districts did earlier, non-Hellenic tongues survive.

Here, however, we can clearly observe that major quality of Greek civilization — diversity within an over-all unity — which we shall notice again and again. All across the Aegean the language was Greek, but local Greek dialects differed as much as do the types of English spoken throughout the world today. Greek dialectal variations were most evident in matters of pronunciation, secondarily were visible in vocabulary, and were least important in grammatical constructions.

In Asia Minor (and generally in the islands) from north to south men spoke Aeolic, Ionic, and Doric. On the mainland of Greece the dialectal distributions were more complicated. Throughout the south and east parts of the Peloponnesus, including Sparta, Argos, and Corinth, Dorians were dominant and, to give an example, pronounced the word for "people" as *damos.* In the Attic dialect, akin to Ionic, the same word was *demos;* and since Attic was the root of literary Greek in later days we talk today of *democracy.* Thessalian was closely related to Aeolic. But there were also such dialects as the Arcadian, in the hills of the Peloponnesus, which resembled the earlier Mycenaean speech, and a group called Northwest Greek, spoken from Boeotia westward and also in Elis and Achaea in the Peloponnesus.

The many local dialectal pockets of Greece had normally also distinct cultural and social institutions. Yet Dorians, Ionians, and others are not to be visualized as distinct races; they were all Greeks and shared in the common qualities of the mother tongue. This was a remarkably supple speech which possessed from early days characteristics of keen logical analysis, a tendency to abstraction and to causal constructions, and a poetic outlook. The languages of the Near East could not begin to rival the ability of Greek to set forth clearly and briefly a chain of ideas and to balance in one sentence, by means of a host of qualifying particles, a complex concept.

Political and Social Institutions. During the dark ages the men of the Aegean basin also evolved a fundamentally common set of political and social institutions which underlay in many vital respects the later course of Greek development. To what extent these institutions were handed down from the second millennium it is difficult to determine, but in at least some cases we can see that the Dorian invasion brought real changes.

Politically, for instance, the wide-ruling lords of the Mycenaean palaces vanished, together with their bureaucracies. Greek lands turned decisively away from this imitation of Near Eastern monarchy to a far simpler system. Local leaders, who called themselves "kings," ruled only tiny areas; and though in Homer these kings boasted their descent from Zeus, they were little more than war chiefs. Powerful in battle, in peace they liked to eat and drink and hear bards chant ancestral tales of warfare and cunning heroes; but kings as well as followers spent much of their time in agriculture and herding. All were bound together by a web of ancestral custom, which was applied in problems of justice by the elders. The kings offered sacrifices to the gods on behalf of the whole community, but each man could approach the gods on his own; priests, seers, and other religious officials were only technical assistants. The Greek kings, sharply limited in powers, were virtually to disappear in the great changes after 750 B.C.; the minute political subdivision of Greece, however, and the communal sense of unity among the inhabitants of each tiny kingdom were fundamental roots of the later city-states.

Socially the population everywhere was bound together in tight units. A people of Dorian speech was divided into three tribes, which were primarily political and military blocks; Athenians had four tribes; and an Ionian district commonly had six. The warriors were often organized in brotherhoods (*phratries*), much like those of American Indians. Such bands ate and fought together; young males were at times attached to these brotherhoods for instruction and were initiated upon maturity.

The family was the basic social and economic unit, within which the father was dominant. It was very important to have a surviving son, who could carry on the religious ceremonies which marked the unity of the family; if a family had only a daughter, her marriage to cousins or uncles was strictly regulated to make certain that the land and movable property remained within the family. In this primitive world individual "rights" had almost no place, and a man cast out of his local community by reason of self-will, murder, or other social crime was in serious straits unless he could find an alien king to serve as his protector.

Any differences which may initially have existed between invaders and subject populations tended to dissolve in the dark ages, but the Greek countryside was nonetheless fairly sharply divided into two classes. The upper class furnished the priests and other officials, led in battle, and sat with the king at feasts and in council on major problems. It was, by and large, richer in land. The lower classes consisted of the smaller peasants, of day laborers who owned no land and so were on the margin of society, and of the simple artisans and tradesmen who provided the non-agricultural necessities of life. Occasionally this element met in assembly to hear the decisions of its king or to elect his successor. A few slaves also appear in Homer, usually captives in war, who were shepherds and the like (if male) or concubines, wool-spinners, and household attendants (if female).

To comprehend the rigidity and superstition which marked most sexual and social customs of the early Greeks a modern student might well use for comparison the ways of tribes in Africa and the Pacific islands which have been studied by anthropologists. If the Greeks were to survive the age of chaos which followed the Dorian invasions and were to build up a solid social structure for the continuance of organized life, they could not allow free action by individuals. The remarkable fact, however, is that the need for social unity did not force the inhabitants of the Aegean into a static, fear-ridden structure. Even during the worst of the dark ages the Greeks were beginning to fashion a civilization of remarkable artistic and intellectual potentialities.

THE FIRST SIGNS OF THE GREEK OUTLOOK

Protogeometric Pottery (1050–900 B.C.). For clear evidence that the fundamental qualities of Greek civilization had begun to appear in the dark ages one must look to the physical remains of the era, especially its pottery, and to the burgeoning of myth and epic.

During the Dorian invasions the more advanced skills which had been plied at the Mycenaean palaces disappeared, such as the working of ivory and gold, fresco painting, and architecture. Neither sculpture nor architecture of any serious significance reappeared in the Aegean basin until almost 750 B.C.; but pottery, wood, textiles, and metals continued to be necessary for survival. Throughout most of this period bronze was still the principal metal, though the use of iron slowly grew for weapons and tools.

The changes which took place in the potters' outlooks are particularly illuminating, for pottery was one of the chief products of this poverty-stricken age. Although vases were employed for many purposes in the homes, not much of this ware has survived; what we do have are the burial gifts, that is, the containers for oil, wine, and other provisions which a corpse was expected to need. The Kerameikos cemetery north-west of the Acropolis in Athens, in particular, provides examples of burials all across the dark ages. Here the first graves after the Mycenaean collapse were simple inhumations, for men could spare little to lay away with the dead; the pottery at this stage displayed the tired shapes and weak decoration inherited from the Mycenaean world.

Then, suddenly about 1050, marked changes occurred. Cremation became the almost universal custom in this cemetery; weapons of iron grew more common; the shapes of the safety pins and long, straight pins used on the garments became very different from those employed earlier. Above all a new style of pottery, called Protogeometric, commenced. Although this style was a direct descendant from sub-Mycenaean work, it shows that the minds and fingers of the potters had launched out on a veritably new path. The shapes in the new style are simple but more solidly based; the decoration, which consists of little more than horizontal lines about the vase and a few motifs such as concentric circles and semicircles (drawn by compass), is nonetheless elegantly applied so as to create an artistic unity.[2]

[2] The Protogeometric amphora found in the Kerameikos cemetery (K.1073) which is illustrated on Plate VIII.B shows the new style in fully developed form. In contrast to the Mycenaean *kylix* next to it the Greek vase has a lower center of gravity with solid foot. Its taut decoration is abstract, yet clearly marks off the different zones of the pot while relating them in a logical progression.

It is not improper to emphasize the visible characteristics of the best Attic Protogeometric vases and to note that every one of these qualities was thenceforth a mark of Greek civilization — a synthesis of clearly defined parts, which has a dynamic quality; a deliberate simplification of form and decoration into a structure capable of infinite variation; an emphasis upon rational principles of harmony and proportion (as the western world has understood these principles ever since); a sense of order in which the imagination is harnessed by the powers of the mind. Even if the eleventh century B.C. was dismally poor in most outward respects, it was the era in which a great revolution occurred in every physical respect visible in the Kerameikos graves. One may justly infer that this was the era in which the basic qualities of the Hellenic outlook appeared as a coherent, enduring synthesis.

Several aspects of this change deserve emphasis. As the indebtedness of the Protogeometric style to earlier pottery suggests, Greek civilization was ultimately based on the rich Minoan-Mycenaean background; yet the historic Greek outlook differed fundamentally from that which had existed earlier. The revolution of the eleventh century, again, was surely home-born, for in this era Greece had the scantiest of foreign relations. Significantly enough the heartland of the new outlook lay in the southeastern districts of Greece proper, such as Attica, Argos, and neighboring territories, which were to remain the main cultural centers of Greek life thenceforth.

From this kernel the Protogeometric style spread widely over the rest of Greece, the islands, and the coast of Asia Minor in the tenth century B.C. Despite its poverty the Aegean world was closely interlinked, and artisans seem to have had wide freedom of movement. "For these men," said a character in the later *Odyssey,* "are bidden all over the boundless earth." [3]

Development of the New Outlook (900–750 B.C.). Once the Protogeometric style had struck roots, the course of progress in pottery flowed continuously. By about 900 life had become sufficiently secure for the potters to spend more time and attention on each vase; they now evolved an ever more complex decoration, still drawn mainly by ruler and compass, which we call the Geometric style.[4] Attica stood generally in the

[3] *Odyssey* 17.386; tr. A. T. Murray.
[4] Plate VIII.C illustrates a Kerameikos amphora (K.2146) of about 850–800 B.C. Both in its elongated shape (as compared to the Protogeometric amphora above)

lead, but all over the Greek world the common style was applied in a host of local variations — another example of that fruitful blend of unity and diversity which manifested itself in the Greek dialects.

The Geometric style in its turn gave rise to a remarkable series of pottery products, still generally Geometric, which flourished especially in Athens in the eighth century B.C. Since the chief pieces of this type were found near the later great western gate of Athens called the Dipylon, it is named the Dipylon style. Here artists finally broke out of the narrow range of abstract motifs which could be drawn by ruler and compass and began to sketch human beings. As the Dipylon vases were intended to accompany the dead or to stand on top of their funeral mounds, they commonly show corpses on biers, mourned by the survivors; funeral corteges with chariots and marching warriors; or scenes of battle by land and by sea.

Some Dipylon vases stand five to six feet high; both technically and artistically they are masterpieces. In shape and pattern of decoration their indebtedness to Protogeometric and Geometric work is evident, but they reveal the great growth of artistic imagination and logical sense over the three centuries 1050–750. The surface of the amphora on Plate IX is a mass of interrelated bands, built up from simple, repeated patterns which are subtly varied and balanced; so too did the roughly contemporary poet Homer vary his simple hexameters to create the great epic of the *Iliad*. In the inserted scene of death on the shoulder of the vase, the drawing of human beings is schematic, yet the meaning is poignant:

> Viewed as a rendering of life it is a solemn scene reduced to its barest terms, terms telling from their very bareness. Here is an artist who has not attempted more than he could exactly perform; an art not childish, but planned and austere.[5]

and in its far more elaborate decoration, this vase shows the changes taking place in Attic workshops. Although the rich variety of the design is made up of a very few motifs, these are combined in a far more complicated manner than in Protogeometric work; coordination and subordination are conjoined. The meander, a dynamic motif to be used for centuries in Greek art and architectural decoration (our Greek key pattern), has now appeared. The concentric circles are placed in a "picture" frame; soon artists were to begin showing animals and human beings in this frame.

[5] J. D. Beazley, *The Development of Attic Black-figure* (Berkeley: University of California Press, 1951), p. 3.

Artistically the great Dipylon vases demonstrate that Greek civilization was capable of major achievements by the middle of the eighth century b.c. Intellectually considered, they attest that such fundamental qualities of the Greek outlook as concentration, balance, and proportion were already comprehended and expressed. Further testimony to this fact can also be gained from the rise of Greek mythology and the epic, which perhaps show more clearly some important aspects of the Greek conceptions of man and the gods.

MYTH AND EPIC

Myth. Many peoples of the world have created stories about gods and heroes, and these tales, whether coming from India, Greece, or Scandinavia, often have the same basic plot or theme. The most influential mythology of western civilization, however, has been that created by the Greeks. This stands out above all others for its rich, yet disciplined imagination; for its humane quality, which rarely emphasized the cruel or frightening aspects of life; and for its esthetic nature. Throughout Greek history it was a fertile source of ideas for dramatists, artists, and philosophers, as it has been ever since.

In some few cases Greek mythology borrowed Near Eastern tales; but for the most part it was of native root, and may even at points have had Mycenaean origins. Myths at times were no doubt created to entertain; frequently they had the more serious ends of releasing the tensions of human fallibility, of explaining natural (or unnatural) phenomena, and of crystallizing religious views. The making of myth was a simple, unconscious process which continued on down into historic times, though then efforts were largely devoted to systematization and rationalization. The major tales seem clearly to have been known by the time of Homer, who refers to several of them.

Throughout Greek mythology there runs a consistent view of the world as dominated by gods who were like human beings save in being more powerful and undying. Essentially these gods were favorable to men, especially to the great heroes. One such hero was Theseus, revered about the Saronic gulf but particularly absorbed in later days by Athens as a legendary king who brought order and civilization. Another figure, born in Thebes but appropriated by the Dorians, was Heracles, who labored to rid the Peloponnesus of various monsters. Most popular among all mythical heroes in early days, Heracles symbolizes the still simple, half-civilized character of the era, which imagined for him a violent end. His wife Deianira, angered by his infidelity, gave Heracles a poisoned shirt; driven into torment, Heracles had himself placed on a funeral pyre but was rescued by the gods to become an immortal.

Both in the great Panhellenic tales and in the minor stories treasured only in one small district of the Greek world a host of motifs of simple origin was elaborated by people who looked out on the surrounding world with deep curiosity but without superstitious fear.

The Epic and Homer. The same views which created Greek mythology were also present in the Greek epic, but there they were developed even further into one of the world's greatest literary achievements. The subjects of the greater epics were largely the wars and the other adventures of heroes who lived far in the past, in the generations before, during, and just after the Trojan war. This war itself was launched by all the Greeks under the leadership of Agamemnon, wide-ruling king of Mycenae, to regain the beautiful Helen, who had been stolen from his brother, Menelaus of Sparta. Beside Agamemnon and Menelaus fought a great galaxy of Greek heroes such as the old, wise Nestor of Pylos; the wily Odysseus from the western island of Ithaca; and Achilles of Thessalian Phthia, son of the goddess Thetis and the mortal king Peleus. Against the Greeks stood the seducer Paris, his brother Hector, and other warriors under king Priam of Troy, together with allies drawn from Asia and Thrace.

Mycenae existed; so too did Troy. Behind the epics there probably lies a kernel of truth in that we may assume Mycenaean freebooters did once attack the citadel of Troy. To some extent memories of the political geography of the second millennium were preserved by epic bards, and a few treasured physical objects described in the epics can only be Mycenaean. Some modern scholars, indeed, argue seriously that the Trojan epics preserve a detailed picture of the late Mycenaean world. On the whole, however, it appears far safer to conclude that the epics evolved both in subject matter and in technique over several centuries. That all Greece actually waged a war of 10 years below the walls of Troy seems most unlikely, and the plots of the *Iliad* and the *Odyssey,* in particular, must be fictional in virtually every respect.

Throughout the dull centuries of the dark ages, when kings and upper classes lived at home and raided each other's lands for cattle and slaves, bards recited lays of the great days when Mycenaean leaders had roamed more widely. As they did so, an oral epic technique was built up. Stock phrases such as "far-shooting Apollo" or "the well-greaved Achaeans" and also whole passages of several lines which described the washing of hands before a dinner, the ceremony of sacrifice, and the like were fixed as pegs which a poet could recite while his mind was recalling the next action of the plot. An epic vocabulary and dialect were also created, which were based largely, but not exclusively, on Aeolic. The verse form of the epic was always the hexameter, a simple six-foot line which could be varied subtly but was admirably suited for oral delivery. In this, as in all later Greek verse forms, the meter was built upon due succession of long and short syllables, not on accent as in English poetry.

This development and elaboration went on for centuries, just as the Protogeometric and Geometric potters of the Aegean evolved an ever more complex system of pottery decoration. Then, early in the eighth century, a great poet called Homer pulled together one cycle of stories into the *Iliad* and poured into his epic its dramatic drive and impact. In all probability he lived on the coast of Asia Minor, and he may have composed his work for recitation at the international festivals which were then rising. The date of Homer, incidentally, is a fiercely debated subject, on which opinions vary all the way from the twelfth to the sixth centuries; but his achievement and his outlook must remind one principally of the parallel triumphs of the Dipylon potters in Athens. Since Homer's intention was to recount great deeds of the past, he gives no contemporary references, yet in the main the religious, psychological, and social tone of his poem accords with what we know of the eighth century.

In each generation since then the *Iliad* has charmed men for its story, for its simple yet beautiful style, and above all for its view of life. The plot itself is laid in the tenth year of the Trojan war and covers only six weeks. At the outset the hero Achilles feels himself insulted by Agamemnon, who takes away a woman he has gained in battle. Achilles retires to his hut to sulk and, by prayer to his goddess mother, secures the displeasure of Father Zeus on the Greeks. During his absence the Greeks are worsted and are driven back to their ships. The death of

Achilles' closest friend Patroclus in the effort to halt the Greek defeat brings Achilles back to the fray, and with the aid of the goddess Athena he kills the great Trojan warrior Hector. In the end the aged Priam, father of Hector, comes by night to Achilles and ransoms the body of his dead son, which the Trojans burn on a funeral pyre.

Significance of the Iliad. The tale of the wrath of Achilles is a story of passion, of bloody warfare, and of strongly defined, proud heroes. Yet its ultimate lessons are far deeper: Achilles learns the folly of blind anger; the poem is infused with a penetrating sympathy; and man, while great in his military glory, is subject to higher authority.

The action of the epic took place on two planes, the divine and the human; and of the two the divine was far more important. When men deserted their reason either for acts of folly or for superhuman deeds, they were felt to be divinely impelled. The gods gave foreknowledge of the future through dreams, the flight of birds, thunder, and actual messengers; at times the gods even came down into the battle, and could be wounded. Quarrelsome, adulterous, and skilled in trickery, the gods were human beings writ large; Homer cast the religious views of the upper classes of his day in a form which remained dominant through the rest of Greek religious history. Yet the gods bowed before the master of all, Zeus of Mt. Olympus, and Zeus himself was bound by the laws of the universe. The divine world thus was a meaningful, orderly structure within which men felt free to work and to create, and the cult of the great Olympian gods in Homer had a rational cast from which superstition and magic had largely been stripped.

In Homer the men who fill the earthly plane are not consciously visualized as self-moving nor as true individuals. Odysseus, Achilles, Agamemnon, and the other heroes are more types than individuals — an idealistic attitude which remained powerful in Greek philosophy of later days. Yet the view of mankind which Homer expressed is a landmark in the progress of civilization. To understand the significance of the *Iliad* in this respect one can do no better than compare it with the greatest epic of Mesopotamian literature, the tale of Gilgamesh. There are many similarities, as we saw in considering the earlier epic; but the differences are equally sharp.

The heroes of the *Iliad* know as well as does Gilgamesh that the gods rule the world and that men must die, but while alive they throb with delight in the world about them. In reflection of the growing pride and individualism of the upper classes who were slowly becoming self-conscious in the eighth century, Homer fashioned a dream of emancipated heroes, competing for honor in the eyes of men, which was thenceforth to be a polar companion to the equally strong Greek feeling for cooperation of the group. From Gilgamesh and Enkidu there stemmed no fructifying development of man's understanding of his own nature; from the men of the *Iliad* came a steadily onrushing exploration of the qualities of mankind.

Only a great poet could have infused the *Iliad* with its majestic interpretation of life which leads inevitably to death and yet is the stage of man's glory. Achilles knows beforehand that if he goes to Troy he will die there, but his honor drives him to go, once his mother's effort to hide him fails. He knows full well that the gods determine all, but he is free to act as he wills. When the goddess Athena, inspired by Hera, descends to calm him, she must begin carefully: "I came to check your passion, if you will listen"; and Achilles reluctantly but freely decides: "I must observe the bidding of you both, goddess, angry though I am indeed. It is better so. What the gods command you, do, then the gods will listen to *you*." [6] Here the ultimate dominance of reason, though forced to strive with elemental passion, stands sharply defined. In the *Iliad* as a whole the basic differences between Greek (and western) civilization and the Babylonian view of life cannot be mistaken. If this epic were to mean as much to later Greeks as the Bible and Shakespeare together have meant to modern English-speaking peoples, the reasons lie far deeper than in its stirring plot; the poetic genius of its author, his psychological sensitivity, and his glowing picture of men and gods had enduring appeal.

Other Epics and the Alphabet. Other groups of epic tales existed besides those revolving about Achilles. The second great epic of early Greece, the *Odyssey*, recounted the wanderings of Odysseus after the fall of Troy for 10 years and his return to Ithaca to kill the arrogant suitors of his wife Penelope; interwoven in this are the adventures of his son Telemachus, who sought support against the parasites on his ancestral inheritance. This story also passes under the name of Homer, but it was

[6] *Iliad* 1.206ff.; tr. W. H. D. Rouse.

probably composed close to the end of the eighth century. The pattern of the *Odyssey* is more discursive, less concentrated, less stylized than is that of the *Iliad;* yet the structure of the plot is more involved in attendant variety. The psychological and religious temper of the younger poem is also different. The physical world about man now begins to appear in real hues — one consequence is the virtual lack of similes in the *Odyssey* as against their frequent use in the *Iliad*. Qualities of determination and calculation are the hallmark of the much-enduring Odysseus, who makes his way through his troubles by wily lies and the assumption of disguised identity rather than by blazing forth in childish wrath like Achilles.

Yet other Trojan epics were composed within the next century or so, though the lesser tales could not stand the test of time and have not survived. Beside them stood stories of the Seven against Thebes, laid in a legendary war of Mycenae and Thebes, which were to be drawn upon by later tragedians; but by the middle of the seventh century B.C. men's interests and literary abilities had passed on to the stage of lyric poetry, which ended the epic outlook.

If the *Iliad* and *Odyssey* survived virtually as they were composed, the principal reason lies in the fact that the Greek world again knew how to write before 700 B.C. At some point in the eighth century Greek visitors to the eastern Mediterranean became acquainted with the Phoenician alphabet, decided that it had utility, and adapted the script for their own language. In doing so they invented some new letters and systematically employed signs for the vowels, more important in Greek than in Semitic tongues. Thus the Greek alphabet was a supple tool capable of setting down all types of thought precisely and clearly.

As in the case of the Greek dialects, so in the alphabet there appeared many local varieties; the one which eventually won out was basically the Attic form with some Ionic influence. Well before 700 B.C. the Greek alphabet was being borrowed by peoples in Asia Minor and was taken over by the Etruscans in Italy, who passed it to the Romans. When and how the great epics were written down, we do not know; but once this step had occurred, they could circulate easily over the whole Greek world as a source for artists, as a stimulus to poets, and as a powerful statement of Greek views on man and the gods.

THE GREEK WORLD IN 750 B.C.

By 750 B.C. the Aegean basin was again resuming contacts with the outside world. From the Near East it borrowed the alphabet, motifs in pottery, and a few mythical tales; the ivory which now began to appear in Greek graves was of eastern origin. Traders, as we shall see in the next chapter, were moving both eastward and also into the western Mediterranean. The population of the Greek world seems to have been expanding at a rapid rate, and the consolidation of local political and social institutions had proceeded so far that Greece was ready to colonize widely abroad from its firm Aegean base.

Even more important, the basic qualities of the Greek outlook had also become set; and the fact that this had been achieved out of native resources deserves repetition. Anyone who reads the *Iliad* or who sympathetically considers the masterpieces of Dipylon pottery can easily infer that Greek civilization was already capable of tremendous achievements. In these works the hallmarks of the Greek genius — disciplined order and concentration, logical analysis, confidence, to name no others — are incarnated in a dynamic form.

So impressive, indeed, are the first fruits of Greek civilization that we are too likely to forget how dull an era had been most of the dark ages. Even in 750 Greek life was still extremely primitive. Greek culture, architecture, and philosophy were yet to begin; and the Hellenic views about the nature of man and the world were still to be developed remarkably. Only the basic guidelines for Greek civilization had thus far been set.

BIBLIOGRAPHY

Sources. For the dark ages the only sure guide is the physical evidence; and in this poverty-stricken era the best clue is the development of the pottery. In assessing the meaning of the styles of pottery shapes and decorations the historian must be careful not to slip into mysticism; but the existence of consecutive change and its direction, both important facts, are clearly demonstrable for the pottery. We have as yet no excavated villages and towns of this period except for some Cretan eyries, inhabited by men afraid to dwell in the plains, and one town on the coast of Asia Minor, Smyrna. Graves, as a result, provide most of the material. Archeological work over the past three decades has given us the beginnings of the evidence needed to reconstruct the story presented in this chapter.

In many modern accounts much use is still made of myths, legends of city foundations, and inferences from the epics. This is a very dangerous procedure. Myths were not created to be history, nor did their makers necessarily try to allegorize historical events — even though modern scholars soberly reconstruct a fanciful tale of Athenian expansion from the legends of Theseus. In assessing this material the historian must remember that much of it was orally transmitted for generations; only in its broadest outlines, as in the memory of the Dorian invasions, can it safely be employed.

This warning is particularly applicable in the case of Homeric epics. The Greeks considered the *Iliad* and the *Odyssey* as true and as the work of one poet, Homer; so too did the modern world down into the eighteenth century. Then various scholars began to have their doubts, most influential of whom was F. A. Wolf. His *Prolegomena ad Homerum* (1795) contained an argument that the epics were a composite of earlier lays. Ever since, fierce debate has raged over the authorship, date, and method of composition of the epics; the conclusions in the text are the personal views of the author, with which many would disagree. Recently the translation of Linear B tablets, which contain as personal names Hector and other epic names, has led some scholars to assert once more that the epics were essentially created in the Mycenaean era; but the diametrically opposite view, that they were a pastiche of earlier tales woven together in the seventh or sixth centuries, still has adherents. Among the many translations of Homer, which attest the enduring popularity of the epics, W. H. D. Rouse's *Iliad* (New York: Mentor MP484, 1950) and *Odyssey* (New York: Mentor MD92, 1949) are lively versions.

Further Reading. The development of early Greek civilization I have discussed in greater detail in *Origins of Greek Civilization, 1100–650 B.C.* (New York: Knopf, 1961), varying points of view may be found in T. B. L. Webster, *From Mycenae to Homer* (Totowa, N.J.: Rowman, 1977), and M. I. Finley, *World of Odysseus* (rev. ed.; New York: Viking, 1978). The most important physical evidence is discussed by A. M. Snodgrass, *The Dark Age of Greece* (Chicago: Aldine, 1972), and by J. N. Coldstream, *Greek Geometric Pottery* (New York: Barnes and Noble, 1968), and *Geometric Greece* (London: Methuen, 1979). See also A. J. B. Wace and F. H. Stubbings, ed., *Companion to Homer* (London: Macmillan, 1962), and P. A. L. Greenhalgh, *Early Greek Warfare* (Cambridge: Cambridge University Press, 1973).

John L. Myres, *Homer and His Critics,* ed. Dorothea Gray (London: Routledge and Kegan Paul, 1958), is a good introduction to the Homeric question. Recent studies which are suggestive if not entirely sound in all respects are Denys L. Page, *History and the Homeric Iliad* (2d ed.; Berkeley: University of California Press, 1966); G. S. Kirk, *The Songs of Homer* (New York: Cambridge University Press, 1962), and *The Nature of Greek Myths* (Penguin, 1974); J. V. Luce, *Homer and the Heroic Age* (New York: Harper & Row, 1975); H. T. Wade-Gery, *Poet of the Iliad* (Cambridge: Cambridge University Press, 1952); and Cedric Whitman, *Homer and the Heroic Tradition* (New York: Norton, 1965). An introduction to mythology may be found in H. J. Rose, *Gods and Heroes of the Greeks* (Cleveland: Meridian M59, 1958). On the Greek adaptation of the alphabet, see David Diringer, *The Alphabet* (Topsfield, Mass.: Newbury, 1977), and Lillian H. Jeffery, *Local Scripts of Archaic Greece* (Oxford: Oxford University Press, 1969), who illustrates the fascinating variations within the common pattern.

10

RISE AND SPREAD OF
THE GREEK CITY-STATE

The century following 750 B.C. was one of the most fruitful in all Greek history. The main qualities of the Hellenic outlook had already emerged; now they became much more clearly defined, and the scope of Greek culture was greatly enlarged. Virtually every aspect of life underwent tremendous change in this age of revolution. For purposes of analysis the historian of the era must take up each strand in the complicated web by itself, but the several aspects did not exist neatly and tidily in separate cubbyholes; during the throbbing flow of great ages many changes run concurrently, so closely interlocked that one can hardly define which is cause and which is effect.

Politically, the period witnessed the rise of the Greek city-state, a form of government which expressed a noble set of political values still fundamental today. On the one hand the political and military strengths inherent in this organization permitted the Greeks to expand abroad widely; but on the other hand local patriotism and mutual suspicion divided the homeland into a host of tiny, absolutely sovereign units. While these states were bound together by a common culture and could occasionally cooperate against an outside enemy, their continuing rivalry eventually was to destroy Greek freedom.

Socially, the power of ancestral groupings diminished enough to allow a significant though limited assertion of individuality and the consolidation of a truly aristocratic outlook, which stamped all later Greek life and from which aristocratic values in western civilization derived in large part their origin. Yet the lower classes, though sorely oppressed, did not quite lose their independence in most areas; and the better aristocrats became ever more aware of the problems of justice.

An economic spirit of conscious rivalry and search for gain produced one of the greatest examples of economic growth in all Western civilization; attendant thereon were the rise of market economies, unknown in the Near East, the use of coinage, and major technological improvements. In the fields of arts and letters there appeared colonnaded stone temples, large-scale sculpture, freehand styles of pottery decoration, and new lyric and choral forms of poetry.

It is impossible to consider in one chapter all these aspects, so important both for Greek history and for western civilization. The present chapter will be devoted to the major political, social, and economic changes; the next, to the intellectual and religious progress. Although the age of revolution may be said to cover the century 750–650, it is apparent in arts and letters that the truly great jump occurred virtually in one generation, that group of men who were active about 700. Sometimes human history evolves at a steady, even pace; sometimes, though, it virtually leaps.

NATURE OF THE "POLIS"

Introduction of the City-State (750–650 B.C.). Much later, in the fourth century B.C., the great political theorists Plato and Aristotle discussed the nature of an ideal political unit. Both of them took it for granted that all truly civilized men would prefer the *polis* or city-state. Aristotle, indeed, went so far as to assert, "Man is by nature an animal intended to live in a *polis.*" [1] Yet even at this date not all Greeks were so organized, and in the dark ages there had been no city-states at all, as we understand the term in Greek history. The *polis* evolved out of the tribal kingdom in the late eighth century and continued to consolidate its institutions over the next 300 years. Basically it was the unit of conscious political history in Greece and of the great Greek colonization.

---

[1] Aristotle, *Politics* 1.2.9 (1253a.2–3); tr. Ernest Barker.

The city-state, in simplest terms, was a small but sovereign political unit, in which all important activity was conducted at one spot and in which communal bonds — expressed in terms of law — were more basic than personal ties. In all these respects the *polis* grew out of the political organization of the dark ages.

Geographically, thus, Greek peoples had often met together from wide areas at religious shrines, and some religious leagues, such as the Amphictyony of Delphi, long continued to play an important role. But on the whole Greeks had been accustomed to act politically and religiously in tiny units, and these were to jell into the separate city-states of historic times. Athens, which was the largest unified city-state of mainland Greece, covered only 1000 square miles; the ordinary *polis* was far smaller and numbered its adult male citizens as a few thousands at the most. The historic Greek world consisted of some 200-odd absolutely independent states.

In the earlier tribal kingdoms two mutually antagonistic political principles had existed. One was that of personal leadership; the other, that of collective unity and basic equality of the tribesmen. A modern observer might expect that, as the Greeks came together in tighter political unity, they would have done so under the direction of the kings. This was the course which the evolving national states of western Europe followed in the Middle Ages. If Greece did not follow the same path, the reasons were several. The tribal kings were weak financially; new military techniques made the kings less important as war chiefs; the isolation of the Aegean limited serious foreign threats; and, above all, the enduring simplicity of Greek life (materially speaking) permitted a survival of the principle that all tribesmen had rights.

During the age of revolution, in consequence, kings virtually disappeared in most Greek states, though they lingered on in Sparta, Argos, and a few other areas. Instead the Greeks improved their political and military machinery for collective action and underwrote this unity by guarantees of common justice and by patriotic symbols especially in the field of religion. This more perfected, more conscious union was the *polis*.

Physical Qualities and Government of the Polis. The average Greek *polis* was no larger than a small American county. Its frontiers were usually natural boundaries such as the sea or ranges of hills, but a state like Athens comprised several plains and valleys while the open country of Boeotia was divided into several states. As a result of its smallness, the citizens of a *polis* could assemble fairly easily at a central point for major political and religious activities.

This central point usually was a grouping of villages, far enough inland to be safe from sudden seaborne raids. At times there was a hill, like the Acropolis at Athens, which could serve as a refuge and on which a temple could be erected to the patron divinity of the *polis* (Athena at Athens). Below it lay an *agora,* an open place where the citizens met in political assembly and also engaged in trade. The upper classes perhaps more commonly lived here, though they had also relatively large rural estates; more surely, the artisans and traders would dwell at the focal point. But the modern equivalent of *polis,* "city-state," is somewhat misleading, for only as trade and industry grew after 700 did true city clusters begin to appear in the Greek world. Most of the citizens in an ordinary state always dwelt in farming villages over the countryside, where they carried on their basic economic, social, and even minor political activity.

The citizens of a *polis* assembled periodically to vote on major issues and to elect officials. The role of the assembly tended to grow as the city-states coalesced, and a mark of this growth was the creation of a steering committee or council to prepare its business. Such councils had appeared by about 600 B.C. at Sparta and Athens. Elsewhere, however, the council represented the developing aristocracy and really ran the government; in these cases its members were chosen in one way or another virtually for life. Even in those states where the assembly had genuine powers, membership was limited in early days to landholders or was otherwise restricted.

Generally the single office of king was replaced by a number of officials. One such officer might still be called "king" so as to conduct the ancestral religious rites which the gods expected from kings; another would be the general (*polemarch* at Athens); another, the civil head (*archon* at Athens); others directed the judicial machinery and supervised state cults. Since the problems of these small states were simple, so too was their machinery; but over the next several centuries the Greeks were to meet and face, in a host of interesting solutions, some of the basic political problems which rise in any developed community. Both by subdividing the executive power and by commonly electing officials for only one year the Greeks seriously weakened the principle of personal leadership in favor of forms of collective action; but at the same time they took other steps which increased the power of the state as a whole as against local social and religious groups.

Moral and Ideal Qualities of the Polis. In its earliest stages the Greek *polis* was not a democracy, but spiritually it rested upon political ideals of great significance. "A state," observed Aristotle, "aims at being, as far as it can, a society composed of equals and peers"; [2] and we can understand neither the origins nor the long endurance of the *polis* unless we keep in mind its moral and ideal qualities. The Greek city-state originated in a very simple world, where rich and poor were not too sharply distinguished and where both upper and lower classes felt themselves bound together in a communal unity. The lower classes were willing to see the kings disappear and to permit the upper classes to take over the day-to-day direction of activities so long as they felt they were justly treated — and, as we shall see later, personal leaders in the form of the famous tyrants reappeared whenever that condition was violated.

Theoretically, thus, all citizens were equal members of the *polis* in the sense that they were protected in the possession of fundamental private rights. Slaves continued to exist, elements of the farming population might be serfs (as in Sparta, Crete, and Thessaly), women were considered politically incompetent; but the citizen body proper had its rights as well as its duties. Ultimately the *polis* was based on the principle of justice, and this in turn rested upon the mastery of law over arbitrary action. Very early in the seventh century, as will appear in the next chaper, the great poet Hesiod called out loudly for the need for justice; a later Greek poet was proudly to proclaim, "The law-abiding town, though small and set on a lofty rock, outranks senseless Nineveh." [3] By the middle of the seventh century Greek city-states were beginning to set down law codes as summations of ancestral customs, so that all might see their rights on public display.

The *polis* incarnated the principles of basic equality, even-handed justice, participation in public activities (by all citizens who met certain

---

[2] Ibid. 4.9.6 (1296b.25–26).

[3] Phocylides, in Dio Chrysostom, *Oration* 36.13. Or, as Aristotle, *Politics* 4.4.7 (1292a.32) puts it, "Where the laws are not sovereign, there is no constitution."

requirements), and government by law. Two other qualities were also implicit in the new system. One was local patriotism, which was marked in the religious field by the growing worship of state heroes and the veneration of one great god or goddess as patron of the community; in the mythological field old tales were reworked to celebrate the glories of this or that city. Aristocrats still intermarried widely and traveled easily in the seventh century, but the tendency lay toward exaltation of local loyalties.

The other, concomitant quality was the burden laid upon the citizens to maintain their political unit. As Aristotle later asserted, "we must not regard the citizen as belonging just to himself; we must rather regard every citizen as belonging to the state."[4] The naïve individual self-assertion of the Homeric heroes was to become more powerful when Greece grew more civilized, but as its complement there stood a stern insistence upon the unity of all citizens. Local social and religious groups lost some of their power to the growing state, though this process was a long and hard-fought battle. In some city-states public officials watched over the conduct of citizens and in Sparta and Crete were to go far in directing the patterns of life. "The city teaches man," as a later poet tersely summed up the educative quality of the city-state.[5]

Military Reorganization. The growing political unity was especially visible in the military field. Whereas the Homeric heroes fought individual duels, by about 700 B.C. Greek citizens were beginning to troop out for battle in a tight block of infantry called the phalanx. The members of a phalanx were heavily armored with bronze helmet, breast plate, greaves, and round shield, and carried a long spear as well as a short sword. In battle these *hoplites* stood several men deep so as to give greater weight and moral support when one phalanx pushed at another on level ground. The role of the general now was to determine when his troops were ready to give battle. Before the fray he encouraged his soldiers by proper religious rites and exhortation, but in the action maneuvers were almost impossible. Since each man provided his own armor, the men of property, both aristocrats and the middling farmers, formed the major defense of the state. They were aided by a few light-armed troops on the flanks, and the richer nobles were proud of their horses;

---

[4] Aristotle, *Politics* 8.1.2 (1337a.27–29).
[5] Simonides, fragment 53 (Diehl).

but cavalry remained very weak in the absence of good forage. In coastal communities simple warships appeared and were rowed by the lower classes.

Initially both the style of armor and the pattern of fighting were adaptations of military development in the Near East, but the spiritual cohesiveness of a Greek *polis* as well as the intellectual ferment of its civilization gave its warriors a strength far beyond their numbers. "It is not stones nor timber nor the craft of craftsmen, but wherever there are men knowing how to defend themselves, there are walls and a city." [6]

Beginnings of Greek Political History (750–600 B.C.). During the dark ages there had been no political history as such. Not only do we lack any written records for the era, but also conscious political organization was absent. At the most, legends give some hints as to the migrations of the era 1100–750. Dorian-speaking peoples, for example, were said to have moved into Sparta, into Epidaurus, and into Megara later than into Argos and Corinth.

Once the *polis* had emerged, its firmer political and military organization permitted more deliberate political action, and the growth of population made states more contentious over prize bits of farmland on the frontiers. The first great war of which we know was fought just before 700 by Chalcis and Eretria to determine possession of the small but rich Lelantine plain. Many states far afield from Euboea, such as Samos and Miletus in the eastern Aegean and Corinth and Megara on the Saronic gulf, were drawn into this clash by their commercial rivalries and local antipathies; in the end Chalcis was successful.

In other wars Megara vied now with Corinth, now with Athens; Sparta conquered its western neighbor, Messenia; and Argos, under its greatest king, Pheidon, held temporary power over much of the Peloponnesus. These events, however, cannot be woven into a continuous pattern of international relations in the seventh century.

Down past 500, fortunately, the Greek states did not press severely and continuously upon one another. Internally, at least, the rise of the *polis* brought order and security, though piracy on the seas and brigandage in the mountains remained enduring problems; and the states of Hellas rarely pushed their wars, in view of the difficulty of sieges, to the total

---

[6] Alcaeus, fragment 426 (Lobel-Page; tr. C. M. Bowra). This truth was widely felt; cf. Sophocles, *Oedipus the King,* 56–57; and Thucydides 7.77.7.

destruction of a defeated foe. In times of emergency, such as the Persian wars, some of the major states — but not all — were able to group themselves in a common bond for the moment of peril. In the long run, however, the division of Greece into many sovereign units, each jealously patriotic, was a terrific burden to which its fall was partly attributable. To understand Greek history it must be remembered that "Greece" was a geographical expression, not a united country. All the Hellenes worshiped the same gods, shared the same basic culture, and met periodically in great international festivals and games; but this cultural unity meant no more politically than has the common cultural outlook of the western European states in modern times.

Consecutive internal development also began slowly to be evident, once the *polis* had emerged and the writing of laws and other documents became customary. The *polis* incarnated noble ideals, but each state was inhabited by men who were moved by passions and were divided into classes. The richer farmers, who controlled the political machinery, did not always treat their weaker neighbors justly; in the tremendous economic and intellectual expansion of the era, tensions and explosions were inevitable.

At Athens and Sparta, where our evidence is fuller, we can see something of the constitutional evolution of these states going back into the seventh century, but this story will be better taken up as a whole in Chapter 12. Sometimes the stresses became so severe that regular constitutional processes were interrupted by the rise of dictators, who were called tyrants. Tyrants appeared chiefly in the more advanced states and gained their dominance usually when an oppressive aristocracy was badly split into factions.

The tyrant himself was an ambitious member of the upper classes, but once in power he tended to curtail the economic and social privileges of his peers. While his position rested upon force, exhibited in a standing bodyguard, such a leader needed popular support. Tyrants accordingly favored the peasants by dividing up big estates, and by other means; also they often aided the growth of the newly rising industrial and commercial classes. Camouflage for their position could be gained by emphasizing patriotic festivals, building temples, and favoring poets and artists. Most tyrants preferred not to take the hazards of war against their neighbors, though they might have gained their initial renown as generals; but they were not averse to colonial expansion.

Among the more famous and lasting houses of tyrants were three: that of Orthagoras and Clisthenes at Sicyon (*c.* 655–570), the latter of whom reorganized the political and religious structure of his state to reduce Argive influence and also helped to destroy Crisa, the master of Delphi; that of Cypselus and Periander at Corinth (*c.* 620–550), which spread Corinthian rule far up the west coast of Greece, curbed the aristocracy, and encouraged the great pottery industry of Corinth; and that of Pisistratus and his sons at Athens (546–10), which is discussed below in Chapter 12. In these examples tyranny lasted more than one generation, but in most cases more stable and constitutional governments had been resumed by the sixth century.

GREEK EXPANSION OVERSEAS

The Mediterranean in the Eighth Century. Although city-states had been known in earlier Mesopotamia and existed in the eighth century along the coasts of Syria and Phoenicia, the Greek development seems to have been purely local. The spread of the Greeks abroad, which now began to take place by sea, was likewise primarily a reflection of the tremendous energies that had been built up in the Aegean world, but its remarkable speed was much facilitated by the growing unity of the Mediterranean world at this time (see Map 8).

In the Near East trade and culture were being consolidated on a broad plane, which was soon reflected in the Assyrian political unification of the region. The Phoenicians had begun to trade in the western Mediterranean, where considerable progress had already occurred in the early first millennium B.C.; and a mysterious people called the Etruscans were importing eastern civilization into Italy (see below, Chapter 21). Both to the east and to the west venturesome Greeks found the paths of the sea more open than had ever been true before.

As in Mycenaean times the Greeks were deeply attracted eastward to the center of civilization. Here, however, the political and economic structure was so developed that they came in the role of traders, not as conquerors. A trading post at Al Mina, by the mouth of the Orontes

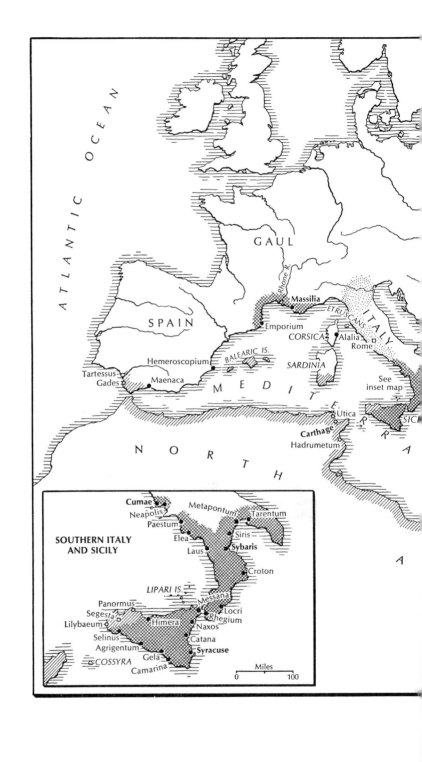

ATLANTIC OCEAN

GAUL

Rhone R.

Massilia

ETRUSCANS

ITALY

Emporium

CORSICA Alalia
Rome

SPAIN

BALEARIC IS.

SARDINIA

Hemeroscopium

See
inset map

Tartessus
Gades   Maenaca

M E D I T E R R

Utica

Carthage

SIC

N   O   R   T

Hadrumetum

H

**SOUTHERN ITALY
AND SICILY**

Cumae
Neapolis   Metapontum   Tarentum
Paestum
Elea   Siris
Laus   **Sybaris**

Croton

LIPARI IS.

Panormus   Messana
Segesta   Locri
Lilybaeum   Himera   Rhegium
Selinus   Naxos
Agrigentum   Catana
COSSYRA   Gela   **Syracuse**
Camarina

A

Miles
0   100

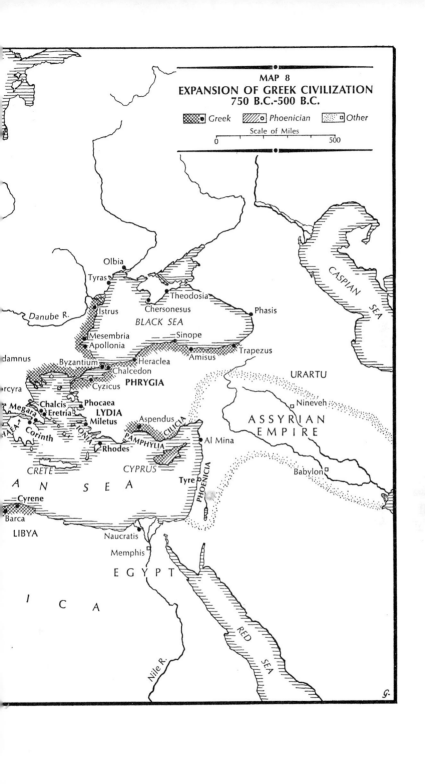

MAP 8
EXPANSION OF GREEK CIVILIZATION
750 B.C.-500 B.C.

Greek   Phoenician   Other

Scale of Miles
0   500

Olbia
Tyras
Theodosia
Danube R.   Istrus   Chersonesus   Phasis
BLACK SEA
Mesembria   Sinope
Apollonia
damnus   Byzantium   Heraclea   Amisus   Trapezus
rcyra   Chalcedon   URARTU
Cyzicus   PHRYGIA
Nineveh
Chalcis   Phocaea
Megara   Eretria   LYDIA   ASSYRIAN
Miletus   Aspendus   EMPIRE
Corinth   Al Mina
Rhodes
CRETE   CYPRUS   Babylon
A   N   S   E   A   Tyre
Cyrene   PHOENICIA
Barca
LIBYA   Naucratis
Memphis
E G Y P T

I   C   A

Nile R.   RED SEA

CASPIAN SEA

G-river in Syria, has recently been excavated, and attests that Greek merchants, primarily from the Aegean islands but also from Corinth, Rhodes and elsewhere, were settled there by the early eighth century. At this and similar points the Greeks became acquainted with the polished products of Near Eastern workshops and also picked up such ideas as the alphabet. Eastern technological skills and objects can be detected in Euboea and at Athens in the ninth, even the tenth century; but the Eastern connection grew steadily after 700 down to the time when Alexander the Great conquered the Near East.

The first contacts, with which we are here alone concerned, were mainly with Syria and proceeded chiefly by the great sea road below the south coast of Asia Minor. In Pamphylia and Cilicia local conditions were still sufficiently primitive so that the Greeks could occasionally settle; but even in Cyprus, where Greek-speaking peoples had secured a foothold at the end of the Mycenaean era, they did not gain cultural domination until the sixth century and later. Politically the Greeks both of Cilicia and of Cyprus were subject to the Assyrians.

Trade with Egypt began later than with Syria and was restricted by the pharaohs of the Twenty-sixth Dynasty to selected ports, such as the new settlement of Naucratis about 610. From this time on Greek traders and learned men, such as Solon and Herodotus, were to be deeply impressed by the antique wisdom and monuments of the land of the Nile. The Egyptian rulers were particularly glad to make use of the semicivilized Greeks as mercenaries; far inland, at Abu Simbel in Nubia, warriors of Ionian origin scratched their names on a statue of Ramesses II in 594–89 B.C. Other Greeks served in the armies of Babylon after the fall of Assyria.

The Westward Movement (750–500 B.C.). Mycenaean traders had reached the coasts of Italy and Sicily; so too did the Greeks from the eighth century onward. Here they came first to sell their own wares and luxuries of Near Eastern origin; in return they gained slaves and, above all, metals to supply the growing industries of the Aegean world. Almost immediately the Greeks discovered that they could dominate these western shores, and a great wave of colonization ensued.

Neither the precise causes of this colonization nor its methods of operation are easily ascertainable in the lack of contemporary literary evidence. During the confusion at the end of the Mycenaean age some Greeks had moved across the Aegean islands to the coast of Asia Minor, but throughout the dark ages the Hellenic world did not have the energy for further expansion. By the eighth century, however, Greek civilization and society were advancing rapidly, and there clearly seems to have been a surplus of discontented population in the homeland. Since this surplus came largely from the countryside, the sites for Greek colonies were chosen mainly with an eye to agricultural possibilities; but settlers also sought easily defensible hills or promontories close to the sea for their main settlement. Good harbors, interestingly enough, were not always selected.

Among the many home states only a relatively few along the coasts served as focuses for the great wave of colonization. Athens founded no colonies; neither did the Boeotian cities. Both areas probably had enough farmland for their growing population; both, moreover, seem to have fallen culturally into a backwater in the age of revolution. Sparta sent out only one colony, to Taras (Tarentum) in southern Italy; for the Spartans were finding local vents for their population and energy. But other states of more advanced economic interests and limited homelands, such as Corinth, Chalcis, Eretria, Miletus, and others, made up for this lethargy, and their colonizing leadership probably drained off some discontented elements from nearby areas.

When a home *polis* decided to found a colony, various preliminary steps were necessary. Colonists had to be sought and sometimes were drafted, one per family, under penalties if they did not stick to the new settlement. Undoubtedly volunteers had to be inspected to be sure they were physically strong and had enough resources to carry them through the first year. A site, too, had to be selected beforehand. On this point the advice of traders was useful; in later days the priests at the great oracles of Didyma and Delphi, who heard much about the world from travelers, also could be consulted. Then the colonists, probably not more than a very few hundred families, embarked and made their way to the new site, where they "built a citadel wall, threw up houses and temples for the gods, and allotted out the fields." [7] The leader, called the *oikistes,*

---

[7] *Odyssey* 6.9–10 (describing the settlement of Scheria, the fairy-tale city of Alcinous and Nausicaa).

was a noble, often probably an ambitious man who was thwarted at home by his fellow aristocrats. He bore a heavy responsibility and if the colony were successful was worshiped by later generations.

Nonetheless each colony was founded as a *polis*. As a result it usually was entirely independent of the home state, though the fire on its sacred hearth and its principal cult were brought from the mother *polis*. The modern connotations of the word "colony" as meaning a subject territory are misleading, especially for the new states in Italy and Sicily; some settlements in the Black Sea by Miletus and elsewhere by Corinth did remain more or less dependent upon the parent state. And, once established, a new *polis* rarely accepted later colonists except in an emergency.

To explain the success of this wave of Greek expansion one must look principally to the dynamic quality of Hellenic civilization and to the happy blend of individual initiative and communal loyalty of the *polis* structure. Military and naval considerations also played a part. By the eighth century Greek sailing ships had been much improved, and a style of long warship, called the *pentekonter*, since it was rowed by 50 men, had been evolved. In their phalanx organization the Greek settlers were able to bowl over much larger numbers of more poorly organized natives along the western coasts. The climate in these districts, also, was sufficiently like that of Greece to permit the transfer of agricultural techniques and living habits without serious alterations.

Areas and Extent of Colonization. The principal areas of Greek colonization and the major mother states are indicated on Map 8. Most of the colonists made their way to southern Italy and eastern Sicily, which were in later times called Greater Greece. The first enduring colony in this area was Cyme, normally known by its Latin name of Cumae; this settlement was a joint foundation about 750 by Chalcis (with Eretria) and the city of Cyme in Asia Minor. Cumae, situated on a hill at the neck of a peninsula, was easily defensible; it also lay as close to the Etruscan mines of copper and iron as the Greeks ever settled. In a great rush during the next two generations men from Chalcis, Achaea, Ionia, and other areas took most of the desirable Italian coastal points to the south, and the Corinthians established themselves at the mouth of the Adriatic, as at Corcyra (733). Paestum (Greek Posidonia, 700) still has a marvelous set of Greek temples; Sybaris (720) was so wealthy as to give rise to a new word, "sybarite." Tarentum (Greek Taras, 706) was unique in being a Spartan colony.

In Sicily the Greeks probably began to colonize the east as soon as the Phoenicians entered the western parts of the island. The greatest Greek colony here was Corinthian Syracuse founded in 734 or 733; but the other city-states marked on the map, founded by Chalcis, Megara, and Corinth, were also wealthy and cultured. Unlike Italy, where colonies remained hemmed in by mountains and native tribes, the Greeks of Sicily extended their power far inland.

Not until about 600 could the Greeks vault on beyond the Etruscans and Phoenicians to make lasting bridgeheads in France and Spain. The Phocaeans of Asia Minor then founded Massilia (c. 600), which in turn set up trading posts along the Spanish coast.

By this time the civilized peoples originating in the eastern Mediterranean were beginning to rub on each other more severely in the west. In the sixth century wars of critical importance broke out among the Phoenicians, Etruscans, and Greeks; and some of the natives, such as the Romans, began to rise to civilized levels. Since these events are closely connected with the rise of Rome, their consideration must be postponed until later; but the establishment and progress of Greater Greece also had significant economic and cultural effects on the homeland.

The other areas settled in the great wave of Greek expansion may be noted more briefly. In north Africa the hump about Cyrene was available and was settled from 630 on by Dorian-speaking colonists from Thera. Colonization of the north coast of the Aegean was conducted mainly after 700, partly from Chalcis, Eretria, and Corinth, partly from the islands and coastal cities of Asia Minor. The main colony here was Potidaea (c. 600), but the area called Chalcidice was a mass of settlements. Then came settlement in force in the Propontis (Cyzicus from Miletus, 675; Byzantium from Megara, a little after 660; and others) and in the Black Sea proper, where Miletus eventually had some 100 colonies and trading posts. Among these the chief were Sinope (before 600) and Trapezus (traditionally 756, but probably later).

The climate in this last area differed too much from that of the Aegean to encourage a full flowering of Hellenic civilization, but the trade which passed through the Hellespont was vital in many respects. Wheat, slaves, gold, and other essential materials came from south Russia; iron and manufactured metal objects were derived from the eastern end of Asia Minor, where the kingdom of Urartu lay; fish were sent to Greece from many points. In return the Greeks exported wine, olive oil, incenses, and other objects including the fine pottery which has turned up in abundance in the great mounds where Scythian lords of the south Russian plains were buried.

ECONOMIC AND SOCIAL CHANGES

Economic Progress (*to* 600). Colonization was the product of so many local and general factors and was so widely launched that it continued on through the sixth century and even into the classic period. The effects of this expansion were far-reaching and long-lasting, as far as the homeland was concerned. Greece was already moving forward rapidly when colonization began; but the geographical enlargement of the Aegean world helped to speed its development.

Economically most men in the homeland continued to be farmers. As the population of the city-states expanded, its pressure led to an expansion of the cultivated area; and in the more advanced districts production for sale in city markets became significant. In particular wine and olive oil were important "cash crops." As a result of this basic agricultural revolution, which went on down through the sixth century, the landscape in the progressive states of Greece grew ever more domesticated, and the lions and other wild animals prominent in the mythical age retreated far into the mountains, where shepherds still watched over their flocks. Sometimes small farmers were able to secure independent positions; elsewhere they fell into debt to their richer neighbors or were even depressed into serfdom.

Industry and commerce grew even more obviously in this era. Abroad, Greece gained access to many sources of raw materials — food, metals, timber (on the north coast of the Aegean), and the like. In return it shipped out both to the colonies and to the hinterlands manufactured items, which were made in the home states or were acquired from the even more advanced workshops of the Syrian coast. Increasing demands by the upper classes had already paved the way for this expansion of industry, which one can see most clearly in the potteries.

To secure the necessary increase in production some specialization of activity took place as one man, for instance, made a vase, another painted it, and others fired the kiln. Almost all techniques of working stone, metals, etc., were borrowed from the Near East; throughout the rest of Greek and Roman history very little further innovation took place. But above all an increase in output required more hands. Some men were available from the nearby countryside in the form of dispossessed or discontented peasants; others were acquired by purchase as slaves from abroad. Industrial slavery never became the backbone of Greek economic life, but the more advanced states had thenceforth extensive slave elements.

Improvements in trade also occurred. Better ships were already available and were built and used in greater numbers; efforts to improve harbors were under way by 600. Some traders took the risks and chances of great profits in long-range trade. We are told of Colaeus from Samos, who was blown by a storm to Spanish Tartessus (c. 630) and made extremely profitable sales of his wares. Other merchants became settled traders in the central kernels of the city-states, a form of economic specialization which surpassed anything known in the Near East. As a result places about the isthmus of Corinth, such as Corinth, Aegina, and Megara, were real cities by about 600. Athens lagged behind until about this date, and the great period of the Ionian cities was to be the sixth century.

If commerce were to be conducted efficiently, it required a better means of exchange than the silver bars common in the Near East. The result was the invention of coinage. The earliest coins, that is, pieces of precious metal stamped to indicate origin and to guarantee value, were issued about 650 by the kings of Lydia in Asia Minor. These were made of electrum, a natural mixture of gold and silver, and were so valuable that they must have been used in wholesale trade. Before 600 the more advanced city-states of Asia Minor and Greece were issuing coins of silver in various weights, though local trade, fines, and other payments were still reckoned in terms of agricultural produce or on a basis of barter.[8]

---

[8] Plate XVIII.A illustrates an Aeginetan silver *stater*, with the distinctive badge of a turtle; the earliest coins were simply made and marked, in accordance with the limited technology of the era. Aegina was the first state of Greece proper to issue coins.

Thenceforth capital could be mobilized and economic activity conducted in a more supple fashion than had ever before been possible.

Behind the specific evidence of development in agriculture, commerce, and industry lay, as an impelling force, a revolution in economic attitudes. During the dark ages, when men struggled to survive and to hold together the tissue of society, the idea of economic gain or profit had small scope. When the Aegean world grew richer from the eighth century onward and its men became more mobile, the conscious effort to gain economic advantage entered Greek life. Thenceforth the economic spirit, as it may be called, was an enduring force of considerable importance in Hellenic civilization, free as it was of absolute kings and powerful priesthoods.

Early in the seventh century the poet Hesiod graphically portrayed the contest of potter with potter and endorsed rivalry, so long as it was conducted fairly. By the end of the century the great reformer Solon of Athens could catalog in one fragment of his poetry the ways of making money and concluded that those who are richest "have twice the eagerness that others have." [9] That the growth of these attitudes helped to spur economic progress is obvious; that their exhibition caused serious social stress is also perceptible.

Consolidation of the Aristocratic Outlook. The upper classes had long been important; when the kings disappeared, they became outwardly dominant. "Haughty, adorned with well-dressed hair, steeped in the scent of skilfully-prepared unguents," as a later poet scornfully indicted the purple-clad lords of one Asiatic *polis*,[10] the rich everywhere sought ivories, bronzes, and the latest vases of Corinth; and boasted their ownership of horses, which they raced in local and international games (see Plate XVII.B). In the Greek landscape horses were hard to feed and economically were useless, an example of Thorstein Veblen's "conspicuous consumption." Luxury, to be sure, is always a relative concept, and the monarchs of the Assyrian palaces would have scorned a noble Greek home as a hovel. Yet the visible distinctions between rich and poor grew more obvious in the Aegean world.

This was a factor both for good and for evil. The upper classes of Greece were remarkably enthusiastic about culture and employed that

[9] Solon, fragment 11 (Diehl).
[10] Xenophanes, fragment 3 (Diels); tr. Kathleen Freeman.

part of the rising Greek surplus which they garnered to support not only their own luxury but also the great outburst of arts and letters which we shall consider in the next chapter. The aristocrats shared, too, a relatively free and sane approach to life which later permitted the rise of philosophy. The temptations of power, however, all too often led them to oppress the poorer, weaker parts of society. The product was political tension which often threw up a tyrant.

These stresses were serious, but they did not reduce Greece to chaos. Colonization funneled off some of the discontented elements, both aristocratic and plebeian. The expansiveness of the Greek economic system, again, permitted the upper classes to have more worldly goods without necessarily exploiting all other elements; indeed new social classes were rising which sometimes were as wealthy as the old aristocrats. Above all, the old sense of communal loyalty was still strong enough to lead the more discerning aristocrats, such as Solon of Athens, to check the excesses of their fellows in a spirit of *noblesse oblige*.

By the seventh century, indeed, the upper classes of Greece were erecting a distinct set of standards and values. The roots of this attitude may be found in the warriors' code of bravery, mutual respect, and rivalry which Homer depicted; meetings at the great festivals and international marriages facilitated a general consensus on the values of life, as people came to reflect more consciously on their nature. This noble view was to affect deeply all later Greek culture.

A Greek aristocrat did not disdain wealth, which permitted him an easy life; but he tended to frown upon industrial and commercial pursuits, as against the profits of agriculture, politics, and warfare. Above all, the aristocrat must know how to make proper use of his leisure existence. As a youth he learned to be physically supple, to play the lyre, and to read and write. Beauty and external grace were qualities closely associated with virtue in an aristocrat's mind.

The aristocratic man became accustomed to a refined pattern of daily living and absorbed the fundamental virtues of justice, class loyalty, and a rational approach to the world. This education was inculcated within the family circle, and in the aristocratic clubs, which were made up solely of men. The position of women sank sharply, and one hears more both of prostitutes and of masculine homosexuality thenceforth. Later, in classic times, the patterns of aristocratic virtue were woven into the system of formal education which then appeared. When the Romans took over the Greek educational scheme, they absorbed these inherent values and passed them on to medieval and modern Europe.

The aristocratic scale of values was not that of the peasants, though in many basic respects the aristocratic outlook incarnated the general views of early Greek society. Nor did the Greek upper classes esteem the virtues of humility, brotherly love, and meekness which Christian preachers were later to proclaim. Beside the cardinal qualities of courage, temperance, justice, and wisdom went proper greatness of spirit, due magnificence of living, and especially a fierce competitiveness for honor and glory in games and public life. "Speak your enemy fair," said the aristocratic Theognis, "but when you have him in your power be avenged without pretext." [11]

Other Classes. The consolidation of this aristocratic outlook, as the possession of a special circle, was partly a reaction to the appearance of other classes. On the poorer level were the increasing masses of industrial and household slaves, of free artisans and small traders, and of rowers and sailors; but some elements involved in the new industry, commerce, and agriculture grew wealthy. Those who were aristocrats by birth began thus to face the unpleasant fact that "new men," especially able middling farmers who seized the advantages of a market economy, were sharing the new wealth and luxury of Greece.

To enhance their position the aristocrats placed greater emphasis upon the legends by which noble houses derived their inception from a union of god and mortal maid. But even so the aristocrats were not able to maintain their dominant position everywhere. Some aristocrats themselves engaged in overseas trade and mercenary service, and the tyrants who arose in the era tended to admit the *nouveaux riches* to upper levels. Before the end of the seventh century the poet Alcaeus of Lesbos was fulminating at this situation: "For, as they say, Aristodemos spoke no foolish saying once in Sparta, 'Money makyth Man,' and no poor man is noble or held in honor." [12] In the middle of the sixth century came Theognis of Megara, who sounds like a hopeless conservative in his insistence that birth, not wealth, should be primary; for even he had to admit that poverty was one of man's worst curses.

[11] Theognis, lines 363–64; tr. by J. M. Edmonds.
[12] Alcaeus, fragment 360 (Lobel-Page; tr. C. M. Bowra).

The student of ancient Greek history, however, must be careful not to call these rising elements a "middle class" in the modern sense. The new well-to-do groups strove to make themselves as much like the aristocrats as possible in the social sphere and usually united with them politically, if given the chance. Greek states remained essentially divided into the rich and the poor, though each side was now far more complicated than in the dark ages. The communal unity of the *polis* was only partially successful in restraining the mutual hostility which tended to result.

THE NEW GREEK WORLD

By the last decades of the seventh century the Greek world had progressed far beyond its simple state of 750 B.C. A tremendous outrush of colonization had thrown nuclei of Greeks, organized in city-states, widely over the shores of the western Mediterranean and the Black Sea. As commercial connections between colonies and homeland intensified, every event, internal or external, thenceforth reverberated throughout the Mediterranean; every pressure or intrusion from outside affected in some degree the whole of the Greek world. "Greece lies scattered in many regions," rightly observed a later orator.[13]

Internally the Greek homeland had largely crystallized into city-states, first in the more developed regions and then by imitation or in self-defense in the neighboring districts. The Greeks, however, who lived along the northern and western edges of Greece proper still remained on a tribal basis. The citizens of the city-states were united in the search for the good life, but they were subdivided economically and socially in a far more complicated fashion than previously. From this subdivision rose dynamic pressures for internal political development, which eventually led to democracy or to more conscious oligarchy. Security of life nonetheless grew within each *polis,* the citizens of which no longer went armed on all occasions; but external war and piracy remained threats of serious dimensions.

The enduring effects of the new political world can hardly be overestimated. Once established, the *polis* protected, accelerated, and confined the genius of Greek thinkers and artists like a hothouse. The first fruits of this swift development will appear in the next chapter. Already by 600

[13] Dio Chrysostom, *Oration* 36.5.

B.C. the outside, non-Greek world was beginning to draw heavily upon the ever more attractive Hellenic civilization, which as a result was to be the base of western culture.

BIBLIOGRAPHY

Sources. If one compares an archeological site of the dark ages with one of the age of revolution, the great physical growth in Greek production and the ever more refined artistic quality of its objects are at once visible; much of this will concern us in the next chapter. Literary evidence also becomes far more abundant as lyric, choral, and other poetry is added to the epic strain. Truly political documents, however, remain rather rare. We have only fragments of the first law codes drawn up by Zaleucus of Italian Locri (*c.* 660), Draco of Athens (*c.* 620), and Charondas of Catana (perhaps sixth century); a major *rhetra* or law of seventh-century Sparta will be noticed below in Chapter 12. The earliest treaties which have survived come only from the sixth century.

The date of the first coins is still disputed; after the Lydian beginnings came coins of the Asia Minor cities and of Aegina. The localism of the Greek world is evident in the fact that not all coins were struck on the same standard. In Greece proper the two most common weights were the Aeginetan and the Euboic.

Traditions grow more useful to the historian in this period insofar as they are connected with institutions, buildings, and families which remained active or extant into the classic period. Greek chronological tables, for instance, have some inherent validity back into the seventh century; lists of Olympic victors go back to 776 B.C. but cannot be trusted in their earliest stages. Yet so famous a king as Pheidon of Argos can be placed by modern scholars anywhere from the beginning to the end of the seventh century; and the first political date of which most students feel reasonably sure is the archonship of Solon at Athens in 594 B.C.

Further Reading. The most famous classic on the nature of the *polis* is Fustel de Coulanges, *Ancient City* (New York: Anchor A76, 1956). Besides works on Athens and Sparta listed in General Bibliography, Kathleen Freeman, *Greek City-States* (New York: Norton N193, 1963), describes the varying patterns in nine other states. Early political difficulties are illustrated in A. Andrewes, *Greek Tyrants* (New York:

Harper Torchbook 1103, 1963); and, on the agricultural side, in W. J. Woodhouse, *Solon the Liberator* (New York: Octagon, 1965). An effort to weave a continuous pattern of political history may be found in the very factual *Lyric Age of Greece* by A. R. Burn (New York: St. Martins, 1960). Werner Jaeger, *Paideia,* Vol. I (New York: Oxford University Press, 1939), and H. I. Marrou, *History of Education in Antiquity* (New York: Mentor MQ 552, 1964), are good on the consolidation of an aristocratic ethos.

Overseas expansion is treated, for the western Mediterranean, by T. J. Dunbabin, *Western Greeks* (Oxford: Oxford University Press, 1979), and A. G. Woodhead, *Greeks in the West* (New York: Praeger, 1962); for other areas by T. J. Dunbabin, *Greeks and Their Eastern Neighbours* (Westport, Conn.: Greenwood, 1979), and J. Boardman, *The Greeks Overseas* (New York: Thames & Hudson, 1980). A. J. Graham, *Colony and Mother City in Ancient Greece* (Manchester: Manchester, 1964), is a careful study. See also L. Casson, *Ships and Seamanship in the Ancient World* (Princeton: Princeton University Press, 1971). Economic and social changes are described in my *Economic and Social Growth of Early Greece* (New York: Oxford University Press, 1977), and A. M. Snodgrass, *Archaic Greece* (London: Dent, 1980). The origins and spread of coinage are thoroughly treated by C. M. Kraay, *Archaic and Classical Greek Coins* (Berkeley: University of California Press, 1976).

11

GREEK CIVILIZATION IN
THE AGE OF REVOLUTION

By the middle of the eighth century B.C. Greek civilization had already
revealed that it had magnificent potentialities. A mighty surge of human
life and passion had welled forth in the *Iliad;* the potters of the great
Dipylon vases had created stiff but poignant pageants of war and death.
These twin products were the summation of what had gone before and
the herald of the onrush which was immediately to follow.

Although the basic qualities of the Greek outlook had thus been
demonstrated, a tremendous elaboration and crystallization took place in
the succeeding decades from 750 to 650. The media of architecture and
large-scale sculpture made their appearance; potters moved from the
tradition-bound Geometric style into ever more supple, freehand decoration, in which scenes of epic, myth, and daily life became clearly identifiable. Literature broke out of its narrow boundaries into a richer expression of the poet's feelings.

This development was facilitated by, and its course in part was determined by, the parallel revolution in economic, political, and social institutions. Greek colonization throughout the Mediterranean gave the
homeland greater resources; the ever wider contacts with the Near East,
in particular, stimulated Greek artists in many visible and invisible ways.
The political consolidation of the city-states was reflected in the rise of
patriotic poets and the rich development of local artistic styles; the
seventh century saw more artistic diversity than was ever again to occur

in Greece. Both in art and in literature the rise of the aristocratic point of view had great effects, though artists and poets expressed a basically homogeneous Greek outlook on life rather than a narrow class outlook.

By 650 the Aegean world had essentially created a new set of artistic and literary forms and techniques, far more complex and supple than those of epic poetry and Geometric pottery. This great development we shall consider in the present chapter, together with the changes in religious views; the full bloom of the new styles, which occurred in the sixth century, will be taken up in Chapter 12.

PROGRESS OF THE ARTS

Orientalizing Pottery. A modern student receives his sharpest visual impact from the changes which occurred in the age of revolution when he looks at the remarkable progress of the pottery. Early in the eighth century all was serene and beautifully ordered in the Geometric style. Then suddenly a riot of curvilinear decoration, floral, animal, even human, burst into view and swirled over the entire surface of the vases; in the exuberance of the age all sense of Greek logic and restraint disappeared in some of the wildest experiments of the potters. The vases themselves changed shape: many of the new types were smaller and were carefully studied, even dainty in effect. And finally the very technique of drawing was elaborated as simple outlining of the decoration gave way in many workshops to solid black-figure painting. This was picked out and enriched by the use of supplementary color (white, red, and purple) and of incision to render more specific detail than Geometric potters had ever deemed necessary.[1]

This pottery is conventionally called Orientalizing, a term which is useful in suggesting the partial liberation from Geometric conventions which artists gained by observing the more naturalistic styles of the Near East (that is, Orient). In this process specific motifs were borrowed such

---

[1] The Protocorinthian *oenochoe* (pitcher) on Plate VIII.D was found at Cumae—an example of the rising export of Corinthian pottery to the Italian colonies. Its neck zone still reflects the Geometric inheritance of the potters in its schematized birds and wiggly lines (to avoid a blank space); but the floral decoration which sprawls over the belly of the vase admirably illustrates the freedom and naturalistic impulses of Orientalizing pottery. The rays at the base, which visually support this design, are characteristic of Protocorinthian work.

as rows of animals, palmettes, rosettes, mythical animals, and rich, tapestry-like patterns. But apart from such detailed indebtedness the term Orientalizing is very misleading. The ancient Near East never produced anything like Greek vases; and, in reality, the Greek artistic outlook was at this very time crystallizing along lines which were fundamentally different from those of the Near East. Basically in their intellectual and esthetic attitudes the potters of the seventh century did not forget their Geometric inheritance; and they were also indebted to the epic and mythical tradition, which they now began to express in clearly defined scenes drawn from the tales of Heracles, the *Odyssey,* and similar sources.

The leaders in the ceramic revolution were the Corinthian workshops, which created in the generation 720–690 B.C. the famous Protocorinthian style. This lasted to about 640; then after a transition came the Corinthian style proper (620–550). Protocorinthian and Corinthian vases were sold all over the Greek world, either empty or filled with incenses, perfumes, and other products; and other potters hastened to absorb the lessons in freehand drawing and rich decoration visible in the wares of Corinth. The seventh century was the golden age of distinctive pottery styles all over the Greek world, such as the Spartan, Argive, insular, and east Greek.

In this period Attic potters, who had previously led Greece, held little place except at home. Their great background hampered free development, and when they struck out on the new paths they often lost their touch in bizarre experiments. These difficulties suggest a very important aspect of the age of revolution. For, though Greek civilization was driving forward toward a new level, its progress was not automatic; many men clung to old ways in fear of the stress and change, and not all innovations were successful.

The experiments of Protoattic pottery (*c.* 710–610) are nonetheless important, for in the end Athenian artists evolved a distinctive style of black-figure pottery which began to vie with and then supplant Corinthian ware in the sixth century. By this date a new artistic synthesis of pottery shapes and forms of decoration had been achieved, and within these well-defined patterns potters harnessed their imagination (see Plate XVII).

Large-scale Sculpture. Another great triumph of the age was the rise of significant sculptural activity. Pottery is the main source from which one may measure the speed and character of artistic development, but in sculpture one can gain clearer conceptions of contemporary views of man and the gods. The audacity which led the Greeks to the creation of large-scale sculpture is a mark of the intellectual strength of the era; the speed with which three-dimensional modeling in clay, wood, bronze, and stone developed attests the extraordinary openness of men to experiment in the decades just on either side of 700.

A very thin tradition of sculpture had survived throughout the dark ages in the form of naïve clay and bronze statuettes of animals and men. In the eighth century there came new factors which at once encouraged the Greeks to essay sculpture on a broader scale and also suggested the patterns to be followed. Among these factors were acquaintance with Near Eastern art, where life-size or larger statues had long been made; the increasing crystallization of Greek views of the gods as forces in human shape; and a growing interest of man in his own nature. The Greek figurines of the eighth century seem crude and stiff, but by at least 680 a more developed style, called Dedalic, had emerged, in which statues began "to open their eyes and take a step with their legs and stretch out their arms." [2] This formal style seems to have originated in the northeast Peloponnesus and swept over much of Greece. Truly monumental sculpture followed by at least 650, when a certain Nikandre dedicated a (still surviving) female statue at Delos. Thereafter statues of gods and men in marble, bronze, and other materials were erected in shrines all over Greece in a host of locally distinct styles.

In their achievement Greek sculptors proceeded much as did their confreres in architecture and pottery; that is, they limited the number of types within which they worked and refined these forms in ever more exquisite detail. From the beginnings of large-scale stone sculpture only three main types of gods and men — the standing nude male (*kouros*), the standing clothed female (*kore*), and the seated female or male figure — were to busy the sculptors. In the minor decorative arts a similar concentration can be found in the marvelous development of such mythical or real animals as the griffin, sphinx, lion, and horse (see Plate X). Besides this limitation and concentration of their energies the sculptors exhibited another enduring quality of Greek civilization, that is, its bent

[2] Diodorus Siculus 4.76.

toward intellectual abstraction which rose directly out of physical reality. In the aristocratic *gymnasia,* where men now engaged in physical exercise unclothed, sculptors could observe physical anatomy carefully; and yet archaic sculpture, while reflecting ever sharper observation of reality, was definitely abstract and idealistic in effect.[3]

Greek Architecture. In the field of architecture the political and spiritual differences between the Mycenaean world and the historic Greek age were sharply evident. Whereas Mycenaean kings had manifested their autocratic power in the erection of great fortress palaces, the functions of the new city-states did not demand major secular public buildings for a long time. The one bond of mankind which now required visible architectural commemoration was the worship of a common divine force, under whose protection the population of the incipient *polis* grouped itself in divine guidance. As this link grew in potency and as the Greek world became richer, men turned to house their gods in ever more magnificent fashion.

The root of the temple form was extremely simple. From the earliest days of Aegean villages a common house plan had been that of the *megaron,* a squarish room with a hearth in the center which was flanked by posts to hold up the roof; in front of the room a porch was supported on its outer edge by two posts or columns. Well-known in the Mycenaean palaces, this form continued through the dark ages as virtually the only remnant of architectural order. At some point before 800 B.C. simple chapels began to appear in this shape, either rectangular or with a rounded rear wall. Basic building techniques had also survived which employed stone or mudbrick with timber posts for walls; roofs, either flat or pitched, were made of brush, covered with mud and a watertight coat.

By the eighth century the chapels grew bigger, and around them architects came to add a colonnade of wooden columns, as at the sanctu-

---

[3] One of the earliest *kouroi,* of about 615–590 B.C., was found at Sunium in Attica (Plate XI). Over nine feet high, its head is cubic, its body four-sided; anatomical detail is merely suggested on the chest by grooves in an abstract fashion; the ears and eyes are stylized, as is the falling hair. If one compares the stance of the *kouros* with an Egyptian statue (see Plate IV, of the Old Kingdom; Saite art was similar), indebtedness is apparent in the advance of the left foot and the fall of the arms into clenched fists. But the Greek sculptor has separated the legs from each other, and the arms from the body; the nude *kouros* has a sense of inner life which was to be made ever more apparent in later Greek sculpture.

ary of Hera on the island of Samos. Then, suddenly, true temples of the historic Greek type appeared in the early seventh century; first they were built of wood, but soon those areas that could afford the added expense turned to more lasting stone. Roofs now were made of tiles; and sculptural decoration was added in the form of figures on the rooftree, metopes along the sides between the triglyphs (which represented in stone the ends of the earlier wooden beams), and complicated scenes in the triangular pediments at the ends of the structure. Minor decorative motifs such as the palmette, rosette, and spiral were adapted from Near Eastern models in the architectural trim.

Balance and restraint are visible in the basic simplicity of the developed form of the temple, upon which Greek architectural genius was to lavish its growing skill over the next three centuries until the Parthenon was built. In the interplay of the vertical columns and the horizontal lines of base and roofline a sense of dynamic action was harnessed. Even in the details of the columns (originally Doric, then also Ionian) the Greeks exhibited their gifts of logical analysis and then synthesis of clearly defined parts. The temple, as has often been observed, was essentially a jewel box, set on a platform to encase the precious statue of the god, for most of the religious activities took place outside at an open-air altar before the shrine. Yet in looking at such a finished example as the Parthenon, a sensitive observer can perhaps best feel one of the greatest gifts of Greek thought to subsequent civilization, the concept that man can reduce the physical world to orderly terms comprehensible in rational, human modes of expression.

Beyond the temples, which have survived to some degree thanks to their stone construction, it is scarcely possible to discuss Greek architecture in the age of revolution. Houses remained simple structures for the basic needs of life; villages and the growing cities showed as yet virtually no trace of planning. City walls were unknown except at Smyrna in Asia Minor until the sixth century; at the most the *polis* might have a central refuge. In all the arts Greece was still a simple land, if one contrasts its products with those to be found in the magnificent palace complexes of the Assyrian empire. By the mid-seventh century, nonetheless, the Greeks had achieved forms of artistic activity and esthetic attitudes which underlay the future triumphs of the ripe archaic and classic periods.

NEW FORMS OF POETRY

Changes in Literature. Like the arts, Greek literature developed new and more varied forms during the age of revolution. The Greek language itself steadily became more supple; new meters were perfected, which were to be used throughout later ancient poetry; and in particular poets expressed a more conscious view of man. In literary forms and techniques the Greeks seem to have owed nothing to the Near East, though some of the ideas they expressed had at times affinities to Near Eastern thinking. Down past 600 Greek literature was poetic and was composed primarily to be chanted or sung aloud, but it was also written down in the alphabetic script which was now widely used by aristocrats and other leading elements.

By 750 b.c. the *Iliad* had already been created, and the *Odyssey* came soon thereafter. Then followed the minor epics of the Trojan cycle and the so-called Homeric Hymns in praise of various great gods, which were written in epic hexameters on into the sixth century. Nonetheless this style was too impersonal, primitive, and restricted to please the more advanced poets who arose from 700 onward.

Hesiod: The Works and Days. The great step across the divide between the dark ages and archaic Greece is represented in literature by Hesiod of Ascra, a hill-town overlooking the Boeotian plain. He tells us, in the poem called *Works and Days,* that he had crossed to Chalcis to sing a song in the funeral celebration of a king killed in the Lelantine war; this would place his active days just about 700 b.c. His verse form (the hexameter) and his vocabulary were very akin to Homeric style; but Hesiod's outlook, unlike that of the epic poets, was intensely personal.

The *Works and Days* was poured out in bitterness at the injustice by which his brother Perses had deprived the poet of his inheritance. So too, Hesiod proclaimed, had acted many men, dishonoring their parents, violating their oaths, plotting in envy together with "bribe-swallowing kings" (lines 38–39). His demand for justice, which rings in one's ears like the outcries of the Hebrew prophets, seems an early outburst in the political unrest which was producing the organized city-state. Yet Hesiod, like a true Greek, moved from his own personal grief to generalize about the state of the world. To account for the presence of injustice he had a threefold explanation: first the myth of Pandora (sent down by the gods with a pot full of tribulations); second, a fable of the hawk seizing the nightingale; and third, a quick sketch of earlier history as divided into five stages of decay from a primitive paradise. In labeling four of the stages gold, silver, bronze, and iron he drew apparently on Near Eastern concepts, but in adding to these an era of heroes he reflected folk memories of the Mycenaean age.

In the myth of Pandora, however, Hesiod had already shown that hope remained as a blessing among the plagues given to men by the gods. To Hesiod, as to Homer, mighty Zeus raised and lowered men as he willed — "there is no way to escape the will of Zeus" (line 105). The reiteration of the powers of the deathless gods is an incessant theme from the opening to the closing lines of the *Works and Days;* but in Hesiod, unlike Homer, the gods were coming to be conceived as ethical forces, as principles which could restrain the complete overturn of all standards threatened by the innovations sweeping over Aegean society. Although Hesiod was bitter, he was not hopeless. Zeus "fails not to mark what sort of justice is this that the *polis* keeps within it" (line 269); and men could prosper if they were just. Much of the poem, accordingly, was given over to detailed advice on farming and on the virtues of work. In passing, he warned his hearers against flaunting women, for "the man who trusts womankind trusts deceivers" (line 375).

The *Works and Days* is a fascinating poem. It is pungent and blunt; true poetic genius shimmers in its swiftly shifting kaleidoscope; for almost the only time in Greek literature we can hear the voice of the peasant. In his social and economic views, however, Hesiod expressed the general standards of Greece, and in such a succinct line as "observe due measure: and proportion is best in all things" (line 694) a famous axiom of later Greek ethics rang loud and true. Hesiod was the first poet in Greek history to speak for himself.

The Theogony. A considerable volume of other epic-type poetry, ranging from a description of the feats of Heracles to astronomical lore, clusters about the name of Hesiod. Prominent in this collection are the *Theogony,* dealing with the origins of the gods, and the *Eoiae,* describing the unions of gods and mortal beings which produced some of the great aristocratic families of Greece. In the *Theogony* the primeval substance of the world is called Chaos, whence came the ordered parts of nature; the process of development was that of physical generation between divine figures, which often produced opposing forces. Eventually the gods who ruled on Mt. Olympus were thus created and, led by Zeus, overthrew the earlier Titans. Sufficient hints of this scheme of thought appear in Homer that we may be sure Hesiod (if he wrote the *Theogony*) inherited his views. Ultimately the whole pattern may be due to Mesopotamian or Egyptian reflections.

In its Hesiodic form, nonetheless, this basically primitive view has become definitely Greek. The anthropomorphic gods are sharply conceived; poetic imagination vivifies the mass of names; and the mental outlook is quite different in tone from the Marduk tale of creation. While a truly critical, rational approach could not be expected so early in a work of pious intent, the *Theogony* lies in the background of Greek philosophic speculation, which began in the sixth century. The first philosophers placed great weight on the play of opposites, conceived physical substances in divine terms, and personified into real entities such abstract forces as Law and Strife. Above all, they too sought to explain the world in terms of order, causation, and unity.

Archilochus. The first great poet who stands entirely within the new outlook of the seventh century was Archilochus of Paros. Born to a noble by a slave woman, Archilochus was an aristocrat by early Greek rules of descent, albeit poor. References in his poem to king Gyges, the founder of Lydian power (d. 652), and to other events fix his date firmly toward the middle of the century. During his career he helped to colonize Thasos, traveled over the Aegean, and eventually died in battle for his homeland.

In both poetic techniques and outlook Archilochus broke with the epic background. The hexameter of Homer and Hesiod was too stately and limited for his purposes, and Archilochus developed out of simple, popular verse forms a great stock of supple meters. At first sight he looms up as a magnificent individual. In his poetry both the aristocratic sense of human freedom and also the liberation of this class from the more superficial bonds of convention are evident.

Yet in reality Archilochus was linked closely to his warrior associates and to the framework of the rising *polis*. Basically the world he saw remained an area where the gods ruled all, though the poet might still feel a naïve independence. His poems, which are mostly short, reflect directly his loves, his hates, his military mishaps, and his involvements in political strife; or rather, they give his feelings born of the actual events of life — for the world of which he sang was always the present. Archilochus had no time to spend on the legendary heroes of the Homeric past; unlike Hesiod, he did not seek to cast his thoughts in a mythical dress. Even the new *genre* of animal fables which he shared with Hesiod and the later Aesop (sixth century) was simply a piquant device by which he could make concrete his passions.

Lyric and Elegiac Poets. Homer and Hesiod were the first great poets in Greek literature, and Archilochus came very closely after Hesiod. Then followed an ever-widening stream of poetry, all of which we cannot hope to consider. The work of the other poets of the middle and later decades of the seventh century, indeed, has survived — like that of Archilochus — only in more or less extensive fragments quoted by later authors.

The bulk of these poets composed songs, either choral or individual, to be sung to the newly improved lyre (at least initially), and so a large section of the poetry of the seventh and sixth centuries is called lyric in contrast to the earlier, chanted epic. Alongside this form went poetry in elegiac couplets; this form was a straightforward meter, good for stories and moral advice, which was often sung to the accompaniment of a woodwind instrument like the oboe, the *aulos*. While personal expression bulked ever larger in songs of love and drinking, most of the poetry was connected directly with religious and patriotic occasions and often gave ethical and other advice; the poet thus was a representative of his community.

Among the early elegiac poets were Callinus of Ephesus (active before 650), who exhorted his countrymen to fight against a wave of Cimmerian invaders, and the highly patriotic Solon of Athens, who will appear more fully in Chapter 12. Mimnermus of Colophon (active about 630), on the other hand, expressed the rising sophistication of the aristocratic classes in his praise of youth and his loved Nanno. At Sparta, which was outstanding in the era for its support of music and choral songs, two principal poets flourished. One was the lyric Alcman of Sardis (active just after 650), who composed lighthearted pieces for choirs of maidens;

the other, the elegiac Tyrtaeus, perhaps of Spartan origin, became the moral leader of Sparta in the Second Messenian war (about 640). His praises of courage, which celebrated the virtues of dying for the father-land and identified aristocratic virtue with valor in battle, became virtu-ally national anthems at Sparta. In Sicily, Stesichorus of Himera (*c.* 632–556) retold epic and mythical tales in long choral odes in lyric meter; this type of poetry, sung in honor of Dionysus, was eventually called a *dithyramb.*

By the end of the century the famous Lesbian lyric poets, Alcaeus and Sappho, were active, but these figures will fall more properly in a discus-sion of the main currents during the sixth century. It may, however, be observed that music was an inseparable companion to much of this poetry and was a highly esteemed art in Greece. Unfortunately we know no more of its progress than some details of the evolution of the lyre, woodwinds, and other instruments and of the growingly conscious prin-ciples of musical composition which underlay the lyric outburst.

GREEK RELIGION

Importance of Religious Belief. At various points in the preceding pages the Greek gods have made their entrance, though more briefly than their importance warrants. Religion was interwoven with every aspect of Hellenic life from earliest days. Choral poetry was composed principally for religious festivals, as were later the great Attic tragedy and comedy; works of sculpture either depicted the gods or were dedi-cated in temple precincts; architecture became a conscious art in the building of temples. Industrial workshops were under the protection of special divinities, and traders gave great bronze caldrons and other testi-monials of thanks to the gods who safeguarded their perilous journeys. Every aspect of political and social life, from the daily round of family activities to the most important decisions of the city-state, was marked by religious rites; the *polis* was equally a religious and a political unit.

Unlike most modern religions the aim of Greek cult was to protect mankind during its life and to secure continuation of the group. Prob-lems of individual survival after death, of individual ethics, or even of the origins of the world emerged only partially and were not always to be answered in religious terms.

PLATE I PALEOLITHIC AGE

Flint hand-ax of middle Acheulian type, from second interglacial deposits along Thames river. See p. 10.

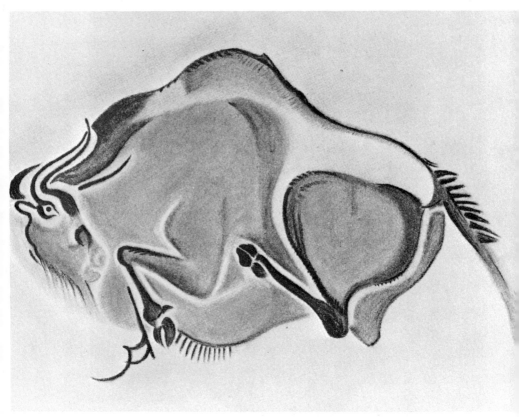

PLATE II PALEOLITHIC AGE
Crouching bison, from Altamira, Spain. See pp. 12, 437.

PLATE III EARLY MESOPOTAMIA

Sumerian gods and worshipers, from temple of Abu at Tel Asmar. See p. 37n.

PLATE IV   EARLY EGYPT

King Menkaure and his wife (Fourth Dynasty), from his valley temple. See pp. 57n, 232n.

PLATE V   MINOAN CRETE
Throne room with griffins, at Cnossus (restored). See pp. 107n, 110n.

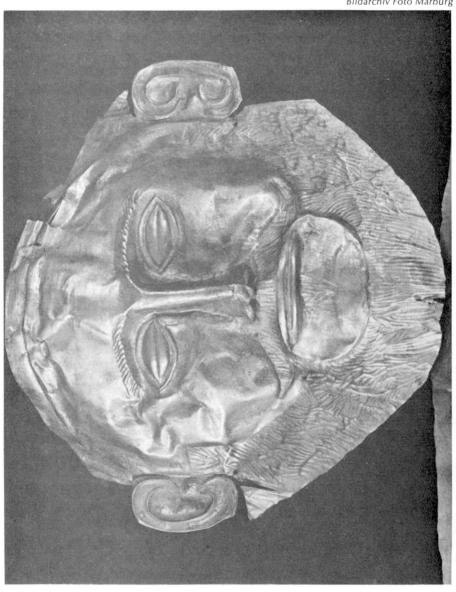

PLATE VI   MYCENAEAN GREECE
Gold face mask, found in shaft graves at Mycenae (National Museum, Athens).
See p. 108n.

PLATE VII

Ashurbanipal killing a lion, relief from Nineveh (British Museum). See pp. 135, 652n.

A. Mycenaean *kylix* (Metropolitan Museum of Art, New York, 12.229.7 [14614], Rogers Fund, 1912). See pp. 110n, 193n.

B. Protogeometric amphora, from the Kerameikos, Athens (Kerameikos Museum K. 1073). See pp. 193n, 194-5n.

C. Geometric amphora, from the Kerameikos, Athens (Kerameikos Museum K.2146). See pp. 194-5n, 248.

D. Protocorinthian *oenochoe* from Cumae (Naples Museum). See p. 229n.

PLATE VIII   EARLY GREEK POTTERY

Friedrich Hewicker

PLATE IX   DIPYLON POTTERY
Dipylon amphora (National Museum 200, Athens). See pp. 195, 248.

PLATE X   ARCHAIC GREECE
Bronze griffin head, from Olympia (Olympia Museum). See pp. 231, 241n.

Alison Frantz

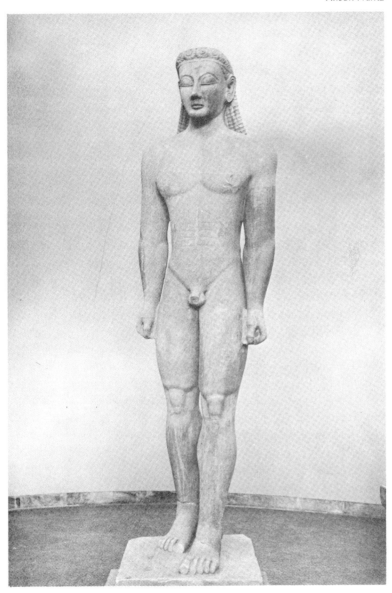

PLATE XI   ARCHAIC GREECE
Kouros, from Sunium (National Museum, Athens). See pp. 232n, 336n.

PLATE XII   ARCHAIC GREECE

Peplos kore, from the Acropolis (Acropolis Museum 679, Athens). See pp. 254, 264n, 450n.

PLATE XIII   CLASSIC GREECE

Bronze Poseidon (or Zeus), found in the sea off Cape Artemisium (National Museum, Athens). See p. 336n.

PLATE XIV   CLASSIC GREECE

Heracles bearing the world, with Athena and Atlas, metope from temple of Zeus
at Olympia (Olympia Museum). See p. 335n.

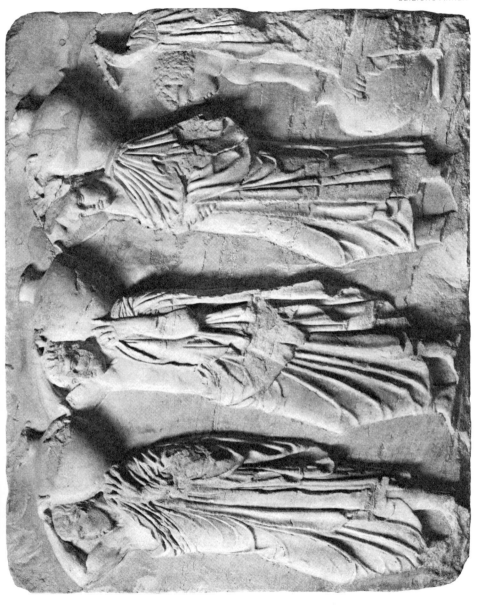

PLATE XV   ATHENIAN CITIZENS
Water carriers, from the Parthenon frieze (Acropolis Museum, Athens). See pp. 281n, 333n.

PLATE XVI   PERSIAN SUBJECTS

Tribute-bringers, from the *apadana* staircase at Persepolis. See p. 281n.

Levels of Greek Religion. Although the religious views of the Greeks were thus a fundamental influence on their history, we cannot hope to understand the subject until literary evidence appears in some quantity to supplement the ambiguous testimony of the physical remains — and at any time the innermost secrets of men's hearts are not easily penetrable. By the seventh century, moreover, many different levels of religious thought existed, some of which were essentially incompatible, yet all of which flourished.

The level which is most visible is that of the gods of Mt. Olympus. At least some of these great gods went back to the Mycenaean era and were the subjects of many varied mythological tales, but in the poetry of Homer and Hesiod they stood sharply individualized as superhuman, undying creatures which yet had human shape and human passions. From the seventh century on artists were to create canonical representations of the Olympians (see Plates XIII, XIX, XXI). Since they were, so to speak, divine aristocrats they appealed particularly to the upper levels of Greek society and bulk large in our literary evidence.

Among the Olympians 12 eventually were grouped as the greatest gods: Zeus, the father; Hera, his wife; Poseidon, Hestia, and Demeter, his brother and sisters; and his children in various ways, Athena, Artemis, Aphrodite, Apollo, Hermes, Ares, Hephaestus. Commonly a city-state revered one of this group for its particular patron, the worship of which was incumbent upon all the citizens; yet all Greeks were united in a common reverence for the great gods of their civilization. Certain shrines, such as that of Apollo at Delos, drew wide audiences to their ancient festivals; and at four points major athletic contests emerged. The Olympian festival and games, held every four years in honor of Zeus, went back to the beginning of the age of revolution; the other three great Greek games, the Pythian of Delphi (to Apollo), the Isthmian (to Poseidon), and the Nemean (to Zeus), began to be significant or were founded only after 600.

Besides the great gods there were many local divinities of the same type. These sometimes were equated with greater forces as loyalty to the city-state became more powerful than local attachments; but sometimes the minor deities maintained their independence. On a lower plane of divine manifestation were the heroes, men who had achieved great deeds and were worshiped at their graves both as protectors and as ghosts.

Throughout the countryside, in forests, springs, or hills, dwelt a host of nameless nymphs, satyrs, centaurs, and other figures to whom the simple folk offered worship as embodiments of the unpredictable forces of nature.

Particularly with regard to the success of his crops, his animals, and his own reproduction an ancient Greek had to think religiously, whereas we today would think scientifically. The level of fertility cults plays virtually no part in Homer, but the physical evidence and later references show abundantly that it was significant throughout Greek history. The earliest figurines and clay plaques are often of a goddess who holds wild animals by their necks, nurses a baby, unites with a god, or stands alone. This female force at times evolved into the historical Artemis, Athena, or Demeter; but elsewhere she continued to be revered simply as the Mistress, the reproductive element in life. The events of the agricultural year underlay the calendar of religious ceremonies, and farming was attended by a great deal of magic and superstition, as was most of life. Hesiod, thus, warned his reader not to use an uncharmed pot in cooking or to cut one's nails with an iron tool. Here and there ritual execution of a human being took place once a year to appease the crop-bringing divinities; even at Athens two unfortunate scapegoats were driven out of the city or burned every year as bearers of the sins of the community.

In general the worship of the gods was a matter of the proper cult observances. The greatest of these was the sacrifice of an animal, partly offered up to the proper divine spirit, partly eaten by his earthly followers. These ceremonies were conducted by the father for his family, by the leaders of the clan for its members, or by the king for the whole state; specialized priests, seers, and other religious functionaries did exist but had only a subsidiary place in Greek civilization. While religion was as important in Greece as in the Near East, its officials and rituals held a far less dominant place.

Religious Stress and Its Release. As we have seen, the age of revolution was one of almost incredible achievements. An inevitable concomitant to such rapid change was great social stress and individual tension as men reluctantly observed their old, stable framework of life and thought yield to a new system. Nowhere can we detect this double-faced aspect better than in the religious development of the era.

Fundamentally men were confident of divine support, and at times might even dare to feel that their future lay in their own hands. Naïve pride, audacity, and self-will are visible in Archilochus and other poets; the rich reveled in their new luxuries and all too often used their political power to oppress the weak. Yet fear was never far removed from pride, and the increasingly self-conscious analysis visible in Greek civilization led men to express also a sense of guilt and alarm.

This fear is particularly visible in the arts of the period. Monsters and wild animals were molded in bronze and stone, and sat fiercely in rows on many Orientalizing vases; in some scenes lions tear men to pieces. In these creatures of nightmare the unpredictability and the savagery of the physical world which still enfolded the Greeks in the age of revolution looms up sharply.[4]

The important aspect of religious progress in the era, however, was its manifold provision of vents and reassurances for the stresses and fears of life. The artistic reflection of the wildness of life itself helped to exorcise fear, and such popular figures as lions grew less fierce by the sixth century. Cults of heroes, who stood halfway between fallible man and the immortal gods, became widespread. Although Greek religious thought never proceeded as far as did that of the Hebrew prophets in connecting ethics with the gods, the poets and other spokesmen of the community firmly asserted that justice must be an ideal of the *polis* and even reinterpreted the Olympian gods themselves, in part, as guardians of this ideal. As men followed the paths of justice or injustice, so were they rewarded by Zeus in visible physical terms: in peace, prosperity, and health; or in plague, famine, and toppling walls. Or, in more general terms which were to be famous throughout all Greek thought, man was inevitably punished by divine jealousy when he grew too proud (*hybris*); the true course was a life of reason and moderation, called *sophrosyne*.

New Cults. While the elaboration of Greek religious and ethical views was very largely connected with the rise of the *polis* and with other

[4] The wicked force of the bronze griffin head illustrated on Plate X suggests the demonic force encompassing mankind in the view of seventh-century Greeks. This imaginary creature originated in the Near East; but the Greek smiths stylized the type, changing a topknot of hair into an abstract knob. Originally it stood, with other griffin heads, on the rim of a great caldron which was dedicated at Olympia, now rising as an international shrine.

communal activities, the individual human beings who lived in this society came to need methods of personal reassurance and of relief from their problems and tensions. This issue helped to shape some major religious developments.

One was the rise of the cult of Apollo, an ancient deity who stepped forward as law-giver, patron of music and poetry, oracular counselor, and healer of guilty consciences. He had long been worshiped by the Ionians at Delos and at Didyma (near Miletus); but his main shrine in the respects just noted came to be that of Delphi, a majestic site below great cliffs and overlooking a deep valley. Here Apollo had an oracle, to which both states and individuals could resort for advice; the lines of his ethical prescription were summed up in the famous mottoes, Know Thyself, and Nothing in Excess. By the sixth century Delphi was becoming a powerful international center and was made into a neutral site after the First Sacred war, in which its previous master, the state of Crisa, was utterly destroyed by Sicyon and Thessaly. At numerous other sites as well, the cult of Apollo came to supersede earlier divinities.

As the figure of Apollo developed, he came to stand as an embodiment of Greek rationalism. A more ecstatic, emotional outlet lay in the worship of Dionysus, who was also an old god. Already "the joy of mortals" in Homer, Dionysus was a god not merely of relaxing wine but of vegetation as a whole (see Plate XVII.A), and his worship was conducted at least partly in frenzied revels by women. At times they broke out by night to dance in the hills and devoured raw flesh to unify themselves with a savior; at other times men and women joined in daytime festivities of Dionysus, some of which led later to the development of the great Attic drama.

Yet a third vehicle for release lay in the cult of Demeter at Eleusis near Athens. At this site an ancient fertility cult in connection with the fall sowing had been built around the story of the rape of Persephone, daughter of Demeter, by Pluto of the underworld. As a result, Demeter had refused to carry out her duty of promoting the growth of man's grain until her daughter was restored for part of the year. Each fall voluntary participants had themselves initiated into the secret rites of the cult, called "mysteries," and thereby gained the promise of life after death. By the sixth century the hall of the mysteries had received a noble architectural dress; the annual initiations continued to draw great crowds until far down into the Roman Empire, when Christianity drowned out the cult. No part of Greek religion was more sacred or secret than the Eleusinian mysteries.

Nor were these all. In later days, especially, we hear of a cult of Orphics, so-called from their legendary founder, the poet Orpheus of Thrace. This dimly lit, rather legalistic faith revolved about the murder of Zagreus (or Dionysus) by the Titans and his marvelous rebirth. Since man sprang from the ashes of the Titans, he was partly evil, partly divine; a famous Orphic jingle asserted that the body (*soma*) was the tomb (*sema*) of the soul. Those who failed to enter the Orphic mysteries and lead the good, vegetarian life would lie in mud in Hades; the initiated and purified "shall dwell with Gods." [5] Cretan seers were also famous communers with the divine, and one such seer purified Athens from its pollution after a bloody uprising late in the seventh century. Other men turned ascetic and talked of transmigration. It must be emphasized that these latter elements, the Orphic mystics, seers, ascetics, and the like, were far removed from the main line of Greek religion and flourished perhaps more in the western colonies than in Greece proper; yet their presence suggests the wide range of religious experiment.

The Greeks were far too earth-centered, keen of thought, and materially successful in the age of revolution to yield themselves utterly to religious preoccupations, however sharply they recognized human frailty. Yet both as individuals and as members of various groups they shared in a rich religious pattern by 600 B.C. Much of this religion remained primitive, for it was crystallized early amid a simple folk. The picturesque Homeric view of the gods as being numerous and as sharing all basic human qualities could never be removed, even though a great philosopher was later to emphasize that "there is one god, among gods and men the greatest, not at all like mortals in body or in mind." [6] The most practical test of religion, however, is perhaps whether it consoles and inspirits men in their daily battles with the world, and this test the many strands of Greek faith satisfied on the level of the individual, of the family and clan, and of the state. Above all Greek religion had an

[5] Plato, *Phaedo* 69C.
[6] Xenophanes, fragment 23 (Diels); tr. Kathleen Freeman.

optimistic, confident quality which rose above gross superstition and fostered the continued development of the arts and letters.

THE GREEKS IN 650 B.C.

Chapters 10 and 11 have considered some of the many interlinked changes of the age of revolution, 750–650 B.C. Through the door of religion we can see, if only partially, the very fundamental psychological and spiritual problems of the era, perhaps the most turbulent which Greek civilization underwent down to the fourth century B.C. The great advances in every field were bought only at the price of individual uneasiness and serious social unrest. The important point, nonetheless, is that the Greeks were in the end able to crystallize a clearer, more rounded outlook which was based squarely upon the main lines of the culture which had appeared in the dark ages. And now that change had become more rapid, the Greeks were remarkably free to experiment and to evolve new forms of thought and art. Among these the rise of philosophy was soon to be a striking phenomenon.

In this advance the Greeks had been successful partly because they limited themselves. Politically they had bound themselves together within the more perfect union of the *polis,* without thereby yielding all freedom of the individual. Intellectually poets and artists took a very few forms and concentrated their energies in perfecting these basically simple patterns. Psychologically they admitted only restricted freedom to themselves and viewed human life in terms of generalized, idealized concepts rather than conceiving men as absolutely individualistic atoms. Nonetheless Hellenic civilization was deeply humanistic in the sense that it concentrated upon the human being and considered him as an object of infinite worth.

Through trade and the movement of aristocrats and artists the Greek world shared the same outlook, yet each area had its own flavor to a greater extent than was ever again to be true. In this happy blend of internationalism and localism, in the growing contacts with Near Eastern culture, and in the tensions between individual human beings and organized society lay some of the forces which pushed Hellenic civilization toward continuing change and a host of great achievements.

BIBLIOGRAPHY

Sources. Both the literary and the artistic products of the age of revolution reflected so distant an era that they were not consciously preserved, for the most part, by later generations. The works of the poets who flourished in the seventh century could still be read in Roman times, for scholars of this period (as well as earlier) sometimes quoted from Archilochus and other figures. Papyri found in Egypt during the last century, which came from Hellenistic and Roman times, have occasionally provided further material. But in the transition from ancient to medieval (or Byzantine) times a great process of selection occurred, and in the transmission of early Greek authors from the Byzantine world to western Europe more was lost. Apart from the works clustered about the names of Homer and Hesiod the poetry of no author has survived intact from the seventh century. Hesiod and the Homeric Hymns are best available in the Loeb Classical Library, where the fragments of other early poets can be found in the volumes *Lyra Graeca* and *Elegy and Iambus*. From this evidence the historian can secure some light on the subjects considered in this chapter, but many figures once great are no more than names to us.

So too archaic art and architecture were replaced by more perfected work in the classic period, save insofar as religious conservatism led to their preservation or later archaistic interests produced copies occasionally. Bronze statues were commonly melted down, once they were no longer thought useful, and have rarely survived; stone statues were sometimes discarded or used as fill. To reconstruct early buildings architectural historians must rely upon their foundations (often under later edifices) and utilize fragments of terra-cotta roof materials and of columns and architraves, where these were made of stone rather than of wood. Thus we can reconstruct in general terms such temples as those of Hera at Samos; some of the superstructure of the temple of Hera at Olympia (though replaced in later times) still stands. Pottery on the other hand is available in considerable quantities, particularly the very popular Corinthian style; and the dating of all artistic progress, as well as of much of the political history, depends primarily upon the dates which have been established for the pottery sequences. Relatively the dating is secure, but specific dates can only be approximate.

Apart from some walls and the tombs, which grew more luxurious in the era, there is little evidence for the life of men. The cities proper were still small; Thucydides (1.10) later described the Sparta of his day as "a straggling village like the ancient towns of Hellas."

Further Reading. The main lines of cultural development are suggested in Chester G. Starr, *Origins of Greek Civilization, 1100–650 B.C.* (New York: Knopf, 1961); see also Werner Jaeger, *Paideia,* Vol. I (New York: Oxford University Press, 1945), and Bruno Snell, *Discovery of the Mind* (New York: Harper Torchbook 1018, 1960). Beyond the histories of Greek art listed in General Bibliography, see the interpretive work of Georg Karo, *Greek Personality in Archaic Sculpture* (Westport, Conn.: Greenwood); the catalog by Gisela M. A. Richter, *Archaic Greek Art* (New York: Oxford University Press, 1949); and on pottery R. M. Cook, *Greek Painted Pottery* (2d ed.; London: Methuen, 1972). T. B. L. Webster, *Greek Art and Literature, 700–530 B.C.* (New York: Praeger, 1960), is a good comparative study; on the literary side see C. M. Bowra, *Greek Lyric Poetry from Alcman to Simonides* (2d ed.; Oxford: Oxford University Press, 1961), and *Early Greek Elegists* (New York: Cooper Square, 1969). For Hesiod, see Friedrich Solmsen, *Hesiod and Aeschylus* (New York: Johnson reprint). H. D. Rankin, *Archilochus of Paros* (Park Ridge, N.J.: Noyes, 1978), is adequate.

E. R. Dodds, *Greek and the Irrational* (Boston: Beacon BP2, 1955), is a superb study of the religious tensions in archaic Greece. The obscure Orphic sect is discussed by I. M. Linforth, *Arts of Orpheus* (New York: Arno), and W. K. C. Guthrie, *Orpheus and Greek Religion* (2d ed.; London: Methuen, 1952); George E. Mylonas, *Eleusis and the Eleusinian Mysteries* (Princeton: Princeton University Press, 1961), is best on the archeological side.

12

THE SIXTH CENTURY

The sixth century B.C. was an era of fruition and of relative calmness in Greek civilization after the stresses and tensions of the age of revolution. Sculptural and architectural forms were further elaborated and resulted in products which marked the height of the archaic style; the wild fantasies of Protoattic pottery gave way to the disciplined Athenian black-figure ware, which began to conquer the Mediterranean market. Lyric and other forms of poetry were widely composed over the Greek world. The most notable testimony alike to the solid foundations of this age and to its freedom of outlook was the appearance of the first philosophers.

The social, economic, and political forces which had already produced great changes in the preceding era were still at work. Many of the religious reassurances noted in the last chapter gained their popularity principally in the sixth century, and the political organization of the Aegean world underwent very significant development. By 500 B.C. Athens and Sparta had developed those markedly different points of view on internal government and foreign relations which were to be their lasting hallmarks. Sparta was by this date the greatest state in Greece, but Athens was rising rapidly; besides these two a number of other city-states played their part in the complicated interplay of Aegean history, which was now more continuously connected.

Abroad, the Greek states in the western Mediterranean fell into conflict with the Phoenicians and Etruscans, and those on the coast of Asia Minor were subjected first to Lydia and then to Persia. The archaic period is the last phase of Greek history in which one can consider the Aegean basin essentially by itself. Thereafter the historian of Greece must also take into account first Persia, then Macedonia, and finally Rome.

INTERNAL EVOLUTION OF ATHENS

Athenian History through the Seventh Century. The course of Greek constitutional development over the centuries was from an early state of simple tribal communities which probably differed very little (in the dark ages) toward ever more complicated political institutions, which varied greatly from one area to another. By 500 b.c. many different types of states existed side by side in Greece. Athens, which may be considered first, had perhaps developed the furthest and was exhibiting democratic tendencies along with overseas naval interests. To understand this unusual course we must look carefully into earlier Athenian history.

With respect to the main economic activity of early Greece, that is, subsistence agriculture, Attica was not favored. Its rainfall was relatively scanty for the raising of wheat, though adequate for vines and olive trees; and the summer winds blew down hot and dusty from the northeast. The commercial and industrial potentialities of the land were more promising. Attica was near alike to the islands, to the Boeotian plain, and to the Saronic gulf; its harbors were good; and it had excellent natural resources, such as good clay, the marble of Mt. Pentelicus, and the silver mines of Laurium (see Map 10).

Athenians later boasted they were autochthonous, and certainly settlement can be traced uninterruptedly from Neolithic times. A Mycenaean palace had stood atop the Acropolis, and settlement of Attica had been thick in Mycenaean times. According to tradition the land had been spared the Dorian invasion and had even been a refuge for fugitives from other districts, many of whom had sailed thence to found colonies of very similar customs and dialect in Ionia. Although these tales are more than doubtful, cultural connections did stretch from Attica across the Aegean; and Athenian potters had stood in the van of Geometric progress (see Plates VIII and IX).

From the dark ages on Attica constituted one relatively large state, which possessed considerable attractive power over frontier districts; Eleusis thus was absorbed, probably in the seventh century. By about 700 another important step had been taken in the replacement of the kings by elected magistrates. These were the nine archons, chosen eventually for one year only: (1) archon proper, the general civil head and protector of property; (2) "king" archon, for ancestral sacred rites; (3) *polemarch* or general; (4–9) six *thesmothetae,* keepers of the law and recorders of precedents. Deliberative and judicial functions were in the hands of the council of the Areopagus, representing the aristocracy and composed of the ex-archons. Whether an assembly (*ecclesia*) had any real place is unknown. Many aspects of this aristocratic system are not entirely clear, but since we have more information for early Athens than for any other Greek state some of its main problems can be seen.

In the seventh century Athens suffered serious troubles. Economically its potters lost their earlier pre-eminence to Corinthian competition, and the aristocrats treated the weak harshly. The poor farmers who owned land could not be dispossessed, but when they fell into debt they often became virtual serfs of the rich, bound to pay one-sixth of their meager produce to their creditors. Landless men could be enslaved and were sold abroad. Socially and politically local territorial groups and noble factions were ill controlled by the weak machinery of the state. Aristocratic leaders vied ruthlessly for power and repute, and one discontented aristocrat, Cylon, made an unsuccessful attempt to establish a tyranny about 632. Draco set down a law code about 620 but this failed to check the unrest.

Solon the Idealist (594 B.C.). As men of judgment assessed the gravity of the situation, they felt the need for wider reforms. The remarkable ability of the Athenians at compromise, which marked much of their history, led in 594 to the election of Solon as single archon or as "reconciler." Solon was an aristocrat who had a broad outlook. He had traveled widely on business and also had been a military leader of Athens in its struggle with nearby Megara for the offshore island of Salamis. Fortunately, for our understanding of his career, he also wrote elegiac poetry, the sober idealism of which made it a treasured inheritance of later generations.

During his year as virtual dictator Solon rescued many of the Athe-

TABLE 4
Greece and the Near East 1100–500 B.C.

B.C.	Political	Greece Economic and Social	Cultural	Near East
1100	Tribal kingdoms	DARK AGES		Era of small states Phoenicians Arameans Israelites
1050		Farming and nomadic tribes	Protogeometric pottery	
1000				David
950				Solomon Israel–Judah
900			Geometric pottery	RISE OF ASSYRIA
850				Ashurnasirpal II Ahab, Elijah
800		Revival of eastern trade	Adoption of alphabet Iliad/Dipylon ware Olympic games (776?)	
750	Rise of *polis* and phalanx Spartan conquest Messenia Lelantine war	Beginning of colonization Rise of aristocracies	Orientalizing pottery Odyssey Hesiod	Amos, Hosea, Isaiah Beginning of Phoenician colonization Tiglath-Pileser III Sargon II: fall of Israel (722)

		AGE OF REVOLUTION		Sennacherib
700				
650	Rise of Lydia: Gyges	Invention of coinage	Archilochus	Psammetichus I
	Second Messenian war	Growth of commercial–industrial classes (slavery)	Developed temple form	Ashurbanipal
	Tyranny at Sicyon, Corinth, etc.		Large-scale sculpture	Josiah
			Alcman, Mimnermus, Tyrtaeus, Stesichorus	Fall of Nineveh
				CHALDAEAN AND MEDIAN EMPIRES
600	Solon archon		Solon, Sappho, Alcaeus	Nebuchadrezzar
	Spartan expansion	Expansion of Athenian trade	Thales	Jeremiah
			Attic black–figure	
550	Croesus		Theognis, Simonides, Ibycus	Ezekiel, 2d Isaiah
	Pisistratus		Anaximander, Anaximenes	PERSIAN EMPIRE
	Western wars with Etruscans, Phoenicians		Attic red–figure	Cyrus
	Polycrates		Pythagoras, Xenophanes	
	Hipparchus, Hippias			Cambyses
	Cleomenes		Hecataeus	Darius
	Clisthenes			
500				

nians sold abroad, abolished agricultural debts of the "sixth-part men," and forbade future bondage of the poor. He favored the production of olive oil but banned the export of cereals, needed by the growing population of Athens. Trade and industry were also promoted by a number of detailed enactments, including the shift of weights and coins to the Euboic standard, which was one-third lighter than that used before and more widely employed in Mediterranean trade. Socially he limited the exercise of aristocratic luxury and subtly reduced the power of the aristocrats by his political reforms.

Solon thus regrouped the citizenry into four classes on the basis of wealth, measured in terms of agricultural produce: the "500-bushel men" (*pentakosiomedimnoi*); the "cavalry" (*hippeis*), those whose property yielded 300 *medimnoi* of produce; the "men of the line" (*zeugitae*) of 200 *medimnoi*, who fought on foot; and the "laborers" or *thetes*. Only men in the first two classes could hold major offices, but all had a voice in the Athenian assembly and in the courts of law (*heliaea*). The latter heard appeals from the officials and eventually came to audit and inspect the activities of officials. The assembly now was to become more effective, and to secure this end Solon established a new council of Four Hundred, a standing committee chosen to prepare business for popular debate and vote. Extensive reorganization and codification of the religious and civil law of Athens were also achieved.

As Solon repeatedly emphasized in his poetry, he stood in the middle. "I gave the common folk," he proclaimed once, "such privilege as is sufficient for them . . . I stood with a strong shield thrown before rich and poor, and would have neither to prevail unrighteously over the other." [1] His aim, in other words, was to remove the immediate sources of stress and to give the weaker elements safeguards while yet leaving general control in the hands of the rich.

Beneath his specific steps lay his sober assessment of the close interrelations of the state and the individual. The *polis* must be based on justice, for any evil anywhere in a state eventually affected all its members. The world, moreover, was one where law in the sense of regular order prevailed through the will of the gods. It was not accidental that Solon reformed Athens so that it might exhibit this ethical law at the

[1] Solon, fragment 5 (Diehl); tr. J. M. Edmonds.

same time as the first philosophers were finding natural law in the physical universe.

Tyranny of the Pisistratids (546–10 B.C.). Solon was the first great statesman who consciously began to point Athens toward the social, economic, and political road it was to follow, but his detailed solutions were too moderate to end the Athenian unrest. Aristocratic rivalry and general tensions soon brought renewed political difficulties, as a result of which the regular constitution broke down and gave way to a tyranny. The ambitious aristocrat who gained complete power was Pisistratus. Twice he seized control briefly (561, 556/5), but finally in 546 he came back from abroad with an army and remained ruler until his death in 527. His sons Hippias and Hipparchus succeeded him and held mastery until 510.

This line of tyrants made no extensive theoretical changes in the Athenian constitution, but the 36 years of their rule brought important developments in other respects. Many of the aristocratic clan leaders, especially the great Alcmeonid family, were generally in exile, and citizens tended to turn for guidance and decisions to the state machinery, which was expanded and improved.

To encourage patriotic unity the tyrants engaged in a remarkably wide range of religious and cultural activities. Both the Acropolis and the lower city were embellished by new temples, and the secular center of politics and trade, the Agora, began to be systematized. Local cults, such as the Eleusinian mysteries, were brought under state control. An annual festival, the Panathenaea, had long been celebrated in honor of the patron goddess Athena, whose statue received a new gown after a great procession; from 566 on every fifth year saw a specially magnificent display of the festival with games, to which Hipparchus added a competition in the public reading of Homer's epics.

Each year at the Dionysia in honor of the gods of wine dramatic performances now became customary. The first tragedian, who separated an actor from the chorus, was Thespis, who received a prize from Pisistratus in about 534. Among foreign poets who sang in the tyrants' halls were Anacreon of Teos (active 550–500), a limpid poet of drink and love; and Simonides of Ceos (*c.* 556–468), so versatile a composer of dithyrambs (choral songs with a narrative content), epigrams, funeral dirges, victory odes, and other poems that he made his living by his art. Sculpture also gained extensive patronage, and a host of beautiful marble maidens (*korai*) in the latest Ionian and other styles appeared on the Acropolis (see Plate XII). This religious center of Athens was also adorned with an entry-gate of limestone, a stone from which pedimental sculptures were made for several temples erected on the hill in the sixth century.

While the tyrants thus favored poetry and the arts, they tended to maintain peaceful relations with their neighbors. Only toward the Hellespont did Athens show aggressive tendencies, partly through state action to take Sigeum, partly through the private initiative of adventurous men like Miltiades of the Philaïd clan. Pisistratid encouragement promoted the consolidation of an independent peasantry, which had an ever better market for its olive oil and wine and so could pay a tax of one-tenth (later one-twentieth) of its produce to the state. Trade and industry, too, became ever more active, both in agricultural products and especially in pottery. By at least 525 B.C. Athens had begun to coin its famous "owls," silver coins with the head of Athena on one side and her owl on the other.[2]

The rule of the Pisistratids is our best known example of early Greek tyranny, but like the tyrannies at Sicyon, Corinth, and elsewhere it eventually fell. Hipparchus was murdered in 514 by two young nobles, Harmodius and Aristogeiton, for purely private reasons; after this event Hippias became more ruthless. The Alcmeonids secured the support of the oracle of Delphi, which in turn urged the Spartans to root out the Athenian tyranny. Sparta, as we shall see shortly, had become the greatest military power of Greece, and its great king Cleomenes was more than eager to do the bidding of Apollo. In 510 he led an army north across the isthmus of Corinth and forced the abdication of Hippias, who went into exile at the Persian court.

Clisthenes and Democracy. Once the tyrant and his mercenary army had been removed, Athens fell once more into dissension, but the basic situation was now far different than it had been earlier in the century.

[2] So standard a medium of exchange in the Greek (and non-Greek) world did Athenian "owls" become that the Athenian mint was not free to change its types easily. For centuries, accordingly, the archaic designs were copied; the example on Plate XVIII.B comes from the late fifth century. This 4-drachma piece was worth almost a man's wages for a week.

The power of the state had been exalted by the Pisistratids at the expense
of local loyalties and clan ties; nonnoble social and economic groups had
gained a sense of independence. When Isagoras, a noble preferred by
Sparta, set up a new oligarchy, his effort to turn back the clock shattered. A rival Athenian leader, Clisthenes of the Alcmeonid family,
gained power in 508 with wide popular support. Although king Cleomenes himself came back with a small Spartan force to restore the
situation, it was in vain; for the populace of Athens rose and besieged
the Spartans on the Acropolis until they agreed to retire.

Clisthenes then recast the political machinery of Athens in a mold
which proved basically satisfactory over the next two and one-half centuries. Essentially his aims were, first, to break the power of local social
units in favor of the state as a whole, a process which had been going on
since Draco first brought homicide under state jurisdiction; and, secondly, to lodge the essential power of the state in the hands of the people. Whether Clisthenes had an idealistic predisposition toward democracy may be doubted; but the exigencies of practical politics at the time
led him to court the support of the populace and so to exalt its role.

Thenceforth the building blocks of Athenian political life were the
small territorial units called the *demes*, eventually about 170 in number.
The citizens were those people registered on the rolls of the demes;
Clisthenes seems to have gone farther than had the Pisistratids in admitting many of the foreigners resident in Athens to citizenship at this time.
The demes had some power of local self-government; for purposes of
general elections their residents were grouped into 10 new tribes.

To ensure, however, that each tribe or electoral district reflected all of
Attica rather than local interests, a tribe consisted of demes located in
three different areas: the countryside proper, the city of Athens, and the
coast. One or more demes from each area formed a *trittys,* and three
trittyes made up a tribe. This complicated grouping attests the advance
in political thinking which had taken place in Greek constitutional
thought and admirably fulfilled its purpose of organizing the citizens on
a public, rather than a social base. The older units — phratries and the
like — continued to exist but operated primarily as social and religious
entities.

The dynamo of the whole government was now definitely the assembly. Clisthenes established, in place of Solon's council, a new council of Five Hundred, consisting of 50 men from each tribe chosen by lot from candidates elected by the demes, to prepare business for the assembly and to supervise from day to day the execution of public business by the officials. Archons continued to be elected and to pass after their year of office into the council of the Areopagus, which still had considerable ancestral power. At the time of the reforms Clisthenes and his adherents spoke of *isonomia,* equality of rights, and his reforms had the great virtue of uniting all elements of the state in a solid political system. The term *demokratia,* rule of the people, was soon to become popular; and further democratic steps were taken in the next 50 years.

The new system proved its popular support and its effectiveness within two years, when the Boeotians and Chalcis tried to attack Athens in 506. Both were defeated, and the Athenians took a part of the territory of Chalcis. Here they settled 4000 colonists, called *cleruchs,* who continued to be Athenian citizens though living abroad. By 500 Athens had achieved a satisfactory internal political system. Abroad, its influence was expanding both commercially and politically, but it was still a minor state in comparison to Sparta.

SPARTAN IMPERIALISM

Spartan History through the Seventh Century. The evolution of Sparta had followed a different course, which on the whole had been less troubled than was that of Athens. In folk-memory the Dorians were said to have come down rather late into Laconia, the rich valley of the Eurotas river with its surrounding hills, tucked off in the south Peloponnesus. Contrary to the usual pattern, the invaders amalgamated on even terms with the earlier population centered at Amyclae. To this union perhaps may be attributed the strange fact that Sparta always had two royal houses, that is, two kings, at the same time.

The kings and nobles of Sparta enjoyed the developing luxury of the age of revolution much as did similar classes elsewhere. Some of the earliest ivories in Greece have been found at the Spartan shrine of Artemis Orthia; music and choral poetry were so esteemed that such experts in the fields as Terpander of Lesbos (*c.* 675) and Alcman of Sardis were drawn to Sparta in the seventh century. Along with other poets from all over Greece they competed at the great Spartan festival of the Carneia (in honor of Apollo), held in early fall.

The kings, as war chiefs, and the nobles also delighted in war. In contests with Argos, which was the greatest state of the Peloponnesus down to 600, the Spartans were long unsuccessful: a seventh-century oracle of Delphi praises the maids of Sparta, no doubt as singers of Alcman's songs, but the warriors of Argos! To the west the Spartans had greater scope and at an uncertain date in the eighth century conquered the most fertile part of Messenia, which lay beyond the great bulk of Mt. Taygetus.

The crucial step in Spartan development came when the Messenians revolted about 640 and held out bitterly over perhaps two decades. In the reconquest the Spartan armies were encouraged by the martial poetry of Tyrtaeus, but more than poetry was needed. Immediately the political system of Sparta seems to have been drastically reorganized, and over the long run the social and economic structure of the state was reordered. The guiding principle of Spartan thought over the next two centuries was to remain militarily strong to as to keep the unwilling subjects under control.

Spartan Government. Politically Sparta had become a *polis* in the eighth century, the full citizens of which lived in four adjoining villages and also Amyclae in the Eurotas valley. In the hills were subsidiary villages of *perioikoi* (dwellers-about), who were also citizens or Lacedemonians and fought in the army, but did not have the vote. The third layer of Spartan society was the small peasants, especially of Messenia, who were depressed into the status of *helots* or serfs.

At the time of the Second Messenian war Sparta took some of the earliest steps toward democracy which occurred anywhere in Greece. Distinctions of class among the full Spartan citizens were outwardly erased so as to gain their loyalty to the state; thenceforth this group was called the "Equals." By a famous decree, the great *rhetra,* the assembly of men over 30 was formally acknowledged as the ultimate authority, though a later amendment permitted the kings and elders to dismiss it if it decided improperly. Reorganization of military and voting districts also took place so as to reduce the power of the old social groupings.

The generals and religious heads of the state continued to be the two kings; but detailed direction of public activities was largely in other hands. A council of elders, the *gerusia,* consisted of the 2 kings and 28 men of 60 years or more, elected for life by acclamation in the assembly. Each year five *ephors* were elected to supervise the social system of Sparta; by the fifth century the ephors also checked the kings. Once established, this structure of "arrested democracy" endured without serious change until the fourth century B.C.

Spartan Life. The Spartan social system was a famous model in antiquity because of its emphasis upon state service, physical training, and stability. In tradition it was established by a legendary figure, Lycurgus, but in actuality it seems to have evolved out of the communal life of the early warrior brotherhoods. Very similar patterns developed in several Cretan districts but there were less harnessed to the conscious needs of the state.

Upon birth Spartan children were inspected by state officials to determine whether they were physically fit to be raised. At the age of seven boys left home and were trained in groups under teen-age leaders. At the age of 20 they passed into the brotherhoods or squads of 15 each, where they ate common meals once a day and perfected their military skills. Until they were 30, men could not dwell permanently with their wives, who lived both as girls and as women a far freer existence than was common elsewhere in Greek society.

To support the "Equals," who numbered up to 9000, the land was divided into plots, cultivated by helots so that the citizens would be free for military training and warfare. Trade and industry were largely conducted by the *perioikoi.* In many ways the Spartan structure was thus one where the citizen body as a whole formed an aristocracy, but in which the old family groups had been broken down for the benefit of the state.

The virtues of this system appealed greatly to many conservative thinkers in later ages, for rather than pursuing wealth and learning the Spartans devoted themselves to their country and thus made "the attainment of a high standard of noble living a public duty." [3] It was not difficult for philosophers such as Plato to idealize Spartan education and society into a system which no earthly men could ever have upheld; in particular, many of the famous stories about the rigors of Spartan life are either legend or reflect much later conditions. Other observers, an-

[3] Xenophon, *Constitution of the Spartans* 10.

cient and modern, have scornfully compared Sparta to the democratic, national ideal of Athens and have noted that after the mid-sixth century Sparta played a very minor role in the development of Greek art and literature. Here too thinking is often fuzzy; Athens was not perfect either, and if Spartan cultural independence dwindled, so too did that of most Greek states from the late sixth century onward. In its chosen fields of political and military activity Sparta was long highly successful and produced a number af outstanding leaders.

Spartan Conquest of the Peloponnesus (to 490 B.C.). The political and social system of Sparta was focused upon one primary aim, that of securing the domination of the Spartan "Equals" at home. The military machine that resulted was so far superior to that of the neighbors of Sparta that it was used by the kings of the sixth century to extend Spartan rule over virtually all the Peloponnesus, except for Argos, which was nonetheless crippled in the decisive battle of Thyrea in 546. In this extension the Spartans did not try to reduce conquered peoples to the level of the Messenian helots, for this would have extended their direct responsibility far too widely. Instead, the Spartans made their neighbors dependent allies, and since they threw out tyrannies in favor of oligarchies the upper classes in many districts welcomed Spartan protection.

Cleomenes, king *c.* 520–*c.* 490, was one of the greatest leaders in this expansion, but in 506 he failed to carry the Spartan allies into a full-scale attack on Clisthenic Athens. The result was a major reorganization of the Spartan alliance into an organization of two parts: the regular Spartan assembly on the one side and a congress of representatives from the allies on the other. Only a policy approved by both sides could be executed; Megara, Corinth, Tegea, Elis, and other states in the alliance thus might feel that they had a voice in common decisions.

By 500 Sparta had become the greatest military power in mainland Greece, and its aid was widely sought by the islanders and overseas Greeks as well. On the whole Spartan leaders followed a consistent policy of opposing outside intervention in Greece by Persia or by any other power; of maintaining their own dominance within Greece; and of fostering generally stable political conditions. The expansive tendencies of Athens were as yet too weak to present any real threat, and so Sparta and Athens were able to cooperate against the great Persian onslaughts which followed shortly after 500. As that struggle was to prove, Greece needed both the quick-witted, maritime genius of the Athenians and the firm, stable leadership of the Spartans.

The Mainland and Islands. From the sixth century onward Sparta and Athens are the states which we can best follow, but never in Greek history is it proper to concentrate solely upon these two leaders. Greece was divided into many independent units, on varying levels of cultural and political evolution. Each part in its own way played a role in the progress of the whole; from time to time now one, now another state had a considerable effect.

The Acarnanians, Aetolians, and other Greeks dwelling in the forests and fertile plains of northwest Greece remained backward tribal peoples. To their east lay the large but weak kingdom of Macedonia. This was not counted as Greek, though its stock was closely related; from Macedonia and Thrace came timber, ship's stores, and other materials to the Greek cities along the Aegean coast (see Map 11).

Just south of Macedonia lay the fertile plain of Thessaly, farmed by serfs for the great landlords. In the seventh century Thessaly grew powerful, not as a *polis,* but as a virtual kingdom under a war chief or *tagos.* During the First Sacred war, which resulted in the internationalization of Delphi, the Thessalians drove southward into central Greece, and for a time in the sixth century it appeared as if two powers from north and south, that is, Thessaly and Sparta, would gain mastery over all the intervening states. But the early promise of Thessaly was not so solidly based as was that of Sparta. The Thessalian cavalry, though good, was not supported by a solid infantry and was beaten several times in the sixth century by the stubborn natives of Boeotia and Phocis; the jealous Thessalian nobles refused to support their war chief; and the office of *tagos* was passed from one house to another. In the decline of Thessaly one can see how much strength the *polis* structure gave the other Greeks.

Throughout southern and central Greece most areas were organized as city-states, but various religious and political groupings tended to mitigate the inherent tendencies of the Greeks to local particularism. The Phocians formed a federal league of city-states and tribes; in Boeotia a league of city-states, more or less under the control of Thebes, existed throughout most of Greek history. One fringe state of Boeotia, Plataea, was allied to Athens; and another, Oropos, actually joined Athens. Many states and tribes belonged to the major religious league, the Amphictyony of Delphi. Very close cultural links, as between Boeotia and Attica or between Corinth and Argos, can also be detected.

Each of the Greek islands commonly formed a single state. Crete, which fell ever more into a backwater, was too large to be united, and Rhodes was divided into three states until much later. As trade and industry grew from the eighth century on, the islanders flourished. Aegina, in the Saronic gulf, was one of the earliest states to coin money (see Plate XVIII.A) and was as powerful on the sea as Athens down to 500; Naxos was outstanding under a tyrant Lygdamis, who was aided by Pisistratus; and Lygdamis in turn helped Polycrates to become tyrant of Samos c. 540.

Although attacked by a Spartan and Corinthian fleet, Polycrates held his position and dominated much of the Aegean until he was caught and crucified by the Persians about 523. His example of naval imperialism, the first in Greek history, suggests the growing commercial unification of the Aegean. The tunnel of Polycrates for a water supply, his harbor works, and the completion of a new temple of Hera on the largest scale ever attempted for an Aegean temple were the greatest physical works in Greece down to the end of the sixth century; to his lavish court he drew from Teos Anacreon and from Italy the poet Ibycus (active shortly after 550), a great composer of choral songs and love poetry. Famous jewelers, doctors, and other skilled men also graced Samos in its apogee.

The Western Greeks. Colonization of the shores of the central and western Mediterranean continued on into the sixth century, then slowly came to a halt. In Africa, in western Sicily, and in Spain the Greeks by this time were encroaching upon the preserves marked by Phoenician trading posts. These posts were collected into one great maritime empire by Carthage when Tyre fell under Assyrian control, and Carthage allied itself with the Etruscans of central Italy to stop the Greek expansion. One of the greatest battles took place off the new Greek settlement of Alalia in Corsica about 535; though it was won by the Greeks, they had to evacuate the colony. By 500, as we shall see more fully in studying the rise of Rome, the Carthaginians, Greeks, and Etruscans had battled each other to a standstill. In their stalemate they left the way open for a native power to conquer each separately.

The major Greek states of eastern Sicily and southern Italy, however, flourished magnificently. They built huge temples, some of which still survive at Paestum, Selinus, and Agrigentum (Acragas), and made statues of terra cotta and stone in patterns essentially like those of Greece but sometimes of a provincial or realistic flavor. Stesichorus, Ibycus, and other poets contributed to the growth of archaic literature; philosophic thought, introduced from the Aegean in the middle of the sixth century, took root quickly and fired native geniuses like Parmenides and Empedocles in the next century. The wealthy Etruscans had turned eagerly to Greek culture since the middle of the seventh century, and by 500 such native states as Segesta in Sicily and Rome in Italy were borrowing extensively from the attractive ideas and products of Hellas.

Like the home states the Greek cities of the west quarreled incessantly with each other regardless of the outside threats. Sybaris, the greatest *polis* of south Italy, turned toward democracy and fell into internal dissensions, which permitted its jealous rival Croton to destroy it utterly *c.* 510. Throughout the sixth century control of these Greek cities lay largely in the hands of landed aristocracies, but by 500 the Greeks of the west were progressing beyond this state. The result was a wave of tyrants, who employed the resources of their subjects in large mercenary armies and imperialism in the fifth century.

The Eastern Greeks. Even more prosperous — and even more seriously threatened — were the states at the other pole of the Greek world, the east coast of the Aegean. These began to rise in significance as the interior of Asia Minor became pacified and as Greek colonization penetrated the Black Sea. After the fall of Hittite civilization Asia Minor had been as backward as was Greece in the dark ages, but by the eighth century a consolidated kingdom of Phrygia had appeared, with a capital at Gordium. King Midas (Mita in Assyrian records) was the first foreign king to make dedications at Delphi and married the daughter of the king of Greek Cyme. About 705 Midas and the Phrygian kingdom fell victim to the invasion of the Cimmerians, a nomadic people forced out of south Russia by the Scythians. After crossing the Caucasus, the

Cimmerians threatened as far west as the Greek cities of Ionia and were beaten off by the Assyrians and the Lydians with difficulty.

The place of Phrygia was taken by the more southerly kingdom of Lydia, centered about Sardis. Under the Mermnad dynasty of Lydia, begun by the usurper Gyges (c. 687–52), Greek trade and ideas penetrated inland to a considerable degree. In return the Lydian kings cast envious eyes on the growing wealth of Miletus, Ephesus, Colophon, Smyrna, and other coastal city-states. By the reign of Croesus (561–47) all but Miletus had been subjugated. When Croesus was taken prisoner by the great Persian conqueror Cyrus, Persian generals took all the coastal towns and set up pro-Persian tyrants.

During much of the sixth century down to this event Ionian merchants traded their products of pottery, textiles, and metalwork from the Black Sea to Egyptian Naucratis, and from the Syrian coast to the colonies in Sicily. The heights of archaic architecture, sculpture, and poetry as well as the appearance of philosophy and history were also closely linked to the wealth of the cultured Greeks in Asia Minor, but by the close of the century leadership in most respects was passing back to mainland Greece.

ARCHAIC CIVILIZATION

The Arts. Some monuments of sixth-century architecture have already been noted in connection with Pisistratus of Athens and Polycrates of Samus. By land taxes, harbor tolls, and other dues the tyrants increased the revenues of the state, and this income they used in part to embellish their cities. So too, but on a lesser scale, did aristocratic circles.

All over the Greek world men were growing rich enough to rebuild wooden chapels into stone temples. These were still generally made from limestone or other easily worked stone which was stuccoed and painted in vivid colors. The form of the temple was that evolved in the age of revolution, but architects steadily refined its esthetic and optical principles. The great international shrines of Olympia, Delphi, Delos, Eleusis, and others also began at this time to assume a monumental dress which included gateways, porticoes, treasuries, many monuments, and even theaters about the temples and their altars; a sacred precinct thenceforth was an extended area, filled with the riches of the Greek world.

As the urban centers of the city-states grew larger and more complex, secular public buildings became necessary. The most expensive item was that of walls for the whole city; market places received fountain buildings, council chambers, and the like; harbors were improved and were guarded by moles.

The temples and the temple precincts were increasingly embellished by reliefs and statues. On the Acropolis at Athens stood a host of elegantly gowned maidens (*korai*). Fourteen of these have survived inasmuch as they were later discarded and used as fill after the Persian destruction of Athens in 480; this collection admirably illustrates the firm Peloponnesian, soft Ionian, insular, and local forces at work in Pisistratid workshops.[4] Statues of nude male athletes (*kouroi*) have also been found in quantities all over the Greek world. Sometimes these may have been used as grave monuments, as were also stone lions; in Pisistratid Athens the wealthy nobles erected great shafts, carved with reliefs and crowned by a sphinx, over their tombs. While this work manifested the growing skill and freer outlook of the sculptor, archaic conventions in pose and a basically abstract analysis were still dominant; one famous attribute is the inward-brooding smile on many archaic faces.[5]

Among the increasingly varied minor arts the work of goldsmiths, sealcutters, and others became more refined, but the leading elements of Greece still appreciated handsome pottery. Corinthian pottery, dominant at the beginning of the sixth century, sank away into sterile repetition of old patterns, and most other local forms of pottery likewise declined. In their place rose ever higher the Athenian styles. By 550 Attic black-figure ware had replaced Corinthian vases in most markets; then, from about 530, Athenian potters produced red-figure vases. In these the figures were left in the basic wash color of the vase while the rest of the surface was covered with a heavy brown slip which became black in the skillful

[4] The finest Acropolis *kore* is No. 679 of 540–30 B.C., a little less than life-size (Plate XII). This lovely lady is known as the "peplos kore," since she is dressed in a Doric peplos over an Ionian chiton; but under her attire one senses a body vibrant with life, which was mastered by a dignified repose. Some of the original paint (red hair, irises, lips, black pupils, eyebrows, eyelashes) has survived; generally ancient sculpture was painted, or in later days waxed in the flesh parts.

[5] The famous "archaic smile" appeared from about 580 B.C. onward (see Plate XII and the Etruscan imitation on Plate XXI), and expressed a sense of life and greater interest in three-dimensional modeling of the face.

firing. As a result minute details could be picked out on the red figures by black lines. This style of pottery, which flourished on across the classic era, was the most famous ever produced in Greece.[6]

Letters. Although most of archaic literature, like the Acropolis *korai,* did not please the tastes of later ages, we know the names of a great number of poets from the sixth century. In the fragments that survive, the aristocratic outlook is visible in both its good and its bad aspects. The most famous of all poetesses, Sappho of Mytilene on Lesbos (active about 600 B.C.), poured out her love for the maidens who lived with her and celebrated their marriages to suitors from as far afield as Lydia. Her contemporary and compatriot, Alcaeus, illustrates the bitterly conservative and factional spirit of many nobles in his scurrilous attacks on Pittacus, an elected reformer of Mytilene who was much like Solon at Athens. Both Sappho and Alcaeus were lyric poets, as were Anacreon, Ibycus, and Simonides at the courts of Polycrates and the Pisistratids.

An even fuller view of the aristocratic spirit wells forth in the elegiac work of Theognis of Megara (active shortly after 550), who wrote down for a beloved younger man the counsels he himself had learned from his forebears. This collection of didactic sayings was much expanded after his death and has survived entire inasmuch as it was enduringly popular. The 1388 lines attributed to Theognis show that the well-born no longer always controlled public life and were not necessarily as rich as were upstarts; but the poet asserted fiercely that only the "good" had true virtue. Theognis was bitter, suspicious, even pessimistic; yet he was a true Greek in his clear view of life, his forceful outlook, and his attention to the human plane. These qualities Solon shared but tempered with a firmer hope in justice.

The Ionian Philosophers. In the sixth century some of the intellectual leaders of Greece began a great rational analysis of the natural world as governed by comprehensible law and a deliberate study of man as a self-

---

[6] On Plate XVII.A Dionysus sails across a fairy sea; from his ship grow grape-heavy vines (note the eye on the prow, customary to help a ship find its course). This cup was painted by Exekias (active 550–30 B.C.), one of the greatest masters of the Attic black-figure style. Plate XVII.B illustrates a red-figure cup by Euphronius, about 510 B.C. The legend reads, "Leagros is beautiful (*kalos*)"—a term applied to noble youths. The more realistic tone of the later cup suggests the great change which took place between the archaic and the classical outlooks.

moving, thinking agent within that world. This analysis was called *philosophia,* or "love of wisdom," and it embraced in one unified approach what we today distinguish as philosophy and science.

Basically the concepts of the philosophers, and still more their logical, analytical attitude, were a refinement of the fundamental qualities of Greek civilization as exhibited from Protogeometric pottery onward. Yet not until the sixth century were the Greeks sufficiently self-conscious, confident, and venturesome to concentrate directly and openly upon the problems of philosophy. It is not accidental that the trail-blazers lived in Ionia, rather than in Greece proper; for the conventional bonds of ancestral views probably had less weight overseas. To a limited extent, too, the thinkers of Ionia may have had closer contacts with the vast body of factual knowledge built up in the Near East, but this was secondary. Greek philosophy incarnated the Hellenic outlook and appeared at the time and place it did as an almost necessary consequence of the free and logical qualities developed during the archaic age.

The first philosopher was Thales of Miletus, who lived at the beginning of the sixth century. He seems only to have talked about his ideas, rather than writing them down, and much which was later told of him was mythical. The one sure point is that he believed the earth floated on water, and that water was the primary substance from which all else was made. This concept perhaps came from Egypt originally and had appeared in the *Theogony* ascribed to Hesiod; the important aspect of Thales' treatment is that he viewed the development of the world as due to natural, rational causes.

Equally significant is the fact that with Thales there began an ever more logical and critical analysis of the problems thus raised. His successor, Anaximander of Miletus (active about 550), wrote in prose and presented a far more complicated view of the origin of things. The world, to Anaximander, evolved out of an "unlimited," infinite substance by the interaction of the opposing forces of hot and cold, wet and dry. His successor in turn, Anaximenes, refined the motive forces of Anaximander's theory by introducing the quantitative difference of thickening and thinning of a primary substance which he called air.

In many of their assumptions the first philosophers of western civilization jumped at once to views popular today. They argued, for instance, that the world was created from one primary substance and (in

Anaximander) that living matter had evolved through stages including fishes. In other respects their views seem to have been naïve reflections of primitive superstitions and were expressed in such figurative language that they cannot always be easily understood. These men were not scientific experimenters; rather they proceeded by applying native logic and intuition to the factual evidence and presumptions which happened to be on hand. Yet the Ionian philosophers, living as they did in a rapidly changing world where deep-rooted convention and religious shibboleths were singularly powerless, have been justly reverted by later ages for their inception of a naturalistic, man-centered, rational analysis of the physical world.

Pythagoras and Xenophanes. Once begun, the philosophic approach jumped first to the other fringe of the Greek world. This transfer was the work particularly of two men, Pythagoras and Xenophanes, who migrated from Ionia to the western colonies.

Pythagoras of Samos, then of Croton from *c.* 530 on, broadened the field of philosophy more than any other thinker in history was to do. Some of his work we should call scientific. He is, thus, famous for his demonstration that the sum of the squares on two sides of a right-angled triangle is equal to the square of the hypotenuse. The fact had long been known and understood in the Near East; but Pythagoras provided a rational demonstration of the general reasons for its validity. Thenceforth Greek geometry progressed rapidly as an abstract analysis. Pythagoras also discovered a basic principle in harmonics, that the pitch of a string depends on its length.

These concepts were minor aspects of his great philosophic-religious view of the world, which he preached to a band of devoted disciples striving to improve their souls. Those on a lower plane avoided certain foods, like beans, and improper actions; the more advanced contemplated the divine, "tuneful" order of the world through the medium of geometry and harmonics. Thus they could escape transmigration of their souls, a concept which may have made its way across the Persian empire from India. In Pythagorean thought the soul and body of man were distinct, and Pythagorean mysticism was to affect many later Greek thinkers.

Xenophanes of Colophon, then of Sicily and perhaps of Elea from *c.* 545 on, was a biting critic of many aspects of the aristocratic outlook, including the luxury of his homeland and the Greek emphasis upon athletics. He was deeply skeptical of man's ability to reach certain truth, a skepticism which applied particularly to the conventional religion of his day. Homer and Hesiod, he averred, had "attributed to the gods all things that are shameful and a reproach among mankind: theft, adultery, and mutual deception"; [7] but in an even more pregnant criticism he noted that if oxen and horses and lions could make works of art, they would make their gods like oxen, horses, and lions. Nonetheless Xenophanes had strongly positive and ethical views about the nature of the divine, unknowable force which moved the world.

In these latter figures the strongly religious undercurrent of Greek civilization is apparent. Most men in 500 B.C. undoubtedly lived their days in the traditional patterns handed down from their ancestors; and even on higher intellectual levels Greek philosophy was always to combine scientific, religious, and other strands of thought to a degree scarcely comprehensible today. By the early fifth century, however, geometry, astronomy, and medicine assumed the quality of independent, rational disciplines, and philosophers were forced deeper beneath the visible surface of life to brood on its fundamental metaphysical problems. Formal logic, too, was much advanced by the increasingly rigorous analyses which made use of mathematics, induction, and even experiments at points.

Each sage, it may be observed, tended to be dogmatic in his pronouncements, and Pythagoreans were long to quote "He said" with reference to their master Pythagoras. Yet in the wide distribution of Greek cultural centers and in the wide freedom allowed to thought the ideas of any one man lay exposed to the relentless criticism of the market place.

THE GREEK WORLD IN 500 B.C.

By the end of the sixth century the main qualities of Hellenic civilization were well developed, and stood in clear contrast to those of the Near East. In saying this one must remember that the Greeks owed much to the first home of ancient civilization and that the economic, social, and religious frame of life was very similar in both areas. Yet the fundamental tone of Greek culture was a new achievement for mankind.

[7] Xenophanes, fragment 11 (Diels); tr. Kathleen Freeman.

Everywhere men firmly believed in the ultimate mastery of the gods, but Greek artists, poets, and thinkers now expressed a concept of man which gave him far more dignity. Economically, thus, the Greek commonly had an independent place, even though his homeland remained poverty-stricken in contrast to the centers of the Near East. Politically, too, the highest form of organization in the Aegean basin was the city-state, built upon principles of earthly justice as safeguarded by basic views of the duties and rights of the citizen body; in the Near East power lay in the hands of imperial autocrats. A famous, though fictitious, story of an interview between the Greek sage Solon and the Lydian monarch Croesus points the moral: when Croesus, after showing Solon all his treasures, triumphantly asked him who was the happiest man in the world, Solon gravely replied, "Tellus the Athenian." When pressed for his reasons by the irate ruler, Solon said, "He had been an honest man, had had good children, a competent estate, and died bravely in battle for his country." [8]

The dead weight of ancestral custom, which bound men together tightly into units and governed them by superstition, was only slightly less powerful in Greece than in the Near East, but the qualification is all important. Greek civilization was sufficiently dynamic to continue to progress and change, though within a fundamentally solid framework. For example, the average inhabitant of Greece was a farmer, whose object in life was simply to raise enough food for his existence; still, an economic spirit of progress motivated many elements in the growing Greek cities. Greek political evolution had produced such developed city-states as Athens and Sparta, a process which was accompanied by abundant turmoil and stress but not by utter breakdown. So too culturally a dynamic drive led the Greeks to create virtually new logical and esthetic attitudes.

If a completely dispassionate observer had calculated the chances for further advance in Greece as against those of the Near East in 500 B.C., he might nonetheless have awarded the palm to the latter. Firmly organized in one imperial state, the Near East had a much older, more deeply rooted, and polished civilization. The Greeks, on the other hand, were split into many jealously independent political units. Internally they

[8] Plutarch, *Solon* 27.4 (tr. Dryden-Clough); the same story appears in Herodotus 1.30.

tended to factional and class strife. Intellectually as well as socially the spirit of competition and mutual criticism was rife.

Only as one probes beneath the boiling surface of sixth-century Greece can one recognize the vigor and vitality of the civilization which the Greeks had created during their long centuries of virtual isolation. Outwardly amazing as the Greek victory over the forthcoming Persian assault was to be, it was only another testimony to that vigor; and the Greeks were to go on after defeating the Persians to expand their culture to even greater and more widely attractive attainments.

BIBLIOGRAPHY

Sources. The earliest stone temple in Greece proper of which some columns are still standing as originally constructed is the Doric temple of Apollo at Corinth, built to replace an earlier temple about 540 B.C.; not long thereafter the so-called Basilica (probably a temple of Hera) was built at Paestum. Ground plans, architectural members, and sculptured fragments have survived for a good many temples, including the Ionic structure of Artemis at Ephesus (with sculptured drums given by Croesus), the Doric Hekatompedon on the Acropolis at Athens, the Doric temple of Artemis at Corcyra, and the Doric temple of Hera near Paestum. We have also good evidence for the Pisistratid hall of the mysteries at Eleusis and a number of other religious and secular buildings, particularly the dainty marble treasuries of the Siphnians and the Athenians at Delphi. Sculpture and pottery became ever more abundant; Attic red-figured wares were buried alike with Etruscan lords in Italy and with Scythian chiefs in south Russia.

Although writers of history began to appear in the sixth century, none of their works has survived. Only for Hecataeus of Miletus (active about 500) do we have some fragments of his geographical studies and collections of early legends. Herodotus, the historian of the Persian wars, tapped memories going back to Pisistratus and Polycrates; but, careful researcher that he was, refused to give much credit to earlier legends. The next great historian, Thucydides, commented on the sixth century more sparingly.

Centuries later Plutarch of Chaeronea (c. A.D. 46–after 120) composed an invaluable series of parallel lives of Greek and Roman worthies. His lives of Thesus and Lycurgus have some useful information alongside a great deal of legend; his life of Solon contains very important quotations from Solon's poetry. Aristotle's *Constitution of Athens* (tr. K. von Fritz and E. Kapp [New York: Hafner paperback, 1950]) collected a great deal of what was known of early Athenian constitutional development; other bits were preserved by the Atthidographers, or writers on Athenian history and antiquities. We have thus a list of archons going back to 683 B.C., which was used for dating purposes inasmuch as the archon proper or *archon eponymos* gave his name to the year, as "the year of Themistocles."

Inscriptions are still scarce in this period but include such material as a democratic reorganization of Chios (M. N. Tod, *Greek Historical Inscriptions,* I [2d ed.; Oxford: Oxford University Press, 1946], No. 1) and a probably Pisistratid settlement on Salamis (Tod No. 11). By the end of the century most Greek states of any commercial significance were issuing coins. Egyptian papyri have increased our knowledge of Sappho and Alcaeus, but the work of all the poets except Theognis has come down in very fragmentary state. See Loeb Clasical Library, *Lyra Graeca and Elegy and Iambus.*

Further Reading. A. R. Burn, *Lyric Age of Greece* (New York: St. Martins, 1960), sums up political developments. For Athens, see also C. Hignett, *History of the Athenian Constitution to the End of the Fifth Century* B.C. (Oxford: Oxford University Press, 1970); and on Solon, Kathleen Freeman, *Life and Work of Solon* (New York: Arno, 1976), and W. J. Woodhouse, *Solon the Liberator* (New York: Octagon, 1965). For Sparta see W. G. Forrest, *History of Sparta 950–192* B.C. (New York: Norton, 1969); several more recent works add nothing of value. The Greeks in the west and east are discussed in the works noted in Bibliography, Chapter 10; for Cyprus, a meeting place of Greek and Near Eastern culture, see G. F. Hill, *History of Cyprus,* Vol. I (Cambridge: Cambridge University Press, 1940), though Swedish and other excavations have since broadened our knowledge.

Denys Page has a detailed but good discussion of *Sappho and Alcaeus* (Oxford: Oxford University Press, 1980). Greek art in this period is discussed by J. D. Beazley, *Development of Attic Black-figure* (Berkeley: University of California Press, 1964); J. Boardman, *Athenian Black Figure Vases* (New York: Oxford University Press, 1974), and *Greek Sculp-*

ture: The Archaic Period (London: Thames & Hudson, 1978), both excellent; Gisela M. A. Richter, *Kouroi* (3d ed.; New York: Phaidon, 1970), and *Korai* (New York: Phaidon, 1968); and Humfry Payne and G. Mackworth-Young, *Archaic Marble Sculpture from the Acropolis* (2d ed.; New York: Morrow, 1951). Probably the best introduction to early Greek philosophy is G. S. Kirk and J. E. Raven, *Presocratic Philosophers* (Cambridge: Cambridge paperback, 1960); John Burnet, *Early Greek Philosophy* (New York: Barnes & Noble, 1963), though much older, is somewhat simpler.

V

THE CLASSIC AGE OF GREECE

13

THE GREEKS AGAINST
THE PERSIANS

To describe in measured tones the Greek achievements in the fifth century b.c. is well-nigh impossible, for never in the history of the world have so few people done so much in the space of two or three generations. Impressive in itself, the classic era was also a seminal influence for all later western civilization.

The potentialities of Hellenic culture were gathered together at this time in a great, many-sided outburst. In literature the forms of tragedy, comedy, and history were evolved. Philosophers deepened their views of the basic qualities of the physical world, sharpened the tools of formal logic in their bitter debates, and came more clearly to grips with the ethical problems of human life. The first true science appeared in the field of medicine; education became a subject of conscious debate and practice. The triumphs of the classic arts, especially at Athens, enshrined standards of harmony, proportion, and beauty which have recurrently been the envy of subsequent eras. Beside these cultural advances went great economic progress and political evolution, the latter of which produced at Athens the first great democracy the world had ever seen.

The boundaries of the fifth century are marked by two great sets of wars — quite different in type and, unfortunately, markedly dissimilar in their effects. At the beginning of the period the westward march of Persian might finally brought its armies and navies into Greece proper, where they suffered shattering and amazing defeats. The victory of the small Greek city-states over the mammoth Persian empire is a mighty testimonial to the great powers stored up in Hellenic civilization during the archaic period, and the self-confidence which resulted from the victories was an important element in the spirit of the classic era.

As the decades of the fifth century wore on, the two greatest states of Greece, Athens and Sparta, stood more and more at odds. The upshot was a series of bitter struggles collectively called the Peloponnesian war (431–04 B.C.), which ended in the complete defeat of Athens. Few wars have had more devastating results. By the close of the fifth century long, somber shadows were falling across its sunlit glow. But even in the height of the classic age men could be passionate, vindictive, and irrational. The cities which fell in the path of Athens were sometimes punished by the execution of all male citizens, and superstitious barbarism lurked not far below the surface throughout the Greek world. The period to be surveyed in this part is a remarkable revelation of the potentialities of the human mind for good and for evil.

RISE OF THE PERSIAN EMPIRE

Persian Conquest of the Near East (559–486 B.C.). From the beginnings of agricultural life in the Aegean basin the Greek world had been repeatedly in contact with the Near East and had profited culturally from those contacts. The dark ages saw an important break in this tie; then, from the eighth century onward, economic and cultural interchange had been resumed on an ever larger scale. Serious political connections came only late in the sixth century, but from that point the history of Greece and the Near East began to mesh more closely.

The Greek development to this date has concerned us in previous chapters; it is now time to review what had been happening in the Fertile Crescent. As noted in Chapter 6, the Near East suffered seriously in the wave of invasions and the general breakdown at the close of the second millennium B.C. Small states such as the Phoenicians and Hebrews had then had a brief opportunity for independent action. When commerce and industry revived, the Near East achieved an urbane, superficially attractive, cosmopolitan culture which was eventually matched in the political field by the rise of the Assyrian empire. This had fallen in 612 to the Medians of Iran and the Chaldaeans of Babylonia.

The resulting split was only temporary, for an obscure Persian king,

Cyrus (559–30), gained the support of the warrior nobles of Iran and led them in a great, sudden outrush which created the Persian empire. Few conquests in history have been so swift. Media fell in 550, Lydia in 547, Babylon in 539; Cyrus died in central Asia, defending his northeastern frontier on the Jaxartes river against the Massagetai nomads. Egypt, the last part of the Near East proper, fell to his son Cambyses in 525. To explain the Persian success one needs to take into account the ever growing cultural and economic unity of the Near East, but some weight must be assigned also to the cohesiveness and vigor of the Iranian nobil-ity and to the ability of the Persian kings.

After the suicide of Cambyses, who seems to have become mentally deranged, a bloody civil war broke out in 522–21. The victor was a collateral member of the Achaemenid royal house, Darius (521–486). In his long reign the Persian realm was extended to the fringe of the Indus river on the east and into Europe on the west. More important yet, Darius organized the Persian empire along lines which it was to follow down to 330 B.C., when the last Persian king fell before Alexander of Macedonia (see Map 9).

Organization of the Persian Empire. The Persian empire was an au-tocracy under "the great king, king of kings, king of the countries pos-sessing many kinds of people, king of this great earth far and wide."[1] In sculptured reliefs which have survived, the monarch looms out, sharply distinguished by his square beard cut off at the waist and dressed in tiara, purple robe, and white or crimson trousers. He sits on a high throne with a stool to protect his feet from contact with the ground; a parasol shades his head; and a fly-flapper guards his sacred majesty. In boastful inscriptions, including the famous Behistun trilingual procla-mation by Darius, the Persian kings underlined their absolutism, their justice, and their belief that they held their powers by divine grant. In Egypt the Persian king succeeded the pharaohs and was a god on earth; in Babylon, Marduk, according to Cyrus, had sought a righteous prince and found his choice in Cyrus; among the Persians themselves Darius, who was a Zoroastrian, proclaimed that "by the grace of Ahura-Mazda Darius is the king."[2]

This divine-right monarchy was necessarily tempered in practice. Six

---

[1] Erich F. Schmidt, *Persepolis,* I (Chicago: University of Chicago Press, 1953), p. 65 (gate inscription).
[2] *Persepolis,* I, p. 63 (terrace inscription).

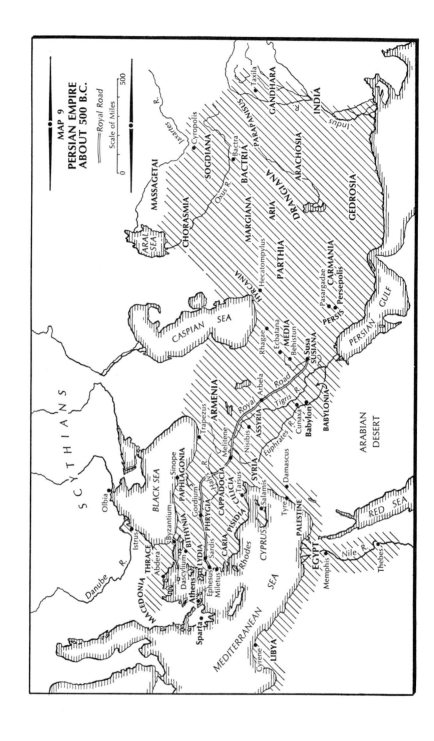

MAP 9
**PERSIAN EMPIRE
ABOUT 500 B.C.**

— Royal Road
Scale of Miles

0   500

of the great Persian noble families, which had helped Darius during the civil war, had special rights; and the Persians as a whole formed a privileged group. The nobles, in particular, were advisers, officials, and cavalry in time of war; young nobles were taught in cadet schools "to ride, to draw the bow and to speak the truth." [3] Persian commoners were exempt from taxes and furnished the most solid block of heavy infantry, including the king's bodyguard of "Immortals"; as garrison troops and as officials the Persians were scattered widely over the empire.

The empire itself was divided into tributary kingdoms and great provinces, called satrapies from the Median word *satrap* or governor. Under Darius, whom the Persians termed a "huckster," each of the 20 satrapies at that time was required to yield specific quantities of tax in money, horses, and other items and provided contingents of ships or soldiers to the Persian navy and army. The satraps were virtually local kings, who often inherited their positions and had wide powers in local government and foreign affairs; but they were checked by royally appointed secretaries, garrison commanders, and traveling inspectors, called the king's "eyes and ears." Roads radiating from the central capital of Susa, along with Ecbatana and Babylon, were much improved and carried the imperial post. The most famous of these roads was the Royal road from Ephesus on the Aegean coast to Susa, three months long, which was much traveled over the centuries by Greek ambassadors, traders, learned men, and captives of war.

On the whole it may be doubted that the Persian empire was more efficiently organized than the Assyrian state had been, or that the Persian army was more effective. The Persians had to contend with repeated rebellions in Egypt, among their Greek subjects, and elsewhere, but they were able to maintain general control over the largest state yet created in the Near East. Much of the area had been broken to the yoke by the Assyrian imperialists, and the fact that the Persian rule was of a more easy-going nature perhaps promoted loyalty. Local styles of government and local customs were generally tolerated, as among the Jews, who created a temple-state about Jerusalem. Economically the more advanced parts of the empire do not seem to have progressed markedly, but they had the benefits of peace, good communications, and a stable coinage of gold darics and silver shekels, which served as a medium of exchange

[3] Herodotus 1.136.

especially for the Greek subjects and for mercenaries. The northern and eastern districts of the empire, which already had begun to develop irrigation systems and towns in the major oases, progressed further on the path of civilization, a development which reached on down into the independent states of India.

Persian Culture. The most valuable contributions of the Persians to the Near East were political unification and military defense against the nomads of central Asia. Culturally the Persians were far less civilized than most of their subjects of the Fertile Crescent, and they showed originality only in the field of religion.

From early days the Indo-European masters of the Iranian uplands had worshiped *daevas* or spirits, akin to those known by the Aryans of India; the priests of this cult were called *magi*. At some uncertain date in the sixth century the fiery reformer Zoroaster rose in eastern Iran to reject the purely ritual quality of contemporary worship, its magic, and the belief in many gods. Instead, he stressed an ethical faith centered about the god of light and truth, Ahura-Mazda, who was opposed by the evil force Ahriman. All men in this world must support the good by their deeds or else serve the spirits of darkness. In the end would come a Last Judgment which would send the good to heaven and the bad to hell. Zoroaster's powerful views became an enduring part of Iranian religion, though not to the exclusion of the main polytheistic tradition preserved by the magi priests. Darius above all other rulers adhered to Ahura-Mazda and in a great inscription at Naqsh-i-Rustam boasted, "What is right I love and what is not right I hate . . . the man who decides for the lie I hate." [4]

Apart from the Zoroastrian writings of the *Avesta* and the boastful inscriptions of the kings the Persians seem to have had no literature. Their own language, for which they had constructed a simple cuneiform syllabary, began to yield even for purposes of administration to Aramaic, which became a common tongue across the lowlands of the Near East. In science the main achievements of the era were due to Babylonian astronomers and mathematicians, who came to be able to predict lunar eclipses and perfected a place-value notation; their knowledge was tapped both by the Greeks in the west and by the Indians in the south-

[4] A. T. Olmstead, *History of the Persian Empire* (Chicago: University of Chicago Press, 1948), p. 125.

east. The arts in the Persian period derived from the many earlier cultures of the Near East and were marked more by magnificence and polish than by originality.

The best preserved Persian monument is the secluded royal fortress and treasury of Persepolis. Here, on a majestic site over a mile high, Darius built a great terrace from 512 on; this he and his successors adorned with a maze of staircases, palaces, colonnaded audience halls, and other buildings. The whole structure was about twice the size of the Acropolis at Athens, and the contrast between Persepolis and the sacred hill of Athena illuminates sharply some fundamental differences between Greeks and Persians. While the Parthenon and other temples of the Acropolis were erected in honor of the patron deities of a free citizenry, the complex of Persepolis celebrated the greatness of the king of kings. His titles appeared on the window sills; he himself was depicted on his throne on the doorjambs, supported by figures representing the satrapies; the staircases were adorned with repetitious scenes from the New Year's festival — especially processions of lively Persian and Median courtiers and guards and also lines of envoys with the taxes and tribute of the empire.[5]

The art of Persepolis is, at first sight, impressive in its majesty; but beside the graceful, dynamic, humane feeling imparted by the Parthenon reliefs the spirit of the Persian work is solemn, static, and purely decorative. On the Persepolis reliefs, true, there is a rich diversity of local costumes, befitting the great variety of the Near Eastern peoples, whereas the Athenian men and women of the Parthenon frieze — unified in the spirit of the *polis* — are externally alike; yet these latter figures are moved by a spiritual force which is totally absent in the Persian parades. The grandeur of Persepolis nonetheless manifests the mammoth strength of a great empire, which was a serious threat to the disunited Greeks.

[5] The great audience hall (*apadana*) of Darius was approached by 2 staircases, each with exactly the same decorated surface of some 300 feet. Plate XVI illustrates from these long processions a group of tribute-bearers, presumably Cilicians. The plastic quality of the figures was probably due to Greek influence and even to Greek workmen; but they were not encouraged to enliven the rather tubular, simplified bodies. Originally the relief glittered with such bright colors as turquoise blue, scarlet, emerald green, purple, and yellow. For the Parthenon reliefs, compare Plate XV.

First Contacts with the Greeks (547–490 B.C.). When Cyrus conquered Lydia, his general Harpagus drove on to the Aegean coast and annexed all the Greek cities of the area, which were unable to form a united front against the threat; their appeal to Sparta brought no practical help. The citizens of Phocaea and Teos abandoned their homes and settled in the western Mediterranean and the north Aegean coast; individual poets, philosophers, and artists sought freedom in Greece or south Italy; but the bulk of the Greek population clung to their old homes. To supervise the cities the Persians installed tyrants, who were subject to the Persian satraps at Sardis and Dascylium. In the building inscription of the royal palace at Susa, Ionians are named as workers alongside Egyptians, Babylonians, Medes, and others; and Greek artistic styles had a powerful influence from the inception of Persian royal building. Along the African coast other Greeks, settled in Cyrene, paid tribute to Persia after its conquest of Egypt, as did the Greeks in Cyprus.

The strength of the Persian realm soon led it to extend its rule across the Hellespont into Europe proper. In particular, Darius himself conducted a great expedition northward across the Danube in 513, but his effort to conquer the Scythians shattered on the great open plains of south Russia, where the nomads could avoid a set battle. Darius' army lost heavily and barely managed to make its way back to the bridge of boats constructed across the Danube. Persian mastery, however, was extended along the north coast of the Aegean as far as the tributary kingdom of Macedonia.

Although the Ionian cities seem not to have been as prosperous under Persian rule and chafed at their lack of independence, the revolt of the Greeks which broke out in 499 B.C. was due principally to the machinations of the ambitious tyrant of Miletus, Aristagoras. To secure wider support in Ionia the rebels proclaimed democracy and expelled the pro-Persian tyrants; then they sought aid from the free Greeks on the west side of the Aegean. Cleomenes of Sparta would not commit his forces so far from home; but Athens was more sympathetic and furnished 20 warships, "the beginning of ills between the Greeks and the barbarians," as the famous historian of the Persian wars, Herodotus, later put it.[6] With this aid and with five ships from Eretria on the island of Euboea the Ionians first seized the offensive in 498 and made a lightning attack

[6] Herodotus 5.97.

inland on Sardis, which they burned. Then the Athenians withdrew, and the Greeks of Asia Minor passed to the defensive despite the advice of the clearer-sighted Hecataeus that they become masters of the sea.

Slowly but inexorably, the Persians reconquered first the island of Cyprus, which had also revolted; then Caria; and finally in 495 defeated the league navy at Lade off Miletus after the Samian and Lesbian contingents deserted. To teach the Greeks a lesson, Miletus itself, the largest city of the whole Aegean, was destroyed the next year. The son-in-law of Darius, Mardonius, consolidated Persian rule along the north coast of the Aegean, though a Persian fleet was lost at Mt. Athos in bad weather; in 490 a moderate-sized expeditionary force under Datis and Artaphernes was dispatched across the Aegean to punish Eretria and Athens.

THE PERSIAN ATTACKS

Marathon (490 B.C.). The expedition of Datis and Artaphernes began the great Persian wars, which were to last without formal interruption down to 449. On the one side stood a huge empire, heir to the ancient civilizations of the Near East, rich in men and wealth, which responded to a single will. On the other side was a congeries of tiny states, each of which numbered its citizen warriors by hundreds and a few thousands. During the first attack, indeed, Athens stood alone save for aid from Plataea; for the Spartans, who promised help against a Persian invasion of Greece proper, could not move until they had completed the festival of the Carneia. Even Athens was not unified in its resistance. It had once, in 508, come close to accepting Persian overlordship to protect itself from Sparta; now Hippias, the ex-tyrant, accompanied the Persian force and could hope to gain treacherous support from the conservative elements of the city, which were discontented with the Clisthenic reforms.

As the Persian expedition moved across the Aegean, it sacked the island of Naxos (see Map 10). Eretria was taken after a six-day siege, thanks to internal treachery, and the captive Eretrians were shipped off to a new home near Susa, three months inland from their native Aegean. Then Datis and Artaphernes disembarked their army of cavalry and infantry, perhaps about 20,000 in all, on the plain of Marathon on the east coast of Attica, to give the Pisistratid faction a chance to raise internal revolt. The Athenians sent off to Sparta their runner Philip-

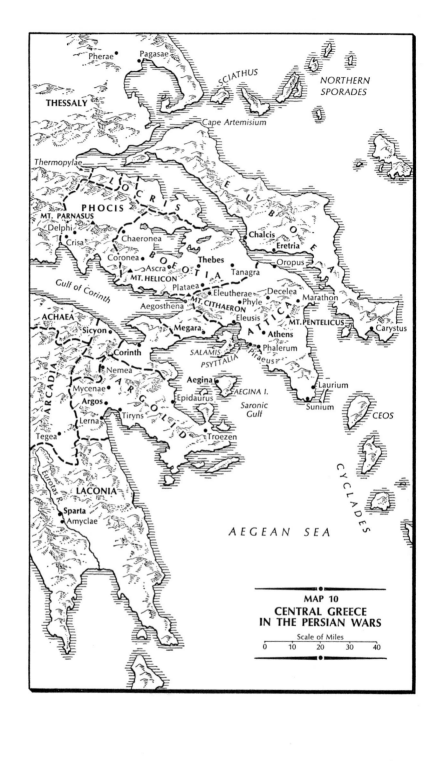

Pherae

Pagasae

THESSALY

SCIATHUS

NORTHERN
SPORADES

Cape Artemisium

Thermopylae

L O C R I S

PHOCIS
MT. PARNASUS

Delphi

Crisa

Chaeronea

Coronea

Ascra

MT. HELICON

Thebes

Tanagra

B O E O T I A

Plataea

Aegosthena

MT. CITHAERON

Eleutherae

Phyle

Decelea

Marathon

Chalcis

Eretria

Oropus

E U B O E A

Gulf of Corinth

ACHAEA

Sicyon

Corinth

Nemea

Mycenae

Argos

Lerna

Tiryns

Tegea

ARCADIA

A R G O L I D

Epidaurus

Megara

SALAMIS

PSYTTALIA

Aegina

AEGINA I.

Troezen

Eleusis

Athens

Phalerum

Piraeus

A T T I C A

MT. PENTELICUS

Laurium

Sunium

Carystus

CEOS

Saronic
Gulf

C Y C L A D E S

Eurotas R.

LACONIA

Sparta

Amyclae

AEGEAN SEA

MAP 10
CENTRAL GREECE
IN THE PERSIAN WARS

Scale of Miles

| 0 | 10 | 20 | 30 | 40 |

pides, who covered 140 miles and delivered their call for help the next day; the Athenian and Plataean army of some 10,000 hoplites marched out to the hills overlooking the plain. Its titular commander was Callimachus, the polemarch, who presided over the council of ten generals; but the leading spirit was the general Miltiades (*c.* 550–489), one of the greatest military geniuses Athens ever produced.

Miltiades persuaded half of his colleagues, including the well-known leader Aristides, that the strategic situation urgently called for an Athenian attack before dissension arose behind them. Tactically, however, the Athenians were hampered by their inferior numbers and lack of cavalry and dared not come down in the open. After several days of waiting a sudden opportunity came when Ionian soldiers of the Persian force secretly sent word by night that the Persian cavalry was gone. Although our source, Herodotus, is far from clear, it appears that the Persian leaders had grown weary of waiting and were embarking their forces, cavalry first, to sail around to Athens proper.

Miltiades at once arrayed the Athenians in a heavy wing formation and weakened center and at daybreak led the hoplites down to battle. The Persians fought bravely and broke the Athenian center, but they were crushed on the wings by the more heavily armored Greeks. Eventually the Persians broke, and the survivors waded out to embark on their ships. Datis and Artaphernes sailed hastily around the Attic promontory to Athens, but Miltiades had swiftly led his army back overland to meet the threat; and the Persian expedition made its way back across the Aegean. It had lost 6400 in the battle; the Athenians, 192 (including Callimachus), who were buried in a mound which still dominates the plain of Marathon today. The Spartan army, finally free to move, came up a few days after the victory, inspected the battlefield, and praised the Athenians.

Gathering of the Full Storm (490–81 B.C.). Although Marathon involved only a limited number of Persians and Greeks, it was of incalculable value to the Athenians and Spartans in proving that the enemy could be beaten. The dramatist Aeschylus wished to be remembered by posterity primarily as having been a "Marathon fighter," and a contemporary epigram praised the dead for saving Hellas from slavery. To the Persians, however, Marathon served only as a warning that a larger force would be needed for what, in the king's eyes, must have seemed merely a matter of punishing a recalcitrant, not very civilized people on one of his far-flung frontiers. Darius accordingly set plans in motion for a full-scale attack but was diverted by an Egyptian revolt. After his death in 486 Xerxes (486–65) first subdued Egypt and a brief revolt in Babylonia, and then renewed preparations. In the fall of 481 he came down to Sardis, where his army assembled. Herodotus gives us the wildly inflated figure of 5,000,000 in all, including camp followers, but the actual fighting force can scarcely have been more than 150,000 or so. The Persian navy, which made itself ready in Ionian harbors, consisted of about 660 Phoenician and Ionian warships.

The Greeks had had 10 years in which to prepare for the next Persian assault. As was their wont, they had spent their time mainly in internecine wars and internal dissensions; but more or less by accident they had forged certain weapons which were to be of decisive value in the approaching battle.

One of these was the unification of Athenian political strength. In the violent contentions of Athens during the decade, democracy became more complete through the introduction in 487 of choice by lot of the archons from candidates chosen by the demes; in 488 the remarkable system of ostracism was first employed. In this unpopularity contest citizens marked on clay sherds (or *ostraka*) the name of the leader they most distrusted, and the man with the greatest number of such votes (out of a total of at least 6000) was exiled for 10 years. Miltiades had already been heavily fined for an unsuccessful attack on Paros and died shortly afterwards; in 485–82 Xanthippus (father of Pericles) and Aristides were exiled. The surviving leader was Themistocles, a man not of full noble birth, who possessed amazing powers of foresight, persuasiveness, and sharp logical ability. Athenian patriotism was, if anything, increased by this political activity and was to count heavily in the grim days ahead.

As sole director of the vigorous Athenian democracy Themistocles prepared a second weapon. Already as archon in 493/2 he had begun to fortify the fine base of Piraeus with its three separate harbors; now (in 483/2) came a fortunate discovery of new, rich silver deposits in the state mines of Laurium. Themistocles persuaded his fellow citizens to forgo the distribution among themselves of the resulting profit of 100 talents and instead to raise the Athenian fleet to 200 triremes. Ostensibly his fleet was to be useful against Aegina, but Themistocles had clearly in mind the Persian threat and also a program of making Athens the major naval power in the Greek world.

As the Persians gathered their huge forces in Asia Minor, some of the leading Greek states began to prepare generally for the attack and assembled at Sparta in 481 to form a league. Their ability to join together was a further basic element in the eventual Greek victory; and the allies, moreover, avoided the serious mistake of the Ionians, 499–94, by settling upon a single leader, the state of Sparta, which was to furnish both generals and admirals. Beside Athens and Sparta stood the Spartan allies, such as Corinth and Aegina, and a number of smaller states, to a total of 31 in the end.

Nonetheless the jealousy and particularism which stamped Greek international relations led far more Greeks to remain neutral or even to go over to the Persians. Argos could not subdue its hatred of Sparta to join a Spartan-directed alliance and remained neutral, once its demand for joint leadership of the Greek forces was denied. Thebes and most other Greek states of central Greece felt themselves directly open to the Persians and yielded in surrender when approached by the Persian army. To make matters worse, those who consulted the oracle of Delphi were given warning omens. The priests of Apollo, in calculating the odds, felt that resistance had virually no chance and discouraged such suppliants as the Cretans from giving aid to the Greek side. Both by land and by sea those Greeks who stood against the Persians were outnumbered about two to one.

The Persian Advance: Artemisium and Thermopylae (480 B.C.). The Persian army was so large that it had to march around the Aegean, rather than sailing across as in 490; indeed, it could not live off the land but had to have shipborne supplies. As a result, the army kept close to the shore in direct contact with the fleet, which for its part needed a protected anchorage each night. Ancient galleys were not seaworthy enough to stay out in storms, and rowers had to stretch their legs on shore after their day's work.

This basic weakness in the Persian plans was seized upon by the sharp mind of Themistocles; if only the Greeks could defeat the Persian navy, the huge army of Xerxes would be a much less serious threat. To secure the proper conditions for naval victory, in turn, two steps were necessary.

First, the maritime powers among the Greek allies, especially Athens, must concentrate all their energies on the sea; and secondly, the Greek admirals must inveigle the superior Persian navy into narrow waters where its numbers and the skill of its Phoenician contingent would be less effective.

In its spring assembly, which convened at the isthmus of Corinth, the Greek league took positive decisions toward implementing this strategic policy. Themistocles was not able to divert all the energies of the Peloponnesians from building a wall across the isthmus itself, a naïve plan which quite overlooked the fact that the Persian fleet could outflank its defense and the likelihood that Argos would join the Persians as soon as they drew near. Yet he secured agreement that the Greeks would send their naval forces north with a small army to delay and, if possible, to cripple the enemy. At first the Greeks selected the vale of Tempe in northern Thessaly as a suitable line of defense but discovered that this position could be turned if the Persians made a short inland detour.

Accordingly they fell back to Thermopylae, where the coastal road was hemmed between sea and mountains to a path only 50 feet wide; the other routes from Thessaly into Boeotia lay so far inland that the Persian strategic necessity of keeping army and navy together prevented their use. Off Thermopylae lay the island of Euboea, which would force the Persian navy to come into a narrow strait; to block its entry the Greek fleet anchored at the northern end of the strait at Artemisium, while a minor detachment guarded its southern exit. Since this was a delaying position, limited forces were committed by land. The Spartan king Leonidas led 300 Spartan "Equals" with allies to total of 9000 men; the Spartan admiral Eurybiades, however, had most of the Athenian and other naval contingents, numbering 271 triremes in the main fleet.

The mighty panoply of Xerxes made its way slowly across the Hellespont via two bridges of boats; along the north coast of the Aegean, where a canal had been dug for his fleet across the dangerous Mt. Athos peninsula; and down into Greece. Everywhere the native peoples and states surrendered. As Xerxes approached Thermopylae, his fleet encountered a violent storm which raged three days and sank many ships; the Greek fleet, in the sheltered lee of Euboea, was not damaged. The enemy navy suffered further damage when Xerxes sent a large naval detachment around Euboea to bottle up the Greek fleet, for another storm blew the 200 Persian ships of this flotilla onto the rocks of the island. The main fleet fought three battles with the Greeks off Artemisium, in which neither side could secure a decisive victory.

While his fleet was trying to force a passage by sea, Xerxes also launched an attack by land at the defenders of the narrow pass of Thermopylae. For two days his Persian "Immortals" died in droves before the stern Greek lines; but on the second night a local traitor revealed the existence of a narrow trail up the mountains behind the Greeks. The movement of the Persian flanking force was detected by Leonidas in time to send off most of his army; he and his Spartans sacrificed themselves to delay the main Persian force. All were killed, and the wrathful Xerxes hung the decapitated body of Leonidas on a cross; the Greek navy had no recourse but to withdraw to Salamis. In later days a proud inscription was erected at Thermopylae, "Stranger, go tell the Lacedaemonians that here we lie obedient to their orders." [7]

Salamis. All central Greece now lay open to the Persians, who advanced to Athens. Since five months had passed, the campaigning year was drawing to a close; supplies for both Greeks and Persians were growing short. The Greeks could draw comfort from their success in whittling down the enemy navy, yet as their naval council of war met at the island of Salamis they could see smoke spiraling up from the Acropolis of Athens, where the Persians had quickly overcome the resistance of the priests and set fire to the temple roofs. All other Athenians had abandoned their city without a fight and were now on the island of Salamis or at Troezen in the Peloponnesus.

Some of the Greek admirals wished to withdraw to the isthmus of Corinth and anchor off the wall which had been constructed by the Peloponnesians. Themistocles argued forcefully that the only Greek hope lay in sticking to the main line of strategy of naval action and in response to a taunt that he no longer had a country or a right to speak threatened to sail off with the Athenian ships and citizens to found a new state in the western Mediterranean. Since all realized the Greeks had no chance without the strong Athenian navy, they yielded once more to his keen analysis and agreed to hold their position. So both sides

[7] Herodotus 7.228.

remained indecisive, for Xerxes could not decide whether to advance by land on the isthmus of Corinth or to deal with the Greek naval force off his flank.

As dissensions arose again in the Greek naval command, the wily Themistocles sent off by night a trusted slave, Sicinnus, to the Persians to tell Xerxes that the Greeks were quarreling, that the Athenians were willing to turn traitor, and that if he wanted a great victory he needed only to attack. Xerxes, a young king desiring glory, fell into the trap and ordered his fleet to advance for the final blow; to make victory doubly sure he sent a detachment around to the west end of Salamis to bottle up the Greeks. He himself sat upon a throne on a hill overlooking the battleground so that he could award prizes to the most valorous of his subjects.

On a morning in late September the Persian fleet of some 350 ships rowed in line abreast from its anchorage at Phalerum toward Salamis. The Greeks, who had about 300 ships in the action, knew they were encircled from the rear and prepared for the decisive battle; Athenian hoplites were embarked on the ships. As the Persians closed in, their line was split by the island of Psyttalia, on which they had stationed troops. The confusion that resulted was heightened by the apparent retreat of the Greeks, who backed water on seeing the Persians enter the narrow reaches of the bay; but this tactical maneuver was designed only to suck the enemy farther in. Suddenly the Greeks rowed forward from front and flanks and threw themselves into hand-to-hand battle with the Persians, who had no chance to use maneuvering tactics. By the close of the day the despondent Xerxes could see his remaining ships streaming away in utter defeat. Some 200 Persian warships, mostly of the Phoenician contingent, were lost, as against only about 40 Greek ships; and Aristides, who had been recalled from exile, had led a crossing to Psyttalia, which wiped out the Persian forces there. Immediately, the Greek victory was due to the military skill and determination of the men who fought in the battle; but behind this factor lay the logical persuasiveness of Themistocles, the doggedness of the Athenians, and the calm, generally accepted leadership which the Spartans provided.

Plataea and Mycale (479 B.C.). Since the surviving ships of the Persian fleet were largely manned by Ionians of doubtful loyalty, Xerxes hastily made his way back to Asia via the Hellespont. With him went a large part of the Persian army, which could no longer be supplied by sea; but a strong force remained in central Greece during the winter, to try once more by land to conquer the Greeks. Before operations began in the spring of 479 the Persian commander Mardonius essayed to detach the battered Athenians from the Greek league, but his ambassadors were rebuffed. To the Spartans, who had hastily sent ambassadors lest Athens be tempted, the Athenians proudly proclaimed their adherence to "our common brotherhood with the Greeks: our common ancestry and language, the altars and the sacrifices of which we all partake, the common character which we bear." [8]

Although the Persians invaded and devasted Attica once more, they soon withdrew into Boeotia upon news that the main Greek army was advancing north from the isthmus of Corinth to protect the Athenians. Under Pausanias, regent for a young king, the Spartans had committed their entire force of some 45,000 Spartans, *perioikoi*, and helots; Athens furnished 8000 hoplites under Aristides, leader of Athens in this year along with Xanthippus. All told, the Greek army consisted of 38,700 hoplites, some 70,000 light-armed infantry, but virtually no cavalry. This army, the biggest ever assembled in Greece, lay at Plataea on the slopes overlooking the Boeotian plain; but even here its supply lines were seriously threatened by the Persian cavalry. Mardonius' force may have been somewhat larger, reinforced as it was by the Greeks of Boeotia, Phocis, and Thessaly.

For three weeks each side waited. Then Pausanias was forced to shift his position by night when the Persian cavalry blocked his main water supply, but one Spartan unit proudly refused to desert its place. At daybreak the Greeks were spread out in disarray, and Mardonius seized the opportunity for an attack. The battle of Plataea, which ensued, was a haphazard affair in which the Greek contingents, led by the Spartans, finally carried the day, sacked the enemy camp, and killed Mardonius.

On the same day, according to tradition, occurred the battle of Mycale on the east coast of the Aegean. A Greek fleet had assembled in the spring of 479 and moved eastward to prevent reinforcement by sea to Mardonius; the Persians, however, sent their Phoenician ships home and placed their Ionian ships on shore in a fortified camp. This was reinforced by the Persian garrison army of Asia Minor. The Spartan ad-

[8] Herodotus 8.144; tr. G. Rawlinson.

miral, king Leotychidas, skillfully spread dissensions among the Ionians; and, when he eventually attacked the camp, the Greeks in the enemy force rose against their masters. The victory of Mycale wiped out Persian naval strength in the Aegean and led to the revolt of most of the Greek cities on the coast of Asia Minor; by themselves the Athenians and Aegean states took Sestos, the main Persian base on the Hellespont, through a protracted siege into the winter.

THE GREEK OFFENSIVE

The Delian League (478/7 B.C.). After their victories the Greeks awarded prizes of valor. The Hellenic spirit of competitive egotism is nowhere better illustrated than in the story that after Salamis the Greek admirals each voted for himself as the most outstanding but that all voted for Themistocles in second place. Following Plataea, the Athenians set up at Delphi the cables of Xerxes' bridge; the Greek allies dedicated there a bronze stand formed of 3 intertwined serpents, on which were inscribed the names of the 31 states which withstood the Persians, beginning with the Spartans and the Athenians. This supported a golden tripod which was melted down long ago, but the stand still exists in modern Istanbul, where it was moved in later days. The Greeks agreed that Plataea should be dedicated to Zeus the Liberator as a sacred land, and every year for centuries to come the archon of Plataea drank a solemn toast to "the men who died for the liberty of Greece." [9]

So far, so good; but what next? The Ionian revolt had achieved spectacular successes in 499–98 but had been crushed after it had passed to the defensive. The Persians held a bridgehead in the north Aegean as well as the interior of Asia Minor; from the Phoenician and other seacoast peoples they could form a new navy in time. Thus far the Spartans had led the Greeks admirably. Their generals had succeeded in the always difficult task of holding together an allied force on a common plan; the firmness of the Spartan outlook and the training of the Spartan soldier had proven invaluable. But now the defects of the Spartan system began to show. The losses among the Spartan "Equals" had been so serious that their control at home was endangered; the parochial views of the Spartan government discouraged it from overseas

[9] Plutarch, *Aristides* 21.

commitments to the Greeks of Asia Minor, whom it urged to evacuate the mainland settlements; and, finally, the Spartan leaders in the continued activity of 478 showed themselves liable to corruption and arrogance. Leotychidas, sent to punish the defectors in Thessaly, was exiled for life when he was only partially successful; Pausanias, who took Byzantium, was recalled on clear evidence that he was adopting luxurious ways and had intrigued with Persia. On the whole the Spartans were glad to turn over further conduct of the war against Persia to another leader.

This was Athens, which had been increasingly active in the Aegean since the Pisistratid era. During the winter of 478/7 the Athenians stepped forward to form an alliance with most of the islanders and some of the seaboard states of Asia Minor. At a meeting on the island of Delos the allies swore oaths of alliance which were to last until lumps of iron, thrown into the sea, rose again. Their common objective was to secure their liberty and to drive back the Persians, but once this end had been achieved, one may doubt if the allies visualized a continuance of the association.

In the Delian league policy was to be established by an assembly of representatives but was to be executed by an admiral and 10 treasurers appointed by Athens. The chief Athenian leader, Aristides the Just, was entrusted with the ticklish task of dividing among the allies an assessment of 460 talents per year, which the member states paid either in cash to the treasury in the temple of Apollo at Delos or in the form of ships. In setting up the Delian league its members drew upon all the experience of the Spartan league, the Ionian league of 499–94, and the league of 481–78; and under the firm leadership of Athens they pressed forward in a great offensive against Persia. Although all swore to respect the internal independence of one another, Athens was soon to convert the voluntary alliance into a forced submission to her will, but this development, which led on into the Athenian naval empire, may be postponed to the next chapter.

The Attack on Persia (477–49 B.C.). Down to 449 the Delian league (or, as it soon became, the Athenian empire) waged war almost continuously against Persia. Throughout most of this era its main admiral was the Athenian aristocrat Cimon, son of Miltiades and a Thracian princess (*c.* 512–450), who was an inspiring commander and an able diplomat. Although his actions are not known in detail, he drove the Persians out of Europe, eliminated possible Persian naval bases on the west coast of Asia Minor, and about 469 shattered the restored Persian fleet at the battle of the Eurymedon river in Pamphylia.

As Athens moved more and more toward a rupture with its erstwhile ally and leader, Sparta, Cimon's political power at home fell. Early in 461 he was ostracized. His successors, especially Pericles, continued to press the war with Persia and boldly spread league forces from Cyprus to Phoenicia and on to Egypt, where the Libyan leader Inarus had raised a standard of revolt. In this latter zone of action the Greek expedition was eventually encircled by the Persians and wiped out in 454 with the loss of almost 100 warships; Cimon, who was once again given naval command after being recalled from exile, died in 450 while besieging the Persian base of Citium in Cyprus. Although the Athenians went on to defeat the Persians off Salamis in Cyprus, they were by now so involved at home against Sparta, Boeotia, and other powers that they were agreeable to peace.

Whether their main negotiator, Callias (brother-in-law of Cimon), actually concluded a formal peace in 449 is uncertain; but at least tacitly the Persians agreed not to send naval forces into Greek waters or to trouble the Greeks of Asia Minor, many of whom continued to pay taxes to the Persians on their agricultural lands. In return the Athenians dropped their offensive. For the next generation there was peace between Persians and Greeks until finally the Athenian empire began to totter in the Peloponnesian war.

THE GREEK VICTORY

When the great historian Herodotus, alive in these latter days, looked back on the stirring events of 480-79, he viewed the war between the Greeks and the Persians as one between freedom and tyranny. The Spartans, as an exiled Spartan king told Xerxes, were free men, but not in all respects free: "Law is the master whom they own, and this master they fear more than your subjects fear you." [10] So the Persian forces at Thermopylae had to be driven by the lash, while the Spartans voluntarily laid down their lives. Yet the Greek victory was due to more than the bravery of free men or the skill of good leaders; in the end Herodotus

[10] Herodotus 7.104.

attributed Hellenic success to the will of the gods, who thus punished the overweening pride (*hybris*) of Xerxes.

Much the same view may be found in the one historical Greek tragedy which has survived, the *Persians* of Aeschylus (produced 472). Although Aeschylus had fought at Marathon and at Salamis, he viewed the Persians dispassionately. The defeat of Xerxes was to him an occasion, not for open eulogy of Greek valor, but for demonstration anew of the retribution for *hybris* by the gods, who governed Greeks and Persians alike.

To a modern observer who cannot believe in the will of Zeus Hellenios the victory of the Greeks is a superb testimonial alike to the powers of Hellenic civilization and to the strengths inherent in the city-state form of organization. True, not all Greeks had rallied to the cause, nor had traitors been absent; but those who fought had been sufficient in numbers and unified enough to carry the day and to prosecute the wars until the Persians gave over any immediate ideas of revenge.

From the Persian point of view the defeats at the hands of the Greeks were perhaps relatively minor matters, which did not shake their rule over the heartland of the Near East. Yet from this point onward the Persian empire was essentially on the defensive and was eventually to fall before an attack led from the Aegean world by Alexander the Great.

To the Greeks the victory over Persia was immediately important in many respects. That Greek civilization would have continued to progress under Persian rule seems more than doubtful; but the victory had some part in inspiring artists and authors to achieve the masterpieces of the classic age. Athens, in particular, drew courage and strength from its salvation and from its position as leader of the Aegean to become the center of Greek culture, the first great democratic state, and also the first truly imperial power in Greek history. These developments will concern us in the next two chapters.

BIBLIOGRAPHY

Sources. Apart from some inscriptions of kings and the Avesta, we have little written evidence from the Persian side; the Gathas are translated by J. Duchesne-Guillemin, *Hymns of Zarathustra* (Boston: Beacon LR19, 1963). Archeological exploration, except at Persepolis, Susa, and a few other sites, has been restricted to a considerable degree by modern political conditions. Both for relations between Greeks and Persians and for much of the history of Persia itself Greek sources are primary. Unfortunately the most influential of these was the imaginative *Persica* by Ctesias, court physician in Persia 415–398 B.C.; Xenophon's *Cyropaedia* is essentially a fictional account of Cyrus' youth.

The first great Greek historian, Herodotus, was born about 484 in Halicarnassus; reared in the Ionian tradition, he was critical of men's actions and deeds, deeply interested in the physical world, and withal deeply pious. His curiosity led him to travel to Babylon, to Egypt, to the Black Sea, and to the western Mediterranean, where he joined in a new colony at Thurii (443 on); but for a considerable period he dwelt and expounded his story at Athens. His history perhaps began as an account of his travels but was developed into a majestic account of the interrelations of Persians and Greeks which led to Salamis and Plataea. Since he viewed history as a very broad subject, embracing geography, ethnology, and much else, he devoted his first five books to the political and social background; the last four, to the war itself.

Herodotus entertains his readers with stories, which have long been famous, but he does not necessarily believe "it all alike" (7.152); his accounts of Egypt and Persia have been proven surprisingly accurate in many points, while subject to a traveler's errors in others. He was biased in favor of Athens and did not entirely understand the tactical operations he described; but in his critical approach and truly historical outlook he fully deserves his title, the Father of History. A good translation is that by A. de Selincourt (Harmondsworth: Penguin L34, 1954).

Other written evidence is preserved on the lives of Themistocles, Cimon, Aristides, and others by Plutarch; in the lives of Themistocles and Pausanias by the Roman writer Cornelius Nepos (Loeb Classical Library); and in the history of Diodorus Siculus (Loeb Classical Library). In the play, the *Persians,* by Aeschylus we have eyewitness evidence, but the historian will find here, as so often, that poetic, dramatic, or fictional literature has serious limitations as a historical source. In Aeschylus' description of the battle of Salamis there are only three geographical indications, none of which is precise.

Some inscriptional evidence is available; but a purported decree moved by Themistocles, which was discovered only in 1959 (M. H.

Jameson, "Waiting for the Barbarian," *Greece and Rome,* 2 ser. 8 [1961], pp. 5–18), is generally considered to be a later forgery. On the north wall of the Acropolis today one can still see column drums and other architectural members which had been intended for a temple but were used after the Persian sack as raw material for the new wall; and the archaic statues of the Acropolis were preserved by being used as fill to level off the top of the hill.

Further Reading. A full but detailed survey of our knowledge of Persia is A. T. Olmstead, *History of the Persian Empire* (Chicago: University of Chicago Phoenix P36, 1960); see also Richard N. Frye, *Heritage of Persia* (Cleveland: World, 1963), and René Ghirshman, *Iran* (Penguin, 1978), the latter of which must be used with caution. Erich F. Schmidt, *Persepolis,* Vols. I–II (Chicago: University of Chicago Press, 1953–57), is beautifully illustrated; see more briefly D. N. Wilber, *Persepolis* (New York: Crowell, 1969); D. Stronach describes the first Persian capital in *Pasargadae* (Oxford: Clarendon Press, 1978). On Zoroastrianism, see M. Boyce, *History of Zoroastrianism* (Leiden: Brill, 1975); J. Duchesne-Guillemin, *Western Response to Zoroaster* (Oxford: Oxford University Press, 1958), which gives a history of modern study of the subject; and Rustom Masani, *Zoroastrianism: Religion of the Good Life* (New York: Macmillan, 1968), by a modern Parsee.

All general histories of Greece (General Bibliography) treat of the Persian invasion and its effects; A. R. Burn, *Persia and the Greeks* (New York: St. Martins, 1970), considers the interplay as a whole, and C. Hignett, *Xerxes' Invasion of Greece* (Oxford: Oxford University Press, 1963), seeks to uphold Herodotus' reliability in general; A. J. Podlecki, *The Life of Themistocles* (Montreal: McGill-Queen's University Press, 1975) is careful. A. de Selincourt, *World of Herodotus* (London: Secker and Warburg, 1962), describes the era; Herodotus himself is more fully treated by J. L. Myres, *Herodotus, Father of History* (Chicago: Regnery, 1971). The background in which history developed is discussed by Chester G. Starr, *The Awakening of the Greek Historical Spirit* (New York: Knopf, 1968).

14

ATHENIAN DEMOCRACY AND
IMPERIALISM

The victories of 480–79 B.C., which checked the Persians, had been won by only a few of the Greek states under the leadership of Sparta. Yet all Greece had been saved, and many parts of the Aegean world went on in the next few decades to unparalleled heights of prosperity and culture. Above all others towered the state which had suffered most in the Persian invasions, Athens, for this was the *polis* best fitted to draw profit from the Greek triumph.

Before the Persian invasions Athens had attained a democratic pattern of government under Clisthenes and had shown naval and commercial leanings under the Pisistratids and Themistocles. During the critical years of 480–79 the men of Athens, even when tempted by Mardonius on the one hand and plagued by the slowness of Sparta on the other, had stood firm. The great Boeotian poet Pindar had rightly praised them for "laying the bright foundations of liberty" in the first naval actions off Artemisium, which gave the Greeks the confidence they needed for the later battle at Salamis.[1] Thereafter Athens was both in a mood and in a position to become the leader of the islanders and the Greeks of Asia Minor through the Delian league. The allies soon discovered that they could not break this initially voluntary bond; for Athenian statesmen ruthlessly expanded and consolidated the hold which the alliance gave them over the smaller Aegean states into an overseas empire.

At home the power of the people became ever more direct. The fer-

[1] Quoted by Plutarch, *Themistocles* 8.

ment of life in Athenian streets, the prosperity of shops and shippers, and the concentration of lines of communication at the port of Piraeus made Athens a dominant cultural center, to which artists, philosophers, and thinkers were drawn from all the Greek world. This one state so swallowed up the fifth-century scene that one sometimes tends to forget that there were many other political units in Greece.

In this chapter we shall investigate primarily Athenian democracy at home and imperialism abroad down to 431 B.C., together with the economic development of the fifth century. From the modern point of view the city-state of Athens was a tiny, simple system; but within its framework there took place a great debate on the merits and the defects of political equality and of external domination. Most of the arguments for and against democracy and imperialism which can still be made today had already been advanced boldly and openly in this debate.

ATHENIAN DEMOCRACY

Expansion of Democracy (487–61 B.C.). In 508 B.C. Clisthenes had reorganized Athenian political groupings so as to break the strength of local factions. He had also lodged the main constitutional power in the hands of the assembly, but its range of action was still checked both by the elected archons, almost always of aristocratic origin, and by the council of the Areopagus. During the next 50 years these checks were removed one by one; "equality of rights" (*isonomia*) yielded to "rule of the people" (*demokratia*).

Several steps were taken in the 480s which gave the leader of the popular majority a wider role. From 487 on the archons were chosen by lot from 500 candidates elected by the demes; the result was to emphasize the place of the board of 10 generals, who continued to be elected. The use of ostracism from 488 on had permitted the majority to exile minority leaders and so to concentrate power in the hands of Themistocles. During and immediately after the main Persian attacks there was no room for constitutional change, and the main leader of the 470s and 460s, the popular general Cimon, was too conservative in internal politics to favor further alterations.

Finally, in 462/1, more radical politicians, Ephialtes and Pericles, felt strong enough to clip the powers of the council of the Areopagus, de-

TABLE 5
The Greek World 500–323 B.C.

B.C.	Political	Literary	Artistic	Philosophical-Scientific
500	Ionian revolt	*Hecataeus*	*Attic red-figure*	*Alcmaeon*
	Marathon	*Pindar, Simonides, Bacchylides*	*Classic sculpture*	*Heraclitus, Parmenides, Zeno*
	Themistocles	*Aeschylus*	*Temple of Aphaia at Aegina*	
	at Athens: fleet			
	Persian invasion:			
	Salamis, Plataea, Mycale			
	DELIAN LEAGUE			
	Cimon			
	conversion into Athenian empire			
	Pericles at Athens		*Temple of Zeus at Olympia*	*Empedocles, Anaxagoras*
450	Delian treasury moved to Athens	*Sophocles, Euripides*	*Parthenon, Propylaea Phidias, Myron, Polygnotus, Apollodorus*	*Leucippus, Democritus*
	Peace of Callias	*Herodotus, Hellanicus*		*Meton*
	Athens vs. Sparta (to 446)			

	Literature	Art	Philosophy
Peloponnesian war:	Antiphon (orator)	Erechtheum	Socrates
death of Pericles	Sophocles, Euripides,	Decline of red-figure	Protagoras, Gorgias,
peace of Nicias	Aristophanes		Hippias
expedition to			Hippocrates
Syracuse	Thucydides	Polyclitus	
Spartan navy	Andocides, Lysias	Parrhasius, Zeuxis	
Fall of Athens			
400 DOMINATION BY SPARTA	Isocrates		Death of Socrates
Expedition of Cyrus	Timotheus		Plato, Euclides,
Revival of Athens	Xenophon	Praxiteles, Scopas	Antisthenes
Leuctra		Rise of Corinthian	
DOMINATION BY THEBES		order	
Epaminondas			
Mantinea			
350 RISE OF MACEDONIA	Ephorus, Theopompus	Mausoleum	Aristotle, Diogenes,
Philip			Aristippus
	Demosthenes, Aeschines		
Chaeronea		Apelles	
Alexander the Great		Lysippus	
300 HELLENISTIC AGE			

spite the great credit it had gained by wise direction of the mass evacuation of Attica in the Persian invasion. Precisely what took place we do not know, but in general terms the functions of this body were restricted to trials of homicide, a role which it played in Aeschylus' *Eumenides* (458). Supervision of the conduct of government passed to the council of Five Hundred, and judicial activity was concentrated in the popular courts. Cimon was ostracized in 461 for his pro-Spartan policy; Ephialtes was murdered by a foreign thug; Pericles, accordingly, loomed ever higher. During the 450s other generals and politicians stood beside him in independent roles, but thereafter Pericles gained that pre-eminent position which he generally held down to his death in 429.

Leadership of Pericles (*to* 429 B.C.). Pericles (b. *c*. 495) was of aristocratic lineage. His father was Xanthippus; his mother Agariste was a great-niece of Clisthenes and so came from the great Alcmeonid clan. He himself was reserved, even haughty, and associated chiefly with thinkers and artists like Anaxagoras, Sophocles, and Phidias. Nonetheless his name is indissolubly connected with one of the world's great democracies, for the people of Athens generally hearkened to Pericles' advice and re-elected him annually for many years as leader of the board of 10 generals. Pericles was incorruptible — a rare quality among Athenian politicians — a masterful speaker, and a clear thinker. Reason and emotion lived together in his breast in remarkable harmony; for he was fired by a great vision of the perfectibility of man in general and of the political greatness of Athens in particular, a vision which has perhaps led later students of his career to disregard some deep defects in his political programs.

Abroad, Pericles capitalized on the military successes of Cimon to make Athens the open master of the Aegean. This policy, which produced glittering success for a time, eventually produced that terrific collapse which will concern us later. At home Pericles fostered patriotism and essayed to uplift his fellow citizens intellectually through encouragement of plays, art and music. He had stood beside Ephialtes in the democratic reform of 462/1; during the 450s he pushed for further actions calculated to give every citizen a role in the government. One measure which helped to assure his popularity was the introduction of pay in 452/1 for jurors and magistrates so that no one could be barred by poverty from public service. Since citizenship was now a privilege, he also carried in 451/0 a law that only children born of Athenian parents on both sides could be registered as citizens. The relative openness with which Athenian citizenship had been granted under the Pisistratids and Clisthenes thus came to an end. If such a law had been in force earlier, neither Themistocles, Miltiades, nor Cimon could have served Athens; and Pericles' own son by his mistress Aspasia of Miletus had to be enfranchised later by special enactment.

By the 440s some 20,000 Athenian citizens drew pay from the state each year, though only for those days actually spent on public service and generally only at the minimum subsistence rate of 2 obols. There were, thus, 6000 registered on the jury panels; 500 served on the council; 1400 were magistrates at home and abroad; and every spring and summer 10,000 rowers served in the navy at the pay of 3 obols a day.

Democratic Machinery of Government. The dynamo of the Athenian constitution now was unmistakably the assembly or *ecclesia*. The assembly embraced all male citizens over the age of 18, a group of probably about 43,000 in the 440s; but a quorum of only 6000 seems to have been needed at its sessions. These were held several times a month on the slopes of the Pnyx north of the Acropolis. Since women, slaves, and foreigners were excluded, a very small part of the 300,000-odd residents of Attica determined public policy. "Democracy," however, is a flexible term in practice; for example, Jacksonian democracy in the United States in the 1830s was attended by equally severe limitations on voting rights, and elections in many democratic modern states are determined by a minority even of those who are entitled to vote. Certainly those people whom Athenian political theory considered capable of political action had as unfettered a role as has ever been true in any system. The assembly listened to such leaders as it would tolerate, and voted decisions which were final.

Even a group of several thousands could not conduct business on an impromptu basis. The governor on the dynamo, accordingly, was the council (*boule*) of Five Hundred, chosen by lot each year as a steering committee from citizens over 30 years of age. The council proposed the agenda for each session and made recommendations as to action. When the assembly had expressed its will, the council then supervised the magistrates in executing policy, checked expenses (at times, every month), maintained public buildings and religious festivals, and in the fifth century could even punish by death such misdeeds as treason. To prevent so powerful a body from becoming an aristocratic stronghold no citizen could serve two consecutive years as councilor or more than two years in his lifetime; as a result about one-fourth to one-third of the citizen body at any time had served on the council. While the whole council met on important matters, it was divided into 10 subcommittees of 50 *prytaneis* each; and for one-tenth of the year (called a *prytany*) 1 subcommittee met and ate together every day in the *tholos* on the west side of the Agora. One-third of this subcommittee in turn had always to be in the building day and night. Each day a chairman was drawn from the subcommittee by lot, and if the assembly met on that day he also served as moderator for the whole citizen body.

Routine administration was in the hands of a large body of city magistrates, numbering about 700 in Pericles' day. Usually a group of 10 men was assigned to a specific, limited job, such as supervision of the markets, so that they could check each other. Most magistrates were chosen by lot; the major exception which was elected was the board of 10 generals, who served also as admirals and as general directors of policy.

The courts (*heliaea*) were, in essence, a committee of the citizen body, consisting of volunteers over 30 years of age to a total of 6000. This group was divided in the fifth century into panels of 600 each, which could be combined for very important cases; later, juries were chosen each day by lot through a very complicated procedure to limit corruption. An actual jury consisted of an odd number of jurors (usually 501), for decision was by majority vote. Each suitor had to serve as his own lawyer, though he might get a skilled orator to write his speech; there was no appeal. In addition to judging cases the courts also audited and inspected the activities of every official at the end of his year of office.

In its belief that all citizens were fundamentally equal and in its willingness to place power in their hands via the assembly and choice by lot, the Athenian democracy has had few equals in history. Yet the system worked reasonably well. The problems of government were far simpler than those on which a modern citizen must express his opinion, and important practical safeguards limited possible abuses. Pericles and his contemporaries had an infinite faith in mankind but very little trust in actual men. Those who were chosen by lot were scrutinized by the council to make sure they had the requisite capacities, and every official who dealt with money was checked carefully. Positions were rotated rapidly; no one could tell beforehand who would form his jury or who would preside over the assembly on a certain date.

Even the assembly was checked by a general rule that no matter not already considered by the council should be taken up, and by the institution of *graphe paranomon*. Under this principle the proposer of a law could be sued in the courts on the grounds that it was unconstitutional. If the jury (composed of older citizens than the assembly) agreed, the law was abrogated; its sponsor was also heavily fined, provided that less than a year had passed since its enactment.

Unlike most modern systems, moreover, a large part of the Athenian citizen body had had actual experience in the processes of government and, in the fifth century at least, took an active interest in politics. Sobriety, confidence, basically good judgment, and balance of outlook — all these qualities stamped Athenian democracy in its halcyon days under Pericles.

The Debate on Democracy. The greatest defense of the Athenian democratic system which has survived is the funeral oration delivered by Pericles over the dead of the first year in the Peloponnesian war (431 B.C.), as reported by Thucydides (2.35–46). Here Pericles praised the equal justice allotted to all while arguing that the more able were given public preferment regardless of class or poverty. In private life, he asserted, each man was free to do as he willed; but in public life citizens were "prevented from doing wrong by respect for authority and for the laws, having an especial regard to those which are ordained for the protection of the injured." All men, even if engaged in business, had a very fair ideal of politics and took their due part in public life. Through such statements Pericles built up a majestic, idealized picture of the freedom, public interest, and intellectual quality of Athenian life. "To sum up: I say that Athens is the school of Hellas and that the individual Athenian in his own person seems to have the power of adapting himself to the most varied forms of action with the utmost versatility and grace." [2]

More prominent in our literary sources, which were generally conservative, is a vein of criticism of Athenian democracy. Some thinkers

[2] Tr. Benjamin Jowett.

accepted democracy as a theory but criticized its practical operations. During the Peloponnesian war the comic poet Aristophanes leveled barbed shafts at the willingness of the people to follow leaders who promised rewards, played on superstitions, and otherwise appealed to baser instincts so as to gain power. After that war had reached its bitter end in the defeat of Athens, the great historian Thucydides penned a mighty indictment of popular ruthlessness and pictured the people as overly optimistic at some points, at others too reluctant to admit its own faults or to change policies as foreign relations and the ebb and flow of war dictated. Modern scholars have been particularly inclined to point out the fact that almost every great leader of democratic Athens was eventually cast off by the people. Miltiades was fined; Themistocles was ostracized about 472/1 and lived his last days as a pensioner of the Persian king; Cimon was ostracized; even Pericles felt the displeasure of the masses on occasion, though he died in office. In view of Pericles' promotion of arrogant imperialism and his serious mistakes in foreign policy, which in the end ruined Athenian power, his reputation may well be overrated.

The aristocratic temper of Greek civilization was so strong that some Athenian observers openly denied the validity of the democratic premises. About 430 an anonymous aristocrat, who is called the Old Oligarch, wrote a bitterly satiric tract against the exploitation of the rich for the benefit of the ignorant, disorderly, rascally multitude; the slowness and poor judgment of popular action; and the democratic zeal for imperialism. The speech of Pericles just quoted was in part his defense against the contemporary charges that more able men were kept out of office by popular suspicion, that minority interests were trampled by the majority, and that an iron conformity was clamped even on private life by the dictates of the masses. By the fourth century political philosophers such as Plato and Aristotle were to attack on theoretical grounds the concept that well-born and poor should be politically equal.

In the first great democracy of western civilization, in sum, the theoretical exploration of the defects of popular government was conducted with remarkable openness and intellectual acuteness. A philosophical defense of democracy does not seem to have been made; the true defense was its practical acceptance. In victory and in defeat the Athenians clung to their system. Theoreticians might generally prefer the stability of

Sparta; but only twice, once in a temporary despair during the Peloponnesian war (411) and again in the bitter days after their collapse in 404, did the Athenians briefly abandon its principles. Otherwise the masses had enough confidence in themselves and their shifting leaders to preserve the democratic system from the days of Clisthenes on past the reign of Alexander.

ATHENIAN IMPERIALISM

Rise of the Naval Empire (478–54 B.C.). The evolution of democracy at home was intimately connected with the increasing imperialism of Athens abroad during the fifth century. The commercial and industrial elements, which benefited from the growth of seaborne trade, were a bulwark of the assembly. In turn the general unity of all classes made it possible for Athens to exert greater strength abroad. To some extent the profits of empire also supported the poor of Athens, particularly in public works; but the Athenian economy was basically strong enough to underwrite the expenses of democracy even after it had lost its overseas dominance.

Athenian interests in the Aegean had begun to be significant by the days of the Pisistratids and had been directed toward controlling the Hellespont, the great artery for trade with the grain-growing regions of south Russia. Miltiades had held a virtually independent principality on the Chersonesus, and the islands of Imbros and Lemnos had been under Athenian control. After the Persian attacks had ebbed, Athens eagerly took up the leadership of the Delian league. In its first years the Athenians were recovering from the Persian devastation and needed all the assistance they could get in their crusade; in the process they converted voluntary allies into involuntary subjects.

The basic force which led to this result was the energetic, self-confident enthusiasm of the Athenians, men "born neither to have peace themselves nor to allow peace to other men"; [3] but their leaders seem fairly clearly to have had a positive program of expansion in mind. Cimon himself compelled all the states which he liberated from the Persians to join the league. About 475 he attacked the pirate community of Scyros, though it was not under Persian rule; the inhabitants were

[3] Thucydides 1.70 (speech of the Corinthians in 432).

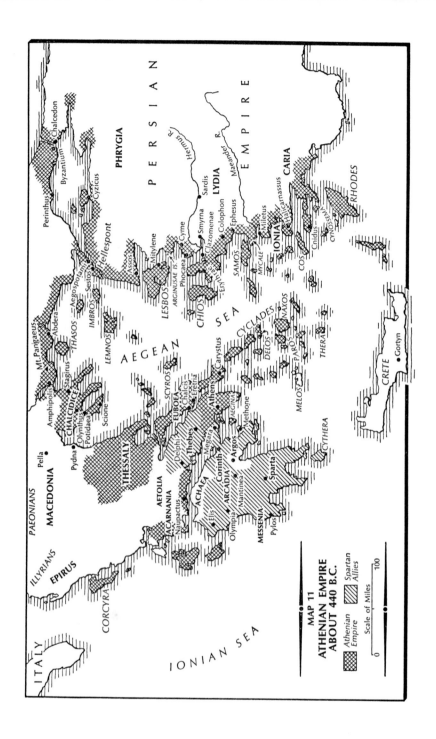

MAP 11
ATHENIAN EMPIRE
ABOUT 440 B.C.

Athenian Empire

Spartan Allies

Scale of Miles

0   100

sold into slavery, and Athenian colonists replaced them. During this minor action the bones of a dead giant were discovered, were acclaimed to be those of Theseus, and were brought to Athens to the enhancement of Cimon's reputation; more and more Theseus became a patron hero of Athens.

Soon afterwards Carystus, on the island of Euboea, was coerced into joining the league; and when states already members grew weary of the continued Persian war or suspicious of Athenian ambition they were kept in the league by force. Naxos was the first to revolt and then to be "enslaved contrary to the law of the league"; [4] even more critical was the secession of Thasos in 465. When this island was reconquered after a two-year siege, its walls were destroyed, and its fleet was confiscated. Thenceforth Thasos was virtually an Athenian subject.

The original proviso that Athens was to furnish the generals and the treasurers of the league aided its conversion into an empire. In 454, after the great defeat in Egypt, the league treasury was moved from Delos to the Acropolis, where it would be safer. From this date, certainly, the erstwhile allies may be considered as tribute-paying subjects of Athens; but in actuality they had no longer had freedom to determine their own policies by the 460s.

Athenian Failure by Land (478-46 B.C.). During the same decades Athens moved from a close alliance with Sparta, which had brought the Greek victory in 480-79, to open antagonism. Already in 478 Sparta had attempted to dissuade the Athenians from rebuilding their walls lest the Persians come again and use Athens as a base; but Themistocles had persuaded his fellow citizens that this task was more important even than rebuilding their homes. While they set to work hastily to fortify the city — at the Dipylon gate one can still see today how old tombstones were used as building materials — Themistocles went to Sparta as ambassador and temporized until news came that the walls were defensible.

Sparta had remained quiescent, though increasingly suspicious, while Cimon turned Athenian energies into the naval war. In 464 a violent earthquake killed a great number of Spartans and led to a great revolt of the Messenian helots, whom the Spartans finally besieged on Mt. Ithome. After two years the Spartans in 462 came to ask Athenian assistance. Against the opposition of Ephialtes, Cimon won a vote of

[4] Thucydides 1.98.

cooperation with the passionate plea that the Athenians "ought not to suffer Greece to be lamed, nor their own city to be deprived of her yoke-fellow." [5] So he led an expedition to aid in the siege of Ithome; but when the distrustful Spartans learned that the radical leaders had gained control in Athens during Cimon's absence they dismissed the Athenian troops. This insult led the irate Athenians to ostracize Cimon and to break their alliance with Sparta.

Thereafter Athens embarked on an ambitious offensive to expand its empire by land in Greece. The wars that ensued involved Athens and now one, now another of the Greek mainland states and lasted down to 446/5. At one point Athens held virtual control over Megara and much of Boeotia, but its military strength in citizen hoplites was inadequate to maintain so wide a suzerainty, particularly when it was also fighting by sea in Cyprus and in Egypt. In 447 the Athenian army suffered a crushing defeat at Boeotian hands at Coronea; in the next year came a brief Spartan invasion of Attica and a revolt of Euboea. Pericles then realized he could not hold both land and sea and made a 30 years' peace with Sparta (winter 446/5). Athens yielded its claims by land, and Sparta admitted Athenian mastery in the Aegean save for contracting that Aegina be an autonomous member of the Athenian empire.

Government of the Empire. Since peace had already been made with Persia in 449, democratic Athens could now consolidate its overseas empire. Immediately after the peace of Callias, which presumably ended the main reason for the existence of the Delian league, there had been a moment of hesitation. Pericles had called a great conference of all Greek states to meet at Athens so as to arrange for the rebuilding of temples destroyed by the Persians, sacrifices for the victory, and a permanent system to police the seas. These agenda had been rejected by Sparta and its allies as likely to lead to Athenian domination over all Greece, and the conference never met.

Pericles then persuaded his fellow citizens to move ahead deliberately as imperial master of the Aegean islands and of many strongpoints on the east and north coasts. The population of this Aegean empire has been estimated at 2,000,000, but all the way from Sicily to the Black Sea Athenian power was a serious factor in local calculation.

Only Chios, Samos (to 439), and Lesbos now provided ships of their

[5] Plutarch, *Cimon* 16; tr. Dryden-Clough.

own to the imperial navy; all others sent tribute every spring to Athens, where it was deposited in the care of the goddess Athena. The islands had to pay quite heavily; those coastal states of Ionia which were in the empire were assessed at a lower rate, partly because they seem to have remained economically weak, partly because the Athenians did not wish to drive them back into Persian hands. One mina of every talent of tribute (one-sixtieth) was paid to the priests of Athena as safekeepers, and since this religious due was normally recorded on stone we have fairly complete accounts of the Athenian tribute from 454/3 to 415/4. Down to 432 about 400 talents were collected as the total yearly tribute, paid by 134 to 173 states. These were organized in five groups — Ionia, Hellespont, Thrace, Caria, the islands — though the Carian was reduced by Athenian policy and in 438/7 was amalgamated with the Ionian. Traveling inspectors and magistrates supervised the collection of tribute and watched over the loyalty of the subjects. In various places garrisons were placed, especially after 440; or colonies of Athenian citizens (called *cleruchs*), who numbered in all about 10,000, were settled on land forcibly taken from local owners. Independent colonies were also sent out to Thurii in south Italy and to Amphipolis in Macedonia.

Athens paid little respect to its initial promise of autonomy for the members of the league. Laws passed by the Athenian assembly required universal use of standard weights and measures and of Athenian coinage. Although the Athenians were willing to tolerate any form of government among their subjects, even tyranny, so long as it was loyal, the internal political systems of the dependent states tended to be democratic under Athenian favor. In the case of Erythrae, Colophon, and others, members of the local councils were required to swear oaths of loyalty to the Athenian democracy. Expulsion of dissidents, the taking of hostages, fines, and other ingredients of imperialism all appeared at one place or another; after crushing the Euboean revolt of 446 Athens required, besides an oath of allegiance from every citizen, that Chalcis permit appeal in major lawsuits to Athenian courts, a step which incidentally benefited Athenian hotels as the Old Oligarch wryly commented.

Under the leadership of Pericles, Athens boldly and openly exploited its imperial position. When the congress of the Hellenes failed to convene, he took 5000 talents from the league treasury for the treasury of Athena proper. Part of this was placed in reserve, but much was used for the beautification of the Acropolis — the Parthenon is a monument to Athenian imperialism as well as to the confidence and artistic taste of classic Athenian culture. Thereafter 200 talents were allotted yearly to Athena beyond her one-sixtieth of the tribute, and the dues of the subjects paid the wages of some 10,000 Athenian citizens who rowed on the benches of that navy which kept the subjects under control.

The Debate on Imperialism. Just as Athenians examined the virtues and defects of democracy, so too they openly canvassed the rewards and liabilities of imperialism. A conservative party, made up largely of Athenian rural elements, stood on the side of conscience; this group opposed Pericles' use of league funds for Athenian buildings and deplored his imperial harshness. The political contention rose to its height in 443, when the citizen body voted whether to ostracize Pericles or the conservative leader Thucydides, son of Melesias (not the historian). The material interests of the Athenians in the prosperity born of empire and their patriotic pride in Athenian magnificence carried the day for Pericles; thereafter imperialism was no longer a political issue.

The moral problems of imperialism, however, were not so easily exorcised. During the Peloponnesian war, thus, the conservative playwright Aristophanes poked fun at the pomposity of Athenian inspectors and the imperial pride of his fellow-citizens. The sophists, who will be discussed later, seriously explored the nature of justice as against the rights of power. Once the war had been lost, an even more searching critique of the moral effects of imperialism upon the masters was leveled by the historian Thucydides; this bitter indictment will be considered below in Chapter 16.

The subjects were not so free to speak. Economically they benefited from the suppression of piracy and the improvement of the sea lanes, and the lower classes, which were fostered by the Athenian bias toward democratic government, seem to have favored Athenian rule. If Athenian cleruchs took some of the land of local farmers, commercial elements on the other hand could move to Athens and share its prosperity. Yet the alien mastery, though exercised with more considerable restraint than was later to be true of Greek imperialists, offended the basic principle of the *polis* as an independent, self-contained unit. Repeated revolts against "slavery," including a great secession of Samos in 441–39, studded the course of the empire. When finally the Peloponnesian war broke out,

Sparta could stand before Greece as the champion of liberty, and Athenian strategy in that conflict had always to consider first the necessity of keeping its subjects under control.

Economic Place in Athens. By the fifth century the great wave of Greek colonization into new areas of the Mediterranean had largely come to an end. Although this cessation closed one of the principal vents for internal social and economic tensions, the Greek world exhibited an unparalleled prosperity in the vigorous decades after the Persian defeat. The maritime states especially profited, and among these Athens led the way.

For the first time in history a state now appeared that could not feed its citizens from its own lands, for Periclean Athens became so large and so specialized in economic activity that the farms of Attica could not provide the city-dwellers with enough grain. Since the days of Solon, moreover, Athenian farmers had turned more and more toward the production of olive oil and wine, which were widely sold abroad. Along with these processed foods Athens exported a wide variety of manufactured items, the most visible of which in our archeological evidence was its fine red-figured pottery (see Plate XVII.B). In return, Athenian merchant shipping and the war fleet required timber, pitch, and other ship's stores, which came largely from Macedonia; and the industrial population of Athens lived off grain drawn from Thrace, Libya, and south Russia. As Pericles said, "All the good things from all over the world flow in to us, so that to us it seems just as natural to enjoy foreign goods as our own local products." [6]

Although this specialization made Athens the commercial hub of the Aegean, it also placed the state in a dangerous strategic position. In 437 (probably) Pericles made an impressive cruise into the Black Sea, where he unseated a tyrant at Sinope and concluded a treaty with the native ruler of the Bosporan kingdom (in the modern Crimea) which controlled the export of Russian wheat. To safeguard Athenian access to Macedonia he settled a large colony at Amphipolis in the next year. Already in 461–56 the city of Athens proper had been connected by the fa-

[6] Thucydides 2.38; tr. Rex Warner.

mous long walls, nearly four miles in length, to its ports of Phalerum and Piraeus so that it could be sure of getting food, whoever held the countryside; but command of the sea remained an absolute necessity for Athenian security.

The busy city-state of Athens was composed of several social elements. Although reliable statistics cannot be obtained, the most reasonable guess would give Periclean Athens 172,000 citizens in all plus 28,500 resident foreigners (*metics*) and 115,000 slaves. Of these groups the latter two deserve some comment.

The metics were formally registered, paid a small head-tax, and were liable for military service in Attica; in return they were free to ply trades and engage in commerce. Only a few favored foreigners (*isoteleis*), however, were allowed to own land, and metics normally could appear in Athenian courts only through a citizen sponsor. Such resident aliens were an element in many commercial states of Greece, for citizens commonly remained attached to agricultural pursuits and their civic duties.

Athens undoubtedly had more slaves than any other Greek state. Servile labor was of primary importance in the silver mines of Laurium, where it was ruthlessly worked to a speedy death; some factories employed slaves by the tens or fifties; the well-to-do were waited upon by personal servants, partly enslaved Greeks but more often from Thrace, Scythia, and Asia Minor. But the direction of economic life and most of the manual labor in industry, commerce, and shipping came from the bustling metics and citizens; when the Erechtheum was built in 421–06, to give one example, epigraphic evidence attests at one point that 20 citizens, 35 metics, and 16 slaves were being employed. While the institution of slavery distorted human values in Attica as elsewhere, one must keep in mind the comments alike of the Old Oligarch and of the orator Demosthenes that slaves at Athens generally acted and appeared like the common citizens. Manumission was occasionally granted for faithful service, and in the next century a famous banking house was run by two freedmen in succession, Pasion and Phormio.

Character of Greek Economic Life. Although it is difficult for modern observers to comprehend the tight communal life of a Greek city-state, no aspect is more alien to our own experience than its simple economic machinery. Farming was almost everywhere carried on by hard hand labor with simple tools and was devoted to providing the individual

farmer's subsistence. Only in Attica and a few other regions was specialized production for the market common. In the workshops, grouped in
quarters according to their products, the major source of power was that
of human muscles — it is small wonder that aristocratic reflection refused to endorse work as a virtue — and techniques were extremely
simple and conservative. Some technological improvement was occurring, as in the milling of grain and baking of bread; but the swift
changes common in the western world since the industrial revolution
were totally absent throughout ancient history.

Retail commerce was conducted on a very small scale by peddlers and
by stall keepers in the Agora or elsewhere; most objects were locally
made, though metals, luxury items, and other imports were required by
most Greek states. Piraeus and similar major ports had warehouses,
docks, and other harbor works, for long-range trade was conducted
almost entirely by sea in vessels of less than 100 tons, which ventured out
only from March to October. Roads were primitive, and land transport
by men or donkeys was fearfully expensive. Bottomry loans, in which a
shipper could borrow usually at 20 to 33⅓ per cent a year, were known
by the end of the fifth century, as was also banking; but the latter
consisted of little more than money-changing, pawnbroking, or acceptance of deposits.

To make economic activity even more difficult, Greece was split into a
host of fiercely autarchical states which had very little concept of sound
public finance. Apart from fines, tolls, and fees, major expenses of cult
and war were usually borne by impositions on the rich, called "liturgies,"
and at times by confiscation or by inflation of the currency. In these
respects the unification of much of the Aegean under Athenian rule
eased commercial interchanges, and the Athenian "owls" were famous as
a stable coinage (see Plate XVIII.B).

Within such systems the surplus of economic production over basic
human needs was not great, and society was commonly divided into a
relatively small rich class and a large group of the poor. At Athens a
middle group of commercial and industrial origin could exist in some
numbers and gave balance to the political structure; but even here an
ancient class of rural landlords tended to lead the peasants in grumbling
discontent over Pericles' expansionist policies. Elsewhere the aristocratic
elements were more firmly in control, often in conjunction with such

commercial elements as existed, and bitter hostility between rich and poor lay close below the surface. Damped down by the general prosperity of the mid-fifth century, this antagonism was to break out widely in the Peloponnesian war, when the rich or poor in various states made common cause with external enemies to gain power at home. Even in 464–61 the great revolt of the Spartan helots had alarmed much of Greece, which supported the Spartan citizens in restoring their mastery.

Shifts in Greek Lines of Trade. During the fifth century very important changes occurred in the routes along which Greek trade and culture penetrated the Mediterranean world. Within the Aegean the port of Piraeus became a focus, largely replacing the more scattered centers of Miletus, Aegina, Corinth, and so on; Ionia, in particular, fell into a slump very early in the century. Attic trade, however, spread from south Russia to Egypt, as is shown in coin hoards, and Greek culture began to have an appreciable influence in Syria. This eastward expansion became even more significant in the next century, but already by the fifth century the island of Cyprus had swung firmly into the Greek cultural orbit.

The old predominance of Corinth in western markets continued but was now challenged by Athenian expansionism. The helots who finally evacuated Mt. Ithome under guarantee of safe exit were settled by Athens at Naupactus on the gulf of Corinth, which remained an Athenian base. A new colony was begun under Athenian auspices in 443 at Thurii in south Italy, near the old site of Sybaris; Athenian diplomatic activity was noticeable in Sicily by the 450s. Here the Greek states were wealthy enough to build huge temples, but they warred incessantly among themselves.

Early in the century the archaic patterns of aristocratic control had broken down in the western states. First came a wave of tyrants, the most notable of whom were based on Syracuse. Gelon of Syracuse had thrown back a great Carthaginian invasion at the battle of Himera in 480. Later Greek tradition connected this attack with the Persian onslaught on Greece proper, but the two invasions seem to have been independent; the Carthaginians had been encouraged by another Greek tyrant, Theron of Acragas. Gelon's brother and successor at Syracuse, Hiero, held brilliant court and attracted some of the greatest poets of Greece. Then Syracuse adopted a democratic constitution from 466 on but continued, like Athens, to build up its power over a large area.

Beneath the surface Greek power in the west was ebbing. Militarily the states were still able to hold back Carthage, the Etruscans, and the natives; a great rebellion of the inland Sicels in Sicily, which extended over 459–40, was completely crushed. Yet Greek cultural influence at Carthage markedly declined in the fifth century, as it did also in central Italy. The latter region had little contact with the great days of classic civilization in the Aegean, but within that dull backwater Rome was fixing those institutions and qualities which were to be of tremendous importance thereafter as it began to exploit the stalemate of the other powers in Italy and Sicily.

THE GREEK WORLD IN THE MID-FIFTH CENTURY

In the fifth century, as earlier, the Greek world was a complex structure, formed of many states which were increasingly connected with a host of non-Hellenic neighbors. Theoretically each *polis* sought complete independence, but in practice the Greeks were grouped in a number of blocs, for example, Syracusan, Corinthian, Spartan, and Athenian. The latter bulks the largest in our sources and shows, accordingly, most clearly the remarkable political ferment of the era after the Persian defeats. The great Athenian experiments in democracy and imperialism, together with the debates over their merits, have influenced western thought ever since.

As the Athenians looked out on this world, they might be pardoned an almost smug attitude of self-satisfaction. Internally they had closed their ranks in the Persian wars and, despite minor grumbling from the right wing of conservatives, had advanced far on the path of democracy. Externally they had been checked in an effort to gain control of the Greek mainland, but their naval empire stood firmly, accepted alike by Persia and by Sparta. Their daily bread depended upon sure control of the sea lanes, yet thus far economic specialization had brought them marked prosperity. In keeping with that prosperity and self-confidence went a superb efflorescence of the arts and letters.

BIBLIOGRAPHY

Sources. For the period from 478, when Herodotus closed his history, to 432/1, when Thucydides' account begins, we have no significant story of Greek history. Thucydides 1.89–117 gives a brief survey of the rise of the Athenian empire, and Diodorus Siculus, Books 11–12, is of some use; Plutarch wrote lives of Cimon and Pericles. Many events, however, can be given only approximate dates, and the chain of events which led to actions is often obscure.

It is accordingly fortunate that epigraphic evidence rises markedly all over the Greek world, and especially at Athens. In addition to formal decrees and treaties with such subjects as Chalcis and Erythrae the tribute lists from 454/3 were carved on stone, and have been painstakingly reconstructed by B. D. Meritt, H. T. Wade-Gery, and M. F. McGregor, *The Athenian Tribute Lists,* 4 vols. (Princeton: Princeton University Press, 1939–53). When one examines such an inscription as that of 459 or 458 listing the 177 men of one Athenian tribe who "were killed in Cyprus, Egypt, Phoenicia, Halieis, Aegina, and Megara in the same year" (Tod, *Greek Historical Inscriptions* I, No. 26), the heavy costs of Athenian imperialism and its wide range of activities become evident.

The coinage provides the most continuous record (Plate XVIII.B); Chester G. Starr, *Athenian Coinage 480–449* B.C. (Oxford: Oxford University Press, 1970), classifies it and suggests its importance.

Further Reading: A classic treatment of political and economic conditions in the fifth century is A. E. Zimmern, *Greek Commonwealth* (5th ed.; Oxford: Oxford Paperback 13, 1961). Very useful is Russell Meiggs, *The Athenian Empire* (Oxford: Oxford University Press, 1980); see also V. Ehrenberg, *Sophocles and Pericles* (Oxford: Blackwell, 1954). *Athenian Tribute Lists,* Vol. IV, has a detailed discussion of the financial structure of the empire and its history.

A. H. M. Jones, *Athenian Democracy* (Oxford: Blackwell, 1957), is excellent; some of the essays in A. W. Gomme, *Essays in Greek History and Literature* (Oxford: Blackwell, 1937), are pertinent; see also P. J. Rhodes, *The Athenian Boule* (Oxford: Oxford University Press, 1971), and E. S. Staveley, *Greek and Roman Voting and Elections* (Ithaca: Cornell University Press, 1972). Economic life is sketched generally by G. M. Calhoun, *Business Life of Ancient Athens* (New York: Cooper Square, 1968); in greater detail by Hendrik Bolkestein, *Economic Life in Greece's Golden Age* (new ed.; Leiden: Brill, 1964), and A. French, *Growth of the Athenian Economy* (London: Routledge and Kegan Paul, 1964).

15

FIFTH-CENTURY CIVILIZATION

Few stages in history have been so clearly stamped with a common spirit as the civilization centered in fifth-century Athens. In the character of Pericles, in the structure of democratic Athens, in the majestic Parthenon, and in a play by Sophocles the same harmonious, even austere quality appears. Much was demanded of its citizens by Periclean Athens, but for a brief span of time men were fired to an amazing, many-sided outburst of human genius.

Fundamentally this brilliant achievement rested upon a happy blend of old and new forces. From the past, men inherited a deep religious belief in the power of basically benign, just gods; a patriotic unification of energies in the *polis;* and an aristocratic social pattern. Rising within these beliefs were an ever greater sense of the importance of the individual human being and a rationalistic, questioning spirit which considered none of the inherited structure free from challenge. The great triumphs of the period stood at the point where these forces were in balance, where men shared a self-confidence in taste and judgment and an exaltation of spirit which admitted almost no limits. Passion ran deep in the art and literature of the fifth century, but for the moment it was firmly harnessed and purified.

Although Athens had failed to unite all Greece under its political sway, culturally it stood unchallenged. The trade routes of the Aegean world brought men and ideas from everywhere to the great port of

Piraeus. Its own economic drive and the fruits of empire provided Athens greater wealth than any Greek state had ever enjoyed, and this wealth was generously dispensed by Pericles, who dreamed of uplifting his fellow citizens culturally as well as politically. Statesmen and artists, however, can proceed only so far as their public permits; behind the Athenian triumphs in tragedy and in art stood an unusually receptive and stimulating citizen body.

Yet classic civilization was not solely an Athenian product. Many of the great figures who were drawn by the challenge (and profit) of Athenian life had been educated elsewhere, and not all of the achievements of the era were located in ˙Attica. Pindar, for instance, was born in Boeotia and wrote his poetry on commissions from all Greece; besides the Parthenon, a large number of great temples arose at other sites in the fifth century. If we concentrate our gaze on Athens, this must not lead us to forget those great thinkers and artists who lived elsewhere.

THE ATHENIAN DRAMA

Performance of Tragedies. The literary form which shows in most succinct and brilliant fashion the qualities of fifth-century civilization is the Athenian drama, especially its tragedies. Unlike modern plays, which are performed commercially under private auspices, the tragedies and comedies of the fifth century were commissioned by the state and were presented at religious festivals in honor of the god Dionysus. Here they were given only once, though the more successful works might be performed again in later years.

By the sixth century B.C. popular, improvised songs in honor of Dionysus at the god's festivals had been turned into a more artistic form of lyric narrative and dance called a dithyramb. It became customary to produce dithyrambs at Attic celebrations for Dionysus, in which poets such as Simonides, Pindar, and Bacchylides competed; but besides these purely choral works, veritable plays with action also seem to have emerged under the Pisistratids. The first victor in a dramatic contest was said to have been Thespis about 534. The origin of the term "tragedy," derived from the word for goat (*tragos*), cannot be explained satisfactorily.

In the fifth century there were three occasions on which plays could be

produced. One was the Lenaean festival in January, when two tragedians presented plays. Five comedies also were performed by the later
decades of the century. Another was the Rural Dionysia, a local celebration in Attic demes, many of which came to have their own theaters;
here plays already given in the city received a second performance,
though Euripides at least presented some of his tragedies in the demes.
The great ceremony was the City Dionysia in late March or early April,
at a time when navigation was resumed and ambassadors and tribute-
bearers from the Athenian empire thronged the city. The main events of
this festival, which was a city holiday, covered six days and included a
great parade, the performance of dithyrambs, and the presentation of
plays by three tragedians and three to five comedians.

Well beforehand the authors who wished to compete submitted their
plays to the archon. Each comedian offered one play; the tragedians had
each to prepare a set of three tragedies, which might or might not have a
common theme, plus an afterpiece called a satyr play. The archon
chose the best three sets and allotted to each tragedian his actors, paid
at state expense, and a producer (called the *choregus*). The producer
was necessarily a wealthy citizen, for he bore the expenses of the chorus,
12 to 15 men, and provided the costumes as his contribution to the glory
of Dionysus. On the appointed days the Athenian public trooped out to
the theater of Dionysus on the south slope of the Acropolis, a structure
with wooden seats; paid their two obols apiece to the lessee who kept up
the theater; and witnessed one play after another. Judges drawn by lot
awarded prizes: a crown of ivy to the poet, the right to set up a triumphal tablet to the *choregus,* and an inscription on a state list in the
Agora to the best actor.

The stage consisted of a circular orchestra with an altar of Dionysus,
about which the chorus marched or solemnly danced, and a permanent
backdrop representing a temple or palace. The actors proper performed
on the shallow steps in front of the scenery or, if they depicted gods,
might appear on an upper balcony.

In the earlier popular celebrations the chorus had stood alone, and
even after actors had individual parts the chorus still played a main role,
as in Aeschylus' earliest surviving play, *Suppliants.* Aeschylus introduced
a second actor, which permitted deeper dramatic action; and Sophocles
added a third about 468. While the chorus still took part in the plot at

times, it tended ever more to shrink to the position of ideal spectator. In Aeschylus' plays it marched in, at the beginning, with a musician who played a type of oboe, and set the scene of the plot in an opening song; in the other playwrights it appeared later. Along the way the chorus voiced in lyric odes the thoughts of the audience as it watched the tragedy unfold, and in Sophoclean tragedy it held the stage alone at the end to reflect on the somber meaning of the scenes just witnessed.

A play might have any number of parts, but no more than three actors appeared on the stage at once. Since the actors wore masks, they could slip from one role to another easily; feminine parts were played by men. Some speeches were sung as odes, others were swift debates. An Athenian tragedy was in many ways like a modern opera, but we can judge it only as a play; for the musical accompaniments have not survived.

Tragic Subjects and Authors. The subject of a tragedy was usually a legend of the heroic age, such as the war of Argos and Thebes or the tales clustered about the great galaxy of Homeric heroes; but plays might also rise from historic events. The one surviving example of this latter type is Aeschylus' *Persians,* performed in 472 with Pericles as *choregus.* Narration of a story or legend, however, was only the vehicle by which the author might explore the nature of mankind; and for this purpose Greek dramatists turned firmly away from realistic depictions of average citizens to an ideal plane of heroic men and women, where the gods themselves might properly appear on occasion. However great, the human figures of tragedy had flaws which brought them to ruin; the authors who enlivened and brought these heroes before the men and women of Athens sought not so much to explain the workings of the universe as to illuminate the greatnesses and defects of mankind. As the critic Aristotle later defined the effect of tragedy, it gave a *catharsis* or purification to its spectators.

Although many authors vied in the annual competitions, the three adjudged the greatest then and by later ancient scholars were Aeschylus, Sophocles, and Euripides, who form an intellectual progression across the great days of Athenian tragedy. Aeschylus (525/4–456) wrote over 80 plays of which only 7 survive. Three of these constitute our one extant trilogy, the *Oresteia* of 458 on the career of Orestes, who slaughtered his mother Clytemnestra in vengeance for her murder of his father Agamemnon, but then in turn was pursued by divine wrath until he secured trial and pardon from the ancient court of the Areopagus at Athens. In another great and puzzling play, *Prometheus Bound,* Aeschylus presented the benefactor who gave fire to man, chained to a rock in punishment by Zeus; the whole action took place about this static figure and showed Zeus as still a tyrant. Presumably Zeus was depicted in the sequel as turning into a divine protector who treated mankind with wisdom and mercy, for Aeschylus was a deeply religious thinker, though at times he exhibits the strong hold of inveterate superstition. The plays of Aeschylus are deeply brooding dramas of inevitable, catastrophic ruin, in which passion was still ill-restrained and in which the religious and aristocratic qualities of archaic Greece were still powerful. His characters, accordingly, stand almost outside the human world, and his poetry rumbles with the thunder of bold images.

Most balanced and serene of the great triad was Sophocles (496–06), who was a friend of Pericles and on occasion an elected general of the Athenian democracy. He is said to have written 123 plays and won first place 24 times; but only 7 are preserved. The greatest of these is generally considered to be *Oedipus the King,* performed shortly after 430. Oedipus, son of King Laius and Queen Jocasta of Thebes, was born under a prophecy that he would kill his father and marry his mother; exposed on a rocky hillside as a result, he was saved by a shepherd and grew up in Corinth ignorant of his parentage. Near Delphi he did unwittingly murder his father and then came to Thebes, where he married Jocasta and had children by his own mother.

The play itself opens at the point where a plague has descended on Thebes, and Oedipus, as defender of his subjects, promises to rescue them. When a messenger from Delphi reveals that Apollo has bidden Thebes to punish the murderer of Laius, Oedipus fiercely calls down curses on the culprit; the audience, which knew the truth, must have shuddered at his self-confident vehemence. "It is," says a modern critic, "the action of Oedipus proceeding from the character of Oedipus and recoiling upon Oedipus which is the whole theme of the play." [1]

Step by step, Oedipus draws closer to the truth. The blind seer Tiresias is goaded by the king into hinting at the actual facts, which Oedipus does not comprehend. Thereafter a messenger from Corinth and the shepherd of Laius' house, who once had taken the babe to the hills,

[1] H. D. F. Kitto, *Greek Tragedy* (New York: Anchor A38, 1954), p. 76.

reveal all. Jocasta, a rationalist who disdains the seers, first detects the truth, rushes into the palace, and slays herself. When Oedipus realizes that he had actually fulfilled the prophecy, he too rushes off and blinds himself. The chorus holds the stage at the end as it sings:

> You that live in my ancestral Thebes, behold this Oedipus, —
> him who knew the famous riddles and was a man most mas-
>   terful;
> not a citizen who did not look with envy on his lot —
> see him now and see the breakers of misfortune swallow him!
> Look upon that last day always. Count no mortal happy till
> he has passed the final limit of his life secure from pain.[2]

In *Oedipus the King* Sophocles portrayed, in a more balanced view than that of Aeschylus, the greatness of man and his inevitable flaws. Sophocles was pious and accepted the world as grand, yet tragic in structure; but he reflected also the increasingly man-centered outlook of Periclean Athens. In another play, the *Antigone* of 441, Sophocles explored the tension between religious duty, which called Antigone (daughter of Oedipus) to bury the body of her dead brother Polynices, and the demands of the state; for her uncle Creon, ruler of Thebes, had forbidden the burial of Polynices as a traitor. Modern critics are inclined to treat this great work as a protest against the secularization of Periclean Athens, which emphasized material prosperity and brooked no bars to communal patriotism. The last play of Sophocles, *Oedipus at Colonus,* was performed after his death and is an amazingly powerful creation for a man in his eighties. It presented the doubtful reception of the blinded Oedipus at Athens, his pardon by its King Theseus, and his eventually serene death.

With Euripides (485–06) we step almost outside the confines of classic balance. In his lifetime Euripides was rarely successful, for he won first prize only five times. Before his death he had abandoned the tottering, bitter Athens of the Peloponnesian war and withdrew to Macedonia, where he wrote his *Bacchae* and some other plays. Yet his questioning of divine government and his sympathetic exploration of human passion in such female figures as Medea, Alcestis, and Iphigenia made him a favor-

[2] Tr. David Grene. The concluding sentiment was a famous one, which appears also in Aeschylus, *Agamemnon* 928; Euripides, *Trojan Women* 509–10.

ite of later ages, which preserved no less than 19 of his plays (1 of doubtful authenticity). When we return in the next chapter to the great intellectual shifts of the late fifth century, marked by the appearance of the sophists, Euripides must claim our attention once more.

Classic Qualities of Tragedy. The classic view of mankind is nowhere better displayed than in the Attic tragedies. Again and again a great man or woman stepped forth upon the stage, only to be stripped of pride and often to die violently in ruin. The vehicle for the ruin was man's own flaws, for man was free; and yet behind all lay the immortal gods, who thus punished undue pride (*hybris*). In tragedy the moral lesson was to cultivate *sophrosyne,* a proper balance and awareness of one's true position. Nonetheless the tragedians shared a humanistic pride in man's achievements and independence of action. Most noble of all is the great paean of the chorus in Sophocles' *Antigone,* which begins, "Wonders are many, and none is more wonderful than man." Man crosses the sea, harnesses the earth, teaches himself word-swift thought and speech; "cunning beyond fancy's dream is the fertile skill which brings him, now to evil, now to good." [3]

The balanced view of man; the serene, even severe temper of tragedy; the welling passion which is restrained almost unconsciously by a sense of proper form — all these are qualities of the classic outlook. In such a play as *Oedipus the King* the tempo is slow and deliberate at the outset, but speeds up inexorably; the reflective chorus which gives occasional relief in its lyric odes, the hot-headed Oedipus, his wife and mother Jocasta — calm and consoling at first, then ever more horrified — and all the other characters are pitted against each other in subtle rhythms. Like classic art and architecture the play has an outwardly simple, austere treatment which omits the insignificant diversions and the by-plots so evident in Shakespeare's plays. The whole development of *Oedipus the King* takes only 1530 taut lines. Yet the tight logical construction of the plot, its skillful proportions, and its artistic quality are a superb example of the developed Greek mind. When Oedipus fiercely proclaimed, "I must not hear of not discovering the whole truth," he expressed the consistent effort of the Greek thinker to plunge to the heart of a problem, no matter what the cost.

Attic Comedy. If the grim world of the tragic heroes seems appropri-

[3] *Antigone* 332ff.

ate to a great religious festival, it may appear surprising that the same audiences also witnessed Athenian comedies, which were rowdy, frank, even grossly obscene by modern standards. Greek religion had many levels, and the cult of Dionysus in particular was intimately connected with human interests and concerns in the field of nature's fertility. Whereas tragedy was a specifically Attic development, comedy emerged widely over Greece out of rural revels of disguised singers. In the Peloponnesus *mimes* or skits evolved from this root; the first writer of comic plays proper seems to have been Epicharmus of Syracuse (early fifth century). At Athens itself comedy was added to the City Dionysia in 486, to the Lenaea probably in 441/0.

While many men competed for the comic prizes, we have only 11 plays, all by Aristophanes (*c.* 450–*c.* 385), plus some fragments from his major rivals Eupolis and Cratinus. Unlike the tragic form, Aristophanic comedy is a loose structure of choral mockeries (including "patter song" like those of Gilbert and Sullivan), witty dialogue, and apostrophes to the audience, which is pictured as eating, drinking, even sleeping. All of this is held together by a wildly improbable, often slapstick plot. The boldness with which Aristophanes attacked the political leaders of the Peloponnesian war or censured the public for its poor judgment has rarely been equaled on any stage. Athenian tragedy never engaged in such topical references, though the attacks on war in some of Euripides' plays have a clear connection with contemporary conditions.

Yet Aristophanes had an amazing breadth of interest, which essentially reflects the broad interests of his audience. While in 424 he attacked, in the *Knights,* the popular leader Cleon as a corrupter of the assembly to his own profit and glory, in the next year it was the turn of Socrates, who was brilliantly if unjustly pilloried in the *Clouds* as an example of the new learning of logic and rhetoric which could make the worse appear the better cause. Later on Euripides was to suffer, by comparison with Aeschylus, in the *Frogs* of 405; how often has comedy turned to a comparison of literary styles? Most popular in modern revivals is his *Lysistrata* (411), in which the women of Athens deny themselves to their husbands until peace is secured.

As these examples suggest, Aristophanes was deeply conservative but had the gifts of turning his fears of Athenian democratic, imperialistic, and materialistic tendencies into ribald mockery. When an audience left the rocky hillside of the Acropolis after watching tragedies by Sophocles and Euripides, and comedies by Aristophanes, its view of life had been enlarged on many levels.

LETTERS, PHILOSOPHY, AND SCIENCE

Classic Literature. Apart from the Athenian poets who wrote in tragic or comic form, a host of other authors flourished in fifth-century Greece. The most famous of these was the poet Pindar of Thebes (*c.* 518–438). From his varied output there survive principally the choral odes in praise of athletic victors, which were great, serene celebrations of aristocratic virtue and ancestral religion. These commissioned odes began with a general praise of the victor, then passed to a myth connected with his homeland, and concluded usually with a few general observations on the nature of mankind. Pindar's poetry, which shimmers in its Doric Greek, is not easily translated; but in three glowing lines he summed up the clear-headed classic view of man:

> A changeable creature, such is man; a shadow in a dream.
> Yet when god-given splendor visits him
> A bright radiance plays over him, and how sweet is life! [4]

Beside Pindar stood Simonides of Ceos (*c.* 556–468), virtually the poet laureate of Greece in the time of the Persian war, who composed epitaphs for its heroes, choral celebrations of its battles, and also a host of dithyrambs, dirges, and odes for victors in the games. His nephew Bacchylides of Ceos (mid-fifth century) was notable for his odes and dithyrambs, some of which have been found on papyri in Egypt.

Prose had also become a distinct literary form by this time, particularly for the use of historians, philosophers, and scientists. In the writings of Hecataeus of Miletus (active about 500) history, geography, and ethnology had been mixed together; but in Herodotus the historical framework became dominant (see Bibliography to Chapter 13). Hellanicus of Mitylene (*c.* 491–06) concentrated upon building up a consecutive chronological arrangement of earlier Greek history, especially centered on Athens; and in a great account of the Peloponnesian war Thucydides

---

[4] *Pythian Ode* 8.95–97, tr. H. D. F. Kitto, *The Greeks* (Harmondsworth: Penguin A220, 1951), pp. 174–5.

created a stripped, deeply penetrating investigation of the meaning and causes of historical events as a model for all later historians. The thought of Thucydides, however, is so interconnected with that of the sophists that it must be reserved for the next chapter, along with the appearance of rhetoric and kindred subjects as distinct literary forms.

Philosophy in the Fifth Century. Throughout the sixth century thinkers in Ionia and in Italy had evolved many views of the nature of man and the world, sometimes fantastic in their details but all exhibiting a great logical and rational drive to fathom the universe as an orderly structure. By 500 the time had come for searching criticism of the unconscious assumptions in these earlier theories, for a statement of fundamental issues, and for a more conscious concentration upon philosophic as against scientific problems. This was the work of two almost utterly opposed thinkers, Heraclitus and Parmenides.

To Heraclitus of Ephesus (most active about 500–490) the world was one of infinite flux, as suggested in his famous statement that one cannot step into the same stream twice (since the water ever changes). Proud, deeply conservative in politics, Heraclitus scorned the follies of earlier poets and philosophers and dogmatically proved his views by the assertion, "I searched into myself." [5] Beneath all the flux, however, was a basic force of the world which he conceived as fire, sometimes literally, sometimes metaphorically in the shape of the *logos,* the divine spirit or world-reason. To Parmenides of Elea (about 480), on the other hand, the world was essentially unchanging, for it was of one primary stuff; and that which existed could not have come into existence out of nothing. The evidence of the senses which suggested the presence of motion must yield before the deeper knowledge of the reflective mind. Drawing from the skill of the earlier Xenophanes, Parmenides greatly sharpened Greek views of logic, a process continued by his pupil Zeno, who constructed some famous paradoxes between sensory and theoretical perception. In one paradox, for instance, Achilles races the tortoise but gives the tortoise a head-start of half the distance to the goal. Since a line consists of an infinite number of dots in the Pythagorean view, the tortoise will always be moving ahead while Achilles tries in vain to catch up and pass his slow competitor. Outwardly absurd, this logical argu-

[5] Heraclitus, fragment 101 (Diels).

ment nevertheless could not be countered on rational grounds until very recent times.

Through the work of Heraclitus and Parmenides the logical gifts of the Greek thinkers were elevated to a conscious level. Questions involved in man's ability to know the world were advanced, and some of the most basic philosophical problems involved in the nature of change and of being were apprehended. Throughout the middle decades of the fifth century a variety of more sophisticated answers was evolved.

Empedocles of Acragas (c. 493–33) gave up the idea that the universe consisted of one uniform material and secured the possibility of change in his hexameter poem *On Nature* by postulating four cardinal elements, fire, water, earth, and air, which were moved by two forces, love and strife. Although a powerful thinker on natural problems, Empedocles was also a mystic, who seems to have considered himself divine and wrote on transmigration in his other work, *Purifications*.

Anaxagoras of Clazomenae (c. 500–c. 428) was drawn to Athens, the first major philosopher to live in the city, and dwelt there for three decades as a friend of Pericles. To Anaxagoras the building material of the universe was tiny, discrete blocks of substances or "seeds," which were rationally assembled through the force of mind (*nous*); here matter and spirit were first clearly distinguished.

More fascinating to a modern mind, but of less effect at the time, was the theory of Leucippus of Miletus (active about 440) and of Democritus of Abdera (c. 460–370) that the world consisted of atoms, that is, of "uncuttable" units of matter in various shapes, positions, and groupings, which moved through the void by purely natural processes. Later on this atomic theory was to be seized upon by the philosopher Epicurus as the basis for the most materialistic ethical system evolved in antiquity.

To the average man much of this physical and metaphysical speculation, which drew ever farther from the realm of the senses, was nonsensical; but some conservatives could dimly scent its dangers in upsetting the old religious views of life. Although Pericles had called Athens the school of Hellas, Democritus discovered that its citizens cared little for his theories; Anaxagoras was mocked as "Old Nous" and finally was expelled for asserting that the sun was a molten rock as big as the Peloponnesus. Yet before the end of the fifth century the sophists were to draw upon some of the basic philosophical discoveries when they advanced a more individualistic concept of man, and the cosmological schemes of Plato and Aristotle were built squarely on the great rational debate of the fifth-century thinkers.

The First Sciences. As philosophy became a more penetrating study of various theoretical problems involved in a rational understanding of the world, so too the scientific approach began to rise in some areas. A rational, analytical attitude which strove to generalize knowledge was perceptible in mathematics from the days of Pythagoras onward; and geometry made great strides in the fifth century, as in the origin of solid geometry by Democritus. Another basically theoretical study, which entailed only very simple observations, was astronomy. Empedocles, Anaxagoras, and others demonstrated the causes of eclipses, and Meton (active about 433) devised a 19-year calendar which correlated the conventional lunar months with the solar year. Yet this work all remained theoretical. Even statesmen still continued to believe that eclipses were of divine origin.

Although experiments were occasionally suggested by the physical thinkers of the fifth century, the empirical collection of facts and the clear view that generalization could rest only upon carefully assessed data appeared first in medicine. The remarkable concepts created in fifth-century medicine had an influence far afield. Thucydides the historian and Socrates the philosopher, as well as the sophists, drew heavily on the medical principle that man had a proper character of his own (or *physis*). Among the doctors themselves, Alcmaeon of Croton (about 500), a pupil of Pythagoras, studied the human sense organs and was said to have been the first Greek to operate on the eye. Empedocles was also a physician, who saved Selinus from malaria by draining its swamps; his view that the heart was the seat of life led to study of the circulatory system by which the *pneuma* or vital spirit was distributed to the body.

Hippocrates of Cos (469–399), the patron saint of the medical profession, emphasized simple, rational treatment of sickness as a natural, rather than as a God-inflicted phenomenon. In the large collection of writings which later passed under his name (but none of which was probably written by him) there appears the theory that the vital forces in man were four "humors" (yellow and black bile, blood, and phlegm), which must be kept in balance by proper diet and conduct of life. This principle underlay medical concepts down to the eighteenth century. One Hippocratic tract, *On the Sacred Illness,* bluntly asserted that epilepsy was not of divine origin; another famous essay *On Airs, Waters, and Places* rationally analyzed the effects of different climates and other elements on the health of men. In the Hippocratic *Precepts* the common Greek tendency to theorizing was abruptly rejected in terms which sound almost like those of a modern scientist:

> In Medicine one must pay attention not to plausible theorizing but to experience and reason together . . . I agree that theorizing is to be approved, provided that it is based on facts, and systematically makes its deductions from what is observed . . . But conclusions drawn by the unaided reason can hardly be serviceable; only those drawn from observed fact.[6]

CLASSIC ART

Athens: Acropolis, Agora, and Piraeus. Among the greatest glories of the fifth century were its artistic and architectural triumphs, the best known of which were at Athens. The city itself remained a maze of narrow, dirty streets, bordered closely by blank-walled houses of sundried brick and without running water. In a climate where much of life could be passed communally out-of-doors, homes were not so significant, though aristocrats were housed in somewhat greater style. The women in such families had their own secluded quarters and were in theory somewhat restricted in social activity; men, however, engaged in reciprocal dinners and drinking parties (*symposia*). The evidence of gems, pottery, bronze candelabra, and representations of furniture on vases show that the minor arts of household life were inspired by the same standards of harmony, proportion, and external serenity as those of the greater arts.[7]

Above the simple abodes of the citizens rose the great rock of the

[6] Tr. W. H. S. Jones.
[7] See, for example, the famous 10-drachma coin from Syracuse (Plate XVIII.C), designed by Kimon about 405 B.C. and depicting Artemis Arethusa; this is only one of a variety of handsome pieces issued by fifth-century Greek mints.

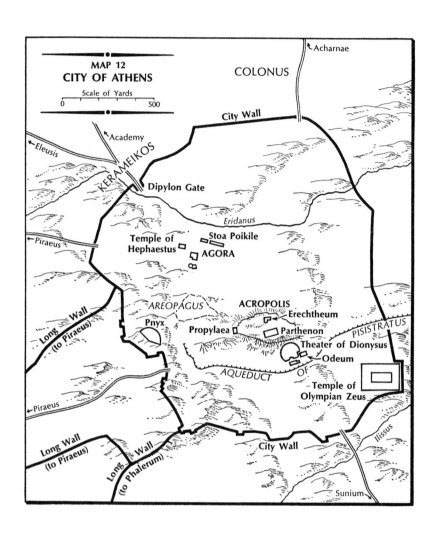

MAP 12
CITY OF ATHENS

Scale of Yards
0   500

Acharnae

COLONUS

City Wall

Academy

Eleusis

KERAMEIKOS

Dipylon Gate

Eridanus

Piraeus

Temple of
Hephaestus

Stoa Poikile

AGORA

AREOPAGUS

Pnyx

ACROPOLIS

Erechtheum

Propylaea

Parthenon

PISISTRATUS

Long Wall
(to Piraeus)

Theater of Dionysus

Odeum

AQUEDUCT   OF

Piraeus

Temple of
Olympian Zeus

Long Wall
(to Piraeus)

Long Wall
(to Phalerum)

City Wall

Ilissus

Sunium

Acropolis, the home of Athena and other divine protectors. After the Persian wars the top of this hill was enlarged and supported by a great wall, and from 448 onward the resources of Athens and the empire were poured into its embellishment. By the end of the century a visitor would have climbed the winding path up which came sacrificial beasts and would first have reached the Propylaea. This was a marvelous Doric and Ionic entry-gate with wings on either side, designed by Mnesicles. Begun in 437, this structure was still unfinished at the beginning of the Peloponnesian war and remained so thereafter (see Map 12).

Beyond, as one entered the sacred precinct, were various minor shrines to the right. On the very top of the softly bluish-tinted limestone hill rose the golden-hued marble columns of the Parthenon, dedicated to Athena the Virgin (Parthenos) and built 447–38. In this Doric temple, generally considered the most perfect example of the temple form, the architects Ictinus and Callicrates subtly curved or bent almost every line so that at a distance it would appear straight; and the workmen finished the Pentelic columns and other members on the site with utmost precision. Few temples were so superbly decorated as was the Parthenon by the sculptor Phidias and his workshop. At either end were great pedimental sculptures representing, on the east, the birth of Athena and, on the west, the contest between Athena and Poseidon for control of Attica. The metopes depicted battles of centaurs and lapiths. High up on the wall of the cella proper ran an almost hidden frieze, which showed the great procession of men and women bringing Athena her new robe.[8] Within the cella was the standing statue of Athena, 40 feet high, made by Phidias of ivory and gold plaques attached to a wooden framework. This is long since gone, but the Parthenon survived virtually intact as a Christian church and then a Moslem mosque until 1687. Then a Venetian bombardment blew up a powder magazine inside it; most of the sculpture was later bought by Lord Elgin, British ambassador to Turkey, in 1801–03 and transported to the British Museum in London.

---

[8] One scene of the Panathenaic festival celebrated in the Parthenon frieze, the youths carrying vessels, is shown on Plate XV. The frieze, 525 feet long, was carved in very flat relief, but monotony either in pose or in tempo was skillfully avoided. Shapes, thus, cut across one another to give a sense of depth, further heightened by the use of color against a blue background. Designed by Phidias, the sculptures were executed by stone cutters who "vied with one another that the quality of their work might be enhanced by its artistic beauty" (Plutarch, *Pericles* 13).

To the left, or north side of the Acropolis, as one looks from the Propylaea, once stood a great bronze statue of Athena the Defender (Promachos) by Phidias, the spear-point of which was visible to Athenian war-fleets entering Piraeus harbor. Behind this lay the Erechtheum, a remarkably complicated building in honor of Athena and various legendary heroes of Attica. The Erechtheum was built in 421–06 as a foil to the Parthenon and was given additional bulk for this purpose by the projecting southern Maiden Porch, the six columns of which are serious Athenian maidens (the caryatids). Unlike the Parthenon, it was of Ionic style, with a finely designed door on the north side; the temple of Athena Nike (Victory) built on a spur by the Propylaea in the same period was also Ionic. Although the buildings of the Acropolis honored the gods and heroes who protected the Athenian state, the human beings who really made Athens great cannot be far absent from the observer's mind as he sees the semiruined buildings which still stand.

On the south slopes of the Acropolis, among other buildings, lay the precinct of Dionysus, where the Athenian drama had its home, and the Odeum, a music hall constructed at the direction of Pericles. Music was an integral part of the plays and otherwise held as important a place as it does in modern life, but the achievements of Damon and other classical musicians are irretrievably lost. Below the northern edge of the Acropolis stretched the Agora, which was adorned with various public buildings in the age of Pericles. Among these was the famous Painted Colonnade (Stoa Poikile), which had paintings of the sack of Troy and the battle of Marathon by Polygnotus of Thasos and other artists. These too, unfortunately, could not survive; for Aristotle later placed this great painter beside Sophocles as showing "men as better than they are" and as revealing the qualities of character.[9] Polygnotus expressed emotion in his faces and engaged in foreshortening; later Apollodorus exploited the use of shading and mixed colors to create a more real world. Only in the decoration of small clay votive plaques and vases and Etruscan imitations can we detect the qualities of Greek painting at this time.

Surrounding the city and reaching down to Piraeus were the great walls of Athens, which made it virtually an island on land. Piraeus itself was redesigned by Hippodamus of Miletus, the first great city-planner, whose ideas embraced both a rectangular grid of streets, already known

[9] Aristotle, *Poetics* 1448a.

in Ionia, and the harmonious arrangement of various parts of a city in accordance with their economic functions. Hippodamus also laid out the colony of Thurii in southern Italy, and principles akin to his were employed in the new city of Rhodes as also in city foundations in the age after Alexander.

The Rest of Greece. Although Athens was ennobled during the fifth century more than any other single city, the prosperity and artistic genius of the classic age brought fruits to many great temple precincts of the Greeks. Almost all the temples were in a perfected Doric style but usually were not so refined as those of Athens, partly because of the expense and partly because marble was not often used except for sculptural decoration.

At Aegina the Doric temple of Aphaia, a local goddess, was erected in stuccoed limestone early in the fifth century and was decorated with sculptures which showed the first stages of the classic outlook. Other great temples were erected in the west at Selinus, Acragas, Posidonia, and Segesta. In the Peloponnesus a Doric temple to Apollo was built at Bassae, high and remote in the Arcadian hills; the architect was Ictinus, the designer of the Parthenon, and the temple has the first known Corinthian capitals (on the inside). The great Doric temple of Zeus at Olympia came in the middle of the century.

The pediments and metopes of this latter temple are perhaps the greatest sculptural achievements of the century.[10] Their creator is unknown, but Phidias made the ivory and gold statue of Zeus which, to later Greeks, ranked as his greatest creation. Beside Phidias stood, as the major sculptors of the age, Myron and Polyclitus, who represented an independent Argive tradition. Since both worked primarily in bronze, their works have not survived except in later marble copies; Polyclitus in particular created a canonical type of the male, nude athlete with gently twisted torso, as in his *Doryphorus* (spear-bearer) and *Diadumenus* (youth binding his hair), relaxed yet capable of supple vigor, physically

[10] In the metope from Olympia illustrated on Plate XIV Heracles is bearing the world on his shoulders, while Atlas (to the right) returns with the golden apples of the Hesperides. The Greek sense of divinity is superbly suggested here in the form of the goddess Athena (left), who merely raises her hand in order to help Heracles with the burden which is obviously straining his human frame. The artistic sense of composition, which interlinked these three vertical accents without any background, is noteworthy.

perfect yet endowed with spiritual grace.[11] In his sculptures and in a treatise on the principles of proportion called the *Canon*, Polyclitus greatly influenced subsequent sculptors and so helped to set the classic style.

In general terms archaic sculpture had still been largely abstract, even symbolic. Now sculptors represented a more naturalistic outlook. Their figures had more freedom to turn and twist while exhibiting an inner life which was often grave and thoughtfully conscious of the world, and controlled in its passionate energy.[12]

THE GOLDEN AGE

Throughout the wide range of literary and artistic activity in Greece during the fifth century there runs a common spirit. To a modern student its qualities are most evident in sculpture and in the Attic drama, which concentrated upon man and depicted him simply yet idealistically. Although we have busts labeled with names of Themistocles, Pericles, and other great figures, they are not fully realistic representations, and in what remains of Greek painting there seems to have been no interest in nature for itself. So too in philosophy the emphasis lay upon rational, theoretical analysis. The Greek outlook, which had been developing since the first Protogeometric pottery and the epics of Homer, had now reached a very advanced level. Together with the companion classics of the next 100 years the marvelously coherent and rounded achievement of the fifth century has had a great influence on western civilization.

While the classic spirit was a common possession of all Greece, it was exhibited in many local forms. Athens could not swallow up the rest of Greece either politically or culturally. The local attachments and political subdivisions of the Aegean world were a saving grace in Hellenic

---

[11] The pose of the *Doryphorus* was adapted by the sculptor of the famous Prima Porta statue of Augustus, shown on Plate XXV.
[12] The bronze statue of Plate XIII, slightly over life-size, is one of our most perfect examples of the classic style. Found in the sea off Cape Artemisium in 1926, it represents either Zeus with his thunderbolt or Poseidon with his trident. Although its sculptor is unknown, he was a master of about 470–50 B.C.; the progress of Greek civilization in a century and a half is sharply evident if one compares this work with the Sunium *kouros* of Plate XI.

civilization; for from this situation sprang first the possibility of cultural variations and secondly the ability of artists and thinkers to migrate until they found their proper intellectual home. Freedom of thought was not an abstract virtue in the city-states of Greece. Democratic Athens, which fostered the outpouring of so much genius and boasted much of its freedom of speech and customs, was perhaps the most insistent in practice that its citizens accept the standards of the majority; Anaxagoras and Phidias both suffered punishments on grounds that were not only political, that is, friendship with Pericles, but also intellectual and emotional. Greek civilization may rightly be revered by later ages, but its molders were imperfect human beings.

BIBLIOGRAPHY

Sources. Among the many literary masterpieces of the fifth century, the one work which perhaps best incarnates the classic virtues is the tragedy *Oedipus the King* by Sophocles; but to read any of the Athenian tragedies and comedies is a rewarding experience. Among English translations, recent good versions are *The Complete Greek Tragedies,* ed. David Grene and Richmond Lattimore, 4 vols. (Chicago: University of Chicago Press, 1959); the Penguin versions by P. Vellacott and E. F. Watling; or *Greek Plays in Modern Translation,* ed. D. Fitts (New York: Dial, 1947). The translations of Aristophanes by B. B. Rogers are also lively (Loeb Classical Library). Pindar has been well translated by Richmond Lattimore (Chicago: University of Chicago Phoenix P33, 1960); Herodotus, by A. de Selincourt (Harmondsworth: Penguin L34, 1954); Thucydides, by Rex Warner (Harmondsworth: Penguin L39, 1954), though the famous translation by B. Jowett, now often despised, is frequently the most quotable. Hippocrates is available in the Loeb Classical Library.

The modern world, unfortunately, has made its acquaintance with Greek sculpture mainly through plaster casts or copies from Roman copies of Greek originals. Far more illuminating is a study of the Parthenon marbles or the great sculptures of Olympia. The best preserved temples of the fifth century are those of Hephaestus (or Theseus) at Athens, Apollo at Bassae, Hera at Posidonia, "Concord" at Acragas, and the lonely, unfinished structure at Segesta.

Further Reading. The studies on Greek civilization, literature, and art listed in General Bibliography pay extensive attention to the classic period. T. B. L. Webster, *Greek Art and Literature, 530–400 b.c.* (Oxford: Oxford University Press, 1939), is thorough; see also his *Athenian Culture and Society* (Berkeley: University of California Press, 1973). G. F. Else, *The Origin and Early Form of Greek Tragedy* (New York: Norton, 1972), treats a difficult subject.

An excellent introduction to Greek tragedy is H. D. F. Kitto, *Greek Tragedy* (3d ed.; London: Methuen, 1966). A. W. Pickard-Cambridge, *Theatre of Dionysus in Athens* (Oxford: Oxford University Press, 1946), and *Dramatic Festivals of Athens* (2d ed.; Oxford: Oxford University Press, 1968), show the staging and occasions for tragedies; T. B. L. Webster, *Greek Theatre Production* (2d ed.; London: Methuen, 1970), is complementary.

G. Thomson, *Aeschylus and Athens* (3d ed.; London: Lawrence and Wishart, 1967), seeks to put the drama in an ancient social context; on Aeschylus see also J. H. Finley, *Pindar and Aeschylus* (Cambridge, Mass.: Harvard University Press, 1955). Sophocles is well treated by C. M. Bowra, *Sophoclean Tragedy* (London: Oxford University Press, 1965); T. B. L. Webster, *Introduction to Sophocles* (2d ed.; London: Methuen, 1969); and C. H. Whitman, *Sophocles: A Study of Heroic Humanism* (Cambridge, Mass.: Harvard University Press, 1951).

On comedy, see Francis M. Cornford, *Origin of Attic Comedy* (Magnolia, Mass.: Peter Smith), or Gilbert Norwood, *Greek Comedy* (Magnolia, Mass.: Peter Smith). Aristophanes is discussed by K. J. Dover, *Aristophanic Comedy* (London: Batsford, 1972). For Pindar, see Gilbert Norwood, *Pindar* (Berkeley: University of California Press, 1974), and C. M. Bowra, *Pindar* (Oxford: Oxford University Press, 1964). The works on Greek philosophy noted in Bibliography, Chapter 12, cover the fifth century.

Besides the general studies of Greek art and architecture (General Bibliography), J. Boardman, *Athenian Red Figure Vases* (London: Thames & Hudson, 1975), and P. E. Corbett, *Sculpture of the Parthenon* (Harmondsworth: King Penguin, 1959), are illustrative.

16

END OF THE GOLDEN AGE

So magnificent was the political and cultural flowering of fifth-century Greece that one might have wished this golden age to last forever. Yet it ended, and the historical observer can see why it was fated to end. For several decades very fundamental changes in men's attitudes had been developing beneath the outward balance of the era. The serenity, communal dedication, and exaltation of spirit which had fired both the creators of the classic masterpieces and the keen-witted Athenian audiences could not endure forever. Nor could the underlying political and cultural tensions of Greece be enduringly repressed.

Politically the Greek world was divided into great blocs — the Athenians and their subjects, the Spartans and their allies, Corinth and her trading empire, Syracuse and the other Sicilian states — which rubbed on each other. Outside the Hellenic state system lay such powers as the suspicious Persian empire, which was seeking to regain the coast of Asia Minor; the large if still weak kingdom of Macedonia; and the imperialistic, commercial state of Carthage. Within several of the Greek blocs themselves there lurked further sources of trouble, for external domination of a city-state accorded ill with its fundamental principles. Athens in particular grew ever more openly imperialistic and displayed a pride or *hybris* which, if the tragedians spoke true, must bring retribution. But men were not as sure as their grandfathers had been that the gods ruled all; Pericles had done much to secularize the state, and his successors

339

tended to equate might with right. Inside most of the advanced city-states a smoldering opposition of rich and poor needed only a suitable opportunity to blaze up in civil strife.

Culturally too men were divided. An advanced group of thinkers, called in part the "sophists," flourished especially at Athens; while the individualistic, openly critical attitudes of these men attracted the youth, they frightened the more pious and conservative part of the population. The harmony and proportion visible in classic literature and art were not likely to last, and in fact the scales tipped ever more decisively against the older temperament.

In 431 a great war broke out between Athens and Sparta, which raged intermittently to 404. Virtually every political tension was drawn into and fed further this terrific holocaust so that its effects were the more destructive; the intellectual and emotional stresses of this era also shattered many institutions and inherited attitudes which previously had limited cultural change. Thereafter Greek civilization entered upon a new phase.

THE PELOPONNESIAN WAR

The First Phase (431–21 B.C.): *Stalemate.* The fact that we call the war between Athens and Sparta the Peloponnesian war reflects the bias of our sources, which are almost entirely Athenian. The greatest of these is the history of Thucydides, an Athenian statesman and general who was convinced from the outset that the war would be the most important ever recorded in Greece and therefore made great efforts to establish the exact truth. Since he was exiled early in the war for failing to relieve a besieged Athenian dependency, he had ample leisure to travel and to talk to both Spartans and Athenians.

By 449–46 Athens had secured peace with both Persia and Sparta, at the price of giving up its efforts to expand into the eastern Mediterranean and to conquer its land neighbors in Greece. Thereafter it had concentrated under the leadership of Pericles in consolidating its naval empire in the Aegean; but even so discontent mounted. Although Athens was not as ruthless as many another imperialist has been, its domination chafed particularly the upper classes among the subject states, who made secret appeals to Sparta for liberation. Corinth and Megara, which were important members of the Peloponnesian league, suffered commercially from Athenian competition. Sparta itself was ever more suspicious of the swelling power of the Athenians, and to Thucydides this fear was the fundamental cause of the war.

If we carefully assess Athenian policy 433–31, it may appear that Pericles deliberately brought matters to a head; for he banned Megarian traders from Aegean markets, aided the Corinthian colony of Corcyra in its controversy with Corinth, and forbade the subject state of Potidaea to draw its annual magistrate from Corinth, as had been the custom. At extended conferences in Sparta during the winter 432/1 the Corinthians and other Spartan allies made it clear to the reluctant Spartans that they must go to war or face the unpleasant probability that their league would break asunder. So the Spartans assented, confident at least that they were fighting the Athenians "for the liberties of Hellas"; [1] besides their league they had also the support of Megara, Boeotia, Locris, and Phocis.

The ensuing war from 431 to 421 was a contest of the elephant and the whale. The Peloponnesian league had only limited naval strength and did not possess the funds either to build a large navy or to hire the necessary rowers. Although its powerful army invaded and laid waste Attica, it could not attack Athens proper, which was safe behind its stone walls and drew much of its food from overseas; nor were the Spartans able to keep their army active throughout the agricultural season. Sparta stood for liberty, yet it could not aid Athenian subjects overseas to secure their freedom. When Mitylene rebelled in 428–27, the Athenian fleet inexorably reduced it once more to obedience.

On the other hand Athens could not force Sparta to surrender, for it dared not meet the invincible Spartan hoplites by land. When the enemy did invade Attica in 431 and subsequent years, the helpless countryfolk had to evacuate their ancestral homes and pour into Athens itself. Although they raged against Pericles and even temporarily removed him from office, he calmly adhered to his cautious, outwardly indecisive policy of wearing down the enemy by naval raids about the Peloponnesus. Above all, Athens must keep its fleet intact, on which rested its imperial revenues and its overseas supplies of grain; Thucydides represents him as saying in a speech to the people, "You must not be extending your

[1] Thucydides 4.85.

empire while you are at war or run into unnecessary dangers. I am more afraid of our own mistakes than of our enemies' designs."[2] Pericles himself died in 429, a victim of the great epidemic akin to typhus which broke out in 430–26 in the overcrowded city of Athens and killed tens of thousands, but his successors over the next decade continued his policy with only occasional deviations.

In general the Athenians had the better of the widely scattered actions in the first round of the war. Sparta itself they could not touch, but at such points about the Peloponnesus as Methone, Cythera, and Pylos they set up coastal forts to which disaffected helots and others might escape (see Map 11). Corinth, however, suffered severely. The Athenians secured naval mastery in the gulf of Corinth through the brilliant battles of their admiral Phormio (429); and from their base of Naupactus they virtually prevented Corinthian trade to the west. By a chance of war the Athenian fleet cut off a whole battalion of Spartans on an island at Pylos and forced it to surrender (425). The Athenian leaders, Demosthenes and Cleon, took among other prisoners 120 Spartan "Equals," a sizable proportion of the Spartan citizen body, and the Spartans thereafter dared not invade Attica lest these hostages be executed.

Athenian operations against the neighboring Megara and Boeotia miscarried and produced at Delium in 424 the one large-scale land battle in the first stage of the war; the Athenians were soundly beaten by the Boeotian army. The last major actions in the war took place along the coast of Macedonia, where a brilliant Spartan leader, Brasidas, was able to get at Athenian subject states by land and incite them to rebel. In a battle at Amphipolis both he and the Athenian Cleon were killed (422).

Thereafter both sides were ready to call a halt to the inconclusive struggle. By the peace of Nicias (421), named after the chief Athenian diplomat, Athens returned its hostages and was to evacuate its coastal forts in the Peloponnesus, though this was not actually done. Sparta relinquished its posts in the north Aegean and essentially deserted its allies, who got nothing. To reassure Sparta, Athens actually contracted a formal alliance with its erstwhile foe and promised to aid it in the event of a rising by the sorely oppressed helots.

Interlude (421–13 B.C.): *Sicilian Disaster.* Athens had done as well, or better, than could have been expected. The Aegean empire was intact; in

[2] Thucydides 1.144; tr. B. Jowett.

western waters its power had risen; the Peloponnesian league had been sorely shaken. Throughout history a naval power has usually been able to defeat a land power only if it secures a powerful land ally; but no major Greek state had been willing to link itself to Athenian imperialism. Argos, the one possibility, had been bound to neutrality by a treaty with Sparta which expired only in 421.

Yet the Athenians were far from satisfied inasmuch as their eager expansionism had been essentially checked. During the strains of the war the temperament of the assembly became steadily harsher, especially after the calm hand of Pericles had been removed and the more vengeful rabble-rouser Cleon had become its main adviser. The epidemic and overcrowding had affected everyone; the devastation of the countryside and the losses of the army damaged especially the rural classes. After the revolt of Mitylene the assembly, under the leadership of Cleon, had first voted the execution of all male Mityleneans; and only with difficulty had more sober heads secured a reversal of the sentence.

Now that the war was over, Athenian opinions were sharply divided, and so was Athenian leadership. Nicias (c. 470–13), a conservative aristocrat, was a second Pericles, save that his religious piety and high sense of duty were not matched by equal firmness and clarity of thought. Far more radical was the erstwhile ward of Pericles and pupil of Socrates, the young, handsome, and popular Alcibiades (c. 450–04). First Alcibiades persuaded the Athenians to ally themselves with Argos and to attempt land operations in the Peloponnesus; though the upshot was a defeat of the Argives and a small Athenian force by the Spartan King Agis at Mantinea (418), the peace was not formally broken.

Then came a tempting opportunity to intervene once more in the affairs of Sicily. During the war the Athenians had made some diplomatic and naval gestures toward unseating Syracusan power; now an appeal from the native state of Segesta promised more extensive local support. Nicias stood in opposition and pointed out the basic strategic requirement that Athens remain powerful in the Aegean, but Alcibiades successfully rallied the spirit of excitement and possible economic profits among the citizens. The assembly not only voted to send an expedition but also set its size on the large scale which Nicias had proclaimed necessary; and it placed in command a triumvirate consisting of Alcibiades, Lamachus (a professional general), and Nicias. In June of 415, some 100 triremes and troopships rowed out of the harbor of Piraeus in gala array, met a further contingent off Corcyra, and set course for Sicily. Never had a Greek state engaged in so great an amphibious operation, with such hopes, and with such inevitable and disastrous failure.

First the Athenian commanders disagreed among themselves and wasted valuable time in which the Syracusans could begin to prepare themselves. Then Alcibiades was recalled by his enemies in Athens, on grounds that he had profaned the Eleusinian mysteries during a drunken revel. Rather than return to face the probability of death, Alcibiades fled to Sparta where he urged the Spartans to aid Syracuse and to resume the war against Athens. Although Sparta sent only the general Gylippus to command the Corinthian relief expedition to Syracuse, this leader invigorated the Syracusans to withstand a great siege by the Athenian force.

Lodged in a swampy corner of the great harbor of Syracuse, Nicias grew more and more despondent and called for help, which was provided by a further expedition under Demosthenes in 413. When the Athenians still failed to carry the city, their commanders decided to retreat; but since an eclipse of the moon had just occurred Nicias refused to leave for 27 days. During that period the Syracusans strengthened their ships and in a hand-to-hand naval battle in the great harbor cut off Athenian retreat by sea. When finally Nicias led off his dejected army by land, they were cut to pieces by Syracusan cavalry. Nicias and the other Athenian leaders were executed, the Athenians died of hunger and thirst in the quarries where they were imprisoned, and the Athenian subjects were sold into slavery. All told 50,000 men and over 200 triremes were lost.

The Last Phase (413–04 B.C.): *Athenian Disaster.* By this time Athens was once more at war with Sparta. Many of its subjects in the Aegean, deeming that Athenian naval strength was irretrievably committed in the west, were ready to rebel, and Sparta seized the favorable juncture to close with its enemy. In tragic terms the Athenians had shown their *hybris* in their increasingly ruthless imperialism; then they had been blinded by the gods and had rushed into the Syracusan disaster; now came the inevitable punishment.

The Spartan leaders had taken lessons from their earlier failures and doggedly pursued a more active strategy in the last phase of the struggle. On the advice of Alcibiades, King Agis of Sparta established in the spring of 413 a fortified post in Attic territory at Decelea. This garrison cut off Attic land communication with the fertile fields of Euboea, hampered Athenian farming, and served as a point of refuge for Attic slaves, 20,000 of whom deserted to the enemy. The Spartans also built a fleet and became active on the east coast of the Aegean, where widespread revolt resulted among the Athenian subjects.

Yet the Athenians struggled on valiantly. They abolished the tribute of their subjects and imposed a flat 5 per cent customs tax at all harbors, which they themselves also had to pay; they refurbished the fleet; and for a time their admirals were able to reconquer some of the rebel states as well as dealing with the inexperienced Spartans. In 411–10 the Athenians defeated the Spartan fleet at Cynossema and then at Cyzicus; the survivors of the latter battle sent a laconic message home, "Ships gone; Mindarus [the admiral] dead; the men starving; at our wits' end what to do."[3] The Athenian leader at Cyzicus had been Alcibiades, the wily turncoat, who had contrived to return to the Athenian side and was made an admiral once more.

The end, however, was foreordained as soon as Persia decided to take sides. From 412 on its satraps in Asia Minor furnished money to the Spartans for the construction of ships and the payment of rowers. In return the Spartans, who stood for Greek liberty, had to make a devil's bargain by promising to return the Greeks of Asia Minor to Persian rule. In 406 their new fleet was ready and blockaded the Athenians at Lesbos. When the news came to Athens, the desperate citizenry launched every old hulk in the shipyards, manned the 110 ships with elderly aristocrats, boys, and even slaves, and rowed out to defeat the enemy spectacularly at the battle of the Arginusae islands. Immediately after the battle the sea turned rough, and 12 disabled Athenian ships sank with their crews; by a vote of the vengeful assembly, which overrode all traditional safeguards, all the Athenian admirals who had won the battle, including the younger Pericles, were condemned to death for not saving the shipwrecked.

With the Persian financial resources at their command, the Spartans restored their fleet and entrusted it to one of the most notable command-

[3] Xenophon, *Hellenica* i.i.2; tr. H. G. Dakyns.

ers they ever produced, Lysander. In 405 he struck at the jugular vein of Athens by seizing command of the Hellespont. The Athenian fleet hastily came up and encamped on the opposite shore of the narrow strait at Aegospotami; but despite the warnings of Alcibiades, once more in exile and living nearby, the Athenian admirals could not maintain enough discipline over their motley crews to secure proper watch. After lulling the Athenians into negligence, Lysander suddenly darted across the strait while the Athenians were on shore, foraging for their food, and seized 160 of the 180 Athenian warships. Then he swept down through the Aegean, driving Athenian colonists, officials, and traders ahead of him to Athens, which he and King Agis besieged by land and — at last — by sea. Although their situation was hopeless, the proud Athenians starved through the winter until finally they had to surrender in the spring of 404. The elephant had shown greater staying power than the whale, and had won in the end by joining naval to land supremacy.

At a council of Sparta and its allies, most voices were raised in favor of the complete destruction of Athens just as it had destroyed other cities during the war; but the Spartans refused to wipe out a state which once had defended Greece and which, moreover, might be a useful tool under Spartan control. The Athenian navy, however, was surrendered, and the long walls between Athens and Piraeus were demolished. As they worked at this task, the Spartans were accompanied by the music of flutes and believed "that day the beginning of liberty to Greece."[4] The Athenian empire had fallen, true; the question now was, to what extent would Sparta or Persia permit the Greeks to be free?

Internal Strife during the War. The great conflict of 431–04 had released a host of vengeful forces on the international plane; but it had also given opportunities and causes for internal strife. The Athenians had done everything in their power to stir up the Spartan helots, who became seriously disaffected; the Spartan masters, who poured out their blood on battlefields by land and by sea, were accordingly driven to treat their serfs in ruthless fashion. In return the Spartans promoted desertion and unrest among the Athenian slaves, who furnished a considerable part of the necessary manpower in Athenian workshops and markets.

Worse yet were the outbreaks of hostility between rich and poor citizens. One notable example among many was analyzed by Thucydi-

[4] Xenophon, *Hellenica* 2.2.18.

des, who gave a graphic picture of the *stasis* or civil war at Corcyra in 427. With Corinthian aid the oligarchs of Corcyra murdered democrats; then came an Athenian fleet, and the democrats took bloody revenge on the upper classes, disregarding even the sanctuaries of the gods. These internal struggles were linked with foreign war, "in every city the chiefs of the democracy and the oligarchy were struggling, the one to bring in the Athenians, the other the Lacedaemonians." [5]

At Athens itself the lower classes usually dominated the assembly under leaders such as Cleon and Cleophon, who were able but dema-gogic, and became ever more tyrannical with respect both to Athenian subjects and to the upper classes at home. In their despair in 411, how-ever, they yielded temporarily to an oligarchic revolution, which set up for a time (411–10) a limited franchise and abolished pay for public service. Thereafter the masses were even more radical and secured a regular pension for the poor, who were afflicted by the economic stresses of the war. Superstition, too, and emotional fears grew powerful in politics as the violence of war warped sane judgment. When the war came to its disastrous end, the democratic system of Athens was wiped out by Spartan ukase, and a tight tyranny, called the Thirty from the number of its leaders, was established which executed democratic leaders and dissidents by the hundreds.

The inhumanity and spilling of blood which were marked here and in other internal fights had their precedent in the general course of the war, which had become ever more unlimited. The Athenians had executed the leaders of the Mitylenean revolt early in the war, but the first utterly vindictive act had been the massacre of all the male inhabitants of Plataea after a two-year siege (429–27) by the Spartans and Thebans, on the sole ground that they had stuck by the Athenians. From 421 on the Athenians too had killed male captives and enslaved the females, as at Scione and above all at Melos, which they attacked in time of peace (416–15) because it had shown pro-Spartan sympathies beneath a surface neutrality. Before the end of the great war brutality was the custom, and large masses of Greeks had been enslaved. Militarism too had become a way of life for thousands of virtually homeless mercenary soldiers and sailors.

In every respect, thus, the outward serenity and confidence which had

[5] Thucydides 3.82; tr. B. Jowett.

marked much of Greek life in the middle of the fifth century had dissolved by 404. Once again Persia had entered Greek affairs. Sparta had been cruelly tried by the long war — unfortunately Thucydides does not describe for us in detail its internal development — and had decided to exercise open suzerainty over all Greece; the catastrophic results that ensued will concern us in the next chapter. The Spartan bloc, nonetheless, was far less firmly knit than before; the Athenian group had been dissolved; and even in Sicily, Syracuse could no longer claim control. As the international structure of Greece had disintegrated, so too had the internal loyalties of the citizens deteriorated in many of the states.

THE NEW INTELLECTUAL OUTLOOK

The Sophists. Not all of the great intellectual changes occurring in Greek civilization were solely the product of political and economic conflicts. One important force in Greek culture of the fifth century was its practical, man-centered quality. In the earlier part of the century this aspect had been muffled by ancestral views, best expressed in Pindar and Aeschylus; but particularly at Athens individualistic, critical attitudes became ever more obvious. Both for themselves and for their children the leaders of this dynamic, democratic society wanted skills and intellectual training which would fit them for the hurly-burly of actual life and, above all, for the task of gaining the voluntary support of other men.

This need was met by learned teachers who were called "sophists," that is, those who made a business of being wise. The term sophist had earlier meant one who was wise in any craft or art; but from now on it was commonly applied to "those selling wisdom to pupils for pay." [6] The wisdom thus taught to students who had already had their primary education was of a practical, earthly order, and its exponents mainly popularized ideas created by others. Yet taken as a whole the sophists had a tremendous effect. The conscious development of Greek higher education was their work; the concomitant concept of Greek culture as a measurable quantity, which separated Greeks from non-Greeks, also became evident at this time; and many specialized aspects of "wisdom" became more academic, less generalized studies.

One of the principal tools needed by a leader of men was rhetoric.

[6] Xenophon, *Memorabilia* 1.6.13.

After the end of the period of tyrants at Syracuse this great Sicilian city had become democratic and gave more scope to rhetoric. As an art useful in courts of law (forensic rhetoric) it was formally taught by Corax and Tisias. Gorgias (*c.* 483–376) came from Sicily to Athens in 427 and amazed the Athenians with his artificial, ornately exuberant style, exhibited in display or epideictic oratory. Thenceforth rhetoric rose ever higher as a main study in ancient education, and soon its popularity as a practical art surpassed the interest in philosophy. The earliest native Athenian orator of whom speeches survive was Antiphon (*c.* 480–11), who took part in the oligarchic revolution of 411 and was executed after its collapse despite his skillful plea of defense.

Along with rhetoric grammar was systematically expounded, and dialectic or formal logic was developed on the basis of work by Zeno and Parmenides. These three subjects were to remain the backbone of formal training on into the Middle Ages; to these were added "mathemata," that is, geometry, arithmetic, musical theory, and astronomy as exercises in pure thought.

While the great sophists such as Prodicus, Hippias, or Protagoras primarily imparted training in specific tools, their profession led them to share a common interpretation of the nature of man which differed sharply from views inherited from the archaic era. Proud of their abilities, they were cosmopolitan of outlook, moved freely from city to city, and viewed mankind as basically similar everywhere. "We are all by nature," said Antiphon the sophist, "born the same in every way, both barbarians and Hellenes. And it is open to all men to observe the laws of nature, which are compulsory . . . We all breathe in the air through mouth and nostrils, and we all eat with hands." [7] The ultimate inference from this point of view, that all men were essentially equal, was to be drawn later by the Stoics; at the time other devastating consequences arose.

The sophists, thus, sought to illuminate for their eager students the wellsprings of human action and to seek out the general rules that moved men in their social setting. As they considered their fellows, they also placed mankind more firmly in its natural environment but analyzed the quality of man, his *physis* (a concept borrowed from medi-

---

[7] Antiphon, fragment 44 (Diels); tr. Kathleen Freeman. This is a different Antiphon from the orator mentioned above.

cine), in reaction to nature. Politically, in consequence, they distinguished between the basic laws of nature and the artificial laws of the man-made *polis*. Antiphon the sophist, for instance, proclaimed that "the majority of just acts according to law are prescribed contrary to nature."[8] And since men should live by and develop their own nature, relativism became fashionable. Protagoras of Abdera (*c.* 481–11), one of the most well-rounded sophists, enunciated a famous opinion that man is the measure of all things; and the comic poet Aristophanes bitterly ridiculed in his *Clouds* the practical result that rhetoric was taught independently of ethics. The skilled speaker, that is, could take either the good or the bad side of a case at his will.

The thought of the sophists was not content merely with indirect assaults on the old foundations of communal loyalty to the gods and the laws of the *polis*. Some men went on to fashion the principle that in international affairs might made right, a doctrine which Athens was applying in practice; and others even questioned the conventional views of the gods. In his funeral oration Pericles paid no attention to the role of divine guidance, while eulogizing the secular qualities of the ideal democracy; Protagoras began an essay *On the Gods* by stating he was uncertain whether the gods existed, though he tried to replace the rule of the gods by the laws of the state as norms for public behavior. In the end Critias (*c.* 460–03) openly proclaimed that the gods were clever inventions of the politicians to gain respect for their laws — an ancient forerunner of the Marxist dictum on religion. Xenophanes had been no less skeptical in the previous century but on an essentially theoretical level; now the terrific reversals of men's fortunes in the Peloponnesian war made them more likely to apply the corrosive skepticism of the sophists in practice toward their own selfish, ruthless ends.

Conservative thinkers were horrified by many of the views boldly proclaimed by the sophists. Their contemporary, Socrates (469–399), separated himself sharply from the often ethically indifferent and baldly practical outlook of the sophists; the "virtue" which the sophists taught as a way of influencing men and gaining friends had little in common with Socrates' effort to direct men toward the pursuit of the true and beautiful. Since his career and death are closely connected with the fortunes of his great pupil Plato, Socrates will be considered more fully

[8] Antiphon, fragment 44 (Diels); tr. Kathleen Freeman.

in Chapter 18; but it should be noted that Socrates himself was scarcely less critical of inherited beliefs and placed his own personal views of man's duty ahead of the prescriptions of state and conventional religion.

Whether the young men of Athens such as Alcibiades listened to Socrates or to Protagoras, they absorbed attitudes which were sharply at variance with the standards of their elders, and which sapped the ancestral strengths of the city-state. Both the intellectual revolution of the late fifth century and the political upheavals of the great war led men on to a new plane of Greek civilization. Two great figures who show this change in its first days are Thucydides and Euripides.

Thucydides, the Political Critic. Thucydides (*c.* 460–*c.* 400) was of aristocratic stock and played an active part in Athenian life until he was exiled in 424 for failing to relieve Amphipolis from an attack by Brasidas. Thereafter he lived away from Athens and traveled widely in search of evidence on the Peloponnesian war, which he described down to 411 B.C. Like Herodotus he refused to turn back to the legendary history of Greece, apart from giving a quick sketch of early conditions at the beginning of his work; but even more than Herodotus he concentrated upon contemporary history. In other respects as well Thucydides stood in an entirely different generation from that of the genial historian of the Persian wars.

While Herodotus presented a widely elaborated, leisurely story, which paid attention to many aspects of life and dealt with each one as a rounded whole, Thucydides concentrated his vision upon political and military events and divided his treatment rigidly by campaigning seasons. His aim was not primarily to chronicle these events but far more to illuminate the forces at work so as to aid leaders who might meet "like events which may be expected to happen hereafter in the order of human things." [9] Thucydides' history, in other words, was intended to be as practical as was the teaching of the sophists and to illumine general truths or laws. Although he could give sharp character sketches of men like Themistocles and Pericles, the latter of whom was perhaps his only hero, he was far more interested in men as a whole, and here he was a sober, impersonal, ruthless judge.

Since Thucydides worked on his history after the war was over, he particularly sought to discover why his native Athens had lost. The basic

[9] Thucydides 1.22; tr. B. Jowett.

responsibility he laid squarely upon the fickle, overconfident people, which showed poor judgment in its choice of leaders and in its blind decisions on foreign policy. Here his thinking squared with that of Aristophanes, but it was expressed more openly and in analytical terms. The growingly ruthless imperialism of Athens is underlined in two famous passages, one the debate in the assembly over the punishment of Mitylene; and the other a probably fictitious interchange between the Athenian generals and the leaders of Melos in 416, in which the former laid down the principle that "the powerful exact what they can, and the weak grant what they must." [10] Not only in his scheme of thought but also in his dialectical skill, in his involved, antithetical prose style, and in his rhetorically polished speeches, which were invented to give the meaning of events, Thucydides revealed the interests and technical advances of the sophists.

This history is one of the most masterful studies of war ever penned. Thucydides repeatedly noted how no one could foretell the course of a war, once it was unleashed, and depicted its brutalizing qualities. His view of the world, unlike that of Herodotus, had no place for active intervention by the gods, and he scoffed at the popular belief in oracles and omens, which rose high along with magic in the stresses of the great war. History to Thucydides was the product of human nature, and more of mass movements than of individual leadership.

Yet, though his account was man-centered, he could not precisely identify the forces moving man. One leader of Syracuse suggested the problem Thucydides faced: "Nor am I so obstinate and foolish as to imagine that, because I am master of my own will, I can control fortune, of which I am not master." [11] Thucydides' tale of the Athenian downfall unrolled almost like a Greek tragedy. Immediately after the Melian expedition, in which the Athenians killed their male prisoners, followed the Syracusan expedition, in which the same fate befell the Athenians themselves.

Euripides, the Social Critic. Although Euripides (485–06) was only a decade younger than Sophocles and died in about the same year, he stood almost as a man of another generation in his dramatic and personal outlook. In keeping with the sophistic movement Euripides was inter-

[10] Thucydides 5.89; tr. B. Jowett.
[11] Thucydides 4.64; tr. B. Jowett.

ested more in the forces animating mankind as a whole than in the qualities of individual human beings. Since his characters tended to be symbols, his plots were often loose but gave him more room to reflect the advances in rhetoric and dialectic. Above all, he was deeply critical of inherited religious and social standards.

As Euripides searched for the basic qualities of mankind, he was impressed by the emotional, nonrational elements, though he essentially believed in reason as a guide to life. In his first great plays, the *Medea* and *Hippolytus,* internal emotion placed the main character in opposition to conventional ideals and morals; the *Hippolytus,* in particular, is a study in sexual passion in conflict with the demands of marriage.

Then came the Peloponnesian war, which weighed heavily on his sensitive spirit. He was proud of Greece itself and in a famous line pronounced the view that Greeks should rule barbarians; but he was more bitter, as a result, over the fratricide of the day. In a series of tragedies drawn from the Trojan war he attacked without direct reference the Spartan enemy (*Andromache*); praised Athens, the home of freedom, but warned it against injustice (*The Suppliants*); and finally slashed bitterly at the horrors of war itself (*Trojan Women*). In this last play the hopeless yet dignified women of Troy, who have survived the murder of their husbands, mourn in one harrowing scene after another as they wait to be taken off in the Greek ships and to serve as grinders of grain, weavers, nurses, and concubines. Astyanax, the infant son of Hector and Andromache, is taken from his mother and killed lest he rebuild Troy; and Andromache is not even permitted to stay and bury her son, who is interred by his grandmother Hecuba. Yet from the beginning scene the audience knows that the Greek victors will be punished on their homeward trip for their *hybris*. When one reflects that this play was presented in the spring of 415, just after the Melian expedition, its powerful lesson seems the more bitter. "If death were visible in the casting of the vote, Greece would not be destroying herself by her warlust." [12]

Throughout the many plays of Euripides that have survived there runs a far more questioning outlook than in those of Sophocles. Aeschylus, true, had spoken as harshly of the gods as Euripides did; but the reader must feel that, while Aeschylus still believed, Euripides had

[12] *Suppliant Women* 484-5; tr. H. D. F. Kitto.

doubts of divine control. "By convention we believe in the gods and define justice and injustice." [13] When Helen, in the *Trojan Women,* essayed to place the blame for her abduction on Aphrodite, Hecuba firmly enunciated the principle of personal responsibility.

Although Euripides was not entirely successful at Athens and finally withdrew to Macedonia, where he composed the *Bacchae* as an exploration of the wild forces driving men, he reflected admirably the new temperament born of war's violence and the more subtle intellectual analyses of the sophists. The product was at once a greater sense of independence for man and a concern over the social and moral grounds on which he might base his life. Since Euripides also possessed a true poetic genius, his plays were enduringly popular in later ages.

THE GREEK WORLD IN 404 B.C.

In virtually every respect the Greek world of 404 was markedly different from that of 431 or, still more, of 500. The great figures of politics, arts, and letters who had created the classic synthesis were all dead, though their work survived in plays, in sculpture, in architecture, and in political theory as an enduring force in all later centuries. The happy balance of conflicting political and intellectual views which had permitted this great outburst had been shattered; yet the Greeks had still remarkable energies and were proceeding onward to a new level of activity.

Politically the shadows grew longer over the Greek world. In the western Mediterranean, Carthage and Rome were beginning to rise, and the Greek states there were divided by bitter hostilities. From the east Persia had reached out a hand, laden with gold, to the desperate Spartans and had thereby regained its position on the coast of Asia Minor. Commercial and intellectual contacts with the vast Persian realm were growing more extensive, as a result of which the Greeks were becoming more aware both of the riches and of the inner weaknesses of their old enemy. Within the Aegean itself Sparta held a more commanding position than Athens had ever been able to achieve, but the loyalties of the citizens to their individual states were weakening.

[13] *Hecuba* 499.

Intellectually a new outlook was emerging. Some of its major aspects have been noted, and two authors have been considered in some detail as illustrations; but the same qualities can be found in many other men of the era. The conservative Aristophanes borrowed his logic from the sophists and reflected their individualistic spirit; so too Socrates floated on the same tide.

An even more intriguing example is that of Alcibiades. Early in the century the unified Athenian citizen body had withstood the Persians and had not allowed even Themistocles to rise too high. Then came the age of Pericles, where the leader and the led were for the most part closely in accord. But Alcibiades, though a convincing speaker and a sharp thinker, was yet unprincipled, that is, he placed his own good ahead of that of the state. And whereas Pericles dreamed a mighty vision of a noble Athens, Alcibiades buffeted about the Greek world until finally he took refuge in the Persian domain, where he was killed in Spartan vengeance for having deserted them and for seducing the wife of a Spartan king during his stay in Sparta.

To some modern observers the fall of Athens in 404 was the most critical event in ancient times and marked the turning point from progress to decline in ancient civilization. This is to attribute too much significance to a single event and to overemphasize the unique quality of the classic age; but certainly the end of the fifth century was a great landmark in the evolution of Greek culture. Thenceforth the road ran straight toward a more cosmopolitan, individualistic world in which the Mediterranean shores were tied together in a common civilization and eventually in a common political rule.

BIBLIOGRAPHY

Sources. The principal source for the Peloponnesian war is Thucydides, whose connection with the sophistic movement was noted in the text. Thucydides is often taken as the model historian of the ancient world in view of his scrupulous effort to establish the facts and his outward objectivity; and he does deserve a high standing in these respects. Nonetheless his account shows that he really preferred the Athenians over the Spartans and that among Athenian leaders he much disliked Cleon. Since his work broke off in 411, Xenophon later finished the story of the war in his *Hellenica* (see the bibliography to Chapter 17).

Nor does Thucydides deign to give all the information we should like to have on internal Spartan stresses, economic conditions, and the like. Only from the Athenian tribute lists (Bibliography, Chapter 14) can we discover that in 425 a great increase in the imperial dues was levied. Other useful information was preserved in Plutarch's lives of Pericles, Alcibiades, Lysander, and Nicias. The plays of Aristophanes and Euripides throw indirect light on current Athenian opinion. Translations of these authors are noted in Bibliography, Chapter 15.

Further Reading. Detailed studies of the Peloponnesian war may be found in the general histories of Greece (General Bibliography). Its outbreak is debated by Donald Kagan, *The Outbreak of the Peloponnesian War* (Ithaca: Cornell University Press, 1969), and in a provocative study by G. E. M. de Ste Croix, *The Origins of the Peloponnesian War* (Ithaca: Cornell University Press, 1972).

The best introduction to Thucydides is J. H. Finley, *Thucydides* (Cambridge, Mass.: Harvard University Press, 1963); see also J. de Romilly, *Thucydides and Athenian Imperialism* (New York, Barnes and Noble, 1980). The standard commentary is A. W. Gomme, *Commentary on Thucydides,* Vols. I–V (Oxford: Oxford University Press, 1945–80). In *The People of Aristophanes* (3d ed.; New York: Schocken SB27, 1962), V. Ehrenberg draws an interesting profile of the Athenians at this time; see also A. W. Gomme, *Population of Athens in the Fifth and Fourth Centuries* B.C. (Oxford: Blackwell, 1967), whose estimates are generally sound. W. R. Connor, *The New Politicians of Fifth-Century Athens* (Princeton: Princeton University Press, 1971), illuminates their rise.

Euripides is discussed by P. Vellacott, *Ironic Drama* (Cambridge: Cambridge University Press, 1975), and C. H. Whitman, *Euripides and the Full Circle of Myth* (Cambridge, Mass.: Harvard University Press, 1974). The sophists were partially rehabilitated by George Grote, *History of Greece,* ch. 67 (New York: Dutton reprint, 1934); see also Werner Jaeger, *Paideia,* Vol. I (New York: Oxford University Press, 1945).

VI

THE BROADENING OF GREECE

17

DECLINE OF THE CITY-STATE

The political framework within which the Greeks lived and developed their civilization had been that of the city-state since the eighth century B.C. Down to 400 this political system proved essentially satisfactory. Its requirements of communal loyalty merged religious, social, political, and economic attitudes and institutions under an overriding unity; the *polis* both channeled and supported Greek art and literature.

This success had been possible partly because Greece was still a simple land. The city-states did not press too closely upon one another and, though distinct, had usually been able to sink individual differences in critical times, as during the Persian wars. When the Greek political system was emerging, the Aegean had been free from outside threats, and by the time the Persians rolled forward the Greeks had had strength enough to repel the Great King. Internal cleavages and dissensions had normally been mitigated by colonization, by the ensuing economic progress of the homeland, and by an inherited spirit of loyalty to common goals.

During the fifth century these favorable factors had begun to weaken, and during the next 100 years Greece experienced ever more serious political difficulties. On the one hand the threats to local freedom which were advanced by Persia from outside and by ambitious city-states from within made each *polis* more jealous of its autonomy. Yet on the other hand the tiny political units of Greece became closely interlinked. Politically they contracted alliances; culturally they shared an ever more cosmopolitan civilization; economically they grew dependent upon foreign trade.

The internal political climate of these states also changed markedly in the fourth century. The *polis* had been largely secularized in the materialistic, yet patriotic spirit of the Periclean age; thereafter came the corrosive questioning of the nature of justice and the assertion of individual standards by the sophists. In the fourth century the changing economic and intellectual attitudes led to the professionalization of government and armies and to a concomitant weakening of the attachment of the individual citizen to his state.

The years from 404 to 336, which will be considered in their political aspects in this chapter, were a difficult age, marked both by chaos and by vigor. In its opening decades efforts were made to change the character of the *polis,* either by forcible unification under the aegis of a leading city-state such as Sparta and Thebes or by federal experiments. The efforts failed, and eventually an outsider, Philip of Macedonia, entered the scene to conquer all the Greeks. Taken as a whole, the developments of the age led the Aegean world straight toward that great explosion in which it conquered the Near East under the leadership of Philip's son, Alexander.

RIVALRIES OF SPARTA, THEBES, AND ATHENS

Aftermath of the Peloponnesian War. Visible signs of political distress in Greece appeared during the Peloponnesian war. Long protracted, it devastated many parts of the Aegean and left Athens too weak to maintain that naval peace which had protected commerce and had kept the Persians at bay; many men had grown used to military life and to military solutions to political problems; and the ugly specter of civil strife had been unleashed in many states.

Upon the final victory in 404 Sparta might have been expected to retire once more within its Peloponnesian stronghold, for the primary requirement of Spartan policy was to maintain the strength of its citizens at home. But the world was now much changed. The bitter struggle just concluded must have suggested to Lysander and other Spartan leaders that they could no longer be safe even in their ancestral domain unless they controlled Greece; and the general moral support which Sparta had enjoyed in its war against Athenian "tyranny" may well have misled it as to the ease of this task. The principle, too, that "rule belongs by nature to the stronger" had now become a conscious belief in Greek international politics.[1] Without much debate the Spartans decided to retain and consolidate their mastery by land and by sea, a fatal decision which eventually produced the complete ruin of Sparta by 371.

Spartan Hegemony (404–371 B.C.). Within the Greek states Sparta encouraged the conservative element. In some cities it installed a governor, or *harmost,* with a garrison; often it instituted a governing board of 10 oligarchs, a decarchy. Athens was placed in the hands of 30 such leaders, who varied from moderates to extreme conservatives. With the aid of the Spartan *harmost* whose garrison held the Acropolis, the extremists, led by Critias, gained power and proceeded in the next year to execute some 1500 dissidents and to exile about 5000 others. Very quickly the narrow vision of the Spartan government became evident, as did also its vacillation between ruthlessness and inaction as one wing or another of Spartan leadership dominated. Public opinion, even among the old Spartan allies, soon swung against its swelling power, especially inasmuch as Sparta forcibly collected tribute to maintain its fleet.

In those states held by Spartan representatives and local henchmen the situation often became tense. At Athens, for example, the rule of the Thirty was challenged by an exile, Thrasybulus, who first seized the frontier fort of Phyle with the connivance of the Thebans and then took Piraeus in the late spring of 403. Critias was killed in an attack on the port, and by September the extreme right had taken refuge in Eleusis. Although Lysander moved up to repress the resurgence of Athenian democracy, he was superseded by the Spartan king, who felt that blind Spartan support of the ultraconservatives was hopeless. The democrats then coalesced with the more moderate oligarchs, though the remnants of the Thirty held out at Eleusis until 401.

To make the Spartan situation worse, open war with Persia soon broke out. Immediately after their victory the Spartans had yielded to Persia the Greeks of Asia Minor, as they had promised to do in return for the subventions which had produced their fleet; but the cities of Asia Minor had supported the viceroy Cyrus, brother of the new Persian king Artaxerxes II Memnon, who made a bid for the throne.

[1] Democritus, fragment 267 (Diels); tr. Kathleen Freeman.

With Spartan tolerance Cyrus raised a force of 13,000 men and in 401 marched inland to Mesopotamia. In battle with his brother at Cunaxa, Cyrus was killed, though the Greeks defeated the Persian left wing; thereafter the Greek mercenary generals were seized in an interview with the Persians. The surviving common soldiers, the famous Ten Thousand, elected new generals, including the Athenian Xenophon, and made their way back through Armenia to the Black Sea by the spring of 400. This exploit suggested to many Greeks over the next decades that they had the strength, if united, to conquer the whole Persian empire, "a country so vast and so vulnerable . . . [which] will easily accommodate all the people among us who are in want of the necessities of life." [2]

Immediately, however, the Greeks of Asia Minor, fearful of punishment for their support of Cyrus, begged aid from Sparta; and the Spartans, encouraged by the military lessons to be drawn from the expedition of Cyrus, tried to redeem their reputation as defenders of all Hellenes against outside control. After some skirmishing they sent a new king, the lame but popular Agesilaus (398–60), to Asia Minor in 396 with a large army of Spartans and mercenaries, the latter largely drawn from the Ten Thousand. Rather than fighting a full-scale war by land, the Persians began to construct a navy and also sent a wily Rhodian agent, laden with gold, to play upon the dissensions of Greece itself.

By 395, less than 10 years after the close of the Peloponnesian war, the Spartans once more faced war at home, which was led by Thebes, Corinth, Argos, and even Athens. Lysander was killed at the outset, and in 394 the Spartans had to recall Agesilaus from Asia Minor. Spartan naval supremacy was ended off Cnidus in the same year by the Persian fleet, which was commanded by the Athenian Conon and was partly manned by Greek rowers; thereupon the islanders seceded from Spartan rule and formed an alliance of their own.

The course of the hostilities in Greece was complicated and indecisive. One fruit was the resurgence of Athens, which rebuilt its long walls to Piraeus 394–91, reoccupied the Aegean islands of Lemnos, Imbros, and Scyros in 392, and launched a new navy in 390. Eventually the warring

[2] Isocrates, *Panathenaicus* 14; tr. George Norlin. Compare the advice of Xenophon to his fellow-soldiers after the Persian seizure of their generals, "We must first try to reach Hellas and our own people, and show the Hellenes that they are poor only because they want to be, when they could bring their paupers over here and see them rich" (*Anabasis* 3.2.26; tr. Rex Warner).

states sent ambassadors to the Persian satrap at Sardis, who proclaimed the terms which the Great King thought desirable:

> . . . that the cities in Asia, with the islands of Clazomenae and Cyprus, should belong to himself; the rest of the Hellenic cities he thinks it just to leave independent, both small and great, with the exception of Lemnos, Imbros, and Scyros, which three are to belong to Athens as of old.[3]

This was the famous King's Peace of 387.

Execution of the peace was entrusted to the Spartans, whom the Persian king now trusted more than he did the Athenians; and the Persians promised to war against anyone who did not accept the terms. The chief leader of Sparta, Agesilaus, brutally used this dominant position to destroy all politically dangerous alliances. The Arcadian state of Mantinea was split up into villages; the Chalcidian league, grouped about Olynthus, was dissolved; the citadel or Cadmea of Thebes was seized by a Spartan commander in time of peace. After three years a small band of Theban patriots liberated their city in 379 and resumed the war anew. Little by little Spartan power in Boeotia was broken, and finally in 371 the main Spartan army was defeated in the decisive battle of Leuctra.

Sparta had ruled Greece more or less completely for 30 years. The consequences were that Greece was largely splintered, that Persia held many Greeks directly under its sway and served as arbiter for the rest, and that Sparta was utterly ruined. Whereas an Athenian orator shortly after 404 had praised Sparta "because of her innate worth and military skill," [4] Thucydides had been very doubtful of the Spartans' ability to adapt their narrow ways to foreign rule. Later on the great analyst Aristotle looked back and observed that the Spartans "collapsed as soon as they had acquired an empire. They did not know how to use the leisure which peace brought; and they had never accustomed themselves to any discipline other and better than that of war." [5]

The body of full Spartan hoplites had thus shrunk from about 5000 in

---

[3] Xenophon, *Hellenica* 5.1.31; tr. H. G. Dakyns.
[4] Lysias, *Oration* 33.7.
[5] Aristotle, *Politics* 2.6.22 (1271b.1ff.); tr. Ernest Barker. Compare Plato, *Laws* 630E, and Thucydides 1.77.

479 to less than 2000 at the time of Leuctra, partly through losses in war, partly through disfranchisement of those "Equals" who lost their land. All efforts to admit inferiors to the rank of "Equals" were refused by such conservatives as Agesilaus, who preferred to organize the Peloponnesian league into tax-paying districts so as to hire mercenaries. Worse yet, the Spartans became luxury-loving and corruptible. One token of the ever freer transfer of land which horrified Athenian thinkers was the fact that two-fifths of the Spartan farmlands passed into the hands of women. Through their petty and vindictive policies the Spartans had lost their great reputation even at home, and the Peloponnesian league dissolved as soon as the Thebans entered the Peloponnesus.

Hegemony of Thebes (371–62 B.C.). Thebes stepped into Sparta's place and held it for nine years. The strength of Thebes rested ultimately upon its leadership of the Boeotian league, which had been reorganized into a truly federal state embracing a number of democratic Boeotian city-states. This method of countering the separatist tendencies of the small political units was also favored abroad by Thebes. Either at this time, or earlier, similar leagues appeared in Thessaly, Aetolia, Acarnania, probably western Locris, Achaea, and above all in Arcadia, where a new center, Megalopolis ("Great City"), was built with Theban support to protect the northern neighbors of Sparta.

Theban power was also in large part an expression of the genius of its two great leaders, Epaminondas, a brilliant general and far-seeing, moderate statesman, and his collaborator Pelopidas. The latter secured Persian support, which resulted in a new peace of 367 in favor of Thebes; but in fighting in Thessaly Pelopidas was killed in 364. Epaminondas then had to face a coalition of Sparta, Mantinea, Elis, Achaea, and Athens, which resulted in the major battle of Mantinea (362). The Thebans won the day, and through the victory might have hoped to control all Greece. Epaminondas, however, had been killed. Thereafter the Greeks made peace and formed an ephemeral league to safeguard order; the real result was "ever greater confusion and indecision in the Greek world." [6]

Exhaustion of the Great Powers. By 355 the major Greek city-states were politically exhausted. Sparta stubbornly refused to admit its loss of

[6] Xenophon, *Hellenica* 7.5.27 (the concluding remarks of his study of Greek disintegration).

prestige but no longer had any influence. Thebes was by this date at war with its western neighbor, the Phocians, who had seized Delphi and were using the gold and silver of the sanctuary to hire whole mercenary armies. Athens, which had by land first supported Thebes against Sparta and then Sparta against Thebes, had by now lost its renewed naval position in the Aegean.

For a time, as long as its naval efforts were devoted primarily toward securing order, Athens had been able to count on wide support from the commercially oriented states; and in 378 its leader Callistratus had even formed the Second Athenian Confederacy to oppose Sparta, but not Persia. The terms of alliance included rigid safeguards against a repetition of the Athenian imperialism of the fifth century. Yet the temptations of power were too persuasive, and after the Theban collapse in 362 Athens began to abuse its position. The more liberal statesman Callistratus was condemned to death while in exile, and when he later returned to Athens was dragged from an altar and executed. The more important of the Athenian allies accordingly revolted in 357–55 and made good their independence, shattering the strength of the Confederacy.

While the Greek homeland had been searching in vain for political unity — and pulverizing itself in the search — much the same course of events had taken place in western waters. Here an extremely able and ruthless Syracusan noble, Dionysius, had seized control of Syracuse in 405 and remained master, with some vicissitudes, to his death in 367. During his autocratic rule Dionysius had beaten off great Carthaginian attacks, the first of which had enabled him to gain power, and expanded his realm to include most of the south Italian colonies as well as points in the Adriatic Sea; at various times he was allied with Sparta or Athens. But while he made Syracuse the greatest city of the west, he destroyed many Greek states and sowed dissension in others; his rule rested always on cruelty and on the employment of mercenaries drawn from native peoples as much as from the Greeks. After his death his son Dionysius II soon lost control, and Carthage once more took the offensive. Only the arrival of Timoleon, a general sent from Corinth on the appeal of Syracuse, saved the day. During 344–36 Timoleon defeated the Carthaginians, especially at the Crimisus river in 341; restored democracy in Syracuse; and rebuilt several destroyed Greek cities.

Both in Greece and in the west the political contentions of the city-states were opening the way for outside powers. In Italy the state of Rome was by this time striding forward with ever-surer steps; in the Aegean, Philip was already king of Macedonia. Nor had the developments of the first half of the fourth century B.C. all been negative. The military art, for example, had made tremendous advances in an era of incessant war. Strategic views had been much sharpened so that generals saw more clearly the main objectives and key points in a campaign; tactics had progressed as mercenary generals and soldiers became more common. Epaminondas, in particular, had made action on the battlefield more mobile and commonly had concentrated his infantry strength on a deeply massed left flank, which carried the day while the other flank was refused or conducted a holding action. Another general, the Athenian Iphicrates, had much improved the light-armed infantry (*peltasts*), armed first with javelins and then with short spears, which could in broken terrain defeat even the best Spartan hoplites.

Another factor of importance was the growing sense of Panhellenic unity, conjoined with a horror at the way the Greek states were tearing themselves to pieces externally and internally. The cultural aspects of this feeling will bulk large in the next chapter, but politically as well there were notable effects. In those parts of Greece where the *polis* had not struck deep roots, federalism grew; the savagery of war was somewhat limited at times; and men of good will came ever more to feel that the Greeks must unite. A prominent spokesman of this group was the Athenian Isocrates (436–338), who first advanced in his *Panegyricus* of 380 the idea that the Greeks should ally themselves in a holy war against Persia, which was both rich and temptingly weak. To this theme he resorted repeatedly in the next 40 years and gained a wide audience.

Rise of Philip (359–52 B.C.). Isocrates had turned in vain first to Sparta and Athens, then to Dionysius of Syracuse in his effort to find a noble, self-sacrificing leader for the Greek crusade. By the middle of the century, it is clear at least to a modern observer, the major city-states had battled each other to a standstill. If any force were to unite the Greeks, it must come from without the Hellenic state system. Two ambitious dynasts, Jason of Pherae and Mausolus of Caria, had already appeared, but each died early. The third, and successful, leader was Philip of Macedonia.

Macedonia was essentially a tribal kingdom, far larger than any Greek state but so loosely organized and so beset by even more barbarian neighbors that it had never been important. Its kings had fostered Greek culture at their courts and were accepted as Greek by the officials of the Olympic games; but the peasantry and nobles, though akin to the Greeks, were considered distinct. The growth of trade in the early fourth century promoted the rise of several cities, yet when Perdiccas III, king of Macedonia, fell in 359 while fighting the Illyrians the seaboard of his state was largely under Athenian control or in the hands of the Chalcidian league, grouped about Olynthus.

Philip (382–36), brother of the dead king, was made regent for the infant heir, soon set aside his nephew, and became outright king. In his early twenties at this sudden elevation, Philip had spent three years (367–65) as hostage at Thebes, where he had gained a great love for Greek civilization and had carefully observed the tactical and political skills of Epaminondas. The student, however, surpassed the teacher; a contemporary historian, Theopompus, was not far wrong in asserting that Europe had never produced a man like Philip. Although his ambitions soon extended to the mastery of all Greece and eventually envisaged the possibility of invading the Persian empire, few men were able to divine his aims before they were accomplished.

Philip's policies were magnificently tailored to his ambitions and were utterly unscrupulous. If he had to fight, he did so and himself led his men; at the siege of Methone he lost his right eye and was several times wounded. But fighting left lasting animosities and Philip preferred to flatter, to bribe, to promise, even to contract alliances with his intended prey before swallowing it up. A true Machiavellian, he was politic or harsh as the occasion demanded; and above all he was patient in worming his way forward through the intricacies of Greek rivalries by setting states at odds and encouraging pro-Macedonian elements.

In 359 Philip's position was perilously weak. Five contenders claimed the throne, and his loose realm was beset by enemies on all sides. First he bought off the barbarians and secured the favor of Athens by withdrawing the Macedonian garrison from the important town of Amphipolis. Then, in the next two years, he turned about and defeated first the

Paeonians, then the Illyrians; regained Amphipolis; and made an alliance with the Chalcidian league, the enemy of Athens. The seacoast
towns of Thrace fell to him one by one; in 352 Philip took advantage of
Thessalian disorder to intervene in the affairs of his southern neighbor.
When he moved on in that year toward central Greece, the Athenians
and Phocians hastily sent expeditions to Thermopylae and the inland
passes. Since Philip was not yet ready to venture full-scale action in
Greece proper, he calmly turned about and went home.

By this date his mastery of Macedonia was assured. Philip's reorganization of the Macedonian kingdom and amalgamation of the frontier
districts were processes which occupied him intermittently throughout
his reign, and the stages cannot be clearly identified. In the end Macedonia was much enlarged, and royal power was greatly strengthened. New
cities — which were kept under the king's control rather than being full
city-states — were founded in numbers; the capital of Pella was beauti-
fied. His revenues were increased by the growth of trade, the mastery of
the seacoast, and the opening up of major gold mines at Mt. Pangaeus;
Philip was the first European ruler to imitate the Persian king of kings
by coining gold "philippics." This money was used partly for bribery;
Philip boasted that he could take any fortress up to which he could drive
an assload of gold. His revenues were also spent on his army, which was
amazingly improved. The cavalry continued to be provided by the Macedonian nobles, who called themselves the king's "companions" and
were used by Philip for the decisive blow. To hold the enemy, however,
a solid infantry of advanced Greek training was formed from the burghers of the cities and the Macedonian peasantry and was equipped with
spears about 13 feet long, far longer than the average Greek spear. This
was a national army, well trained, continuously exercised in the field,
and directed by a single mind.

Duel with Athens (352–38 B.C.). The Greeks had little chance against
such a persistent, able monarch. The states of Hellas were divided by
inveterate rivalries, and their citizens were less willing than of old to
sacrifice lives and property for the common good. Much of central
Greece was preoccupied by the Sacred war against the Phocians; the
Athenians had just lost their naval league. To make matters worse, the
citizens and leaders of Athens were deeply concerned over internal politics, particularly with regard to the provision of state funds to the poor

through paying them for attending the assembly, serving as jurors, or partaking in the festivals. Probably in 358 the festival (*theoric*) fund had been set up as a separately administered unit, and its principal commissioner from about 354, Eubulus, secured a rule that all surplus monies of the state should be assigned to this fund.

Nonetheless Athens kept up and even increased its navy and might still hope to gain considerable support among various parts of Greece if it took a firm stand against Philip. It had also the greatest orator produced by ancient Greece, Demosthenes (384–22), who was eager that his native state should be powerful under his leadership. By at least 351, when Demosthenes probably delivered his first Philippic oration, he had settled upon Philip as the foe, and more than any other Greek he divined Philip's ambitions. Unscrupulous in his attacks on rival politicians and not overly concerned about the facts of a situation, Demosthenes battered away at the blindness of the Athenians. His orations reveal at once the reluctance of the democracy to go to war and his increasing success in alerting it.

The first open rupture between Philip and Athens came when Philip decided to absorb his last independent neighbor, his ally the Chalcidian league. Olynthus swallowed its pride and begged for Athenian aid; Demosthenes supported the request in his three Olynthiac orations of 349; and the assembly voted assistance. Its attention, however, was diverted by a revolt of nearby Euboea, engineered by Philip; and the Athenian expedition was both too little and too late — its general was ill-provided with money and was forced to ravage as he went to get food for his mercenaries. The Olynthians had to give battle by themselves (348) and were betrayed by traitors both in the battle and in their efforts to shut the town gates after the defeat. Philip destroyed the city as a warning to the other Greeks; the Athenians tried in vain to secure allies for a large-scale, joint Hellenic effort.

Even Demosthenes had to concede by 346 that Athens could do no other than conclude peace, in which all the major Greek states joined. The Phocians, however, were excepted, and Philip next conquered Phocis. Although he destroyed the political union of the Phocians, he rejected the vindictive advice of the Boeotians that they all be sold into slavery; for himself he took the seats of the Phocians on the Delphic Amphictyony, the most sacred meeting of the Greeks. While Demos-

thenes, Aeschines, and other politicians brought suit against each other
in the Athenian courts on political charges, he continued to consolidate
his positions in Thrace and Thessaly and made futile gestures to secure
the friendship or at least the acquiescence of Athens in his expansion.

As the Greeks considered the rise of Philip, some adopted a favorable
attitude. Isocrates addressed his *Philippus* to the Macedonian king in 346
and urged him to unite the Greeks in an attack on Persia. Others,
however, grew alarmed and turned toward Athens. The final round of
hostilities began in 340, when Philip moved against the vital lifeline of
the Greek commercial states, the Hellespont, and laid siege to Perinthus
and Byzantium. In both assaults he was repelled, largely because Athens
furnished naval support to the two cities; then he declared war on
Athens and invaded central Greece late in 339.

This was Demosthenes' finest hour. First he persuaded his fellow
Athenians to ally themselves with their old foe Thebes; most remarkable
of all, he journeyed to Thebes and convinced it that it should reject the
overtures of Philip and stand for Greek freedom beside Athens. Then he
persuaded his fellow Athenians to devote the festival fund to war purposes. Some other Greek states gave support, but the whole of the Peloponnesus remained virtually neutral.

In 338 the Athenian and Theban citizen armies, led by a host of
generals, moved to bar Philip's path, and on August 2 the decisive battle
occurred at Chaeronea between the 2 foes, each somewhat over 30,000
men. Philip led his right wing against the less-experienced Athenians
and by a feigned retreat threw them into disarray and defeat; his left
wing under his son Alexander crushed the Thebans. The surviving
Athenians, including Demosthenes, ran for home. They prepared to
stand siege, but Philip wished neither to crush the great home of Greek
culture nor to commit himself to a long blockade without naval power.
When he offered very favorable terms of alliance, the Athenians accepted with alacrity. Thebes, on the other hand, was stripped of all
power in Boeotia and was garrisoned by Macedonians.

League of Corinth (337–36 B.C.). Demosthenes had failed, and Philip
was master of all Greece. Some modern critics accuse the Athenian
orator of being blind to the real drift of fourth-century politics, of narrow chauvinism, and of outworn patriotism; to others Demosthenes is a
heroic figure, fighting (as he himself put it) for freedom against tyr-

anny. In the final struggle, which Philip only just barely won, the strengths of city-state loyalty and the weaknesses of Greek international division stand clear. The *polis* form of organization was long to continue to be important in the Aegean, but thenceforth the main power and impetus in Greek civilization were to lie in other hands, first those of Philip and Alexander, then of the Hellenistic monarchies, and finally of Rome.

After his victory Philip convened the Greek states at the isthmus of Corinth and formed a league, which all mainland states (save for stubborn Sparta) and many islanders joined. The legislative body was a council of representatives; the *hegemon* or executive was "Philip and his descendants," who contracted a joint alliance with the league of Corinth. Within Greece the members swore to protect the liberty of each member, to suppress brigandage and piracy, and to withstand local upheavals for the redistribution of land and abolition of debts. Externally they declared war on Persia in 337 to avenge the devastation of Greek temples by Xerxes, and commissioned Philip to lead their joint army.

In the spring of 336 Philip sent the advance guard of his army across the Hellespont, but before departing himself he prepared to marry his daughter to the king of Epirus. Earlier Philip had married a new queen, whereupon his first wife Olympias and their son Alexander had left the court in anger. Alexander soon returned, only to be present when his father was murdered by a dissatisfied Macedonian noble; a rich tomb, which some scholars think is Philip's, was discovered several years ago at Aegae, the old Macedonian center. Alexander succeeded without difficulty to the throne at the age of 20.

GREECE IN THE FOURTH CENTURY

Internal Unrest. The fact that the league of Corinth was designed in part to maintain stability within Greece suggests the degree of economic and social unrest which beset the city-states of the period. Since the dark ages there had been a cleavage between rich and poor, but the split had normally been mitigated by a sense of common loyalty as well as by such safety valves as colonization. From the time of the Peloponnesian war, which weakened the bonds of society, the strife between upper and lower classes became more widespread and keener.

At Athens the legacy of the civil strife in the days of the Thirty lingered after the restoration of the democracy. Socrates, the teacher of Critias and other oligarchs, was condemned to death in 399 on the charges that he had corrupted the youth, had introduced religious innovations, and did not worship the gods of state. Rich men were milked for the expenses of state pay and were not always given fair trials if they came into court. The powers of the council of Five Hundred were much reduced, and charges of treason or *graphe paranomon* were hurled at each other by rival orators.

Athens enjoyed sufficient economic activity that the rich could normally stand their burdens, and those traditions of public moderation which went back to Solon also helped to mitigate conflicts. Elsewhere, however, the rich and the poor at times fell into open war (*stasis*). The battle cry of the oppressed was redivision of land and abolition of debts, but the wealthy could also expect murder and exile. On the other hand the upper classes naturally formed oligarchic clubs and circles to maintain their control. Aristotle incidentally comments that an oligarchic oath ran, "I will be an enemy to the people, and will devise all the harm against them which I can." [7]

What the underlying economic position of Greece was in the fourth century is difficult to determine in the absence of statistics. Trade into the western Mediterranean had already dropped off in the fifth century and did not revive. Commercial activity in south Russia and along the Persian-held seaboard of the eastern Mediterranean seems to have expanded down to about 350, when it too apparently declined. Within the Aegean proper traders were hampered by the lack of peace but on the whole became more specialized and skillful in their operations. The Ionian cities were far more prosperous than in the fifth century, and a number of new or refounded cities rose in Greece. Despite local attacks the rich men of this world clearly grew richer. Through a considerable price inflation, however, the poor became poorer both in the cities and in the country, where big estates grew at the expense of the peasantry. In this distortion there was ample seed for internal discontent, for the willingness of men to take up the life of a mercenary soldier, and for the great migrations into the Near East which were to follow Alexander's conquests.

---

[7] Aristotle, *Politics* 5.7.19 (1310a.9–10); tr. Ernest Barker. Aristotle devoted no less than two books of this work on counsel as to how to avoid civil strife.

As important an element in the background of *stasis* as the economic and social troubles was the growingly evident decline in civic attachment. The increasing individualism of Hellenic culture is visible wherever one turns in the art and literature of the fourth century; one fine example appears in the famous *Apology*, which Plato set down as being the defense of Socrates at his trial in 399. The great philosopher bluntly proclaimed that if his city gave him the choice between death and giving up his speculations, "I should reply: Men of Athens, I honor and love you; but I shall obey God rather than you, and while I have life and strength I shall never cease from the practice and teaching of philosophy."[8]

The individualism that Socrates justified on an ethical plane other men exhibited more unconsciously. Rich and poor alike sought personal profit from public office; in the more advanced states citizens tended to hire mercenaries rather than to fight themselves — the Athenians who faced Philip at Chaeronea had fought for only one month of the previous 24 years. At Athens and elsewhere the job of running the machinery of state was accordingly turned over in large degree to virtually professional financiers such as Eubulus. The public budget and business of a *polis* were tiny matters, but in this school were trained the Greeks who went out under Alexander and his successors to manage the huge bureaucratic structures of the post-Alexandrian Near East.

Theories of Political Reform. While Socrates himself concentrated upon the problems of truth and good conduct for the individual, his successors, Plato and Aristotle, concerned themselves seriously with the problems of the fourth-century *polis*. Their general philosophical schemes of thought will be considered in the next chapter, but the political treatises of the two thinkers throw interesting light on the changes that were actually occurring within the city-state of the age.

Plato and Aristotle both were able to conceive of political life only in terms of the city-state, a unit small enough for all citizens to know each other; and both placed the Greeks in a different category from "barbarians." Their solutions for the ills of their world were largely to put back the clock by dreaming of an ideal *polis* which would have no foreign ties and which would absorb all the loyalties of its citizens.

The famous Platonic dialogue of the *Republic* presents Socrates and

[8] Plato, *Apology* 29; tr. B. Jowett.

some friends as conversing in an effort to establish the nature of justice. Socrates enunciates the principle that justice can best exist within a perfect state — an excellent illustration of the tendency of the Greeks to connect ethics with the state rather than with religion — and this in turn leads to a consideration of the ideal *polis*. Its directors would be philosophers, who were trained in the search for the Good. Its protectors would be a soldier caste, who would be served by the lower orders, and these latter elements would be kept rigorously in their dependent place. To Plato, as to Xenophon and various other conservative thinkers, the Spartan ideals of state service were far more attractive than the ever-shifting, egotistical practice of Athenian democracy. In the dialogue *Menexenus,* Plato directly satirized even the Periclean ideal of democracy.

Shortly before his death Plato came back anew to the problems of the ideal state and wrote the *Laws,* a long, didactic dialogue on laws that such a state would require, particularly to assure its religious basis. Here the dictation of the state over the individual was clearly spelled out in the formulation of religious and public machinery to enforce conformity, for all aspects of life had their political and social effects (an idea more theoretically treated in his *Protagoras*). Dissidents were to be imprisoned, reformed by persuasion, and even executed if they were stubborn. Already in the *Republic* Plato had seen the necessity of censoring Homer, whose epics gave too individualistic a picture and portrayed the gods as immoral; now in the *Laws* state control of thought was prescribed in ruthless fashion. The Platonic political ideal has remarkable resemblances to that of totalitarianism, and, like its modern parallel, it was produced by an almost desperate fear of change.

The second great political theorist of the fourth century, Aristotle, wrote a study called the *Politics*. Beforehand he and his pupils surveyed the internal development of some 158 Greek and foreign cities; the one surviving treatise of this great accumulation of facts is the *Constitution of Athens*. The *Politics* itself is so rich a study of the many variations and complex issues in Greek political theory and practice that it is not easily summarized. To Aristotle slavery and the dependent position of women and children were justified by nature as fundamental principles of the household; and in turn the organization of the state rested upon the qualities of the household. On the public level there were three possible forms of good government: kingship, aristocracy, and democracy, and a perversion of each form in tyranny, oligarchy, and ochlocracy (rule of the masses). In earlier Greek history Aristotle detected a progression from the good to the evil form of each type, which ended in the ochlocracy of his day in Athens. While Aristotle went on to give prescriptions for the maintenance of each good form, he also speculated on the form of a perfect state, which would harmonize all elements, and discussed at length the educational systems which would thereby be required to give its citizens the good life. In keeping with the general distinction between the two great philosophers of the fourth century, Plato constructed a purely theoretical utopia, in which women and property would be held in common; Aristotle kept far closer to the realities of ancient political life and sought to improve its defects.

The Situation in 336. It is difficult to see that either Plato or Aristotle had any practical effect on the political developments of their era. Plato journeyed twice to Sicily to advise Dionysius II, but his counsels were of little avail. In tutoring Alexander, Aristotle seems to have had his main effect in stimulating the youth's love of Greek civilization. To halt the internal strife of the day Aristotle argued that the middle classes between rich and poor must be fostered, an excellent piece of advice in the abstract but not easy to carry out in reality.

Of more importance were the essays in federalism which we have already noted and the improvements in the techniques of government achieved by the professional administrators. On the international level the efforts first of Sparta and then of Thebes to unite the Greeks under the rule of one state had failed, but the new, more easily marshaled strength of Macedonia had succeeded where the *polis* could not. By 336 the Aegean at last had peace, but at the expense of the real independence of its units and as a preliminary step to a great external war against Persia.

The outwardly saddening record, however, of civil strife and international war during the period 404–336 is a testimony, nct to a real collapse of Greek civilization, but to the inadequacy of its inherited political framework. In cultural respects, as we shall see in the next chapter, individualism, specialization, and cosmopolitanism of the fourth-century Greeks supported continued vigorous activity.

BIBLIOGRAPHY

Sources. Whereas the historian must rely for the fifth century B.C. largely upon two uncontrollable sources, first Herodotus, and then Thucydides, the volume of evidence for the next century increases greatly. Since the complexity of international politics also grows, we are not always necessarily able to obtain the entire picture.

The one formal history of the period that has survived is the *Hellenica* of Xenophon (*c.* 430–354), covering the era 411–362 (Loeb Classical Library). Although Xenophon imitated Thucydides, his insight and impartiality were far inferior; and his account grew steadily weaker as he proceeded. Xenophon also wrote the *Anabasis,* a vigorous account of the expedition of Cyrus and the retreat of the Ten Thousand, to which he was an eyewitness (trans. Rex Warner, Penguin L7, 1949). Among many other essays from his pen are a praise of Sparta (*Constitution of the Lacedaemonians*), a eulogy of *Agesilaus,* and the *Memorabilia* concerning his teacher Socrates.

Two other major historians came from the rhetorical school of Isocrates, but their works survive only in fragments and in the use made of them by such later historians as Diodorus Siculus. Theopompus of Chios (*c.* 378–05) wrote a *Philippica* and other studies; Ephorus of Cyme (*c.* 405–330) composed a universal history from the Dorian invasion to his own day. (See G. L. Barber, *The Historian Ephorus* [New York: AMS Press, 1977]). An extensive fragment on papyrus, called the *Oxyrhynchus Historian* (I. A. Bruce, Cambridge: Cambridge University Press, 1967) continues Thucydides and is far superior to Xenophon in judgment. Plutarch wrote lives of Artaxerxes Memnon, Agesilaus, Demosthenes, Timoleon, and Pelopidas.

Further light comes from the Athenian orators. Of the 61 orations ascribed to Demosthenes that survive, not all are surely his (Loeb Classical Library). A considerable body of the work of Lysias and Isaeus also survives; for Aeschines, Hyperides, Lycurgus, *et al.,* only a few are left out of a great many (Loeb Classical Library, *Minor Attic Orators*). In one case we have orations by Demosthenes and Aeschines, delivered in 343, on the same subject, the Athenian embassy to Philip in 346. Both men were present, but the speeches are so contradictory that the historian cannot hope to reconstruct the issues involved. The abundant physical evidence will be cited in the next chapter; among the many useful inscriptions are those giving terms of alliance of the Second Athenian Confederacy (Tod, *Greek Historical Inscriptions,* Nos. 118, 121–3) and of the league of Corinth (Tod, No. 177).

Further Reading. The fourth century, long unjustly neglected, has begun to get due attention. C. Mossé, *Athens in Decline, 404–86* B.C. (Boston: Routledge & Kegan Paul, 1973), is thin; more detailed are J. Buckler, *The Theban Hegemony 371–362* B.C. (Cambridge, Mass.: Harvard University Press, 1980), J. Cargill, *The Second Athenian League* (Berkeley: University of California Press, 1981), D. M. Lewis, *Sparta and Persia* (Leiden: Brill, 1977), and my *Greeks and Persians in the Fourth Century* B.C. (*Iranica Antiqua,* XI–XII, 1976–77). Military innovations are discussed by J. K. Anderson, *Military Theory and Practice in the Age of Xenophon* (Berkeley: University of California Press, 1970), and J. G. P. Best, *Thracian Peltasts* (Groningen, 1969).

A truly magnificent portrait of Philip is drawn by G. T. Griffith in N. G. L. Hammond and Griffith, *History of Macedonia,* Vol. II (Oxford: Oxford University Press, 1979); J. R. Ellis, *Philip II and Macedonian Imperialism* (New York: Thames & Hudson, 1977), is briefer. On his major opponent, Demosthenes, little is available in English; see Werner Jaeger, *Demosthenes* (Berkeley: University of California Press, 1938). M. I. Rostovtzeff, *Social and Economic History of the Hellenistic World,* Chap. II (Oxford: Oxford University Press, 1941), is a good survey of conditions before Alexander. H. C. Baldry, *The Unity of Mankind in Greek Thought* (Cambridge: Cambridge University Press, 1965), is reflective; T. T. B. Ryder, *Koine Eirene* (London: Oxford University Press, 1965), takes up efforts to secure peace by international agreements.

Works on Plato and Aristotle are listed in Bibliography, Chapter 18; on their political theory two books by Ernest Barker, *Political Philosophy of Plato and Aristotle* (New York: Dover, 1959), and *Greek Political Theory: Plato and His Predecessors* (4th ed.; New York: Barnes and Noble, 1960), may be cited.

18

GREEK CIVILIZATION IN THE FOURTH CENTURY

Men of the fourth century changed their cultural views as much as their political structures. Although there was very evident continuity in the forms and concepts of Greek civilization, the spirit expressed by fourth-century philosophers, authors, and artists was strikingly different. If one assesses this alteration in terms of the classic balance and poise of the fifth century, one may speak of "decline"; a fairer judgment, however, must stress the enduring fertility of Hellenic culture, which led its creative thinkers to establish new standards of art and literature.

The decisive point in this respect had come at the very beginning of the century or even late in the fifth century, as in the rise of the sophists and the reflection of their views in Thucydides and Euripides. Yet much in the new outlook remained to be worked out in the fourth century and even in the age succeeding Alexander, the Hellenistic period.

In many respects a man of the modern world will feel less difficulty in understanding the products of the fourth century than the austere, impersonal, uncompromising art and literature of the Periclean age. Henceforth Hellenic civilization assumed a more urbane, consciously polished, and cosmopolitan flavor. Nonetheless the basic forces which moved thinkers and artists of the fourth century were Greek, and their masterpieces entered into the Greek inheritance of later ages.

378

FOURTH-CENTURY PHILOSOPHY

The Contribution of Socrates. Most students of the fourth century would agree that among its greatest figures were two philosophers, Plato and Aristotle. The remarkable advances in philosophic thought, moreover, show perhaps more clearly than any other aspect the main qualities of the period. The philosophers continued to draw inspiration from earlier political and intellectual principles; yet they also manifested phenomenal abilities to strike out on new lines. Particularly impressive were their advances in ethics and in more generalized analyses of the fundamental problems of knowledge.

To begin this story one must go back to the great, if somewhat dim figure of Socrates (469–399), who spent his life in questioning the standards of his fellow Athenians. In doing so he developed the famous Socratic method, which consisted of probing a man's beliefs and showing their inconsistency so as to reduce the victim to an admission of his own ignorance, the first step toward true wisdom. The brilliance of his cross-examination with its paradoxes and swift analyses attracted many young nobles, such as Alcibiades, Critias, Xenophon, and Plato. It also deeply angered their materialistic elders, who lumped the gadfly Socrates together with the equally critical sophists. In this respect the legacy of Socrates to fourth-century philosophy was a far broader understanding of the issues involved in rational understanding, a less dogmatic approach than that of men like Heraclitus, and a sharper logical sense, particularly on the side of inductive logic.

Yet Socrates, unlike most of the sophists, was interested primarily in ethical questions, and his views did not constitute a purely negative criticism of older beliefs. In his youth he had studied the contemporary theories of physics, which at first sight had promised him a key to the nature of wisdom; but he turned away from their mechanical, scientific character. In that turn he also directed Greek philosophy decisively away from the Ionian tradition of poorly grounded physical speculation. From artisans and from medicine, the only science based on real experience and exact knowledge of man, Socrates learned far more; as Cicero later put it, Socrates brought philosophy down from the skies. His primary effort, as it is stated in Plato's *Apology of Socrates,* was to persuade his

fellow citizens "not to take thought for your persons or your properties, but first and chiefly to care about the greatest improvement of the
soul." [1] This would be achieved if men gained inner certainty through
self-knowledge; men, to Socrates, were bad only if they did not know
the good.

The great distinction between pre-Socratic and post-Socratic philosophy lies in his critical, systematic concentration upon ethics; but there
are other significant differences. Although the philosophers of the fourth
century were to address themselves largely to the problems of the individual human being, they went beyond Socrates in positive construction
of metaphysical systems; for human life and the world must have some
purpose. Wherever they touched upon the sciences, they embraced these
aspects too within a broadly and tightly argued scheme of thought.
Their work, accordingly, was far more widely attractive than had been
that of the Ionian thinkers.

Since Socrates himself wrote no philosophical treatises, we can only
speculate as to whether he had deeply based views on virtue or divine
governance, but on the whole it appears probable that he was a practical
genius. As noted in the previous chapter, he was executed in 399, partly
because some of his pupils had played an evil role in the preceding
decade, partly because he refused to bow to the will of the Athenian
state. He thus became the greatest martyr produced in pagan antiquity, a
martyr to the freedom of reason. His dynamic personality, however, and
still more his logical effort to establish universal truths by which individual men might live, stimulated such varied schools as the Cynics, the
Cyrenaics, and those of Plato and Aristotle.

Plato. Of his direct pupils, Plato (428/7–348/7) was the greatest. Plato
was an Athenian noble, who initially had planned to be a statesman; but
the conduct of public life both by his friends, the Thirty, and then by the
restored democracy left him disinclined to enter the political arena. After
the execution of his master he traveled abroad several times for about 12
years. Although Plato, like Confucius, never succeeded in putting his
political ideas into practice at home or at Syracuse, which he visited
three times under Dionysius I and II, the political problems of Greek life
bulked large in his thought.

Nonetheless even these aspects were integrated into his wide meta-

[1] *Apology* 30; tr. B. Jowett.

physical and moral outlook. Plato's philosophical views were not a closed system, and we can follow the evolution of his thought through a marvelous set of 26 essays, almost all in dialogue form, which he composed during a long creative life. In his youth Plato wrote tragedies, none of which survive, and also composed poetry. His polished dialogues represent perhaps the greatest Greek prose down to his day and are not easily matched for literary grace and clarity by any subsequent philosophic treatises.

Some of his earlier works revolved about the last days of Socrates (*Apology of Socrates,* which is not a dialogue; *Crito, Phaedo*) or attacked the sophists (*Protagoras, Gorgias, Hippias*). Others gave the results of his thought upon a certain subject; but in most of his works their dialogue form permitted Plato to show the search for truth, as the characters tossed a subject back and forth, sometimes humorously, but always with driving, relentless logic on a high moral plane. The *Symposium*, which had Alcibiades and Aristophanes among its participants, considered the nature of love as rising to the ideal of Beauty; the *Phaedo*, life after death; the *Theaetetus*, knowledge; the *Timaeus*, the origin of the world. In the last occurs the famous fable of a lost continent in the west, called Atlantis, which appears also in the fragmentary *Critias;* in several other works Plato created further fables or myths as symbols of the truth.

To set down in a few words the complete scheme of thought of a great philosopher, who was always pressing forward to new insights, is impossible, for a philosopher's principles mean little without his proofs. In general terms Plato's approach may be described as idealistic and transcendental. In the *Republic* and another early dialogue, the *Phaedo*, he sketched a view that the basic entities of the world are abstract universals or "forms" (often called *ideas*) such as justice, truth, beauty, and — highest of all — the Good. Earthly, particular examples of these eternal concepts are necessarily imperfect, just as the human body is less perfect than the soul. This latter concept Plato drew, along with many other principles, from the Pythagoreans, who had almost as great an effect upon him as did his master Socrates.

Later, in the *Parmenides* and other essays, Plato criticized defects in his early theory and came to form his universals as numbers or mathematical concepts; but always he considered that the philosopher must proceed from the transitory particulars to comprehend the transcendental forms. His primary tool was reason, which acquired knowledge of the eternal truths by recollection in the mind's eye (*Meno* and *Phaedrus*) or by search of one's own soul; mathematics, required of all students, allowed them to contemplate abstract concepts. Yet to comprehend the Good, Plato averred, required virtually mystical communion, and such comprehension could not be expressed in writing. In seeking to establish eternally true and unchanging principles, Plato stood in opposition to the rapid changes which marked his era.

After his return from his first Sicilian trip to the court of Dionysius I Plato established an association of kindred souls, like a Pythagorean brotherhood, about 385 in a wooded plot just outside the city, by the *gymnasium* of the hero Academus. To this joint school and research institute able young men came to absorb the master's views and, at times, to conduct their own thinking for decades; the Academy went on after Plato's death to the sixth century after Christ. In this vehicle, and still more through his dialogues, all of which continued to be preserved, Plato's ideas had a great influence. In Hellenistic and Roman times, both liberal Jews, like Philo, and cultivated Romans, like Cicero, were much affected by his theories. Christian scholars made very great use of Plato's idealistic concepts, which accorded well with Christian theology; and the last great pagan philosophy, Neoplatonism, expanded the more mystical aspect of his views.

Aristotle (384–22). Plato's greatest pupil was the son of the Macedonian court doctor, Aristotle of Stagirus. While the teacher was a genius who pressed his abstract ideas relentlessly, the pupil was a master of common sense who brought order and system to many fields of knowledge.

Aristotle came to the Academy when he was 17 and remained there for 20 years, to the death of Plato. Then, since he was not chosen head of the Academy through jealousy and through the fact he could not, as resident alien (metic), hold title to the Academy grounds, he moved to Assos in Asia Minor and then to Mitylene. Here he had an opportunity to engage in extensive marine biological studies. Aristotle was picked by Philip to be tutor of Alexander in 343/2, and returned to Athens in 335 under Alexander's protection to found his own school, the Lyceum or Peripatos (covered walk). After the death of Alexander in 323 the anti-

Macedonian reaction in Athens forced Aristotle to move to Chalcis, where he died the next year.

Like the Academy, the Lyceum was a research institute and was equipped with library, maps, specimens, and so on; but Aristotle engaged in formal instruction of students, many of whom then went out into active life. The influence of the Peripatetic school, as it was often known, thus spread widely over the Greek and then the Hellenistic world. Aristotle himself wrote a number of dialogues in his youth, which imitated Plato's style and to some extent his thought; but these were lost in antiquity. Far more important were his later works, which are bare, unadorned studies often resembling lecture notes. These were taken by Theophrastus, Aristotle's chief student, to Asia Minor and lay neglected in a cellar for 200 years; not until the Roman general Sulla moved them to Rome in 84 B.C. were they adequately published.

This tremendous volume of specialized studies was virtually an encyclopedia of learning, all infused with Aristotle's approach and concepts. Aristotle codified in the *Organon* (a series including the *Categories*, *Prior* and *Posterior Analytics*, etc.) the logical achievements of the earlier Greeks so well that Aristotelian logic and philosophic terms remained the framework of thought down to the past century. His essay on *Poetics*, though a fragment, likewise became a manual of literary criticism; the *Nicomachean Ethics, Metaphysics, Rhetoric, Politics,* and other treatises are equally masterful. Unlike Plato, Aristotle was only passingly interested in physics and mathematics, and his work in this field was marked by fundamental errors; in the area of science he excelled especially in biology, a field in which he and his pupils compiled a number of classificatory and analytical studies of some 500 animal species.

In these latter works Aristotle sought to collect and to test all available information, then to form hypotheses, and finally to apply these hypotheses. This is, in sum, a scientific method, and in the first generations of the Hellenistic world there came the greatest outburst of Greek science, as we shall see in Chapter 20. Both Aristotelian biology and Aristotelian mechanics reigned supreme down through the Middle Ages, when the scholastics, especially St. Thomas Aquinas, took Aristotle as an authority second only to the Bible. In the Renaissance, unfortunately, this use of Aristotle as an ultimate test of right and wrong stood in the way of the free investigation of physics and mechanics by Galileo and other leaders of the modern scientific revolution; but his biological work remained virtually unchallenged until the appearance of Linnaeus in the eighteenth century.

Behind the detailed analyses in every field lay Aristotle's general views. Aristotelian science was teleological, that is, it postulated that everything in nature had a purpose and that certain "causes" made oak trees, for example, become oaks as they grew from acorns. Chief among the causes was the "formal" cause, for the end of every creature or action was the appropriate form. The connection between this view and that of Plato's forms or *ideas* is clear; but whereas, to Plato, the transcendental element was primary and distinct from its earthly incarnations, Aristotle moved always from the actual world in framing his more general concepts. The Aristotelian and Platonic views stood opposed much as did nominalism and realism in medieval thought, but one must not make the mistake of considering the two greatest philosophers of the fourth century as completely contradictory. Both shared much the same political outlook, as we saw in Chapter 17, and the general framework of post-Socratic thought stamped alike the work of Plato and of Aristotle. Their concentration upon the problems of the individual, again, led straight into the great ethical philosophies of the Hellenistic world.

Other Philosophies. The ferment of philosophic thought stirred up by the corrosive criticism of the sophists and of Socrates was not exhausted in the work of Plato, Aristotle, and the disciples who grouped themselves about these giants. One pupil of Socrates, Euclides of Megara (*c.* 450–380), founded the Megarian school, which combined the monistic ideas of Parmenides with the ethical views of Socrates.

Another pupil of Socrates was Antisthenes of Athens (*c.* 455–*c.* 360), who founded the Cynic school and inspired its most memorable figure, Diogenes of Sinope (*c.* 400–325). In going about the world with a lantern looking for an honest man and in living in a tub, Diogenes expressed Cynic skepticism and indifference to external luxuries, but Antisthenes and Diogenes both had a positive concept of the nature of virtue as expressed in a simple life of self-sufficiency (*autarkeia*) which disregarded formal conventions and followed natural ways. The shamelessness of Diogenes in this latter respect led to his being called "the dog" (*cyon*), whence came the name Cynic.

Far to the other extreme were the Cyrenaics, so-called from their origin in Cyrene. The Cyrenaics, who traced their view of life to Aristippus, the grandson of a friend of Socrates, favored pleasure as a principle to govern man's life; for to them the present moment was the only reality, and sensation the only road to truth. Eventually this strain was to be swallowed up in the Epicurean philosophic school. The fact that such diverse views, along with those of Plato and Aristotle, claimed their origin in Socrates' teaching suggests the tremendous reverence felt in later days for the bulb-nosed, heavy-set Athenian who placed ties of family and state below the pursuit of truth. The diversity also suggests the freedom and tremendous vigor of thought in one of the most fertile philosophic centuries in western civilization.

NEW LITERARY TRENDS

Poetry and Drama. No century of Greek civilization from the time of Homer to the end of the Hellenistic age was so weak in poetic production as the fourth century B.C. The archaic aristocratic tradition which had earlier encouraged such a great galaxy of poets as Archilochus, the Lesbians, Theognis, and Pindar had lost its creative strength by the fifth century; even the close religious and political union between the individual creative thinker and his community, which had supported the tragic poets of Periclean Athens, was now dissolving.

After Euripides tragedies continued to be written for the Athenian festivals, but apart from one play, the *Rhesus,* which was attached to the body of Euripidian tragedies, none was later considered worthy of preservation. The diminished fertility, indeed, of the tragic vein is perceptible in the fact that many of the masterpieces of the Periclean age were now presented again. Comedy continued to be more vigorous, partly because its form was less defined and could change as the temper of life altered. Whereas the Old Comedy of the fifth century had relished personal attacks on politicians, Middle Comedy of the fourth century moved toward a study of domestic manners. The last plays of Aristophanes, the *Women Assembly-goers* (*Ecclesiazusae* of 391 B.C.) and *Wealth* (*Plutus* of 388), show this change as well as the reduced place of lyric songs by the chorus. Thereafter stock characters like courtesans, gluttons, and philosophers, and the problems of love and lost children took the stage and led toward the New Comedy of the early Hellenistic age.

The very closely allied art of music was also undergoing a revolution in this period. Toward the end of the fifth century the old musical conventions broke down, and a new, freer style emerged. The results we cannot directly judge inasmuch as ancient music has survived only in tiny fragments, but the text of a lyric cantata or *nomos* by Timotheus of Miletus (*c.* 450–360), the *Persians* (at Salamis), suggests a greater emphasis on realism, emotionalism, and varied meters. Here, as in poetry and drama, the fourth century was a transitory era between classic and Hellenistic styles.

The Rise of Prose. The true vigor of this era displayed itself, from the literary point of view, in the development of Greek prose. The first great prose work had been the history of Herodotus, written in the Ionic dialect and in a straightforward manner. Then came the history of Thucydides, which reflected the conscious analysis of grammar and rhetoric by the sophists. If the style of Thucydides was stiff and almost crabbed, this was perhaps due as much to his mental precision as to the difficulties of creating an artistic prose, for certainly the writers of the fourth century advanced rapidly to a supple elegance.

One product, the dialogues of Plato, we have already noted. Isocrates (436–338) wrote a host of pamphlets and orations over his long life with even greater, studied skill; in these works Isocrates combined an involved periodic structure and artistic effects into an apparently simple, flowing prose which set a standard for later generations in its precision and dignity. In his *Evagoras,* an encomium of a late king of Salamis in Cyprus, Isocrates wrote the first real biography in Greek literature. History, too, was now couched in a more polished, emotional style; the works of Xenophon, Theopompus, and Ephorus have been noted in the bibliography of Chapter 17.

Virtually all this fourth-century prose was written in the Attic dialect; and Isocrates went so far as to argue that only those Greeks who partook of Attic culture could truly be called Hellenic. Doric was used in literature solely for some forms of poetry, including the mimes or skits. As the cosmopolitan tongue of Aegean culture, however, Attic lost some of its local peculiarities and became more urbane and graceful, while yet keeping its native strength. From this unifying tendency sprang a common dialect, the *koine,* which was to be used all over the Hellenistic world, though polished work was still to be written in the purer Attic.

Attic Rhetoric. The greatest single triumph of the new prose was the Attic oratory of the fourth century. The law courts of Athens were kept busy by commercial contentions and by famous legal attacks of the major politicians on each other; the assembly was a sounding-board for all the alarms of international and internal struggles. These opportunities, however, had largely been present in the fifth century, when Themistocles, Cimon, and Pericles had swayed the public; what was new was the more conscious elaboration of the oratorical art.

In the Athenian courts litigants spoke for themselves, but there was no ban on hiring a skilled rhetorician to prepare one's speech. The greatest masters of this art, who had to adapt their orations deftly to the character of their client, were Lysias (*c.* 459–380); and Isaeus (*c.* 420–350); the latter taught Demosthenes, who also wrote speeches for others and taught rhetoric. Virtually all the Athenian politicians of the century were by necessity orators. Andocides (*c.* 440–390), at the beginning of the century, had a loose, somewhat untutored style; then came the more polished orations of Aeschines, Lycurgus, Hyperides, and others. The greatest by far was Demosthenes, a master of invective and irony in his private speeches and of the most skillful, outwardly simple, and lucid analysis in his public orations.

Beside the practical experts stood the masters of rhetorical theory. Aristotle considered some psychological aspects of the subject in his *Rhetoric;* more significant was Isocrates, who studied under Tisias, Gorgias, Protagoras, and Socrates, then wrote speeches for others, and opened his own school about 393. While Plato was a more original theorist on the subject of education, Isocrates had a far greater influence on his own day. For 40 years young men came from all Greece to study rhetoric and the liberal arts under Isocrates and then went out to become generals, statesmen, and historians.

In his emphasis upon a broadly rounded education Isocrates consolidated the educational ideals of the sophists, though he opposed their radical overturn of standards. Philosophy, that is, did have its uses as a guide to practical life, for right conduct must be the basic aim of education; but the study of literature and still more of rhetoric was the principal key. The general principles of his system accorded well with the aristocratic standards of Greek civilization and underlay Hellenistic education, whence they passed to Rome as it grew great. Few men of the fourth century agreed with the sophistic view that "we are all by nature born the same in every way, both barbarians and Hellenes," [2] but the spread of Greek civilization over the Near East after the conquests of Alexander was to owe much to Isocrates' interpretation of Hellenism as a matter of culture rather than of blood.

FOURTH-CENTURY ART

Pottery and Painting. In the field of pottery the fourth century became as poverty-stricken as in that of poetry, for the long chain of painted pottery stretching across Protogeometric, Geometric, Orientalizing, and Attic black-figure and red-figure ware now reached its end. The potters of Athens, in particular, had lost their ability to create fresh masterpieces in the severe classical style by the end of the fifth century and turned to crowded compositions which used white, yellow, and even gilding.

These florid, emotionally charged red-figured styles went on into the fourth century, but the most interesting efforts to decorate vases with figured scenes were made in southern Italy (Apulia, Campania, etc.), where a complicated technique was used to reproduce scenes from tragedy and comedy as well as myth. Before the end of the fourth century figured ware had virtually disappeared in the Greek world. This great change was due in part to the growing wealth of the upper classes, which could more easily afford metal ware. To satisfy the needs of the poor the new pottery styles commonly had metallic shapes, plain black or other glaze, and at times relief ornament.

Another reason for the abandonment of vase painting lay in the great advance of painting itself. The new artistic sense of anatomy and of relation of figures to space could no longer be adequately reproduced on the small, curved sides of pots. The great masterpieces of the painters have long since vanished, but from literary references we can sense some of the lines of their development. In the closing decades of the fifth century, Parrhasius of Ephesus and Athens, and Zeuxis of southern Italy had moved beyond Polygnotus' creation of techniques to express depth,

[2] Antiphon, fragment 44 (Diels); tr. Kathleen Freeman.

and depicted more realistic scenes. Zeuxis was said to have painted grapes so that birds flew down to peck them. Then, in the fourth century, came another great master, Apelles of Colophon, whose painting of Aphrodite rising from the sea was praised for its naturalistic realism.

Architecture and Sculpture. Architects found it difficult to develop new forms or to improve further the temple. Notable among Doric temples were those of Athena Alea at Tegea, designed by Scopas, and of Zeus at Nemea; thereafter the Doric order steadily lost strength. The great temples of Ionia, as those of Artemis at Ephesus and of Apollo at Didyma (near Miletus), were Ionic in style but barren of true originality; perhaps the most notable was that of Athena Polias at Priene, designed by Pythius and dedicated by Alexander the Great in 334. The new Corinthian order differed from the Ionic only in its more luxurious, naturalistic, and intricate capitals, the first examples of which came late in the fifth century. Scopas used Corinthian half-columns in the interior of the temple at Tegea; other architects employed the style in the interior of the Doric, round sanctuaries (*tholoi*) constructed at Delphi and Epidaurus.

More significant was the rising prominence of secular buildings. Cities developed their market places with fountain houses, council chambers, and the like; converted their primitive theaters into noble stone edifices, as at Epidaurus and Athens; and paid great attention to their walls. Some of the most remarkable stone work of the century has been preserved in the fortresses of Eleutherae (Attica), Aegosthena (Megara), and the new center of Messene in the Peloponnesus. The most famous single architectural monument of the period, one of the later Seven Wonders, was also secular, the Mausoleum of the dynast Mausolus (d. 353) at Halicarnassus, which Pythius designed.

Sculpture reflected the new spirit of the fourth century with remarkable clarity. The balanced serenity and almost austere restraint that had stamped the great work of the preceding age was no longer possible or desirable. A mannerist style in which external form was developed at the expense of internal content had already begun to appear in the last decades of the fifth century; now even the statues of the gods must be graceful and elegant. In the *Hermes* of Olympia, which is probably the original work by Praxiteles of Athens (active 364), the remarkable improvement in technique, which permitted a more realistic portrayal of the human body, is evident.[3] So too is a loss of majesty and intellectual content, replaced by soft, sweet languor; another great Praxitelian work was the nude Aphrodite of Cnidus, which made that island famous.

Alongside the purely formal approach there arose a more realistic tendency. True portraiture of men emerged, so that we can visualize through Roman copies the faces of Isocrates, Plato, Demosthenes, and other notable figures. Freer depiction of emotion was encouraged; Scopas of Paros was famous for his statue of a maenad with head tossed back in ecstasy. Satyrs, unclothed Aphrodites, and other popular works were created in abundance, and also (at Athens) grave reliefs showing the deceased and family in sorrowful yet calm resignation.

The height of the new style was achieved by Lysippus of Sicyon (active about 328), who alone was permitted by Alexander the Great to create his portrait bust; since he worked solely in bronze, we have only later copies in marble of his great works. His *Apoxyomenus* presented an athlete in more advanced, three-dimensional fashion than any previous work; not only did Lysippus thus place sculpture in space, but he also formulated a new, more lifelike canon of proportions for the human body, in which the head was smaller and the body more slender than in the earlier canon of Polyclitus. From this level Hellenistic sculpture moved forward steadily.

THE EDGE OF A NEW WORLD

The fourth century B.C., down to the accession of Alexander, has been considered in the preceding two chapters primarily as a watershed between the archaic-classical structure, centered in the Aegean basin, and the broad Hellenistic world which embraced all the Near East. In many respects the most basic point of division lies in the closing decades of the fifth century. From that time onward philosophy, literature, the arts, and

---

[3] This statue, illustrated on Plate XIX, was found at Olympia in 1877 in the temple of Hera where Pausanias, author of a description of Greece, saw it in the second century after Christ; the right ankle and left ankle and foot are restored. The skin of Hermes originally was stained red, then wax-impregnated; since his hair was painted, it was only roughed out. Presumably he held out a toy or bunch of grapes to the infant Dionysus, whom he was taking to be reared by the nymphs of Nysa.

the political system itself began to turn toward a new spirit, but the full dimensions of the next great phase of Greek civilization did not generally become apparent until the generation of Alexander.

Then came the conquest of the Persian empire and the establishment of great Greco-Macedonian monarchies over most of the Near East. The same era saw the consolidation of a new sculptural style, the rise of the New Comedy, a great outburst of science, and the creation of the Stoic and Epicurean philosophies.

The forces that had driven Greek civilization in this direction had operated in many fields which it has not been possible to consider here. In religion, to give only one example, new gods appeared from Thrace and Asia Minor, and previously minor deities gained new significance. Asclepius, one of the most famous, was formally received at Athens in 420, with Sophocles as the public official in charge of the event; but the principal home of the god of healing was at Epidaurus, which was magnificently embellished in the fourth century as a center for faith cures. The emotional, personal devotion of this cult, as that of other new divine figures, suggests the need for spiritual outlets and for individual reassurance in an age of great changes. Other expressions of these needs lay in the wider use of magic, as attested by lead tablets of curses which were buried in the ground; in more graphic views of Hell, shown on Apulian vases; and in a variety of superstitions which the horrified Plato tried to ban in his *Laws*.

The changes of the fourth century, taken as a whole, represented a liberation from the rigid forms of earlier generations. Men felt themselves more to be individuals and brooked less easily the ties of state, of the Olympian religion, or of the old patriarchal family. In philosophy they sought personal ethical guidance and reassurance; in literature and in art they favored a more emotional, realistic approach. A counterpart of increased individualism was greater cosmopolitanism, which led some men to more mobile life and promoted the integration of Greek culture into a perhaps more superficial but certainly more uniform structure. "To a wise man," said Democritus, "the whole earth is open; for the native land of a good soul is the whole earth." [4]

In showing the existence of change and estimating its direction in any era, the historian must run the danger of seeming to exaggerate the

[4] Democritus, fragment 247 (Diels); tr. Kathleen Freeman.

degree of alterations so that they appear to be a revolution. The great Panhellenic enthusiast, Isocrates, composed as his last major work at the age of 97 the *Panathenaicus,* a diffuse eulogy of his own city; and most men remained patriotic even if they would not lay down their lives and property for the sake of complete local independence. So too authors, artists, and philosophers turned away from the patterns of earlier Greek civilization only in their formal aspects. The main qualities of the Greek spirit, including its human-centered, rational, harmonious instincts, continued their sway and were, if anything, more evident in the new developments of the fourth century and of its child, the Hellenistic age.

BIBLIOGRAPHY

Sources. The first Greek philosophers whose works have survived in quantity are Plato and Aristotle. The major works of each are noted in the text (and, for the political treatises, in Chapter 17). A beginning student might well read, from Plato, the *Symposium* and the *Phaedo* before essaying the *Republic;* in the tremendous body of Aristotle's works the *Poetics, Politics,* and *Nicomachean Ethics* are a good, if stiff introduction. To determine the views of Socrates is a difficult problem; the main evidence is Plato's *Apology of Socrates* and Xenophon's *Memorabilia, Apology,* and *Symposium,* with some comments by Aristotle. Both Plato and Aristotle are available in a variety of paperback translations (Penguin, Mentor, Bobbs-Merrill, and others).

The major historians and orators were cited in the bibliography of Chapter 17. The most famous orations of Demosthenes are his *Philippics* and the defense of his career in *On the Crown* (330), which led to the defeat and retirement of his opponent Aeschines. The smooth, almost monotonous style of Isocrates appears well in his *Panegyricus;* his views on education are largely given in his *Against the Sophists* and *On the Antidosis* (Loeb Classical Library).

Apart from the *Hermes* of Praxiteles and surviving fragments of the Mausoleum, on which Scopas and other sculptors worked, we have very few original works by fourth-century sculptors; the violently emotional pediments of the temple of Athena Alea at Tegea were at least designed by Scopas. Many masterpieces, however, were copied so repeatedly in Hellenistic and Roman times that their general nature can be assessed.

Further Reading. The great philosophers of this period have been considered in many popular works, of which the following are good. Socrates: A. E. Taylor, *Socrates* (Westport, Conn.: Greenwood, 1975). Plato: J. C. B. Gorling, *Plato* (Boston: Routledge & Kegan Paul, 1973); T. Irwin, *Plato's Moral Theory* (Oxford: Oxford University Press, 1977); N. P. White, *A Companion to Plato's Republic* (Indianapolis: Hackett, 1979); Paul Shorey, *What Plato Said* (Chicago: University of Chicago Press, 1978); A. E. Taylor, *Plato: The Man and His Work* (3d ed.; New York: Meridian, 1956). Aristotle: W. Jaeger, *Aristotle* (2d ed.; Oxford: Oxford Paperback 37, 1962), a fundamental study; W. D. Ross, *Aristotle* (New York: Barnes & Noble, 1965); G. E. R. Lloyd, *Aristotle* (Cambridge: Cambridge University Press, 1968). As a rule novels are not cited in these bibliographies, but Margaret Doody, *Aristotle Detective* (Penguin, 1981), deserves mention for its vivid picture of Athenian social and legal relations (as well as being a gripping detective story). See also F. M. Cornford, *Before and After Socrates* (Cambridge: Cambridge Paperback, 1960). Isocrates, who had at least as much influence in the era, is discussed by H. I. Marrou, *History of Education in Antiquity* (New York: Mentor, 1964), a standard work; and W. Jaeger, *Paideia,* Vol. III (New York: Oxford University Press, 1944).

T. B. L. Webster has a good comparative study in *Art and Literature in Fourth Century Athens* (London: Athlone, 1956). Changes in fourth-century architecture are noted in A. W. Lawrence, *Greek Architecture* (New York: Viking, 1975). M. Bieber, *Sculpture of the Hellenistic Age* (rev. ed.; New York: Columbia University Press, 1961), is full on Lysippus, who is also treated by F. P. Johnson, *Lysippos* (Westport, Conn.: Greenwood, 1968); B. R. Brown, *Anticlassicism in Greek Sculpture of the Fourth Century B.C.* (New York: New York University Press, 1973), briefly but clearly sums up the great cultural changes of the era.

19

ALEXANDER AND THE
HELLENISTIC WORLD

Alexander, son of Philip, has always been regarded as one of the greatest individuals in history, for under his leadership the Macedonians and Greeks conquered all the Persian empire. So began a new age of history.

Yet Alexander did not achieve this great deed all by himself, nor were the changes that ensued merely the product of the men who immediately accompanied him. In a broader view Alexander's meteoric conquests were an explosion of the Greek world. Earlier in the fourth century Persia had appeared strong and Hellas weak; but this situation, born of Greek disunity, had actually been the reverse of reality. Once Philip had forcibly drawn the Greeks together, his son could move forward swiftly.

Although Alexander died young, his marshals maintained Macedonian-Greek supremacy in the Near East and encouraged an outpouring of Greek settlers as bureaucrats, traders, soldiers, and scholars. This new world is called Hellenistic (or "Greek-like") to distinguish it from the earlier, Hellenic era. Chronologically, the Hellenistic period may be taken as beginning with the death of Alexander in 323 and ending with the suicide of the last major Hellenistic ruler, Cleopatra of Egypt, in 30 B.C.

This era is fascinating in itself, but it is also intriguing in its many superficial similarities to the modern world. The spread of Greek civilization into the Near East will remind one of the extension of European culture over the world in modern times; and just as European colonists faced quite different patterns in China and India, so too the Greeks met alien ways in Mesopotamia and Egypt. Political history now became a complicated interplay of the policies of the major Hellenistic rulers, who used diplomacy and war much as has been the practice in modern Europe. Various social and economic aspects of European overseas domination, or colonialism, find parallels as well in the Hellenistic world, for this was basically a system in which a small minority of Greeks and Macedonians dominated great masses of natives. The social and cultural domination of the Near East which Alexander's conquest gave to the Greeks was to last in most respects until the great Arab expansion in the seventh century after Christ, but here we shall consider only the first and most prosperous stage, politically and economically, down to about 200 B.C.

ALEXANDER THE GREAT

Preparations for Invasion (336–34 B.C.). When Alexander (356–23) became king at the age of 20 in 336, he inherited a unified kingdom, a well-trained army, and mastery over the mainland Greeks. The latter took the accession of the young ruler as an opportunity for disaffection, but they were overawed by his swift appearance in their midst. In 335 Alexander suppressed the barbarians along the northern frontier of Macedonia in brilliant campaigns which showed to Philip's veteran generals and to the Macedonian army the mettle of their leader. At one point a rumor that Alexander had been killed swept into Greece and led the Thebans to revolt. Alexander raced down, took, and destroyed Thebes as a warning to the other Greeks; his admiration for Hellenic culture, however, induced him to leave standing the house of the famous Boeotian poet Pindar.

Alexander inherited also a major policy, the invasion of the Persian empire. That the Persians could be defeated had been shown in the famous expedition of the Ten Thousand of 401–400 and had been preached as a Greek duty by the Athenian publicist Isocrates. So long as the Greeks had been disunited, the Persian king had been able to maintain an outwardly strong position by the use of diplomacy and gold; but in truth the empire had weakened steadily during the fourth century.

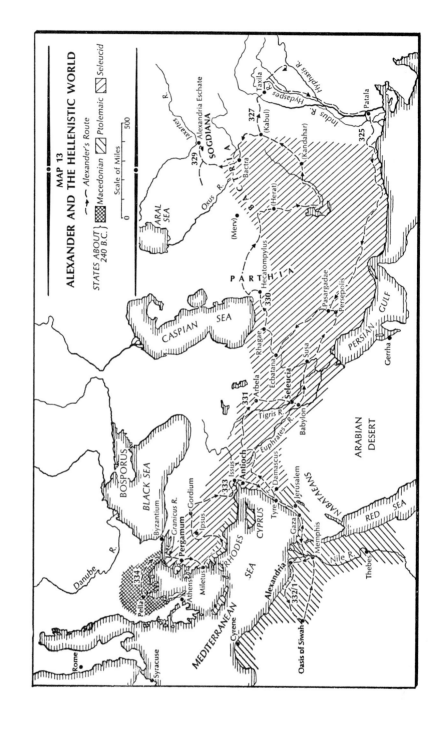

MAP 13

ALEXANDER AND THE HELLENISTIC WORLD

STATES ABOUT 240 B.C.
— Alexander's Route
▨ Macedonian   ▩ Ptolemaic   ▨ Seleucid

Scale of Miles
0   500

Rome

Syracuse

MEDITERRANEAN SEA

Cyrene

Oasis of Siwah   332/1

Alexandria

Memphis

Thebes

Nile R.

RED SEA

NABATAEANS

Jerusalem

Gaza

Tyre

Damascus

CYPRUS

RHODES

Miletus

Athens

Ipsus

Pergamum

Gordium

Granicus R.

Byzantium

Pella   334

BOSPORUS

BLACK SEA

CASPIAN SEA

ARAL SEA

Danube R.

Antioch   333

Issus

Tigris R.

Euphrates R.

Babylon

Seleucia

ARABIAN DESERT

Gerrha

PERSIAN GULF

Susa

Ecbatana

Arbela   331

Rhagae

Pasargadae

Persepolis

PARTHIA

Hecatompylus   330

(Merv)

(Herat)

Oxus R.

SOGDIANA   329

Alexandria Eschate

Jaxartes R.

B A C T R I A

Bactra   327

(Kabul)

(Kandahar)

Taxila

Indus R.

Hydaspes R.

Hyphasis R.

Patala   325

The central court was repeatedly split by harem intrigues, the last of which elevated a new king, Darius III, in 336. The Persian rule on the fringe of India was lost, the Iranian nobles became less attached to the throne, and Egypt maintained its independence from 404 down to 343. More and more the Persian rulers had turned to Greek mercenaries, who formed the bulk of the infantry.

Nevertheless the Persian empire was vast, and its navy, led by the Greek admiral Memnon, controlled the seas. In invading Asia, Alexander faced the threat that his opponent might stir up revolt in Greece itself. To counter the danger Alexander left behind a sizable part of his Macedonian infantry under the grizzled general Antipater; the expeditionary force which finally crossed the Hellespont in the spring of 334 consisted of 30,000 infantry and 5000 cavalry — small in modern terms but very large when measured by ancient means of supply. The backbone was composed of the Macedonians, who fought the battles; but Alexander had also Greek contingents from the league of Corinth, who were employed in garrisons and as line-of-communications troops, and also important bands of mercenary Cretan archers and other light-armed troops. A regular staff, secretaries, scientists, and philosophers accompanied the king.

Conquest of Hither Asia (334–30 B.C.). Alexander is the first general in history whom we can see thinking out answers to his strategic problems and then doggedly executing his plans. For the first three years of his conquest his operations were designed to crush the Persian navy by taking all its ports from Asia Minor to Egypt, a simple but brilliant idea which required two major battles and many sieges. Whether he actually saw ahead to the entire conquest of the Persian realm we cannot determine, though as he crossed the Hellespont Alexander threw his spear into the opposite shore in symbolic gesture that he would win the enemy land in battle.

Immediately thereafter he moved to Troy, where he offered libations to the Greek heroes of epic legend and took a sacred shield which had traditionally been dedicated by the Greeks; under his pillow there was always a copy of the *Iliad,* corrected by his tutor Aristotle. In the first action of the invasion he met the satraps of Asia Minor, with their local forces, at the Granicus river; charged boldly across the river at the head of his cavalry; and scored a smashing victory. Although wounded himself, Alexander visited his wounded soldiers and publicized the success in Greece as a victory of the league of Corinth. During the remainder of the campaigning season of 334 he took the coast of Asia Minor and drove inland to Gordium, where he cut a famous knot; in tradition anyone who could master the knot would become ruler of the world.

In 333 Alexander advanced into Syria. Darius III, leading the main Persian army, moved to the same district and accidentally came in behind the Macedonians at Issus. Although the situation was dangerous, Alexander pointed out to his troops that the Persians had exposed themselves in flat terrain, whereupon his men enthusiastically retraced their steps and secured another major victory. At Issus Alexander wiped out the Greek infantry of his foe, but even though he seized the family of Darius the Persian king himself escaped.

Rather than follow the fugitive king of kings inland, Alexander continued his strategic plan and marched on down the coast. At Tyre he was held up by a seven-month siege. During its course his men made a causeway out to the island city, fought from ships, and even battled under the sea with Tyrian divers; but in the end Alexander's marvelous command over his troops led them to conquer a fortress which the Assyrians had besieged in vain for 13 years. Egypt received Alexander as a deliverer, and here he rested his men through the winter of 332/1. Ever energetic himself, he founded a new city, Alexandria, to serve as a great Macedonian port for his realm and marched out to the oasis of Siwah, where he consulted the famous oracle of Zeus Ammon. What the oracle promised him he never divulged; but an important event occurred at his entry, when the priests hailed him as Son of Ammon. As he moved on through the Near East and wrestled with the problem of being master both of the Aegean world and of the erstwhile Persian empire, Alexander was to turn more and more toward assuming a divine position as a means of binding all his subjects to his rule.

Alexander's first major strategic problem had been solved, for the last remnants of the Persian fleet had fallen into Macedonian hands. Now he could concentrate his attention on Darius. In the spring of 331 he returned along the Syrian coast and plunged inland to northern Mesopotamia. Here he met the Persian army near Arbela. During the respite of two years since Issus, Darius had frantically prepared for the decisive battle; but, unable to reach Greece for new mercenary infantry, he had to depend primarily upon his Iranian cavalry. To weaken the enemy he laid waste the route by which Alexander would approach and poisoned the wells, but Alexander learned of this in time to take another road.

Unlike his speedy action at the Granicus and Issus, Alexander this time halted four days at a safe distance from the enemy and reconnoitered the battlefield, while his men prepared themselves. His army had been enlarged to 40,000 infantry and 7000 cavalry by reinforcements from home; the Persian force was considerably larger. Finally Alexander gave his officers his plan of action in a firm speech which emphasized the need for obedience, went to bed, and slept so soundly that his second-in-command, Parmenio, had to awaken him on the morning of the battle (October 1, 331).

Since the Persian infantry was weak, Darius had devised a new weapon, scythe-bearing chariots which were to slice up the Macedonian phalanx; these stood in front of the infantry, while his cavalry was on the wings. Alexander likewise placed his infantry in the center and cavalry on the wings, but to avoid the danger of being outflanked by the numerically superior enemy he threw out flying wings on either side and stationed Greek infantry in the rear as a reserve — the first major occasion in Greek military history when such a tactical formation was adopted.

The battle of Arbela opened with heavy cavalry engagements on either flank. Alexander directed the action on his right flank, which drew in more and more men and attracted the left elements of the Persian center. The remainder of the Persian center, however, tended to drift to its right, a common phenomenon in ancient battles where every soldier sought to cover himself with his neighbor's shield (to his right). Alexander saw his tactical problem clearly, which was to allow this stress in his enemy to develop as far as possible without letting his own cavalry wings be crushed by the Persian hordes of cavalry; at just the right moment he hastened to his infantry and led most of its battalions in an assault straight at the weakening Persian center. Darius, on the other hand, sadly misjudged the tactical development of the battle. He launched his scythe-bearing chariots before the Macedonian infantry was deeply involved; so they harmlessly galloped through the openings made by the steady Macedonian hoplites in their ranks. As Alexander's center advanced, Darius fled in fright with his infantry. The day was won, but

Alexander, instead of pursuing, had to turn about to relieve Parmenio on his left wing, which had almost collapsed. As a result Darius once more escaped.

After the battle of Arbela Alexander marched to Babylon, where he gave his men a month's leave in the metropolis of the Near East. Then he drove up into Persia proper and spent two months at the treasury-fortress of Persepolis, which was burned in vengeance for Xerxes' treatment of Athens. In the spring of 330 Alexander once more took up the chase of Darius and followed the foe past Ecbatana to the south coast of the Caspian Sea. In the relentless chase the Macedonian infantry wore out; but Alexander and his cavalry continued the pursuit, fired by the news that the Persians had virtually deposed their weak king and held him prisoner. Finally, as dawn began to break on a day in mid-summer, Alexander caught up with the fugitives at Hecatompylus and charged. The Persian conspirators about Darius did not dare meet the attack, though Alexander had only 60 men immediately with him; they put a dagger into Darius and fled eastward. As Alexander stood over the body of the last Persian king, he could rightfully claim to be master of the Persian empire.

Campaigns in Central Asia and India (330–25 B.C.). Much in Alexander's realm insistently called for attention. Antipater was ruthlessly maintaining peace in Macedonia and Greece, but the sullen Greeks grew more uneasy the farther Alexander marched away from the Aegean. In the newly conquered provinces Alexander for the moment continued the Persian satrapal organization; yet this could not be a permanent solution. Alexander, however, plunged on into central Asia to curb the murderers of Darius and to assert his authority over Bactria, Sogdiana, and other satrapies up to the Jaxartes river.

Since these campaigns took place in areas the Greeks had never before seen and did not thereafter know well, the geography of his eastern operations is at times hazy. It is, nonetheless, clear that Alexander met protracted resistance, which often assumed guerrilla forms, and his military ability showed itself in his remarkable ability to adapt his tactics to the new conditions. Rather than marching in one body, he fanned his troops out in many columns. To counter the mounted archers of the steppes Alexander remounted most of his cavalry on fast Sogdian horses and even enlisted native archers. Everywhere he founded military garrisons to hold down the major lines of communications; and in the end his persistence put an end to the resistance.

By 327 he was ready to move down the Khyber pass and neighboring mountains from Afghanistan to northern India, parts of which had at times been Persian. In India he encountered one of his most dangerous foes, the giant King Porus, who held the Hydaspes river (the modern Jhelum, a tributary of the Indus) against him with elephants, cavalry, and infantry. For a time Alexander made feints at crossing the river so as to reduce the wariness of his enemy; then one dark, stormy night he stealthily moved upstream, crossed undetected, and came down to meet the Indian force. Since his cavalry could not face the elephants, Alexander had to keep his horse well out on the wings while his infantry desperately battled in the center. Once again the Macedonians won, but their losses were as great as in all the major battles of Hither Asia put together.

By this time Alexander's men, "conquerors of the world covered by rags of barbaric and Indian booty, miserably patched together," [1] were utterly weary, but Alexander drove on to take, as he thought, the rest of India, the great size of which was not known. In July 326, in the monsoon rains, his troops balked at the river Hyphasis (the Beas) and refused to go farther. Finally their commander yielded and marched back to Babylon via the lower Indus and then the desolate coast of the Persian Gulf, where three-quarters of his army perished for lack of food; the summer monsoon, of which Alexander was unaware, prevented his fleet from coming up the Gulf to bring supplies.

On Alexander's return to Babylon in 324 he was forced to spend a year reorganizing and tightening up his administration; but he was also planning an invasion of Arabia to round out his realm from India to Egypt. Amid his work and carousing he caught a swamp fever (perhaps malaria) and died on June 10, 323, at the age of 33.

Alexander's Place in History. Judgments on Alexander's career vary widely. Some students consider him little more than a military adventurer, who secured release from his tensions in drunken bouts, in one of which he killed his close friend Clitus, who had saved his life at the Granicus. Others feel that Alexander began a new age and that, perhaps

---

[1] Diodorus 17.94.2.

more than any other secular individual, he changed the course of western history in its ancient phase. In popular imagination Alexander soon became a great hero who was the subject of ever more fantastic folk tales; under the name of Iskander and other corruptions he turned into a legend from Albania to Afghanistan. Even in Greek memory he became a romanticized figure.

To penetrate to the reality of his aims is difficult. On one point, that of his military ability, it can safely be said that in all history there is scarcely a more model general than Alexander. During his 11 years of campaigning he covered over 22,000 miles and never lost a battle. Usually he knew more of the terrain than even the natives did; he led his men with physical bravery and moral courage; tactically and strategically he displayed a sound, quick judgment and carried out his well-formed plans relentlessly.

In other aspects as well Alexander had boldness of vision. Economically he planned to unite his realm by means of great new ports, Alexandria in Egypt and Patala at the mouth of the Indus. He reorganized the tax system of the Persian empire into new districts independent of the satrapies. Mints at Amphipolis, Babylon, and elsewhere issued a coinage on the Attic standard which was intended to be an empire-wide means of exchange.

Politically and culturally he had a romantic dream of uniting his great realm on broader lines than any of his successors were to essay. He himself was to be the master. In Greece he ordered his deification in 324 so that he could stand above the cities; for his army and his aides he tried after the death of Darius to introduce Persian royal court practices, but only with limited success. Beneath his absolute control Macedonians, Greeks, Persians, and other elements were to serve side by side.

In the cosmopolitan spirit of the succeeding Hellenistic age Alexander was at times interpreted as a man who planned to unite east and west into one world; after a mutiny of his troops at Opis (near Babylon) we are told that he prayed at a reconciliation feast "for harmony and fellowship in the empire between Macedonians and Persians." [2] Yet Alexander was not simply an idealistic theorist. The mutiny at Opis, for instance, had been caused because he was training Persians to serve in his army

[2] Arrian, *Anabasis* 7.11.9; tr. E. I. Robson.

— but they were being trained in the Macedonian-Greek fashion. So too he and many of his officers and men married Persian women, but there is no evidence Persian nobles secured Macedonian wives. Alexander did have a much broader view of his empire than Aristotle, who "advised Alexander to treat the Greeks as if he were their leader and other peoples as if he were their master, to have regard for the Greeks as for friends and kindred, but to conduct himself toward other peoples as though they were plants or animals." [3] Nonetheless he sought primarily to promote Hellenic culture. His some 70 military colonies, mostly in central Asia, were founded as Greek cities, though often they supplanted earlier towns. In the economic bloom of the Hellenistic world, such points as Kandahar and Herat long continued to radiate Greek influence. Alexander's conquests, in sum, represented an outpouring of Aegean energies and resulted in Greco-Macedonian domination over the Near East.

THE HELLENISTIC STATES

Wars of Alexander's Successors (323–280 B.C.). Alexander left as his heirs a half-wit half-brother and a posthumous son, born to his new Persian wife, Roxane. Both were soon swept aside, along with his mother Olympias and all other members of Philip's house; for Alexander's marshals and satraps showed themselves to be extremely ambitious and also extremely able. Since the great bulk of his realm had long been united in the Persian empire, there was no reason why it should not have continued to enjoy political unity, save that the rival generals balked each other of securing over-all mastery. The most notable, Antigonus the One-Eyed (*c.* 382–01) and his brilliant but erratic son Demetrius the Taker of Cities (336–283), came close to downing the others but met final defeat at the battle of Ipsus in 301, in which Antigonus was killed. By this time the division of the Hellenistic world into several great monarchies was well advanced, though one of the victors at Ipsus, Seleucus (*c.* 358–280), who held the territory from Syria to India, continued to seek the mirage of universal rule until his murder in 280.

The Hellenistic state-system which emerged during the wars of Alex-

---

[3] Plutarch, *On the Fortune of Alexander* 329B.

ander's successors was as complicated as that of modern Europe. Of the
three major powers the longest enduring was the realm of the Ptolemies
in Egypt. The Seleucid dynasty was the most important in many respects,
for it held the great bridge of land from inland Asia Minor through
Syria and Mesopotamia to Iran. Its eastern provinces, however, fell away
in the third century; a native dynasty, the Parthian, rose in Iran from
247 on, and the Greek settlers in Bactria revolted and maintained their
independence into the middle of the second century (see Plate XVIII.D).
The third major line was that of the Antigonids in Macedonia, founded
by Antigonus Gonatas (c. 320–239), the grandson of Antigonus the One-
Eyed.

The Antigonids also generally exercised suzerainty over Greece, but
the homeland of Hellenic civilization was far from exhausted. Although
Athens and Sparta now rarely played active roles, the Aetolian league in
western Greece and the Achaean league in the Peloponnesus grew steadily
stronger as the greatest federal structures of antiquity. Rhodes, Byzantium, and other commercially important city-states continued to be free.
Among the many smaller kingdoms of the age Pergamum in western
Asia Minor was influential in promoting Roman political entry in the
Hellenistic world (see Chapter 23), but its kings also successfully supported artistic and literary activity, based on an economic system modelled
after that of Egypt.

Political Division. Superficially the political history of the Hellenistic
world is one of tremendous complexity and incessant wars. The greater
monarchies were not firmly united territorial states, as the Greek city-
states had been; rather, they were held together by the political and
military abilities of the kings of the three major lines. This situation in
itself led to wars to secure the necessary prestige for survival.

Under the surface there were more fundamental conflicts among the
monarchies, for example, the need to keep lines open to the Aegean so as
to secure Greek mercenaries, colonists, and administrators; and the competitive struggle to control the Mediterranean ends of the great trade
routes. The Ptolemies and the Seleucids, thus, waged a series of Syrian
wars for mastery of the coast of Syria and Palestine.

Throughout the third century the Ptolemies generally held the upper
hand, not so much because their armies were efficient as because they

were masters of the sea and had tremendous financial resources through their exploitation of Egypt. Yet the Hellenistic statesmen understood fairly well the principle of the balance of power, and so other major and minor states tended to unite against any dynasty which seemed overly powerful. Treaties of alliance, of dynastic marriage, and of financial subvention succeeded one another in the ever-shifting lines of diplomatic activity much as in eighteenth-century Europe. In such a system warfare was not pushed to the bitter end of wiping out rival states, and for a time in the third century its practice became more humane as kings sought to make use of, rather than exterminate, the cities they conquered and as holy places secured formal grants of immunity from the horrors of war.

Quite apart from the contentions of the kings themselves, other forces tended to pull the Hellenistic world apart. The Greek cities of the Aegean world sought to free themselves from royal yokes; and the Iranian east, at the other geographical extreme, never reconciled itself to Hellenic mastery. Everywhere, but especially in Egypt, the natives murmured; both by land and by sea, where Rhodes sought desperately to check piracy, security was difficult to maintain. By 200 B.C. the Hellenistic monarchies had battled each other to a standstill. The way thus was open for Parthia from the east and for Rome from the west to be called in by dissatisfied elements and to absorb ever larger parts of the Near East.

Common Political and Military Patterns. Despite its political divisions the Hellenistic world formed a social, economic, and cultural unit which at times was called the *oikoumene,* or "inhabited world." Even politically its institutions had a common stamp, in which were blended Near Eastern and Greek elements. The greater kings, who had won and held their realms by the sword and by cunning, were as absolute monarchs as any Sargon or Thutmose; indeed, they were less confined by the prescriptions of ancestral tradition inasmuch as they had entered the Near East from the outside. Native aristocracies disappeared or were shoved to one side; but no Greek aristocracy came in with the kings to serve as checks.

To help them in keeping their vast realms together the kings had three main programs, spiritual, administrative, and military. Spiritually the monarchs could not build upon any sense of patriotism, nor did they venture to follow Alexander's rather bold schemes for uniting natives and Greeks. In all cases, accordingly, they relied principally upon the positive support of Greeks, though natives who became Hellenized found the way open to royal favor; but in their effort to create a more general spiritual bond several royal lines, including the Ptolemies and Seleucids, came to deify their rulers as earthly benefactors and saviors. The ancient Near Eastern political ideal of kingship by divine right thus rose above the Greek ideal of the free citizen and passed into the stream of western civilization. Some Greek philosophers went so far as to justify royal absolutism in theoretical terms.

While local structures of government largely remained as they had been before, a developed bureaucracy was swiftly created as a second bond in each of the new states. The Greeks thus brought Hellenic rational calculation into the traditional society of the Near East. This administration used the Greek language, calendar, and principles of law; state finances were conducted with coinage on the Attic standard. Only in Egypt was a Phoenician standard employed, in order to isolate its internal economic system from the outside world. The kings were much interested in economic development, as we shall see below; and state control of commerce and industry went far beyond the relatively free principles prevalent in earlier Greek times.

Militarily the Hellenistic state-system rested upon Greeks and Macedonians. Each of Alexander's successors had cajoled into his own service as many of Alexander's veterans as he could. Thereafter the rulers sought to build up dependable forces of Greco-Macedonian background. In Egypt military colonists were dotted over the land; the Seleucid kings relied more upon settled clumps of soldiers who could be summoned in war; both sought to keep open avenues by which they might recruit mercenaries in the Aegean world. Natives could be used very rarely both because of language problems and also from the fear that they might revolt. During the Syrian war Ptolemy IV turned in desperation to native Egyptians and trained them in the Greek fashion (217 B.C.), only to suffer serious internal disturbances thereafter. In military and political respects the Hellenistic world was administered in a Greek manner, though under the control of absolute monarchs; and in both respects organization was more skilled and professional than ever before.

SOCIAL AND ECONOMIC ASPECTS

Greek Social Domination. Beside the kings, the administrators, and the soldiers stood a host of other Greeks in most of the Hellenistic states, who set the cultural tone of the world and dominated its social and economic system. These Greeks came largely of their own accord as traders, artisans, scholars, and others to seek the economic advantages of the new, "colonial" world; but the kings welcomed them enthusiastically.

The Seleucid line particularly sought to build up a solid Greek framework in its far-flung domains and performed yeoman service in establishing Greek cities, either old settlements which were reorganized under Greek control or entirely new centers such as the capitals of Antioch and Seleucia-on-the-Orontes. In Asia Minor some 80 colonies were founded by rulers of various houses, and a dense network of Greek cities was built up in Syria. Both areas thenceforth had a Greek veneer down to Arab days; but other cities appeared in profusion as far as Bactria and India. The Ptolemies were more loath to upset the patterns of life they had inherited, and in Egypt only three Greek cities existed: the great capital of Alexandria, a façade for the country; the old Greek trading colony of Naucratis; and one city up-country at Ptolemais. In Egypt, accordingly, the Greeks lived in more scattered fashion but grouped themselves in religious, social, and educational units based on the local *gymnasia.*

The Greek cities of the Hellenistic world were at least as important as the kings and long outlasted the major monarchies. To the kings the loyalty of the cities was vital, for they were the economic centers and provided significant revenues to the royal exchequers. The local leading classes were heavily burdened to meet the king's demands and also to keep up the physical elegance of the urban centers. Nonetheless most citizens were deeply attached to their communities and preserved earlier Hellenic political attitudes at least on the local level. From the kings, in return for their support, they expected protection from outside foes and also assistance in maintaining their locally privileged position; when the Hellenistic monarchs eventually failed them in these respects, the Greeks turned to Parthia and to Rome.

Socially and economically Hellenic elements formed a dominant level over great masses of natives. In Alexandria, Antioch, and the great Babylonian center of Seleucia-on-the-Tigris alike, groups of relatively few Greeks constituted an upper crust much as did the English masters of Bombay, Singapore, or Hong Kong in the nineteenth century. Culturally, as we shall see in the next chapter, these Greeks clung to their ancestral inheritance, though they were willing to admit wealthier natives to their ranks so long as these men Hellenized themselves.

The Economic Bloom. During the century following Alexander's death the Hellenistic world appeared remarkably prosperous. Alexander had put into circulation the great masses of silver and gold stored in Persian treasuries, so that prices rose considerably down to 270. The demand both for Greek emigrants and for Greek products, however, relieved for most of this period the serious stresses that had afflicted the fourth-century Aegean world. Abroad, the new Hellenistic cities were burgeoning in their first decades. Caravan and local trade supported many inland cities; Alexandria, Seleucia-on-the-Orontes, and other ports grew rapidly. Rhodes became a main clearing house for Mediterranean trade, which spread out northward via Byzantium and Cyzicus into the Black Sea and westward via Corinth to Sicily and southern Italy.

Within the Hellenistic heartland, which extended from Sicily to Mesopotamia and from the Black Sea to southern Egypt, the conduct of trade became ever more professional. Ships grew larger; harbors, such as the famous port of Alexandria with its lighthouse (*pharos*) nearly 400 feet high, were systematized; banking became more widespread. Items of trade included slaves from backward areas; Attic pottery, which was exported for a time more widely than ever before, such luxuries as incense, perfume, glass, art objects, and jewels made or processed largely in Syrian and Egyptian workshops; metals, wood, papyrus; and great quantities of wine and olive oil, largely of Aegean origin, and wheat from the Black Sea, Egypt, and Sicily. Rhodian jars which served as shipping containers for these latter bulk items turn up in numbers all the way from the Carpathian mountains of central Europe to Carthage and Susa.

Exploration and trade moved even farther afield to distant corners of Eurasia. In the west the daring Pytheas of Massilia just before 300 circumnavigated Britain, where he observed the long summer days and heard of a distant island called Thule (Iceland or Norway); Carthaginian adventurers reached the Cape Verde islands. In the east Patrocles, a Seleucid official, explored the Caspian about 285, and an ambassador of Seleucus I, Megasthenes, wrote a treatise on India. Trade in spices, jewels, and other luxuries grew between India and the west, partly overland through Afghanistan, partly by sea up the Persian Gulf (through the intermediaries of the Gerrhaeans) and around Arabia to the Nabataeans and to Egypt. The polyglot nature of this trade is suggested by a surviving contract drawn up on the Somali coast by a Carthaginian, a Massiliote, and a Spartan. Overland trade to China, though never more than a trickle, began in the second century B.C.

A notable characteristic of Hellenistic economic activity was the large part played in it by state machinery, especially in Egypt. The Ptolemies of Egypt inherited a centralized system of government, which went back to the days of the pharaohs. As far as possible they maintained this structure but animated it by dextrous application of Greek rationalism so as to increase and garner the production of the peasants. The roads were improved; new crops and animals were introduced; the use of iron tools became common for the first time.

But all was regulated by the Ptolemies for their own benefit. In each village a secretary made an elaborate census of land, animals, property, and persons, which was consolidated on the nome registers and forwarded to the central administration at Alexandria. Each year peasants were directed what to produce and were issued seed grain for that purpose; at harvest time careful watch ensured that they turned over their due rents and taxes. From tax receipts it has been calculated that no less than 218 taxes were imposed; and for each receipt the taxpayer had to pay a small sum in addition. Monopolies processed and sold oil, salt, wine, beer, and other staples at great profit, which was protected by high customs duties. The peasants had also to yield labor to keep up the canals and roads and to move the state-owned grain to Alexandria, where it was sold abroad to secure the revenues with which the Ptolemies assured their pre-eminent international position. No ancient structure ever surpassed the complexity of this machinery, though it was never as tidy and uniform over the whole land as sometimes pictured.

The Situation in 200 B.C. From about 250 onward prices rose again in the Hellenistic world as international stresses and inflation grew more prominent, and by the end of the third century the great economic expansion of the Hellenistic world had drawn to a close. The Ptolemies could not heal the division between the exploiting bureaucracy and the peasants. The former learned how to defraud the king despite elaborate checks; the latter reacted to their terrific pressure by dragging their feet and at times by scattered strikes. In Greece the conflict of rich and poor again became intense in the later decades of the third century. Overseas migration was no longer so feasible as earlier, and the countryside continued to be absorbed into great estates. Open civil war broke out sporadically, as in Sparta.

Politically the kings wore themselves out in incessant, inconclusive wars. The over-all pattern of Hellenistic history was one of ever-greater splintering, as Alexander's unified empire yielded to the great monarchies and these in turn lost outlying districts. Between the international disintegration and the growth of internal dissidence the Hellenistic powers became too weak to maintain themselves against attacks by less-civilized but more firmly united states from the outside.

Nonetheless the conquests of Alexander had been one of the greatest turning points in ancient history. The remarkable vitality of Greek civilization, which had earlier led the Greeks to throw out scattered colonies all over the western Mediterranean and Black seas, had reached such a level that under Alexander the Greeks and Macedonians overthrew the native political system of the Near East itself. In this tremendous expansion Greek intellectual and artistic leaders were inspired to a new wave of cultural achievements which had great effects on neighboring peoples from Rome to India. The Greeks, moreover, had set themselves so firmly in social and cultural mastery of the Near East that Hellenistic civilization survived the terrific political and economic unrest which beset the last two centuries B.C.

BIBLIOGRAPHY

Sources. For the career of Alexander we have almost no contemporary materials, and the growth of legend about his exploits soon made his life a subject of romance. The best account of his military operations is the *Anabasis* of Arrian, who wrote in the second century after Christ but used such solid sources as the work of Ptolemy I, one of Alexander's marshals (tr. A. de Selincourt, Penguin L81, 1958). Plutarch's *Life of Alexander* contains both legendary and factual material. Quintus Curtius Rufus' account (Loeb Classical Library) is more dramatic and romantic, and with other similar accounts led to a variety of Alexander-romances in the Middle Ages.

The history of Diodorus Siculus, Books 18–20 (Loeb Classical Library), gives a detailed account of the wars of Alexander's successors to 302; and Plutarch has lives of some of the greater generals of the era, such as Eumenes and Demetrius, as well as of some later Greek leaders, such as the reforming Spartan kings Agis and Cleomenes and the Achaean statesman Aratus. But for the era 281–11 we have no connected ancient history of the Hellenistic world except for a skeleton in Justin's abridgement of the history of Pompeius Trogus; the rhetorical or dramatic histories by Timaeus, Duris, Phylarchus, and others are gone. Polybius began his story of the rise of Rome in 221 (see Bibliography, Chapter 23). As a result the mid-third century in its details is one of the most obscure of all ancient history.

Other types of evidence throw light on certain aspects. Greek papyri from Egypt illuminate its administrative and economic activity on the village and estate level. The records of Zeno, a local manager for the state treasurer in the mid-third century, for instance, are discussed by M. I. Rostovtzeff, *A Large Estate in Egypt in the Third Century* (Chicago: Ares, 1980); a good selection of papyri is available in A. S. Hunt and C. C. Edgar, ed., *Select Papyri*, 2 vols. (Loeb Classical Library). Only rarely, as in the *Revenue Laws of Ptolemy Philadelphus*, ed. B. P. Grenfell (Oxford: Oxford University Press, 1896), on the collection of oil and wine, does this material give the general rules laid down by the Alexandrian central administration.

Inscriptions are abundant for some Greek cities of the Aegean world, but the new cities of the Near East rarely furnish much epigraphical evidence. Another source is that of the coins issued by the rulers, which often provided a skeleton of dynastic succession; for the Greek rulers of Bactria and India this numismatic material is all-important (see Plate XVIII.D).

Further Reading. The standard survey of the Hellenistic age is W. W. Tarn and G. T. Griffith, *Hellenistic Civilization* (3d ed.; New York: Meridian 121, 1961). On the political side this may be complemented by

Max Cary, *History of the Greek World from 323 to 146 B.C.* (5th ed.; London: Methuen, 1968); M. I. Rostovtzeff, *Social and Economic History of the Hellenistic World,* 3 vols. (Oxford: Oxford University Press, 1941), is one of the greatest works of a major historian of the past generation.

On Alexander, a famous, romantic study is W. W. Tarn, *Alexander the Great,* 2 vols. (Cambridge: Cambridge University Press, 1979), which inspired Mary Renault's novels. Among more recent biographies the only useful one is by J. R. Hamilton (Pittsburgh: University of Pittsburgh Press, 1974), but see also U. Wilcken, *Alexander the Great* (New York: Dial, 1932), and the collection of essays in G. T. Griffith, *Alexander the Great: The Main Problems* (Cambridge: Heffer, 1966). R. E. M. Wheeler, *Flames over Persepolis* (London: Weidenfeld & Nicolson, 1968), is well illustrated; E. W. Marsden analyzes *The Campaign of Gaugamela* (Liverpool: Liverpool University Press, 1964); D. W. Engels, *Alexander the Great and the Logistics of the Macedonian Army* (Berkeley: University of California Press, 1978), shows that something significantly new can be said of his career.

Expansion of city life is treated in detail by A. H. M. Jones, *Greek City from Alexander to Justinian* (Oxford: Oxford University Press, 1940). W. S. Ferguson, *Hellenistic Athens* (Chicago: Ares, 1974), is still useful; J. A. O. Larsen, *Representative Government in Greek and Roman History* (Berkeley: University of California Press, 1976), is a good guide to the Hellenistic leagues. For the kingdoms and their rulers see P. G. Elgood, *Ptolemies of Egypt* (Bristol: Arrowsmith, 1938); H. J. Bell, *Egypt from Alexander the Great to the Arab Conquest* (Oxford: Oxford University Press, 1948), who comments on the papyri; E. V. Hansen, *Attalids of Pergamum* (2d ed.; Ithaca: Cornell University Press, 1971); G. H. Macurdy, *Hellenistic Queens* (New York: AMS, 1976); and W. W. Tarn's brilliant, if somewhat hypothetical restoration of the *Greeks in Bactria and India* (2d ed.; Cambridge: Cambridge University Press, 1966). The military structure of the kingdoms is to be found in W. W. Tarn, *Hellenistic Military and Naval Developments* (Chicago: Ares); G. T. Griffith, *Mercenaries of the Hellenistic World* (New York: AMS, 1977); B. Bar-Kochva, *The Seleucid Army* (London: Cambridge University Press, 1976).

20

HELLENISTIC CIVILIZATION

When Alexander's conquests threw Greeks and Near Easterners into close and continuing contact, each side represented a quite different system of thought and art. True, all parts of the ancient world shared many fundamental qualities of religious, social, and economic organization; moreover, Greek development had been indebted to Near Eastern models since Neolithic times. Yet the existence of fundamental differences in outlook between conquerors and conquered was obvious to both.

The Hellenistic world, which thus represented a meeting of two major civilizations, affords interesting parallels to the modern contact between European and Asiatic cultures. In many subtle ways the conquering Greeks and Macedonians were affected by their entry into the Near East. They had, for instance, a broader geographical outlook and far more wealth than in the days of Pericles; and they were now under the political domination of absolute monarchs. But the Greeks borrowed directly from their subjects only to a very limited degree.

Hellenistic civilization was not a fusion of two different outlooks; rather it adhered to the Greek way of life, especially as this had been developed in the fourth century B.C. The values of Hellenistic culture, however, came to be expressed in a more urbane, polished, and superficial fashion. The leading thinkers of the Hellenistic age may be termed cosmopolitan, specialized, and professionalized. Often they were erudite to the point that only the intelligentsia of the age could follow contemporary poetic or philosophic utterances; for popular and intellectual levels tended to grow apart. Both levels, nonetheless, shared a greater interest in the individual human being and in the natural world enfolding him, and tended to speak in more emotional and realistic terms than had been true in Hellenic times.

As a consequence the bright and gay ideas of the Greeks were more widely attractive than had ever been true before, and the Mediterranean world began to come together as one unified cultural sphere. This great achievement will concern us in later chapters, for it underlies the rise and endurance of the Roman empire. At this point the Hellenistic bloom itself must be considered down to about 200 B.C., though to round out developments in literature, the arts, philosophy, and science we must at points go on into the second century.

CITIES AND SCHOOLS

Hellenistic Cities. The royal courts of the Hellenistic world were important forces in many aspects of art and poetry, but the main vehicles of Hellenistic culture were the Greek cities and schools. Wherever it was possible to do so, Greeks lived in cities or, at the least, formed separately administered corporations, called *politeumata,* in native communities. The cities were organized in the Greek fashion with council and assembly but at times had a royal governor in residence; they were commonly laid out on the Hippodamian plan, with central *agora,* rectangular street grid, temples, and walls. One excavated example, Dura-Europos on the Euphrates, maintained its Greek quality on down into Parthian and Roman times, though only 20 to 40 Macedonian families then persisted to form the upper crust.

The natives formed almost all the farming population and must normally have furnished the bulk of the city inhabitants. Yet this proletariat does not often appear in our sources; what we can see, rather, is the governing level, that class which exhibited Greek polish. Through its classical background this group inherited a fundamentally aristocratic spirit, but in many aspects of its life it showed a more bourgeois flavor than ever occurred anywhere else in the ancient world. Economically men sought to live off inherited capital, which was invested in land, in shops and stores, and in slaves to provide the labor and day-to-day management. Socially the leading circles were selfish, materialistic, and firmly intent upon maintaining their privileged position. Individual families now lived more for their own pleasure, as against the claims of the clans, and limited the numbers of their children at least in the upper levels; women, too, were more emancipated in the Hellenistic world than in earlier Greek society. Since the city-dwellers were usually subject to the wills of monarchs, political interests tended to sink in significance as against economic outlets for their energy.

Nonetheless the Greek upper crust was of great social importance, as noted in the previous chapter, and remained strongly attached to its local cities. Physically it sought to beautify the cities with fountains, statues, gymnasia, and the like; culturally it supported the writing of local chronicles and poetic treatments of the origins of the cities.

Generally the local upper classes did not themselves travel widely, but they were continuously affected by ideas which seeped in via books and the more mobile elements of this wide world. Among the latter were doctors, artists, professional athletes, philosophers, and the international guilds of "Dionysiac artists," that is, repertory companies which moved all over the Hellenistic world under royal guarantees of immunity. Through patronage of these elements and through the school system the Greeks maintained Hellenistic civilization and did more than any other element to set its standards.

The Schools. Primary schools had been known in the Greek world since at least the sixth century B.C., and the sophists had done much to make more advanced education a conscious subject. Now an integrated system of education became widespread, for schooling had two vital functions: to ensure that the young learned the Greek culture of their forebears and to meet the cultural needs of a more fluid, individualistic world.

Literacy seems to have been more common among rich and poor Greeks alike than ever before, but only the sons — and sometimes the daughters — of the governing classes could hope to go through a full course of instruction. Education was almost wholly private, though endowments were occasionally made and public supervision was frequent on the top level, that of the *gymnasium*.

From the age of 7 to 14 children learned to read, to write, and to count; physical education (in the form of individual competition rather than team sports) was a very important element. Instruction on the primary level was largely through rote memorization and endless repetition, and failure to do well resulted in physical punishment. Ancient educators showed little interest in child psychology, and teachers were a very poorly paid, almost menial element of society.

Those students who could afford to go beyond primary instruction studied from the ages of 14 to 18 under the *grammatikos*. Here they read and memorized Homer, Euripides, Menander, and other authors; learned grammar and composed moral essays; and studied geometry, the theory of music, and kindred subjects. The capstone was the *gymnasium*, where the future leaders of the cities, called "ephebes," spent a year or two in learning some military skills and maturing their sense of Hellenic solidarity. Even in Egypt, where the Greeks of the countryside could not live in cities, the *gymnasium* was a widespread focal point for the maintenance of ancestral moral values.

Hellenistic education was clearly designed to inculcate the fundamental virtues and skills of a governing class. Much of it was conducted orally, both because books were scarce and because leaders needed the tool of rhetoric. Athletics were also fostered, though in an ever-decreasing degree, as a means of promoting individual self-confidence and bearing. Vocational skills as such played no part; ethical training was, on the other hand, heavily emphasized. Above all this educational system was designed to produce deep acquaintance with inherited standards rather than to lead the young toward questioning experiment.

Those able men who wished to become specialists went on after their formal education to study with leading philosophers, rhetoricians, doctors, and the like. Medicine was centered mainly at Cos and Cnidus; philosophy and rhetoric were studied at Athens and Rhodes. Athens, in particular, became almost a "university town," deeply respected on into Roman times for its inherited monuments and the concentration of learned scholars.

The most attractive center without question was Alexandria, tied by its overseas trade to all the Mediterranean. In this city flourished the greatest research institute of the Hellenistic age, the famous Museum, the scholars, poets, and scientists of which will appear repeatedly in the next several pages. Here too was a botanical garden, zoo, and the great libraries of Alexandria. There were two libraries, called the Great and the Smaller; the former, begun by the Peripatetic Demetrius of Phalerum about 295, numbered 400,000 volumes in the third century. Libraries also existed in Pergamum and other cities, for Hellenistic learning was not focused exclusively in any one center.

LITERATURE AND THE ARTS

The New Scholarship. Hellenistic civilization was not only widely based but also covered more varied fields than had ever before been cultivated. One important area of study, the results of which had much to do with shaping our own classical inheritance, was that of literary scholarship. Since the days of the Athenian tyrant Pisistratus, men had tried to establish the proper text of Homer, and Hellanicus had begun to coordinate earlier Greek chronology. Now, scholars became far more methodical, more numerous, and more influential; in the usual fashion of professionals they also engaged in amusingly bitter controversies with each other.

Much of Hellenistic scholarship revolved about the great Homeric epics. The *Iliad* and *Odyssey* were divided into the 24 books which have been standard ever since, and successive critical editions of the *Iliad* by Zenodotus, Aristophanes, and Aristarchus, all librarians of the Great Library, were issued at Alexandria in the third and second centuries. The last editor, Aristarchus (*c.* 217–145), made a careful study of Homeric language and usage to determine the proper readings in disputed passages. Other men wrote commentaries and assembled antiquarian lore; one such work, analyzing the list of Trojan heroes comprised in 60 lines of the *Iliad,* ran to 30 books. Similar editing and commentary was devoted to Pindar, Hesiod, and other poets. Lists of the major works within each literary form were drawn up for the benefit of educators and the reading public; and those plays and orations not on the lists began to disappear from circulation.

Out of this study emerged a great mass of bibliographical work, as by Callimachus of Cyrene (*c.* 305–240); definitive studies of Greek chronology by Eratosthenes of Cyrene (*c.* 275–194) and Apollodorus of Athens (to 119 B.C.); treatments of punctuation; and the first Greek grammars.

The work of Aristophanes of Byzantium (*c.* 257–180) on *Analogy* defined the Greek declensions; Aristarchus isolated the eight parts of speech; and the latter's pupil, Dionysius of Alexandria, called "the Thracian," wrote the first extant grammar.

The products of the many Hellenistic scholars illustrate the backward-looking quality of its civilization, but their effect for the future was more than that of simply consolidating the achievements of earlier Greek culture. In their labors they created a basically rational and critical approach which was to underlie Christian scholarship and Biblical study throughout the Middle Ages and which was in modern times to spur the development of history and other humanistic subjects.

Hellenistic Literature. Not all writers, moreover, were content to comment upon the past; the era from Alexander through the third century B.C. witnessed one of the most remarkable outbursts of Greek letters. After the hiatus of the fourth century poetry again became a significant subject. Poets often took as their subject obscure mythological legends, especially of the unhappy love of mortal beings or a mortal woman and a god. These authors, who are commonly called "Alexandrian," sought avidly to strike out on new paths and to dazzle their cosmopolitan audiences by virtuosity and polish, though they could rarely speak deeply from the heart. Most commonly their product was learned and complicated in references, and was couched in hexameter or elegiac meter; prominent were the narrative *epyllion* and the terse *epigram*.

One of the most famous poets was Callimachus, whose *Aitia* (or "Causes") was a narrative elegy of the poet's inquiry of the Muses about early myths; other products of his pen were satirical *Iambi*, hexameter and elegiac *Hymns*, epigrams, and lyric poems. His bitter opponent, Apollonius Rhodius (born at Alexandria *c.* 295), was librarian of the Great Library until his retreat to Rhodes; Apollonius wrote a major epic, the *Argonautica*, about Jason's search for the Golden Fleece. This work was unusual in the normally cold pattern of Hellenistic literature in that the figure of Medea was sympathetically and romantically developed.

The third great poet of the third century, Theocritus of Syracuse (*c.* 310–250), was attracted to Cos and then to Alexandria. While he wrote *epyllia*, he was most famous for his *Idylls* or celebrations of pastoral life, which merged realism and romanticism and were written in a literary

Doric hexameter. Other men versified discussions of the heavenly bodies and of weather signals, as in the *Phaenomena* of Aratus of Soli (*c.* 315–240); or treated of snakebites and their remedies and of poisons, as in the *Theriaca* and *Alexipharmaca* of Nicander of Colophon (second century); Lycophron (perhaps also second century) described the prophecies of the Trojan Cassandra in his *Alexandra,* which he filled with obscure references and words never found elsewhere. Perhaps the most appealing works of the age are its brilliantly polished, terse epigrams, which were eventually collected in anthologies. One of the most poignant, yet restrained, of these is by Callimachus:

> They told me, Heraclitus, they told me you were dead,
> They brought me bitter news to hear and bitter tears to shed.
> I wept, as I remembered, how often you and I
> Had tired the sun with talking and sent him down the sky.
>
> And now that thou art lying, my dear old Carian guest,
> A handful of grey ashes, long long ago at rest,
> Still are thy pleasant voices, thy nightingales, awake,
> For Death, he taketh all away, but them he cannot take.[1]

Besides the learned poetry there flourished a great variety of popular poetry, including ballads and realistic skits dealing with brothel-keepers, unruly schoolboys and the seamy side of life, as in the *Mimes* of Herodas (third century). Rising above this ephemeral work was the New Comedy at Athens, the greatest figure of which was Menander (342–291). Menander, who was a contemporary of the philosophers Zeno and Epicurus, sensitively observed the dissolution of old ways and beliefs about him and turned his observation into more than 100 comedies. These comedies of manners had love plots involving prostitutes, and parents and children at odds; the life they portrayed was materialistic, even brutal. Yet Menander had a sympathetic, keen-sighted view of the world; and many of his brilliant lines became famous quotations. St. Paul cited two of his observations, including "Evil communications corrupt good manners"; and one famous passage sums up his view of life:

[1] *Greek Anthology* 7.80; tr. William Cory, *Ionica* (London: George Allen, 1905), p. 7.

Think of this lifetime as a festival
Or visit to a strange city, full of noises,
Buying and selling, thieving, dicing stalls,
And joy-parks. If you leave it early, friend,
Why, think you have gone to find a better inn;
You have paid your fare and leave no enemies.[2]

Very little Hellenistic literature survived intact to enter directly into the main stream of western literary inheritance, for not one work was adjudged by later ages to be a real masterpiece on the plane of the epic, dramatic, historical, or rhetorical achievements of earlier centuries. Much of Hellenistic prose and poetry was marked by jargon, obscure references, and a style which departed from the classic Attic models. Much, too, was superficial, for the age as a whole lacked deeply rooted standards. Yet, besides its weaknesses, Hellenistic literature also reveals the interest of its authors and readers in the romantic, the realistic, and the individual human being; these forces led to the beginnings of biography and romance.

So far as we can discern, this work was entirely Greek, both in language and in attitudes. Its polished urbanity and skillful technique made it, nonetheless, deeply attractive to men of Near Eastern background, such as cultivated Jews, and also to the Romans. Through translation and adaptation by Roman authors, indeed, Hellenistic poetry has had a wide influence on modern poetry, particularly in respect to meter and the use of mythological conceits.

Hellenistic Art. The same qualities that stamped the literature of the era are also visually evident in its art and architecture. While the *polis,* the Olympian cults, and the aristocratic outlook — all creative forces in earlier art — were losing their powers of inspiration, the Hellenistic world yet inherited esthetic forms and a spirit from the fourth century which supported its own arts in new triumphs. The Hellenistic world, moreover, was relatively wealthy and had an abundance of patrons in the form of the absolute monarchs, the wealthier citizens, and the cities.

---

[2] Paul, I Corinthians 15:32–3. Gilbert Murray, *New Chapters in the History of Greek Literature,* II (Oxford: Oxford University Press, 1929), p. 10. Other famous lines are "Whom the gods love die young," and the succinct, realistic view, "We live not as we will, but as we can."

The result was a vast volume of art and architecture that was technically competent, often emotional, and superficially attractive to neighbors of the Hellenistic world.

The creation of many new cities, supported by the wealth of the Near East, gave rise to a great volume of building. About the market places colonnaded porticoes called *stoas* were erected; one of the best known, which has recently been reconstructed, was that commissioned by Attalus II of Pergamum at Athens (*c.* 150 B.C.). The other civic buildings and port structures were built in a flamboyant style, richly decorated with a free use of color, and at times several stories high.

Sculptors took their line of departure from the naturalistic, emotional approach, which had evolved in the fourth century, especially in the workshop of Lysippus. His famous depiction of Alexander encouraged a more realistic, yet romantic treatment of portraiture, some of the masterpieces of which are the tiny portraits of the Hellenistic kings on coins.[3] Beside royal representations stood symbols of the cities. One influential model of this type was the *Tyche* (or Fortune) of Antioch, a female seated on a mountain with turreted crown and the personified river god Orontes below, by the chief pupil of Lysippus, Eutychides. Religious sculpture tended to be conventional, but two works in this field may be singled out. One was the bronze Colossus of Rhodes, representing the local patron deity Helios (the sun); created by Chares of Lindus, it fell in the earthquake of 225 some 60 years after its erection. The other was the statue of the god Sarapis, made by Bryaxis, which was the canonical representation of this new Greco-Egyptian deity.

Two of the major artistic centers were Rhodes and Alexandria; besides these appeared later a very influential style at Pergamum. In the late third and the second centuries the kings of Pergamum celebrated their victories over the barbarian Celts or Gauls, who invaded Asia Minor in 278, by erecting monuments at Athens and at Pergamum. The Great Altar of Pergamum, depicting the battle of Giants and Olympian gods as a symbol of the Pergamene defense of civilization against barbarism, reflected at once realism in its details and a highly emotional treatment of the conflict. Through the political and intellectual connections

---

[3] See the coin of Antimachus of Bactria about 185 B.C. (Plate XVIII.D). This was struck with a realistic portrait in Greek style, generations after the small Greek ruling class of Bactria had broken away from Seleucid rule.

of Pergamum with Rome in the second century this style was to have a great influence in Roman art.[4]

A great deal of Hellenistic art was modeled on a smaller scale for a citizen market. The beauty of the female body was now displayed in partly clad or nude forms, such as the Aphrodite of Melos and other statues, which were later copied en masse for the Roman market. These were, in part, designed for public display; but private homes could have small bronze and marble figurines. Some of these represented in brutal reality old fishermen and market women; others were purely decorative renditions of satyrs and the like. Those inhabitants of the cities who were too poor to afford bronze or marble could buy terra-cotta figurines, made at Tanagra (in Boeotia), Myrina (in Asia Minor), and many other places.

Wealthy burghers also adorned their homes with mosaic floors and painted walls; and gold jewelry and gems were made on a scale previously unknown in the Greek world. Poorer citizens could buy glass gems and gold-appearing bronzes; before the end of the Hellenistic age the blowing of glass had been invented for goblets, vases, and other objects. For all levels, from kings to simple folk, the Hellenistic arts provided graceful, polished products, even though the spirit animating this work rarely rose above a rather superficial blend of the romantic and the realistic, and reflected more the ephemeral and decorative interests of the age than the timeless, ideal quality of classic Greece.

HELLENISTIC PHILOSOPHIES

New Guides to Ways of Life. In the Hellenistic world philosophy and science often remained linked, as they had been conjoined in the thought of Aristotle and earlier Greek students. In both areas there were also many specialists, who made remarkable advances.

The great Hellenistic philosophers furnished guides to personal conduct in the day-to-day flow of an uncertain life. Both in their aim and in their prescriptions they descended directly from Socrates and his disci-

[4] The Gaul killing himself after he has stabbed his wife, shown on Plate XX, is a Roman copy of a bronze original which was dedicated in the sanctuary of Athena at Pergamum (probably shortly before 200 B.C.). Other Gauls who sink realistically to the ground in suicide are known through Roman copies, and originally were probably placed about this central group.

ples, but Hellenistic thinkers no longer paid very serious attention to the political side of man's life. Rather, they addressed themselves to those individuals, increasingly numerous, who felt themselves poorly anchored in the cosmopolitan Hellenistic world. With respect to the absolute monarchs the new philosophies at best held an uneasy truce and, at worst, counseled their adherents to maintain internal independence of spirit regardless of external pressures. With respect to the cities the Stoics at least advocated performance of urban duties, but their center of interest did not lie in the tie of citizen and city.

It is small wonder that both Stoicism and Epicureanism arose first at Athens, the point where the breakdown of civic loyalty and of old religious and social ties was most keenly felt. Although these individualistic philosophies appeared in the first generation after Alexander, they gained their widest adherence as the material prosperity and political strength of the Hellenistic world later waned. Such philosophic consolations, it should be noted from the outset, were basically rational and fundamentally negative; the best they could offer was peace of mind in this life.

Stoicism. The founder of Stoicism was Zeno of Cypriote Citium (335–263), who came to Athens on business as a young man, hearkened to the preachings especially of the Cynics, and remained at Athens all the rest of his life. His favorite haunt was the Painted Stoa of the market place, where, from 302 on, he walked up and down with his disciples, advancing his views in terse, dogmatic statements. Thereafter came Cleanthes of Assos (331–232), who was more poetic of temperament and religious in spirit; his Hymn to Zeus, in praise of the merciful governance of the world, has survived. The third leader of Stoicism was Chrysippus of Soli (280–07), who tightened up Stoic doctrine in response to serious criticisms by other schools.

Stoicism was not an absolutely fixed system of thought. Nonetheless its basic postulate was the concept that the world was divinely governed on rational principles and that man must seek to understand this plan so that he could truly assent, "Thy will be done." To support this view Stoicism created a physics based on the views of Aristotle and Heraclitus; the supreme power or Zeus was divine reason or fire (*logos*), a spark of which resided in each human being. When one died, his spark returned to the eternal divine spirit — though later Stoics, like the

Roman Seneca, were to feel on occasion that the soul lived forever in the Isles of the Blest. In the revolution of time the world periodically underwent great conflagrations, when all was destroyed to begin again in another cycle of exactly the same events.

Men, accordingly, were best advised to use their freedom of will to live in conformity with the divine plan. What happened to the body was a matter of indifference, though some external events might be "preferred" over others; but wealth or poverty, sickness or health, affected only the body and not the "autarky" of the mind. The Stoic cardinal virtues, which were later taken over by Christianity, were temperance, judgment, bravery, and justice. The ideal Wise Man exhibited these qualities in perfection and was emotionless (*apatheia*). This pitiless doctrine, which condemned all imperfect men regardless of the degree of their faults, was subject to much criticism and was mitigated by later Stoic thinkers. Another theoretical quality of Stoic thought stressed by Zeno was "that we should consider all men compatriots and fellow-citizens," [5] that is, that all men were equal citizens of one great city under the skin though their external role might be that of king or slave. This view reflected the cosmopolitan, individualistic tendency of the Hellenistic world, but it led to little in the way of humanitarianism or other practical results.

To justify their views, often couched as paradoxes, the Stoics constructed an all-embracing scheme of thought. Zeno himself discussed metaphysics, logic, physics, ethics, and rhetoric; later there arose a distinct Stoic grammar and a Stoic logic. Eventually Stoicism absorbed so many strands of ancient thought that it may be called "the philosophy" of the ancient world. Its broad view of mankind and its virtually monotheistic concept of the divine power illustrated the broadening and the unification of Mediterranean civilization. Yet its narrowly rational emphasis could not eliminate a great dross of superstitious beliefs and even mysticism. In Roman times Christianity was to borrow much from Stoicism, but was to go far beyond its doctrines.

Epicureanism. While Zeno walked the Stoa, another, gentler soul was living in a suburban house at Athens, where, after 306, he talked in his garden with his brothers and friends (including both men and women)

---

[5] Plutarch, *On the Fortune of Alexander* 329B. Eratosthenes (cited in Strabo, *Geography* 1.4.9, C66) asserted that men should not be classified as Greek or barbarian but as good or bad.

about the grossly superstitious fears of mankind. This was the Athenian Epicurus (342–271), the founder of Epicureanism.

The Stoics endorsed, with some reservations, the reality of sensation; Epicurus accepted completely this principle. Upon it he erected one of the most marvelously coherent systems of thought ever advanced by any philosopher. Men, that is, sought physical pleasure and disliked pain, so the object of life should be to secure this desirable end: "Pleasure we call the beginning and the end of the blessed life." [6] First, however, one could not remove one's fears of death and of divine interference unless one knew the nature of the universe; "without the study of nature there is no enjoyment of unmixed pleasure." [7] To this end Epicurus turned back to the atomic theory of Democritus and reshaped it to show that the universe was a collocation of atoms, though in his mechanical world — as critics have always pointed out — Epicurus permitted the atoms some free will to move on their own as they fell through the void. Yet when a man died, his soul dissolved so that he had nothing further to fear. The gods did exist, and one might worship them as a convention; but they had no active role in this almost purely materialistic scheme.

Although men sought pleasure, they must avoid excesses which led to pain. The result has been neatly summed up as a hedonistic calculus, in which an Epicurean carefully balanced probable delights in any act against its possible discomforts. In the end a follower of Epicurus should lead a simple life and should avoid all outside ties, as in marriage, public ambition, or pursuit of wealth. Only thus could the truly happy man secure *ataraxia*, imperturbability or absence of distress. In Epicureanism virtue was a meaningless concept except insofar as an outwardly virtuous life might ease one's relations with one's fellow men; and friendship was utilitarian.

This selfish doctrine was so systematically elaborated by Epicurus that it could undergo very little change after his death. In many respects its practical advice for life debouched at the same point as did Stoicism, though on such bluntly materialistic and egotistic grounds that relatively few men could accept the doctrines in their entirety. One who did so, the Roman Lucretius (*c.* 99–55 B.C.), wrote an impassioned poem, *On the Nature of the World (de rerum natura)*, which survives as our prime

[6] Epicurus, *Letter to Menoeceus,* in Diogenes Laertius, *Lives of the Philosophers* 10.128.

[7] *Principal Doctrines* 12, in Diogenes Laertius 10.143.

exposition of Epicurean physical theory. Other men of the Late Roman Republic, including Caesar, were strongly tinged by Epicurean ideas; but thereafter its influence waned. Epicureanism stood far removed from the fundamentally religious cast of ancient thought, a position which was reflected in its attacks on astrology, religious quackery, and mysticism.

Other Philosophies. In so widely spread and diverse a world as was the Hellenistic period, Stoicism and Epicureanism could not stand alone as the poles of philosophic thought. From earlier days there survived other views. One was expressed in the Lyceum of Aristotle, which exercised its Peripatetic influence mainly in scientific and literary circles. Another was the Academy of Plato, which continued to discuss and to preserve Plato's dialogues. These works were more widely spread in the Hellenistic world than any of the technical treatises of the contemporary philosophers.

The leadership of the Academy, however, was soon seized by skeptics. Pyrrhon of Elis (*c.* 360–270) was the founder of systematic skepticism or Pyrrhonism, which moved into the Academy under Arcesilaus of Pitane (*c.* 315–241), a bitter critic of Stoic dogmatism. Intellectual aristocrats were much attracted by the critical ability of Academic skeptics, who denied the certainty of knowledge and defined action as a choice of probabilities.

The masses, on the other hand, were moved by popular philosophers, often called Cynics. At the beginning of the Hellenistic age this wing had a genuine program of simple life, as advanced by Diogenes of Sinope; but soon it became a home for wandering preachers. These men took ideas from the other schools and discussed them in popular places in *diatribes,* that is, lively, conversational treatments of themes such as wealth, marriage, and the like, which included little mimes, proverbs, and striking antitheses. Free of tongue and hostile to accepted social conventions, the Cynics yet were no more interested in stirring up social revolution than were the conservative Stoics and Epicureans.

HELLENISTIC SCIENCE

Biology. The field in which Hellenistic civilization broke the freshest ground was that of science. The discoveries of Aristotle and other Greeks in the century after Alexander set views of the natural world which were to survive virtually unchallenged until the sixteenth century after Christ.

The rational, logical approach of earlier Greek thinkers formed the background; but the immediate impetus came from Aristotle's remarkable scientific advances. His successor at the Lyceum, Theophrastus of Lesbos (c. 372–288), wrote two fundamental works, *Enquiry into Plants* and *Causes of Plants* (on plant physiology); and the next head of the Lyceum, Strato of Lampsacus (d. 270–68), engaged in physical speculation, which included deliberate experiment. Even more important, however, in spurring scientific study were the broadening of the geographical world after Alexander's conquests, a fuller acquaintance with Babylonian mathematics and astronomy, and the more realistic treatment of mankind and interest in the physical world, which were also apparent in Hellenistic art. Much, though not all, of the scientific research was conducted at Alexandria, where the Ptolemies supported study through the Museum.

Apart from the work of Theophrastus, little theoretical progress was made in most fields of biology, though a great deal of applied advance took place in agricultural botany. Manuals on scientific farm management were written in numbers to aid the proprietors of the increasingly numerous great estates; this material was later tapped by the Romans.

The one biological study which did see notable advance was that of medicine. Two doctors, Herophilus of Chalcedon and Alexandria and Erasistratus of Ceos, began the dissection of corpses about 300 B.C. and made great advances in identifying the nervous system, the liver, pancreas, and the veins and arteries. These founders of the sciences of anatomy and physiology came, indeed, very close to discovering the concept of the circulation of the blood.

Medical treatment of the sick had already become rational in the fifth century B.C., and Hippocratic doctrines continued to predominate. The school of Empirics tended to dismiss the anatomical observation of the period as useless in the practical problems of curing the sick, but the great research doctors did contribute the concepts that the pulse was a useful indication of illness and that fever was only a symptom of disease, rather than being a disease in itself. Doctors were often honored for their services in epidemics, and public medical care existed in some cities and in all Egypt.

Physical Sciences. Among the physical sciences chemistry remained a purely practical skill in industry, but those studies that were connected with mathematics made great progress. In mathematics itself Euclid (fl. *c.* 300) assembled earlier geometric knowledge into his systematic treatise, the *Elements,* one of the most influential textbooks ever written. Archimedes of Syracuse (*c.* 287–12) developed geometry to its highest ancient levels and in mathematical physics wrote the first scientific works on statics and hydrostatics. He also made a careful calculation of the value of *pi* (later improved by Apollonius), devised a way to express numbers to any magnitude, and became a legend for his hobby of mechanics. During the Roman siege of his city he developed several famous military machines that delayed the Roman advances; he was killed when the Romans took the suburb in which he lived. Apollonius of Perge (*c.* 262–190) developed the theory of conic sections. Beyond this point, however, ancient mathematics advanced but little further because of the clumsy Greek numerical system, which much hampered algebraic thought.

In astronomy the Hellenistic age could draw upon a valuable collection of observations and theories in Babylonia. At the outset Heraclides Ponticus (*c.* 390–10), a friend of Plato, discovered that Venus and Mercury were satellites of the sun and that the earth rotated daily on its axis. The natural conclusion, that the earth also rotated about the sun, he may also have suggested; but the most famous argument to this end was advanced by Aristarchus of Samos (310–230), a pupil of Strato. The heliocentric theory was so at variance with Greek religious beliefs that the Stoic Cleanthes urged Aristarchus be prosecuted for impiety. Worse yet, when astronomers came to check his theory, casually advanced without detailed argument, they found its postulates of circular orbits and uniform motion of the earth did not fit the evidence or Greek principles of mechanics. The greatest astronomer of the Hellenistic age, Hipparchus of Nicaea (*c.* 190–26) sought "to save the facts of observation" by constructing a new, far more complicated pattern of celestial movements about the earth which essentially did agree with the evidence then known.[8] This system, adapted by the astronomer Ptolemy about A.D. 150, remained dominant until Copernicus picked up Aristarchus'

[8] Thomas Heath, *Aristarchus of Samos* (Oxford: Oxford University Press, 1913), p. 308.

idea (preserved by Archimedes) and elaborated it in the sixteenth century after Christ.

Although modern scientists regret the wrong turn of astronomical theory, the truly scientific grounds on which it took place deserve our respect. Hipparchus went on to draw up a scientific star catalog of some 850 stars visible to the naked eye so that later ages could check if stars did move. He measured the lunar month and solar year with remarkable accuracy; and discovered the phenomenon of the precession of the equinoxes. Hipparchus even advanced a proposal for determining longitude by joint observation of a specific lunar eclipse all over the Mediterranean area, but this proposal was barred by the wars of his age.

Along with greater knowledge of the heavenly bodies went a spectacular development of geographic understanding of the earth. The Greeks had long since accepted our planet's being a sphere, but now they gained a far more extensive and detailed knowledge of its Eurasian parts. Eratosthenes, a scholar in many fields, made a more detailed map than had ever before been possible, and estimated the circumference of the earth by an entirely correct method. Since one of his fundamental data was slightly erroneous, he missed the correct circumference by apparently some 200 miles. Hipparchus proceeded further in mathematical geography, developing trigonometry for the purpose.

Decline of Hellenistic Science. From the late second century on geography was mainly a descriptive subject. So too astronomy became more and more a field for astrological speculation and prediction, and medicine ceased to make theoretical advances. After 200 B.C., indeed, the one major Hellenistic scientist was Hipparchus. This turn away from science has much exercised modern observers, in view of the ever greater weight placed on science in our life; but many reasons can be advanced for the decline of Hellenistic science.

Ancient science lacked almost all the instruments used in the great growth of modern scientific measurement and observation. The mathematics used in daily life consisted of little more than simple counting. The technological base, moreover, was so primitive that it was impossible, for instance, to apply practically the knowledge of the properties of steam; only simple machines could be devised for spectacular ends like shutting doors without human intervention or raising tables in banquet halls. In other words the modern fructifying connection between scientific discovery and technical exploitation of the results could not exist. Hellenistic science was very largely a theoretical study, except in some aspects of agriculture and fortification.

More important as limits to science than these technical defects were the spiritual qualities of ancient civilization. Archimedes tinkered in mechanics for his own amusement and devised the famous Archimedes screw for lifting water, but when he was asked to write a handbook on engineering he refused: "He looked upon the work of the engineer and every art that ministers to the needs of life as ignoble and vulgar." [9] The gulf, that is, between the gentleman and the lower classes, who lived and died by using their muscles, was a significant bar to any practical application of scientific ideas; the existence of slavery, it may be noted, was only an incidental, not a major aspect of this distortion. Perhaps most important of all as an invisible check to scientific study, however, was the generally held view that the natural world, no less than mankind, was fundamentally alive and was divinely governed. To understand its character one could better turn to philosophy and to religion than to science, which was little more than a hobby; and in the disasters of life prayer or rational resignation to the will of God were the principal props for man.

MAJOR CHARACTERISTICS OF HELLENISTIC CIVILIZATION

The Hellenistic world is an intriguing one both in the complexity of its political organization and in the new flavor of its widely spread culture. This civilization was fundamentally Greek. Literary works were produced in Greek, albeit in the standardized *koine* dialect as a rule, and drew almost exclusively from Greek forms, poetic styles, and concepts. Art and architecture were Greek in idiom; so too was philosophy. Only in the sciences can indebtedness to Near Eastern knowledge be clearly established.

The Greeks of the Hellenistic world were influenced by the new environment, but that influence was displayed more in the scale and lavishness of products and in the tone of the era than in direct borrow-

[9] Plutarch, *Marcellus* 17.4; tr. B. Perrin.

ings or cultural amalgamations. Even in the field of religion the Greeks continued to worship their old gods, though at times in a new spirit. The one cult of Near Eastern background which gained some Greek support, that of Sarapis and Isis, was cast in a Hellenized form by Ptolemy I.

Frequently, as one looks at the religious, philosophic, and political patterns of this age, one feels that the Hellenistic era stood as a preparation for the Roman world; as will appear in Chapters 23 and 24 men such as Cicero, Caesar, and Virgil were deeply indebted to Hellenistic models and its educational system. In contrast to the great triumphs of archaic and classical Greece the works of the post-Alexandrian era seem, on the one side, pedantic and professionalized; on the other, overly romantic, emotional, and purely decorative. The audience of the age, which helped to set its tone, consisted not only of kings and their courts but also of a rather smug, conservative leading class in the cities.

Yet the products of the era may not be depreciated too far; western civilization down to very recent times built directly on Hellenistic science, arts, and letters. One must also be careful not to visualize Hellenistic culture as monolithic; Pergamene and Alexandrian artistic styles, for example, were very different. At the time, moreover, Hellenistic models were popular not just in Rome; the Parthians and Indians also borrowed heavily, and Judaism was much affected by the urbane, polished influences of its Greek neighbors. The most advanced civilization in the world of Jesus and of Caesar alike was Hellenistic.

If one notices the dates of the greater Hellenistic thinkers and artists, it is quickly obvious that almost all of them flourished before 200 B.C. In every aspect the greatest bloom occurred in the century following Alexander's death; then the Hellenistic world declined politically, economically, and culturally. The student of this age must always keep in mind that it represented a thin, though powerful governing layer of Greeks (and some Hellenized natives) on top of a great mass of subjects.

Nonetheless the Greek element was tenacious and maintained itself under Parthian and Roman rule. In doing so it preserved and consolidated earlier Greek achievements; and after a long period of chaos Greek civilization was to revive in the peace and prosperity that eventually resulted from the Roman conquest of the Mediterranean basin.

BIBLIOGRAPHY

Sources. In Hellenistic literature only a few works, such as the *Argonautica* of Apollonius Rhodius (tr. E. V. Rieu, Penguin L85, 1959), *Alexandra* of Lycophron, *Hymns* of Callimachus (both Loeb Classical Library), and *Idylls* of Theocritus (tr. A. S. F. Gow, 2 vols. [2d ed.; Cambridge: Cambridge University Press, 1952]) survive intact in the original Greek; others were translated into Latin or paraphrased by Roman authors. In this respect the finds of literary papyri in Egypt, which attest the generally cultivated level of the Greek administrators under the Ptolemies, have been very helpful. To this source we owe the *Aitia* of Callimachus, the *Mimes* of Herodas (Loeb Classical Library), and a number of plays by Menander (Loeb Classical Library); only recently was the *Dyskolos* or *Bad-tempered Man* of Menander found. Much of the Greek Anthology comes from the Hellenistic period; see the translations by Kenneth Rexroth (Ann Arbor: University of Michigan Paperback AA63, 1962) and Dudley Fitts (Westport, Conn.: Greenwood, 1978).

The works of Hellenistic philosophers were voluminous; Epicurus alone wrote 300 volumes in a technical, obscure style. These disappeared, and we must rely mainly upon summaries or discussions by Roman thinkers from Cicero and Lucretius in the Republic to Seneca, Epictetus, and Marcus Aurelius in the Empire. Some original quotations appear in Diogenes Laertius, *Lives of the Philosophers,* Book 10 (Loeb Classical Library).

Apart from the *Elements* of Euclid and some treatises by the other mathematicians mentioned in the text, we are in the same difficulty with respect to science. The handbooks of Philo and Hero dealt especially with military siege engines and mechanical curiosities, and have survived in part.

Very few Hellenistic cities have been excavated for their own sake. In Mesopotamia, Dura-Europos on the Euphrates was carefully explored by French and American expeditions after World War I. Priene and Pergamum in Asia Minor have also been well excavated and published; other material of value comes from Athens, Ephesus, Delphi, etc.

Since Alexandria and most of Antioch are still covered by modern cities, it is difficult to gain a clear idea of the greatest Hellenistic centers.

Hellenistic sculpture was popular among the Romans. Chief among the originals are the Victory of Samothrace (early second century), Aphrodite of Melos (second century probably), and the great altar of Pergamum, which was re-erected in the Berlin Museum. Hellenistic painting and mosaic work has been found at Delos and elsewhere; one great painting, Alexander's victory over Darius at Arbela, was copied in mosaic for a rich Pompeian.

Further Reading. Hellenistic education is best described by H. I. Marrou, *History of Education in Antiquity* (New York: Mentor MQ 552, 1964); the resulting scholarship is discussed in detail by R. Pfeiffer, *History of Classical Scholarship* (New York: Oxford University Press, 1976); P. M. Fraser, *Ptolemaic Alexandria* (Oxford: Oxford University Press, 1972). See also J. Onians, *Art and Thought in the Hellenistic Age* (London: Thames & Hudson, 1979), and T. B. L. Webster, *An Introduction to Menander* (Manchester: University Press, 1974). John Ferguson, *The Heritage of Hellenism* (New York: Harcourt Brace Jovanovich, 1973), is a clear survey, as is also T. B. L. Webster, *Hellenistic Poetry and Art* (London: Methuen, 1964).

M. Bieber, *Sculpture of the Hellenistic Age* (rev. ed.; New York: Columbia University Press, 1961), is fully illustrated; see also C. M. Havelock, *Hellenistic Art* (Greenwich, Conn.: New York Graphic Society, 1971). N. Davis and C. M. Kraay, *The Hellenistic Kingdoms: Portrait Coins and History* (London: Thames & Hudson, 1973), is well illustrated.

A. A. Long, *Hellenistic Philosophy* (London: Duckworth, 1974), is technical but comprehensive. The materialistic approach of Epicurus has attracted many scholars, including Cyril Bailey, *Epicurus* (Oxford: Oxford University Press, 1926), and other studies; N. W. DeWitt, *Epicurus and His Philosophy* (Westport, Conn.: Greenwood, 1973); and A. J. Festugière, *Epicurus and His Gods* (New York: Russell, 1968). On the other schools see Donald R. Dudley, *History of Cynicism* (New York: Gordon), and Edwyn Bevan, *Stoics and Sceptics* (New York: Arno, 1979). Works on Lucretius, Seneca, and other Roman adherents of the Hellenistic philosophies will be found below, in Bibliographies, Chapters 25 and 27. Virtually all the works on Greek science listed in General Bibliography treat of its great Hellenistic period.

Sources on Hellenistic religion are assembled by F. C. Grant, *Hellenistic Religions* (Indianapolis: Bobbs Merrill LLA134, 1953). Moses Hadas, *Hellenistic Culture: Fusion and Diffusion* (New York: Norton, 1972), is mostly concerned with the interactions of Hellenistic and Jewish culture, on which see also Victor Tcherikover, *Hellenistic Civilization and the Jews* (New York: Atheneum, 1970).

VII

THE RISE OF ROME

21

THE EARLY WESTERN
MEDITERRANEAN

The ancient history of the Mediterranean region, after the first foundations of civilization in the Near East, falls into two major periods. One is
the rise of Greek civilization in the east; the second is the emergence of
Rome in the west and its military conquest of the Mediterranean world.
Thereafter came a political and economic unification of east and west,
which was attended by a great cultural consolidation.

The first of these periods we have already followed through the
merger of the Fertile Crescent into the Persian empire, the development
of Greek civilization, and the meteoric career of Alexander the Great,
who initiated the Hellenistic age by his conquest of the Near East. But it
is not possible to go far down into the Hellenistic world without turning
to see what had been happening in the western Mediterranean, for by
200 B.C. Rome had mastered these shores and was beginning to exert a
potent influence on the Greek east. To set the stage for Rome, in turn,
requires that we jump back to the Paleolithic and Neolithic eras and
follow once more the first stages of human development, this time with
special reference to western Europe.

In the Paleolithic period the inhabitants of western Europe seem to
have been as advanced as those in any other part of Eurasia; indeed,
there are few parallels to the wide array of well-made tools from Magdalenian times in France or the famous cave-paintings of France and
Spain (see Plate II). When men progressed into the Neolithic level,

however, western Europe dropped behind. It remained an obscure, backward region for several millennia while the focus of human development lay in the Near East and the eastern Mediterranean.

The men of the west, thus, were slow to move beyond the food-gathering stage into the practice of agriculture. They did not achieve civilization, that is, the creation of firmly organized states which used writing and had economic specialization, until 700 B.C. and later. On each level of development the main stimuli to progress came always from the eastern Mediterranean. Yet it is important to note that west and east were far separated in space and in spirit; the inhabitants of western Europe did not slavishly copy in detail the eastern institutions but evolved local ways of life, which were significantly different from their models.

This chapter will consider the general background of evolution in the western Mediterranean and adjacent parts of Europe down to about 500 B.C. By that date Rome had emerged out of this slowly moving world; and its rise was to link the backward west and the more civilized east into one great realm. From the second century B.C. onward all Mediterranean shores followed the same political and cultural path.

PREHISTORIC DEVELOPMENT OF ITALY AND THE WEST

Appearance of Agriculture. The history of western Europe after the glaciers began their last retreat about 8000 B.C. can be sketched only on the basis of archeological discoveries down to 700 B.C., together with some linguistic evidence from later times. This material is relatively abundant and shows the presence of a great number of cultures, which existed side by side or followed consecutively; but even so it is not easy to discern the movements of ideas and peoples that produced the structure we see in early historic times. The main stages are the adoption of agriculture, the height of the Bronze age in the second millennium B.C., and the crystallization of cultures and linguistic distributions, which immediately preceded the entry of civilized peoples from the east.

As the ice melted, the flora and fauna of Europe changed in accordance with the improving climate, and men were able to live ever farther north. Before 4000 B.C. the general rise in the level of the Atlantic Ocean finally separated the British isles from the continent and Scandinavia proper from Denmark; most of western Europe thenceforth had a wetter, warmer climate than it now experiences. In this Atlantic era, which lasted into the early second millennium B.C., deciduous forests and marshes were extensive; but the great rivers, including the Danube, Rhine, Elbe, and Rhone, as well as the indented coastline permitted the flow of ideas along and through the mass of western Europe.

The practice of agriculture certainly came into Europe from the Near East, for men raised basically the same crops and domesticated the same animals as did the early farmers of the Fertile Crescent. The chronology of the spread of the new ideas is not yet altogether clear, but there seem to have been two main lines by which they advanced westward.

One avenue lay through Greece, where Neolithic villages had appeared perhaps by 7000 B.C., and up the Balkans into central Europe. Since the climate and terrain of this latter area differed greatly from the semidesert regions of the Near East, agricultural practices had necessarily to be extensively altered. Early Danubian farmers, who existed in the sixth millennium B.C., tended to move from one site to another in the loess lands by the river, burning the oak forest in an area and mining the soil until it was exhausted.

Outthrusts from this region eventually reached the Low Countries; in Denmark and Sweden there were by 3000 B.C. farmers who raised cattle and opened up the forests with ax and fire. From that time onward agriculture was commonly practiced over central and western Europe, though hunting tribes continued to exist. Among the many cultures distinguished by archeologists, the Battle-ax cultures of the third millennium, so named because a favorite weapon was the stone battle-ax, seem to have been widely spread from Holland to Russia, partly because their members pastured animals as well as sowed cereals. These peoples have attracted a great deal of modern speculation, for apparently they spoke Germanic tongues.

A second avenue by which Neolithic achievements entered Europe lay westward by sea through Italy and Sicily. Inasmuch as the coastal districts of western shores shared generally the same flora and climate as the eastern Mediterranean, though with greater and more assured rainfall, agriculture here required less adaptation than it did in the heavy forests of continental Europe. This thrust passed through Italy from the sixth millennium, perhaps in several waves as we shall see in a moment; but to complete our survey of the general advance of farming in western Europe it may be noted that the seaborne influence reached on to Spain and north Africa. Eventually agricultural customs made their way across France and around the Atlantic coasts to England before 3000 B.C.

So ideas and perhaps people moved northward from the Mediterranean to meet the other main current flowing up the Danube. One visibly impressive wave, of religious import, was the spread of the practice of building megalithic monuments from Spain and Portugal, where the custom began in the late fourth millennium, as far as Scandinavia. Sometimes men placed a flat stone on top of two or three other stones and encircled it by a ring of as large boulders as brute strength could move. This form (called a dolmen) and another, underground type (the passage-grave) were largely associated with collective burials under the protection of a great mother. A solar cult, however, was perhaps celebrated at such megalithic shrines as Carnac in Brittany, where long avenues of stones were erected, and at Stonehenge in England, where a famous circle was created about 1660 B.C. This was one of the latest megalithic achievements; by this time the Bell-beaker people, named from their characteristic pottery beer tankard, were trading from Spain up along the Atlantic coasts of Europe. They settled in Brittany, England, and the Low Countries and pushed far inland to meet the Battle-ax cultures (see Map 5).

The Geography of Italy. The Italian peninsula, in which Rome eventually emerged, must interest us particularly and can serve as a more detailed example of the lines of progress in the western Mediterranean. Italy itself falls into two distinct parts. Continental Italy, comprising the Po valley in the north, is about 320 miles east and west by 70 miles from the Alps on the north to the Apennines on the south. This district shares much the same climate as does Europe proper and is richer both in ever-flowing rivers and good farmland; but since it lay far from the eastern Mediterranean, it remained backward throughout ancient times.

Peninsular Italy, 650 miles long by not more than 150 miles wide, has a rocky backbone in the Apennine mountains, which run across the upper end to the Adriatic, then generally down the east coast to a point south of Rome, where they turn across the peninsula toward Sicily (see Map 14). Subsidiary ranges and hills rise everywhere, so that peninsular Italy is divided into many compartments. Although three-quarters of this area is hilly country, the plains are more extensive than in Greece and have always supported a heavy farming population — one of the greatest resources of later Roman expansion. Rainfall, too, is more regular and heavier than in Greece, particularly in the western coastal districts known as Etruria, Latium, and Campania, which had an inheritance of rich soil from their prehistoric volcanoes. The plains of Apulia, on the east side of the Apennines, have less rain and in historic times were useful primarily as pastureland. In the peninsula proper rivers are short and often dry up in the summer. Only the Tiber could be accounted a major geographical factor, but the masses of silt brought down by this yellow-brown stream made the creation of a harbor at its mouth a major undertaking in later days. The best harbors of Italy in antiquity lay on the southern coasts and on the bay of Naples.

Although Italy as a whole was cut off by the Alps to the north and by the Adriatic and Tyrrhenian seas on east and west, it could be reached without great difficulty both by peoples moving from southern France, the Balkans, or Africa (via Sicily) and by traders from the eastern Mediterranean. Yet this land varies so widely from ever-green plains to rocky wastes or to rolling land brown in summer droughts that its inhabitants have always tended to fall into very distinct cultural groups. The achievement of the Romans in uniting it politically is clearer if one remembers that after the fall of the Roman Empire Italy was never again completely unified until 1870.

Neolithic and Bronze Age Italy. Men have lived in Italy since Paleolithic times, but the population increased with the advent of agriculture. From that point onward the racial stock has been mainly of Mediterranean type, short, lithe, long-headed, swarthy, and dark of hair — Caesar was a good example of this body-form. Farming appeared first along the southern coasts, where early farmers often lived in caves; the presence of a type of pottery which was decorated by impressions of the *cardium* shell suggests affinities to very similar pottery in the eastern Mediterranean. Next came, likewise from the east, the use of painted pottery, which spread no farther than Sicily.

Eventually the hunters of the interior took over the practice of agriculture; and by the third millennium B.C. most plainsmen in Italy lived primarily by farming. Air surveys have shown that at this time Apulia, for example, had nearly 200 settlements, varying from single buildings to

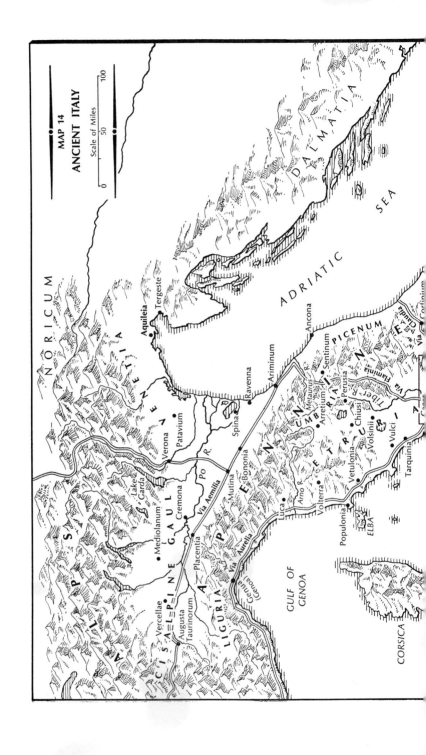

MAP 14

ANCIENT ITALY

Scale of Miles

0   50   100

NORICUM

ALPS

VENETIA

Aquileia
Tergeste

CISALPINE GAUL

Vercellae
Augusta Taurinorum
Mediolanum
Cremona
Verona
Lake Garda
Patavium

ADRIATIC SEA

DALMATIA

Ravenna
Ariminum
Ancona

Po R.

Placentia
Via Aemilia
Mutina
Bononia
Spina
Via Aurelia

APENNINES

LIGURIA

(Genoa)

GULF OF GENOA

Luca
Arno R.
Volterra
Populonia
Vetulonia
Tarquinia

ELBA

CORSICA

UMBRIA
Via Flaminia
Metaurus R.
Sentinum
Arretium
Perusia
Chiusi
Volsinii
Vulci

ETRURIA

PICENUM

Tiber R.

Corfinium
Via Claudia

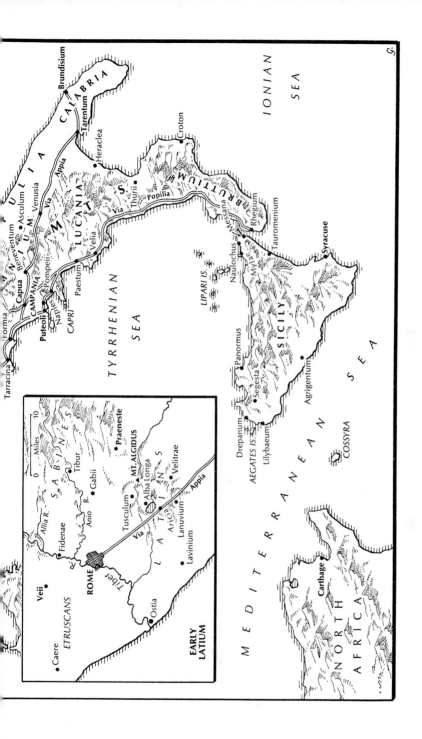

6.

IONIAN SEA

CALABRIA

Brundisium

APULIA

Tarentum

Heraclea

Via Appia

Croton

BRUTTIUM

LUCANIA

Venusia

Asculum

Via

M. Benevenum

SAMNIUM

Capua

Napes

CAMPANIA

Pompeii

Puteoli

CAPRI

Paestum

Velia

Thurii

Via

Popilia

Messana

Rhegium

Tauromenium

Naulochus

Mylae

Syracuse

LIPARI IS.

TYRRHENIAN SEA

Panormus

SICILY

Segesta

Agrigentum

Drepanum

Lilybaeum

AEGATES IS.

COSSYRA

MEDITERRANEAN SEA

Tarracina

Formia

EARLY LATIUM

Carthage

NORTH AFRICA

SABINES

Praeneste

Tibur

Gabii

MT. ALGIDUS

Alba Longa

Velitrae

LATINS

Tusculum

Aricia

Lanuvium

Anio R.

Via

Appia

Allia R.

Fidenae

Veii

ETRUSCANS

Caere

ROME

Tiber

Lavinium

Ostia

0   10
Miles

villages of round houses surrounded by ditches, in an area 50 by 30 miles. Other cultures entered Italy from the northeast as offshoots of Danubian and Balkan progress and from the northwest as outliers of Swiss lake-dwellers and Bell-beaker peoples.

During the second millennium B.C. the consolidation of Aegean culture which produced first the Minoan period in Crete and then the Mycenaean era in southern Greece had a potent influence on the neighboring peninsula to the west. Minoan writing and other evidence of Minoan trade have been found in the Lipari islands (north of Sicily) and in Sicily itself. In the subsequent Mycenaean period traders from the Aegean made their way often to southern Italy and Sicily, but not beyond. A major route ran from the Adriatic across the Alps by the Brenner pass and so into central Europe via the Elbe river. Down the famous "amber route" came amber from the Baltic; up it bronze smiths made their way into Europe. The growing demand for copper led to extensive mining in Austria and to the use of bronze for weapons throughout continental Europe.

While southern Italy and Sicily shared cultures which were considerably affected from the Aegean, the rest of Italy was occupied by peoples who can be divided into two main strains. In the Po valley there developed by about 1700 B.C. a style of agricultural villages called *terremare* sites; the inhabitants had horses, made glossy gray and black pottery, and were skillful in working bronze. The men of these sites were affected by central European currents, and in turn their ideas spread on down the east coast of Italy. Along the central mountain ridge lay the second form, or Apennine culture, whose members relied more upon hunting and pasturing animals. The use of wagons now appeared in Italy, and bronze was extensively employed for weapons and for tools.

Italy in the Early First Millennium. Toward the end of the second millennium very extensive movements of peoples occurred all over Eurasia. Their shattering blows reduced Asia Minor and the Aegean to barbarism; the old homes of Near Eastern civilization were seriously affected and only recovered after several centuries of localism. Europe, which was not yet civilized, perhaps bent more easily before the migrations of the period; but evidence of destruction can be seen in Italy as far south as Sicily, where many villages fortified themselves in vain about 1250 B.C.

Thereafter Italy and central Europe had few relations with the east for half a millennium. Nonetheless the tempo of development speeded up greatly after 1000 B.C. in the western Mediterranean and in Europe. Historic linguistic distributions were apparently set in this period; considerable cultural advance took place; and eventually the peoples of Italy were, as a result, ready to profit from renewed contacts with the civilized east.

Quite generally in Europe speakers of Indo-European tongues became clearly dominant in the era, as part of the great process of movement which spread this group of languages to India and Persia, to Asia Minor and Greece, and to the Italian and Iberian peninsulas. How and when they entered Italy is unclear in the lack of written materials, but by historic times all inhabitants of the land, save perhaps the Ligurians in the northwest and the invading Etruscans, spoke one or another Indo-European tongue. Interestingly enough, the Latins near the future site of Rome had virtually a different language from that common over most of the rest of Italy, which is termed Osco-Umbrian. The word for "fire" in the latter, for example, was *pir*, which is closely akin to the Greek (as in pyromaniac) and even to our English word, while the Latin word was *ignis*, which has cognates in Sanskrit and Balto-Slavonic.

Culturally, Italy moved even more swiftly than did central Europe in the early first millennium. One main form of Italian culture, marked by the use of iron and cremation, is called Villanovan, after a site near Bologna; its main area was the Po valley and the western districts down to Latium. Besides Villanovan culture there were many other relatively distinct local ways of life. Men in the central mountains continued their Apennine culture, but various areas along the Adriatic were noticeably affected by influences from the Illyrian, or Balkan, shore of the sea. In Italy, as in central Europe, an upper, warrior class evolved, which used horses. Particularly in the rock-drawings of the Camonica valley on the edge of the Alps there is revealed in visual form the importance of the horse and of a warrior god on horseback; these pictures manifest also a marked quickening of intellectual perception. By the eighth century B.C. Italy was advanced enough to absorb the new eastern influences which began to come to its shore.

THE ENTRY OF EASTERN PEOPLES

Main Lines of Development. By 800 B.C. the Near East had regained its strength after the shock of the invasions and internal unrest at the close of the Bronze age. Arameans by land and Phoenicians by sea were trading on a wider scale than had ever before been possible, and the Assyrian empire was arising to bring political unity to an increasingly interconnected' cultural and economic entity. Off in the Aegean basin Greek civilization had emerged by this time; the expanding population of the area was ready to explode abroad in a tremendous wave of colonization. Seafaring had at last reached such a point that the natural unity of the Mediterranean basin could begin to manifest itself.

The westward drive of the Greeks and Phoenicians has already been considered as a testimony to the expansive qualities of the civilization in their homelands. Now it is time to examine this same process from the point of view of the western Mediterranean.

The peoples living along the western shores of the Mediterranean were in 800 still villagers who made their living almost entirely by agriculture. Social and economic distinctions, true, did exist on a rudimentary level. Miners and smiths worked iron and copper; potters made vessels which, particularly in Italy, were decorated with geometric designs; an upper class of warrior chieftains was common. But if one turns to see what new ideas were now to be introduced into this simple world, its relative backwardness quickly becomes apparent.

On the political level the city-state, with definite boundaries and conscious internal and external policies, appeared beside the tribal patterns. Writing in an alphabetic script made possible the emergence of literature and the codification of religious ritual and legal views. The Greek practice of erecting temples and carving statues of anthropomorphic deities was borrowed by Italic peoples, who thereby made more concrete their earlier worship of undefined spirits. Both the major arts of sculpture, painting, and architecture and also the minor arts of jewelry-making, gem-cutting and other skilled techniques spread over western shores.

Not all these achievements of the east were taken over at once, nor did the various districts of the western Mediterranean move forward with equal speed. Spain and north Africa remained backward down to the

Roman conquest. Some Celtic peoples in southern Gaul eagerly bought Greek pottery and bronzework and even used the Greek alphabet; but their neighbors to the north and east were affected only in a minor degree. The area which did respond most swiftly was the Italian peninsula, particularly because it lay directly exposed to eastern currents; and so it was the first western area on the stage of written history.

Greeks and Phoenicians. Three peoples transmitted eastern achievements westward: the Greeks, the Phoenicians, and the Etruscans. Of these, the Phoenicians were the least significant, partly because their settlements were mainly trading posts. These centers, which at times went back into the ninth century, were dotted along the coast of north Africa as far as Spain, in western Sicily, and in Sardinia (see Map 8). The major Phoenician clusters at Utica and Carthage seem to have been established in the eighth century.

Phoenician artisans were deft in adapting for mass production the artistic styles of Egypt and Syria, but their merchants were willing to sell anything which could be bartered for the silver of Spain, for slaves, and probably for the wheat of North Africa. Phoenician culture thus had a minor effect in stimulating the native peoples with which it came into contact, save in the district immediately around Carthage. As the home state of Tyre was more and more menaced by the Assyrians and then the Persians, Carthage came to acquire general control over the Phoenician trading empire by the early sixth century B.C. In this centralization of Phoenician power the increasing pressure of the Greeks may have had a role; certainly a situation of lasting tension between Greeks and Phoenicians arose.

Greek colonization in the west followed the lines already marked out by Mycenaean traders, but it was a far more powerful movement than that of the second millennium. The first lasting colony was placed at Cumae about 750 B.C. This site was as far north on the trade route to Etruscan copper and iron as was feasible for the Greeks, and it remained the closest Greek state to the site of the later Rome. Thereafter a host of colonies sprang up on the southern coasts, in Sicily, and eventually in Gaul (Massilia, *c.* 600 B.C.). These colonies were all agricultural settlements of Greeks dissatisfied in their homeland. With them, however, came wares of the Orientalizing period as well as ideas and artistic concepts of the rapidly expanding Hellenic outlook.

Etruscan History. The third people to come from the east, the Etruscans, are one of the most fascinating and puzzling elements in all ancient history. From ancient times there has been a fierce debate on their origin. The Greek historian Dionysius of Halicarnassus considered them of native Italian origin, as do those archeologists who emphasize the continuity of development in Etruria from Villanovan culture into the Etruscan period proper. Herodotus, on the other hand, recounted a tale of their movement from the Aegean in a time of famine, and most modern scholars feel that both their strange language, which is not Indo-European, and also their unusually strong ties with eastern customs support this view. On the whole it appears most probable that bands of Etruscans made their way west, perhaps from Asia Minor, and settled in the rolling country and volcanic uplands of Etruria about 800 B.C. Here they built a number of cities on hilltops, from which they ruled the previous Villanovan stock.

From the beginning the Etruscans seem to have organized themselves in the advanced political form of the city-state, such as Veii, Caere, Tarquinia, Vulci, Vetulonia, and others. Twelve of these states were united in a religious league, but otherwise each state was absolutely independent. Based on their more conscious political structure was a superior military technique, which employed heavy body-armor and bronze chariots. At first under kings and then under the leadership of the aristocrats, the Etruscans spread their power rapidly and extensively.

Since this expansion took place at the very dawn of history in Italy, its stages and methods are not entirely clear. One avenue of conquest, however, led the Etruscans from their southern outliers of Caere and Veii into the Latin territory; Praeneste and Rome were certainly ruled by Etruscans for a time. Etruscan leaders pushed even farther south into Campania, where they held Capua by about 650 and reached to the coast at Pompeii. Other bands drove north into the rich Po valley in the sixth century, where they gained a stronghold even at Spina, the main avenue of Hellenic influence in the north of Italy.

Both the disunion of the Etruscans at home and the rise of native Italic peoples eventually produced the loss of this early hegemony. The first check was administered by the Greeks, as we shall see below. Then, about 500 B.C., the Romans and Latins regained their independence; and mountaineers of Oscan speech, akin to the Samnites of the central Apennines, wrested Capua from the Etruscans about 440. The critical blow was delivered by the invasion of uncivilized Gauls, or Celts, from central Europe in the late fifth century, who took over the Po valley and ravaged central Italy until the Romans stopped them. Eventually the Etruscans were conquered in their homeland, state by state, by the rising power of Rome. From the third century B.C. onward they played no further major part in Italian history, though Etruscan lords long continued to live in luxury from the products of their fields and mines.

Cultural Place of the Etruscans. Politically the Etruscans were important both in introducing the city-state form of government to much of central Italy and also in forcing the native peoples to better cohesion in order to maintain their independence. The Etruscan place in the early history of Rome will concern us in the next chapter.

Even more significant was their cultural role. The Etruscans brought civilization to central Italy generally and to the Romans in particular. To give one clear example, the alphabet we use today was borrowed by the Romans from the Etruscans, who in turn had taken it by 700 B.C. from the Greeks. In the process the Etruscans stripped off some of the Greek vowels, which were not necessary in their own peculiar language, and changed various consonantal values. Both were steps which impoverished the suppleness of the script for all later ages.

As serious a debate rages today over the cultural place of the Etruscans as over their origins. While admitting their great role in introducing eastern civilization to Italy, some critics deny that the Etruscans had any originality; others, on the other hand, ascribe notable inventiveness to Etruscan craftsmen. The best judgment on this highly subjective issue probably lies in the conclusion that the Etruscans originated very little on their own but did nonetheless give a certain local stamp to their borrowings. Etruscan culture in the main shows the remarkable fructifying power of Greek civilization, though the Etruscans were less able to create a continuous, self-moving cultural spirit than were the later Romans. Besides this outside influence, however, there was also a substratum of continuing Villanovan concepts; the names of Etruscan persons and gods, for instance, are a mixture of Indo-European words with more specifically Etruscan words.

Initially the Etruscan lords bought largely from Phoenician merchants, but by 675 Greek influence began to rise to predominance. Etruscan sculpture, which began in the last decades of the seventh century, imitated each successive stage of Greek development, largely through the intermediary styles of the Greek colonies in southern Italy. The regional diversity of the Etruscans is evident in this sculpture, which was made in different areas from terra cotta, stone, or bronze; and in the best statues there is an independent technical ability and an intriguing interest in the human body itself.[1] A naïve realism is particularly evident in depictions of the dead, placed on top of sarcophagi as full-length figures or as busts on funerary urns (at Chiusi primarily); this realistic interest was to be a potent force in Roman art. Later on, Etruscan bronze work, including candelabra, polished mirrors incised with Greek myths, and ornamented boxes, showed considerable technical skill. Goldsmiths perfected the unusual technique of creating designs incrusted with fine drops. At Populonia the iron ore of Elba was smelted; copper for much of the west came from Vetulonia and Volterra.

Etruscan painting, which is preserved in underground tombs particularly at Tarquinia, gives many fascinating reflections of daily life in scenes of boating and fishing as well as in solemn portrayals of the dead man and his wife in banquet scenes. Here again the Greek artistic influence is unmistakable, but the tone is more earthly and realistic than in Greek vase painting; the player on the double pipes from the Tomb of the Leopards about 480/70 B.C. (Plate XXII) is a fine example of the best period of Etruscan painting. In pottery itself the Etruscans largely bought their painted vases from Greek merchants or patronized Greek potters who settled in Etruria; some of the most famous examples of Attic black-figure and red-figure ware have come from the tombs of well-to-do Etruscans. Yet, alone among all peoples of the west with whom the Greeks came into contact, the Etruscans developed a native style of some artistic quality, the black-glazed *bucchero* ware, which was even exported to Greece.

Etruscan architecture displays the same mixture of eastern inspiration and local adaptation. The walls of Etruscan cities still stand at Perugia and Volterra; in their gates as in their tombs the Etruscans made use of

[1] The most impressive early Etruscan statue is the terra-cotta Apollo of the late sixth century found in the ruins of Veii (Plate XXI); the head reflects the contemporary archaic style of Greece (see Plate XII), but the physical rendition—as in the legs—is of a different spirit. A much later Etrusco-Roman work of the second century B.C. is the realistic "Brutus" of Plate XXIII.

arches and vaults from the third century on, a form to be taken over by the Romans. Temples were built with columns in the Greek style and adorned with terra-cotta revetments and other decorations which were likewise of Greek origin; but the basic Etruscan plan of placing the temple on a high platform or *podium* and of omitting columns on the sides and rear was not Hellenic. The Etruscan temple, moreover, continued to be partly wooden. Although most of the older Etruscan cities show no regular planning, the later settlement of Marzabotto near Bologna had a gridiron pattern of streets, an eastern system; here too can be seen a close interpenetration of religious and political principles in town-planning, as in the Etruscan (and later Roman) custom of tracing a sacred boundary (*pomerium*) for a town.

Throughout all the physical remains of Etruscan culture the importance of religion is evident. Unlike the Italic peoples, the Etruscans worshiped gods in human form; their great triad Tinia-Uni-Menrva (the latter with an Italian name) was to be taken over by the Romans. Ascertainment of the will of the gods was the subject of an extensive religious machinery of experts. *Haruspices* listened to the thunder, assessed prodigies like unusual births, or inspected the liver of a sacrificial animal in a technique borrowed from Mesopotamia. After the Roman conquest the Etruscans seem to have developed a morbid fear of death, which is reflected in tomb paintings of Hell and of the god of death, Charun, with hammer poised to strike an unfortunate mortal. Human sacrifice was practiced in the form of duels, which the Romans developed into gladiatorial combats. At this time, too, foretelling the effects of a proposed action became an ever more complex art from which the Romans borrowed extensively.

Although one may survey various aspects of this civilization, the Etruscans remain a most peculiar element in early historic Italy. We can read the words of Etruscan inscriptions, but usually we do not know what they mean, inasmuch as Etruscan has never been satisfactorily translated. So too the Etruscan outlook on life seems far removed from that of the Greeks or the Romans. Women had so high a place among the Etruscans that descent was sometimes traced through the female side; and the emphasis on the physical aspect of life and mere enjoyment was unusually marked. During the period of Etruscan political and economic predominance in central Italy their upper classes surrounded themselves with the pleasures which merchants brought to them or their own artisans manufactured; by the late fifth century their greatest days were over, culturally as well as politically. The Etruscans could attain neither the intellectual, dynamic quality of Hellenic civilization nor the political and military structure of the Romans. The latter, their next-door neighbors, were much indebted to the Etruscans, as will appear later; but they never appreciated the hedonistic quality in Etruscan life. The sober Roman outlook, indeed, developed partly in reaction against the Etruscan model of the physical enjoyment of the delights of luxury.

THE WESTERN MEDITERRANEAN IN THE SIXTH CENTURY

Wars of Etruscans, Phoenicians, and Greeks. The expansion of civilized peoples from the eastern Mediterranean into the western shores has interesting points of similarity to the expansion of Spain, France, and England into the New World after the days of Columbus. Both expanding civilizations enjoyed sufficient superiority in military techniques and social organization to be able to set up trading posts and other settlements wherever they wished along the new coasts. In both periods of history the colonizing powers seem at first tacitly to have respected each other's zones of action. Although Phoenicians or Etruscans probably dealt as roughly with a stray Greek ship as Englishmen did a Spanish vessel, Greek merchants traded with both of their neighbors and even settled down in Etruria and at Carthage.

By the sixth century, however, the eastern peoples found themselves at loggerheads in the western Mediterranean just as European powers came into serious conflict in the Americas in the seventeenth and eighteenth centuries. These troubles emerged not so much over questions of trade as over territorial possessions; and the Greeks were the element which brought on the wars by reason of their unceasing expansion. In north Africa they tried to settle near Tripoli just after 520; in Sicily they colonized Acragas on the south shore in 580 and essayed to establish a post on the far western tip at Lilybaeum; in Spain they moved as far south as Maenaca from their base at Massilia; in Campania Greeks and Etruscans now stood opposed to each other (see Map 8).

The step which seems to have sparked war was the Phocaean settlement about 560 at Alalia in Corsica, a port which lay on the route from

Sicily to Massilia. Since this colony also menaced Etruscan shores and trade from Carthage to Etruria, the Etruscans and Carthaginians joined their forces and fought a great naval battle with the Greeks off Alalia about 535. The Greeks won, but were so seriously reduced in numbers that they yielded their post. Corsica fell to the Etruscans, and Sardinia to the Carthaginians.

Thereafter the Carthaginians pushed the Greeks out of southern Spain and eventually gathered their strength to launch a great attack in Sicily in 480. The Greek homeland at this time was distracted by the Persian invasion which led to Salamis and Plataea, and the Greeks of Sicily were sadly divided; but the tyrant of Syracuse, Gelon, scored a decisive victory at Himera on the north coast. From this time onward, however, Greeks and Carthaginians were to fight each other in Sicily for two centuries until eventually the Romans conquered both.

The Etruscans, by themselves, had as limited success against the Greeks. In 524 Cumae halted an Etruscan attack by land. In 474 Syracuse and Cumae joined hands to fight a great naval battle off Cumae in which the Etruscans were defeated; an Etruscan helmet was dedicated by Hiero of Syracuse at Olympia. Nevertheless Greek expansion in Italy was halted, both because of Etruscan opposition and because of the bitter divisions among the Greek city-states themselves. Already in 510 Sybaris had been destroyed by its rivals; the surviving city-states of southern Italy remained as split as were their parent states in Greece proper.

Results of the Wars. The native peoples of the western Mediterranean took no independent part in these wars, though they furnished by necessity men and money to their respective masters. The results of the conflicts, nonetheless, went far toward establishing the framework within which they lived thereafter.

The way, thus, was open for the rise of a local power — which was to be Rome — which would conquer each of the more civilized peoples and could do so by reason of their division. The fact, again, that Carthage was able to maintain its bases in Sicily and Spain against the Greeks led to an enduring tension which helped eventually to invite Rome's expansion outside Italy proper. Thirdly, within Italy itself the predominant cultural influence was to remain Greek. Politically and socially Rome developed a remarkable set of institutions and outlooks, which helped to assure its mastery; but culturally it was very heavily indebted to Greece.

The rise of Roman civilization, indeed, was to be the most amazing revelation of the fructifying power of Hellenic culture.

In studying the rise of Rome, however, one must always remember that Rome faced west toward the less civilized regions of Europe as well as eastward toward the ancestral home of ancient civilization. The fact, moreover, that Italy and the west long remained backward culturally — though not politically — means that people like the Romans were able to develop ways of life which were not purely copies of Near Eastern culture.

BIBLIOGRAPHY

Sources. For the prehistoric period in western Europe, which runs in its Mediterranean districts down to 700 B.C. and on the continent proper almost to the time of Christ, we must rely primarily on the archeological evidence, assisted by linguistic survivals, some folk memories, and, in later days, references by the Greeks. Since the area has been well explored by archeologists, there is a considerable body of evidence by which a number of distinct and interlacing culutres can be established. The megalithic monuments, in particular, are largely still visible; see Glyn Daniels, *Megalith Builders of Western Europe* (New York: Praeger, 1959).

Archeology is again of great use in dating the Greek and Phoenician settlements of the west and in showing the transmission of eastern wares; but here we can also draw to some extent upon the references in Herodotus, Thucydides (especially 6.3-4 on the colonization of Sicily), and local legends. In Etruria the physical evidence from the tombs is abundant.

Written Etruscan materials consist of some 9000 inscriptions, mostly brief and often on tombstones, as well as an Etruscan religious text of 1500 words which somehow made its way to Egypt (the Zagreb mummy-binding). Many efforts have been made to decipher the Etruscan language, but at best we can identify some numerals, titles, and other words to a total of about 120. Companion texts in Phoenician and Etruscan have been found on some gold plates; long known are apparent parallels in inscription from the island of Lemmos in the Aegean, a point which tends to support the theory of eastern origin for the

Etruscan language. Greek references to the Etruscans are few, though valuable; the Romans did not write extensively until after Etruscan power had waned, and had little interest in describing their peculiar neighbors except with respect to religious practices.

Further Reading. J. Briard, *The Bronze Age in Barbarian Europe* (Boston: Routledge & Kegan Paul, 1979), is solid; see also J. Murray, *The First European Agriculture* (Edinburgh: University Press, 1970). Works on the Celts are noted in Bibliography, Chapter 25. For the Mediterranean proper, see L. Bernabò Brea, *Sicily Before the Greeks* (New York: Praeger, 1957), and D. H. Trump, *Malta* (London: Faber & Faber, 1972); for Italy proper, Trump's *Central and Southern Italy before Rome* (New York: Praeger, 1966), and L. Barfield, *Northern Italy before the Romans* (New York: Praeger, 1971).

General development of the Phoenicians is noted by Donald Harden, *The Phoenicians* (New York: Praeger P128, 1963); but the best book on Carthage is by B. H. Warmington, *Carthage* (London: Hale, 1960). The western Greeks are well treated by T. J. Dunbabin, *Western Greeks* (Oxford: Oxford University Press, 1968), and A. G. Woodhead, *Greeks in the West* (New York: Praeger, 1962). The Etruscans have attracted great attention in recent times. The most sensitive introduction is D. H. Lawrence, *Etruscan Places* (New York: Viking Compass, 1957); more factual are Jacques Heurgon, *Daily Life of the Etruscans* (New York: Macmillan, 1964), and Massimo Pallottino, *The Etruscans* (Harmondsworth: Penguin A310, 1955). Pallottino has also written a summary *Art of the Etruscans* (New York: Vanguard, 1955), and *Etruscan Painting* (Geneva: Skira, 1952); see also E. Richardson, *The Etruscans* (Chicago: University of Chicago Press, 1964), and J. D. Beazley, *Etruscan Vase-Painting* (Oxford: Oxford University Press, 1947). A beautifully illustrated and enthusiastic volume is *Etruscan Culture: Land and People* (New York: Columbia University Press, 1962), by various Scandinavian scholars.

22

ROME IN ITALY

In tradition Rome was founded as a city-state in 753 B.C. This date, historians now feel, is too early; and the ancient accounts of early Rome are legendary in many respects. Since history must concentrate on the actual course of events, it cannot tarry over Horatius at the bridge, Brutus' vengeance for Lucretia, and other famous tales of Roman heroes and villains. Yet these stories had a very real significance, for the view which any people has of its past helps in turn to shape its future. In their fierce emphasis upon loyalty to the state the legends of early Roman days provided a counterbalance to the many forces dividing the Roman people in historic times; and a model of serious, upright men was provided in these tales for each new generation.

The ideal qualities of the Romans are at points strikingly similar to those which we today ascribe to the early settlers of the American colonies. The historical rise of Rome fell, in truth, into stages which generally paralleled the evolution of the United States. First came the period of the Roman kingdom down to 509 B.C. During this era Rome was created and set many of its basic patterns of social organization. In these respects, as also culturally, the Romans pursued rather different paths from the Greeks; but politically and economically Rome seems to have progressed for a time almost as rapidly as did such states as Athens.

Then, from 509 to 264, Rome expanded its control over the Italian peninsula and at the same time underwent very considerable internal political development. Finally Rome, like the United States after 1898, was ready to look abroad, and in doing so was to step onto a stage of complex international relations. Fundamentally, however, the qualities which Rome manifested from that point onward were already firmly established.

THE ROMAN KINGDOM

Creation of the City-State (800–575 B.C.). Although the legends of early Rome are unreliable in their details they do reflect historical reality when they connect the founding of Rome with the Latins. The site itself may have been inhabited continuously from the time of Apennine culture: by the middle of the eighth century B.C. men dwelt in two hut villages on the steep-sided Palatine hill near the best crossing of the lower Tiber, where they were safe from river floods and could protect themselves easily from outsiders. A cemetery in the later Forum had cremation graves, perhaps from another village. The grave goods have obvious Latin ties in the use of urns shaped like huts and in the styles of *fibulae* (safety-pins). Yet Rome saw from earliest times a mixture of all the peoples and currents of western Italy, for by 700 Sabines from the central mountains, who buried their dead in log coffins, were settled on the Esquiline hill. This elevation, like the Quirinal, Viminal, and Caelian hills, was an outlying finger (see Map 15).

During the seventh century the population of the Roman villages grew to the point that some men built their houses down in the Forum area proper. Some of the most ancient religious festivals of later Rome probably go back to this period. One of these was the primitive fertility rite of the Luperci, who ran about unclad on February 15 each year; another was the ceremony of the Palilia on April 21 which was designed to protect the livestock of the community as it went out to summer pastures. At least a religious union of all the villages in the area is suggested by the traditional festival of the Septimontium, though the "seven hills" of this ceremony were only parts of the Palatine, Esquiline, and Caelian hills; another festival, of the Argei, reflects the addition of the Quirinal settlements in the stage called "Rome of the four regions." Testimony to increasing contact with the civilized neighbors is afforded by the appearance of Greek vases and Etruscan *bucchero* ware and by the construction of temples. Probably at some point in this development Rome crystallized into a city-state.

The archeological evidence shows a tremendous physical change about 600 B.C., which unified this Roman nucleus into a true city; interestingly enough, Athens was becoming an urban center at about the same time. Burials in the Forum ceased, and the area was drained by the *cloaca maxima* and was paved so that it could serve as a focus of political and economic activity. Streets such as the Sacred way were regularized, and

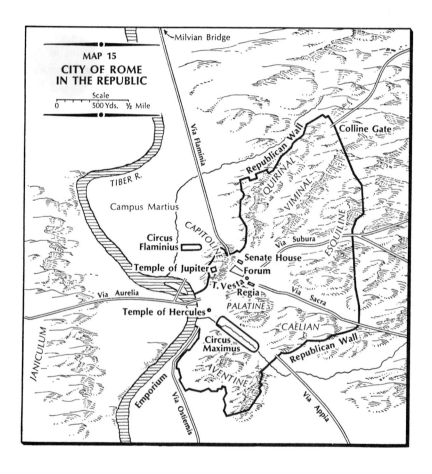

an impressive number of sanctuaries and other buildings were erected over the next 100 years.

This development, which really marks the beginning of Roman history, was a reflection of the growing economic activity and cultural consciousness of western Italy as it passed under civilizing influences. While other Latin centers became city-states and developed urban centers in the same era, Rome was peculiarly favored. It stood on the main river of western Italy, 15 miles inland at the junction of Etruscan, Sabine, and Latin districts, where major trade routes crossed below its hills. Its people and leaders, moreover, seem to have moved from the simple level of families and clans to that of a city-state with unusual political skill. Whether the city-state of Rome was a purely local product in reflection of the advanced Etruscan and Greek models, we cannot say; but certainly Rome was under Etruscan domination for most of the sixth century. The result was a tremendous explosion of political and cultural activity.

Political Expansion (700–509 B.C.). During this period Rome was ruled by kings. The traditional number of seven is suspect, and the deeds ascribed to Romulus, Numa, and other rulers are in large part an effort in later ages to explain the origins of Roman religious — and other — customs. The memory, however, that the last kings were Etruscans, especially the two Tarquins (who may be doublets of one original ruler), seems solid, particularly when we remember that the Etruscans were expanding south at this time as far as Campania.

As an Etruscan base Rome enlarged its rule considerably in the sixth century. Legends recount the destruction of the old Latin religious center at Alba Longa, a conquest up the Tiber as far as the neighboring community of Gabii, and the consolidation of Roman mastery down to the seacoast at Ostia, where salt works provided a vital commodity to much of central Italy. Although these steps cannot all be attested archeologically, the Etruscan kings and their aristocratic supporters gave Rome a tradition of military expansion and made it one of the strongest centers in western Italy. The army on which this activity was based was called the legion, grouped in phalanx formation and composed of warriors armed in hoplite style.

Since the king was primarily a war chieftain, he was elected. As military leader he was also a religious head, for he must be able to secure the support of the gods and found their will by taking the *auspices*. In time of war he levied taxes and drafted men, and had powers of life and death in the field. These powers were the root of the Roman concept of the highest executive power, or *imperium*. Many aspects of law were in the hands of the fathers of the families or were settled, as between families, by private arbiters; but the king enforced public and religious order.

Beside the king stood an advisory body, the Senate, composed of the men of authority whom he called into council. The third part of the early Roman constitution consisted of the assembly of freemen, who were grouped into 30 wards or *curiae*. In this *comitia curiata* a majority of wards carried a vote. Only matters presented by the king could be decided, and only those whom the leader called upon to speak had a voice. Among many of the basic principles of the later Roman government set in the period of the kingdom were the absolute power or *imperium* of the executive in the field; the ambigious position of the Senate as an advisory group, which yet comprised the men of standing; voting by wards in the assembly; and the lack of independent voice for the citizens in their assembly.

Other early units included three tribes, which served as units for taxation and drafting, and perhaps contributed each two Vestal Virgins to carry on the state cult of Vesta at the hearth of the city. The aristocrats or patricians were grouped into clans (*gentes*), from which a member took his name (*nomen*) such as Cornelius, Fabius, and Julius; in later days some clans were subdivided so that a man like Gaius Julius had also the *cognomen* of Caesar. These clans always remained powerful socially and through intermarriage and other ties were bases for political manipulations, as at elections; but from early times they were subordinate to the state. The problem at the end of the kingdom and in the Early Republic, however, was whether they would remain so or would split apart the community in their own interests.

Among the lower class of plebeians there were dependents of the patricians, called "clients"; this mutual relationship, in which clients gave political support to their patrons, was long to be a powerful force in Roman social organization through which ex-slaves, foreigners, and other weaker elements were integrated into public life. Other plebeians, both among the rural population and in the city proper, seem to have had an independent, if minor, place and were also organized into *gentes* from early times. Patricians and plebeians were sharply divided in economic, social, and even political standing; for only patricians could attend the Senate or serve as priests. On all levels, however, families were organized on a strongly patriarchal basis. The father had very extensive powers over his sons so long as he lived; and the mother, though honored, was firmly subordinate in the eyes of the law.

Cultural Development. Equally important was the cultural expansion of the Roman kingdom. Throughout the sixth century and on down to about 480, Rome formed part of a close-knit cultural sphere reaching from central Latium up into southern Etruria (as at Veii and Caere). Athenian black-figure and red-figure ware appears in the tombs of the era to attest Roman contact with the outside world, but local crafts and trade also grew. During the kingdom a bridge was built across the Tiber where an island made crossing easier, and Rome began to be a focal point for the roads both east-west and north-south in central Italy.

At the end of the bridge emerged the "Etruscan quarter," and Etruscan inscriptions have been found within the city. Etruscan influence brought some ceremonial trappings of the majesty of government, such as the curule chair on which officials sat in meetings, the *fasces,* and other items; and the Romans borrowed the concept of a sacred boundary or *pomerium* for the city proper. On the whole, however, the main political effect of Etruscan connections was to stimulate native progress.

In the cultural and religious fields as well there was swift advance on native roots, which clothed itself partly in forms derived from Etruscan and also Greek models. If we may judge from a law set up in the Forum in archaic Latin (under the *lapis niger*), this tongue remained the official language of government even under Etruscan kings; yet the Latin alphabet, originally of 21 letters, was probably derived from the Etruscan adaptation of the Greek alphabet. The system of Roman nomenclature (personal name and clan name) seems also to have been of Etruscan origin, as was the calendar of 12 months (Aprilis and the term Ides for the middle of the month were both of Etruscan roots).

Military expansion and economic progress permitted the construction of some 14 to 15 public religious buildings during the kingdom, more than Rome was to be able to produce for centuries after the kings departed. A temple to Fortune in the Forum had Etruscan terra cotta decorations; nearby were the round temple of Vesta and the Regia or house of the kings. Most impressive of all was the great temple erected on the Capitoline hill in honor of Jupiter Optimus Maximus, together with his female companions Juno and Minerva. The Capitoline temple was 200 feet square — larger than any temple known in Etruria during the period. Since its columns were spread far apart, the temple always had to have a wooden superstructure and often burned down. The statue of Jupiter was made of terra cotta by Etruscan workmen, as was the chariot placed on top of the roof.[1] Henceforth Jupiter was the patron god of the Roman city-state until Christianity gained mastery; and for centuries to come triumphal processions, marking the expansion of Rome, were to wind through the Forum and up the Capitoline slopes to his temple.

Whereas earlier Italic peoples seem to have worshiped their divine protectors as spirits in the open air, Rome had now taken over the civilized custom of building temples and erecting cult statues. Besides its great triad, which reflects Etruscan practice, Rome also adopted the worship of Hercules (centered in the cattle-market), Castor and Pollux, and others from the Greeks. Increasingly in later centuries Roman religious concepts were to be influenced by Greek anthropomorphic views, but the simple Romans remained deeply attached to the gods of state and home, whom they worshiped in almost legalistic exactitude of prayer and sacrifice. Not only did their religious calendar preserve some of the earliest cults of the city, but also their basically animistic approach survived particularly in the family cults of Vesta (guardian of the hearth), of the Lares and Penates (guardians of the land and the storehouses), of Janus of the door, and of the Genius or procreative power of the father. Roman poets could never create an independent religious mythology, though in its place they did fashion a political mythology of early Roman heroes. While magic and gross superstition played a very minor part at least in public worship, taboos and that belief in a superhuman, abstract force which anthropologists call *mana* can be found repeatedly in Roman religious thought.

End of the Kingdom. The importance of the first stage of Roman history in setting its later political, cultural, and religious patterns cannot

[1] The Apollo from Veii (Plate XXI) of about 500 B.C. must suggest what the original statue of Capitoline Jupiter was like; the latter was made by the sculptor Vulca from Veii.

be overestimated; but this extremely active period was brief. In Roman legend the patricians, led by Brutus, expelled the last Tarquin king in 509 and established a republic. Although an actual expulsion may well have taken place, the general decline of Etruscan power in central Italy was a fundamental factor in permitting the changes at Rome. The Latins, thus, are said to have defeated the Etruscans in a battle shortly after this event, and in 474 Etruscan naval power was crushed off Cumae by the Greeks. By the early fifth century all the western Mediterranean was losing its earlier close contact with the advanced centers in the east, a phenomenon attested by the marked decrease of Greek pottery alike at Carthage, in Etruria, and in central Italy (though not at Spina in the Po valley).

As far as Rome is concerned, we may accept the date of 509 B.C. as marking a great constitutional change, which put control in the hands of the patricians. To reduce the dangers that the leaders might usurp kingship again, the *imperium* was lodged in two consuls of equal authority, who were elected for only one year; from this point on for a thousand years each year was dated by the consuls then in office. Very soon, however, the new Republic lost its political power in central Italy in battles with the Latins, who formed a league of their eight major states. Economic activity also declined. In the fifth century B.C. Rome faced crucial problems, both abroad, where the hungry hillsmen threatened its survival, and internally, where the plebeians groaned under the oppression of their patrician masters. Culturally, as a result, the Romans failed to prosecute their earlier artistic and architectural activity after at least the middle of the fifth century; not until the third century were they again to move forward in this area and also develop the arts of oratory and history on a truly literate plane.

ROMAN CONQUEST OF ITALY

External Expansion to 264 B.C. While the Romans culturally fell into a backwater, their political and military abilities were never more marked than from the era from 509 to 264 B.C. During this dimly lit period they recovered from their collapse at the beginning of the Republic and went on to conquer all the peninsula. Internally they hammered out, slowly and with many false starts, a reorganization of their political system which eventually produced technical democracy.

Down to 340 B.C. the wars of the Early Republic took place in a narrow strip of western Italy, 30 miles from the sea to the central mountains and 90 miles from the Ciminian hills of south Etruria to the jutting promontory of Tarracina at the edge of the Latin districts (see Map 14). The main opponents were initially the expanding hill tribes of the Aequi and Volsci, who pressed on both the Latins and the Romans. After the Latin league had secured its independence from Rome at the battle of Lake Regillus (*c.* 496 B.C.) the two powers nonetheless found themselves forced to join 'in a treaty of equal alliance to oppose the hillsmen, the *foedus Cassianum* of 493. The critical battle appears to have been that of Mt. Algidus in 431, after which the tide turned in favor of the plainsmen.

The Romans were also at odds on their own with the neighboring Etruscan center of Veii, which traded southward across the Tiber via Praeneste. The direct route was cut by Roman advance up the Tiber in 426–25, but reduction of Veii itself was a bitter struggle. In the end Veii was taken in 396 and was utterly destroyed by the general M. Furius Camillus after a continuous siege over several years. During the last stage the Roman state had to institute regular payment for the soldiers thus kept away from their farms.

Then came the worst blow Rome was ever to suffer until its final collapse in the fifth century after Christ. Uncivilized Celts, called Gauls, had been moving down into the Po valley from central Europe and launched a series of great raids into central Italy. In 390, according to conventional Roman chronology, the Roman army marched out to meet the Gauls north of Rome at the Allia river, but was wiped out. The city itself was almost totally destroyed.

The dogged Romans, however, rose nobly to the threat. They appointed Camillus dictator and raised a new army. In 378–57 they built a stone wall five and one-half miles long about the city, far larger than that of any Etruscan city. As defenders of central Italy Rome gained extensive support and by 350 was virtually master of the neighborhood.

To lay a solid basis for further expansion had required almost two centuries, but now the Romans blazed forth. During the period 340 to 264 they conquered all the rest of the Italian peninsula. The initial stimulus came from a revolt of the Latin league, which chafed at its increasingly dependent postition; in a brief war, 340–38, the Romans defeated and dissolved the league. During the hostilities with the Latins, their southern neighbors, the wealthy Oscans who had become civilized in Campania appealed again for assistance against their Samnite kinsmen of the central mountains. Capua, Cumae, and other cities were accordingly added to Roman control.

This latter step brought the Romans by 326 into serious conflict with the Samnites, who were far more numerous but less well unified. Although the first phase ended in 321 when the Samnites trapped a Roman army at the Caudine forks, the wars flared up again and again. It was probably in this long-protracted struggle that the Romans reorganized their basic military unit, the legion, into a more supple structure. During the Samnite wars they had also to face from time to time Etruscan and Gallic foes; but they skillfully divided and conquered their enemies, while their own subjects generally remained loyal. The Roman victory at Sentinum in 295 delivered the crucial blow to an army of Samnites and Gauls; final settlement, however, scarcely came until 282.

There remained southern Italy, where the Greek cities of the coast were barely maintaining themselves against inland Lucanian tribes. In 282 Rome sent an army south at the request of Thurii and dispatched a few ships to the gulf off Tarentum, in violation of an old agreement with that state. The Tarentines sank the ships and invited into Italy the king of Epirus, Pyrrhus (319–272). This skilled Hellenistic general defeated the Romans at Heraclea (280) and Asculum (279), partly through using the new tactical weapon of elephants.

Pyrrhus then essayed to make peace. The Senate almost approved his terms; but the Carthaginians hastily offered Rome naval and financial aid, and an aged Roman leader, Appius Claudius, had himself carried into the Senate House to speak against compromise. Since Pyrrhus could not hope to conquer all central Italy from the Romans, he turned to Sicily upon the invitation of the Greeks in the islands and fought the Carthaginians. When he returned to Italy in 275, the Romans checked him at Beneventum; Pyrrhus withdrew to Epirus; and the Greek cities of the south had to admit Roman garrisons. Thenceforth the Romans were masters of the Italian peninsula (for chronology, see Table 6 in Chapter 24).

Causes of Victory. The Roman conquest of Italy was not a process the Romans deliberately planned, for it took over two centuries of almost haphazard actions. If the Romans fought so continuously, the reasons lie partly in the ill-stabilized conditions. In Italy at this time strife between plainsmen and hillsmen was unending and opened the way for the Gauls; the Greeks quarreled among themselves and tempted intervention by their Italic neighbors. The Roman system of alliances, which made Rome responsible for protecting each ally, also involved Rome in an ever-widening circle of external entanglements.

Potent forces of expansion existed within Rome itself. The Romans remembered their days of greatness in the kingdom; their leaders sought military glory, which would enhance the honor of their families and bring them booty; and the population of Rome seems to have increased at a rapid rate. Beside looting their victims of movable property, the Romans commonly took about a third of conquered lands on which they settled colonies of Roman and Latin farmers.

To explain their victories, the Romans had one fundamental answer: "We have overcome all the nations of the world, because we have realized that the world is directed and governed by the gods."[2] Divine support was gained by scrupulous attention to religious vows by the leaders and by rewards of booty to the temples; the Romans, too, had a ceremony conducted by the *fetiales* which ensured that their wars were just defenses of the Romans and their allies. This religious machinery undoubtedly had a considerable effect in heartening the troops and generals to their tasks, but more earthly factors also had a potent role both in bringing victory and in aiding the maintenance of Roman rule.

Tactically and strategically the Romans hammered out ever more supple principles of organization and operations. Most of their enemies, who were not civilized, could be divided and met in detail by Roman forces, which were kept concentrated and had a central geographical position. Even skilled opponents like Pyrrhus could win only battles, not wars, against the abundance of Roman manpower and the dogged persistence of Roman leadership. Initially the Romans organized their legions into phalanxes, but during the Samnite wars they developed a more articulated division of the legion into blocs or *maniples,* grouped in three lines which operated independently; most soldiers were now armed with short swords and javelins.

As far as possible, the Romans fought only on ground of their own

[2] Cicero, *On the Responses of the Haruspices* 9.

choosing and at the time when they were ready. To aid them in refusing battle under unfavorable circumstances they picked up from Pyrrhus the habit of fortifying their camp every night. Roman commanders were mostly experienced veterans, and since they were also the chief officials of the state they normally could decide on their own judgment when and how to give battle.

Holding down the conquered called for skills of a more political nature. The establishment of colonies provided bases and points of control over conquered areas, and by the late fourth century the Romans had begun to build all-weather roads to link the capital with other districts. Appius Claudius laid out the first great Roman road, the *via Appia,* to Capua in 312. More important, however, was the treatment of the defeated. A Roman conquest was not in itself a gentle matter, and a considerable part of conquered lands was taken for Roman settlers. Yet the Romans generally were fighting peoples of similar culture and language, and after the destruction of Veii they commonly spared the vanquished from utter destruction.

Across the fourth century the Romans developed a very deftly arranged set of varying positions for their subjects. Most defeated states became "allies" (*socii*), who paid no tribute and retained local self-government; they furnished a set number of troops upon call and surrendered foreign policy to Rome. After the Latin league was dissolved in 338, many Latin states received "Latin status," holders of which could gain citizenship if they settled in Rome; most colonies also received this status. Dating from the annexation of Tusculum in 381, however, some Latin communities were absorbed down the years into the Roman citizen territory but retained their legal existence as local *"municipia."* Yet a fourth status, that of Roman citizenship without the right to vote, was given to areas in Campania and elsewhere. By 225 B.C., as we know from a list of Polybius, about 1,000,000 male inhabitants of Italy were Roman citizens (either full citizens, full citizens having a local center in their *municipium,* or citizens without a vote), 500,000 were Latins, and 1,500,000 were allies, grouped in some 120 to 150 small states.

Thereby the Romans bound particularly the upper classes in the subject territories to their rule and divided Italy so that it could not feel a sense of common opposition to a tyrannical master. Unwittingly the Romans began thus to enlarge the concept of Rome and so took great

steps toward solving the problem of welding conquered to home territories, a problem which had shattered the Athenian empire. One of
Rome's opponents was later to praise this liberality in granting citizenship, by which the Romans "have not only enlarged their own city, but
they have also sent out colonies to nearly seventy places." [3] Eventually in
A.D. 212 Roman citizenship was to be given to virtually all free men of the
entire Mediterranean basin.

POLITICAL EVOLUTION OF THE REPUBLIC

Expansion of the Government. A very major factor in the Roman
ability to conquer and to hold Italy was the fact that at the same time
they reorganized the primitive form of republican city-state with which
they began in 509 B.C. Although Roman tradition records many violent
internal dissensions, the citizens were able to close their ranks during
external crises. In the end they constructed a political system and a civic
spirit which united all major elements of the state in support of its
military expansion.

The aspect of this internal development which we can see most clearly
is the enlargement of the governmental machinery. Throughout the
period down to 264 the two annually elected consuls remained the chief
magistrates at home and served as the generals abroad. In the field each
consul usually operated independently with an army of two Roman
legions plus allied còntingents; but at home both had to concur if any
serious action was to be taken. In critical emergencies the consuls stepped
aside to make way for a single dictator, whom they appointed for six
months; but this office fell into disuse by the end of the third century.

In 366 a praetor was added with the *imperium,* initially with the task
of commanding the urban defense forces if the consuls were absent. Additional generals could be secured by continuing the term of outgoing
magistrates as proconsuls or propraetors. This device for continuing able
generals in their posts, which had appeared in the Samnite wars, was

---

[3] King Philip V of Macedonia, letter to Larissa in 214 B.C., in Naphthali Lewis and
Meyer Reinhold, *Roman Civilization,* I (New York: Columbia University Press,
1951), pp. 386–7.

much used in later days when the military needs of Rome could no longer be met by annually changing commanders.

By 264 there were eight quaestors, as financial officials; four aediles, who supervised public markets and roads; 10 tribunes of the people, who protected the lower classes; and 10 judges of liberty, who tried suits involving legal freedom. Minor officials and also the lictors and scribes attendant on the major magistrates carried out routine matters. State religious officials, including nine pontiffs, nine augurs, and others, supervised public sacrifices and festivals; these were aristocrats who might well continue their other political activities.

At intervals, which finally came to be every five years, two censors were elected to let state contracts for temple maintenance, roads, and the like; to draw up a list of citizens for tax and draft purposes; and to set the roll of the Senate. Usually old members were appointed anew to the Senate, and gaps were filled from the ranks of ex-magistrates; but the censors, as senior aristocrats of great reputation, could expel senators on grounds of undue luxury, immorality, or incapacity.

Although the Senate continued to be an advisory body, summoned by consul or praetor, its voice as a continuing body of experienced men was potent, and it had virtual control over finances; by this time it numbered usually about 300 men. True legislation, however, was passed by the citizen body. The old organization of the *comitia curiata* gradually became a fossil, and by 264 citizens met in either of two groupings. In the Centuriate assembly (*comitia centuriata*) men voted in wards or "centuries" on the basis of their wealth. This mode of assembly appeared some time in the sixth or fifth century in connection with military reforms, for each of the five classes of centuries was obligated to furnish soldiers with more or less armor depending on its wealth. Above the five classes were the 18 equestrian centuries, the men who could provide a horse; then came the first class of 80 centuries, the men who could provide full armor; the second and third, each of 20 centuries of the less-well armed; the fourth, of men with javelins, 20 centuries; and the fifth, of slingers, 30 centuries. Five other centuries included carpenters, trumpeters, and others. Since the 18 equestrian centuries and the 80 centuries of the first class furnished a majority of the 193 wards and, moreover, voted first, the Centuriate assembly was weighted in favor of the more well-to-do part of the citizen body. In each class, moreover, half the centuries were assigned to the *seniores,* men from 47 to 60, and only half to the *juniores,* men from 17 to 46, so that the older part of the population had greater power than its numbers warranted. Officials with *imperium* called together the Centuriate assembly to elect major magistrates, to pass "laws" (*leges*), to ratify treaties, and to declare war or peace.

Citizens could also be assembled by tribunes in the Tribal assembly (*comitia tributa*). Here they were grouped by 264 in 33 tribes or geographical wards (from 241 on in 35 tribes) to elect the 10 tribunes and two of the aediles and to pass legislation called *plebiscita.* The Tribal assembly had appeared as an extralegal voice of the plebeians early in the fifth century, and then had another name (Tribal council) as embracing only plebeians; but by 264 the Tribal assembly was a full part of the state machinery. Neither assembly, it should be noted, met frequently; the operation of the government was largely in the hands of the executive, advised by the Senate.

By 264 the city-state of Rome still possessed a relatively simple government, partly because subject territories were allowed to govern themselves, partly because the fathers of the families exercised many functions. Nonetheless the citizens had gained a rich political experience and had shown remarkable pragmatic ability to throw up new solutions to meet the problems that appeared in the tensions of growth. Especially notable is the interconnection of political and military capacities: citizenship itself was closely tied to the ability to bear arms, and the Romans were the more willing to grant citizenship to others because of their military needs; and aristocrats had to prove their abilities on both the military and the civil level from the minor posts of youth on up to the consulship.

Patricians versus Plebeians. At the beginning of the Republic the patricians had controlled the government in every respect. They alone could be elected to office or serve as priests; and through the principle of "authority of the senators" (*patrum auctoritas*) their approval had to be secured for any legislation. Indeed, the some 50-odd patrician clans controlled voting in the *comitia curiata* through their clients, although they constituted only a tenth of the population at the most; one clan, the Fabian, was said to have mustered a sizable army for an independent war against Veii. The plebeians, no longer protected by the kings, were

much oppressed economically and politically in the grim days of the
Early Republic.

The resulting struggle between patricians and plebeians involved
many issues. Plebeians who fell into debt became virtual serfs or even
could be sold into slavery; marriage between the classes was virtually
forbidden; and control of the courts lay in patrician hands. According to
our sources for the period, however, the controversy was focused chiefly
in the effort of the plebeians to gain a voice in the government. This
privilege the patricians were loath to give, but after two centuries of
struggle the plebeians won.

A basic reason for their success was the fact that Rome needed them
for its ever-widening wars. The regular draft quota rose from 3000 at the
beginning of the Republic for each year's campaign to 8400 by 366, and
thereafter swelled even more markedly; and since the patricians admitted no new families to their ranks after the Appius Claudius clan and a
few others in the Early Republic, the additional warriors were virtually
all plebeians. As the wars went on, the Roman annexation of land
gave more and more opportunity for the plebeians to secure economic
independence.

Another significant factor was the ability of the plebeians to gain
leaders. Some of their spokesmen seem to have come from the commercial and industrial elements located on the Aventine hill within the city
proper. Others consisted of the well-to-do agricultural families in those
districts which gained Roman citizenship after the patrician order closed
its ranks.

The twists and turns of the constitutional struggle are a famous, if
partly legendary, story. The first step in the plebeian progress was the
creation of a Tribal council, the root of the Tribal assembly, and the
election of tribunes "of the people," as distinguished from the military
officers called "military tribunes." Initially the tribunes protected their
fellow commoners in matters of taxes and the draft, but eventually they
arrogated to themselves the power to veto any unjust action of the
government except when a dictator was in office. Although this was
highly illegal, the plebeians backed their leaders and protected them
against patrician violence; long before 264 a tribune was considered sacro-
sanct, that is, anyone interfering with a tribune or injuring him was made
outlaw. As the great historian Theodor Mommsen observed, this office

was a "wretched compromise," [4] which did not lead to a complete voice of the plebeians. During the decline of the Republic its powers were often to be used to block action designed to help the people, for usually the aristocrats could influence one of the 10 tribunes to stop his fellows by a veto. Yet at the time the tribunes and their assembly gave cohesion and direction to the plebeian struggle.

Next, traditionally in 451–50, the laws of the state were codified in the Twelve Tables by two successive boards of 10 officials under Appius Claudius, which were elected especially for the purpose. The laws were written in terse sentences and reflect a far simpler community than is visible in Hammurapi's code in Babylon. Yet in the first Roman code all free citizens possessed rights as well as duties within the state. In providing for wills and contracts, the Twelve Tables gave room for a fair amount of individual decision and economic activity; and wives and children had legal means of securing emancipation from the father's power.

Thereafter the plebeians pressed for admittance to the state magistracies. At times, if our tangled sources are correct, plebeians did serve as "military tribunes with consular power," a replacement for the regular office of consul; but on the whole the patricians held control of the executive offices until two tribunes, C. Licinius and L. Sextius, forced through an extensive set of political and economic reforms in 367 which added a praetor and two more aediles. In the next year Sextius himself was elected consul, and soon thereafter it became a convention that one consul was plebeian. In 351 a plebeian was censor, in 337 praetor; and in 300 the Ogulnian law opened the major priesthoods. After a particularly violent struggle in 287, during which the plebeians seceded to the other side of the Tiber, the Hortensian law removed the *patrum auctoritas* and thus gave full power to the *plebiscita* of the Tribal assembly.

From this time onward, Rome must technically be called a democracy, in which the people were the final source of constitutional power. In the army they were still subject to the life-and-death authority of their general, but the more extreme powers of the *imperium* stopped at the sacred boundary of Rome. Within the city citizens could appeal to the tribunes for aid, and had the right of appeal to the Centuriate assembly in capital cases. Enslavement of citizens for debt was banned by the Poetilian law of 326 or 313.

[4] Theodor Mommsen, *History of Rome*, I (Chicago: Free Press reprint, 1957), p. 356.

In practice the Roman government was not conducted as democratically as had been that of Periclean Athens. The old patrician and the leading new plebeian families essentially amalgamated during the third century into a "senatorial aristocracy," that is to say, a group which furnished the magistrates and therefore served in the Senate. Only a man with strong family backing had, as a rule, any chance to enter on the ladder which led from minor training posts like military tribune through the great state officers. Relative freedom of expression obtained solely within the Senate, and throughout the political system the "authority" (*auctoritas*) of elder citizens, ancestral custom (*mos maiorum*), and reverence for law were conservative forces.

Yet the eventual surrender by the patricians of their exclusive position without a shattering revolution attests the political sense of the Romans, and the new governing class long conducted state policies so as to keep the general citizen body satisfied at home and the subjects throughout Italy reasonably loyal. It is easy to idealize those grave Roman aristocrats who loom up dimly as heroic figures in the dim history of the centuries from 509 to 264, for their tenacity in adversity, political wisdom, and patriotic spirit provided Roman leadership with truly great qualities.[5] Yet the historian must always be on his guard against undue idealization. Aristocrats were quite capable of violent contention for the glory of public office and even bought votes, a practice forbidden by law as early as 358; they yielded only because of the needs of the state and, after absorbing the new plebian leaders, were to remain an exclusive group in subsequent centuries. The general simplicity of Roman life down to this point had also an effect in holding the patricians and plebeians together in a fundamental sense of communal loyalty; for within the aristocratic group there was a tendency to factional division which must have caused trouble in the early centuries whenever foreign pressures did not damp it down. In later times this dissolvent effect was to recur in more serious form.

ROME IN 264 B.C.

By 264 B.C. Rome had reorganized its internal system of government and had conquered all the Italian peninsula. At this point it began to look abroad and strode forward with relative swiftness to conquer first

---

[5] The so-called "Brutus" of Plate XXIII, probably of the third century B.C., admirably suggests the firm severity of Roman aristocrats.

the western Mediterranean and then the coastal districts of the Hellenistic world.

By this time Rome was one of the biggest cities in the Mediterranean with two aqueducts and a population of some 80,000. Such an agglomeration required seaborne grain, which was brought up the Tiber; in return Roman artisans created metal work such as the famous Ficorini cista (jewel box) which could be sold outside the city and a variety of pottery certainly made at Rome which turns up from Spain to western Sicily and Carthaginian Africa. Slaves were already present in numbers in the shops and factories of Rome by the mid-fourth century; at its close Appius Claudius tried the experiment of admitting rich sons of freedmen to the Senate, but his successors as censors revoked this break with tradition. Aristocrats were beginning to enjoy luxuries of Hellenistic type, and the triumphant city was putting on a new dress of temples and statues.

The conventional view of Rome at this time as purely land-oriented is not justified in fact. We know of Latin-speaking traders in eastern Mediterranean waters before 250; Hellenistic embassies had been coming off and on to Rome for several decades. Roman senators like "Brutus" knew a great deal about the Mediterranean world, and Roman state policy now involved naval activity in limited dimensions. True, Roman aristocrats and citizens alike were still rooted in the land, as was true of all Greek and Roman states in antiquity; but this does not necessarily imply public disinterest in commercial matters. The *foedus Cassianum* of 493 and the pacts with Carthage safeguarded the legal treatment of Roman traders; coinage had begun at Rome by 300, partly in silver to advertise the growing power of Rome but also in large copper pieces designed for market use. The very fact that Rome went to war with Carthage in 264 is not necessarily the accidental, inexplicable blunder which it is often portrayed as being. In the great expansion which followed, the political and military strengths developed in the conquest of Italy were to stand Rome in good stead.

[6] Livy, *History of Rome*, Preface; tr. A. de Selincourt.

BIBLIOGRAPHY

Sources. The early history of Rome has been set on a much firmer footing by recent excavations, which have carefully observed stratigraphic levels; but the existence of the great modern city of Rome limits the freedom of archeological exploration. Down to the end of the period considered in this chapter no building save the so-called Servian wall (built after the Gallic invasion) still stands above ground in Rome today.

The traditional account of early Rome is best preserved for us in the famous history of T. Livius (59 B.C.–A.D. 17). Any historian who reads his eulogy of his ancestors, "I do honestly believe that no country has ever been greater or purer than ours or richer in good citizens and noble deeds . . . nowhere have thrift and plain living been for so long held in such esteem," will immediately suspect that Livy's account is subject to distortion. Even though Livy was essentially honest, he was not deeply critical and engaged in very little research beyond reading earlier histories. His account, however, was so polished from the literary point of view that these earlier accounts, written back to about 200 B.C., have not survived. Even for Livy we have only Books 1–10 on the period covered in this chapter, which run down to 293 B.C., together with abridgments of later times, available in Loeb Classical Library; the first five books are translated by A. de Selincourt (Penguin L104, 1960) with a commentary by R. M. Ogilvie (Oxford: Oxford University Press, 1965).

For the Early Republic Livy and his predecessors had available only scanty materials. These include family and folk memories, which were often exaggerated; a list of consuls (the *fasti consulares*), which was engraved in Livy's day on an arch in the Roman Forum and has survived in part in this form as well as in the historians; the *annales maximi,* a list by years of the events and prodigies which the pontiffs thought worthy of record; and a few documents. Among the latter are early calendars, the *foedus Cassianum,* some early treaties with Carthage, and remnants of the Twelve Tables, which fell into practical disuse by the second century B.C. and so did not survive intact (fragments in *Remains of Old Latin,* Loeb Classical Library). For the Roman kingdom sources were even fewer.

In addition to Livy's reconstruction of Roman history there is also some evidence in Virgil's great epic poem, the *Aeneid;* the Greek histories of Dionysius of Halicarnassus and of Diodorus Siculus (both Loeb Classical Library); and Plutarch's lives of Romulus, Numa, Poplicola (colleague of Brutus), Camillus, and Coriolanus (a fifth-century figure, largely legendary). The picture given by these sources has been so seriously attacked since the beginnings of historical criticism in modern times that some scholars have refused to credit any Roman history before the third century B.C. So severe an attitude is unwarranted, but certainly we must be ever more cautious as we plunge back further and further before 264 and are forced to rely upon tradition, religious survivals, and linguistic evidence.

Further Reading. Raymond Bloch, *Origins of Rome* (New York: Praeger, 1960), places the rise of Rome in the context of Italian history; see also R. M. Ogilvie, *Early Rome and the Etruscans* (London: Fontana, 1976). Einar Gjerstad's views may be found in his *Legends and Facts of Early Roman History* (Lund: Gleerup, 1962). See also Jacques Heurgon, *The Rise of Rome* (Berkeley: University of California Press, 1973), and E. T. Salmon, *Samnium and the Samnites* (Cambridge: Cambridge University Press, 1967). L. R. Palmer, *Latin Language* (London: Faber and Faber, 1954), is good.

General treatments of Roman expansion may be found in H. H. Scullard, *History of the Roman World from 753 B.C. to 146 B.C.* (4th ed.; London: Methuen, 1980); W. V. Harris, *Rome in Etruria and Umbria* (Oxford: Clarendon Press, 1971). In my Walker-Ames lectures, *The Beginnings of Imperial Rome* (Ann Arbor: University of Michigan Press, 1980) I have sought to revise the conventional picture of Rome in the mid-Republic. L. P. Homo, *Roman Political Institutions* (New York: Knopf, 1962), is perhaps the most useful introduction to this complicated subject; one important aspect is carefully studied in A. N. Sherwin-White, *Roman Citizenship* (Oxford: Oxford University Press, 1973).

23

ROME IN THE MEDITERRANEAN

During the period 264–133 B.C., Rome strode out of Italy into the broad Mediterranean world. This expansion was not deliberately planned; many Roman leaders, indeed, spoke against foreign entanglements and commitments in terms we might well call "isolationist." Yet internal expansive forces were strong and were further intensified by the unstable political conditions which existed elsewhere in the Mediterranean.

First the Romans fought two great wars with Carthage, which gave them control of the western Mediterranean by 201. Thenceforth Rome had the enduring problems of pacifying and civilizing districts which were less civilized than itself.

After 200 the Romans also looked eastward, where the Hellenistic political structure was falling to pieces. The wars of the great monarchies after Alexander had by this time worn down their strength, and the lower classes grew ever more restive at the exploitation by the Greek bureaucrats and by the city-dwellers. From the Iranian plateau a new dynasty, that of Parthia, expanded by land into Mesopotamia; from the west Rome advanced swiftly to take control of the coastal districts of the Hellenistic world. By 133 the state on the Tiber held virtual mastery over all the Mediterranean world, though it was not yet ready to assume direct responsibility for the governance of this empire.

The expansion of Rome had other than military aspects. The continuing economic, social, and internal political developments of Rome must be considered in the next chapter, in connection with their enduring effects after 133. Culturally, as we shall see toward the close of the present chapter, the Roman upper classes became ever more receptive to the attractive, if somewhat superficial, qualities of Hellenistic civilization. Some dogged Romans were deeply suspicious of these foreign ways, but Roman society as a whole accepted sophistication with enthusiasm. In every respect the period witnessed a growing unification of the Mediterranean world, which was to produce the last great phase of ancient history.

THE DUEL WITH CARTHAGE

Opening of Hostilities. By 264 Rome had developed a system of government which was technically a democracy but in which the actual exercise of power was primarily in the hands of a landed aristocracy, accustomed to military activity. It had also gained mastery over the Italian peninsula and had bound its allies, or subjects, to it by a pattern of varied privileges and responsiblities.

Across the Mediterranean in north Africa, Carthage had also been expanding. Its constitution, which was praised by the Greek political expert Aristotle for its stability, allowed popular expression of opinion; but administration lay in the hands of two annually elected *suffetes* and a council of 300 with its important inner committees (council of 30, supreme court of 104). The aristocratic families of Carthage held extensive lands in the neighborhood but also had commercial interests' to a greater degree than did their peers in Rome, for Carthage dominated a great trading empire in north Africa, south Spain, western Sicily, and Sardinia and Corsica. Some of the products which it sold for metals and other raw materials were made in Carthage; others came from the east or from Campania. Like the Romans, the Carthaginians were more and more influenced by Greek culture from the fourth century onward.

To maintain its position Carthage relied largely upon a mercenary army, some naval power—though its navy had fought no battles for a long time—and diplomatic guarantees of its closed commercial sphere. Whereas the Romans exacted troops rather than money from their subjects in Italy, the Carthaginians required from their dependents a heavy tribute in grain and precious metals in order to defray the expenses of their empire. The population of the Carthaginian domains is estimated at about 3,000,000, approximately the same as that of Roman Italy.

At the very beginning of the Roman Republic, Carthage and Rome had contracted a treaty which banned Roman traders from most of the Carthaginian shoreline, while Carthage agreed not to interfere in the Roman sphere of interest in Latium. Other treaties of similar nature had been made later, in 348 and 306. In the war with Pyrrhus Carthage had offered financial and naval assistance to Rome. Between Roman and Carthaginian interests lay a buffer of Greek states, that is, Massilia and its dependencies in Gaul and north Spain and the Greek cities of Sicily. From these states, however, were to spring the conditions which led Rome and Carthage into decisive struggles, called Punic wars because the Greek name for Carthaginians was "Poeni."

The spark which kindled the first struggle came from an attack by Hiero, king of Syracuse, on some Campanian mercenaries who had seized Messana at the northeast tip of Sicily. In their plight these "Mamertines" appealed to both Carthage and Rome. The former sent naval aid at once; the Roman Senate debated the issue in a quandary. If Rome allowed Carthage to have a foothold so close to Italy, it could hamper the trade of the south Italian subjects of Rome; but Roman naval interest had always been so slight that the Senate hesitated to move into Sicily. An answer to the appeal, which was one of the most critical decisions in all Roman history, was referred to the assembly. The people, spurred by the consuls, voted to protect the Mamertines.

An advance Roman detachment threw out the Carthaginian garrison already in Messana; but when the Roman consul Appius Claudius appeared, he found himself in open fighting with Carthaginian reinforcements. The war which thus resulted was to lead to the beginning of Roman overseas empire (see Map 16).

The First Punic War (264–41 B.C.). Initially the Roman army scored great successes in Sicily, for the Carthaginians had no nearby naval bases to check Roman troop movements across the Sicilian straits. Hiero joined the Romans in 263; Agrigentum fell in the next year after a siege of seven months. But the other coastal towns in Carthaginian hands could not be easily taken so long as the Punic fleet supplied them by sea, and coastal raids on Italy itself pointed to the dangers of a Roman naval weakness.

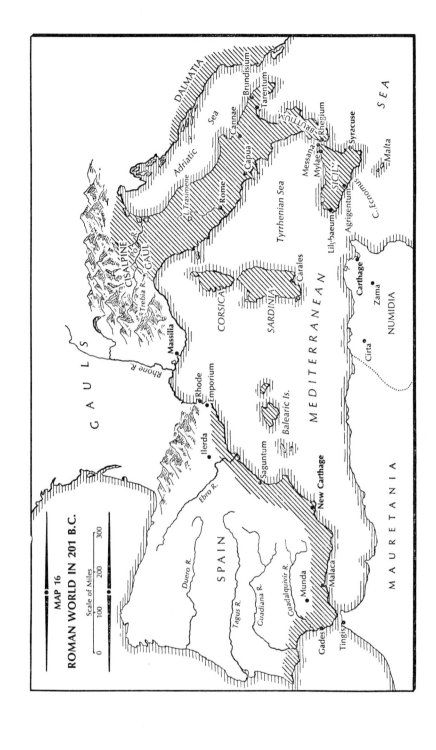

MAP 16

ROMAN WORLD IN 201 B.C.

Scale of Miles

0   100   200   300

GAULS

SPAIN

Duero R.

Tagus R.

Guadiana R.

Guadalquivir R.

Ebro R.

Rhone R.

Gades

Tingis

Malaca

Munda

New Carthage

Saguntum

Ilerda

Rhode

Emporium

Balearic Is.

Massilia

CISALPINE GAUL

Trebia R.

L. Trasimene

Rome

Capua

Cannae

Tarentum

Brundisium

DALMATIA

Adriatic Sea

Tyrrhenian Sea

CORSICA

SARDINIA

Carales

MEDITERRANEAN

Lilybaeum

Agrigentum

SICILY

Messana

Mylae

Rhegium

BRUTTIUM

Syracuse

Malta

C. Ecnomus

Carthage

Zama

Cirta

NUMIDIA

MAURETANIA

SEA

The clear-headed Roman strategists saw the need and in 261 set about building a fleet of 20 *triremes* and of 100 heavier *quinqueremes,* in which each oar was pulled by five men. Crews were trained in mock-up ships on land, and the Romans devised a secret weapon, the "crow" (*corvus*). This was a gangway held upright until a Roman ship was next to its enemy, whereupon it was suddenly lowered so that Roman soldiers could pour onto the foe's vessel. So equipped, the Roman fleet under the consul C. Duilius rowed to Sicily in 260 and won a smashing victory at Mylae over the Carthaginians under Hannibal, whose ships were caught one by one. Soon Carthage held only the base of Lilybaeum in western Sicily.

The triumphant Romans, rather than wasting time here on a difficult siege, decided in 256 to strike directly at Carthage. Their fleet, under the consuls M. Atilius Regulus and L. Manlius Vulso, defeated the Carthaginians under Hamilcar in the great battle of Ecnomus, then landed a Roman army near Carthage. In their desperation the Carthaginians turned to a Spartan mercenary general, Xanthippus, who was versed in Hellenistic tactics. Xanthippus skillfully combined the Carthaginian infantry with Numidian cavalry and elephants to defeat the Romans. Regulus was taken prisoner, and the remnants of his forces were evacuated by the Roman navy.

Thereafter the Romans suffered naval disaster after disaster in storms, which sank all-told about 600 warships and 1000 transports; probably no naval war in all history has seen such casualties by drowning. The Roman state and treasury were close to exhaustion, but finally in 244 the Senate assessed itself for a public loan to build a last fleet of 200 warships, which omitted the top-heavy *corvus*. This squadron C. Lutatius Catulus led down to Sicily to blockade Lilybaeum. In 241 he took his ships out to sea, despite stormy weather to meet and crush the relief fleet sent from Carthage in the battle of the Aegates islands.

Carthage was equally exhausted by the long war and now made peace. It surrendered Sicily to the Romans and paid an indemnity of 3200 talents over the next 10 years. After the peace the Carthaginian mercenaries in Africa, Sardinia, and Corsica rebelled for lack of pay. The Romans initially refused to aid the rebels, but finally in 238 intervened and exacted the surrender of Sardinia and Corsica by Carthage as well as a further indemnity of 1200 talents.

Both Sicily and Sardinia-Corsica were formed into provinces. These were governed from 227 on by two additional praetors, who were assisted by quaestors and an appointed staff of mature "legates" or deputies and fledging aristocrats. Rome also continued the previous Greek and Carthaginian practice of requiring tribute in the form of one-tenth of the grain crop from its new subjects; this tribute was collected according to careful regulations by local bidders or "tax farmers." Both in creating provinces and in demanding tribute, the Romans broke with their Italian policy and began to lay the patterns which governed their further imperial expansion.

Interlude (241–18 B.C.). The expansive forces inherent in the Roman system of government and alliances soon led the Romans into other areas. To the north lay Cisalpine Gaul or the fertile Po valley, occupied by the barbaric Gauls but coveted by the Roman farmers. The popular hero C. Flaminius, tribune in 232, secured a law against the opposition of the more far-seeing Senate, which divided some of the southeastern part of the valley into new farms. After a Gallic rebellion in 225, Cisalpine Gaul was conquered by 220.

To the east, across the Adriatic, a number of minor principalities were engaged in piratical activity which disturbed the south Italian cities. In 229–28 and again in 219 the Roman fleet operated in the Adriatic and established a Roman sphere of influence along the Dalmatian coast. This pacifying activity was generally approved by the Greeks proper, but the kings of Macedonia, just to the east, began to grow suspicious of the Romans.

Internally the Roman noble families continued to vie for public office, which they kept largely within their aristocratic circle. Only 11 consuls in the period 264–01 were "new men," that is, from families which had not supplied consuls in the past. Nonetheless there were signs of political activity by the small farmers which elevated, for instance, Flaminius to the consulship and then the censorship; in the latter office he built the great north road, the *via Flaminia,* and the Circus Flaminius in Rome. Flaminius may also have been responsible for the reorganization of the voting wards in the Centuriate assembly to minimize the power of urban wealth, an event which occurred at some point between the Punic wars. Alone among the senators, he supported the Claudian law of 218 which forbade senators and their sons to own ships of over 225 bushels' burden; whether by intent or not, this provision was to encourage the rise of a separate commercial and industrial class in the growing economic activity of Rome and Italy. As we meet it later, the class in question was to be called the equestrian order.

Carthage, meanwhile, licked its wounds and began to build up a strong position in Spain, which it had virtually lost during the strains of the First Punic war. This purposeful expansion, carried on by the general Hamilcar, then his son-in-law Hasdrubal, and finally his son Hannibal (245–183) from 221, seriously alarmed Massilia, which made representations to Rome. In 226 the Romans dictated an agreement with Carthage which set the limit of its northward expansion at the Ebro river, but the suspicious Romans continued to watch developments in Spain with concern. They contracted an alliance with the native state of Saguntum, though it lay south of the Ebro, and encouraged the Saguntines in anti-Carthaginian activities. The fiery young Hannibal refused to tolerate this interference and took Saguntum after siege in 219. The Romans had done nothing to aid their ally but now sent ambassadors to Carthage with the ultimatum to surrender Hannibal. On its refusal the ambassadors declared war in March 218.

Hannibal's Invasion of Italy. The Romans went into the Second Punic war (218–01) confident of victory. They had retained the naval mastery which they had gained in the previous war and launched two squadrons at once. The first was to take a Roman army under the consul P. Cornelius Scipio to Spain to pin down Hannibal; the second was to ferry an army under the other consul Ti. Sempronius Longus to Africa in order to conquer Carthage itself.

Unfortunately for the Romans, they moved too slowly — their enemy had plans of his own. Hannibal calculated that if he could invade Italy and defeat the Romans their subjects would revolt and so end Roman power. He was confident in his own powers of generalship and in the quality of his veteran army; he could secure a base among the disaffected Gauls of the Po valley; all that remained was to get from Spain to Italy. As early in the spring of 218 as the Pyrenees were open he marched into southern Gaul, dextrously made his way across the Rhône despite native opposition, and crossed the Alps into Italy in September, just after the first snows had fallen. Hannibal had had to march by land both because the Romans held the sea and because he brought with him a large force of cavalry and elephants; but by the late fall he stood among friendly Gauls in the Po valley with an army of 20,000 foot and 6000 horse (see Map 14).

While Scipio was at Massilia, he learned of the Carthaginian march, too late to stop Hannibal. The consul sent his army on to Spain, an important step later in preventing easy reinforcement to Hannibal, and returned to Italy. Sempronius abandoned his attack on Carthage and marched north to meet his colleague in the Po valley. In December 218, in battle in the mists on the Trebia river, the Romans lost two-thirds of their force in a Carthaginian ambush. The Po valley now had to be yielded to Hannibal.

The Roman people, much disturbed by the situation and by a host of unfavorable religious portents, rallied behind the popular hero Flaminius and elected him as one of the consuls for 217. The mission of the Roman generals this year was to hold the line of the Apennines against Hannibal; but the wily Carthaginian moved early across a minor pass west of the modern Florence. Although he lost his eyesight in one eye as a result of disease contracted in the marshes along the Arno river, Hannibal drove his men southward behind Flaminius, who hurried to catch up with his two legions. The result was another Carthaginian trap on the north shore of Lake Trasimene, from which none of the Romans (including their general) escaped. Hannibal released those prisoners who were from the Italian allies and moved south to Campania, awaiting in vain the expected revolt of the Roman subjects.

In their despair the Romans chose a dictator, the conservative senator Q. Fabius Maximus. Fabius sought the favor of the gods by ceremonies and a vow of two temples and took over the remaining consul's army. These troops he kept in the mountain edges of Campania and restored their confidence by harassing any small detachment sent out by Hannibal. While applying these "Fabian tactics," the dictator could count on the certainty that Hannibal would have to move out of Campania by late fall so as to secure winter quarters, for all its cities were fortified. Once Hannibal's cavalry was up in the hills, Fabius planned to strike.

One night the expected alarm came near the modern Cassino as a mass of lights was seen moving toward that exit. The Romans shifted hastily in that direction, only to discover at daybreak herds of cattle which had had torches tied to their horns. Hannibal meanwhile had slipped out by another pass to eastern Italy, where he wintered.

For the year 216 the Romans elected L. Aemilius Paullus and C. Terentius Varro as consuls. Rather than dividing their forces, they sent out an army of at least 60,000 under both consuls, with orders to meet and defeat Hannibal once for all. The consuls had first to train their troops, but by late summer moved down near Hannibal at Cannae, in northern Apulia. On August 2 the Romans arranged their army in compact mass on the south bank of the Aufidus river, in open terrain where no mists would occur. Hannibal, likewise eager for battle, ordered his army, of no more than 45,000 men, in a long line, with his superior cavalry on the flanks. When the battle began, his infantry center of half-civilized Spaniards and Gauls deliberately retreated under Hannibal's personal supervision so as to lure the Romans forward. His cavalry meanwhile won first on the left, then on the right flank. Thereupon his African infantry, farther out in the line, wheeled in, and his cavalry closed behind the close-packed Roman infantry, blinded by the dust of the battle; only about 10,000 Romans managed to break their way out of the trap. This double envelopment of a superior enemy was one of the greatest tactical masterpieces in all military history.

When the news came to Rome of the crushing defeat at Cannae, the Senate convened at once and ordered the wailing women of the city indoors. Slaves were drafted to protect the city, and sacred arms dedicated in the temples were taken down to equip this scratch force. Human sacrifice was ordered, a savage rite almost unknown in Roman religious practice; even mention of the word *pax* was forbidden. As the Greek historian Polybius observed, "the Romans are never more severe than in defeat."[1] All factional struggle was for the moment dropped, and the surviving consul Varro was formally thanked for not despairing of the Republic when he returned to Rome after having helped to lose its army.

Roman Strategy of Exhaustion. After the battle of Cannae Hannibal's basic strategy at last gained part of its objective, for a great deal of southern Italy revolted from Roman rule. Capua, the greatest city in Campania, joined the revolt, as did eventually Syracuse, the principal

[1] Polybius 27.8.8.

city of Sicily. The Gauls of the Po valley had already rebelled, and shortly after Cannae came the news that the Roman army of reconquest in the Po valley had been wiped out. The young king of Macedonia, Philip V, contracted an alliance with the victorious Hannibal and began the First Macedonian war (215–05) against Rome with the object of taking the Roman protectorate on the Dalmatian coast.

Yet most of the Roman subjects in central Italy remained loyal, and the Romans themselves fought on stubbornly. Never again did their commanders allow themselves to be drawn into open battle in Italy with Hannibal. After 216 one Roman army continually watched the great Carthaginian, while others set about the grim task of conquering the Italian rebels. Although Hannibal once drove to within sight of Rome, he could not hope to besiege it; and the Romans continued their investment of Capua until it fell in 211. Syracuse too, though protected by the ingenious military machines of Archimedes, had to surrender in 211. Philip V was kept busy in Greece itself by a Roman fleet, which secured some Greek allies by land, including the Aetolian league. In the year 212, the high point of Roman drafts, some 200,000 soldiers and 70,000 sailors — almost 10 per cent of the available population — were in service under 15 magistrates and promagistrates with *imperium*.

In Spain, meanwhile, the Roman army which had been sent out in 218 continued to put pressure on the Carthaginian domains and pinned down troops that would have been valuable to Hannibal. In 211 the two Roman commanders, both Scipios, were caught and killed; but the next year the son of one, P. Scipio (eventually called Africanus), was assigned as commander in Spain, though he was only 24 or 25. A sudden, brilliant dash in 209 far behind the Carthaginian lines gave him the hub of Carthaginian power, New Carthage (Cartagena), whereafter he began to gain the upper hand. Scipio Africanus failed, indeed, to stop Hasdrubal, the brother of Hannibal, from leading a relief army north across the Pyrenees in 207; but this force was caught and crushed in north Italy at the battle of the Metaurus river. Hannibal, now reduced to the toe of Italy, gained his first news of the defeat when the head of his dead brother was thrown into his camp by a Roman cavalryman.

Now, once again, the way was open for the Romans to return to their initial strategy of crushing Carthage by direct attack. Both the Roman treasury and the people, however, were themselves close to exhaustion.

Their most experienced general, M. Claudius Marcellus, who had taken Syracuse, had been surprised and killed in 208. At this critical juncture the young Scipio Africanus, who had returned to Rome from his Spanish victories, stepped forward and secured the command. His army consisted mainly of volunteers and was equipped by loans.

In 204 Scipio landed in Africa and after some success granted a tentative peace treaty to Carthage, one condition of which was that it evacuate Hannibal from Italy. So Hannibal left in 203 a land where he had never been defeated in battle, yet could not win in war. After his return the armistice was broken, and the decisive battle took place at Zama in 202. This time Scipio had the advantage in cavalry, for the Numidians had joined him; and, using Hannibalic tactics against Hannibal, won.

The peace was harsh. Carthage yielded its elephants and all but 10 of its warships, formally surrendered Spain to Rome, and promised to pay 10,000 talents over the next 50 years. In the further agreement not to wage war in Africa itself without Roman approval lay seeds for later troubles which eventually were to bring the utter destruction of Carthage.

In the end Hannibal had lost. His genius had not been able to overcome the firmness of Roman character and the basic loyalty of the Italian subjects of Rome, but the test he applied to these strengths was never again equaled. Modern observers may feel that the solid Roman people and empire had more to offer the Mediterranean world than did Carthage, which still practiced human sacrifice regularly and had only a weak, derivative culture; this war made it certain that western civilization was to be based on the Greco-Roman outlook.

Yet we need not accept the black picture which the Romans painted of Hannibal's "inhuman cruelty and lack of faith." [2] In his strategic and tactical genius, as in his ability to keep a motley army under discipline in an enemy land for 15 years, Hannibal has few military peers. After the end of the war he became the leader of Carthage and tried to make it a more democratic, unified state. Roman suspicion finally forced his exile, and Roman vindictiveness pursued him in the eastern Mediterranean until he finally committed suicide in 183 rather than fall into the hands of Roman envoys. At the same time, incidentally, his great oppo-

[2] Livy 21.4.9.

nent Scipio Africanus died in virtual exile as a result of internal Roman political rivalries.

Roman Entry into the East. After the Carthaginian peace of 201, Rome had a multitude of problems. Much of Italy had been devastated, and large parts needed reorganization after rebellion and reconquest. The Gauls of the Po valley were virtually independent; the Romans held only the coast of Spain, which was far from tranquil. Financially the Roman state was in weak condition, and the Roman people were exhausted from the long war. During its course the leaders had had to provide entertainments on an even larger scale, and religious hysteria had manifested the strain of the struggle. Nonetheless the Romans at once turned east. Within 13 years Rome had gained virtual mastery over the Hellenistic world.

Both the Roman entry into the east and the speed of its conquest are phenomenal events. The swiftness of the Roman advance can be explained on the grounds of the solidity of its governmental system and the great improvement in its military structure in the war with Hannibal, as contrasted to the growing weakness of the Hellenistic monarchies. In Greek eyes the Romans were still semibarbarians, but even the most cultured Greeks had to admit the raw force and determination of Rome. The involvement of Rome in Hellenistic politics is more surprising, for down to 200 B.C. Rome had had only the scantiest of political contacts with the east though its cultural connections had been growing.

To account for this step we must bear in mind the situation in Rome and in the east just before 200 B.C. The Romans themselves had become ever more militarized by the war they had just concluded. They were, moreover, deeply frightened by the narrow escape from Hannibal and were not in a mood to assess calmly the developments which were being reported from the east. In the Aegean Philip V (221–179), their erstwhile foe, was aggrandizing ruthlessly; farther east the young Seleucid King Antiochus III (223–187) was reviving his ancestral state. This latter monarch loomed up as a new Alexander, thanks to his reconquest of Asia Minor and his reassertion of Seleucid overlordship in Parthia and Bactria. To counter the expansion of these two rulers the other eastern states could no longer engage in the usual Hellenistic principle of balance of power, for Egypt was now in the hands of a boy king, Ptolemy V, who was crippled further by the increasing apathy and even hostility of its peasantry.

The Second Macedonian War (200–196 B.C.). The immediate cause of Roman intervention was a joint appeal in 201 by Rhodes, the major city-state in the east, and by King Attalus I of Pergamum, a small principality in northwestern Asia Minor. They themselves had declared war on Philip V in an effort to halt his conquest of the minor independent states in the Aegean, but had had little success. Since Antiochus III was occupied in wresting Syria and Palestine from the weak Egyptian grasp and was rumored to be in alliance with Philip V, Rhodes and Pergamum saw no alternative but to turn outside the Hellenistic state-system and to seek aid from the "rising clouds in the west," Rome.[3]

Neither Rhodes nor Pergamum was a true ally of Rome in the legal sense, but the Roman leaders looked on Philip with unfriendly eyes since the compromise peace which had ended the First Macedonian war in 205. The Greek ambassadors, skilled in oratory, thus convinced Rome both that Philip was a real threat if allowed to conquer Greece and that the Greeks would heartily support Roman liberation. The Senate was more easily persuaded than were the people, who initially refused to vote war, but in the summer of 200 war was officially declared (see Map 17).

To avoid the dangers of a draft, a largely volunteer army, which was poorly disciplined and poorly led, was sent to Greece. The Greeks, moreover, did not show as much enthusiasm as had been promised. For a time Philip held his own in a cautious strategy designed to weary the Romans, but in 198 the brilliant young T. Quinctius Flamininus (228–174) became consul and took over the Roman army. Fond of Greek culture and speaking Greek well himself, Flamininus cajoled or forced the Greek states into fuller support and met Philip's phalanx on the hillside of Cynoscephalae in 197. In this unexpected battle the Roman legionaries and veteran junior officers won the day. Philip had to make a peace in which he promised to stay out of Greece as well as pay a small indemnity of 1000 talents and yield all but five warships. He was, however, left in control in Macedonia to serve as a bar both against the barbarians

[3] Polybius 5.104.10.

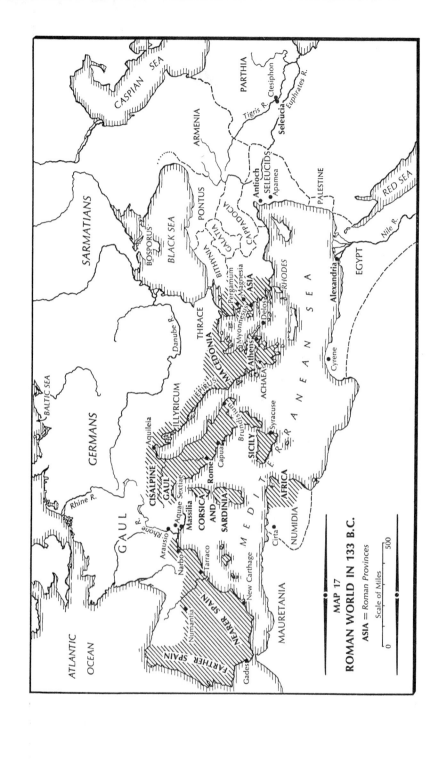

MAP 17

ROMAN WORLD IN 133 B.C.

ASIA = Roman Provinces

Scale of Miles

0   500

ATLANTIC OCEAN

BALTIC SEA

GERMANS

GAUL

Rhine R.

Rhône R.

Arausio

Narbo

Aquae Sextiae

Massilia

Aquileia

CISALPINE GAUL

Rome

Capua

CORSICA AND SARDINIA

Tarraco

New Carthage

Gades

Numantia

FARTHER SPAIN

NEARER SPAIN

MAURETANIA

Cirta

NUMIDIA

AFRICA

SICILY

Syracuse

Brundisium

ILLYRICUM

EPIRUS

MACEDONIA

ACHAEA

Athens

Delphi

Myonnesus

Magnesia

Pergamum

ASIA

Delos

RHODES

THRACE

BITHYNIA

PONTUS

GALATIA

CAPPADOCIA

ARMENIA

PARTHIA

Tigris R.

Euphrates R.

Ctesiphon

Seleucia

Antioch

SELEUCIDS

Apamea

PALESTINE

Cyrene

Alexandria

EGYPT

Nile R.

RED SEA

MEDITERRANEAN SEA

ADRIATIC SEA

BLACK SEA

BOSPORUS

SARMATIANS

CASPIAN SEA

Danube R.

of the Balkans and against any westward expansion by Antiochus III.

The Greek allies now discovered that the Roman Senate was the final arbiter and that it would not allow them all the rewards they wished. Establishment of boundaries in Greece took the efforts of Flamininus for two years, but eventually the Romans evacuated their forces and left Greece "free." Some of the Greeks shared a view which Livy put as follows, at the proclamation of Greek freedom before the Isthmian games:

> There was one people in the world which would fight for others' liberties at its own cost, to its own peril, and with its own toil . . . ready to cross the sea that there might be no unjust empire anywhere and that everywhere justice, right, and law might prevail.[4]

Others, however, were less content. All Greeks might resent the ruthless looting of Roman troops and the humiliation of being freed by virtual barbarians. The lower classes felt no gratitude to a Roman policy which favored the upper classes; these in turn wished to be entirely free to dominate their local areas. Immediately after the Romans withdrew, the tyrant Nabis of Sparta exploited the unrest of the lower classes and had to be quelled by a return visit of Flamininus, but worse was soon to come.

War with Antiochus III (192–88 B.C.). After the defeat of Philip, Antiochus III moved into the power vacuum left in western Asia Minor and even regained the bridgehead in European Thrace which his ancestors had held. The new king of Pergamum, Eumenes I, feared this encirclement and incited the Greek cities of Smyrna and Lampsacus to appeal for aid to Rome on the grounds that they too were descended from Trojan stock. The suspicious Romans virtually ordered Antiochus III to give up either Thrace or Asia Minor. In the usual fashion of Hellenistic diplomacy the Seleucid king felt himself free to retaliate by stirring up trouble in the Aetolian league and elsewhere in Greece against the Romans.

So sophisticated a policy was poorly received by the simple-minded Romans, and very shortly (192) Antiochus III found himself at war. This conflict the Romans treated far more seriously than they initially had viewed the hostilities with Philip V. After their army had driven

[4] Livy 33.33.5–7; tr. E. T. Sage.

Antiochus' small expeditionary force out of Greece by a battle at Thermopylae, it was put under the virtual command of Scipio Africanus for a full-scale invasion of Asia Minor; since Scipio had recently held the consulship, he could not be re-elected so soon, and his brother L. Cornelius Scipio (Asiaticus) was nominal commander.

The Roman army crossed by the Hellespont into Asia Minor; the Roman navy, with Rhodian and other aid, meanwhile defeated at Myonessus the Seleucid fleet under Hannibal, who had fled east in 195. Only one major battle by land was needed, at Magnesia in 189, to wreck Antiochus' field force.

In the ensuing peace of Apamea in 188 Antiochus yielded all but 10 of his warships and his elephants, paid an indemnity of 15,000 talents (the largest ever exacted by Rome), and relinquished all Asia Minor. The liberated territory was given partly to Pergamum, partly to Rhodes. Thenceforth no major state in the Mediterranean world stood in opposition to Roman domination; but to this point the Romans had annexed in the east only a few islands off the western coast of the Balkan peninsula.

Roman Policy (188–33 B.C.). As this last fact suggests, the Romans were reluctant to take over direct responsibility for the position that their armies had secured so swiftly. A strange mixture of philhellenic idealism, suspicion, unreasoning fears for their safety in Italy, and ignorance of the complicated problems of the Hellenistic world pulled the Romans in opposite directions.

A conservative wing of Roman opinion, led by the self-made M. Porcius Cato (234–149), wished to have as little as possible to do with the Hellenistic world, though these men were willing to see Rome rule the barbarian west. Another wing, in which stood Scipio Africanus, Flamininus, and Scipio Aemilianus (185–29), the adoptive grandson of Africanus, felt that Rome must supervise the Mediterranean world and should take the fruits of the more advanced culture of the east; yet even this group favored no more than a general Roman protectorate over the civilized world. The results were perhaps the worst possible both for the dependent states and peoples of the Roman world and for Rome itself, which moved in the era to 133 B.C. through the stages of toleration, irritation, and violent arrogance.

In the east the suspicious Romans hamstrung the Seleucid monarchy.

The Jews of Palestine, who rebelled under the Maccabees in 167 against a policy of Hellenization instituted by Antiochus IV, were supported by Rome; when this king invaded Egypt in 168 and appeared likely to conquer the decrepit Ptolemaic state, he was halted by a Roman ultimatum. Internal dissensions over the succession to the throne after his death continued to weaken the Seleucid power. The Parthians, a nomad people who had entered Iran in the early third century, had asserted their independence in 247 but expanded only as the Seleucids declined. In 141 the Parthians took Mesopotamia, and thenceforth ruled the Near East from the borders of Syria to India.

The Third Macedonian war (171–67) was occasioned by the ambitions of Philip's son Perseus (179–67) and by an appeal to Rome by Eumenes of Pergamum. It resulted in the abolition of the Macedonian monarchy and the division of Macedonia into four republics; but both Pergamum and Rhodes had not shown the loyalty that Rome expected during this war and thenceforth lay under Roman suspicion. The kings of Pergamum dared do nothing without Roman consent, and Rhodes suffered financially from the Roman erection of Delos as a free port for the booming trade between east and west.

Even yet Rome avoided direct responsibilities, but finally renewed trouble in Macedonia in 149–48 forced the creation of the Roman province of Macedonia. Greece itself chafed ever more under the arbitrary, haphazard, indirect Roman control; finally the Achaean league led a revolt of desperation. The league was thereupon dissolved, and the Roman consul L. Mummius destroyed Corinth (146) as an object lesson. Greece remained technically independent but was supervised by the praetor in Macedonia.

The west was no more tranquil. The Sardinians rose in revolt once, and repeated rebellions broke out in Spain, which often took the form of guerrilla opposition. The difficulties in drafting troops to meet the nasty wars in Spain from 154 onward were to have an important effect in paving the way for the reforms of Tiberius Gracchus. Roman suspicion of the reviving prosperity of Carthage led to the Third Punic war (149–46), in which the Romans determined to wipe out Carthage. Although its citizens bitterly withstood the Roman siege, conducted by Scipio Aemilianus, their city was taken and destroyed in 146, and salt was symbolically sown on its site. Thenceforth Rome had six provinces:

Sicily; Sardinia (with Corsica); two provinces in Spain named Nearer and Farther, as measured from Rome; Macedonia; and Africa. A full solution to the problems of organizing the Roman empire, however, was to take another bitter century in which the Mediterranean world came close to chaos.

HELLENISTIC CULTURE IN ROME

Renewed Links to Greek Civilization. From its earliest days Rome had been deeply affected by Greek culture, either directly or via Etruscan intermediaries. In the early fifth century this tie had weakened in central Italy. The Romans lived within a narrow world, culturally speaking, during the period in which they built up their own system of government and conquered Italy. Rome thus had no direct contact with the great days of classic Greek culture; its ties were resumed only from the early third century onward. By this time Greek civilization had passed into its Hellenistic phase, more superficial but far more widely attractive. While the Romans needed no lessons in political or military skill from the east, they showed ever greater interest in its culture.

Roman armies and generals brought back much of the physical achievement of this world from southern Italy, Sicily, and the Hellenistic east. Marcellus, the conqueror of Syracuse, returned with cargoes of statues which he erected in public places to embellish Rome; Aemilius Paullus, who defeated Perseus, brought the Macedonian state library to Rome; Mummius sacked Corinth before destroying it.

Men, too, came in tremendous numbers; the Roman conquest of Epirus alone netted 150,000 slaves in 167. Many of these went to man Roman farms and ranches, but some men who were enslaved were cultured, like the comedian Terence (P. Terentius Afer, *c.* 195–59). Polybius and other Greek leaders were brought in 167 to Rome as hostages. Others, including the philosophic leaders of Athens in 155, came as ambassadors or were drawn by the increasing wealth and power of the new Mediterranean capital. The Romans themselves, who had no developed culture of their own, proved amazingly receptive to many aspects of Hellenistic civilization.

Much of what they took was on the level of entertainment or physical

A. Dionysus in his ship, black-figure by Exekias (Antikensammlungen 2044, Munich). See pp. 242, 265n.
B. Leagros on his horse, red-figure by Euphronius (Antikensammlungen 2620/1, Munich). See pp. 222, 265n, 313.

PLATE XVII   ATHENIAN POTTERY

A. "Turtle" from Aegina. See pp. 221n, 261. B. Attic "owl". See pp. 254n, 315.

C. Arethusa from Syracuse. See p. 331n.

D. Antimachus of Bactria. See pp. 404, 412, 421n.

PLATE XVIII   GREEK COINS

PLATE XIX   FOURTH-CENTURY GREECE

Hermes and the infant Dionysus, from temple of Hera at Olympia (Olympia Museum). See p. 390n.

PLATE XX HELLENISTIC AGE

Dying Gaul and his wife, Roman copy of Pergamene school (Terme Museum, Rome).
See pp. 422n, 509.

PLATE XXI   THE ETRUSCANS

Apollo, terra cotta statue from Veii (Villa Giulia Museum, Rome). See pp. 264n, 450n, 462n.

PLATE XXII   THE ETRUSCANS

Player on the double pipes, painting from Tomb of the Leopards, Tarquinia. See p. 450.

PLATE XXIII   ROMAN ARISTOCRACY
"Brutus," a Roman noble of the Republic (Conservatori Museum, Rome). See pp.
450n, 473n, 509n.

PLATE XXIV   ROMAN CITIZENRY

"Cato and Porcia," tombstone busts probably of the Late Republic (Vatican Museum, Rome). See pp. 549n, 568n.

PLATE XXV   AUGUSTAN AGE

The emperor Augustus, from Prima Porta (Vatican Museum, Rome). See pp. 336n, 568n.

PLATE XXVI

Pont du Gard, an Augustan aqueduct near Nîmes in southern France. See pp. 564, 568n.

PLATE XXVII   IMPERIAL ROME

Interior of the Pantheon, from G. B. Piranesi (1720-78), *Vedute di Roma*. See p. 597n.

PLATE XXVIII

Philosopher sarcophagus, in the Lateran Museum, Rome. See p. 662n.

PLATE XXIX   EAST AND WEST
A Buddha head of Gandhara type (Victoria and Albert Museum, London). See p. 634n

PLATE XXX   SASSANIAN PERSIA

Sassanian silver dish of the fourth century (Freer Gallery of Art, Washington). See p. 652n.

PLATE XXXI

The emperor Valentinian (?), bronze statue in Barletta. See pp. 662n, 686n.

PLATE XXXII   LATER ROMAN EMPIRE
The empress Theodora, mosaic in San Vitale, Ravenna. See pp. 662n, 703n.

pleasure. The first barber came from Sicily to a Latin town in 300; professional cooks soon made their appearance in Rome. Aristocrats began to build more luxurious mansions, equipped with the best of Hellenistic furniture and comforts; to improve their taste in one respect the poet Q. Ennius (239-169) composed a manual *On the Art of Pleasant Eating*.

For the masses, public entertainments grew in numbers. During the early third century the Etruscan custom of giving gladiatorial games was introduced at noble funerals. At the conclusion of the First Punic war another means of pleasing the public appeared in the state production of comedies at religious festivals; these were adapted from the New Comedy of Menander and other Greek authors. L. Livius Andronicus (*c.* 284-04) was the first to do so; then came T. Maccius Plautus (*c.* 254-184) in the Second Punic war, and Terence in the second century. Beside comedies appeared tragedies, partly on Greek models but also on Roman themes; Cn. Naevius (*c.* 270-199) and M. Pacuvius (*c.* 220-*c.* 130) were the leaders in this field.

The first major poets in Latin had also the function of celebrating the great deeds of Rome's nobles and the glories of Rome's past. Naevius wrote an epic on the First Punic war; Ennius, the greatest early poet, composed the *Annales* as a summation of Roman history to 172. Just before the close of the third century Q. Fabius Pictor wrote the first prose history of Rome, but in Greek. In the second century Cato the Censor produced a history in Latin (the *Origines*), written in large letters for the benefit of his son. In this history, incidentally, Cato refused to support the growing individualism of his day by naming any figures in Roman history save the elephant which had carried Hannibal across the Arno marshes and so had done more than any elephant could rightfully be expected to do.

Hellenistic educational principles also came to Rome. To replace the archaic Twelve Tables, the earlier primer, Livius Andronicus translated the *Odyssey* into Latin; and Greek rhetoricians and grammarians began to be sought by noble families as tutors for their sons. Rhetoric thus was a principal vehicle by which Greek ideas spread in Rome. Grammarians ameliorated the roughness and the poverty in vocabulary of the Latin language and improved its fundamental qualities of conciseness, sonority, and logical directness. By 133 Latin had become a literary tongue, and its aristocratic speakers at least were at home in the artistic, literary, and intellectual heritage of the Hellenistic world.

Limits on Roman Borrowing. During the first waves of Hellenistic influence through the third and second centuries the Romans appear almost entirely as borrowers from the riches of the east. Yet it would be incorrect to infer that Roman culture was thenceforth simply a branch of Hellenistic civilization, though this inference is often made by modern scholars. In reality ideas and motifs underwent a subtle, but significant change in their sea passage from east to west.

Down to the late second century Roman independence showed itself primarily in the refusal of the Romans to surrender completely to alien ways. The hardheaded Roman citizenry was quite willing to take over what it deemed useful, but it showed little interest in the abstract or theoretical achievements of Hellenistic civilization. In science the Romans were attracted principally by the practical manuals on agricultural management, which led Cato to produce the first surviving monument of Latin prose, *de agri cultura.* Cato bitterly opposed the use of Greek doctors and stood generally against the introduction of Hellenistic culture into daily life. As he wrote his son,

> Concerning those Greeks, son Marcus, I will speak to you in the proper place. I will show you the results of my own experience at Athens: that it is a good idea to dip into their literature but not to learn it thoroughly. I shall convince you that they are a most iniquitous and intractable people, and you may take my word as the word of a prophet: whenever that nation shall bestow its literature upon us, it will corrupt everything.[5]

Serving as censor in 184, Cato tried to cut down the scale of luxury in Rome, even going so far as to rip out water mains laid into private houses; earlier he had struggled against the growing emancipation of women.

Cato probably helped to secure the expulsion of two Epicurean thinkers in 173 and certainly tried to expel the Academic leader Carneades in

[5] Pliny, *Natural History* 29.1.14; tr. Lewis and Reinhold, *Roman Civilization,* I, 491.

155; for this philosophic skeptic shocked Rome by arguing on one day that justice was a fundamental principle in the world and then on the next exploding this view. One would hesitate to call Cato a fraud, but certainly he was more a creature of his age than he admitted — in fact, he was as thoroughgoing an individualist as his opponents. He learned Greek himself, and many of his famous aphorisms were filched from the Greek.

Other aristocrats were sufficiently self-conscious and open-minded to be ready to accept Greek ethical thinking as a basis for their lives. The Stoics, in particular, had a view of the universe as divinely ordered which appealed to the Romans especially after the great second-century Stoic Panaetius (c. 185–09) reformed his school's doctrines on the inevitability of a world conflagration and the hopeless imperfection of all men save the pitiless and perfect Wise Man. Stoic ethical and political theory, as taught by Panaetius at Rome, accorded well with the Roman sense of duty, though it also reinforced the growing individualism of the aristocrats. The more abstract ideas of Stoic logical and physical theory, however, gained little attention. In assessing the increasing polish of Roman aristocrats we must always remember that the cultured friend of Panaetius, Polybius and Terence, the high-born Scipio Aemilianus, was also the leader of the Roman army in the ruthless destruction of Carthage.

In the arts and architecture too little survives for us to see clearly the process of Roman adaptation, though the remains of Pompeii suggest that this minor Italian town was shifting from Greek to Roman styles by the end of the second century; by this date Roman builders were using travertine limestone and also concrete, both of which were to permit bolder experiments in architecture. In literature, however, the course of events is clearer. Plautus and Terence both adapted Greek plots for Roman production, the former in more slapstick manner, the latter in more sophisticated delineation of character; yet their plays have an undoubted Roman spirit. They wrote, moreover, in Latin — of all peoples with whom the Greeks came into contact the Romans were the only ones to create an independent literary speech.

Before the end of the second century Roman authors and, increasingly, Roman thinkers and artists were to begin to show the fruits of the entry of Hellenistic civilization into Rome. The product was a synthesis of

Greek forms and techniques and Roman spirit into what must be termed a Greco-Roman culture, or perhaps better, a general Mediterranean upper-class culture. The full fruits of this synthesis were to be attained only after the Romans and their subjects had both come to accept the responsibilities and the yoke of empire. That acceptance required a terrific upheaval and reorganization covering a full century and a half.

BIBLIOGRAPHY

Sources. Once Rome moved into the eastern Mediterranean, the volume of sources increased greatly. The historian Polybius came to Rome as a hostage during the years 167–51 and bent his efforts toward explaining to his fellow Greeks the reasons by which "the Romans in less than fifty-three years have succeeded in subjecting nearly the whole inhabited world to their sole government — a thing unique in history." [6] To do so, he sketched the course of the First Punic war, but began his full discussion in 220–16 B.C. Polybius was perhaps the most scrupulous of all ancient historians and ruthlessly attacked the errors of other historians; as an Achaean statesman and friend of Scipio Aemilianus he had an unparalleled opportunity to observe the rise of Rome. Unfortunately we have only the first 5 books of his work complete, with fragments of the other 35. From Book Six there survives especially his famous, though not accurate, description of the Roman constitution as one of checks and balances. This concept greatly influenced the political theorist Montesquieu and, through him, the leaders of the American Revolution. For translation, see Loeb Classical Library; F. W. Walbank, *Historical Commentary on Polybius,* Vols. I–III (Oxford: Oxford University Press, 1957–79), and his more general study, *Polybius* (Berkeley: University of California Press, 1972).

From Livy's history we have Books 21–45 covering 218–167 B.C. (Loeb Classical Library). Often Livy drew directly from Polybius, but he preserved the annalistic tradition at many points. Cornelius Nepos (Loeb Classical Library) wrote lives of Hamilcar and Hannibal; Plutarch, of Fabius Maximus, Aemilius Paullus, Marcellus, Flamininus, and Cato

---

[6] Polybius 1.1.5.

the Censor. Plutarch's life of Cato throws in a vivid light the beliefs of the main conservative leader which are visible also in fragments of his history and in his manual *de agri cultura* (E. Brehaut, *Cato the Censor on Farming* [New York: Columbia University Press, 1933]). Further information is available in the works of Appian and Dio Cassius noted in later Bibliographies.

Most of the early Latin poets survive only in fragments, which are fairly extensive for Ennius (see *Remains of Old Latin,* Loeb Classical Library). There remain, however, 21 plays of Plautus and 6 of Terence, available in Loeb Classical Library and various paperback editions. These have little contemporary political reference, for the Roman governing circles did not favor political discussion on the stage.

Further Reading. The duel with Carthage is described by T. A. Dorey and D. R. Dudley, *Rome against Carthage* (New York: Doubleday, 1972), and J. F. Lazenby, *Hannibal's War* (Warminster: Aris & Phillips, 1978). Good lives of Hannibal are those of Gavin de Beer (New York: Viking, 1969), and Harold Lamb (New York: Pinnacle, 1976); for his opponent see B. H. Liddell Hart, *A Greater than Napoleon: Scipio Africanus* (Boston: Little Brown, 1927), and H. H. Scullard, *Scipio Africanus* (Ithaca: Cornell University Press, 1970). The latter has also written a study of internal factions in *Roman Politics, 220–150* B.C. (Oxford: Oxford University Press, 1973). A. E. Astin has lives of Scipio Aemilianus (Oxford: Oxford University Press, 1967), and Cato the Censor (Oxford: Oxford University Press, 1978). P. A. Brunt, *Italian Manpower 225* B.C.–A.D. *14* (Oxford: Clarendon, 1971), is thorough.

For the Roman conquest of the eastern Mediterranean see the works on Hellenistic political history in Bibliography, Chapter 19, and F. W. Walbank, *Philip V of Macedon* (London: J. Grant, 1967); W. V. Harris, *War and Imperialism in Republican Rome 327–70* B.C. (Oxford: Clarendon, 1979), argues for deliberate expansion.

The Roman comedians are treated by W. Beare, *Roman Stage* (Totowa, N.J.: Rowman, 1977); G. E. Duckworth, *Nature of Roman Comedy* (Princeton: Princeton University Press, 1972); and G. Norwood, *Plautus and Terence* (New York: Cooper Square). See also H. I. Marrou, *History of Education in Antiquity* (New York: Mentor, 1964), on the reception of Hellenistic culture in Rome.

VIII

THE CONSOLIDATION
OF ROMAN RULE

24

DECLINE OF THE ROMAN REPUBLIC

The year 133 B.C. marks a visible turning point in Mediterranean history. During the preceding era, 264-133, Rome conquered the uncivilized western shores and the cultured east, but neither master nor subjects had made a full adjustment to the complexities of this unification. In growing powerful, the Roman aristocracy became arrogant and sought to cloak its rude simplicity in the elegant dress of Hellenistic civilization. Much greater changes, however, were to be required by the social, economic, and intellectual effects of empire.

During the century and a half from 133 B.C. to A.D. 14 the Mediterranean world groaned under the most widespread wars it ever suffered in antiquity. Subjects desperately sought to throw off the rule of their exploiters; Roman generals ruthlessly expanded the hegemony of Rome both for their own honor and profit and for the benefit of allied financial interests. At home the Roman Republic tottered as a political system and then fell.

Although the storm clouds mounted ever higher on the horizon, a student of the period should always remember that the Romans continued to display tremendous vitality. Amid civil war and chaos at home they proceeded to annex more territory than ever before in their history; and the synthesis of Greco-Roman culture produced the remarkable heights of Ciceronian and Augustan literature and art. In sum, the Mediterranean was being unified both politically and culturally, even though the republican system of government at Rome was no longer adequate. By the death of Augustus in A.D. 14 a new style of political organization under the rule of one man had been consolidated.

So complicated is the history of the last century of the Roman Republic that in this chapter we must first assess at some length the situation in 133 together with the sources of difficulties. Only on this basis can one inspect the unfolding of troubles. First come the idealistic reforms of the Gracchi brothers and then the long-term rivalry of Marius and Sulla. With the death of Sulla in 78 there opens a new phase of the decline of the Roman Republic.

THE ROMAN WORLD IN 133 B.C.

Economic and Social Changes. By the second century B.C. Italy was becoming the economic focus of an interlocked Mediterranean world. Italian traders and capitalists gained a strong place in Aegean economic life and were active on the trade routes running east from Italy to Alexandria and to Syria, the latter largely via the free port of Delos. From the east came slaves and manufactured luxuries such as glass, spices, jewels, and art objects; a physical testimony to the bulk and width of eastern exports exists in the remains of Rhodian jars, used to carry wine and grain, which have been found in great quantities all over the Mediterranean and into Europe as far as the Carpathian mountains. In return Italy sent east olive oil and wine of its own but covered much of its purchases with the tribute of empire. To the more backward west shippers carried metal wares, textiles, and more wine and oil, as attested by the recent underwater discoveries of sunken ships off the coasts of Italy and France.

In reflection of this economic development the towns of Italy grew in size and economic specialization. One example, which can still be studied in some detail, is the growth of Pompeii; but the greatest expansion occurred in the imperial capital itself. Provincials poured into Rome, both slaves and those in search of wealth; rural citizens, too, were drawn from the farms, though in lesser numbers. During the second century two new aqueducts more than doubled the water supply of Rome, and one of Cato's most lasting achievements as censor in 184 was a thorough reconstruction of its sewer system. While noble homes rose on the Palatine hill and other favored locations and public buildings of some pretensions appeared in the Forum, slums multiplied on the Aventine and in the lower parts of the city. Although most of this teeming population worked in shops, in small factories, and in the homes of the nobles, its economic position was always precarious; in particular the food supply of so many thousands was a serious problem. Public festivals to give the masses some diversion had multiplied from only one in 264 to six in 133, but the maintenance of order was ill-secured by the small forces at the command of the aediles.

Equally great changes were occurring in much of the Italian countryside. Scientific agriculture on Hellenistic models had begun to appear before the Second Punic war and expanded markedly in the second century. The growing urban centers gave an outlet for cash crops. Public land increased greatly as a result of the confiscations in areas which fell away to Hannibal, and was largely rented by senatorial aristocrats or wealthy leaders of the Italian towns; private land also tended to come into the hands of these elements through ill-disguised force, foreclosure of loans, and the long-term draft of peasants into the armies with which Rome conquered its empire. Many men moved into the Po valley or spread out widely in south Gaul, Spain, and Africa. In place of the free peasants the sheep ranches of Apulia and the specialized farms of Campania and Latium relied increasingly on slaves, who were available cheaply and in numbers as another fruit of Rome's wars. Never in ancient history did agricultural slavery assume such proportions as in Italy of the Late Republic.

From the economic point of view these conjoined changes in agriculture, industry, and trade must be termed progress, for Italy produced more varied wares and foods in greater quantities than ever before; in the next century Varro could describe it as one vast orchard. It also advanced toward a true money economy. Coinage had begun very late in Rome, just before the First Punic war, and remained limited until almost the end of the third century. During the strains of the Second Punic war the silver *denarius,* equalling 10 *asses* of bronze, was introduced; and in the second century Roman coinage became a standard medium of exchange in the Mediterranean world.

The social effects of these changes, however, were disastrous. Much of the countryside was occupied only by gangs of slaves, who were locked

TABLE 6
Roman Republic 509—44 B.C.

B.C.	Internal	External	Cultural	Greek World
500	ROMAN REPUBLIC Patricians vs. plebeians	WARS IN ITALY Alliance with Latin league		CLASSICAL (see Table 5)
	Centuriate and Tribal assemblies	Wars with Aequi, Volsci, Etruscans	Loss of links to Greek world	Peloponnesian war
450	Twelve Tables			
400		Destruction of Veii Gallic invasion		Philip of Macedonia
	Licinian—Sextian reforms			
350		Conquest of Central Italy War with Latin league Samnite wars begin		Alexander the Great HELLENISTIC AGE Political division: Ptolemies, Seleucids, Antigonids
300	Ogulnian law Hortensian law Development of senatorial aristocracy	Sentinum		Writers: *Menander, Callimachus, Eratosthenes, Apollonius Rhodius, Herodas, Theocritus*
		War with *Pyrrhus* OVERSEAS WARS First Punic war	*Livius Andronicus*	Philosophers: *Epicurus, Zeno, Cleanthes, Chrysippus, Pyrrhon*
250		Acquisition of Sardinia–Corsica Adriatic sphere War in Po valley	Hellenistic education introduced	

	Internal affairs	Wars	Literature / Law	Science & Philosophy (East)
200	C. Flaminius Centuriate assembly reorganized Claudian law	Second Punic war Second Macedonian war	Q. Fabius Pictor Plautus, Naevius	Scientists: Theophrastus, Strato, Herophilus, Erasistratus, Euclid, Archimedes, Aristarchus, Eratosthenes
	Conflict of "isolationists" and "internationalists"	War with Antiochus Third Macedonian war	Ennius, Cato, Pacuvius	Revolt of Maccabees Writer: Polybius
150		Revolts in Spain Annexation of Macedonia	Aebutian law: formulary system	Philosophers: Carneades, Panaetius Scientist: Hipparchus
	Ti. Gracchus C. Gracchus Marius: new army	Third Punic war	Terence, Lucilius	Parthian conquest of Mesopotamia
100	Italian revolt Civil War Sulla dictator Pompey—Crassus cos.	Jugurthine war Cimbri–Teutones Mithridatic war Sertorius' revolt	Ius civile (Scaevola)	
50	Cicero cos. Civil War Dictatorship of Caesar	Pompey in east Caesar in Gaul	Lucretius, Catullus, Cicero, Sallust, Caesar, Varro	Posidonius

into prisons at night and were exploited without mercy until they died. In 133 a great slave revolt was still smoldering in Sicily, and worse outbreaks occurred in Italy itself as the political structure of the Republic deteriorated. The backbone of the Roman military system had been the land-owning peasant, but from the recrudescence of Spanish revolts in 154 onward the draft system was ever less successful in filling the ranks of the Roman armies which fought in Spain, Africa, and the east. One of the consuls of the year 151 and those of 138, indeed, were thrown into jail by the tribunes in contentions over the draft.

Nor was the city of Rome in better shape as a result of its growth in population. Some of the inhabitants of Rome were richer than ever before and displayed their wealth in crude ostentation; by law the aristocrats now were even marked off by a specially reserved section at the theaters. The poor, however, could hope for no more than unceremonious burial in the great pits of the Esquiline hill after a brief and bitter life, and were increasingly discontent.

One notable sign of trouble was the growth of religious emotionalism, which the Senate desperately tried to curtail. In 186 it directed a great inquisition into the worship of Bacchus or Dionysus by slaves and poor free men, on the grounds that it was a source of murders, vice, and revolutionary unrest; a senatorial decree, while not banning the worship entirely, ordained: "Let no one be minded to perform ceremonies in secret . . . [or] in a group larger than five men and women together." [1] Here, as in the expulsion of astrologers and Jews in 139 and of worshipers of Isis at later dates, was established a religious policy of restraining alien cults which could upset the multitude; much later this policy was to be applied to the Christians.

By 133, accordingly, both aristocrats and the erstwhile simple peasantry were changing in character; and in those changes the foundations of the republican system were dissolving.

Roman Culture and Law. The Roman upper classes, as we noticed in the preceding chapter, turned ever more toward Hellenistic civilization. So great a figure as Scipio Aemilianus was a truly cultured gentleman, but many of his peers took from the east mainly a veneer, particu-

[1] *Corpus Inscriptionum Latinarum,* I, No. 581; tr. Lewis and Reinhold, *Roman Civilization,* I, pp. 472-3.

larly of physical pleasures and of philosophic justification for their growing individualistic self-assertion.

From the late second century onward, nonetheless, Roman borrowings led to more sophisticated cultural expression and even to original achievements. C. Lucilius (*c.* 180–102) was the founder of satire, the one literary form that the Romans created essentially on their own (though with some Hellenistic suggestions). Both the greater self-consciousness of the Romans and the controversies of the Gracchan age produced an intensified interest in the Roman past; the pontiffs' records (*annales maximi*) were published, and several annalists wrote more extended and rhetorical histories than that of Cato's *Origines*. In architecture the technical skill and inventiveness of Roman engineers were beginning to display themselves, but in sculpture we have no certain busts of Roman leaders until the first century B.C.[2] Copies of Hellenistic masterpieces however, especially from the emotional Pergamene school, became ever more popular in Rome (see Plate XX).

Above all, Roman private or civil law was now developing on more systematic and thoughtful lines, partly through the stimulation of Hellenistic thought, partly because the needs of empire could no longer be met by the Twelve Tables even as commented upon by the pontiffs and other aristocratic jurisconsults. From about 200 B.C. there begins the "classical" period of Roman law. By the Aebutian law of the mid-second century the praetors were essentially set free of the Twelve Tables and accepted for each case coming before them a "formula." This contained the nub of the legal issues involved and defined the penalty to be assessed by the senatorial *iudex* who heard the evidence in the case and pronounced judgment; although the plaintiff drew up the formula (as amended by the defendant), he had to turn for its preparation to a specialized jurisconsult. The Praetor's Edict, issued anew each year, was a steadily growing body of these formulas.

Beside the praetors stood the other skilled aristocrats who gave "responses" or advice on specific points at issue to suitors, advised governors

[2] The bust illustrated on Plate XXIII is traditionally named "Brutus," that is, the founder of the Roman Republic; dated by art historians all the way from the fourth to the first century B.C., it is probably a third-century product. While Etruscan and Hellenistic elements have been detected in the head, the strength of character and veristic quality (though in idealized form) seem surely Roman.

and praetors, and developed an ever more professional body of legal commentary; the chief work in this field was the *Ius civile* of Q. Mucius Scaevola of the early first century B.C., the last pontiff to be a master of the law. In this evolution of jurist-made law the theories of Greek philosophy had little role, but the training of aristocrats in Greek dialectic had very extensive effect in sharpening their classifications and comprehension of fundamental principles. The trial-lawyers, such as Cicero, formed a quite separate group, who developed their rhetorical skill on Greek models. Here one finds some employment of abstract concepts of law; but the real founders of the Roman law, the jurisconsults, kept their eye always on practical cases and problems and much preferred to avoid even the drafting of statutes.

The Hellenistic East. While Hellenistic civilization struck root in Italy and spurred native development, it was in a sad state of decline in its homeland. After the days of Polybius and Panaetius, only one major Greek thinker appeared in the first century B.C., the Stoic Posidonius (*c.* 135–*c.* 51 B.C) of Apamea, who became a Rhodian citizen. This decline was in part a reflection of the economic and political decay of the Hellenistic world, which permitted the rise of Parthia, of the Jewish state in Palestine, and of other principalities. A more fundamental reason, however, was the weakening position of the Greek and Hellenized upper classes of the cities in the eastern Mediterranean. In 133 these leading elements were still uncertain whether to accept Roman rule and to hope that the Romans would in turn support their local domination or to revolt and seek independence in anger at the arrogance and exploitation they suffered. This uncertainty was to produce many minor explosions and finally a great outbreak in 88.

Political Discords. The tremendous variety of social, economic, and intellectual strains in the Mediterranean world goes far to explain why the last century of the Republic was to be one of the most confused and turbulent of all ancient history. As is usually the case, the stresses manifested themselves largely on the political level; and unfortunately the machinery of Roman government was ill-prepared to stand the strains.

Outside the area directly held by Roman citizens, the Republic provided poor administration and worse military protection. Much of the Mediterranean world was governed by client states. These were hamstrung by the negative Roman policy of weakening any political threat and suffered from the operations by Roman moneylenders and capitalists, largely of the equestrian order.

Two of the greatest cities of the Mediterranean, Carthage and Corinth, had been wiped out in 146 as a token of Roman arrogance and impatience with opposition, yet the Romans refused to bear full responsibility even for their provinces. To these came each year a new praetor and quaestor, attended by a fairly large suite of legates and junior assistants. The attention of these officials was directed in large part toward future political careers in Rome itself, though most governors seem to have taken their responsibilities seriously. There were, however, enough exceptions bent on making as much money as possible to require the creation in 149 of a standing senatorial court to try cases of extortion. The Romans now maintained standing armies in some troubled areas, but these forces were too weak to meet major threats. On the sea Roman policy was to disarm all possible foes in the hope that Rome itself would not need to maintain a navy, a policy which opened the way for pirates. In response to this weak government and exploitation, revolt after revolt broke out in Spain, and many other parts of the Mediterranean world were turning to sullen hatred of their arrogant masters.

The Italian allies held a privileged position inasmuch as they were subject only to the Senate in accordance with their ancient treaties, and the upper classes of the burgeoning towns benefited markedly from their financial and commercial opportunities. The Italians were becoming increasingly Romanized, as in the use of Latin; yet they too were discontent. Their military contingents were not always treated fairly in the distribution of booty and land, particularly in the major colonies settled in the Po valley; and the Romans grew ever more haughty and indifferent to local autonomy. Eventually this dissatisfaction was so exacerbated by the influences of internal Roman politics that much of Italy revolted in 90 B.C.

The Roman Aristocracy. Within the dominant circle of the Roman citizenry itself political problems reflected the social and economic changes noted above among commoners and aristocrats alike. Since the Second Punic war the control of the aristocrats over the government had been less challenged than it had been in the third century; but the governing group grew ever more exclusive politically. Twenty-six clans furnished three-quarters of the consuls between 234–134. Beside the senatorial order, nonetheless, was emerging a layer of important families grouped generally as the equestrian order.

Economically the interests of senators and equestrians ran parallel in their attention to capitalistic agriculture and moneylending, which the senators conducted through agents; but the equestrians were at once more directly concerned with state contracts and the profits of empire and also were virtually barred from public office. If the equestrians should combine with the many voters from rural tribes who now lived in Rome, senatorial control of the assemblies might well be shaken, especially after the introduction of the secret ballot by two laws in 139 and 137.

The aristocratic families themselves contended as fiercely as ever for public office and fell into factions of cliques. Some nobles sought earnestly to maintain the inherited system of government and life; others tended to disregard the public good for their own personal advancement; but in either case the pressure was strong against thoroughgoing reforms to meet the problems of empire. A friend of Scipio Aemilianus, C. Laelius (consul in 140), made some proposals for redistribution of state lands but hastily desisted when he measured the opposition. But Scipio himself, as censor, was said to have prayed that the gods "preserve" the Roman state, rather than using the conventional word "increase," and such troubles as the imprisonment of the consuls over the draft in 138 gave weight to his prayer.

THE GRACCHI BROTHERS

Tiberius Gracchus (133 b.c.). The open outbreak of dissensions coincided with the appearance of a truly idealistic reformer, sprung from the governing class. Tiberius Sempronius Gracchus (163–33) was of the bluest blood. His father had been twice consul and once censor; his mother Cornelia was the daughter of the great Scipio Africanus; his sister was married to Scipio Aemilianus; his own father-in-law was Appius Claudius, a leading politician and head of a famous clan. As Tiberius traveled through the countryside and served in Spain, he became emotionally aware of the problems of the common Roman citizens. Since he interpreted the fundamental cause as being the decline of the free peasantry, which furnished the Roman armies, he reached the simple solution of dividing state lands among the landless. Elected tribune in 133, Tiberius proposed a law which allowed the present renters or holders of state lands to keep up to a maximum of 1000 *jugera* (about 600 acres) and provided indemnification for their improvements; all excess land was to be reclaimed by the state and given to the poor in small plots.

Tiberius was counseled by two Greek thinkers, Blossius and Diophanes; but his ideas probably were more shaped by the Claudian faction, which sought electoral profit for itself. His land bill was written largely by his father-in-law Appius Claudius, P. Licinius Crassus Mucianus (soon to be *pontifex maximus*), and P. Mucius Scaevola (the greatest jurist of the period and one of the consuls for 133). Many other aristocrats, however, were bitterly opposed to the bill and secured its veto by Tiberius' fellow tribune, M. Octavius. Whereas a conservative man would have stopped at this point, Tiberius felt deeply the needs of the people and turned to it to vote Octavius out of office, a completely unconstitutional step. The people so voted, and the land bill was passed.

A commission consisting of Tiberius, his brother Gaius, and Appius Claudius started to reclaim public lands but found itself without funds, due to the Senate's refusal to veto an adequate appropriation; Tiberius thereupon secured from the people a declaration that the treasures of Pergamum, which had just been willed to Rome by the last king, be devoted to the commission's needs. This too was contrary to traditional practice by which the Senate controlled finances, and when Tiberius took the bold step of standing for re-election as tribune a riot broke out. The conservative senators, armed with clubs and legs of chairs, rushed about Rome, killing Tiberius and 300 others. The bodies were thrown in the Tiber.

So the first blood in a century of bloodshed was spilled. The activities of the land commission, however, were not suspended until 129, and then on the grounds that the reclamation of public lands was irritating to the leaders of the Italian cities. These men also held much of the public domain, and we may suspect that the commission had been turning its attention toward them rather than toward the senators.

Gaius Gracchus (123-21 B.C.). Although the conservatives had thus wiped out the challenge to their position, they did not sit easily for long. In 123 Gaius Gracchus (154-21) was elected tribune with the express purpose of carrying out his brother's program. His fellow tribunes were all of his party, and since re-election to the tribunate had now been legally made possible he served also as tribune in 122. Instructed by the fall of Tiberius and implacably opposed to the conservatives, Gaius had a far wider program, on which he drove forward with great dexterity.

Many of his steps were designed to secure a broad base of support. For the people Gaius reactivated the land commission and secured legislation that the state would stabilize the price of grain in Rome; to this end great public granaries were built along the Tiber river.

To attach the equestrians, he secured to this class the valuable privilege of collecting taxes in the new province of Asia, which had been created out of the erstwhile kingdom of Pergamum after a bitter revolt in Asia Minor, 133–29; unlike the tithe collection in Sicily, which was farmed out locally, the taxes of Asia were to be collected by tax-farming groups which bid at Rome for the privilege. Another law gave the equestrians the right to compose the juries which tried accused governors. Thenceforth the equestrians formed an officially distinct group of men, who held a strong club over the head of any senator who tried to check their financial and commercial exploitation of the provinces. The evil which Gaius did lived long after his day, and one cannot entirely excuse him on the grounds he could not foresee the results; he himself cynically observed he had created "daggers with which nobles might lacerate each other." [3]

Although the chronological sequence of his actions is not clear, these measures were all logically preparatory to aid his main program: to build good farm-to-market roads which would aid farmers in selling their grain; to set up urban colonies for the poor of Rome (for Gaius saw more clearly than had his brother the fact that city-dwellers did not always want to go back to the farm); and to give citizenship or Latin status to the Italian allies. On the last two steps, however, Gaius began to lose popular support. One of his proposed colonies was at the recently accursed site of Carthage, which was moreover in a province, not in Italy; and the common people were not eager to admit the Italian allies to their own privileged position.

The conservatives regained their courage and advanced an apparently more radical leader, M. Livius Drusus, who outbid Gaius in promising

[3] Cicero, *On the Laws* 3.9.20.

to set up 12 colonies in Italy and offered to the allies not citizenship but a legal ban on execution or scourging while they were on military service. Gaius was not re-elected tribune for 121, and the Senate proposed revocation of the colony at Carthage. When violence broke out in the assembly, the Senate authorized the consuls to take all measures "lest the Republic suffer" (the *senatus consultum ultimum,* or martial law).

A brief civil war then raged through Rome. Gaius and most of his supporters were besieged on the Aventine; Gaius was killed in trying to escape across the Tiber; and some 3000 others were murdered. When the consul, C. Opimius, was accused of killing Roman citizens without trial, he successfully pleaded the authority of the Senate, which thereby arrogated to itself powers it had never formally held before. He also confiscated the wealth of the slain to build a temple in the Forum to Concord.

Results of the Gracchan Agitation. Although the Gracchi had thus been eliminated from the Roman scene, the Republic was never again to be the same. The equestrians had a new sense of their importance and a class identity, for the senators dared not abolish their position as jurors in trials of extortion. The common people, on the other hand, kept nothing; their right to receive grain at set prices was only spasmodically honored until the last days of the Republic. Yet they could remember, in bitterness, the fiery words of Tiberius:

> The savage beasts in Italy have their particular dens, they
> have their places of repose and refuge; but the men who bear
> arms and expose their lives for the safety of their country
> enjoy in the meantime nothing more in it but the air and
> the light . . . They fought indeed and were slain, but it was
> to maintain the luxury and the wealth of other men. They
> were styled the master of the world, but had in the mean-
> time not one foot of ground which they could call their own.[4]

For the provincials, nothing had been achieved; the Gracchi, indeed, had been quite willing to sacrifice their interests for partisan advantage at Rome. The Italian allies, finally, were increasingly restless thenceforth. Their claim to citizenship had been rebuffed; wealthier Italian elements saw their "right" to public lands sacrificed for the benefit of the senators,

[4] Plutarch, *Tiberius Gracchus* 9.4–5; tr. Dryden-Clough.

and the commercial position of the Italian merchants was ever more challenged by the equestrians.

The conservative wing of the Senate might feel that it had upheld constitutionalism and property rights, but it sat on its throne with a guilty conscience. Twice in little more than a decade Roman blood had been spilt, yet no lasting solution of the many problems had been achieved. The Gracchan brothers, in truth, had not seen all the dimensions of these problems; and their proposals had fundamentally sought little more than to return the social and economic structure of Rome to an earlier pattern. Later reformers were not to be so simple and were to learn from the Gracchan failure that they must have force at their disposal, rather than rest their case solely on a political appeal to the people.

Within little more than 10 years after the death of Gaius, the increasing divisions of the aristocracy and the ineffectiveness of senatorial leadership in its primary field, that of foreign policy, were to give an opening to the first of the great military commanders. Thenceforth the rattle of arms in both foreign and civil war provided martial music for the turbulent reforms by which largely self-seeking individualists met the needs of Rome and the Mediterranean world.

MARIUS AND SULLA

Rise of Marius (to 100 B.C.). The occasion for the rise of C. Marius (157–86 B.C.) was a conflict over the succession in the dependent kingdom of Numidia, long ruled by the aide of Scipio Africanus at Zama, Masinissa (*c.* 240–149). The Italian traders and equestrian elements interested in this growingly civilized area supported, on the death of Masinissa's son in 118, the sons of the dead king, Adherbal and Hiempsal; their cousin Jugurtha, however, was crafty in bribing senators and showed greater energy. In 112 Jugurtha took the capital, Cirta, and killed Adherbal. Unfortunately several hundred Italians fell in the butchery, an affront which the Romans could not overlook.

The war with Jugurtha which followed was militarily minor, but politically it was of great importance. The incompetence and lethargy of the Senate in directing foreign affairs were made manifest, and the generals sent to Africa were unable to bring the struggle to a decisive end. Marius, then military tribune, succeeded in gaining the support of the equestrians and was elected consul in 107, even though he was a "new man." He further secured the transfer of the African command to himself by popular vote, an unprecedented step. Although Marius swiftly put down open opposition after one critical battle, he too was committed to a dragging guerrilla struggle in the Algerian mountains until his quaestor L. Cornelius Sulla (138–78 B.C.) secretly made his way to the ruler of Mauretania and persuaded King Bocchus to betray Jugurtha.

No sooner had Jugurtha been taken than a really critical threat to Rome arose on the northern frontier. From the uncivilized depths of central Europe came a great outpouring of tribes, led by the Cimbri and Teutones, who were probably Celtic in speech. Roman generals sought in vain to check them in southern Gaul and finally, in 105, suffered a catastrophic defeat at Arausio (Orange), the worst since Cannae. In panic the people elected Marius consul a second time in 104 and continued to re-elect him until he crushed the Teutones near Aquae Sextiae (Aix) in 102, and the Cimbri the next year in the Po valley at Vercellae.

Once more Marius was elected consul, the sixth time, in 100, together with radical men like C. Servilius Glaucia as praetor, and L. Appuleius Saturninus as tribune. The year 100 saw a major land law in favor of Marius' veterans and serious riots at the elections in the fall, whereupon the Senate passed the *senatus consultum ultimum* and ordered Marius to arrest his friends. This done, they were murdered during the night in the Senate House itself, serving as temporary jail. The political career of Marius, who was able to cope with neither his friends nor his foes, came to a close for the moment.

Military and Political Alterations. During the years 121–100 a number of significant military and political developments occurred with which we must reckon during the remainder of the Republic. The military needs of the Roman empire and protectorates, thus, became increasingly evident. Roman opposition to the Cimbri and Teutones had been motivated in the first instance by an appeal from its old friend, Massilia, but the life-and-death struggle with the barbarians foreshadowed the enduring role of Rome as defender of Mediterranean civilization against barbarian pressures from northern Eurasia.

Within the Mediterranean sphere itself the Romans found themselves stretched to cope with so minor an affair as the war with Jugurtha, and were compelled to make gestures against the piracy which their policy of naval disarmament had encouraged in the unsettled eastern Mediterranean. In 102 the praetor M. Antonius waged a brief campaign by land and sea and occupied some bases on the south coast of Asia Minor, which were called the province of Cilicia. Yet the Romans still were reluctant to take over direct responsibilities. Upon inheriting the territory of Cyrene through the will of its last king in 96, the Senate failed to provide a governor for 20 years.

Of the major military reforms, many are connected with the name of Marius, who was far more able as a general than as a politician. Marius waived the ancestral requirement that soldiers hold at least a small property qualification and accepted volunteers, who served for the sake of pay and booty. Drafting continued to be employed on occasion, but very commonly armies were raised by specific generals on the appeal of their name and the likelihood of rewards. Whereas troops in the earlier Republic had often been given land at the conclusion of a war, this practice seems to have stopped before 150, and the armies of the Late Republic secured such grants if their generals were politically strong enough to wrest a land distribution from the unwilling Senate. On the top level the connection between politics and war thus remained close, for only an able politician could secure a military post or reward his troops; but the officer class, as a whole, tended to become more professional.

So too the enlisted men, though commonly serving only for six years or so in one enlistment, became more professional in outlook, and could be trained rigorously on methods borrowed from the gladiatorial camps. Their loyalty was increasingly centered on their specific legion, which had its own standard or "eagle." This legion was now organized not into small maniples but into 10 cohorts, or battalions, each approximately 500 men strong; all legionaries were armed alike with short sword and javelin. Beside and before the cohortal legion skirmished auxiliary units of cavalry, slingers, and archers who were recruited from Crete, the Balearic islands, Spain, and other semicivilized regions. In the hands of Sulla, Pompey, and Caesar the new-style army was to prove itself the greatest military machine the world had yet seen. It was also to be less and less bound by abstract loyalty to the Republic or to the senatorial aristocracy which enjoyed the fruits of Roman rule.

Politically, the leading elements of Rome were separating into two ill-defined camps. The conservative wing, called derisively by its opponents the Optimates, or Best, was more clearly organized and stood for maintenance of senatorial domination; generally this group commanded a majority of the Senate, the priests, and commonly the magistrates. Among major leaders only Sulla stood consistently in this camp, though Pompey and Cicero joined it on occasion. Most enterprising, self-seeking men turned rather to join the faction which allowed greater scope for the individual. This was the group of the Populares, including such disparate elements as idealistic reformers, ruthless equestrians, and discontented aristocrats. The Populares generally endorsed the Gracchan reforms but otherwise varied widely in announced policies as their leadership and support shifted. In so divided a political structure compromise and positive action to ameliorate problems became ever more difficult.

Italian War and First Mithridatic War (90–85 B.C.). The consequences of the Roman refusal to face problems either abroad or at home were two great wars, among the many important results of which was the rise of Sulla. The first was the Italian war (90–88), in which Rome staggered under a revolt by many of its Italian allies. These subjects had been increasingly discontent with the arrogance of Rome and were repeatedly rebuffed in their requests for citizenship or other protection from the days of Tiberius Gracchus. In 91 M. Livius Drusus the Younger, as tribune, tried once more to gain their admission to citizenship along with proposing new colonies and a reorganization of the courts; but in 90 he was murdered. The Italians then revolted and created a separate confederacy with its capital at Corfinium, renamed Italia. Rome hastily granted citizenship first to all allies who had not revolted and then even to the rebels, provided they resume their loyalty; but extensive military action was required to put down the central mountaineers who persisted in secession. From this point on, all the Italian peninsula shared Roman citizenship, and Rome was in consequence no longer a city-state. Within the next two generations Italy and Rome were to merge spiritually into a base on which a new order could be eventually established.

In the Italian war Sulla showed himself unusually competent and was rewarded by election as consul in 88. At this point came news that Mithridates VI (120–63 B.C.), the able king of Pontus, had finally been so goaded by Roman interference and open attacks as to invade the Aegean; his persistent wooing of the Greeks in preceding decades led virtually all the Roman-held territory of Greek culture to blaze up. On one day some 80,000 Italians resident in Asia Minor were killed; and even Athens, long sleeping quietly as a cultural center, joined his banner.

Sulla obtained command of the army to meet this grave threat. Marius, eager to enhance his military fame, raised the Populares and secured new orders that he should be commander. Rather than obeying this legal directive, Sulla appealed to his army and marched it back on Rome, the first general in Roman history to do so; most of his senatorial officers left him, but his men obeyed their leader. Marius and others had to flee for their lives, after calling in vain on the slaves of the city to revolt; and Sulla carried out some minor reforms which restricted the liberty of the Tribal assembly. Even though his candidates for the consulship of 87 lost, Sulla then went east to deal with the foreign threat.

Once he was out of Italy, the Populares revived and took Rome by force. Marius killed some of his enemies among the Optimates, was elected consul for the seventh time, and then died. His successor, L. Cornelius Cinna, was consul continuously from 87 through 84 and pursued a somewhat more conciliatory policy. The purity of the coinage, which had suffered in recent years, was improved, and steps were taken to reorganize the government of Italy after the grant of general citizenship; but Cinna was not able to reach any agreement with the absent Sulla.

From 87 to 85 Sulla concentrated on the war with Mithridates, though he operated entirely on his own in the east without support from home. First he took and sacked Athens after a siege of over a year. In reverence for its noble past, the city was not destroyed; but Sulla was ruthless in plundering the treasuries of Delphi and other shrines to get funds. Then he drove the forces of Mithridates out of Greece and himself crossed to Asia with a makeshift navy. Here he resumed Roman sway, but concluded a compromise peace with Mithridates in 85 rather than pushing the war to the complete defeat of the king of Pontus.

The preservation of Roman domination in the east was due partly to

Sulla's energy and skill but also owed much to the realization by the Greek upper classes that their position was more secure under Roman than Pontic rule. As they began to shift back toward Rome, indeed, Mithridates had incited the lower classes to rise against them. Sulla once again put the men of wealth in firm control, though they had to pay dearly for their momentary insurrection by furnishing 20,000 talents to his war chest. Thenceforth the upper classes of the Hellenistic world stuck firmly by Rome through the torment of the civil wars in the dying Republic; that loyalty which was eventually to uphold the Eastern Roman or Byzantine Empire went back essentially to this decision.

Civil War and Sulla's Dictatorship (83–79 B.C.). Sulla was now free to return to Italy. To meet him Cinna had been raising troops, but after his death in a mutiny a great deal of the strength of the Populares vanished. Such leaders as Cn. Papirius Carbo and Marius the Younger secured enough support among the newly enfranchised Italians, who were deeply suspicious of Sulla, to fight a civil war through 83 and 82. Much of south and central Italy was ravaged; a battle at the Colline gate of Rome ended the main fighting. A number of able young aristocrats had joined Sulla by this time, including Cn. Pompeius (106–48 B.C.), the famous Pompey of later decades, who swept up the Marians in Sicily and Africa.

Sulla then had himself appointed dictator to reform the Roman constitution. The first step was to settle scores with the Populares, whose names were posted on whitened tablets in the Forum; anyone thus "proscribed" was outlaw, and his murderer received a reward. Many men whose only crime was the possession of wealth also suffered, for Sulla needed immense quantities of money and land to settle the 120,000 troops who had fought under his banner. Forty senators and 1600 equestrians were on the initial lists; in the end thousands perished.

Thereafter Sulla firmly settled the powers of the Republic in the hands of the reconstituted Senate, to which he added, among others, 300 new members from the ranks of equestrians and wealthier Italians. Thenceforth the 20 quaestors elected each year automatically passed into the Senate so that its membership would be maintained without recourse to the censors. The equestrians lost their place on the juries, the public provision of grain which had been reinstituted was abolished, and the tribunes were curtailed; thenceforth no tribune was ever to hold any other office or even to be re-elected tribune save after an interval of 10 years. The Senate itself received formal power to veto all legislation.

Very little of this was to last even a decade, but in other respects the Sullan reforms began to correct some of the weaknesses in the machinery of government. Criminal jurisdiction was transferred from the assembly to seven standing courts, each with a senatorial jury. Partly to provide leaders for these courts the number of praetors was increased from six to eight, and each praetor thenceforth normally served one year in Rome and a second year as propraetor (commonly called "proconsul") in a province; 2 of the 10 provinces were governed by the ex-consuls. Beside Cisalpine Gaul, which was finally made into a province, the others at this date were Sicily, Sardinia-Corsica, the two Spains, Macedonia, Africa, Asia, Narbonensis Gaul, and Cilicia (Cyrene being not yet fully organized).

To what extent Sulla went beyond Cinna in encouraging the reorganization of local government in Italy along Roman principles is uncertain, but certainly Italy by this time was putting on a civilized dress. At Rome itself Sulla rebuilt the Capitoline temple and the Senate House; the great public records office (Tabularium) arose at the west end of the Forum, where it still stands. On the cliff over Tarracina one can yet see the massive foundations of the temple of Jupiter Anxur; and the temple of Fortune, apparently reconstructed by Sulla after his siege of the city, rose in tier after tier up the hillside, built of concrete faced with marble. From the cultural point of view one of the greatest consequences of Sulla's eastern war was the proper publication of the major body of Aristotle's great works, which had lain almost totally neglected for centuries in Asia Minor.

Having completed his self-appointed task, Sulla resigned his dictatorship in 79 and retired to Campania, where he died the next year. Among all the great figures who blazed out in the Late Republic, he is one of the most remarkable. Although of ancestral lineage, he had risen from poverty by his own abilities; and although he stood firmly on the side of the Optimates in the end, he had terrifically weakened the constitutional practices of the Republic by his own example. Personally, too, he was unusual. A man of lively mind, he preferred the company of actors and had a keen sense of the ironic and unexpected in life; yet he was credulous of dreams and firmly believed he stood under the protection of Fortune, whence came his nickname "The Fortunate."

His solution to the political problems of Rome, though eminently logical, was not to last; and other civil wars soon followed. One of the greatest Latin poets, who grew to manhood in Sulla's days, was then to pray in anguish to Venus,

> . . . that this brutal business of war by sea and land may everywhere be lulled to rest. For you alone have power to bestow on mortals the blessing of quiet peace.[5]

BIBLIOGRAPHY

Sources. Although the books of Livy's history covering the era 133–78 are lost, we have summaries of their contents (the *Periochae*) and various short histories of later date which drew from his book. One of these is the *Epitome bellorum omnium annorum DCC* of Annaeus Florus (second century after Christ), who begins the decline of Rome with the Gracchan period; another is the long history of Rome written in Greek by Dio Cassius in the early third century (Loeb Classical Library). The *Roman History* written by Appian, an Alexandrian Greek in the second century after Christ (Loeb Classical Library), takes up R—— area by area and is useful for the Mithridatic wars as w———— strife from the Gracchi onward; Book I of the ——— ——— W——— valuable, though Appian failed to comprehend th—— ——— problems. Plutarch has lives of the Gracchi, Sulla, and Ma—— ——— ph- let by the contemporary of Caesar, C. Sallustius Crispus, treats the *Jugurthine War* (Loeb Classical Library). Sallust, the greatest surviving republican historian, was prejudiced against the Senate and exhibited a strongly moral tone in his analysis of the decline of public ethics after the Third Punic war. The historian would give much to have Sulla's own satirical *Memoirs*.

In Latin literature the major work surviving from this period is an anonymous treatise on rhetoric, *Ad Herennium* (Loeb Classical Library). Besides the architectural monuments noted in the text, sculpture

[5] Lucretius, *On the Nature of the Universe* 1.29–32; tr. R. E. Latham.

and painting now began to swell in volume and in quality as a presage to the remarkable achievements at the close of the first century B.C. Coinage also grew more varied in types and so becomes more useful to the historian in this era; see E. A. Sydenham, *Roman Republican Coinage* (London: Spink, 1952) and M. H. Crawford, *Roman Republican Coinage,* 2 vols. (Cambridge: Cambridge University Press, 1975).

Further Reading. The political and economic conditions attending the decline of the Republic may be found in F. B. Marsh, *History of the Roman World from 146 to 30 B.C.* (3d ed.; London: Methuen, 1963), and Tenney Frank, *Economic Survey of Ancient Rome,* Vol. I (New York: Octagon, 1972). Richard E. Smith, *Failure of the Roman Republic* (New York: Russell, 1976), is useful, though his thesis is doubtful; his brief essay, *Service in the Post-Marian Army* (Manchester: Manchester University Press, 1958), illuminates the army reforms. G. P. Baker, *Sulla the Fortunate* (Totowa, N.J.: Rowman), is a good life; his opponent, Mithridates, is sympathetically treated by Alfred Duggan, *King of Pontus* (New York: Coward McCann, 1959). There are recent lives of Tiberius Gracchus by D. C. Earl (Brussels: Latomus, 1963), and A. H. Bernstein (Ithaca: Cornell University Press, 1978); see also D. Stockton, *The Gracchi* (Oxford: Oxford University Press, 1979). E. Badian has written a number of thoughtful essays as well as *Roman Imperialism in the Late Republic* (2d ed.; Oxford: Blackwell, 1968), and *Publicans and Sinners* (Cornell University Press, 1972). One aspect is carefully discussed by Wiseman, *New Men in the Roman Senate 139 B.C.–14 A.D.* (Oxford: Oxford University Press, 1971).

25

THE AGE OF CICERO AND CAESAR

During the troubled era from 78 to 43 B.C., the political structure of the Roman Republic finally collapsed into the dictatorship of Julius Caesar. The course of history in these 35 years was the most complicated interplay of political and economic interests that the ancient world had yet seen.

Abroad, Rome settled its accounts with Mithridates and the pirates and significantly expanded its rule outside the Mediterranean watershed into continental Europe. These wars, in part caused by the weakness of the republican system, had in turn potent effects at home, where politicians manipulated the voters in elaborate chicanery which gave scope for the greatest political oratory of Roman times. Beside elections and speeches, however, there were the tools of political murder and gang warfare, which resulted even in the burning of the Senate House.

Partly as a consequence of the great opportunities, the era produced some of the most resplendent individual figures of all Roman history. One, who in Shakespeare's words

> . . . doth bestride the narrow world
> Like a Colossus; and we petty men
> Walk under his huge legs, and peep about
> To find ourselves dishonourable graves,

was C. Julius Caesar (100–44 B.C.), the man who conquered Gaul and died as dictator of Rome. Another was M. Tullius Cicero (106–43 B.C.), the most important single cultural leader in the thousand years of Roman development. Around and below these great figures was a host of others to demonstrate the vitality of Roman civilization even though its old political framework was crumbling. By 43 B.C., it should be noted, the Republic was dead; but a new lasting arrangement of political powers and responsibilities had not yet been arranged.

THE CICERONIAN AGE

Political Evolution (78–64 B.C.). To set the stage for the careers of Cicero and Caesar one must examine briefly the complicated lines of political development during their formative years. Sulla had left the senatorial aristocracy completely in control, and in subsequent decades this element remained an important conservative force. Commonly it dominated the religious machinery; through its circles of clients at home and abroad the aristocracy had considerable weight; matrimonial and other alliances furnished many links between the great houses.

The main conservative leaders, however, were more skilled in short-range manipulation and obstruction than in long-range reconstruction. Many of the major explosions of the period were set off by their obtuse unwillingness to compromise with other powerful elements, their dream of a "liberty" which would give them unchecked power, and their unrelenting suspicion of individual ambition. In private correspondence Cicero scornfully called them "the gentlemen of the fishponds," in allusion to their hobby of raising prize fish. Not a few of the aristocrats who survived Sulla's purge tended to be unpolitical and sought enjoyment in the luxuries of imperial Rome.

Beside the families of ancient lineage there were other important political elements. The provincials scarcely counted as an active force, but silently they pressed their Roman masters to fashion some system which would give stable order. The leaders of the burgeoning Italian towns, now citizens, were a more significant group, which Cicero and others sought to win over because of their ability to deliver large blocs of votes. Although these families of local prominence had social and cultural ties with great Roman houses, they tended to live in more old-fashioned virtue and, by the last years of the Republic, were producing military and political leaders who had to be absorbed within the governing class.

At Rome itself the ever-growing population was sharply divided between the ostentatious rich, to be numbered at only a few thousands, and the hundreds of thousands of poor citizens, often of alien origin. Poorly policed, the commoners were insecure in their daily life despite the state distribution of grain; their close-packed masses in the tenement areas were the stuff of which mobs could easily be manufactured. Among the upper classes the equestrians had in minor part been elevated to the Senate by Sulla but remained on the whole an independent group. They smarted at times in social inferiority but eagerly exploited the possibilities of financial gain through tax-farming, moneylending, and trade. One equestrian friend of Cicero, T. Pomponius Atticus, lent money impartially to radical and conservative politicians alike; others were not so unpolitical. And finally, the armies of the Republic were an increasingly essential, long-term institution more loyal to commanders than to abstract ideals. Junior and senior officers alike were by now often semi-professionals.

Immediately after Sulla's death the Senate falteringly faced the demagoguery of M. Aemilius Lepidus, one of the consuls for 78, which finally produced a minor rebellion and a battle at the Milvian bridge just north of Rome. That the Senate came out triumphant was due in part to the abilities of a young protégé of Sulla, Cn. Pompeius (106–48 b.c.), who secured as a result a command against the Marian insurrection in Spain.

Although Pompey was able to repress the revolt only after its wily guerrilla leader Sertorius had been murdered, he returned to Italy in triumph in 71. Here he helped M. Licinius Crassus (c. 112–53 b.c.) stamp out the last embers of the great servile insurrection which the gladiator Spartacus had initiated in 73. The social unrest illustrated in this insurrection was to be a continuing threat across the last decades of the Republic, and the fear felt by the uneasy masters is suggested by Crassus' brutal crucifixion of 6000 unclaimed slaves along the Appian way.

Both Pompey, who had not held any elected office, and Crassus now sought the consulship. The conservatives opposed their bids and thus forced the two ambitious men temporarily to join hands in order to secure their joint election for the year 70. During their consulship Pompey and Crassus released the tribunes from their Sullan restrictions and gave the Populares freer room for action. Some 64 senators added by Sulla were expelled from the Senate; their efforts to get back via election to public office helped to make the elections of the next few years the most corrupt Rome had ever witnessed.

Crassus remained in Rome during the 60s and built up a skillful political machine embracing such ward heelers as L. Sergius Catilina and Caesar to give him and his equestrian friends a potent voice. Pompey seized the opportunity afforded by the severe piratical incursions throughout the Mediterranean, not excepting the shores of Italy and the port of Rome, and by the Gabinian law of 67 was granted *imperium* over the Mediterranean and authority to operate inland 50 miles. Creating a navy out of all the ships he could commandeer, he swept from west to east, hemmed up the pirates in their bases on the rocky south coast of Asia Minor, and after taking these strongholds either killed or settled inland the masses of desperate men who had been driven to the sea by the disorder of the era.

Next Pompey was given another extraordinary command, by the Manilian law of 66, to deal once and for all with Mithridates, whom L. Licinius Lucullus had already worn down in the Third Mithridatic war (since 74). The king of Pontus was forced to flee to the Crimea, where he committed suicide in 63, but Pompey took the opportunity to annex the Seleucid heartland of Syria and Palestine and to reorganize Roman rule in the east by creating new provinces and founding cities to spread Hellenization (see Map 18). While he moved from triumph to triumph in the eastern Mediterranean, Optimates and Populares alike shivered at home in fear that Pompey might return with his devoted army and navy as a new Sulla.

Political Career of Cicero (*to* 63 B.C.). Against this turbulent background occurred the political rise of Cicero. Born to a wealthy equestrian family of Arpinum, Cicero came to Rome to complete his education and studied law with the great *pontifex maximus* Q. Mucius Scaevola. As a good Roman, he served in the armies which put down the Italian revolt of 90–88, but thereafter avoided military life. Instead, Cicero turned to oratory and the law and gained his first notable success by defending a man attacked by one of Sulla's favorites (the oration *pro Roscio Amerino*). Then, like many Romans of the first century B.C., Cicero took postgraduate work in Greece, where he studied oratory under the greatest Greek rhetorician of the period, Apollonius, and probably philosophy under Posidonius.

On his return he plunged into the combined career of politics and law. In the latter profession he eventually rose to be the greatest defense attorney of the age; and, though no gentleman could directly take a fee, the legacies and presents which Cicero received amounted in modern terms to millions of dollars. Yet he always remained in debt as he bought rural villa after villa and finally attained his dream of owning a house in the most select quarter of Rome, on the Palatine hill. Cicero's financial records are a precious revelation of the tremendous expenses required by a cultured Roman aristocrat.

After serving as quaestor in Sicily in 75 Cicero was a member of the Senate. He next ran for the aedileship, for 70, and adopted a Populares stand; partly in consequence he seized the opportunity to prosecute an unusually rapacious governor of Sicily, C. Verres, and drove Verres into exile without awaiting the verdict. Cicero's Verrine orations form our most detailed picture of the amazingly varied means by which Romans could ruthlessly exploit the provinces. Elected aedile for 69, Cicero moved on to the praetorship in 66 and then dared to run for the consulship in 63. Since he was a "new man" without noble ancestors, his chances were slim; but Cicero dextrously campaigned among the Italian leading classes, paraded a friendship with Pompey to please the people, and at the same time sought to gain the favor of the conservatives. Inasmuch as the other major candidate, Catiline, was even more distasteful to the Optimates, Cicero succeeded. In 63 he was consul with C. Antonius.

The crowning point of Cicero's political career was also one of his most troubled. In an effort to gain popular support against the possible dangers when Pompey should return, Crassus and his lieutenant Caesar proposed a land law which would purchase and distribute state lands among the poor. As consul charged with keeping the treasury solvent, Cicero had to oppose in the orations *contra Rullum* this measure, which he defeated at the cost of his own popularity.

Then, through spies, Cicero gained wind of a plot by Catiline and other bankrupt aristocrats to murder the consuls and to seize control of Rome. By skillful oratory in the orations *in Catilinam,* Cicero drove the conspirators out into the open before their plans were ripe. Catiline fled to Etruria and raised a revolt of the oppressed peasants, which was put down by the other consul Antonius; many of the conspirators in Rome were seized. In a senatorial debate on their fate M. Porcius Cato the Younger (95–46), great-grandson of Cato the Censor, secured a vote for their execution, which Cicero carried out at once. Since all Roman citizens, however, technically had the right of appeal to the people, he had engaged in an illegal step which was to cause him serious trouble in later years.

Nonetheless Cicero could go out of office proud of his achievements in maintaining the Republic. Modern estimates of the dangers in the Catilinarian conspiracy vary widely, but there can be no doubt that Cicero, more than any other great figure of the era, strove to link his career with a reasoned defense of the ancestral system of Roman government. To strengthen his defense he dreamed of a "concord of the orders," that is, the collaboration of the senatorial and equestrian orders; but harnessing the conservatism of the aristocrats and the rapacity of the equestrians was to be beyond his powers, even though Cicero later tried to broaden his program to include all the leading elements of Italy. Eventually Cicero had to witness the utter collapse of the Republic, and died in its ruins.

Literature of the Ciceronian Age. The generation of Cicero and the immediately subsequent Augustan age mark the high point of Latin letters. By this time the Romans were fully at home in their great Greek inheritance; many studied in Greece, and such major Hellenistic thinkers as Posidonius spent time in Rome. While the classic achievements of Greece were revered, Roman writers and artists drew mainly from Hellenistic models, which were more emotional and individualistic.

In the work of Cicero and his contemporaries everything, at first sight, appears Greek — the basic substance of ideas; the methods of expression, for example, meters, oratorical style, and so forth; and even many of the detailed metaphors or commonplaces. Yet, just as American culture is subtly different in tone from its source in Europe, so too the men who wrote and thought in Latin had their own outlook and a just pride. If we look for what is Roman in the culture of the Ciceronian age, we shall find it mainly in the spirit of the period, as in the practical hardheadedness and the fresh enthusiasm with which the Romans enlivened the weary, pessimistic thought of the dying Hellenistic era.

One of the great poets of the Latin tongue, T. Lucretius Carus (*c.* 99–*c.* 55), composed only one poem *On the Nature of the World* (*de rerum natura*). The substance was drawn from Epicurean physical doctrine of the atoms; the six-foot meter and much else of the poetic technique were Greek; but the poem as a whole was infused by an independent power and majesty of spirit. Lucretius was the most forceful missionary of all pagan culture as he preached the materialistic philosophy of Epicurus in an effort to liberate his fellow men from their fears of death and their superstition. Sometimes his lines are aridly scientific, but often they glow in poetic genius; the opening prayer for peace was quoted at the end of the previous chapter.

Most poets of the period wrote very short, learned poems in the Alexandrian style. Chief among these was C. Valerius Catullus (84–54), born in north Italy but sent in his early twenties to Rome to finish his education. Here he fell in love with the wife of his patron, a worldly-wise woman whom he called Lesbia; we know that her real name was Clodia and that she was sister to one of the greatest gangsters of the age, P. Clodius. Finally the scales fell from Catullus' eyes as he realized that Lesbia had many other lovers: and he wrote the famous couplet:

> I hate and love, nor can the reason tell;
> But that I love and hate I know too well.[1]

After going to Bithynia as deputy on a governor's staff, he returned to attack Caesar, but was reconciled by the bland skill of the latter, before he died at 30. Behind him Catullus left 133 short poems, which are often no more than translations from the Greek; yet in their lyric genius the love and hate of a young man throb more clearly than in any other ancient author.

The towering figure, however, was Cicero himself. As a poet he was no more than mediocre, but the Ciceronian oratorical style has influenced the Latin and vernacular prose of modern Europe more than any other single factor. Some of his orations have been noted in the discussion of his political career; in all 58 are still extant, or about one-half his output in this field. During the dictatorship of Caesar, Cicero's golden voice found only ignoble opportunities for employment, and he poured out in swift profusion a mass of essays and dialogues on rhetorical theory, philosophy, ethics, and political theory. His thought was an eclectic mixture of Academic, Stoic, and other Greek schools, but to

[1] Catullus, *Poem* 85; tr. F. A. Wright.

convey it he had to create a philosophical vocabulary in Latin. In the Middle Ages the Latin west learned much of its philosophy through the *Academica, Tusculan Disputations, On Duties (de officiis)*, and other Ciceronian works. In his political treatises *On the Republic* and *On the Laws* we can sense especially his attachment to the principles which had made Rome great. In comparison to Plato's theoretical study in the *Republic*, Cicero's dialogue of similar title was that of a practical student earnestly seeking to fashion a practicable constitution for his beloved country. Throughout his literary output there appears Cicero's broad view of man as a civilized, humane being.

Both Caesar and Cicero reveal in part their inner thoughts in their own works. Caesar wrote *Commentaries on the Gallic Wars*, designed to justify his conquest of Gaul and to magnify his deeds, and later discussed his war with Pompey in the *Civil War*. Modern students of Latin who have painfully construed the *Gallic Wars* sentence by sentence have probably not appreciated how clear and revelatory an account Caesar wrote; for no other great general do we have a similar firsthand report until modern times. For Cicero there is a great body of 931 letters either from his pen or addressed to him. These reveal his abundant egotism and his propensity to fall into black doubt and fear — and all too well his human failings — but they also throw into sharp light his humanistic outlook, his pride in Rome (though also his disinterest in the provincials), and his continuing effort to maintain the Republic. Purely as letters their informal style has rarely been equaled in conciseness and variety.

As attached as Cicero to the Roman past was the greatest polymath of the era, who lived on into the Augustan age, M. Terentius Varro (116–27 B.C.). Part of Varro's *On the Latin Language* and *On Agriculture* have survived. His great study *Divine and Human Antiquities,* his satires, and other works on history, law, geography, music, architecture, and other subjects are unfortunately lost; for Varro was one of the most learned men Rome produced. The other great prose writer of the era, C. Sallustius Crispus (86–*c*. 34), wrote accounts of the Jugurthine war, the Catilinarian conspiracy, and more extended *Histories* on 78–67 B.C.

Spirit of the Ciceronian Age. The literature of the Ciceronian period illustrates well its swirling currents of thought. Under all there was a strength of spirit, reflecting the deep bases of Roman development; yet on the surface we can see the fears of this age. Many elements were willing to seek political peace at the expense of old principles. Others turned to mysticism, particularly to that form called Neopythagoreanism which P. Nigidius Figulus (praetor in 58) preached and which Cicero expressed in part in his *Tusculan Disputations* after the death of his favorite daughter Tullia. Above all, the aristocrats of this world had learned to live as individuals, seeking their own narrow ends of wealth, luxury, or power; even Cicero, though broad in cultural views, had little concept of the problems of the empire or the commoners.

THE RISE OF CAESAR

Caesar's Early Years (*to* 61 B.C.). While the general qualities of the Late Republic help to explain the rise of Julius Caesar, much must be attributed to his own remarkable powers. Caesar was, in truth, the most well-rounded man of the era.

Caesar's clan was so noble that it traced its legendary origin to Iulus, son of the Trojan hero Aeneas, who in turn was the son of the goddess Venus. Nevertheless the Julian clan produced over the centuries only two great men, Caesar himself and his grandnephew, the later Augustus. As a youth, Caesar married Cinna's daughter; Marius married his aunt. When Sulla became dictator, Caesar's life was spared only because of his other family connections. During a year's study 75/4 at Rhodes he perfected his oratory under Apollonius, the tutor of Cicero; in swaying men's minds through the spoken word Caesar was eventually second to Cicero alone.

On his return Caesar plunged into the tangled politics of the post-Sullan period and learned a second art, that of political manipulation. For a time he dallied with the Optimates, but by the 60s he had found a better niche as assistant to Crassus. Quaestor in 69–68, he served in Spain, where he was said to have observed a bust of Alexander and to have realized that he was already the age at which Alexander had died.

His subsequent career, nonetheless, was equally slow. As aedile in 65 he gave magnificent games to win the public's favor, which put him heavily in debt to Crassus. In 63 he stood for the august post of *pontifex maximus,* which was now subject to public election, and to the scandal of the conservatives secured this vital position of supervision over the religious machinery. After his praetorship in 62 he served as propraetor in Spain in 61, where he gained some military experience. In his Spanish posts Caesar perhaps began, unlike Cicero, to be consciously aware of the needs of the empire; but if he were to go further, he must wrest from the suspicious Optimates first the consulship and then a major military command to gain the kind of glory that surrounded Pompey.

First Triumvirate (60–59 B.C.) On his return to Rome in 60 Caesar asked that he be permitted to stand for the consulship while still outside Rome. Normally candidates had to be present in the city, but if Caesar entered Rome he would legally be unable to celebrate, as propraetor, a triumph for his Spanish victory. Since the conservatives of the Senate, led by Cato, haughtily refused him this permission, Caesar had to yield his triumph in order to run for the consulship; and the conservative opposition impelled him into collaboration with the equally discontented Crassus and Pompey. Crassus desired a reduction in the high price his equestrian friends had unwisely bid for the tax collections of Asia. Pompey, who had returned to Italy victorious in 62 but had dismissed his army, found the Senate loath to approve en bloc his reorganization of the east and to grant land for his veterans. Since all three were opposed by the Senate, they joined in an informal ring called the First Triumvirate. Cicero was invited to join the cabal but, though despondent over the quarrels and blunders of the aristocracy, refused.

The ring secured the election of Caesar as one of the consuls for 59. After seeking in vain the support of the Senate and the other consul, M. Calpurnius Bibulus of the Optimates' wing, Caesar turned to direct action. With the aid of Pompey's veterans and the threat of force, he overrode the vetoes of Bibulus and of the tribunes to carry the land law desired by Pompey and then a mass of other legislation for his partners. Bibulus retired to his house and every day issued a decree that the heavens forbade public business that day. Caesar's reward for this year of illegal and violent activity was appointment as governor of Illyricum and Cisalpine Gaul for five years. To this was added Transalpine Gaul upon the death of its governor, one of those accidents which stud the course of history; for thereafter Caesar's attention came to be focused on Gaul.

Nonetheless he continued to keep a wary eye on politics at home and sought to win every possible cultural and political leader. As governor of the nearest province, he could do so more easily; yet as a proconsul he could not legally enter Italy itself without yielding his official *imperium*. Pompey was bound to him by having married his only child, Julia; to remove Cicero's dangerous tongue Caesar made it possible for a personal enemy of Cicero, Clodius, to be elected tribune for 58. As tribune Clodius shipped off Cato to annex and seize the treasures of Cyprus and moved a law that anyone who had put to death a Roman citizen without trial or appeal to the people should be outlaw. Cicero fled before the passage of the bill to Macedonia, where he sadly learned that his pride and joy, the mansion on the Palatine, had been torn down to make way for a shrine of Liberty. As soon as Cicero was gone, Caesar set off for north Italy. Thus far he had been no more than a skillful politician and rabble-rouser; but at the age of 41 his great career was just beginning.

Celtic Gaul. The area to which Caesar now turned was to occupy him for nine years, down to the end of 50 B.C. Cisalpine Gaul (the Po valley) had been settled over the past 150 years by immigrants from Italy proper and was basically civilized. Transalpine Gaul, which Caesar called in his *Commentaries* "the province" (the modern Provence along the Riviera coast), had long been exposed to cultural currents from Massilia. Since it lay along the great Roman road to Spain, it had been made a province in 120, and a Roman colony had been settled at Narbo about 115. Beyond these bases stretched the vast uncivilized districts of Celtic Gaul as far as the Rhine and modern Holland (see Map 18).

The Celts were grouped in bitterly opposed tribes under warrior princes and aristocrats. True cities did not exist, but hillforts called *oppida* dotted the landscape. The culture that particularly distinguished the Celts is called La Tène. This had emerged on the middle Rhine toward 500 B.C. out of the earlier Hallstatt culture as central Europe quickened its pace under Mediterranean influences. To the civilized peoples of Etruria and the Greek colonies the natives exported salt, copper, iron, tin, and slaves; in return they bought wine, Greek pottery, metal wares, and other luxuries. La Tène culture was particularly associated with warrior aristocracies, and its spread southwest over Gaul to Spain and from about 250 B.C. across the English channel to Sussex seems to reflect their conquests over earlier Hallstatt waves. By Caesar's day the more advanced Celts were coining money on Greek and Roman models, and the Druids knew the Greek alphabet. But, as he observes, the Belgae who were remote from the Roman province "have infrequent trade contacts with its high culture and refinement, and thus remain unaffected by influences which tend to effeminate character." [2]

To the archeologist La Tène culture is marked by a recognizable set of artistic patterns blended from Etruscan, south Russian, and native roots, including fantastic stylized animals; common, too, was the use of heavy torques or neck pieces of gold and bronze. Beyond these material similarities the Celts shared a common tongue and a common religious outlook. The Celts believed in life after death by rebirth, had various divinities whom Caesar tried to equate with Roman gods, and were led by the priesthood of the Druids. This group educated the young, practiced divination, gathered mistletoe, and at least at times engaged in human sacrifice in sacred groves. It seems to have been the one unifying factor among the Celtic tribes.

Caesar's Conquests (58–50 B.C.). Caesar took the command of the northern frontier of the Roman world initially for five years, which was extended for another five in 55. His principal intention presumably was to gain the military skill and repute necessary for his further advance in Roman politics; but the opportunities and responsibilities of his command swiftly led him to the conquest of all Gaul. The Gallic tribes themselves, some of which were bound to Rome by treaties of friendship, were at odds as more powerful groups sought to reduce their neighbors; and the outside pressure from German-speaking barbarians, seeking to move west across the Rhine, gave him further excuse for far-ranging expeditions in this very unstable society.

In 58 he halted a migration by the Helvetii from southwestern Switzerland, then threw back the Suebic German leader Ariovistus, and drove up the Rhône, his main supply line, to northeastern Gaul, where his troops wintered. This step so clearly foreshadowed Roman conquest that in 57 he had to face attacks by the Belgae and Nervii in northern Gaul; in the next year he mopped up the Atlantic seaboard. In 55 Caesar reconnoitered across the Rhine and invaded Britain, a step he repeated in 54 though his shipping ran into trouble with the unexpected tides.

As the Celtic tribes of central and northern Gaul began to sense their lasting subjugation, they broke out first in sporadic revolts and then in

[2] Caesar, *Gallic Wars* 1.1; tr. John Warrington.

52 in a great insurrection led by Vercingetorix. Caesar finally penned up the Gallic leader at Alesia and, though himself besieged from the outside, finally forced Vercingetorix' surrender. By 50 one of the most remarkable and significant conquests in Roman history had been accomplished, an advance which can be followed step by step through Caesar's *Commentaries*.

The effects of the annexation of Gaul warrant the judgment that this was Caesar's most important contribution to history. As far as the Celts were concerned, the immediate results were catastrophic, even if we need not believe Plutarch's remark that a million were killed in the wars, a million enslaved, and a million left to populate Gaul. In the long run, however, Gaul entered fully into the orbit of Mediterranean civilization. Here, for the first time, classical culture strode over the watershed into continental Europe. The importance of this development is obvious when one recalls that Gaul later became medieval France, the heartland of western culture in the Middle Ages.

In Rome itself Caesar's star rose high on the horizon. The Romans had never forgotten the bitter memories of the Gallic invasion of 390 and had been further alarmed by the serious attacks of the Cimbri and Teutones in Marius' day. Caesar's victories were officially celebrated at length, even though conservatives like Cato grumbled that he was engaged in offensive war and ought to be handed over to the Gauls for punishment. The riches which Caesar gained in his looting of Gaul, moreover, were lavishly employed to bribe many Roman leaders; even the father-in-law of Cato was won by this maneuver.

Finally, the effects on Caesar himself were significant. The attentive reader of his *Commentaries* can see that at the beginning Caesar made serious mistakes as a general, from which he was saved by the training of his own men and by a lack of discipline of his opponents, brave and reckless though they often were. As time went on, Caesar perfected his skill so that in the subsequent civil wars he never committed a serious blunder save in underestimating the problems of naval logistics. Not only did he gain military confidence; he also won the hearts of his men and increased the strength of his loyal army from 2 to 13 legions. By 50 Caesar had become deft alike in oratory, in politics, and in the military art. Each of his possible competitors — Cicero, Pompey, and the conservative wing — was lacking in one or another field.

CIVIL WARS AND DICTATORSHIP

Outbreak of War. All Caesar's skills were to be needed by 50, for during his absence Roman politics dissolved into chaos. In an effort to imitate Caesar's ascent Crassus, the second of the triumvirate, picked a war with Parthia in 55. Unfortunately Crassus had to march his legionaries out into the open land of upper Mesopotamia and was surrounded in 53 near Carrhae by a smaller but mobile force of Parthian archers who were supplied with never-failing arrows from a camel train. His army was largely destroyed in the rout, and Crassus was killed.

In Rome gang warfare, headed by the rivals T. Annius Milo and Clodius, raged through the streets. Order broke down to the point that the people's food supply was endangered, and elections were occasions of great violence. The course of Pompey, who remained in the city throughout, is not easy to follow; his aim may have been to stand by until the chaos became serious enough to draw all elements voluntarily to seek his leadership as "first citizen." In 57 he was given control of the food supply for five years, and after a meeting of the Triumvirate at Luca in 56 he and Crassus were consuls again in 55. While Caesar's proconsulship was extended five years, Pompey was made proconsul of Spain, likewise for five years; but Pompey was permitted to govern his province (and later Libya) through legates. In 52 Clodius was killed in the gang warfare, and the Senate House was burned in his funeral hysteria; to restore order Pompey was chosen sole consul, the first time in republican history.

Beside Pompey stood the conservatives, who had their own short-sighted plans. This element considered Caesar its main opponent and sought stubbornly to remove him from his proconsulship so that he could be tried for his illegal activities as consul in 59. To do so the conservatives had to win over Pompey, and as the 50s wore on they came ever closer to this goal. The death of Julia in 54 snapped Pompey's main link with Caesar, and Crassus' defeat in the next year removed the last element of balance. Through complicated maneuvers in the year 50 the extremists quashed Caesar's plan to stand for consul *in absentia* and so to return home in office for the year 48; all compromises offered by the more moderate senators were banned.

On January 7, 49, the Senate finally voted martial law (the *senatus consultum ultimum*) and entrusted the Republic to Pompey. The agents of Caesar, Mark Antony, M. Scribonius Curio, and others who as tribunes had vetoed unfavorable measures, fled at once to Caesar. Since the ultimate result would be certain condemnation, Caesar rebelled against the government and on January 11 led the small force which was with him at the time across the Rubicon river, the legal boundary of Italy.

Civil Wars (49–45 B.C.). At this time the calendar, like everything else in Rome, was so out of adjustment that the date of his crossing was actually November 23. Caesar thus had at least a month of campaigning weather; and it behooved him to move swiftly if he were to forestall Pompey's plan to squeeze him in Gaul the following spring between the Pompeian army in Spain and a force then being raised in Italy. Like a whirlwind Caesar sped down the east coast of Italy. The new Pompeian recruits surrendered in masses, a testimony to the disinterest of the Italian countryside in the rivalries of Roman leaders. Pompey and the Senate had to evacuate Rome so quickly that they could not bring away the treasury, and fled to Brundisium whence they crossed the Balkans just ahead of Caesar.

Since Caesar had no ships, he could not follow. Instead he consolidated his power in the west, except for Africa. Sicily and Sardinia he garrisoned so as to safeguard the food supply of Rome; then he took the calculated risk of attacking the Pompeian forces in Spain while Pompey leisurely built up a new army in the Balkans. In a brilliant campaign of 40 days Caesar maneuvered the Pompeian generals in Nearer Spain into a position at Ilerda which lacked water or supplies and by psychological warfare forced their surrender without battle; the scholar Varro, who commanded in Farther Spain, then capitulated too. Caesar spared the enemy troops, as he did with all he conquered, and returned to Brundisium by the fall of 49.

Here some ships had been assembled, though not enough to carry all his force. Caesar put half his army aboard and crossed safely to a point south of Dyrrachium. The ships which he sent back were caught in part by the Pompeian admiral, his old foe Bibulus, and were sunk. Throughout the winter 49/8 Caesar was marooned on the east coast of the Adriatic, but Pompey waited calmly at Dyrrachium to polish him off in the spring. Finally Caesar's lieutenant Mark Antony succeeded in bringing over the rest of the army; in brilliant maneuvers Caesar wound up in the position of blockading Pompey, whose back was against the sea.

Yet Pompey still had naval command and could be fed, while Caesar's men were reduced to living off meat and roots (unlike their usual wheat ration), and even vowed to eat the bark of the trees. In July 48 Pompey broke out by an amphibious operation, and Caesar had no alternative but to withdraw east to the plains of Thessaly. Thanks to Pompey's naval force he was cut off from Italy, and Pompey, who followed, outnumbered him 40,000 to 22,000. Pompey undoubtedly could have won simply through logistical pressure, but in an effort to end the campaign in glory he offered Caesar battle at Pharsalus on August 9. Caesar's command over his men and skill in tactics on the battlefield first halted Pompey's superior cavalry and then produced a threat to Pompey's rear; the Pompeian army broke, and its general fled.

When Pompey reached Egypt, the fearful Ptolemaic government cut off his head and sent it to Caesar. While seeking his own egotistic ends, Pompey nonetheless had done yeoman service in repressing the separatist movement of Spain and in reorganizing the east; though his war against Caesar appears sluggish, one must remember that he was burdened down by a host of quarrelsome senators and that he did show remarkable inventiveness. As Cicero wrote in a letter, Pompey "holds with Themistocles that those who are masters of the sea will be victors in the end";[3] and his emphasis on cavalry at Pharsalus was most un-Roman. But neither as general on the battlefield nor as politician in Rome could Pompey match his opponent. Many of his followers, including Cicero, quickly sought and gained Caesar's pardon; others, however, fled with most of his ships to the west.

Although Caesar had secured the essential victory, against great odds, three more years of fighting were needed to tranquilize most of the Roman empire. He himself followed Pompey to Egypt where he was held over a year, partly by the wiles of the young Cleopatra at odds with her brother-husband Ptolemy XIII, partly because he came with so small a force that he was besieged in the royal palace at Alexandria until outside reinforcements could reach him. Then came the pacification of Asia Minor where he defeated Pharnaces, son of Mithridates, at Zela, the

[3] Cicero, *To Atticus* 10.8.

occasion for his famous dispatch *veni, vidi, vici* ("I came, I saw, I conquered"). After a brief stay in Rome he had two final wars against the fugitive Pompeian lieutenants. In Africa (46) he crushed Q. Metellus Scipio, father-in-law of Pompey, at Thapsus, whereupon Cato the Younger committed suicide in a philosophic gesture at Utica; in Spain (45) he met Pompey's sons and barely won the hard-fought battle of Munda.

Caesar's Dictatorship. When Caesar returned to Rome in 45, it was not to remain long. His own intention was to repay Parthia for the defeat of Crassus, and his troops were already moving east by the spring of 44; but he himself was never to follow.

In all, Caesar spent only 17 months in Rome during the years 49–44. Whatever long-range plans he may have had, accordingly, were not executed, and we would do well not to place too much credence in the ambitious engineering and other projects ascribed to him. Nonetheless, some basic points of his policies can be discerned.

Caesar, in the first place, was absolute master and proposed to maintain that mastery openly. He had himself made dictator in 46 for 10 years and in February 44 for life; he was normally consul; the inviolability (*sacrosanctitas*) of a tribune was awarded him in 44; in 63 he had secured election as *pontifex maximus;* and from 46 he was the equivalent of censor (*praefectura morum*). This miscellaneous assembly of constitutional and semiconstitutional powers, however, does not appear to have satisfied his clear-thinking mind; Plutarch is probably right, though modern students debate the matter, in portraying Caesar as planning to have himself made deified king on the Hellenistic model despite the inveterate hostility of Rome to kings. In his new calendar the month Quintilis was renamed July; his head appeared on coins in 44, an honor usually reserved to kings or gods; and early in 44 what was very close to an official cult of him was established with Antony as priest.

Second, Caesar had an almost un-Roman breadth of view toward his empire. He treated the Senate as a master; new members from the equestrian order and the Italian leading elements were added to the Senate by the hundreds. The number of magistracies was greatly increased, but these were not filled every year on time; those elected were virtually Caesar's nominees. Beyond this forceful amalgamation of old and new elements of the upper classes Caesar did much for the provincials. All Cisalpine Gaul was added to citizen territory, many Greeks were enfranchised individually, the Jews in the Aegean and in Palestine were protected, tax-farming was abolished at least in the province of Asia, and Caesar even founded some 20 citizen and Latin colonies outside Italy.

Third, whatever appeared to Caesar's coolly rational mind as obsolete or inadequate he reformed with little regard to past convention. For example, the disordered calendar was rearranged, effective January 1, 45, in the pattern which still obtains today (with one slight modification by Pope Gregory XIII in 1582). The grumbling reaction of Cicero and other conservatives to the new dates, however reasonable the reform, is a significant testimony to Caesar's failure to appreciate the power of ancient custom over men's minds.

The very rationality, indeed, that marked Caesar perhaps more than any other great ancient politician was at once his strength and his undoing. Although he had come to power on the culminating wave of a revolution against oligarchic control, he did not try to appeal to men's ideals, and he proclaimed that revolution was at an end. Although the aristocracy by and large opposed him, he expected it to accept the award of the battlefield. Liberal in pardons to the defeated, he gave many of them public offices; worse yet, he made the fatal mistake of dismissing his bodyguard. The result was a plot of the conservatives, led by M. Junius Brutus and C. Cassius Longinus, who murdered him by their dagger blows on March 15, 44 B.C. Ironically enough, Caesar fell at the foot of a statue of Pompey in the theater of Pompey, where the Senate was convening.

New Chaos (44–43 B.C.). The assassins burst out into the streets, waving their daggers and crying Liberty; but by the end of the day they had taken refuge from the angry mob on the Capitoline hill. They were a contemptible lot, not least because they had made no plans for the difficult task of restoring constitutional government. Yet on the other hand one must remember that both Cicero and Livy returned unfavorable verdicts on the rule of Caesar. In particular Caesar had not achieved a truly Roman solution to Rome's problems. His unending dreams of conquest, which extended beyond Parthia to Dacia (the modern Rumania) and Britain, were not what the weary empire needed; and his assassination in itself proved that he had not mastered the problem of yoking the very real strengths of the Roman upper classes to his cause. Caesar ended the Republic, but he did not begin the next phase.

The man best placed to succeed Caesar was his main lieutenant, then consul, the bluff roistering Mark Antony (c. 82–30). On the 15th Antony hid until he could assess the situation; then he seized Caesar's private papers, plans, and money, and soon stood as the main figure in Rome. After a public funeral for Caesar which incited the masses to frenzy the assassins found it convenient to leave the city and eventually acquired governorships in the eastern provinces. The more moderate conservatives distrusted Antony, but at the moment their leader Cicero stood despondently quiet in favor of compromise.

All ignored the sole male relative of Caesar, his grandnephew C. Octavius, a sickly, slight lad born September 23, 63 B.C. and therefore only 18 at this point. Caesar had planned to give the youth some military experience and so had sent him part way east to Apollonia in Dalmatia with some of the troops destined for the Parthian war. On the news of Caesar's murder Octavius hastily returned to Rome despite the prayers of his mother, and there found he had been made heir to three-quarters of Caesar's wealth as well as adopted posthumously. Since Antony refused to turn over his inheritance and also failed to pay Caesar's bequest of 300 sesterces to every Roman citizen, Octavius sold all his family property to meet this obligation. Inasmuch as Antony also barred the formal rite of adoption and tried to suppress Octavius by charging the young man with an effort at his own assassination, Octavius turned by October to Caesar's veterans settled in Campania. From these men and from the legions called from Macedonia, Octavius raised a private army.

With this asset he became an object of interest to the Ciceronian faction, which was moving toward a break with Antony. Early in 43 Octavius as propraetor and the new consuls A. Hirtius and C. Vibius Pansa were in north Italy, prepared to fight Antony, who had foolishly left Rome in an effort to seize Cisalpine Gaul from one of the assassins, Decimus Brutus. At home Cicero rose to the height of his career in his 14 "Philippic orations," which blasted Antony ever more directly. In the field the senatorial forces threw Antony out of north Italy in May, though only at the cost of the lives of the two consuls.

The governors of the western provinces, however, rallied to Antony, and Octavius realized ever more clearly that he had no lasting place on the side of the Senate, which refused in July to give him one of the vacant consulships. Cicero, indeed, would have humored him, but a witticism attributed to Cicero asserted the youth was "to be honored, lifted up, and lifted off." [4]

In rebuttal Octavius marched his army, which now included the troops of Hirtius and Pansa, on Rome. He had himself elected consul on August 19 at the age of 19, and was now formally adopted as son of Caesar, whereafter he was called C. Julius Caesar Octavianus or, in modern usage, Octavian. Then Octavian secured the outlawry of Caesar's assassins, but to counter both this element and the Senate he arranged to join with Antony and M. Aemilius Lepidus, governor of Transalpine Gaul and Nearer Spain. This pact of the Second Triumvirate was sealed in a meeting on an island in a river near Bononia (Bologna) in early November.

Thereupon the three moved down on a helpless Rome and on November 27 had themselves officially designated triumvirs "for ordering the Republic" for five years, with virtually unlimited powers for taxation and appointment of officials. Before carrying out vengeance on Caesar's assassins, a few important steps had to be settled in Rome. Caesar was officially made a god; and a proscription more severe than that of Sulla was launched against 300 senators and 2000 equestrians. Antony, in particular, had scores to settle; but the three needed money for their armies. Although Octavian was later to try to hide his part in this blood-bath, there is no reason to think he was any more merciful at this point in his career than were his elder associates.

One of the prime victims was Cicero, who had fought desperately but in vain to prevent the rise of a new dictatorship. Indecisive in flight, he was caught and slain on the Appian way near Formia on December 7. His head was brought back to Rome and nailed to the *rostra* in the Forum. Antony's wife Fulvia mockingly pierced his tongue with her bodkin — no act could have better symbolized the frightful end of the Roman Republic.

BIBLIOGRAPHY

Sources. No period of ancient history before the fourth century after Christ provides so much firsthand evidence as that covered in this chap-

---

[4] Cicero, *To His Friends* 11.21.1; tr. R. Syme.

ter. Caesar's *Gallic Wars* (Penguin L21, tr. S. A. Handford, 1951) and *Civil War* (Loeb Classical Library) carry his account only to the defeat of Pompey; but his lieutenants wrote on the Alexandrian, African, and Spanish campaigns. Cicero's many writings are noted in the text; selections may be found in *Basic Works of Cicero,* ed. Moses Hadas (New York: Modern Library 272, 1951), or *Selected Writings,* tr. M. Grant (Harmondsworth: Penguin L99, 1960). Unfortunately, we have no products of Pompey's pen; but points of view independent of Caesar can be found in Plutarch's lives of Crassus, Cato the Younger, Pompey, and Marcus Brutus. There are also Plutarchean lives of Caesar, Cicero, Sertorius, and Lucullus; the gossipy biographer C. Suetonius Tranquillus (c. A.D. 69–140) wrote *Lives of the Twelve Caesars* (Penguin L72, tr. R. Graves, 1957) beginning with Julius Caesar. He is the first surviving biographer to be deeply interested in personal details and gives a wealth of information. The histories of Florus and Appian noted in the previous chapter carry across this period; Books 36–54 of Dio Cassius' history, which cover the period 68–10 B.C., are preserved intact (Loeb Classical Library). Sallust wrote a pamphlet on the *Catilinarian Conspiracy* which is interesting to contrast with Cicero's own orations (Loeb Classical Library).

Caesar's protection of the Jews is illuminated in Josephus, *Antiquities of the Jews* 14.10 (Loeb Classical Library); his reorganization of local government in Italy and the charter of one Caesarian colony in Spain are preserved in inscriptions, both of laws actually passed under Antony (Lewis and Reinhold, *Roman Civilization,* I, pp. 408–12, 416–28). The best translation of Lucretius is that of R. E. Latham (Harmondsworth: Penguin L18, 1951); several are available of Catullus, including that of Horace Gregory (New York: Norton, 1972) with the Latin text.

The development of the Celts is noted occasionally in classical historians; Posidonius paid attention to them, and others refer to their religious customs. Archeological material is abundant in the graves of the wealthy leaders; one, of a princess found at Vix in 1953, had a huge bronze crater, gold diadem, and Attic and Etruscan pottery of the late sixth century B.C.

Further Reading. The general history of this confused era may be found in F. B. March, *History of the Roman World from 146 to 30 B.C.* (2d ed.; London: Methuen, 1953), and *Founding of the Roman Empire*

(Westport, Conn.: Greenwood, 1975); or W. K. Lacey, *Cicero and the End of the Roman Republic* (London: Hodder & Stoughton, 1978). Some of its hidden forces are exposed by Ronald Syme, *Roman Revolution* (Oxford: Oxford Paperback 1, 1960), and Lily Ross Taylor, *Party Politics in the Age of Caesar* (Berkeley: University of California Paperback 53, 1961). E. S. Gruen discusses in detail *The Last Generation of The Roman Republic* (Berkeley: University of California Press, 1973).

Although there is no first-rate life of Caesar, the following are useful: J. P. V. D. Balsdon, *Julius Caesar* (New York: Atheneum, 1967); M. Gelzer, *Caesar* (Oxford: Blackwell, 1979); and, on his literary ability, Frank Adcock, *Caesar as a Man of Letters* (Cambridge: Cambridge University Press, 1956). Cicero is perhaps easier to assess. H. J. Haskell, *This Was Cicero* (New York: Knopf, 1942), is a favorable study by a modern newspaper editor; a lawyer, R. N. Wilkin, discusses particularly his qualities as *Eternal Lawyer* (New York: Macmillan, 1947); J. Carcopino, *Cicero: The Secrets of His Correspondence,* 2 vols. (Westport, Conn.: Greenwood), is hostile. There are recent lives of Crassus by B. A. Marshall (Amsterdam: Hakkert, 1976), and A. Ward (Columbia: University of Missouri Press, 1977); of Pompey by P. A. L. Greenhalgh (London: Weidenfeld & Nicolson, 1979–81) and R. Seager (Berkeley: University of California Press, 1979); of Brutus by W. L. Clarke (Ithaca: Cornell University Press, 1981).

For the Celts see T. G. E. Powell, *The Celts* (New York: Thames & Hudson, 1979); P. Jacobsthal, *Early Celtic Art* (Teaneck, N.J.: Somerset); S. Piggott, *The Druids* (New York: Praeger, 1975). Caesar's conquest is analyzed in detail by T. Rice Holmes, *Caesar's Conquest of Gaul* (New York: AMS).

Lucretius is well discussed by E. E. Sikes, *Lucretius: Poet and Philosopher* (New York: Russell, 1971); Catullus by E. A. Havelock, *Lyric Genius of Catullus* (Oxford: Blackwell, 1939), and T. Frank, *Catullus and Horace* (New York: Russell, 1965). G. Boissier wrote a very sensitive work, *Cicero and His Friends* (New York: Cooper Square, 1971); W. Warde Fowler, *Social Life at Rome in the Age of Cicero* (New York: Macmillan, 1909), though old, is still useful.

26

THE AUGUSTAN AGE

Although Caesar has conquered the romantic imagination of later ages, his grandnephew had far the greater effect on Roman history. The changes in name of this truly astounding figure signalize the steps in his career: born C. Octavius, he was from 43 B.C. called C. Julius Caesar Octavianus (or Octavian), "the son of the god" Caesar; and after 27 B.C. was known as Imperator Caesar Augustus, the first of the Roman "emperors." Despite his sickly nature Augustus lived on to A.D. 14.

During his 59 years of active political life after Caesar's murder, Octavian-Augustus first gained sole mastery over overwhelming odds, and then brought an end to the whirlwind of revolution which had beset Rome for a century. Immediately, men's sense of relief and joy helped to spur the most remarkable outburst of arts and letters in Roman civilization; in the longer run the new system of government gave lasting peace to the Mediterranean world.

To distinguish the scarcely veiled autocracy of the new system from the republican structure we call the period from 27 B.C. onward the Roman Empire. The Early Empire, in which the Augustan pattern was outwardly dominant, extended down to A.D. 284, at which point a very considerable change produced the Later Empire. In this chapter we shall consider the restoration of order under Augustus; thereafter we can watch the unfolding of the long-range effects on culture and society. Beside the earthly savior Augustus there was, to be sure, another Saviour in these years, but the rise of Christianity needs its own special attention.

The Formative Years (43–36 B.C.). Octavian's career began at the age of 18. His visible assets were his youth and his claim to be Caesar's adopted son; his hidden qualities included a puritanical spirit which reflected his birth and early training in a Latin hill town, an utterly ruthless ambition, a determination to avenge Caesar, and a cold intelligence of rare degree. Withal he was able to win some lasting friends and aides, chiefly of equestrian origin. One, M. Vipsanius Agrippa (*c.* 63–12), was to be his admiral and general; another, C. Maecenas (d. 8 B.C.), his diplomat, patron of letters, and minister of the interior. By necessity and by inclination Octavian looked beyond the senatorial aristocracy for his followers, and the opportunity which his rise gave to these new elements helps to explain his success. Yet in the end one must always come back to Octavian's own qualities.

After using and throwing over the Senate in his first year, Octavian had become triumvir with Antony and Lepidus in November 43. Once scores had been settled in the proscription and money confiscated to pay a huge army, Antony and Octavian marched east to put down Brutus and Cassius, who had gained command of the groaning eastern provinces. In 42 the opposing forces met at Philippi in Macedonia. The sickly Octavian remained in his tent during the two battles except, fortunately, at the point when it was sacked by the enemy. Antony, however, won the day, and both Cassius and Brutus committed suicide.

Thereafter the victors divided the empire. Lepidus, the makeweight, finally received Africa; Antony took over the east (and Gaul) to extort money and to face the Parthians; Octavian was given Spain, Sardinia, and the difficult commission of settling 100,000 veterans in Italy. To do so he had to take away land from its owners over much of the peninsula, including that of a fledgling poet called Virgil; the upshot was a sullen rebellion in 41–40, led by Antony's ex-wife Fulvia and his brother Lucius Antonius, consul of 41. Octavian was ruthless in putting down this rebellion at its last stronghold, Perusia (Perugia).

Then came another critical test. Sextus Pompeius, a son of Pompey the Great, had seized extensive naval strength on the murder of Caesar and now held Sicily and Sardinia as well as blockading Rome's food supplies. Octavian himself was stoned by the hungry populace; slaves, proscripts, and the discontented ran off to join Sextus; but Octavian had no naval strength to meet the threat. A temporary peace was arranged between the two in 39 by Antony, who had married his colleague's noble sister Octavia the previous year; but open warfare between Octavian and Sextus broke out in 38. The first fleets that Octavian built were crushed; he then recalled Agrippa from Gaul to create new flotillas in 37 — a squadron constructed near Naples was trained in an artificial harbor. Finally in 36 Agrippa won decisive battles at Mylae and Naulochus, though Octavian was defeated with the Adriatic squadron off Tauromenium. Sextus fled east and was executed by one of Antony's governors.

Through the fires of foreign and internal war and the bitter problems of mastering the violently disturbed social fabric of Italy, Octavian learned vital lessons in these critical years. From being an avenger of his uncle, ruthless and lawless, he slowly shifted until by 36 he stood as defender of law and order and the old republican virtues. On his victory over Sextus he remitted back taxes, burned the propaganda of previous years, and promised a restoration of constitutional government. The slaves he took on Sextus' rowing benches he returned to their owners or crucified. More and more Octavian's appeal was to the conservative classes and especially to the solidly based, leading elements of Italy.[1] Out of the wreckage of abstract ideals which had taken place in the past 20 years, he was fashioning a new program; his resulting conquest of men's minds can be seen in the fact that first Virgil and then Horace had joined his cause in the early 30s.

Duel with Antony and Cleopatra (36–30 B.C.). It was time that Octavian had reached a clear policy designed to marshal the west behind him, for his relations with Antony grew ever worse. In 36 Octavian had set aside the third triumvir, Lepidus, who had feebly joined in the war against Sextus; and he had already seized Gaul in 40 on the death there of Antony's lieutenant. Antony, meanwhile, had fought a war with Parthia in which he had repelled Parthian efforts to take Syria but in 36 had barely escaped destruction.

---

[1] Some of the qualities of the middle elements in the Roman world at this time can perhaps be detected in the grave busts of Plate XXIV, which are probably to be dated to the last decades of the Republic.

Another actor had entered the scene in the form of the wily Cleopatra. The last Ptolemaic ruler of Egypt had been no more than mistress to Caesar and had born him a son, Caesarion; in 41–40 she played the same role to Antony, who then had turned away to Octavia. Now, however, as Antony was weakened in strength and in need of money, she regained her place with him and conjoined sex with intelligence to obtain a wider role for Egypt. By 34 Antony had made her "Queen of Kings," as overlord of the east beside him.

All this was grist to Octavian's machine for propaganda, which was the most dextrous of ancient times. Octavian could not attack Antony directly because of his old Caesarian ties and his wide circle of friends; but by focusing attention on Cleopatra and by insinuating that Antony had lost his wits in drink and love he subtly moved toward the elimination of his last rival. In the process Cleopatra was magnified into a threat to the survival of Roman ways and Roman mastery, and so assumed the image of *femme fatale* which has ever since been her memory.

By 32 the two were on the point of rupture. The two consuls of the year and 300 of the 1000 senators joined Antony, who finally divorced Octavia. Her brother then baldly seized Antony's will, deposited with the Vestal Virgins in Rome, and published its declaration that Caesarion was a legal son of Caesar (a threat to Octavian's own position), the magnificent legacies to Antony's children by Cleopatra, and Antony's wish that he be buried in Alexandria beside Cleopatra. At the same time Octavian levied an extraordinary income tax of 25 per cent and a 12½ per cent capital levy on the wealth of freedmen. All Italy "voluntarily" swore an oath of allegiance to him as leader of a Roman crusade against the eastern menace, an interesting step both in its suggestion that the master of Rome should be backed by personal loyalty rather than impersonal law and in its revelation that Rome and Italy were coming to be a united concept.

Thus the two warlords prepared to hurl east and west against each other in the third civil war of two decades. During the winter 32/1 Antony and Cleopatra came up to Greece, where many of their rowers died in a plague. Octavian and his general Agrippa moved their navy, the same which had been trained against Sextus Pompey, down to Brundisium; and in the spring of 31 Agrippa quickly wrested the initiative by bold attacks on Antony's supply lines to Egypt. Through the most skillful naval campaign of ancient times he bottled up Antony by the summer on the west coast of the Balkans. On September 2 Antony sought to break out from the gulf of Actium, but his disaffected navy with its poorly trained rowers fought badly. Cleopatra fled, and Antony deserted the battle to follow her to Egypt.

After mopping up in Greece Octavian followed. Since Antony's deputies in the east fell away, Antony could not even defend Egypt and committed suicide on the false news that Cleopatra was dead; she, in turn, soon killed herself when it became clear that the cold Octavian wanted to preserve her only to exhibit in Roman triumph. On August 1, 30 B.C. the victor had entered Alexandria. As he looked down on the embalmed body of Alexander, he could reflect that he had begun his career two years younger than the great Macedonian, with far fewer resources; now, master of the Mediterranean world, he was only 32.

Restoration of Constitutional Government. Although Octavian had risen to dominance over many hurdles, any one of which could have tripped him to destruction, he now faced his greatest challenge. The east was prostrate; conquered Egypt was sullen; the masses and slaves of Italy were barely contained; the frontiers of Europe and Asia alike were insecure. Worst of all, his world was so used to violence, to militarism, and to change that it could not easily forswear this poisonous excitement.

Yet his contemporaries also desperately sought peace and order, and most men now were willing to sacrifice the dubious political liberty of the Republic, which was in any case a faint memory after years of chaos. Through his period of testing in the early 30s and through his meditations on the qualities and defects of Caesar's dictatorship, Octavian was prepared to move forward on a course which would halt revolution, meet the basic needs of his subjects, and at the same time honor the ideals of the society in which he had been reared. To a modern observer his restoration of order may appear simple, almost fated; but a study in detail of his career must leave one in amazement that he could master the plots against his life, the unruliness or incompetence of many of his officials, and the heavy pressures from his subjects to detour him from his chosen path.

Of immediate importance were a lasting disposition of the forces which had won him victory and an at least preliminary arrangement of his constitutional position. Over 100,000 veterans were given land in Italy and the provinces, for which Octavian could now furnish recompense to its previous owners from the confiscated treasures of Egypt; the remaining forces by land and by sea were formed into a permanent army and navy, on lines which will be considered below. The militaristic spirit of the age was diverted into a great program of frontier adjustment and internal pacification. Throughout his life Octavian remained sole master of the armed forces, which took their oath of allegiance to him and which he termed "mine" in his *Res Gestae;* but the unruliness of his troops at various points in the 30s warned him against relying solely on them for mastery.

To secure a more solid constitutional position, a critical problem in view of Caesar's murder, Octavian experimented over a decade and more. In 36 he had received the tribunician sacrosanctity by special grant. In 33 he dropped the title of triumvir as inconsistent with his effort to appear truly Roman, and relied for a time on being chosen consul each year and on his purportedly voluntary support as leader of a sworn party. This position, however, was neither strictly constitutional nor adequate in the long run; and in 28–27, as he stated in his *Res Gestae,* "when I had put an end to the civil wars, having acquired supreme power over the Empire by universal consent, I transferred the Republic from my own authority to the free disposition of the Senate and People of Rome." [2]

On January 13, 27, in a prearranged session of the Senate he offered to lay down his powers, but the Senate insisted that he continue to administer the state and granted him the proconsular *imperium* over three troubled areas of the Empire (Spain, Gaul, Syria) for a 10-year period. Three days later it voted him honors for his virtues of valor, clemency, justice, and piety, and the title of Augustus, a religious term connoting superhuman qualities. The normal functioning of the Senate and the magistracies was re-established so that in a technical sense the Republic once more existed.

This settlement was far from definitive. In 23, for instance, Augustus gave up the consulship after a critical illness, and thereafter stood farther behind the façade of government. Yet historians properly take 27 B.C. as marking the point at which order may be said to have been restored, and the rule of the *princeps,* or "first citizen," was consolidated.

[2] *Res Gestae* 34.

THE AUGUSTAN POLITICAL SYSTEM

The Central Government. The new form of government was one of the most artful blends of old theories and new principles ever conceived by any statesman. Its satisfaction of the needs and aspirations of the important elements in the Mediterranean world underlay two centuries of peace in the Roman Empire. On the other hand, the compromises which the practical Augustus made with an ideally perfect autocracy caused serious trouble in the relations of the rulers and the senatorial aristocracy for the next 100 years.

Technically the organs of republican government continued in their ancient fashion, and the people remained the font of powers, which it granted to Augustus through the assemblies. The Roman Empire was a rule of law, unlike the arbitrary despotisms of its eastern neighbors. In practice this principle became ever weaker as the rulers grew more absolute, yet the Empire passed on to western Europe the great principle of the ancient city-state that a free citizen had rights and duties. In theory the powers of the emperor reverted back to the people on his death, so that there was not true hereditary succession in the system we call "Empire."

Nevertheless Augustus was master. Most of the frontier districts and also the Spains came to be "imperial" provinces assigned to the procon-sular *imperium* of the ruler, who sent out legates of the senatorial class to serve as governors at his pleasure. The other, "senatorial" provinces, to which the Senate assigned proconsuls, were subject to Augustus' overrid-ing power (*maius imperium*). Epigraphic evidence attests his interfer-ence in the senatorial province of Libya to bring peace between the natives and the Greeks, and increasingly the emperor with his judicial advisers served as a court of appeal for all the Empire.

Italy and Rome, as of old, were the responsibility of the Senate and the magistrates, but here too Augustus had sufficient powers to limit ineffi-ciency. The treasury (*aerarium*) remained under senatorial control; yet Augustus' own vast possessions (*patrimonium*), administered by his freedmen and equestrian procurators, provided him independent funds with which he had often to aid the treasury. Each imperial province had its *fiscus* for local taxes, from which its troops were paid.

Both in the provinces and at Rome he mistrusted popular action, which had heightened the anarchy of the past half-century. The Roman populace, however, formed an important constitutional element; while controlling it strictly, he sought also to gain its favor by "bread and games,"[3] that is, by giving magnificent shows and frequent distributions of cash and by supervising the food supply through his Prefect of the Annona, who gave out free wheat to a fixed roll of 200,000 recipients. Sporadically Augustus appointed a Prefect for the City, which later became a permanent post; always he paraded his tribunician power, which he received in 30 or 23, to suggest his popular support and his protection of the common people.

With regard to the aristocracy his position was delicate. Caesar's fate warned him to respect its claim to pre-eminence; and in any case he needed to draw from it the generals, governors, jurisconsults, and advisers required to administer the Empire. Yet the old families were in part dying out or had been decimated by the civil wars; and their contentions for honor and for freedom to misgovern the provinces could not be granted full sway. Augustus purged the Senate on several occasions of its drones and ne'er-do-wells, and reinforced it by heavy drafts from the equestrians; increasingly in the future "new men" could rise to the Senate by imperial patronage. Both of the upper classes now had formal limits, that of the senators the possession of 1,000,000 sesterces, the age of 25, and proper military service; and that of the equestrians 400,000 sesterces. While granting deference to this reformed upper group, Augustus had many levers to control it besides essential mastery over admission to its ranks. Through the tribunician power he had an ultimate veto as well as the power of convening the Senate and presenting legislation to the Tribal assembly. As *pontifex maximus* after the death of Lepidus in 12 B.C. he supervised the religious machinery. In the Senate itself he had the right of first speech, among other privileges; above all, however, he exceeded others in his *auctoritas,* or prestige, that indefinable authority which clusters about great men and smooths their way by the general tendency to accept their opinions.

In general Augustus was successful in winning support, perhaps too much so. In times of food shortage the people clamored for him to translate his mastery into open dictatorship, and even aristocrats were often willing to shirk their responsibilities by referring problems to Au-

[3] Juvenal, *Satires* 10.81.

gustus; but always he clung to his position as *princeps,* after which the imperial system is often called the Principate. Augustus accepted such extraordinary titles as "father of the fatherland" (*pater patriae*) in 2 B.C., but he would not permit himself to be placed in an openly unconstitutional role.

To rally the ancestral strengths of the Roman spirit Augustus not only paraded respect for its constitutional forms but also essayed a remarkably comprehensive restoration of its religious and social ways. This may in part have been calculated, but one must keep in mind also his simple moral background and his deeply conservative spirit. On the religious side, he revived many old rites, while streamlining the cult in general. In Rome he rebuilt 82 temples and built others, including one to his major patron Apollo beside his home on the Palatine hill; as a gesture of Hellenic sympathy he was initiated into the Eleusinian mysteries.

On the social and moral sides he tried to curb luxury among the commoners, to check inhuman treatment of slaves, and by laws in 17 and 2 B.C. and A.D. 4 to limit the number of slaves who were freed for ex-slaves became Roman citizens. Especially he sought by blandishment, by the simple tone of his life with Livia, and by legislation against celibacy and adultery and in favor of child-bearing to restrict the self-destruction of the upper classes. These laws, from 18 B.C. on, were consolidated by the Papian-Poppaean code of A.D. 9 (named after the two bachelor consuls of the year!). Here his success was only partial, for many elements took the new peace and security as an opportunity for unrestrained luxury; but some groups, including the leading families of the Italian towns, furnished him enough able and dedicated men to staff his armies and to supervise the provincial government as major senatorial and equestrian officials.

As a kernel for his own central administration, Augustus made use chiefly of slaves and imperial freedmen. This side of the governmental machinery was to grow continuously in later generations and to evolve from a purely personal staff into a true bureaucracy. Under Augustus much depended on the unremitting attention of the ruler and his immediate relatives. Augustus himself had only one daughter Julia; but his third wife, Livia, had two sons, Tiberius and Drusus. These, together with Agrippa, served as his generals in most of his major wars. Unfortunately Agrippa died in 12 B.C.; Drusus was killed by a fall from his horse in Germany in 9 B.C.; and Tiberius, who was in the end to succeed Augustus, found it difficult to live in harmony with his imperious step-father.

Provinces and Cities. So simple a central structure could not have succeeded had not Augustus continued the republican policy of decentralizing responsibility. The provincial governors were now better checked to prevent the rapacity of men like Verres and, in the imperial provinces, served for longer periods; but basically their functions remained restricted to general supervision of local justice, tax collection, and military protection. The detailed processes of government were almost entirely in the hands of the local units — cities in the more advanced areas, tribes and other groupings elsewhere. On this level Augustus firmly favored the upper classes, which responded joyfully to his introduction of peace.

In many ways the Roman Empire, under Augustus and later, appears as a partnership between the emperors and the local upper classes. The emperors gave peace and order; the local leaders in return furnished the money and the loyalty required to hold together so vast a world. Augustus and later rulers, true, found it necessary at times to interfere to prevent local extortion, but on the economic side at least Augustus promoted a policy of *laissez faire* which led to a quick revival of the economic energies of his subjects.

His main positive steps in this direction were the reorganization of the coinage to provide a sound imperial currency in gold, silver, and base metal; the maintenance of a permanent navy to eliminate piracy; and a simple tax structure which provided enough money at this time without overburdening the subjects. Virtually all landowners, except in Italy, paid a land tax, and another tax was assessed on other forms of property; to give a fair base, assessments were conducted every five years in Roman towns and at intervals in the provinces. Collection of these direct taxes was supervised by an equestrian procurator in imperial provinces, and by the quaestor in senatorial provinces; in the latter tax-farmers still had some role, as was generally true everywhere in the collection of such indirect taxes as customs.

From Caesar's fate Augustus learned to maintain the open distinction between Romans as masters and provincials as subjects. Nevertheless he too granted citizenship on a wide scale, founded military colonies in the provinces, paid deference to Greek culture, and in other ways paraded before the provincials his interest in their welfare. In response the upper classes in the eastern provinces, released at last from the terrific burdens of civil wars, proceeded from 29 B.C. on to deify him in the usual Hellenistic custom and formally to institute a cult of *Roma et Augustus*. This deification Augustus accepted and even promoted in other parts of his realm as a mode of securing patriotic attachment; in many cities the freedmen held a special place in the cult as *seviri Augustales*. In Italy and Rome, however, he remained only the son of a god (Julius Caesar) until his death.

Not only did men deify Augustus and name the month of his greatest triumphs after him; they also erected statues of him in profusion all over the Empire and beyond as far as the Roman trading posts in India. A pattern for enthusiastic praise of the ruler now began, which in later reigns was often purely conventional but under Augustus had real meaning. The preamble to a degree by the council of the province of Asia runs thus:

> Whereas external and deathless Nature has vouchsafed to men, as the greatest good and bringer of overwhelming benefaction, the emperor Augustus; the father who gives us happy life; the savior of all mankind in common whose provident care has not only fulfilled but even surpassed the hopes of all: for both land and sea are at peace, the cities are teeming with the blessings of concord, plenty, and respect for law, and the culmination and harvest of all good things bring fair hopes for the future and contentment with the present.[4]

Peace by Land and by Sea. Thus far we have considered the practical and spiritual means by which Augustus bound the upper classes of the provinces and of Rome to support his rule. Together with this great range of problems, Augustus had also to restore order internally and to protect the Empire against the external threats from the neighboring peoples of Eurasia and Africa. His success in meeting this problem and in forming a military system which could cope with it in the future was one of his most magnificent achievements. Thrice he ceremonially closed the arch of Janus in the Forum to symbolize the presence of complete

---

[4] *Ancient Greek Inscriptions in the British Museum*, IV.1, ed. by Gustav Hirschfeld (Oxford, 1893), No. 894; the translation in part by David Magie, *Roman Rule in Asia Minor*, I (Princeton: Princeton University Press, 1950), p. 490.

peace in the Empire; and his coinage and public monuments celebrate his military and diplomatic activity.

In Rome itself he set up a police force for the first time (the Urban Cohorts) and in A.D. 6 a semimilitary fire brigade (the Vigiles) to repress the disorders of the past century. In the vicinity and throughout Italy lay his own bodyguard, the nine Praetorian Cohorts under their two Praetorian Prefects; for Augustus did not repeat Caesar's foolhardiness in dismissing protection.

The troubled areas of the Empire itself were brought into order (see Map 18). Spain required Augustus' own presence for three years and protracted military action from 28 to 19 B.C., in which the northwest districts were subjugated; thereafter three legions lay in the Iberian peninsula as the heaviest internal garrison anywhere in the Empire. Egypt, too, Augustus did not trust, and he stationed two legions in the province. Senators were barred from Egypt; its governor or Prefect was a trusted senior equestrian. Some minor districts, such as Thrace and Palestine, were left under client kings so as to avoid direct Roman responsibility; but 10 years after the death of Herod the Great in 4 B.C. the Romans reluctantly had to make Palestine itself another equestrian province.

On the southern frontier Augustus launched a rather unsuccessful expedition in 25 B.C. across the Red Sea against the Sabaean kingdom (in modern Yemen). With regard to Parthia, however, he neatly conjoined threats of force and diplomacy to secure a peace in 20 B.C. by which the Parthians returned the standards they had taken at Carrhae and in subsequent Roman disasters. Augustus was particularly proud of this feat, which he celebrated on coins and in other media; but the militaristic spirit of Roman aristocrats was not quite so satisfied with this negotiated arrangement.

To drain off this spirit and to secure defensible frontiers in Europe, Augustus fought most of his wars along the northern boundary, which had been very ill-defined in the Republic. Britain he let go as not worth conquest; but Roman armies majestically rolled forward in Europe itself, usually under the leadership of his stepsons Tiberius and Drusus. The two joined in a pincers attack in 15 B.C. to gain Switzerland and the bulk of modern Austria. Other concentric attacks under Agrippa and then Tiberius, 13–9 B.C., brought Roman power forward to the middle

Danube, and further campaigns under other generals conquered Moesia (modern Bulgaria). Basing his supplies on water transport, Drusus plunged into Germany as far as the Elbe river, which he reached in 9 B.C. before his death. No other Roman leader ever added so much territory as did Augustus.

Conquest, however, was easier than consolidation. By A.D. 6 Tiberius was ready to attack King Maroboduus of the Marcomanni in modern Bohemia, but he had to forgo this rounding-off of Rome's German possessions to meet a great insurrection in Pannonia. While this area was being reconquered, a worse disaster occurred in the forested, loosely held wilds of Germany. In A.D. 9 the governor P. Quinctilius Varus was sucked into a trap in the Teutoburger forest by Arminius, who had learned the military art as a Roman auxiliary commander. Three legions were wiped out, Varus committed suicide, and all Germany was lost. The aging Augustus had neither the military strength nor the energy to launch a reconquest. Tiberius regained Pannonia, but the Roman frontier to the west remained on the Rhine. Historians have often speculated if subsequent European history would have been greatly different had the Germans been Romanized, as were the Celts of Gaul; and certainly the Elbe-Danube defense line would have been shorter than that of the Rhine-Danube. The military and financial strengths of the Empire, nonetheless, had been tested to their utmost in the Augustan expansion, and only minor advances were to seem feasible in later generations.

The pacification and expansion of the Roman world were supported by a great reorganization and consolidation of its military system, largely carried out by Agrippa, but on lines determined by Augustus. A permanent navy was created from the flotillas of the civil wars, with main bases at Misenum on the west coast of Italy and Ravenna on the east coast; minor fleets were established now or later in Egypt, Syria, the Black Sea, and the river frontiers of Europe. Although a junior service in comparison to the army, the navy wiped out piracy for the only time in Mediterranean history before the nineteenth century after Christ, and safeguarded Roman command of the sea — the hub of the ancient world — so well that it had to fight no battles for over 200 years.

A permanent army was fashioned from the great forces of the civil wars. Twenty-eight legions, of 5500 infantry and 120 cavalry each, were formed as the backbone. After the loss of 3, under Varus, 25 remained, which normally were distributed as follows: Spain, 3; Rhine, 8; Danube, 7; Syria, 4; Egypt, 2; Africa, 1. These legions technically were recruited only from citizen volunteers, though some noncitizens were actually used by being given citizenship on enrollment. Beside the legions stood an equal number of auxiliary units of light infantry and cavalry, grouped in much smaller units of 500–1000 men (cavalry *alae,* infantry *cohortes*); the auxiliaries were not Roman citizens but blocks drafted from warlike peoples. Legionaries served 20 years and received a bonus on retirement, which was paid from A.D. 6 by a military treasury fed by a 5 per cent tax on certain legacies and a 1 per cent tax on sales. Auxiliaries spent 25 years under the colors and, from the middle of the first century after Christ, were given Roman citizenship on retirement.

This army, which numbered under Augustus some 250–300,000 men, had to defend 4000 miles of frontier. Its pay and supply were by far the greatest burden on the Empire's financial structure. Coinage was at least partially designed for its needs, and the supply of food required a great apparatus of roads, boats, and collecting points along the frontiers. Since the army was mainly stationed along the uncivilized boundaries, its effects in bringing Roman culture to the edges of the cultivated world were great. Near its posts rose civilian settlements which often developed into cities, such as Köln (*colonia Agrippina*) in Germany. As another example, the advance southward into the Numidian wastes of the main camp of the third Augustan legion, which remained in the same province for 300 years, marked the successive occupation and domestication of new zones in this area.

While its success in defending the Roman world for centuries was to make the army of the Empire one of the greatest ever known, there were inevitable defects in its structure. The centurions (noncommissioned officers) of the legions were experienced veterans, as were often the commanders of the auxiliary units; but the legates (commanders) of the legions and the military tribunes were aristocrats who normally shifted back and forth between civilian and military posts as in the Republic. Some middle-grade officers were actually close to being professional soldiers, but Augustus and his successors were very loath to encourage the appearance of truly professional generals.

The division, again, between legions and auxiliary units, a reflection of the Augustan emphasis on the superiority of Roman citizens, was only slowly and incompletely removed. Worse yet, Augustus and later emperors sought to pacify and disarm the interior districts so that the Empire became ever more an organism with a hard shell and soft interior. Apart from the Praetorian Guard the emperors had no mobile, strategic reserve; in case of war on one frontier, troops had to be shifted from a less threatened sector, a process aided by the interior lines and naval command of the Empire. The size of the army was too small and had to be increased in later years; but the population of the Empire, probably somewhat over 50 millions under Augustus, could scarcely support a much larger military structure either with recruits or with supplies. The Roman Empire has been called "a geographic impossibility" in view of its vast dimensions at a time when men could only walk, ride, or sail; but the careful training, advanced supply system, and pride of its troops born of repeated victories held it together as long as it remained spiritually and economically strong.

THE AUGUSTAN AGE

Its Spirit. Two salient characteristics stamp all the magnificent achievements of Augustan arts and letters, which form the greatest triumph of Roman civilization. Always in this age one comes back to the figure of Augustus, who deftly interwove his policies and his own triumphs into culture to a degree rarely equaled by any political leader. Augustus himself had a native talent of high order, which is only partially suggested by the vigor and clarity of his *Res Gestae,* and genuinely appreciated the work of poets and artists, whom he subsidized directly or through Maecenas with handsome pensions. Usually Augustus was content to make deft suggestions, but as will appear in the case of Ovid he could hurl the thunderbolt of disfavor or even exile against those who angered him.

Yet, though poets and artists alike often took up themes pleasing to their master, it will not do to call them lackeys. For a second aspect of the era is its deep expression of Roman ideals. In the wars between Octavian and Antony, the poet Horace had not been alone in fearing a victory of the east; and the natural consequence of Octavian's triumph had been a restatement of Roman patriotism. Both the poems of Virgil

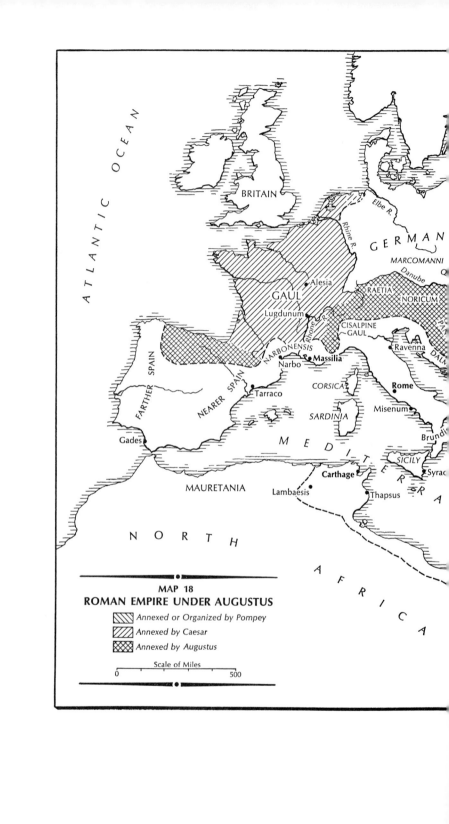

ATLANTIC OCEAN

BRITAIN

Elbe R.

Rhine R.

GERMAN

MARCOMANNI

GAUL

Alesia

Danube

RAETIA

NORICUM

Lugdunum

Rhone R.

CISALPINE
GAUL

NARBONENSIS

Ravenna

FARTHER SPAIN

NEARER SPAIN

Narbo

Massilia

Tarraco

CORSICA

Rome

SARDINIA

Misenum

Gades

M E D I T E R

Brundi

SICILY

Syrac

MAURETANIA

Lambaesis

Carthage

Thapsus

R

A

N O R T H

A

F

R

I

C

A

MAP 18
ROMAN EMPIRE UNDER AUGUSTUS

Annexed or Organized by Pompey

Annexed by Caesar

Annexed by Augustus

Scale of Miles

0   500

GES

SARMATIANS

CASPIAN SEA

DACIA

BOSPORUS

Danube R.

Tomi

BLACK SEA

MOESIA

ARMENIA

THRACE

achium

Philippi

Zela

PHRYGIA

CAPPADOCIA

PARTHIA

rsalus

Pergamum

Carrhae

Tigris R.

Actium

Smyrna

CILICIA

Tarsus

Athens

Antioch

Ctesiphon

SYRIA

Seleucia

RHODES

CYPRUS

Damascus

Euphrates R.

CRETE

PALESTINE

Jerusalem

A N

S E A

Cyrene

Petra

ARABIAN

LIBYA

Alexandria

DESERT

EGYPT

Nile R.

RED SEA

G-

and the altar of Augustan peace, which together form the highest expression of that patriotism, reflect men's love of Roman antiquities and their search for the meaning of Rome to the world.

In great and small things alike — the lofty aqueduct of the Pont du Gard in Gaul (see Plate XXVI) and small bits of sculpture, the majestic fabric of Virgil's *Aeneid* and the lyric odes of Horace — there is that common underlying spirit which one detects in eras of true inspiration. For its expression neither the emotional unrest nor the pedantic sterility of the Hellenistic period could furnish complete patterns. The Augustan age accordingly turned away from Hellenistic models in every field to the achievements of classic Greece, not to imitate blindly but to gain inspiration in forms.

Virgil. The greatest poet of the age or, indeed, of all Roman history was P. Vergilius Maro (70–19 B.C.). Born in north Italy, he received a good education but might have remained a gentleman farmer all his life had not his land been expropriated after Philippi. His early verse, however, caught the attention of Maecenas, and Virgil passed the rest of his life in Rome or near Naples in the circle of this elegant patron of letters. A gentle soul with sensitive spirit, Virgil felt and reflected in his verse many underlying forces of the generation of Augustus.

The earliest poems which we are sure come from Virgil's pen, the 10 *Bucolics,* are short, artificial praises of pastoral life in the Alexandrian mode. Yet they reveal a mind of mixed hope and sadness in the years just after Caesar's murder; the Fourth Bucolic, a vision of a golden age to attend the birth of a babe, was taken in the Middle Ages as a presage of the birth of Christ.

After settling on support of Octavian, Virgil wrote (*c.* 37–29) the four books of the *Georgics* on the practice and glories of Italian agriculture, a theme suggested by Maecenas. To a modern reader the *Georgics* may often seem to drag in their technical detail despite the marvelously turned hexameters and glowing digressions, but even now they convey something of the unremitting toil of peasant farming and the rich pageant of the Italian agricultural world.

For the rest of his life Virgil concentrated on a great hexameter epic, the *Aeneid.* This recounted in 12 books the wanderings and wars of the legendary hero who was directed by the gods to pave the way for Rome. The earlier books, which contain the famous account of Aeneas' dallying with Dido at Carthage and his visit to the underworld at Cumae, are by far the more famous; but the last half had an equally great significance in the poet's scheme, which culminated in the promise of Jupiter to fuse Trojan (or Roman) and Latin into one great race.

The *Aeneid* is much more than the story of Aeneas, for through this device Virgil was able to state his lofty views of the development of the Roman Republic, divinely directed to be master of the Mediterranean. The purpose of this rise is summed up in a prophecy by Aeneas' father:

> Remember, Roman,
> To rule the people under law, to establish
> The way of peace, to battle down the haughty,
> To spare the meek.[5]

The idea was far from new, but as Virgil majestically expressed it the concept was to echo far down the corridors of the Empire.

The height toward which all Roman history inevitably ascended was the poet's own age, the age of Augustus, who was celebrated both directly and in many hidden twists. Yet neither this somewhat blatant praise nor the pomposity of Aeneas must blind us to other, less obvious qualities of the *Aeneid*. As against the gloomy Lucretius, Virgil had an essentially optimistic outlook for mankind; his humanity and pity sounded new notes which did in truth make him a pagan forerunner of Christian thought. The popularity of Virgil at the time and in all later ages was the result not of his celebration of Augustus but of his sensitive expression of human longings.

Horace and Other Poets. Virgil's friend Q. Horatius Flaccus (65–8 B.C.) forms a remarkable contrast. Born in south Italy as the son of a freedman, he was yet well educated in Rome and Athens through the efforts of his self-sacrificing father. As deeply attached to the Roman tradition as was Virgil, Horace had joined the army of Brutus as military tribune, and after its defeat barely made his living as a treasury clerk until Virgil introduced him to Maecenas' patronage. Thereafter he lived in Rome or on a farm in the nearby Sabine hills.

Horace's literary output consisted of several books of short odes and epodes, and longer satires and epistles, all in verse that reflected many kinds of Greek meter. A republican in his youth, he came to support

[5] *Aeneid* 6. 847–53; tr. J. W. Mackail.

Augustus for two reasons: his protection of the "falling empire" against external and internal foes, and his efforts at social reform. The themes reappeared frequently in Horace's verse, as did Augustus himself; but in reading Horace one feels that this poet never yielded his mind so fully to the new autocrat as did Virgil. Horace had a complex character, and in reflecting the luxury and social corruption of the upper classes he displayed also his essential pessimism.

These latter qualities show, in one way or another, in the other poets of the era, who stood farther from Augustus. One was Sextus Propertius (*c.* 50–after 16 B.C.), who made his name by elegies in praise of his mistress Cynthia. Under the blandishments of Maecenas, Propertius engaged in heavy-handed eulogy of Augustus, but never understood his program. To the famous line of Horace, " 'Tis sweet and glorious to die for the fatherland" (*dulce et decorum est pro patria mori*), Propertius replied in covert defiance of Augustan social views, "None of my blood will ever be a soldier." [6] The second Roman elegist of the age, Albius Tibullus (*c.* 48–19 B.C.), never even named Augustus, though he mingled praise of love with happiness at the joy of peace.

The last great poet of the era, P. Ovidius Naso (43 B.C.–A.D. 18), was of the next generation. Born too late to appreciate the sense of relief which attended the restoration of peace, Ovid was nonetheless a successful — too successful for his own good — mirror of the elegance and immorality of the upper classes. After winning note by his love poems, the *Amores* and *Heroides,* he composed the *Art of Love.* This manual of seduction, published in 3 B.C., gained him the lasting anger of Augustus, who had just had to banish his own daughter Julia for profligacy; but not until A.D. 8, perhaps in connection with the revelation of the adultery of Augustus' granddaughter, did the emperor strike and exile Ovid to a bleak Greek outpost on the Black Sea, Tomi. Despite Ovid's desperate efforts to curry favor in his *Tristia* and *Letters from Pontus* and to celebrate Roman tradition in his *Fasti,* a poetic version of the Roman year's festivals, he died in exile. Ovid's poetry, especially the 15 books of his *Metamorphoses* on miraculous changes of shape, remained enduringly popular; but both his facile superficiality and his punishment augured ill for the future of Latin letters.

Livy and Greek Authors. Among the prose writers of the era, the most independent-minded was C. Asinius Pollio (76 B.C.–A.D. 5), whose

[6] Horace, *Odes* 3.2.13; Propertius 2.7.13–14.

lost *History of the Civil Wars* argued that the struggle between Octavian and Antony was merely to determine who would be master. Far more influential was T. Livius (59 B.C.–A.D. 17), who fixed the picture of republican Rome for all succeeding generations in the 146 books of his *History of Rome.*

Livy took over the great mass of legend and elaborated fact which had been created by the Latin writers of the past two centuries and cast it into majestic prose. To say this is not to deny that he possessed some critical acumen and that he had a high view of the historian's role, but the quality which especially stamps his pages is his passionate pride in the greatness of Rome. In this quality and in his eulogy of earlier virtues his views ran parallel to those of Augustus, yet the comment of the later historian Tacitus that Augustus once called Livy a Pompeian suggests his basic independence of outlook. Nor could Augustus have been entirely pleased by Livy's introductory remark that he turned to the past "to avert my gaze from the troubles which our age has been witnessing for so many years." The national character, once so great, had degenerated ever more and had at last tumbled into its present ruin, "when we can bear neither our vices nor our cures," a backhanded compliment to the Augustan social reforms. Livy's history, unfortunately, was so long that later writers epitomized it; there survive only Books 1–10 down to 293 B.C. and 21–45 on the period 218–167.

Beside and slightly earlier than Livy stood Dionysius of Halicarnassus, who taught rhetoric at Rome 30–8 B.C. and composed a history of the Republic down to the First Punic war for the illumination of his fellow Greek subjects and to display his elaborate rhetoric. Three other Greek writers of the era were notable, or at least voluminous. Strabo (64 B.C.–after A.D. 21) compiled a descriptive geography of the Mediterranean world and a lost history; Nicolaus of Damascus (b. *c.* 64 B.C.), secretary of Herod the Great, wrote a *Universal History* in 144 books on which Joesphus later drew; and Diodorus Siculus (d. *c.* 21 B.C.) put together a scissors-and-paste history of the Mediterranean world. The growing consciousness of imperial unity at the time is also reflected in an extensive Latin work, the *Historiae Philippicae* of the Gallic Pompeius Trogus, who concentrated on the Hellenistic and other non-Roman areas of the Empire.

The Arts. From the era of Sulla onward, architecture, sculpture, and painting bulked ever larger in Rome. The models here as in literature were Greek, and many of the artists in first-century Rome had Greek names; but they worked within a fundamentally Roman spirit. The chaos of the civil wars limited building, though Caesar began a new forum and reconstructed one of the main basilicas. Augustus, however, could boast allegorically that he found Rome in brick and left it in marble (that is, marble veneer). The Campus Martius was transformed into a splendid complex of marble buildings. The magnificent forum of Augustus had its center in the temple of Mars the Avenger, and celebrated in its statuary the great heroes of Rome, including Augustus' own ancestors. Only scraps of this remain, but other Augustan buildings, including the theater of Marcellus, the mausoleum of Augustus, and the portico of Octavia, still stand in part; the Pantheon, built by Agrippa, was entirely reconstructed a century later. In keeping with the classic tendency of the era, architects imposed an alien balance and proportion on their structures and thus largely sidetracked the inventive genius of Roman architecture, which recovered its road only later in the first century after the Neronian fire. The one surviving manual of ancient architecture, that of Vitruvius Pollio, comes from the Augustan period and reflects its classicism, though the domination of the Corinthian order led to a more luxurious architectural style than that of classic Greece.[7]

So too in painting the so-called "third style," which took the wall as a flat surface and preferred restful, classically limited expression, seems a step backward from the illusionism popular in the Late Republic and the early decades of Augustus. In sculpture the sharp, clear work of the dying Republic yielded to the needs of imperial idealization, which is marked in the portraits of Augustus and his associates.[8] One great jewel,

---

[7] Plate XXVI illustrates the Pont du Gard, an Augustan aqueduct near Nîmes in southern France, which is one of the most impressive surviving works of the age. The greatness of Roman engineering is shown both in its building techniques and in its ability to create works of art within a functional framework.

[8] The most famous among many portraits of Augustus is that found in a villa at Prima Porta near Rome (Plate XXV). This is probably a copy of a statue set up in Rome itself after 20 B.C., for on Augustus' breastplate a Parthian is returning the lost standards. Among the other allegorical figures the cupid on a dolphin refers to the descent of the Julian clan from Venus. The pose is a direct imitation of the *Doryphorus* of Polyclitus; the expression of the face is idealized (compare Cato and Porcia on Plate XXIV); but the sure power of the master of the world is nonetheless well reflected.

which has been reconstructed in modern times, is the altar of Augustan peace, completed in 9 B.C. Its sculptural decoration is a superb testimonial to the artistic skill of the era and to the deft interweaving of Augustan into Roman traditions; the lower panels are restful, marvelously worked floral designs, above which are rows of Roman dignitaries, including Augustus and his close associates, as well as symbolic representations of the Roman past and the present peace.

To sense the revival and stabilization of the age, however, one must widen one's gaze far beyond Rome. All over the Empire, but especially in its eastern sections, old centers were embellished, and new cities were founded. The latter were frequently named after Augustus or members of his family; and much of the public building everywhere was linked with Augustus. Throughout the world, says the later Jewish writer Philo, he was honored with temples, porticoes, sacred precincts, groves, and colonnades; both at Alexandria and at Caesarea in Palestine his temple looked down on the harbor as a "hope and beacon of safety to those sailing in or out." [9]

Meaning of the Augustan Age. In Augustus the Mediterranean world celebrated an earthly redeemer, to whom it yielded liberty but from whom it secured the blessings of peace and prosperity. The rewards of the bargain were obvious in the expansion and the consolidation of the frontiers; in the establishment of economic order which permitted the growth of commerce, industry, and agriculture; and in the proffer of spiritual ideals. For Rome and Italy these latter were an equal union within the old spirit of Rome; for the rest of the world, the sense of fair administration and the universal symbol of the emperor as god on earth.

Beneath the praises of the subjects and the eulogies of the Augustan poets one can also sense the price that men paid. The Augustan system was, in the end, one of artfully veiled autocracy. As the later historian Dio Cassius observed, from this time forward it was no longer easy to find out what was happening; for the imperial bureaucracy clamped a veil of secrecy upon decision-making. Some of the flaws in the military and economic structure which Augustus set up have been noted, and their inexorable working-out in later difficulties will occupy us in subsequent chapters. The political arrangements at Rome were to lead to serious friction between later emperors and the upper classes; worse yet,

[9] Philo, *Legation to Gaius* 151.

the concentration of powers in the hands of one man and his aides accorded ill with the political principles of the Greco-Roman world, on which rested in the end its cultural strength. In this respect the decline in literary vigor in Augustus' own lifetime after the death of Horace in 8 B.C. was as ominous a sign as was the exile of Ovid.

Nonetheless, anyone who studies the rise of Augustus from schoolboy to master of the Mediterranean world and examines his phenomenal skill in changing chaos into order must conclude that his achievements were almost without equal in ancient times. His system was to give the Mediterranean two centuries of peace and prosperity. If classical culture was to prove unable to thrust forward to greater heights, the security of the Roman Empire was yet vital to the rise and spread of new ideas of fundamental importance in western civilization.

BIBLIOGRAPHY

Sources. The only extended historical account of Augustus is that of Dio Cassius, which is preserved intact down to 10 B.C., thereafter in abbreviated form (Loeb Classical Library); Book 52 is an imaginary debate between Maecenas and Agrippa which throws more light on the early third century after Christ than on Augustus' own problems. Suetonius' *Life of Augustus* is very full of valuable detail but is not arranged in strictly chronological order; the history by Velleius Paterculus, written under Tiberius, is helpful on the Augustan wars (Loeb Classical Library). Before his death Augustus revised for the last time a succinct account of his major deeds and benefactions, the *Res Gestae,* which was set up on bronze tablets before his mausoleum in Rome; this was copied at several places, especially in Asia Minor. Our best surviving copy, from Ancyra (modern Ankara), is often called the Monumentum Ancyranum (tr. F. W. Shipley, Loeb Classical Library). The other firsthand testimony to his aims is his extensive coinage; see H. Mattingly, *Coins of the Roman Empire in the British Museum,* I (London: British Museum, 1923), and C. H. V. Sutherland, *The Emperor and the Coinage* (London: Spink, 1977).

The authors of the period have been translated often. For Horace, see *Complete Works,* ed. Caspar J. Kraemer, Jr. (New York: Modern Library 14, 1936), or *Satires and Epistles,* tr. S. P. Bovie (Chicago: University of Chicago Phoenix P39, 1959), and *Odes and Epodes*, tr. J. P. Clancy (Chicago: University of Chicago Phoenix P47. 1960). A verse translation of the *Aeneid* is that of Rolfe Humphries (New York: Scribner SL6, 1951); in prose, by W. F. Jackson Knight (Harmondsworth: Penguin L51, 1956). For the *Bucolics* or *Eclogues*, see the translation of E. V. Rieu (Harmondsworth: Penguin L8, 1949); a fine version of the *Georgics* is that of C. Day Lewis (Oxford: Oxford University Press, 1940). Rolfe Humphries has translated Ovid's *Art of Love* (Magnolia, Mass.: Peter Smith); for the *Metamorphoses*, see the translation of Mary M. Innes (Harmondsworth: Penguin 1955).

Further Reading. An introductory life of Augustus is that of John Buchan, *Augustus* (Boston: Houghton Mifflin, 1937); a fuller treatment, F. B. Marsh, *Founding of the Roman Empire* (Westport, Conn.: Greenwood, 1975); and a detailed study of his rise, T. Rice Holmes, *Architect of the Roman Empire*, 2 vols. (New York: AMS, 1976). Ronald Syme, *Roman Revolution* (Oxford: Oxford Paperback 1, 1960), illustrates the rise of new men, one of whom is discussed in M. Reinhold, *Marcus Agrippa* (Rome: L'Erma, 1965). A recent life of Cleopatra is by H. Volkmann, *Cleopatra* (New York: Sagamore Press, 1958).

The political and military organization of the Empire may be found in the works listed in General Bibliography; see also Mason Hammond, *Augustan Principate* (New York: Russell, 1968), and Lily Ross Taylor, *Divinity of the Roman Emperor* (New York: Arno, 1975). Chester G. Starr, *Civilization and the Caesars* (New York: Norton, 1965), discusses all aspects of the Augustan age; literary and artistic achievements will also be found in appropriate studies in the General Bibliography. Good lives of Virgil are those of Tenney Frank (New York: Russell, 1965), and F. J. H. Letters (New York: Sheed, 1946); of Horace, by A. Y. Campbell (Westport, Conn.: Greenwood), Eduard Fraenkel (Oxford: Oxford University Press, 1966), and L. P. Wilkinson (2d ed.; Cambridge: Cambridge University Press, 1968); of Ovid, by H. Fraenkel (Berkeley: University of California Press, 1969) and L. P. Wilkinson, *Ovid Recalled* (Cambridge: Cambridge University Press, 1955). Livy is admirably assessed by M. L. W. Laistner, *Greater Roman Historians* (Berkeley: University of California Press, 1963).

IX

THE ERA OF EURASIAN STABILITY

27

THE ROMAN PEACE

As Augustus lay dying, August 19, A.D. 14, at the Campanian town of
Nola, he begged those about his bed to pronounce whether he had been
a good actor. Certainly he had so tranquilized his world during 44 years
of sole mastery that it easily accepted the succession of his stepson Tiberius, who was already co-ruler. At Rome, says the historian Tacitus,
"all — consuls, senators, equestrians — plunged into servitude" by taking
an oath of allegiance to the new *princeps*.[1]

The bitter phrase of Tacitus is misleading, for Tiberius sought desperately to maintain the outward compromise of the Augustan system
between *princeps* and aristocracy. Repeatedly during the next century, to
be sure, this compromise broke down; of the first 12 Caesars, 7 met
violent ends. Still, the troubles at Rome rarely had any repercussions in
the provinces. For the Roman Empire as a whole the era from A.D. 14 to
180 (the death of Marcus Aurelius) was the most peaceful and secure
that the ancient Mediterranean world ever experienced.

The *pax Romana* was due in the first instance to the wise arrangements of Augustus, which safeguarded the stability and prosperity of the
Mediterranean and permitted the extension of its civilization far inland.
Yet luck accompanied wisdom. All across Eurasia there was relative
tranquillity for the last time before violent upheavals ended ancient
history. The non-Roman parts of this world will be surveyed in Chapter

[1] Tacitus, *Annals* 1.7.1.

575

29; here we need to observe the political shifts in the Empire itself, its economic bloom, and its growingly sterile culture. The extraordinary combination of economic prosperity and cultural decline must also claim our attention as a presage of the breakdown of the ancient way of life.

THE UNFOLDING OF ABSOLUTISM

The Surface of Political History (A.D. 14–180). The historians and other authors who lived in the Empire were most interested in the series of emperors, particularly their peccadilloes, and in their relations with the upper classes. These varied from open murder and assassination to relieved harmony. As a result, the conventional pictures of many emperors are incredible caricatures: Tiberius (14–37), for instance, is stamped as a gloomy, suspicious old man who is nonetheless capable of the wildest orgies at his retreat on Capri; Claudius (41–54) is the wife-ridden fool; the esthete Nero (54–68) has become an archetype of Satan; Marcus Aurelius (161–80) is the perfect philosopher-king.

Although these surface impressions have had a wide influence in modern literature, they need not be repeated here. Nor is it very useful to take up the emperors one by one, fascinating as they are in their manifold diversity which illustrates the individualistic qualities of the Early Empire. The really important aspects of the political history of the era are of longer duration than the reign of any one figure, but before turning to these developments we may well consider the two sets of political problems which help to produce the conventional views of the early emperors.

First, true hereditary succession was impossible in a system in which the ruler received his power from the people; yet Augustus and later emperors sought to name successors from their own families. The rulers down to 68 came from the Julio-Claudian family, connected with the Julians through Augustus and with the Claudians through his wife Livia. Then the revolts of the provincial armies against Nero cast into vivid relief the fact that the emperor was in the end the man who controlled the military system. Already in 41 the Praetorian Guard had installed Claudius over the opposition of the Senate; now the major armies engaged in quick but violent civil wars which threw up T.

Flavius Vespasianus (69-79). Vespasian's two sons, the spendthrift Titus (79-81) and the dour Domitian (81-96), ruled in succession, until the safety valve of assassination again came into play and removed Domitian. After the Flavians came the "Good Emperors," none of whom had a close male relative and so adopted a leading senator as heir; the last, however, was Marcus Aurelius, who did have a son, Commodus, and unwisely secured for him the throne. Within such a system cliques often formed about potential successors, and emperors had always to keep a wary eye against the creation of military heroes who might mislead the armies.

A second nexus of political difficulties emerged out of the relations of the *princeps* and the upper classes. Tiberius transferred the election of magistrates from the people to the Senate, a step which may be said to have marked the formal end of the Republic; the Senate also assumed the place of a high court to try its own members on criminal matters. Yet steps such as these could not restore to the aristocracy a true sense of importance. No ruler of the first century, save perhaps Vespasian, was able to reproduce the Augustan compromise; and several, including Gaius (37-41), Nero, and Domitian, were seduced by their own predisposition or by the unceasing flattery of their courts into open despotism. During their lifetimes all rulers received fulsome adulation; on their death most were subject to scurrilous attacks.

Beneath the surface, however, the aristocrats stirred up rumor, mob action, and plots. Repeatedly during the first century, sudden arrests and exiles, political trials, and murders of too prominent or wealthy aristocrats revealed the fundamentally despotic quality of the Empire. This unstable relation ended only with the Good Emperors from Trajan (98-117) to Marcus Aurelius. On the one side, these rulers were polite, able, hard-working servants of the state; on the other, the old aristocratic, sin-loving families had largely died out and had been replaced by more sober elements drawn from all Italy and, indeed, from virtually all the Empire.

The reconciliation is evident in the famous *Panegyric* which the civil servant Pliny the Younger chanted before Trajan and the Senate in A.D. 100 in thanks for his consulship. Throughout his speech Pliny maintained a certain dignity, but the adulation of Trajan, covered under the veil of frankness, is remarkable. The Senate, thus, was clearly admitted

TABLE 7

Roman Empire 27 B.C. — A.D. 180

B.C.	Emperors	Major Events	Writers (L = Latin; G = Greek)
27	AUGUSTUS	Pacification: Spain, Gaul, etc. Annexations on northern frontier Constitutional reorganization	Virgil, Horace, Propertius, Tibullus, Ovid, Livy, Asinius Pollio, Vitruvius, Trogus (L) Dionysius of Halicarnassus, Strabo, Nicolaus of Damascus, Diodorus Siculus (G)
A.D. 14	TIBERIUS	Crucifixion Conspiracy of Sejanus crushed	
37	GAIUS		Q. Curtius Rufus (L) Philo Judaeus (G)
41	CLAUDIUS	Elevation of C. by Praetorians Annexation of south England Consolidation of civil service	
54	NERO	Esthetic absolutism Fire of Rome Peter and Paul in Rome Jewish revolt	Seneca, Lucan, Persius, Petronius, Pliny the Elder (L)
68	GALBA	Civil wars	Dioscorides (G)
69	OTHO		
	VITELLIUS		

	VESPASIAN	Annexation of SW Germany	
79	TITUS	Eruption of Mt. Vesuvius	Josephus (G)
81	DOMITIAN	Dour absolutism	Quintilian (L)
		Danubian wars	
96	NERVA	Reconciliation with upper classes	Martial, Juvenal, Tacitus, Pliny the Younger, Suetonius (L)
98	TRAJAN	Annexation of Dacia and Arabia Petraea	Plutarch, Epictetus, Dio Chrysostom (G)
		Parthian war	
		Martyrdom of *Ignatius*	Arrian, Appian, Ptolemy (G)
117	HADRIAN	Imperial tours	
		Codification Praetor's Edict	
		Jewish revolt	
		Hadrian's Wall; Pantheon	
138	ANTONINUS PIUS	Martyrdom of *Polycarp*	Lucian, Aelius Aristides (G) Apuleius, Fronto (L)
161	MARCUS AURELIUS	Parthian war	Pausanias, Galen, Marcus Aurelius (G)
	LUCIUS VERUS (to 169)	Danubian wars	
180	COMMODUS	Plague	

to be second to the emperor, deputy for Jupiter on earth, "a prince most similar to the gods." When Romans, continued Pliny, pronounced their vows for the eternity of the state and the safety of the ruler, they did not put matters correctly; for the endurance of the Empire, yet more its peace, its concord, its security — all were safeguarded by the strength of their ruler. When Trajan swore to obey the laws, the orator asseverated, he learned for the first time that the *princeps* was not above but below the law. The last, most tragic irony was Pliny's observation on the imperial order to the Senate to be free after the Domitianic repression — "He will know when we use the freedom he gave that we are being obedient to him." [2]

The machinery of despotism, true, was not dismantled, but for the following century we hear less of the secret police or of open clashes between the ruler and the classes from which he drew his advisers and administrators. Marcus Aurelius boasted of having been taught by a friend "the conception of a state with one law for all, based upon individual equality and freedom of speech, and of a sovranty which prizes above all things the liberty of the subject." [3]

Unification of the Empire. The problems of the succession and of the relations of rulers and aristocrats were not without their importance, but other political developments less noted by imperial historians rightfully deserve closer attention. Among these are the unification of the Empire, the expansion of the imperial government, the consolidation of Roman law, and the crystallization of the frontiers.

Augustus had based his system on a clear distinction between Roman citizens and provincial subjects, though he had in practice been liberal in granting citizenship and had sought to give the provinces good government. The men of the Republic who had conquered the Mediterranean world had done little to remove its variations in culture, political organization, religious practice, and social customs — variations which were far deeper than one might suspect in looking only at the Greeks or the Romans by themselves. Nor did Augustus himself, wisely, go far even in standardizing the financial and political administration of the provinces. As a result of this tolerance and in consequence of the ever widening admission of provincials to the imperial structure of government, the

[2] Pliny, *Panegyric* 67.2.
[3] Marcus Aurelius, *Meditations* 1.14; tr. C. R. Haines.

divisive forces latent in the Empire were pushed deeper and deeper below the surface. Those areas which the Republic had conquered in brutality and had driven to hatred were now pulled together in common acceptance of Roman rule, even in identification with Rome.

By A.D. 154 a Greek orator whose very name, Aelius Aristides, blends Greek and Roman elements could assert that the term *Roma* included not just one city or the peninsula of Italy but the whole Empire. Outside the Empire was nothing but what must be considered useless; within its firmly marked frontiers lay the "inhabited land" (*oikoumene*), an egotistical term inherited by imperial authors from the Hellenistic world.

Decade after decade of peace and good government thus made their mark in a manner rarely equaled by any imperial power in history, and the long survival of the Roman Empire was more guaranteed by this spiritual unification than by any other factor. In the west this Romanization was normally accompanied by acceptance of the Latin language and of Roman culture; in the east, men remain basically Hellenic in speech and outlook but did adopt such Roman customs as gladiatorial games. As the upper classes everywhere took on a similar political and cultural garb, they rose on the escalator of imperial society. Claudius allowed Gallic senators to stand for offices after a great debate in 48 of which we have his speech. Easterners began to be senators in numbers under Trajan; Africans, under Antoninus Pius. From the time of Hadrian almost half the Senate was of provincial origin; Trajan himself was born in Spain. Citizenship, too, was ever more widely distributed, though not until 212 were virtually all free inhabitants of the Empire to be made citizens.

Limits on Unification. This unification was a truly remarkable achievement; but in assessing the "Roman peace," as contrasted to modern divisions and unrest, one should not fail to note that it had certain limits. Two districts, thus, were enduringly restless. One was Judaea, where the Romans could never establish a *modus vivendi* with Jewish political hopes and religious customs. A great revolt in 66 led to the destruction of the temple in 70, and an even more bitter struggle 132-35 brought an imperial ban on Jewish residence in Jerusalem, renamed Aelia Capitolina. From this point onward Judaism turned ever more away from Hellenic culture, a process evident in the creation of the Talmud. The other dissident area was Egypt. The peasants of the Nile, exploited to produce grain for Rome (though more came from Africa), were already engaging in sabotage and shirking their duties by the reign of Nero; the upper classes, too, of the great city Alexandria continuously grumbled because the emperors kept them under close surveillance.

The satisfaction with the imperial peace, which wells up in laudatory inscriptions and in honorific statues, was, moreover, essentially an upper-class phenomenon. We do not hear much of the lower classes of countryside and city, partly because they too shared, though in minor degree, the prosperity, partly because they were suppressed by all the machinery of state and society. Occasionally, however, they did erupt into view through discontent over particularly flagrant oppression; significantly, unrest rose in scattered districts by the reign of Marcus Aurelius into more extensive insurrection. Yet such pinpricks aside, the Mediterranean world enjoyed internal stability to a hitherto unprecedented degree.

Expansion of the Imperial Government. During the first two centuries after Christ the governmental machinery that formally bound together the far-flung Empire was continuously expanded and centralized. In this process the demands and needs of the subjects had far greater influence than any conscious will of a ruler, and the day-to-day conduct of the administration was as largely determined by the permanent bureaucracy as by its titular masters. Historians of the age rarely noted these developments, which have been ferreted out by patient modern study of inscriptions which give public careers and state edicts.

Under Augustus the central administration had been a relatively small group of aides, freedmen, and slaves; and at this time provincial government was largely an improvisation from republican experience. Governors of major provinces were senators representing either the Senate or the emperor; minor provinces as well as Egypt were assigned to equestrians; most taxes were collected locally under the supervision of senatorial quaestors, or equestrian and freedman procurators. Justice, too, lay largely in local hands, though appeals could be made to governors and their judicial deputies or even to the emperor's court.

As far as the central administration was concerned, much continued to be directly in the hands of the rulers. Military control, in particular, remained too vital to the emperors to be assigned to a special department, even if the Praetorian Prefects occasionally served as advisers on military matters as well as on the conduct of the civil administration.

For general advice the emperors also had an informal council or *consilium* of "friends." Claudius, the first great systematizer of the imperial bureaucracy, grouped major offices in several great departments, which eventually came to be *ab epistulis* (imperial correspondence), *a libellis* (petitions), *a cognitionibus* (judicial matters), *a rationibus* (supervision of financial matters), and *a studiis* (records and reference).

More and more these posts and other major fiscal offices came into the hands of equestrians, rather than of freedmen. Under Hadrian, the military and civil careers of equestrians were largely separated so that men specialized in one or the other field, beginning on the civil side with the position of tax attorney (*advocatus fisci*); and the higher equestrian offices were carefully graded by salary and by titles such as *vir egregius, vir perfectissimus,* and *vir eminentissimus* (a senator was *vir clarissimus*). Special administrations for inheritance taxes, customs (levied at several major customs lines within the Empire as well as on the frontiers), and other taxes grew in size and complexity. Provincial dues now passed through the local *fisci* to the central treasury or *fiscus,* which supervised the emperor's great holdings.

By the second century the imperial administration had become an extensive and detailed structure. Its skill in providing food and water for Rome, the largest city in the world (well over half a million), is impressive; equally efficient, though less praiseworthy in modern eyes, was the maintenance of gladiatorial games and amphitheaters from Britain to Syria. The letters between Trajan and Pliny the Younger, as governor of Bithynia, throw our clearest light on the sincere efforts of ruler and agents alike to secure the welfare of the governed.

Two aspects of this generally beneficial development were less desirable. One was the tendency of the central government to invade the sphere of action of the local communities, both because it was more efficient and because the cities, as we shall see later, were running into financial difficulties. Theoretically it would have been possible for the cities to gain a new function and a sense of importance by having a voice in the centralized government; but this did not occur. Some of the wealthiest men became, as individuals, members of the Senate or imperial bureaucracy; but on an organized level their only vehicle of expression was in the provincial or district assemblies of the imperial cult, which occasionally sent ambassadors and petitions to the ruler. Influence, rather, streamed in the other direction as the imperial government laid down rules for local operations, as the court of the governor became a more important arena for cases, and as municipal posts became assigned responsibilities for wealthy men whether they wished to hold them or not. Since the cities were the essential framework of ancient culture, this loss of local autonomy and local purpose was a dangerous sign for the future.

The second problem was the unceasing expansion of the bureaucracy. More and more officials had to be paid; the imperial court grew more elaborate and expensive; and the functions of the government ever increased. In the latter aspect one interesting development was that of social welfare. Humanitarian views on slaves and women, who became more emancipated than ever before, cost nothing in themselves even when translated into official decrees for the protection of slaves, women, and children promulgated by Hadrian. But provisions for feeding poor children in Italy (the *alimenta,* begun by Nerva and Trajan) did involve expenses, as did occasional public attention to education, libraries, and other social services. So long as the Empire was prosperous, the costs of government were bearable, and the subjects continued to elevate their "father" ever higher in gratitude for earthly blessings. Would they continue to do so if prosperity ceased?

Development of Roman Law. Many types of law existed in the Empire as a result of the diverse backgrounds of its peoples. In Celtic communities as among the nomad tribes on the Syrian frontier, for example, the custom of the ancestors was an unwritten code. The Greek cities relied on the more advanced principles of Hellenic law, which is illuminated for us — with some local variations — in the papyrus records of law suits and contracts. Rhodian sea law, a special field of Greek law, was standard over most of the Empire. But as the Mediterranean world became more unified and as Roman citizenship spread, Roman law came ever closer to being the law of the Empire.

When modern legal historians speak of Roman law, they mean the private or civil law which governed especially property relationships. After the rigid application of the formal code in the Twelve Tables had been broken in the early second century B.C., the praetors and jurisconsults had had wide freedom through the formulary procedure to hammer out a far more developed set of principles in civil cases, but much remained to be done in the Early Empire down to the second century after Christ. While the old courts under the praetors and aristocratic *iudices* continued to be active, more and more the judicial function fell to the administrative machinery, from governors and procurators to the emperors, who employed a very loose procedure called *cognitio extraordinaria* in civil as well as criminal cases.

After Hadrian ordered the codification of the Praetor's Edict by the great jurisconsult Salvius Julianus in 129, innovation in legal principles grew scantier. Interpretation, however, continued, and was primarily the responsibility of the imperial *consilium* (which now had permanent, salaried members), the legal advisers of officials, and the learned experts or *jurisprudentes*. The first major surviving book on Roman law, the *Institutes* of Gaius, was a textbook written in the reign of Marcus Aurelius; a series of great systematizers and commentators followed in the third century.

As far as criminal law was concerned, the institution of several permanent criminal courts by Sulla first allowed the continuous development of the penal side of law. In the Empire all-encompassing charges such as *lèse-majesté* (*laesa maiestas*) were connected with imperial safety to so great a degree that criminal law was often arbitrary and in the hands of imperial functionaries. Interestingly enough, penalties for crimes began by the second century to be different for members of the upper classes and lower classes, and the latter became regularly subject to judicial torture to gain the truth.

Solidification of the Frontiers. Throughout the period to A.D. 180 the Roman army maintained internal and external security. It served also as a potent vehicle for Romanization, both through its recruitment of provincials into the auxiliary units and also, more and more, the legions; and through its camps, roads, and canals along the frontiers. Particularly in modern Algeria and Tunisia we can follow, thanks to air photography, the spread of cultivation southward through the careful husbanding of water supplies as the line of military outposts was advanced.

The Empire inherited a policy of unlimited military expansion in which frontiers were fluid, but by the death of Augustus it had passed to a strategic defensive, in which it sought to hold what it had. Thereafter tributary kingdoms which had become pacified were occasionally annexed, but only minor military conquests occurred. From 43 on, Claudius took southeast England, and subsequent rulers expanded Roman rule into Wales and into southern Scotland. This fringe area, however, never yielded enough revenue to meet the costs of the heavy garrison required to keep down the semicivilized British and to keep out the utterly uncivilized Picts in the Highlands.

The Flavians absorbed without difficulty southwest Germany so as to shorten the lines of communication between the Rhine and Danube, and this area underwent a considerable Romanization. Trajan, the most military of all the emperors in this period, annexed Dacia in two hard-fought wars (101–02 and 105–06) and sought to conquer Parthia (113–17). Although he took the capital of Ctesiphon, attacks on his long supply line were forcing him to reduce his aims before his death; Hadrian wisely gave up the attempt and restored the eastern frontier to its previous location.

Hadrian, moreover, accepted an important, though unconscious shift in military policy which had been evolving in past generations. In the Julio-Claudian period the frontier had been a flexible belt from which the armies went out on tactical offensives to chastise the independent tribes; but as the frontier was moved forward alike in Transjordania, northwestern Africa, and Europe it swallowed up the room for maneuver. The result tended to be a static line, the *limes*. By the second century one could follow this line across the landscape in many areas as a patrolled road studded by watchtowers and minor forts, behind which lay garrisons of auxiliary units and legions. Hadrian built a stone wall across southern Scotland, and in southwest Germany a wooden palisade; the frontiers in Syria and Algeria can still be identified on aerial photographs. These well-defined boundaries, it should be noted, were not intended to be real defense lines but rather served as a base for collecting customs and for watching the free natives beyond.

When the Empire thus passed to the tactical defensive, it did so in complete confidence; the imperial army held full sway along the border zone. Yet the development was both militarily dangerous, inasmuch as the barbarians now held the initiative, and spiritually symbolic of the stiffening rigidity of the Empire in the second century. The civilized Roman world was crystallizing its limits — some modern historians call the process a hardening of the arteries — though one must remember that the barbarian neighbors were deeply influenced by the objects and ideas brought by traders and by military service in the Roman armies. Even battlefield formations became more rigid as Hadrian introduced a phalanx-type organization for the infantry; and movement of whole legions, deeply rooted at their old posts and locally recruited, from one frontier to another virtually ceased in favor of the dispatch of temporary detachments, called *vexillationes*.

By the late second century increasing pressure was evident on several frontiers. Marcus Aurelius had to send his co-ruler Lucius Verus east to meet a Parthian attack (162–66), which was finally checked. From 169 he himself was almost continuously occupied on the Danubian frontier. Here German tribes such as the Marcomanni and Quadi and also the Iazyges, an outlying element of the great Sarmatian masses of south Russia, built up pressure which made this frontier an increasingly important and dangerous spot; in 167 they poured as far as north Italy. Throughout the decade of the 170s, apart from an interruption caused by the revolt of a general in the east, Marcus Aurelius battled the German and Sarmatian tribes. Despite some catastrophes the Roman army still brought its emperor victory, and just before his death Marcus Aurelius was contemplating the annexation of much of modern Hungary across the Danube. His son Commodus discarded these plans and made peace so that he could return to Rome.

THE ECONOMIC PEAK

Growth of Trade and Industry. The archeological evidence for the Roman Empire is the most extensive for any ancient period. Every year new rural villas with mosaics, statues, and baths are found in England, France, and all the western provinces; exploration of great and minor cities in Italy, Africa, and the east can continue for generations. This physical material attests that the Mediterranean world reached the peak of its well-being under the emperors. It also reveals in detail many aspects of life which are muffled in the literary sources.

The most evident economic phenomena are the growth and shifts in industry and in trade. While no radically new ways of making objects were discovered, existing techniques were spread ever more widely. In the west Italy lost the dominant position it had held in the Late Republic, as we can see in the great growth of glass-blowing, metalwork, and pottery manufacture in Gaul and the production of wine and olive oil in Gaul, Spain, and Africa. By A.D. 100 Italy was needing imperial assistance, and the emperor Domitian even tried in vain to ban the production of wine in other western areas. The eastern provinces, badly battered by the civil wars of the dying Republic, revived their ancestral skills and by the time of the Good Emperors had become the economic heart of the Empire. This resurgence carried over into a revival of Greek letters by the early second century, when easterners also began to appear in the Senate; in the third and following centuries the continuing economic and cultural strength of the east was to have ever greater effects.

Shipping remained the main vehicle of exchange. Great grain fleets sailed yearly from Alexandria and Africa to Rome and sometimes comprised behemoth vessels over 1000 tons' burden; but other, smaller craft scurried about the Mediterranean, mostly in the spring and summer. New ports were created, as at Ostia, where the warehouses and market areas have been laid bare in recent years. But especially in the European provinces the Roman roads were steadily improved and permitted wheeled traffic to penetrate many areas. These roads, which were mainly graveled, were designed first for military use but served as arteries for trade and Romanization as well. The luxurious furnishings of a Rhineland villa, thus, might well include marbles from the Aegean, Egypt, and Numidia, glass from Alexandria, and bronze work from Italy.

A fascinating, though quite minor, aspect of the growth of trade was its extension far beyond the frontiers. In Europe Roman traders or free barbarians made their way, especially from the second century on, far into Germany. In Africa a caravan route ran across the Sahara until increasing drought cut off the supplies of ostrich eggs, gold, and other exotic items. To the east venturesome men could go by ship down the Red Sea and across the Arabian Gulf to India; the use of the regular monsoon winds to blow vessels to and from India, with their pepper, spices, jewels, and muslin, was discovered by a sea captain Hippalus, probably under Augustus. Strabo asserted that 120 vessels yearly made the Indian run from Egypt, and Pliny the Elder later grumbled at the loss of precious metals in consequence. Other adventurers could trudge by land to the Parthian trading centers, whither Chinese silks made their way by the Silk Route across central Asia.

Finds of Roman coins and pottery are relatively numerous in south

India; at Kapisa (Begram) in Afghanistan a treasure room contained Syrian glass, Roman bronzes, ivory-paneled Indian ware, and Chinese lacquered boxes. Men who called themselves Roman even made their way once from India by sea around the long Malayan peninsula (where a gold medal of Antoninus Pius and Roman glass have been found at Go Oc Eo in south Vietnam) and reached south China in the reign of Marcus Aurelius (A.D. 166).

By then, unfortunately, the peace of Eurasia was breaking up. The thin lines of trade across Asia either by land or by sea did have some effects in spreading artistic ideas, as will appear in Chapter 29; but they never had a chance of linking together firmly and clearly its major powers. An interesting point about the trade, nonetheless, is the fact that in antiquity, as in early modern times, it was men from the west who took the initiative.

Stratification. The prosperity of town and countryside in the Roman Empire was very unevenly divided. In consequence there developed an economic stratification which was ever more marked on social and political levels as well. In Pompeii, destroyed by the unexpected eruption of Mt. Vesuvius in 79, some wealthy men lived in sumptuous houses; the poor were huddled together in tiny quarters. In Ostia and Rome tenement buildings of several stories were built of brick-faced concrete. Literary sources show clearly the weight of urban oligarchies, which furnished the town councils and magistrates and dominated the religious, educational, and other aspects of life. Beside them were great masses of the poor, who grumbled in low tones or occasionally erupted despite the imperial police structure. If one could get on the escalator of prosperity, it might carry one far upward. Inscriptions attest the pride and achievements of many men of humble origin, especially freedmen; one such parvenu is satirized in Petronius' witty *Satyricon,* a fascinating social revelation. But by the second century this escalator was slowing down, and those who stood on top were distinguished in style of dress, reserved seats in the theaters, and even a different scale of punishments in courts of law.

In the countryside small individual farms do not seem to have been an important element. Much land came into imperial possession through confiscations and was organized in huge estates administered by written rules; several such estates are well known in Africa. Rich men like

Trimalchio invested the profits of trade and moneylending in estates to gain prestige; the erstwhile nobles and chiefs of Celtic tribes in Gaul, Spain, and Britain lived in great villas which by the second century often embraced industrial wings. Although our evidence is very incomplete, it appears that rural slavery diminished from its exceptional prominence in the first century B.C., partly because the wars of the Empire no longer brought in great masses of human flesh for sale.

In its place we hear more and more of *coloni,* that is, free tenants who rented small plots usually as sharecroppers and in some instances at least had to provide labor on the part of the estate kept by the imperial procurator or landowner. In Egypt the small farmers were bound to their land during the agricultural season, and elsewhere too the imperial machinery sought sporadically to return men to their place of origin (*idia* in Greek, *origo* in Latin). Legal freedom meant very little to most men, who lived and died as farmers on lands which their ancestors had tilled. Mobility was a privilege of the educated and commercial classes, and even they could be swiftly seized by the imperial dragnet if they fell at odds with the rulers.

Signs of Trouble. The economic historian has serious difficulty in studying the height of ancient economic development, for usable statistics on any scale are lacking. On the whole students do concur that the Roman Empire witnessed an increase of production down to the middle of the second century. This increase was due primarily to the stabilization of the Mediterranean, which permitted the application of already existing techniques on a wider and more continuous scale, and secondarily to the concentration of buying power largely in the hands of imperial and upper-class circles. Although Pliny the Elder asserted that even the serving girl had her comb and mirror, mass markets were on the level of basic necessities. Of some weight too were the sheer growth of population of the Empire, its expansion in area down through Trajan, and the commercial connections across the frontier.

These factors were not enough to produce a really dynamic growth; and by the second century signs of economic trouble were appearing. In the reign of Trajan, Pliny the Younger was sent as extraordinary governor of Bithynia in northwestern Asia Minor because the cities there were building beyond their means and had run into financial difficulties. This type of trouble, together with a decline in civic spirit, led the imperial administration to interfere more and more in local autonomy. Taxes, too, went up to meet the expenses of the army and of the bureaucracy. When the soldiers of Marcus Aurelius demanded a gift after a victory, the emperor doughtily told them it would have to be "wrung from the blood of their parents and kinsmen"; [4] and to finance his protracted campaigns he at one point had to sell excess imperial furniture and possessions. The weight of both gold and silver coins had been cut about 10 per cent by Nero, but this step was perhaps motivated by a desire to equate the imperial coinage with that of the city mints in the Greek east. Marcus Aurelius, however, increased the copper content of silver coins, and more severe inflation was to follow later.

The most puzzling element is the apparent fact that the population of the Empire, after reaching a peak somewhere in the middle of the second century, began to decline. This disturbing tendency can be ascribed neither to economic depression nor to any mechanical cause. The troops who fought in Parthia under Marcus Aurelius brought back a plague which ravaged much of the Empire; but normally such losses are made up by an expanding society within a generation or two. Marcus himself, however, settled Germans in vacant parts of the Balkans, and the imperial citizenry continued to drift down in numbers. One part of the explanation for this development may perhaps be sought in the loosening of family ties, which is apparent in the legal reforms of the second century; but more fundamental reasons must lie in that surge of individualism which will be considered later in this chapter.

EXPANSION OF CULTURE

Growth of Cities and Schools. The expansion of culture is a major characteristic of the period from Augustus to Marcus Aurelius. The root of ancient civilization was in the city, and the urban framework developed mightily under direct imperial encouragement. Across the Jordan new cities emerged, and other bustling centers appeared in central Asia Minor, in Africa, in Gaul, even in Britain and the Balkans as focuses where Mediterranean civilization met the rural tissues of life. These cities rarely ran over 10–20,000 in population; but older centers such as Alexandria, Antioch, Rome, and Carthage (refounded by Caesar and

[4] Dio Cassius 71.3.3; tr. E. Cary.

Augustus) became great metropolises. In the east, interestingly enough, even so small a city as Chaeronea could absorb the energies of Plutarch; but in the west only Rome stood out as a cultural center.

Everywhere the cities put on the same dress of marble-veneered public buildings — basilicas, *gymnasia*, theaters and amphitheaters, baths, temples — and decorated their fora or agoras with statues of the emperors, of governors, and of local dignitaries. Even though the heart of local attachment was increasingly crippled by dependence on imperial initiatives, urban magnates showed extraordinary generosity in public benefactions; neighboring communities vied in building and in seeking grandiose titles.

The vehicle by which the urban classes passed on their learning was above all the school, and education also throve. A few cities even had public education; generally, however, the school was a private institution built around a single master. Primary education extended from the ages of 7 to 14, and embraced writing, reading, and very simple arithmetic, all taught by rote and well pounded in. Although most men were still illiterate, the housewalls of Pompeii, covered with scribbled jests, love appeals, and election posters, suggest the fact that more could read and write than ever before in the ancient world or again until relatively modern times. Fewer students went on to the secondary level, where the *rhetor* taught oratory and expounded more advanced literature. Specialists studied law, medicine, philosophy, or rhetoric at the major "postgraduate" centers such as Athens. Professors of rhetoric (called *sophists*) had such high repute that cities vied to attract them, both to enhance their reputation and to gain the wealthy students who flocked about the leading sophists.

The effects of this system of education were both good and bad. From Gaul to Syria it was an effective machine for imparting the polish and skills required by a member of the upper classes. The basic principles descended from the Hellenistic world, so that everywhere educated men were imbued with the same ideals. Yet the western provinces taught in Latin, and the eastern in Greek; by the second century learned men who were at home in both languages were growing fewer, and a cultural split between east and west was slowly growing.

The emphasis of this system was ethical and conventional; the aim was not to encourage originality but to give acquaintance with a basic, inherited wisdom and to instill the gentlemanly standards of the upper classes. The weight of educational conventions was a heavy one against innovation and true cultural progress; rarely were its products so free of thought as the biting critic Lucian (*c.* 120–80). Lucian, nonetheless, is a fine example of the practical utility of education; the son of a poor Syrian stone cutter, he managed to secure a good education and thereafter rose to high posts in the imperial bureaucracy.

Writers: Greek. The literature produced by men trained in classical culture was both voluminous and popular. Book publishing served almost a mass market; the poet Martial asserted that his books could be bought in far-off Britain. Literary papyri from Egypt reach their peak in the second century after Christ and embrace the standard works of most of the great Greek authors. Libraries, too, became a common pride even of middle-sized cities.

Greek letters began to revive toward the end of the first century; some of the authors who lived in the next hundred years have been enduringly popular. The genial biographer Plutarch (*c.* 46–after 120) set Greeks and Romans side by side without prejudice, as befitted a citizen of the Empire, and also wrote a host of antiquarian, ethical, and other tracts (the *Moral Essays*). Other prose writers who can be placed generally in the second century are the historian Arrian of Bithynia, who wrote our best surviving account of the wars of Alexander (the *Anabasis*) along with books on Parthia and India; Appian of Alexandria, who set down in 24 books Rome's wars area by area; and Pausanias, who described the antiquities of Greece in loving detail.

Among the orators and teachers of rhetoric the most notable were Dio of Prusa (40–after 112), called "Golden-mouthed" (Chrysostom), who at once advised emperors and urged his Greek countrymen to preserve their Hellenic ways; and also Aelius Aristides of Smyrna (117 or 129–89), perpetually half-sick until cured by the god Asclepius but nonetheless prolific of speeches. The constant rival of rhetoric, philosophy, was in sad shape everywhere as the old schools sank into eclectic mishmashes; but Stoicism could still produce in Greek the plain speaking of the ex-slave Epictetus (*c.* 55–135) and the earnest, if unoriginal *Meditations* of the emperor Marcus Aurelius.

Although scientific inquiry now meant little more than the reworking of past ideas and the collection of curious events, three students who wrote in Greek had tremendous influence. One was the physician Dioscorides of the first century, whose work *Materia medica,* a treatment of drugs, was standard for botanical knowledge well over a millennium thereafter. Ptolemy of Alexandria, active 121–51, consolidated the theory that the earth was the center of the universe and assembled most of the knowledge that the Middle Ages had of astronomy (the *Grand Collection,* or *Almagest* in Arabic) and the earth's surface (the *Geography*). Galen of Pergamum (*c.* 129–99), perhaps the last great doctor of antiquity to engage in dissection, wrote voluminously; some of his many essays remained standard medical handbooks to A.D. 1800.

While only a few pursued the scientific path, many thrilled to the romances which emerged during the Empire. This new literary art appealed to the semicultivated; and, since romances were meant to be read by individuals alone, their rise reflects the growingly individualist quality of imperial life. One type of romance embellished the careers of historical personalities, as the *Alexander Romance* of Pseudo-Callisthenes, though this in its earliest form comes from A.D. 300; a Latin life of Alexander by Q. Curtius Rufus, equally romantic, can be placed in the early first century after Christ. More common was the tale of a youth falling in love with a girl, their separation by a magician, and the pursuit by the youth to the ends of the earth until finally the girl was saved. Although Lucian mocked this kind of tale in his travel fantasy, *A True History,* devoted readers read on, and by the third century could enjoy the *Daphnis and Chloe* of Longus, and Heliodorus' *Aethiopica.*

Writers: Latin. Throughout the Latin literature of the first century there runs a common theme of gloom amid the luxury of imperial Rome, born of the survival of old republican morality. The one author who best illuminates this spirit was L. Annaeus Seneca (*c.* 5 B.C.–A.D. 65). Tutor of Nero and statesman of genuine ability, he sought in his political life to harness despotism to virtue but in vain, and eventually Nero forced him to commit suicide. Seneca composed tragedies which had great influence on modern French tragedy; he surveyed the physical world in his *Natural Questions;* and on the death of Claudius he wrote a cruel but witty satire, the *Apocolocyntosis* (or "pumpkinification" in reference to the deification of the dead ruler). Always, however, Seneca returned to the field of philosophy, where he composed *Moral Essays* at various periods and, after his forced retirement, his *Moral Letters* to

Lucilius. The basis of his writing was a Stoic belief in divine governance, but Seneca accepted also ideas from Academic and even Epicurean
backgrounds.

Seneca's tone, however, was new and heralded important themes in
the great intellectual changes of the Roman Empire. Seneca was compassionate and humanitarian, and bitingly opposed the gladiatorial
games in which even during the intermission "men were strangled lest
people be bored." [5] A highly practical man, he sought to advise his
fellow aristocrats as individuals little attached to any external social or
political units; but their common attempt to set up earthly delights as
the aim of life he assailed with contempt. Seneca, again, was as devout as
any Christian in believing that each man had a spark of the divine
within him:

> God is near you, he is with you, he is within you. This is what
> I mean, Lucilius: a holy spirit indwells within us, one who
> marks our good and bad deeds, and is our guardian. . . .
> No man can be good without the help of God.[6]

As later Christians read Seneca, they felt that he must have known
Paul; and by the fourth century they invented letters between Paul and
Seneca. But his was a purely pagan product, tinged with a pessimism
and rationalism quite alien to Christian doctrine. The static mournful-
ness of Seneca's world was summed up in his cry, "There is, believe me,
great happiness in the very necessity of dying." [7]

Other writers of Seneca's generation included his nephew, the poet
Lucan (39–65), who bitterly assailed imperial autocracy in his *Civil War*
(of Caesar and Pompey); the Stoic satirist Persius (34–62); the novel-
ist Petronius, author of the *Satyricon*; and Pliny the Elder (23–79),
whose vast *Natural History* was a compendium of ancient knowledge
and misinformation. At his death Pliny, as commander of the Misene
fleet, was scientifically observing the eruption of Mt. Vesuvius when he
succumbed to asphyxiation.

The generation that came to maturity about and just after A.D. 100 was
also productive. The epigrammatist Martial (*c.* 40–104) and the satirist

[5] *Epistles* 7.5.
[6] *Epistles* 41.1–2; tr. R. M. Gummere.
[7] *To Polybius* 9.9.

Juvenal (*c.* 50–127) both shed lurid lights on the self-seeking Roman society of their day. Among the prose writers were the bitter historian Tacitus (*c.* 55–after 115; see Bibliography); his friend, the orator and letter-writer Pliny the Younger (61–114); the biographer Suetonius (*c.* 69–*c.* 140); and the slightly earlier Quintilian, whose *Oratorical Institutes* are one of the most sober treatises on education of ancient times. Thereafter Latin letters declined markedly. The most learned man produced in the west in the second century, Favorinus (*c.* 80–150), preferred to write in Greek, as did even the emperor Marcus Aurelius in his *Meditations*. Perhaps the only notable Latin writer of the later second century, apart from lawyers and Christian apologists, was Apuleius (b. *c.* 123), whose *Golden Ass* was a picaresque novel.

Seneca and Lucan were Spanish; Favorinus was Gallic; Apuleius came from Africa, as did Fronto (*c.* 100–166), the tutor of Marcus Aurelius and orator. African also were the two earliest competent Christian Latin writers, Minucius Felix and Tertullian. The more newly civilized areas of Britain, the Rhenish provinces, and the Balkans, however, did well if they lifted themselves to the level of Mediterranean culture; not until after the end of Roman rule did these areas begin again to express an individuality. But then the west as a whole was far less significant than the east by A.D. 200 both culturally and economically.

Imperial Architecture and Art. All the arts, which were heavily patronized by the emperors and aristocrats, flourished in the era of prosperity. In architecture the basic patterns of the past continued to dominate; when Hadrian ordered the completion of the temple of Olympian Zeus at Athens, his architects and craftsmen continued a project begun about 700 years earlier under the Pisistratids. Yet imperial architects grew ever bolder from the time of Nero in the use of concrete as a building material and in designs based on arches and vaults. True palaces emerged, including Nero's vast Golden House which was decorated with plaster painting rediscovered in the early Renaissance and imitated by Raphael; Domitian's architect Rabirius built an audience hall with a vault about 150 feet high. The Colosseum, seating about 45,000, was constructed by Vespasian and Titus; in the next generation Trajan's architect Apollodorus created the impressive new Forum of Trajan with libraries and market-halls. Under Hadrian the Pantheon, rebuilt in its present shape, became the first great ancient building to incorporate internal space as an artistic element.[8]

Sculptors also were busy, turning out elaborate sarcophagi with motifs hinting at afterlife, modeling nude Venuses, and reproducing earlier types such as sleeping hermaphrodites, fauns, and other decorative items. Hadrian, who constructed a great rural retreat just below Tibur (Tivoli), adorned his villa with copies by the hundreds of Hellenistic, classic, and even archaic statues.

The celebration of imperial victories and virtues especially favored the emergence of a great official relief style. On the arch of Titus the scenes of victory over the Jews incorporated a spatial sense to an unprecedented degree; the column of Trajan was decorated with a continuous, cartoon-like spiral of his wars against the Dacians. Later Marcus Aurelius was honored by a similar column, the reliefs of which are impressionistic and, in their stubby figures, incline toward the symbolic. A tendency to turn the figures of a scene outward toward the spectator in a frontal pose, so as to command his respect and absorption, was also appearing in painting and sculpture by the late second century. The significance of this remarkable drift away from classical attitudes will appear when we turn in the next chapter to the religious search of the age.

Cultural Sterility. Despite the volume of literary and artistic output many thinkers observed in their contemporary culture a decline which they rarely felt in political and economic matters. The first marks of this decline are archaism, erudition for its own sake, repetitiousness, affected style, and romanticism. All of these center about men's inability to engage in original, fresh thinking within classical frames and, in our eyes, are made more dangerous by the serious lack of interconnections between cultured and uncultivated classes. Later, but still in the second century, more positive indications were to attest to an unconscious turn by some men from classical culture as a whole.

Writers, that is to say, usually turned out small pieces, though often in

[8] The engraving by G. B. Piranesi (1720–78), reproduced from his *Vedute di Roma* on Plate XXVII, suggests the sense of internal space better than any photograph can do. The Corinthian columns are of the luxuriant style preferred by imperial architects; the great dome is made with ever lighter materials as it rises to the central eye, which also serves as a compression ring to distribute stresses.

quantities, and rarely struck new notes. The eclectic philosophical systems of the second century, while insisting that materialism was not enough and that man had a genuine significance, could not furnish a real substitute for concentration on earthly gain or expound satisfactory answers to the gnawing, sometimes unconscious problems of the subjects of the Caesars. Rhetoric gazed back and too often produced magniloquent, meaningless flights of fancy. The masses of imperial sculpture in modern museums sufficiently attest both its skill and its lack of deep originality; the one new type created within the classical pattern was that of Antinous, the favorite of Hadrian.

A modern observer may well wonder that in the very height of prosperity classical culture showed signs of failing. The explanation cannot be sought in any lack of interest or patronage, either by the emperors, themselves often authors, or by the upper classes. Nor did political autocracy in itself seriously curb freedom of thought. Historians and poets alike eulogized the ruler's virtues, which were celebrated as well on coins and in inscriptions; rhetoricians had precise rules as to how to praise their master; and in this monarchical system, as always, "nearly all of us live according to the standards of one man." [9] Yet the subjects of the emperors did most of this of their own accord in a desire to throw up a lofty, perfect symbol of the man-become-God; for by the second century the compromise between ruler and ruled gave a wide range of freedom, "where we may speak or not, be silent or at leisure, as we choose." [10] Where the political system did enter as a factor was in its very success in maintaining generations of essential security — and dullness — and in tending to break down the allegiance of men to their local communities.

For in the end the Empire represented a final, catastrophic completion to the individualizing movement of the ancient world, aspects of which we have noted in fourth-century Greece and again in Rome of the second and first centuries B.C. Man lost his political significance as an active member of a political group; the social and political units which had enfolded and supported the individual, from which the thinker had gained his vital strength, were broken down. Humanity, thus liberated and made individual to an extent never known before — or again until the present century — could not bear its position; and the initial sign of

[9] Pliny, *Panegyric* 45.5.
[10] Plutarch, *Moral Essays* 469E.

that incapacity was the moribundity of the classical intellectual system. In the third century the decline was to appear also in political, economic, and social areas.

Two superb examples of the effect of this situation are afforded by emperors themselves. One was Hadrian, whose tortured search for a firm foundation to life led him to take up in turn many arts and sciences and to travel more widely over his realm than did any other ruler. Yet this ever-restless master of the world sank finally into morose melancholy, which stamps his one surviving poem:

> O blithe little soul, thou, flitting away,
> Guest and comrade of this my clay
> Whither now goest thou, to what place
> Bare and ghastly and without grace?
> Nor, as thy wont was, joke and play.[11]

The other instance was the last emperor to be truly at home in classical civilization, Marcus Aurelius. A weary, fearful man, crying desperately for certainty, Marcus Aurelius engaged in that self-scrutiny which was practiced by men of the Empire for the first time in history and so produced his aphoristic *Meditations*. As ruler he recognized that his must be the cheery face, independent of help from without and independent of such ease as others could give. Yet the burden of his position was too much for the overworked, despondent man who wrote, "everything above and below is ever the same, and the result of the same things. How long then?" and felt that even his own intimates wished him gone from his imperial post.[12]

In concluding a probe beneath the surface of the halcyon period A.D. 14–180, nonetheless, the observer must note two counterbalancing aspects of the Early Empire. One is the important fact, to which we must revert in the next chapter, that new ideas and concepts of the nature of man were arising in the very era in which classical civilization failed to draw fruit from the prosperity and security of the Empire. Some of these attitudes showed themselves dimly in the pages of Seneca and in artistic developments; but a fuller, more conscious revelation came in the field of religion.

[11] *Scriptores Historiae Augustae, Life of Hadrian* 25; tr. A. O'Brien Moore.
[12] Marcus Aurelius, *Meditations* 6.46.

Secondly, it is the duty of the historian to search out the weaknesses or forces of change in any era, for only thus can he explain what is to come next. The illumination of various political, economic, and cultural signs of difficulty in the Empire, however, must not blind one to the very genuine satisfaction of most vocal subjects of the Caesars in the material ease and tranquillity of this period. While the upper classes benefited most, even the lower classes were generally content not to murmur loudly. Looking back from the England of King George III, the historian Edward Gibbon could see the roots of trouble in the second century but yet justly observed:

> If a man were called to fix the period in the history of the world during which the condition of the human race was most happy and prosperous, he would, without hesitation, name that which elapsed from the death of Domitian to the accession of Commodus.[13]

BIBLIOGRAPHY

Sources. We have only parts of the history of Dio Cassius (Loeb Classical Library: F. Millar, *A Study of Cassius Dio* [Oxford: Oxford University Press, 1965]. Suetonius' *Lives of the Twelve Caesars* (Penguin L72, tr. R. Graves, 1957) extends through Domitian; a much weaker set of biographies called the *Historia Augusta,* written in the fourth century (Loeb Classical Library), begins with Hadrian. The Jewish apologist Flavius Josephus (b. 37-38) wrote the *Antiquities of the Jews* and the *Jewish War* down to the fall of the temple (Loeb Classical Library). Historical writing in the second century was much weaker, and the details even of Trajan's wars in Dacia and Parthia are difficult to establish.

Tacitus wrote the *Annals* (Penguin L60, tr. M. Grant, 1956) from the death of Augustus to the suicide of Nero and the *Histories* (*Complete Works of Tacitus,* tr. A. J. Church and W. J. Brodribb [New York: Modern Library 222, 1942]) thereafter to the death of Domitian. His three shorter works were the *Dialogue concerning Orators,* an idealized

[13] Edward Gibbon, *Decline and Fall of the Roman Empire,* ed. J. B. Bury, I (London: Methuen, 1909), 85-6.

description of the Germans, and a life of his father-in-law Agricola, general in Britain (the last two in Tacitus, *On Britain and Germany,* tr. H. Mattingly [Harmondsworth: Penguin, 1971]). Terse and epigrammatic, Tacitus was the greatest stylist to write history in Latin and gives us enough facts to correct his bitter prejudices. He was much interested in psychological traits, but ancient thinkers generally did not comprehend the possibility of change in character; worse yet, Tacitus was despondently uncertain whether there was any purpose in history. Of his major works we have only Books 1–6 and 11–16 of the *Annals* and Books 1–5.26 of his *Histories.*

Examples of Latin poets may be found in Lucan, *Civil War,* tr. R. Graves (Harmondsworth: Penguin L61, 1957); and Juvenal, *Satires,* tr. Rolfe Humphries (Bloomington, Ind.: Midland MB20, 1958). For novels, see Petronius, *Satyricon,* tr. William Arrowsmith (New York: Mentor MD283, 1959); Apuleius, *Golden Ass,* tr. R. Graves (New York: Cardinal C62, 1952); and *Three Greek Romances,* tr. Moses Hadas (New York: Anchor A21, 1953). Philosophy and criticism may be sampled in *The Stoic Philosophy of Seneca,* tr. Moses Hadas (New York: Anchor A148, 1958); Epictetus, *Enchiridion,* and Marcus Aurelius, *Meditations* (Chicago: Gateway 6026, 1956); and Lucian, *Select Satires,* tr. L. Casson (New York: Anchor A295, 1962). See also *Letters of the Younger Pliny,* tr. Betty Radice (Harmondsworth: Penguin, 1975), and the *Institutes* of Gaius, tr. F. de Zulueta, 2 vols. (Oxford: Oxford University Press, 1946).

The abundance of physical evidence, including coins and inscriptions, makes it possible to reconstruct much of the social and economic history. Modern archeology begins with the start of excavation at Pompeii in 1748, which has gone on almost continuously and is not yet finished. Those fortunate enough to walk down its narrow, sun-baked streets and peep in at shops and houses gain a sense that the Romans really lived which no book can quite present; but besides Pompeii a number of other cities and villas can be inspected all over the Roman world today.

Further Reading. The political development of the Early Empire will be found in the works in General Bibliography; its growing absolutism is analyzed by Mason Hammon, *Antonine Monarchy* (Rome: American Academy, 1959). Tiberius is discussed by F. B. Marsh (Cambridge:

Heffer, 1959), B. Levick (London: Thames & Hudson, 1976), and R. Seager (London: Eyre Methuen, 1972); Gaius, by J. P. V. D. Balsdon (New York: AMS, 1976); Claudius, by A. Momigliano (New York: Barnes & Noble, 1961); Nero, by Michael Grant (London: Weidenfeld & Nicolson, 1970) and B. H. Warmington (New York: Norton, 1969); Hadrian, by S. Perowne (Westport, Conn.: Greenwood, 1976); Marcus Aurelius, by A. Birley (Boston: Little Brown, 1966). M. P. Charlesworth, *Five Men* (Cambridge, Mass.: Harvard University Press, 1936), has fascinating sketches of typical men of the period.

S. Dill, *Roman Society from Nero to Marcus Aurelius* (Norwood, Pa.: Norwood), is a classic; Ramsay MacMullen, *Enemies of the Roman Order* (Cambridge, Mass.: Harvard University Press, 1967), discusses opposition; cultural development is noted in Chester G. Starr, *Civilization and the Caesars* (New York: Norton, 1965). M. Grant describes *Cities of Vesuvius* (Penguin, 1978); see also J. J. Deiss, *Herculaneum* (London: Souvenir Press, 1968). R. Meiggs, *Roman Ostia* (Oxford: Oxford: University Press, 1973), is detailed. Literary figures have been treated by R. Syme, *Tacitus,* 2 vols. (Oxford: Oxford University Press, 1958); G. Highet, *Juvenal the Satirist* (New York: Oxford Galaxy, 1961); M. T. Griffin, *Seneca* (Oxford: Clarendon Press, 1976); and D. A. Russell, *Plutarch* (London: Duckworth, 1973).

Useful for bibliography is A. Garzetti, *From Tiberius to the Antonines* (London: Methuen, 1976); E. N. Luttwak, *The Grand Strategy of the Roman Empire from the First Century A.D. to the Third* (Baltimore: Johns Hopkins, 1976), is a thoughtful analysis by a modern military expert.

28

THE SPREAD OF CHRISTIANITY

When later ages in the western world looked back on the famous Roman peace, they accounted as one of its main blessings the origins and initial spread of Christianity. Jesus was born in the reign of Augustus; by the end of Marcus Aurelius' life the Christian faith was established from Gaul to Syria and Egypt. Viewed purely as a historical phenomenon, this development sheds a clear light on the spiritual needs of the men who lived under the Caesars.

From the historical, as well as the religious, point of view the story of the early Christians is amazing. Their calm yet obdurate adherence to a new standard of virtues furnishes a corrective to the lurid tales of imperial sins. Their fructifying view of the nature of man and of his relations both to the physical world and to God was hammered out by Christian theologians in the very period in which classical civilization was losing its forward momentum. The individual Christian churches furnished to their members and to converts a strong social and psychological unity not to be found anywhere else in the weakening social structure of the Empire. Long afterward, when the imperial political system collapsed in the western provinces, the churches survived with scarcely a falter.

At first sight the Christian view seems entirely different from the pagan outlook, and Christians sometimes boasted themselves as a "third race" distinct alike from pagans and from Jews. Yet beside the few Christian thinkers who really tried to dismiss classical civilization one must place the great majority who were willing to despoil the gentiles. The rapid spread of the Church within the Empire proper was due in part to its Hellenic dress, and Christianity eventually was to be a main vehicle for the passage of ancient ideas to the modern world.

THE PREPARATION FOR CHRISTIANITY

The Search of the Pagan World. A major element in the spread of Chrisitanity was the fact that the pagan world was already moving, though blindly, in the direction that Christian thought was to take more consciously. Neither a Roman poet like Virgil nor a Greek philosopher like Epictetus would have understood the statement that he was a forerunner of Christianity, yet it is true that many thinkers and artists of the Empire reflect the contemporary spiritual uneasiness and the search for meaning in a vast, materialistic world.

Some men turned to skepticism, which was itself a powerful dissolvent of old beliefs as a preparation for new creeds. Late in the second century Sextus Empiricus set down in his *Outlines of Pyrrhonism* a rounded system of skepticism; and it was considered a comfort to men to point out that "nature's chief blessing, death," ended their existence.[1] Others went to an opposite extreme and accepted a black view of predestined Fate via astrology, or sought to blandish its forces by magic. Particularly among the upper classes men used philosophy as a staff of life; true acceptance of the Stoic or other doctrines meant a real conversion to a simple, thoughtful life of self-scrutiny. But philosophers could offer in the end little beyond negative, rationalistic, pessimistic preachings.

The whole drive of imperial culture was in the direction of new concepts of man and of the divine. Virgil had had a serene belief that the world had purpose under the guidance of the gods, and his poetry breathes a sense of humanity and pity which we can find again in Seneca and in the humane and practical Plutarch. Even clearer hints appear in the decisive shifts of sculpture away from the classic ideals of rational presentation of the physical human shape. By the late second century figures tended to turn straight toward the spectator to draw his reverence; their realism was dissolving in a play of lights and shadows.

[1] Pliny the Elder, *Natural History* 7.190.

Human beings were turning into symbols, spiritually connected with each other and charged with moral significance. Thus the eyes of statues often appear to stare at an imaginary world, and their heads tilt upward as if in communion with Heaven. Perhaps earlier than any other form of expression, the art of the Empire points toward the rise of a symbolic, transcendental, yet simple outlook which was bent ever more on a subjective study of man's position and deeds.

The most direct revelation of man's continuing search for meaning in the world is in the field of religion. By the second century most men were seeking to believe; the only question was, in what? The imperial cult remained a powerful focus for political and economic loyalty, and the emperor rose ever higher as a "father" and earthly protector. The old cults of the cities and, beside them, of the gods of Rome as the city-become-Empire received due worship. Yet as men became political ciphers their inner attachment to the state religion weakened; and conventional Greco-Roman polytheism, born in a primitive era and designed mainly to answer the physical problems of life in this world by groups, did not meet new needs.

Significant in this respect were the popularity of oracles, the credit to miracle-workers, and the rise of a host of emotional, personal faiths. Some were brand-new, the product of religious charlatans or "possessed" discoverers of a true creed. Others were drawn from the motley religious background of the great Mediterranean world, particularly its eastern reaches.

From Egypt came the Hellenized cult of Isis, her consort Sarapis, and their child Harpocrates (or Horus), who formed a sacred trinity. Sarapis was ritually killed each fall and resumed life on the third day; Isis was the mother of all, the cleanser of sins, the aide of women in childbirth. Each day the tonsured priests of the faith, clad in white, engaged in regular ceremonies which involved hymns and the sprinkling of the sacred Nile water. Membership was secured by individual baptism, which removed one's sins. The moral requirements of the cult were not extensive, but deep emotion could be evoked by conversion, as Apuleius describes in his *Golden Ass*. On death the true believer in this faith was judged by Sarapis and passed into life everlasting.

A quite different faith was that of Mithras. Derived from the Iranian religion, Mithraism adopted astrology in Babylonia and other ideas in

Asia Minor; but it remained a morally vigorous creed, which appealed especially to men and to the western provinces from the first century after Christ. Each group of his worshipers, usually small, sought to have in its Mithraeum a sculptured centerpiece of Mithras in a cave, killing the bull from which human and other life sprang. Admission to the church was through ritual initiation, followed by progress through seven degrees into ever higher rites; the regular services by priests included a consecrated bread and drink. During life, believers had to fight against the evil spirit Ahriman, and thereafter were assigned by Mithras either to Hell or to Heaven, which was in seven degrees corresponding to the planets. Some 60 Mithraea are known from Rome alone, including one under the later Christian church of San Clemente.

A third cult, that of Cybele or the Great Mother, had been brought to Rome officially in 204 B.C. From Claudius onward, Roman citizens could be priests in her emotional faith, which reached its crescendo each spring on March 25 when the coming of spring was celebrated as the resurrection of her consort Attis. The worship of Cybele spread, perhaps as a result of its official endorsement, more widely over the western provinces than did any other mystery cult.

These and similar faiths are often miscalled the "rivals" of Christianity. They did share some of the same characteristics, such as ritual entry, insistence on a good life, and a judgment after death. The cults, too, offered a daily liturgy and services which bound one individual closely to his brethren and to the god or gods above; these services or "mysteries" were open only to the faithful. From the Christian point of view, however, the worship of Isis, Mithras, Cybele, and other saviors is interesting mainly as an indication of what men of the Empire desired in doctrine and cult ceremonies.

For all the "Oriental" faiths suffered from fundamental defects. They were, on the one hand, too willing to accept the mastery of the state; yet, on the other, were not fully integrated into Greco-Roman civilization. None, that is, was really widely accepted throughout the eastern and western provinces. In the fourth century Christianity settled on December 25 (rather than January 6) as the birth of Christ largely to exorcise the great Sun festival of the winter solstice; but Christian thinkers always remained more worried by the competition of pagan philosophy and the official demands of the state cult of Rome.

Judaism in the Time of Christ. Although Christianity was to be unique in the degree to which it put on a Greek dress, it sprang directly out of Judaism. The Church always kept the Old Testament, partly, but not entirely, because it was thought to foreshadow the coming of Christ; and much in early Christian organization, mode of worship, and doctrine had its roots in contemporary Judaism.

After the return of the Jewish leaders from the Babylonian exile, as was noted above in Chapter 7, came the consolidation of the books of the Old Testament as a historical revelation of God's promise and statement of the Law. This codification, however, did not end the enduring fertility of Jewish religious thought as it faced the problems of life first under Persian and then Hellenistic cultural influence and political control.

Abroad, the Jews spread widely to the cities of the Aegean, to Alexandria, and to the Egyptian and Cyrenaic countryside. These men of the Diaspora, or "dispersal," became intimately acquainted with Hellenic ways and in Alexandria translated the Old Testament into Greek for the daily use of their synagogues (the Septuagint version). In this city rose the greatest Jewish scholar of the Diaspora, Philo (*c*. 30 B.C–A.D. 45), who essayed to reconcile Plato and the Bible, while giving priority in invention to Moses, and developed an allegorical method of interpreting the Old Testament for that purpose. Save for its preservation at times in the Christian tradition, this Hellenizing wing had little influence on later Judaism.

At home political independence was resumed with the revolt of the Maccabees from 167 B.C. but lasted only to the conquest by Pompey in 63; thereafter the Jews of Palestine were especially restless, both politically and religiously. Here Hellenizers and non-Hellenizers, rich and poor, Zealots who wanted independence and those who were willing to accept Roman rule, the supporters of the line of the crafty Herod the Great and the opponents of this foreign dynasty — all wrangled and contended with one another; one revolt on the death of Herod led to three guerrilla leaders' proclaiming themselves king of Israel.

On the spiritual level there were two main groups in Palestine by the time of Jesus. One was the Sadducees, largely of priestly and upper-class character, who were more willing to mix with the gentiles. The other, larger element was that of the Pharisees, who stood for popular education in the Law and its adaptation to meet the needs of society and an inner life of personal consecration. Some of this group had come to accept a concept of resurrection and a Last Judgment, which had ties with Zoroastrian doctrines. On the far left stood the Essenes, inclined to ascetic life and a more emotional approach which is illuminated by several books of the Apocrypha and by the Dead Sea scrolls. Floating amid these richly varied views was the concept of a Messiah, a redeemer who would liberate the Jews from their external domination and bring victory to the world of the Lord.

Whether in Palestine or scattered abroad, the Jews stood within but apart from the pagan world. Their strongly ethical views and the Jewish concept of God as One attracted many men, called "half-Jews" because of their reluctance to accept all the dietary and other requirements of the Law. Far more pagans, however, looked with suspicion on Jewish clannishness and the demands of the Jews for special privileges, as on the Sabbath or in the payment of two drachmas yearly per head to the temple in Jerusalem. The Roman government generally frowned on any local anti-Semitism which proceeded to open violence, but casual comments by Horace and Tacitus as well as official edicts adequately illustrate the dislike by Romans for the Jewish "superstition" and for its enthusiastic proselytizing.

The later persecution of the Christians was to draw heavily from these hostile attitudes, for Christians could claim neither the ancestral position of Judaism as the faith of one particular land nor its *de facto* protection which resulted from the sheer existence of large blocks of Jews in some areas. On the other hand the far-flung network of Jewish synagogues, which had made extensive adjustments to pagan life, and the spread of a view of man and God quite different from Greco-Roman concepts had a considerable role in the first expansion and early character of Christianity.

THE FOUNDATIONS OF CHRISTIANITY

Teachings of Christ. For the historian to discuss in detail the life of Jesus would be both presumptuous and unsound. The source material is almost entirely in the Gospels; and these records of the works and words of Jesus were not written down until the first flush of hope that He would soon return had passed away. The Gospel according to Mark is generally considered to be the oldest, perhaps composed about A.D. 65 by a follower of Peter at Rome. The information which this evidence gives was certainly intended to show the teachings and passions of Jesus as a proof that God had committed Himself to the flow of human life, but it was not rigorously historical. The date of the birth of Christ must be 4 B.C. if He were born under Herod the Great (d. 4 B.C.) — the conventional reckoning of 1 B.C./A.D. 1 we know to be an erroneous product of the sixth century after Christ — yet Luke connects the event with a Roman census when Palestine became a province in A.D. 6. So too the date of Christ's baptism is insecure; the length of His ministry is estimated at one to three years as a rule; the Crucifixion can be set only as probably occurring in A.D. 29, 30, or 33.

The teachings of Jesus are another matter. Their basic line was one in keeping with that of the earlier prophets and had points of contact with the more radical Jewish thought which is shown in the Dead Sea scrolls. But the exhortations of Jesus well up in the Gospels as a unique personal message pitched in terms that, in their simplicity, would enter the hearts of contemporary auditors and yet, in their subtlety, could baffle divines over the centuries. Jesus announced that the Messiah was to come not to bring rule on earth as most of His fellow Jews believed, but to usher in the Last Judgment; and that until that point men must lead a moral life, loving their fellow men and God. The virtues of the Sermon on the Mount — humility, charity, brotherly love — were not those of the Greco-Roman world; but in time they were to become the ethical standards of the western world.

In earthly terms the life of Jesus could scarcely be termed successful. A carpenter of poor education, He was baptized by another religious enthusiast, the ascetic John the Baptist, who preached righteousness and the divine judgment with such power that Herod Antipas had him suppressed. Neither the doctrines of Jesus nor their popularity among common folk were likely to win Him the favor of the upper classes in the uneasy conditions of Palestine. Jesus neatly avoided the trap of being made to appear anti-Roman in the famous story of the tribute money, ending "render unto Caesar the things that are Caesar's"; [2] but once He had entered Jerusalem, the end drew inexorably nearer. The Gospel

[2] Matthew 22:21.

accounts waver between trying to pin the blame on the Jews and on the Romans. No one, however, who was in a position of responsibility wished to allow a possible focus of insurrection, and the equestrian prefect Pontius Pilate passed the final judgment on political grounds.

Crucifixion was a mode of execution reserved for slaves and the poorest elements until Constantine abolished it. The thought that the founder of Christianity had died thus so irked educated men that at times they argued He had suffered only in appearance; and the cross was late in becoming a symbol in Christian art. Yet the voluntary sacrifice by the Son of God for the salvation of His fellow men was a fundamental proof for Christianity. As Paul fiercely put it, "We preach Christ crucified, a stumbling-block to Jews and folly to the Gentiles . . . if Christ has not been raised, then our preaching is in vain and your faith is in vain." [3] The question of the Resurrection on the third day is as little subject to historical judgment as are the miracles reported throughout His ministry; what matters historically is that His followers believed and that the small group about the disciples carried on.

Christ soon became and long remained a theological symbol. Only recent generations have been deeply interested in Him as the Son of Man. His ideas, embodied in the Gospels, have nonetheless repeatedly bubbled up to refresh the Christian Church and to upset the easy conventions of rigid dogma. Christianity, thus, was the only major faith of the Mediterranean world to be grounded in historical events, rather than in the dross of myth; and the Saviour it offered to the Roman world was an individual unconnected either with the upper classes or with the imperial government. His rewards were other than the purely physical or material.

Paul's Mission. At the Ascension the followers of Christ differed from their fellow Jews primarily in the belief that the Messiah had come and would soon come again; but the cleavage was steadily to widen. In Jerusalem the group had to move quietly; the deacon Stephen, a man of the Diaspora, was bolder and was stoned to death for blasphemy. The new ideas, however, spread swiftly to the nearest big city, Antioch, where the half-Jews in particular were attracted. Very soon the primitive Church faced its truly crucial decision: should it, essentially, turn from the Jews who persecuted it to appeal to the gentiles? James, the Lord's

[3] Paul, I Corinthians 1:23, 15:14.

brother, who directed the central organization at Jerusalem, was conservative, as were many others. Peter, the chosen disciple, was bolder; and in about 48 a compromise was reached that Christians might disregard the Law of Moses so long as they abstained from fornication and the meat of pagan sacrificial animals. Yet controversy went on, and the man who took the boldest stand was the convert Saul.

Saul, called Paul, was a Pharisee of the Diaspora, born in Tarsus, where he had learned some Stoic philosophy and enough Hellenistic culture to be able to quote Menander. He was also a Roman citizen by birth, at a time when there were very few Roman citizens in the eastern provinces. But he was foremost a Jew and in some manner became a leading persecutor of the followers of Christ, Whom he never saw until he had his crucial vision on the road to Damascus. The energies he had used against the Church were now employed in its favor, not always to the pleasure of the conservative wing.

After a period of meditation Paul engaged in missionary activity in Syria and eastern Asia Minor; then, from about 48, he made the famous trips through Asia Minor and the Aegean which are chronicled in Acts. Paul's normal procedure was to start preaching in a synagogue and then, after being expelled by the Jews, to address himself to the gentiles. A later tale from Asia Minor perhaps preserves his appearance:

> A man little of stature, thin-haired upon the head, crooked in the legs, of good state of body, his eyebrows joining, and nose somewhat hooked, full of grace: for sometimes he appeared like a man, and sometimes he had the face of an angel.[4]

At every favorable point in this area Paul founded a Christian cell. On his last visit to Jerusalem he was seized by Jewish opponents, but his Roman citizenship saved his life; and the governor sent him to Rome to be judged by the Emperor's court. Here he lived for some years and according to tradition was executed by decapitation (64 or later) after a further missionary trip to Spain.

Among the many active Christian missionaries in the generation after Christ, Paul's activities are the best illuminated. His friend and traveling

---

[4] Acts of Paul and Thekla, in M. R. James, *The Apocryphal New Testament* (Oxford: Oxford University Press, 1953), p. 273.

companion Luke wrote an account of his journeys, stressing his relations to Jews, Romans, and gentiles (Acts); and Paul's own letters are the oldest part of the New Testament. His passionate energy and travels make Paul a figure whom many scholars call the second founder of Christianity. Although his letters were swift, tumbling answers to the specific problems of churches, they rose out of a powerful mind which did not boggle at the new directions in which the Christian promise must carry its adherents.

Thenceforth Christanity became ever more a gentile faith which settled, for instance, on the non-Jewish calendar of Sunday as the day of rest and Wednesday and Friday as fast days. By the early second century Ignatius of Antioch could warn Christians against Judaizing. The Jewish-Christian church at Jerusalem continued under a regular line of leaders from James until the great revolt of 132–35; but the imperial ban on Jewish inhabitation of the city thereafter helped to reduce the Christians of Palestine who fully accepted the Law to a minor sect called the Ebionites.

Christian expansion, too, throughout the Roman Empire was much advanced by Paul, thanks to the ease of communications; but Paul's letters show abundantly that he conceived the Church as one whole, of which the individual groups were each a part. Paul also made the first adjustments of Christianity to Greek thought, though this aspect must not be overemphasized; in construing the teachings of Christ he still moved largely within the Jewish framework.

Paul was not the only missionary, to be sure, nor did he have the greatest influence as far as organization of the early Church was concerned. The disciple Thomas went outside the Empire to Parthia and was said to have reached India; Andrew preached to the Scythians; and Peter is generally agreed to have gone to Rome, where Paul found a church already well in existence on his arrival. In tradition Peter was martyred at the same time as Paul by being crucified upside down in the Vatican circus; recent excavations under St. Peter's have perhaps found the first shrine erected over his body and certainly show that by the second century Christians felt his remains were located there.

The governing center, however, remained at Jerusalem, organized under James, a board of disciples, and seven deacons as administrative officials. James himself was said to have been martyred by the Jews

THE SPREAD OF CHRISTIANITY 613

before the revolt of 66–70, which forced the Christians of Jerusalem to flee for a time; thenceforth the Christian churches over the Empire were virtually independent. The sense of common creed and common unity against the hostile outside world held the churches together, but never again did all Christians turn toward the same focal point.

CHRISTIANITY AND THE PAGAN WORLD

Christian Organization. The century after the deaths of Peter and Paul is the darkest in Christian history. The churches were still small and suffered from the dislike of pagans and Jews alike; disagreements over doctrine grew more intense as the generation which had known the disciples (with whom Paul was reckoned) vanished. Yet the firm promise of salvation offered by the Christian creed and its strongly ethical teachings, reinforced by the close bond of believers in each local nucleus, gave it an ever firmer foothold in the cities of the Empire and even in the countryside in the east; and the prosperity of the Empire permitted its emissaries to travel back and forth with relative ease.

During this period many of the fundamental qualities that marked Christianity through the rest of the Empire, and even later, were established. Of these we may examine those connected with its organization, its relations to the state, and the interplay between Christianity and classical culture down to A.D. 200.

The church in each city — and Christianity was organized on the basis of the cities — was independent. Initially, like the synagogue, it had a fairly democratic organization under a board of elders (*presbyters*) and deacons; often too the ecstatic side of early Christianity was reflected in the presence of local "prophets," who were filled with the divine spirit and communicated with God. As time went on, the general tendency of city government toward oligarchy and the needs of the church itself for self-defense against persecution and heresy led to a concentration of powers. In the reign of Trajan the letters of Ignatius of Antioch assert that *presbyters* must be tuned to their bishop (*episkopos* or overseer) as the strings to a harp, and that a church must be unified under its bishop to be with God. Not all churches thus had single leaders even in the later second century, but by the third century the bishop of each city, though still elected, was the spokesman for and director of his congregation.

Church history came to be organized on the chain of bishops reaching back to the apostolic foundation. The doctrine of Apostolic Succession, that is, that the powers given to the disciples by Christ before His Ascension were handed down from bishop to bishop by the sacrament of ordination, was already explicit by the end of the first century in the letter of Clement of Rome.

The bishop's responsibilities were many. In the first place he oversaw the regular ceremonies of worship or sacraments, which became more fixed and extensive. Baptism by triple immersion in the name of the Father, the Son, and the Holy Ghost came after study in Christian doctrine; only those so baptized could partake in the most sacred rite. This was the eucharist, originally an evening ceremony after a community meal (*agape*) and then shifted to the morning as an independent ceremony; it was accompanied, after the fashion of the synagogues, by prayers, hymns, and the reading of the Bible. At regular intervals the faithful thus commemorated the Last Supper and united in the sacrifice of Christ. Penance, which was not considered by the Epistles to the Hebrews as possible after baptism, slowly became a regular rite as a disciplinary and corrective measure. The sacraments, which eventually numbered seven, thus emerged as formal bonds of Christian brethren and as continuing reinforcement and guarantee of their faith. Salvation was possible only within the framework of the Church.

Second, the bishop administered through the deacons the property of his church, which came to encompass a meeting place, a cemetery, and the bequests of the faithful. From the famous, but brief attempt at communal living which Acts records, the Christian Church had a strong sense of social responsibility to care for the sick, for widows and orphans, and for the unfortunate. This social sense stood in strong contrast to the ruthless, atomistic quality of much of pagan life as did the firm grounding in Christian doctrine of the principle that all the children of God were equally endowed with an individual soul.

Both social principles helped to draw searching individuals into the fold, but the Church was not an egalitarian system in practice. It opposed licentiousness, suicide, exposure of newborn infants, and other social evils; yet it made no effort to preach revolution or even to oppose slavery in principle. Nor were all its members underprivileged. The unfortunate Ananias (Acts 5:1-10) had had property, and thereafter persons of wealth and culture formed a not unimportant element in the Christian community. If tradition can be trusted, even Domitian's cousin, Flavius Clemens, consul in 95, and his wife Domitilla were Christians; more to the point, the bishops and thinkers of the Church were largely forceful, passably educated men.

Third, the bishop kept in contact with his fellow bishops to coordinate Christian belief and policy. To a large extent this communication was by messengers and by letters, following the precedent of Paul. The writer Tertullian, in proving the unity of the Church, commented on its "peaceful intercommunion, the title of brotherhood, and the fellowship of hospitality." [5] In the late second century Avircius Marcellus of Phrygia, probably a bishop, traveled as far west as Rome: "I saw too the plain of Syria and all its cities, Nisibis beyond the Euphrates; and everywhere I found brethren, with Paul in my hands and Faith everywhere led the way" and prepared for him the eucharist, symbol of Christian unity.[6]

Eventually councils of bishops came to meet for better debate. We know of such a council at Rome under Commodus to handle the thorny question of settling the date for the increasingly popular festival of Easter. This controversy, incidentally, produced the first known effort of a bishop of Rome (Victor) to excommunicate those who disagreed with him as representative of the church of Peter and Paul. From the third century such meetings became more frequent as the Church grew stronger and was vexed by problems of heresy.

Since church organization tended to follow imperial divisions, the bishop of the capital city in each province often had pre-eminence; and, indeed, his church might well have been the original center from which Christianity spread to the countryside. After Jerusalem fell, the bishop of Rome, the imperial capital and center of communications, was in a particularly strong position, which was reinforced by the foundation of the Roman church by Peter; for all could read the words of Christ to Peter, "Thou art Peter [*Caipha* in Aramaic]; and upon this rock [*cai-*

[5] Tertullian, *On the Prescription of Heretics* 20.
[6] Monument of Avircius, quoted by Michael Gough, *The Early Christians* (New York: Praeger, 1961), p. 44.

pha in Aramaic; *petra* in Greek] I will build my church . . . And I will give unto thee the keys of the kingdom of Heaven." [7] Yet, though the famous bishop Cyprian of Carthage could hail the Roman church in 252 as "the chair of Peter and the leader whence priestly unity has been derived," his letter was a firm lecture to his fellow bishop at Rome; and in the next sentences he proclaimed the right of his church to set its own course.[8] The implications of the doctrine of Petrine supremacy were only to be worked out long afterward; the phrase Catholic Church (*katholike ekklesia*) used from Ignatius onward meant at this time only the union of all believers.

Christianity and the State. Christianity was at odds with outside society and the state from the days of Jesus. Fundamentally this cleavage arose from the new view of man as a spiritually independent agent, yet bound to his fellow men and to God above; but men rarely sensed the dimensions of the gulf between the basic principles of Christianity and those of classical civilization. To understand the persecution of the Christians one must turn to the practical reasons why they were disliked on the popular level and also by the imperial government.

To the populace Christians were men who defiantly stood apart in secret unions. Pliny the Younger, who encountered Christians as governor of Bithynia, reports but denies the popular tales of their lewd activities after their evening *agape*. Christians were not only exclusive; they also rejected the pagan gods and claimed sole possession of the right path of life. Christians did not often take the unwise step of public preaching, except when being interrogated, but one may suspect they sometimes offered an intolerable model of rectitude. Conversion of one member of a family at times brought strain, as in the case of the wife who kept picturing to her pagan husband the hell-fires in wait for him. As a new creed, Christianity could not claim ancestral privilege but served rather as a whipping stick in case of local unrest. Most of the persecution of Christians was in the form of social and economic ostracism, which must have made potential converts hesitate long.

The imperial government disliked Christianity too because of its unusual scale of values and patterns of life; from the Republic onward the

---

[7] Matthew 16:18–19.
[8] Cyprian, *Letters* 59.15; tr. R. P. C. Hanson.

Romans had been harsh toward any cult which produced popular disturbances. Yet the main grounds of political distrust were of a rather different order. Repeatedly in tales of martyrdom, as in that of bishop Polycarp of Smyrna, the final test was the order to a Christian to sacrifice to the emperor or to the gods for the emperor and his refusal to do so. To the Christian this act was one of pagan worship; to the imperial bureaucrat, simply a profession of patriotism toward the figure who embodied the state. To make matters worse the Christians were organized in an empire-wide net of secret, exclusive clubs, likewise an object of suspicion to the government, which regularly controlled the right of association.

The result was sporadic imperial persecution, but only in scattered localities through the second century. In Rome trouble between Christians and Jews led to the expulsion of the Christians under Claudius. The great fire of the city in 64 produced a brief but intense persecution. by Nero, who sought first to make the Christians scapegoats and then to suppress a "baneful superstition," which could legally be charged with "hatred of the human race" (that is, of pagans).[9] Either then or under the Flavians a general administrative policy became established that the Name alone, that is to say, simple membership of the Church, was enough for execution of these "atheists."

This policy was enforced by Pliny the Younger in Bithynia, but we can see in his letter of inquiry to Trajan both Pliny's sense of duty and his puzzlement at the obduracy of the Christians in disobeying the proper orders of an imperial official. Trajan, in reply, ordered him not to seek out the Christians and to reject anonymous accusations "as a bad precedent and out of keeping with the spirit of our times." [10] In the prosperous contentment of the second century the government frowned on popular violence against the Christians, except in a few instances when the governors (who had fairly wide latitude in their operations) permitted persecutions so as to keep their provinces quiet. We know in detail of one pogrom at Smyrna, thanks to a letter describing the glorious martyrdom of Polycarp in 156, and we have a general account of a similar affair in Vienna (Vienne) and Lugdunum (Lyons) in 177 under Marcus Aurelius, when the burned remains of the Christians were

[9] Tacitus, *Annals* 15.44.
[10] Pliny, *Letters* 10.97.

thrown in the Rhône to prevent their proper burial. The policy of disapproval, nonetheless, continued to hold, and on these principles was to rest the more extended persecution of the third century.

For their part the Christians held firmly to the doctrine of Jesus, elaborated by Paul as "the powers that be are ordained of God." Polycarp, while refusing to sacrifice to the emperor, told the proconsul of Asia, "We have been taught to give honor, as is proper, to rulers and authorities appointed by God, provided it does not harm us." [11] In Revelation a strong sense of hostility to the powers of this world manifested itself, but the lukewarm persecution by the state prevented the Church from sliding into an attitude of total opposition. Nonetheless the imperial and popular condemnation had two great effects: it kept together the members of the local churches in a tight bond and dissuaded the only mildly interested; and, second, the principle of separation of church and state received a first endorsement in Christian thought.

Christianity and Classical Culture. The relations of Christian thought to classical civilization were a significant blend of acceptance and rejection. Christ Himself spoke Aramaic and could have known only such parts of Hellenistic culture as trickled into Galilee. Paul, however, quoted the Stoic Cleanthes to the Athenians (Acts 17:28); and the turn of Christianity away from the Jews to the gentiles almost forced it to cast its literature in the simplified Hellenistic Greek known as the *koine.* Behind the Gospels may lie a lost Aramaic version of the teachings of Christ, but the language of the early Church was to be Greek.

The ramifications of this fact were many. Alone among the so-called Oriental faiths Christianity could have a wide appeal on cultivated levels; its distinction even from the Hellenized Judaism of the Diaspora was sharpened; and its thinkers could draw vigor from the marked revival of Hellenic thought and letters by A.D. 100. Even in Rome the church was Greek until the mid-third century, but in time Christian conquests among Latin speakers became extensive. Latin translation of the New Testament, book by book, began in the second century; and Tertullian (*c.* 160–*c.* 225), who created ecclesiastical Latin, was the first Christian writer of real literary ability in any tongue.

The fundamental doctrines of the new faith, to be sure, were of a new order, and despite insidious temptations to adjust their thought to the

[11] Paul, Romans 13:1; *Martyrdom of St. Polycarp* 10.2; tr. F. X. Glimm.

polished, refined classical outlook Christian thinkers never entirely abdicated these basic principles. Some, indeed, drew the ultimate conclusion from the words of Paul, "Hath not God made foolish the wisdom of this world?" and rejected pagan culture. The Mesopotamian Tatian (late second century) opposed any use of Greek ideas; and the African Tertullian, given to spectacular statements, laid down the superficially antirational view, "We have no need for curiosity after possessing Jesus Christ, nor for inquisition after enjoying the gospel." [12] Yet Tertullian himself, trained as a lawyer, poured out a host of theological tracts which drew on all the skill of classical logic and made considerable use of Stoicism.

The basic disagreement of Christianity with pagan principles, in sum, did not mean in practice its rejection of classical civilization. For this there were several reasons. Not only did the Church exist within the world of the Roman Empire, but also its members in early times came to it largely one by one as adults educated in the classical system. Having accepted the Christian promise, they then turned to lead other pagans to the way of salvation. From the early second century men like Quadratus, Justin, and Minucius Felix composed "apologies" to the emperors in which they sought to explain Christian doctrines in terms that classically trained men could comprehend.

While some Christian leaders continued to feel that their faith ought to be simple, others had come by the late second century to recognize a need for clarification and extension of Christian theology. In doing so, they inevitably drew large drafts on Greek logic, rhetoric, and philosophical doctrines. The western fathers Irenaeus (b. c. 130) and Tertullian cautiously led the way; far more was achieved by the Christian Platonists of Alexandria. The first of these reconcilers of Hellenic thought and Christian principles was Clement of Alexandria (c. 150–211/16), who had received a full classical education before his conversion and proclaimed a secret knowledge (*gnosis*) which enabled him to probe more deeply.

Clement's pupil Origen (c. 185–254) was the greatest early Christian scholar. Origen was saved from martyrdom in 202 by his mother, who hid his clothes and so kept him from rushing out to seek the fate his father had met. Thereafter he perfected his knowledge under Clement

[12] Paul, I Corinthians 1:20; Tertullian, *On Prescription* 7.

on the Christian side and also under the philosopher Ammonius Saccas on the Platonic side; to excise the temptations of this world he had himself castrated. Origen devoted his life to teaching and to the outpouring of a huge volume of work, taken down by stenographers.

In his Biblical commentaries and homilies Origen methodically applied to the Old Testament and New Testament alike the allegorical method used by Jewish scholars like Philo; he also made great use of Plato. After finding that Greek translations of the Old Testament differed seriously, Origen learned some rudiments of Hebrew and employed Alexandrian literary techniques in creating the *Hexapla*, an edition in parallel columns of six texts, Hebrew and Greek, of the Old Testament. His earliest study, *On the Bases*, was the first and for long the only systematic study of Christian theology; another major work, *Against Celsus*, refuted an elaborate attack on Christianity by the pagan Celsus. Once Origen had fully broken the ice, Christian thinkers thereafter continued to use philosophy to expound and systematize their doctrine.

The First Heresies. Christians had a driving curiosity to be certain about every detail of that mode of life and creed which could give them the salvation for which they sacrificed so much in the hostile, pagan world. Christian thought, accordingly, had a purpose and a drive lacking in the weary classical pattern; and the primacy of faith, though basic, did not produce an intellectual numbness. The problem, if anything, was the reverse, that is, that contention over doctrine would go so far as to split the Church into radically opposed camps.

The doctrine that was generally accepted was called orthodox; beside it stood a host of alternatives, called heresies. Some dissident groups opposed the rise of the bishops and of a systematic order which tended to eliminate the mystical and ecstatic; the leading heresy in this regard was the Montanist of Asia Minor, which preached the imminent coming of the New Jerusalem as well as total opposition to the state. Others felt that if a moral life aided their salvation then asceticism would more certainly save them and therefore preached sexual abstinence. One interesting element, grouped about Marcion (d. *c.* 160), pushed the doctrines of Paul to their extreme by denying any connection between Christ and the God of the Old Testament; for a time the Marcionites spread widely and formed an almost independent church.

Yet the most serious threats emerged along the line where Christianity met classical civilization. Origen himself was later accounted a heretic because of his accommodation to pagan concepts; more extensive heresies grew out of Christian contacts with gnosticism. The gnostics were thus called because they claimed a special revelation or knowledge (*gnosis*) and created many elaborate and mystic explanations of life, a potpourri of paganism, Oriental cults, and philosophy which revolved about the redemption of a heavenly spark within mankind. Some gnostics found themselves attracted to Jesus as a savior, but were forced to deny His humanity as an affront to the pureness of divinity; nor could they accept bodily resurrection. Leading Christian gnostics were Basilides and Valentinus of the first half of the second century.

The views of such men, if accepted, would have crippled basic Christian beliefs both about the nature of Christ and about the equality of all believers; for gnostics constructed levels of knowledge through which men could rise to the ultimate contemplation of reality. Some of the earliest apocryphal, or "secret," writings were produced by gnostics who claimed arcane wisdom. In the end, however, the weight of the Church always clung to its guidelines; the gnostic assault, indeed, forced it to distinguish between apostolic writings and apocryphal works. The treatise *Against the Heresies* by Irenaeus, bishop of Lyons, was a refutation from Scripture of the gnostic separation of human and supernatural in Christ, a task which led him to the first systematic exposition of orthodox belief on the point. The battle yet went on into the Trinitarian struggles of the fourth century which we shall inspect later.

Christianity by A.D. 200. The modern student who reads widely in the polished but thin pagan literature of the Roman Empire or examines its elegant, repetitious statuary will experience a shock on turning to the freshness and vigor of Christian thought and belief. When Clement of Rome rhapsodizes:

> How blessed and wonderful, beloved, are the gifts of God!
> Life in immortality, brightness in righteousness, truth in
> full assurance, faith in confidence, temperance in holiness,[13]

his thoughts do not have for us, bred in a long Christian tradition, their due impact; for in their own era they were a gale of new life blowing through old halls.

It is worth repeating an earlier observation that pagan thinkers and

[13] *Letter to the Corinthians* 35.1–2; tr. Kirsopp Lake.

artists were moving in the same direction and exhibited unconsciously a new view of the humanity of man and the divinity of an all-powerful God; for men's minds were not hopelessly sapped by the sterility of imperial civilization. Yet these thinkers were too limited by old conventions to be able to break entirely free. Only Christianity stood independent of the state and of the culture of its day — independent but nonetheless attached to both sufficiently to absorb and pass on to later ages some of the most basic political cultural achievements of the pagan world.

By 200 only a minute proportion of the Empire's population dared or desired to be Christian; and a modern observer may well be amazed at the calm certainty of this little group that it held the right path, regardless of pagan ridicule and the official disapproval by the ever more omnipotent emperor. Yet the Church had sunk its roots across the Mediterranean world, which was still perplexed by the willingness of this novel sect to accept martyrdom in order to gain eternal life. In the troubled, even chaotic century and a half to come Christianity was to meet and overcome its greatest tests from imperial persecution. As pagan views on the one hand changed ever more swiftly in that era and on the other Christian morality adapted itself more fully to the problems of living in this world, the new creed could eventually rise under Constantine to a position of imperial toleration, even favor.

BIBLIOGRAPHY

Sources. In the New Testament the letters of Paul are the oldest element. They illuminate in passing his theology; his travels are in part described in Acts of the Apostles, written by his follower Luke. Among the Gospels, Matthew and Luke seem to draw from Mark and other sources, one of which may have been an Aramaic or Greek collection of the sayings of Jesus (called Q by modern scholars); other material of the same type, which they did not use, turns up in apocryphal Gospels. The Gospel according to John was only accepted by the orthodox after some hesitation; the other material attributed to John presents many problems. Even by the late second century Christian scholars were unsure of the meaning and authorship of Revelation, which is written in a quite different, poorer form of Greek than is the rest of the New Testament. See R. M. Grant, *Historical Introduction to the New Testament* (New

York: Touchstone, 1972); J. A. T. Robinson, *Redating the New Testament* (Philadelphia: Westminster, 1976); and E. J. Goodspeed, *History of Early Christian Literature* (Chicago: University of Chicago Press, 1966).

By about 170 the New Testament, essentially in its present form, was beginning to be regarded as authoritative Scripture rather than simple evidence for the teachings of Jesus. The oldest physical testimony is a papyrus fragment of John 18 of the first half of the second century; this was originally part of a *codex,* or bound book, unlike the normal Greek literary roll. One of the most famous complete texts is the *codex Sinaiticus* of the first half of the fourth century (now in the British Museum except for 43 leaves in Leipzig); the *codex Vaticanus* is also of the fourth century. These are described in Frederic Kenyon, *Our Bible and the Ancient Manuscripts* (rev. ed.; London: Eyre and Spottiswood, 1958).

The very limited number of other early Christian works may be found in *The Apostolic Fathers,* tr. Kirsopp Lake, 2 vols. (New York: Loeb Classical Library, 1912–13) or *Early Christian Fathers,* tr. Cyril C. Richardson (Philadelphia: Wesminster, 1953). These include the letters of Clement of Rome and of Ignatius of Antioch; the *Didache* (*Teaching*) *of the Twelve Apostles;* and the *Shepherd of Hermas,* which for a time was ranked as part of the New Testament even though it dates about A.D. 150. By the second and early third century we have the *Apology* of Justin and the first major Christian works in Latin, the polished dialogue *Octavius* by Minucius Felix and the noble *Apology* and other works by Tertullian. Of other, lost works there is often a valuable notice in the *Church History* of Eusebius in the early fourth century. M. R. James, *The Apocryphal New Testament* (corr. ed.; Oxford: Oxford University Press, 1953) has a full collection of the apocryphal gospels, acts, apocalypses ascribed to the apostles and designed to give secret wisdom, to explain the early years of Jesus or the last of Mary, and to justify gnostic tendencies at times.

Neither pagans nor Christians saw fit to discuss Christianity, save for brief, slighting references, down to *The True World* of Celsus, a lengthy attack about A.D. 180. Christian archeology scarcely begins before the third century inasmuch as believers met in private homes or inconspicuous chapels. The most remarkable find in recent years has been the shrine of St. Peter, erected about A.D. 160–70 on the Vatican hill. When Constantine built the first basilica of St. Peter's, this small monument was its focal point, but we do not know that it was thought to mark his actual grave. See J. M. C. Toynbee and J. B. Ward-Perkins, *Shrine of St. Peter and the Vatican Excavations* (New York: AMS Press). The catacombs of Rome commence about the end of the second century; there is still debate whether Christian symbols appear in Pompeii and Herculaneum before the eruption of A.D. 79.

Further Reading. The religious background of the Roman Empire, often discussed, may be found in J. Ferguson, *The Religions of the Roman Empire* (Ithaca: Cornell University Press, 1970), and Franz Cumont, *Mysteries of Mithra* (New York: Dover T323, 1956); a more recent study of *Mithras, the Secret God,* is by M. J. Vermaseren (New York: Barnes and Noble, 1963). One of the most penetrating studies is A. D. Nock, *Conversion: The Old and New in Religion* (New York: Oxford Paperback 30, 1961). On Judaism, see Emil Schürer, *History of the Jewish People in the Age of Jesus* (Edinburgh: Clark, 1973–79), a famous work well revised by F. Millar and G. Vermes; G. J. Moore, *Judaism in the First Centuries of the Christian Era,* 2 vols. (New York: Schocken, 1971); E. M. Smallwood, *The Jews under Roman Rule* (Leiden: Brill, 1976). The Dead Sea scrolls are sensibly considered by T. H. Gaster, *Dead Sea Scriptures* (New York: Doubleday Anchor, 1976); and R. de Vaux, *Archaeology and the Dead Sea Scrolls* (Oxford: Oxford University Press, 1973). E. R. Goodenough provides *An Introduction to Philo Judaeus* (2d ed.; Oxford: Blackwell, 1962).

Goodenough has a brief, clear study on *The Church in the Roman Empire* (New York: Cooper Square, 1970); Adolf Harnack, *Mission and Expansion of Christianity in the First Three Centuries* (New York: Harper Torchbook 92, 1961), is a classic; R. M. Grant, *Early Christianity and Society* (San Francisco: Harper & Row, 1977), is useful on its subject. Fuller are, from the Protestant point of view, Hans Lietzmann, *History of the Early Church,* 4 vols. in 2 (New York: Meridian MG26A–B, 1961); from the Catholic side, Jules Lebreton and Jacques Zeiller, *History of the Primitive Church,* 3 vols. (New York: Collier BS77–79V, 1962). The idea of the Messiah is treated by a Jewish scholar, Joseph Klausner, in *Jesus of Nazareth* (New York: Menorah Press, 1978); see also S. O. P. Mowinckel, *He That Cometh* (New York: Abingdon,

1956). A. D. Nock (Santa Fe, N.M.: Gannon, 1970), A. Deissmann (Magnolia, Mass.: Peter Smith), and M. Grant (New York: Scribners, 1976), discuss the career of St. Paul; Jacques Maritain, *Living Thoughts of St. Paul* (New York: Longmans, 1941), gives a clear exposition of his views. See also M. Hengel, *Acts and the History of Earliest Christianity* (London: SCM, 1979).

The development of the liturgy is sketched by J. H. Srawley, *Early History of the Liturgy* (2d ed.; Cambridge: Cambridge University Press, 1947), and treated in greater detail by Dom Gregory Dix, *Shape of the Liturgy* (London: Dacre Press, 1945). W. H. C. Frend, *Martyrdom and Persecution in the Early Church* (Oxford: Blackwell, 1965), is thoughtful and wide-ranging. On the gnostics, see F. C. Burkitt, *Church and Gnosis* (New York: AMS, 1977); the important Egyptian discoveries are to be found in W. Foerster, *Gnosis* (Oxford: Oxford University Press, 1972–74), and J. M. Robinson, *The Nag Hammadi Library in English* (San Francisco: Harper and Row, 1977). The archeological evidence is summed up by Michael Gough, *Early Christians* (New York: Praeger, 1961) and *The Origins of Christian Art* (London: Thames & Hudson, 1973). The intellectual development of the early Church will be found in works listed in Bibliography, Chapter 31; but see also W. Jaeger, *Early Christianity and Christian Paideia* (Cambridge, Mass.: Harvard University Press, 1961).

29

THE FARTHER ORIENT

To the Romans their great capital was *caput mundi,* "capital of the world." One orator went so far as to proclaim that "he who does not see the Empire is as one who does not see the sun." [1] Yet the inhabitants of this charmed land knew, in their more sober moments, that it was linked to great land masses in Europe, Asia, and Africa. Although the imperial army and the ever more firmly drawn boundary (*limes*) served as bars between Roman and non-Roman, diplomacy and trade reached out to the neighboring peoples, beyond whom lay more dimly known regions.

During the golden age of the Roman peace the ties among the civilized districts of Eurasia grew closer than ever before, even if these contacts had only limited effects in any one area. The barbarians, who lay about and between the organized states, were essentially quiescent at this time, partly because the great powers were strong enough to man their walls firmly and even to extend their sway. The Germans, Huns, and other peoples to the north will concern us in later chapters; the Arabs blazed out only after the end of ancient history.

Various minor civilized outposts existed, especially toward the east of the Roman Empire. Many were dependent on Rome, including the Bosporan kingdom in the Crimea, the oasis state of Palmyra, and the

[1] Callinicus (under Aurelian), in Polemo, *Declamationes,* ed. H. Hinck (Leipzig: Teubner, 1873), p. 43.

Nabataean realm centered on the rose-red city of Petra (annexed by Trajan in 106). Others, such as Armenia, looked mainly to Parthia or were totally independent, like the Sabaean state in southwest Arabia (modern Yemen). These we must pass over so as to inspect more closely the Parthian Near East, the India of the Mauryan and Kushan dynasties, and Han China; the period to be covered in this survey runs roughly from the third century B.C. to the early third century after Christ (see Map 19).

In general all three shared the prosperity of the Roman Empire, and Han China offers remarkable parallels to the political and cultural development of the Empire. The similarities which exist are worth noting, yet the historian must be wary of establishing a common pattern in great detail for states so thinly linked and based on such different outlooks. It is more important to observe how the individual patterns of each district became consolidated and amplified as bases for the major nonwestern civilizations which have assumed new significance in the modern world.

THE PARTHIAN NEAR EAST

Political Development (247 B.C.–A.D. 224). The Parthians themselves were a nomadic people who had settled in the ancient province of Parthia and rose in power as the Seleucid monarchy declined. Their Arsacid dynasty dated its power from 247 B.C., but Mithridates I (*c.* 171–38) of this line did not take Mesopotamia until 141, after the Romans had hamstrung the Seleucid kings. Thereafter the Parthians ruled from the middle Euphrates eastward to Afghanistan on the southeast and the Oxus river on the northeast. In a geographic sense their capitals of Ctesiphon and Ecbatana and their main commercial center of Seleucia-on-the-Tigris were the crossroads of the Eurasian civilized belt.

The political and cultural currents which meshed here must have been extremely complicated, and the interplay of forces should have had significant results. Unfortunately, however, the history of Parthia cannot yet be written. The Parthians themselves enjoyed the old Iranian lays, which eventually produced the *Shahname* (Book of Kings), but they were not inclined toward historical composition. Written materials of any kind are few; and the backwardness of the Iranian highlands until very recent decades has not encouraged archeological exploration. Our

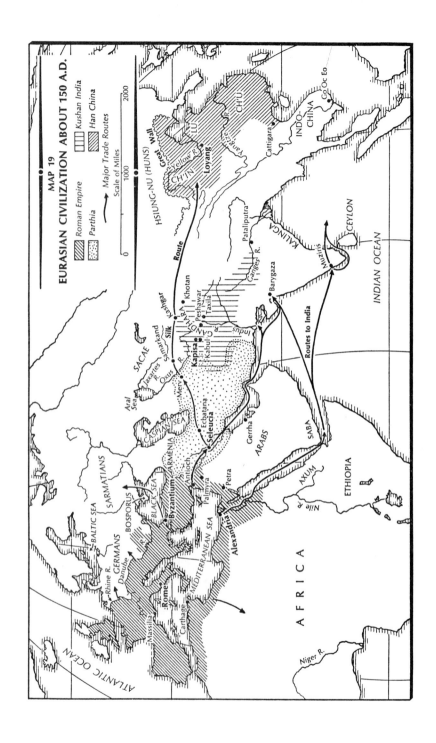

MAP 19

EURASIAN CIVILIZATION ABOUT 150 A.D.

Roman Empire   Kushan India
Parthia   Han China
→ Major Trade Routes

Scale of Miles
0   1000   2000

main information, accordingly, comes from Roman references, which undoubtedly exaggerate the importance of the western frontiers of Parthia.

Actually the Arsacids must continually have faced serious problems on all their frontiers. Two Parthian kings fell in succession in the late second century B.C. fighting the twin nomadic peoples called Sacae (in western sources) and Yueh-chi (by Chinese authors). Eventually the Parthians detoured these nomadic peoples to India, but they had recurring, dimly lit struggles with the resulting Kushan dynasty in India as well as with the barbarian nomads to the northeast.

Parthian relations with Rome began when Sulla, as governor of Cilicia, met a Parthian embassy in 96 B.C.; thereafter wars flared up intermittently, in which the Romans were commonly the aggressors. In the first contest Crassus lost his life at Carrhae (53 B.C.); Antony did little better in the 30s; and Augustus negotiated a peace in 20 B.C. During the Empire there were new hostilities under Nero; and in the second century Trajan, Lucius Verus, and Septimius Severus all penetrated to Ctesiphon. The Romans, however, could overcome neither the logistical problems of supply from their Mediterranean base so far inland nor the tactical difficulties of using infantry on open plains against Parthian cavalry; and so they never made a lasting conquest. On the whole the Arsacid kings maintained the security of the kernel of their realm and gave it a stability which the Seleucids had never been able to achieve.

After their seizure of Mesopotamia, on the other hand, the Parthians did not expand farther; for new additions would have been not only difficult but also a dangerous gamble. Internally the Parthian organization was of a loose type in which the great landlords of the Iranian valleys were virtually independent local princes, who brought their own armies of mailed cavalry and horse-archers to aid the kings if they deemed it to be in their own interest to do so. Five areas, including Armenia, formed major client kingdoms; others were minor principalities; and yet others had satraps. As the Parthian rule grew old, the peasants fell ever more under the power of the landlords, in a process reminiscent of the Roman Empire; and the class structure became more rigid. A further source of dissension was the enduring fratricidal rivalry in the Arsacid royal house; insecure sons often bolted to Rome, where they were maintained as possible pretenders to the throne. From the middle of the first century after Christ these conjoined factors seriously weakened royal power.

Besides the Persian-speaking elements the Greek cities of the Near East continued to exist as important focuses of trade. The Parthian kings themselves remained seminomadic in outlook, and built their western capital of Ctesiphon basically as a camp, which they deliberately placed across the Tigris river from Seleucia. Nevertheless they carefully guarded the interests of their important Greek subjects and on their coinage boasted themselves "philhellene." Spices, incenses, pearls, and other luxuries came from India by land and by the Persian Gulf; silk and lacquer moved from China by caravan across central Asia, initially south of the T'ien Shan mountains to Samarkand on the famous Silk Route. These latter wares were exchanged on the eastern border of Parthia at a place called Stone Tower, for as the Chinese grumbled, "The inhabitants of Ta Ts'in [Rome] always desired to send embassies [or traders] to China, but the An-hsi [Parthians] wished to carry on trade with them in Chinese silks, and it is for this reason that they were cut off from communication." [2] The language of this trade was Greek, which drove out Aramaic.

Decline of Hellenism. The cultural development of the Near East under the Parthians was of such crucial importance that one wishes we could see it more clearly. The Arsacid dynasty represented a political victory of non-Hellenic elements, but, as just noted, it protected the Greeks. The dominant pattern was initially Hellenic on the surface. Greek upper classes continued to govern the major cities; they carefully maintained their *gymnasia* as vital centers for propagating Greek customs; and they duly celebrated their religious and cultural festivals. Greek authors and artists moved with fair ease back and forth between the Roman Empire and Parthia; and on the same routes missionaries spreading Christianity traveled eastward as far as India and, later, China. The kings themselves often possessed a veneer of Greek culture. According to Plutarch, the head of Crassus was brought to the Parthian court just as King Orodes II was hearing a performance of Euripides' *Bacchae;* an actor held the head high on the stage at an appropriate moment in this wild tragedy.

[2] F. Hirth, *China and the Roman Orient* (Leipzig, 1885), p. 42, from the Hou-han-shu.

Yet the Parthian era was the period in which Hellenism began to retreat as the Near East turned more and more to face inward away from the intrusion of Mediterranean culture. At Dura-Europos, which the Parthians had taken in 141 B.C., Near Eastern influences in dress, religion, and architectural styles became steadily more dominant. Under Vologases I (c. A.D. 51–80) coins first bore Iranian legends. The symbol of the fire altar, with a sacrificing priest, appeared at the same time as advertisement of the worship of Ahura-Mazda, and traditionally the Avesta was compiled in this reign. Pure Zoroastrianism, however, had long since disappeared; the principal deity in Parthian times was the goddess Añahita.

Artistically the Parthian period seems the most stagnant in the history of the ancient Near East, but beneath the surface there are clear signs that the Greek esthetic outlook was being rejected. Famous in this regard is a fresco found at Dura, which depicts Conon and others in sacrifice; here the human figures, ruthlessly simplified and unnaturally elongated as symbols, look out in strict frontality at the spectator, commanding his respect to the spiritual meaning of the worship. Another distinctive trait is the flying gallop in which horses and wild animals are shown, especially on metal work, in a highly abstract manner. This style, which had wide affinities with nomad art, serves as a reminder that far more than Greek influences bore on the Parthian world. The Near East abandoned Greek naturalism more easily and more fully than did the Roman Empire, though the same forces were at work in both areas as classic realism yielded to symbolic, almost abstract conceptions.

The full fruits, nonetheless, of the many lines of change in the Parthian kingdom came only after the last Arsacid fell in 224 to the first ruler of the Sassanian dynasty. The Near Eastern resurgence thenceforth led steadily toward the great heights of the later Arab empire.

MAURYAN AND KUSHAN INDIA

The Mauryan Empire. Beyond the Parthians, the Greco-Roman world had only a dim awareness of the Chinese (called the Seres) and but little more knowledge of India. Yet Alexander's invasion of the Punjab did bring direct connections with India for a time, and the ties with the west had more considerable political and cultural effects in India from 300 B.C. to A.D. 200 than ever before.

Immediately after Alexander's departure a notable dynasty, the Mauryan, appeared in north India. Its founder, Chandragupta (322–298), united the Indus and Ganges basins, together with Afghanistan, by force of arms; the Greek claims he bought off in 305 by giving the first Seleucus 500 elephants. Whether Chandragupta drew directly on Hellenistic administrative skills is not clear; but his autocratic, centralized realm, focused on the capital of Pataliputra (modern Patna), had strong resemblances to Ptolemaic Egypt. Irrigation and the distribution of water were carefully regulated, and heavy taxes were exacted for the maintenance of the controllers and inspectors of the bureaucracy and the large professional army. Royal monopolies in metallurgy and mining, based on the copper and iron mines of south Bihar, furnished further revenues; deliberate colonization by the lowest caste of *sudras* was extended in the Ganges basin.

The grandson of Chandragupta, Asoka (269–32), inherited this firm structure and at first carried out further conquests in the Kalinga area of the southeast. Then his revulsion against the slaughter and slavery involved in conquest led Asoka to become a devout Buddhist. Over most of India today his edicts, carved on rocks and pillars, still proclaim his passionate attachment to the doctrines of the Buddha and his efforts to inculcate morality in his subjects. One of these, recently discovered at Kandahar, fulminates against hunting in both Greek and Aramaic; the others are in the Kharoshthi or Brahmi scripts.

Asoka's agents, as these edicts indicate, carried the word of Gautama far afield to Ceylon, Syria, and Egypt. At home the wealth and security of the Mauryans now led to more building in stone and the creation of a court style of art. Since India previously had lacked a strong sculptural tradition, Mauryan carvers were freer to take western influences. A great audience hall at Pataliputra, in Persian style, has left considerable remains; and the highly polished Sarnath capital, crowned with the Buddhist wheel of life and also lions, is a product of Asoka's reign.

Soon after Asoka's death the Mauryan empire fell to pieces. The Greek overlords of Bactria drove down into the Punjab, and the able general Menander set up an independent kingdom about 130 B.C., based on Kabul in Afghanistan. Although cut off from the Greek world by

Parthia, the Greek principalities of north India survived on to the last part of the first century B.C., and some parts of Greek medicine, astronomy, and technical aspects of play production seem to have become accepted by Indian civilization.

The Kushan Dynasty. Soon after the rise of Parthia to mastery of the Near East, its kings had had to confront a serious invasion of the Sacae and Yueh-chi. Both peoples moved on down as far as India; on the way the Yueh-chi ended the Greek line in Bactria about 133 B.C. Eventually the Yueh-chi came under the leadership of the Kushan dynasty. The first major kings of this line, Kadphises I (Kujula) and Kadphises II (Vima), respectively annexed Afghanistan and north India; Kushan capitals were Peshawar in India itself and Kapisa (Begram) in Afghanistan, the latter on a great east-west caravan route.

Since our knowledge of Kushan times relies on the very feeble Indian historical tradition and on the coins of the rulers, much is dark. The dates of the greatest Kushan ruler, Kanishka, thus are extremely uncertain, but may provisionally be set in the early second century after Christ. While it would appear that India proper was really a fringe area in the Kushan empire of central Asia, the relative stability of this far-flung realm is attested above all by the remarkable spread of Buddhist art and thought; the entry of Buddhism into China comes at this time. Trade with the Roman Empire by the sea route to Egypt, which took eight months for a round trip, also reached its peak in the era; and both pagan and Christian authors of the Mediterranean world knew something of Brahman ideas.

In the third century after Christ the Kushans met sterner opposition from the new Sassanian rulers of Persia, and the ground swell of nomad movement wrested other areas from their control. By the fourth century their rule of India had yielded to a new, more specifically Indian dynasty (the Gupta).

Evolution of Buddhism. In the time of Asoka, Buddhism became a missionary faith, and thenceforth it spread widely across central Asia by land and into southeastern Asia by sea. As it expanded, Buddhism developed a powerful mode of artistic expression which has affected the arts of Asia ever since.

Originally Buddhism had been a practical, ethical creed in which only a rare individual could rise to the oblivion of personality in Nirvana. As a world cult it necessarily became more emotional and varied in appeal, yet not all Buddhist thinkers were willing to accept these modifications. Kanishka, who first placed the image of Buddha on his coins and fostered Buddhist expansion northward, convoked a great council at Gandhara to secure a common doctrine, but his efforts failed to heal the split which had been deepening since the time of Asoka.

In the end there arose two major forms of Buddhism. That called the *Hinayana* or 'lesser vehicle' spread mainly by sea and now is to be found chiefly in Burma and Ceylon; the *Mahayana* or "greater vehicle" had more widespread popularity inasmuch as it offered an escape from the earthly round to all. In the *Mahayana* form of Buddhism a principal doctrine was the belief that there were *bodhisattvas,* men who had secured the right to gain Nirvana by their own meditations but who voluntarily remained in this world to aid others toward the same goal. Gautama, in this doctrine, was himself a *bodhisattva,* who had been incarnated in earlier holy men, and the blessed ones who came after him were united with him. Thus the Buddha tended to rise into a divine position and in the famous Lotus *sutra* was transfigured after preaching to his disciples for the last time. By worshiping the "saints" and by self-denial and kindness to others the ordinary man too could gain salvation. *Mahayana* thought became ever more complicated on many levels from the highly philosophical to the grossest superstition.

As Indian art developed, partially under western influences, it initially found a more sympathetic home in the earthly oriented Buddhism than in Hindusim. On sacred Buddhist sites, such at that of Barhut (*c.* 150 B.C.), the faithful erected mounds or *stupas;* the buildings and ornamental railings of these *stupas* were sculptured, often with lively, humorous pictures of life. Originally the Buddha himself was referred to only by such symbols as his footprint or an empty throne, but in the first century after Christ sculptors began to depict Gautama.

Among the several different schools of sculpture the most amazing and influential was that of Gandhara in the northwest, which drew very heavily on Greco-Roman art. The earliest Buddhas of Gandhara are standing, realistic figures, modified by the addition of Buddhist attributes such as long ear lobes, topknot, and a tuft of hair between the eyebrows.[3] Only later did this type melt into the more static, canonical

---

[3] One of the clearest illustrations of the manner in which Buddhist sculptors adapted western styles is the head shown on Plate XXIX.

depiction of the Buddha seated on a lotus in a yoga pose, which spread to China and thence eventually to Japan. In India itself the new style was a leavening force in native patterns; thence sprang eventually a Hindu art proper.

Consolidation of Hinduism. Throughout the Mauryan era Hinduism seems to have been on the defensive in the upper circles of society about such men as Asoka and Kanishka. These rulers, however were tolerant toward Jainism and Hinduism; and Kanishka depicted Siva more than the Buddha and even figured Iranian deities on his coins. As far as the subjects were concerned, most Indians continued to find the most satisfactory answers to the problems of life in the ancestral social and religious views embodied in Hinduism. The wrangling sects of Buddhist monks eventually died out almost completely in India itself; the main lasting effect of its emotional, practical appeal was reorientation and consolidation of the Hindu religion, which really came into focus only in the period under consideration.

The two principal figures thenceforth in this pantheistic cult were Siva and Vishnu. The three-faced figure of Siva, seated in a yoga posture and surrounded by beasts, seems to appear in the Indus civilization, but the historical Siva inherited his quality as a mountain-born, avenging deity from the storm god of the Vedic tradition. Eventually Hindu art created another great representation of him as a dancing god, the master of creation and of destruction. This role of Siva as generative principle led to phallic symbolism and the remarkable frankness which appears in Hindu sculpture. Beside Siva stood his wife Parvati, who was non-Aryan in root as a great mother; sometimes benevolent, Parvati could also be the fierce feminine force Kali. A mystical set of beliefs called Tantrism appeared in later days in celebration of the female energy of Parvati in relation to Siva.

As Siva became a more personalized divine being, so too did Vishnu; and both could be revered by ordinary human beings in emotional terms of love (called *bhakti*) as well as by philosophers in the intellectual approach of the *Upanishads*. Vishnu, a minor figure in the *Vedas* connected with the sun, swallowed up many other forces and was eventually thought to have had 10 major incarnations on earth. Of these the seventh was Rama, the eighth was Krishna; and both figures became the centers of two great chains of Sanskrit epic.

The *Ramayana* is the story of Rama, who saved his wife Sita from the demon Ravana and came back from exile to ascend his proper throne. As a perfect king and spreader of civilization, Rama served as ideal for the warrior Kshatriya caste. About Krishna revolved a set of tales of love and also the extraordinarily long epic *Mahabharata*. This was consolidated between A.D. 200 and 400 and so was somewhat later than the *Ramayana*. It revolved about an ancient war of noble charioteers; within it was incorporated a great speech, the *Bhagavad Gita* by Krishna as a charioteer, to encourage his master in battle. This "Song of the Lord" emphasized the necessity for human action in accordance with one's duty, thus countering the opposing Hindu philosophical doctrine that action in this world is useless. It also urged a loving faith in God:

> Even if a very evil doer
> Reveres Me with single devotion,
> He must be regarded as righteous in spite of all;
> For he has the right resolution.[4]

Although these epics had very early roots, they assumed their present form largely in Kushan times. In the same era, and also in the next or Gupta period, Hindu art also expressed the consolidation of Hindu concepts of the greater and lesser gods into a remarkably varied pattern ranging from crude animism to the most sophisticated philosophical approach. The caste and village structure of Indian civilization helped to carry those views on as the base of all later Indian life.

HAN CHINA

The Unification of China. While the Romans of the Late Republic and Early Empire were conquering the Mediterranean basin and were creating a unified culture as the hallmark of the gentleman and administrator, China was undergoing a very similar political and cultural development over the period 221 B.C.–A.D. 220. This history can be followed in more detail than can that of India or Parthia, for the Chinese developed a powerful written historical tradition.

Politically the Late Chou period (see Chapter 8) was one of outward breakdown as local warlords gained mastery. The chaos born of this

---

[4] *The Bhagavad Gita* 9.30; tr. Franklin Edgerton (Cambridge, Mass.: Harvard University Press, 1944).

wrangling, however, disposed men to seek a more stable political system, and unification as a solution was facilitated by a variety of economic and social changes. The development of irrigation and of water transport by canal and river bound the Chinese ever more closely together; the old local bonds were weakened by the rise of money and markets, which favored purely economic relationships. Socially a class of scholar-rural gentleman grew in strength as Confucian doctrines spread. On the one hand this class served the warlords as administrators; but on the other it replaced more and more on the local level the old nobility and was willing to see, above it, a political unification.

The principalities of the plains declined in the fifth and following centuries, and two states spread down from the western hills. The southern or Ch'u state expanded widely along the ricelands of the central Yangtze river through its use of warships; the northern was led by the Ch'in despots, who abandoned chariots in favor of masses of infantry equipped with iron weapons and crossbows. Eventually, under Shih Huang Ti (221–10), the Ch'in line ruthlessly welded the separate states together. To man the administrative districts he created, Shih Huang Ti laid the first foundation for the great Chinese bureaucracy of later millennia; and to weaken the nobles he gave ownership of the land to the peasants, who paid taxes to the state.

Shih Huang Ti expanded his control southward to Indo-China and joined together the earlier walls built in the north to form the Great Wall, 2500 miles long, designed to keep out the barbaric nomads of Mongolia and to keep in his peasant subjects. This "First Emperor" found Legalism a helpful tool and was implacable against intellectual opposition, which was in part voiced by Confucian scholars conservative of the past and accustomed to freedom of speech. Aided by a great minister Li Ssu, he standardized Chinese writing and set up one body of law; later tradition even asserted that in a famous "burning of the books" he essayed to wipe out both the literary classics of the past and the volumes of Confucian thought.

His magnificent tomb, discovered not long ago, was guarded by an army of over 7000 terracotta warriors — infantry, chariots, and crossbowmen — life-size and individually molded. But the requirements of forced labor on the tomb and his palaces, rigorous laws, and heavy taxes led to a rebellion which ended the Ch'in dynasty three years after his death.

The victor was an erstwhile brigand Liu Pang (206–195), outwardly coarse and simple, who superficially reversed the Ch'in despotism. Yet Liu Pang continued the basic forms of Ch'in organization and so founded the Han dynasty. China thus became a unified political system at a time when the Roman Republic was just setting out on its conquests of the eastern Mediterranean.

Political History of the Han (206 B.C.–A.D. 220). The long Han rule of China falls into two parts. The Earlier or Western Han (206 B.C.–A.D. 8) gained control over the landlords and firmly united their state in 13 provinces, which have survived to modern times. They also expanded Chinese domination widely. The outstanding ruler of this line, Han Wu Ti, the "Martial Emperor" (140–87), warred against the nomadic, ever threatening Hsiung-nu (probably Huns) to the west and secured direct contact with the Yueh-chi beyond them in central Asia; asserted Chinese supremacy in Manchuria and Korea; annexed south China; and exerted lordship over the fringe area of Indo-China to the south. Internally as well he was forceful in revising earlier customs and reduced the power of local lords, as by taking over control of the coinage and extending government monopolies. Although Wu Ti officially recognized Confucianism, not all scholars liked his authoritarianism.

The most extraordinary ruler of Han China was the usurper Wang Mang (A.D. 9–23), an obscure cousin of the previous emperor, who manipulated public opinion to secure his way to the throne. The reign of this fanatic Confucian was marked by a nationalization of the land, which Wang Mang divided equally among the peasants on the payment of 50 per cent taxes to the state. Gold was replaced by bronze currency; prices were fixed; imperial monopolies, already standard in the sale of salt and iron, were extended to other basic commodities. For a brief moment China knew virtually a socialist structure, instituted primarily to assure the absolute position of the emperor. In the last year of his reign Wang Mang, far less deft than his contemporary, Augustus, realized the discontent of his subjects and revoked most of his edicts. His step was too late, for a revolt led to his death and execration.

The line of rulers called the Later or Eastern Han, which ruled from the old Chou capital of Loyang, restored the earlier pattern and maintained its control down to A.D. 220. Chronologically the Later Han corresponded to the first two centuries of the Roman Empire, and in this era the parallels of the two widely separated areas are close in their economic boom and decline, in the growth of bureaucratic government, and in the consolidation and essential sterility of earlier cultural patterns.

Economic and Political Prosperity. The age of the Han, taken as a whole, was a period of internal order and prosperity. Fundamental in China, as in the Roman Empire, was the agricultural level, which in China required irrigation to produce the peasants' food and to provide the surplus to feed the armies that maintained Han order. Both irrigation projects and flood-control efforts on the treacherous Yellow river were vital and were carried out on an extensive scale. In addition agriculture benefited by improvement of techniques and by the introduction of such crops as alfalfa, grapes, oranges, lemons, and, in the third century after Christ, tea. Most of China proper was now domesticated by peasant villages, practically self-sufficient; according to some estimates the population of China doubled in the Han period.

The provincial and national capitals were chiefly centers of culture and grain reservoirs for the political superstructure, rather than focuses of trade, and the rulers and rural gentry often followed anticommercial policies. Nonetheless, trade expanded widely, especially into south China and Indo-China. The first contacts between China and Japan, still on a barbarous level, were made under the Later Han. In silk textiles, in the first stages of porcelain, and in other industrial techniques Chinese artisans made great progress. As already noted, some of these products moved across Asia via the Silk Route to Parthia and the Roman world; and a brief contact between China and Rome was even achieved by sea in the reign of Marcus Aurelius.

Through its state monopolies of vital raw materials, control of coinage, and tax structure, the Han dynasty exercised a considerable degree of control over the internal economy of China. In social and political aspects as well the bureaucracy was a powerful force to ensure uniformity and obedience. Although service in the bureaucracy tended in practice to be hereditary, admission — as in the Roman Empire — depended upon imperial appointment; and, again like the Roman world, imperial officials had to be well trained in the conventional culture of the day and belong to the "gentleman" class, which continued its strength from the Chou period. Increasingly this culture in China entailed learning by heart the major works of the Confucian school, as Confucianism became the official creed of the state from the time of Wu Ti; and the subsequent custom of civil service examinations is usually traced back to Han beginnings. The bureaucracy itself was more carefully organized and graded than in the Early Roman Empire under three major officials, the Imperial Chancellor, the Grand Minister of War, and the Grandee Secretary.

Cultural Consolidation. While local cultural differences, especially in the south of China, were still marked, the form of Chinese civilization that had earlier been evolved in the Yellow river plains was winning the upper hand far more decisively than Greco-Roman culture in the contemporary Mediterranean world. Like the scholars of the Empire, however, Han thinkers concentrated primarily upon consolidating their inheritance, which they did much more thoroughly, systematically, and conservatively.

Sacrifices in honor of Confucius became compulsory in schools under the Later Han, and standard texts of the Confucian literature were officially established in order that prospective bureaucrats might learn them. So too scholars settled the definitive texts of the Chou classics, much as had Alexandrian scholars for earlier Greek literature; in China this process was necessitated by the development of a standard calligraphy executed with a brush pen and, after A.D. 105, using paper. Han scholars also made the first great dictionaries of their language and began a remarkable tradition of historical writing, the only one ever developed by mankind apart from that commenced by Herodotus and Thucydides.

Such an environment did not enourage original philosophical or literary activity, even though in the practical sciences China made advances that were much later to be borrowed by the west; but a solid, stable base of culture was laid down for subsequent ages. Intriguing enough, this consolidation led to evidence of cultural sterility by the second century after Christ, beside which appeared nonorthodox schemes of thought.

Weakening of Han China. Likewise in the second century the power of the central government weakened, and the local landowners increasingly assumed control over their neighborhoods. The free peasants of the countryside, who bore on their shoulders the splendid frame of Han life, had long been heavily oppressed by taxes and by forced labor and dues, legal or illegal. Now they often lost their farms and became day laborers, or to pay their rents had to sell their sons and daughters. Social unrest rose, and produced as one fruit a great revolution in 184, the leaders of which, called the Yellow Turbans, promised a golden age by the aid of Taoist magic. The protest was unavailing, but Chinese production and population turned downhill. Political leaders rose and fell rapidly in court intrigue and civil war; men of intellectual stamp grew despondent and questioned their ability to right matters.

A significant expression of the increasing uncertainty of life was the tendency of men to seek religious reassurance. Taoism, for instance, had already made its appearance as a mystical way of introspection and personal salvation, and had been favored by Shih Huang Ti. Its magical and alchemical side became prominent, and by the third century of Han rule it had developed into a religion. While Taoism was a native answer to the human search for superhuman support, a foreign solution also became available in the first century after Christ. Buddhism had made its way into central Asia and was introduced into China primarily by missionaries from this area; it is possible that other exponents of the Indian faith came by sea to southern China.

Down to the end of the Han dynasty Buddhism remained of minor importance in China, for it had to acclimate itself to the local scene. The necessity of this adaptation suggests the strength of the native Confucian pattern, which bent new ideas into its frame far more than Roman civilization was able to bend its equally new and upsetting force, Christianity. In one respect, however, Buddhism had an effect which the Christian Church could not share, for it brought with it the powerful artistic tradition evolved in Kushan India, which greatly stimulated Chinese sculptors.

END OF THE ERA OF STABILITY

To turn for a moment from the development of Greco-Roman civilization in order to survey the rest of the civilized belt of Eurasia is worthwhile, if only to put Mediterranean history in a broader perspective. Everywhere peace and prosperity were relatively abundant in the halcyon centuries that lay just on either side of the birth of Christ. Products of the Roman Empire have been found all the way from Denmark to Indo-China and to China proper; and an Indian ivory statuette, once a mirror handle, has turned up in the ruins of Pompeii. More significant than these physical interchanges was the propagation of religious and artistic ideas from the Near East to China and from the Mediterranean eastward.

Within the states of this world, well-organized systems of government maintained order, especially in the two poles of Han China on the east and the Roman Empire on the west. Culture throve, if only in terms of quantity; and this vital phase of consolidation produced a base on which rested the later developments alike in western Europe, in the Near East, in India, and in China. Particularly in the better illuminated zones of the Roman world and of China the historian can also observe at once the signs of decline in the old structures and the emergence of new ways of thought.

For by the time of Christ the civilized states had all essentially passed to a defensive attitude, both culturally and politically. Down to A.D. 200 they were able to maintain their major lines of protection against the northern nomads — the Rhine and Danube, the Caucasus, the Oxus, and the Great Wall of China — but interior economic and political decline was sapping their ability to do so in the greater tests of the next centuries.

The barbarians without, indeed, were profiting by the lessons of civilization through constant contacts along their frontiers. By observing the mode of war of their enemies and often by service in the armies of the civilized states they improved their arms and military organization, and at points passed to the creation of larger, more solid political units. Traders, too, in search of amber, fur, slaves, and other commodities introduced the barbarians to the luxuries of civilization and whetted their appetite for more. Soon after A.D. 200 the balance between civilized and uncivilized began a serious shift.

BIBLIOGRAPHY

Sources. Since neither Parthia nor India had an independent historical tradition, our main evidence consists of the coins of the rulers (often in Greek till the time of Christ or later) and references in Greek and Roman literature. These latter are sometimes distorted but at times rest on firsthand accounts such as the *Indica* of the Seleucid ambassador

Megasthenes (fl. 300 B.C.) and the surveys by Nearchus, admiral of Alexander. Arrian's *Indica* and Strabo's *Geography* (both Loeb Classical Library) drew from these. Arrian's *History of Parthia* is lost, but the extensive account of early Parthian history in Pompeius Trogus is preserved in Justin's epitome. Ptolemy's *Geography,* written *c.* 160, shows fair knowledge as far as the Malay peninsula; the *Periplus of the Red Sea* (tr. W. H. Schoff; New York: Longmans Green, 1912) of the later first century after Christ was a coastal guide for sailors.

Parthian and Indian inscriptions are not numerous; N. A. Nikam and Richard McKeon give parts of *The Edicts of Asoka* (Chicago: University of Chicago Press, 1978). Archeological work on these areas is in its beginnings, as in the French exploration of Begram and the Indian studies at Pataliputra. A manual called the *Arthashastra* is an abstract discussion of politics (trans. R. P. Kangle [University of Bombay, 1963]). A full translation of the Sanskrit epic *The Mahabharata* was begun by J. A. B. van Buitenen (Chicago: University of Chicago Press, 1973–); *The Laws of Manu,* tr. G. Bühler (New York: Dover), describe social structures. The *Bhagavad Gita* is available in translations by F. Edgerton (New York: Harper TB 115, 1964), and Juan Mascaro (Harmondsworth: Penguin L121, 1962).

For Han China the archeological evidence is increasing; a preliminary report on the tomb of Shih Tuang Ti is A. Cotterell, *The First Emperor of China* (New York: Holt Rinehart & Winston, 1981). The first great Chinese historian, Ssu-ma Ch'ien (145–86 B.C.), was grand astrologer for Han Wu Ti. His account, *Shih chi,* is largely cast in biographical chapters together with sections on the development of music, sacrifices, and so on, but is marked by independence of thought, historical imagination, and a strong ethical sense (trans. Burton Watson [New York: Columbia University Press, 1961], who also discusses his life in *Ssu-ma Ch'ien* [same press, 1958]). Later came Pan Ku (A.D. 32–92) to write of the Earlier Han dynasty as a whole; see H. H. Dubs, *History of the Former Han Dynasty by Pan Ku,* 3 vols. (Baltimore: Waverly Press, 1938–55) and selections in B. Watson, *Courtier and Commoner* (New York: Columbia University Press, 1974).

Further Reading. M. A. R. Colledge, *The Parthians* (New York: Praeger, 1967), presents our scanty evidence; Parthian art is well illustrated by his *Parthian Art* (Ithaca: Cornell University Press, 1977). See also Richard N. Frye, *Heritage of Persia* (Cleveland: World, 1963), and

R. Ghirshmann, *Iran* (Harmondsworth: Penguin, 1978).

History and Culture of the Indian People, Vols. II–III (Bombay: Bharatiya Vidya Bhavan, 1951–54), covers India through the Gupta era. B. G. Gokhale, *Asoka Maurya* (New York: Twayne, 1966), also translates his edicts. G. Woodcock, *The Greeks in India* (London: Faber, 1966), describes the amazing Greek principalities. J. H. Marshall, *Guide to Taxila* (4th ed.; Cambridge: Cambridge University Press, 1960), sketches the remains of one major site. H. R. Zimmer, *Art of Indian Asia,* 2 vols. (New York: Pantheon, 1955), is lavishly illustrated; see also Benjamin Roland, *Art and Architecture of India* (Harmondsworth: Penguin, 1953). A. L. Basham, *The Wonder That Was India* (3d ed.; London: Sidgwick & Jackson, 1967).

On the Han see Ch'ü T'ung-tsu, *Han Social Structure* (Seattle: University of Washington Press, 1972); M. Loewe, *Everyday Life in Early Imperial China during the Han Period* (New York: Harper, 1970); D. Bodde, *Festivals in Classical China* (Princeton: Princeton University Press, 1975). Owen Lattimore, *Inner Asian Frontiers of China* (Boston: Beacon Press BP130, 1962), illuminates many forces in Chinese development. On Chinese art, see Ludwig Bachofer, *Short History of Chinese Art* (London: Batsford, 1947); L. Sickman and L. Soper, *Art and Architecture of China* (2d ed.: Penguin, 1971); and William Willetts, *Chinese Art,* 2 vols. (Harmondsworth: Penguin A358–59, 1958). Joseph Needham, *Science and Civilisation in China,* 9 vols. to date (Cambridge: Cambridge University Press, 1954–80), is a major, if contentious work; its first volume is particularly illuminating. Arthur F. Wright, *Buddhism in Chinese History* (Stanford: Stanford University Press, 1959), is good; see also K. K. S. Ch'en, *Buddhism in China* (Princeton: Princeton University Press, 1964).

The trade of Eurasia as a whole is suggested by Mortimer Wheeler, *Rome beyond the Imperial Frontiers* (Harmondsworth: Penguin A335, 1955).

X

DECLINE OF THE ANCIENT WORLD

30

THE FIRST SIGNS OF STRESS

By the third century after Christ the political and cultural framework of the ancient world was beginning to totter. Premonitory shivers had occurred in the previous century, but few had noticed their import. Thenceforth, however, almost no area in the civilized belt of Eurasia could continue to feel entirely secure.

In this chapter we shall consider the signs of stress in the region which is best illuminated, the Roman Empire, from the accession of Commodus to that of the great reformer Diocletian (A.D. 180–284). Yet the story of the Empire cannot be told by itself. On the north the Germans were breaking loose in their first serious probes of the frontier, and on the east — too often at the same time — the new Sassanian state of Persia was a serious threat. Behind the Germans, in turn, other peoples were shifting as the long calm of Eurasia cracked.

The external challenges were accompanied by ever more critical internal problems as the deep-seated weaknesses of the Empire, like hidden geologic faults, caused rifts on the surface. Economically the Empire deteriorated abruptly; socially it became openly stratified in an effort to halt change; politically the elaborate veils of the Augustan principate were ripped away to reveal military autocracy. Intellectually, too, one may speak of decline in the sense that the classical outlook weakened; neither arts nor letters could flourish when the era descended to chaos.

Nonetheless the Empire had deep, inherited strengths which could not be dissipated quickly; after cracking apart in the middle of the century it resumed its unity by the reign of Diocletian. Even amid its troubles the third century produced the last great philosophy of classical spirit, Neo-platonism; and Christianity flourished. Once order had been restored, architecture and literature were able to produce new achievements in the fourth century, though on rather different lines than in the Early Empire.

The Germans. Although all frontiers of the Empire were assailed at one point or another in the third century, the most serious blows were delivered by the Germans. The emperor Aurelian yielded Dacia to the Goths; and the south German angle between Rhine and Danube went to the Alamanni about 260; but this was not to end the pressure.

Since the Germans were thenceforth to play a major part in European history, modern scholars have devoted much effort toward determining their ancestry and early movements. Archeologists generally agree that the German-speaking tribes may be traced back to the Battle-ax cultures of central Europe in the third millennium B.C., but even in historic times it is difficult to distinguish them from the more advanced Celtic tribes, whose La Tène culture had an effect as far as Denmark. The somewhat shaky evidence of Germanic legends suggests that they moved from the shores of the Baltic from 500 B.C. onward into central Europe. By the second century after Christ the group called Goths had entered south Russia, where it came into contact with and largely supplanted the Sarmatians of the Eurasian steppe; and other Germans generally occupied Germany. The three main groups of Germanic dialects were the Nordic (the root of Scandinavian tongues), the western (the source of modern German), and the eastern (Gothic).

To the Romans and Greeks the Germans were children in their delight in quarreling and fighting, which alternated with their torpor of drunkenness and gluttony while at peace. The men hunted but generally refused the physical labors of farming. These were left to the women and to the slaves gained in raids. The basic social unit was commonly the clan of some 10 to 20 families; superior groupings were the hundreds and *gaus* as military and judicial units and the tribes. The tribal kings

TABLE 8

Roman Emperors*
A.D. 180—284

Commodus	180-92	Decius	249–51
Pertinax	193	Gallus	251–53
Didius Julianus	193	Aemilianus	253
Septimius Severus	193–211	Valerian	253–60
Caracalla	211–17	Gallienus	253–68
Macrinus	217–18	Claudius II Gothicus	268–70
Elagabalus	218–22	Aurelian	270–75
Severus Alexander	222–35	Tacitus	275–76
Maximinus	235–38	Florianus	276
Gordian I and II	238	Probus	276–82
Balbinus and Pupienus	238	Carus	282–83
Gordian III	238–44	Numerianus	283–84
Philip	244–49	Carinus	283–85

*Inasmuch as the political and cultural events of the period of this table are described consecutively in this chapter, they are not outlined here.

were little more than chiefs in war, elected by a folkmoot, though usually they came from a royal family. Each king had a sworn band of immediate retainers (called the *comitatus* by the Romans), but could summon his tribesmen for larger forays. Unlike the territorial, impersonal organization of the civilized world, the main principle of organization that the Germans brought with them was personal loyalty.

As the Germans came up against the Roman frontier, they were stopped from the days of Caesar onward, though the Roman expansion into continental Europe in turn was halted under Augustus. The effects of this confrontation of civilized and uncivilized across the frontiers of Rhine, Danube, and the north shore of the Black Sea were of great importance, especially for the Germans. The growth of trade may well have helped the German tribes to group themselves in wider political units. By the late third and fourth centuries some peoples were moving into a semicivilized state, as marked by the swift acceptance of Christianity on their entry into the Empire and the translation of part of the Bible into Gothic by Ulfilas (consecrated bishop in 341). The Germanic invasions, in other words, might be devastating; but their leaders were inclined to admire rather than to despise the culture of Mediterranean lands.

Roman diplòmacy, which utilized subventions and force to split up dangerous groupings, had a considerable effect in destroying local chieftainships, but in the long run forced the independent Germans into larger and more consciously organized agglomerations. By the third century there lay along the Roman frontier from west to east the Franks (lower Rhine), Alamanni (southern Germany), Vandals (Hungary and Silesia), and the Goths reaching on into south Russia. The latter, divided generally into the Visigoths on the west and the Ostrogoths on the east, were more nomadic and caused the greatest trouble in the third century. Behind these, in dim darkness, were the Burgundians on the Main river, the Saxons on the Weser, the Lombards in Silesia, and other tribes (see Map 20).

Although the invasions proper tend to draw one's attention, the movement of the Germans into the Roman Empire was a long, continuous process. They came as slaves, for Roman noble households liked to have blond-headed specimens in their service. Others slipped across or, from the days of Marcus Aurelius, were deliberately moved into frontier districts to provide manpower; this policy became ever more common in the later third century. As we shall see later, the Empire itself was losing some of its civilized qualities; by the third century the European frontier was no longer a sharp boundary between civilization and barbarism.

Sassanian Persia. To the east the Roman Empire faced the only civilized state of its acquaintance. In the relations between Rome and Parthia the latter was generally on the defensive, and as Roman strength and interests shifted eastward in the second century the Parthian kings met serious defeats. Trajan temporarily annexed Mesopotamia; in reply to the Parthian attack on Syria under Marcus Aurelius a Roman expedition burned Ctesiphon in 165; and again under Septimius Severus the Parthian capital went up in flames in 198. Septimius Severus even annexed the northern end of Mesopotamia as a Roman province.

Iranian kings were strong only so long as they held the loyalty of their great vassals in the mountain valleys. This loyalty the Parthian dynasty steadily lost until finally in 224 Ardashir, grandson of Sassan, killed the last Parthian king. Thus began the Sassanian dynasty, which ruled down to the coming of the Arabs in 637–51.

Although the change was outwardly a mere replacement of one ruling dynasty by another, Sassanian Persia was to be a far stronger realm in every respect. In their heavy demands for taxes and forced labor, in their acceptance of local rule by the great estate owners, and in their elimination of personal liberty the Sassanian kings operated much as did contemporary rulers of the Roman Empire. Far more than the Parthians, the Sassanians promoted urbanization, and eventually they created an extensive bureaucracy to link the crown and the provinces. This stronger base permitted them to take a far firmer stand against Rome and also to defend or expand their eastern frontiers. Ardashir retook Nisibis and Carrhae in north Mesopotamia. His son Shapur I (240–72) destroyed Dura in 256, raided as far west as Antioch, and made the Roman emperor Valerian prisoner in 260. At the same time Shapur I had strength enough to turn eastward and subjugate the Kushans in Afghanistan and Turkestan, who were definitely annexed by Shapur II (309–79).

In keeping with this political and military revival was the cultural vigor of Sassanian Persia. In part this vigor continued to be expressed in forms derived from Mediterranean culture. Shapur I himself commissioned translations of Greek, as well as Indian works on medicine, astronomy, and philosophy. Both Christianity (eventually in the Nestorian form) and Judaism were strongly rooted in the Near East; the Babylonian Talmud, which became the basic Jewish commentary on the Law of Moses, was essentially complete by the sixth century.

Yet Hellenic influence had already begun to wane in Parthian times; by the third century Iranian and Mesopotamian ideas held the upper hand. Shapur I protected the religious reformer Mani, who adapted Christian and gnostic ideas to the old Iranian principle of the fight of good and evil and created a religion deliberately intended for all the world; but besides and after Mani a religious leader Kartir helped to develop a state church and official creed. The magi of this militant Zoroastrianism secured the crucifixion of Mani about 274–77 and a temporary persecution of his followers, the Manicheans.

Most remarkable was the artistic outburst of Sassanian times, which linked on to old Iranian principles and designs as well as to the Hellenistic inheritance. Silver dishes, tapestries, and other works manifest the heraldic employment of animal motifs, arranged symmetrically in antithetical poses. The monarch, where shown, was always taller than other men, as on the reliefs at Naqsh-i-Rustam where Shapur I towers over the kneeling suppliant, Valerian.[1] In this art the spirit was even more symbolic and static than was becoming the case in Roman art. Sassanian styles had a wide effect over central Eurasia and were carried as far as early medieval Europe both via the Germans and through the Roman Empire.

Like the Roman emperors, however, the Sassanian kings were really on the defensive against the growing pressures of the uncivilized reaches to the north and later in Arabia. Politically and culturally the links between the Roman east and the Sassanian realm were far closer than had been true in the early days of the Roman Empire. Occasionally they even cooperated in trying to hold the Caucasus passes against the nomads; but as so often has been the case in international relations the two civilized powers spent far more time in mutually weakening wars which drew their attention and energies from the outside threats.

Economic and Social Internal Shifts. During the third century the tendency toward economic and social change which had begun to appear dimly in the age of prosperity of the Roman Empire became ever clearer. The speed of alteration accelerated, moreover, under the spurs of the internal unrest and of the heavy burdens which the state imposed to meet the external threats.

The economic output of the Empire plummeted sharply. This fact, which is evident in the remarkable falling-off of archeological evidence, was the product of several conjoined factors. The productive population sank both because of a decline in numbers, accentuated by recurrent

---

[1] See the fourth-century monarch on the Sassanian silver dish illustrated on Plate XXX. The relief was worked separately, then set by tabs into the dish. From Assyrian days on (Plate VII), the hunt was a favorite scene in Near Eastern art; Iranian rulers had vast "paradises" or game parks.

plagues, and because of greater drafts for the army. Especially in the western provinces men had to huddle behind walls to be safe, which reduced their productivity, and everywhere considerable elements turned to brigandage by land and piracy by sea. Roads, too, deteriorated despite repeated road repair programs; the coinage was not to be trusted; and many imperial exactions were simply drafts on capital. Most important, optimism sank into sullenness as the demands of the state rose, so that those who did work had less and less incentive.

The growing interference by the state in social and economic life, which in the second century had been largely altruistic and paternalistic, now passed into arbitrary direction as the leaders thrown up by the army necessarily and ruthlessly seized an ever greater proportion of the dwindling production. One mode of doing so lay in inflation. Already Marcus Aurelius had adulterated the standard silver coin, the *denarius;* Septimius Severus increased the base metal almost to 50 per cent; and Caracalla began the issue of the *Antoninianus* or double *denarius,* which had less than its proper weight. By the middle of the third century this coin became a copper piece coated thinly with silver. Prices rose, and after 250, soared; many economic sectors turned to barter.

Another means open to the state lay in forcible confiscation and requirement of service. The civil population groaned under the military requisition of food and clothing (called *annona*) and of transport (*angareia*), which at times became simple plundering. The guilds (*collegia*) of shippers were legally bound to the task of supplying Rome with grain; and the *collegia* of butchers and bakers at Rome may have been similarly bound by the reign of Aurelian. The upper classes of the towns, especially the town councilors (*decurions*), were more and more saddled with compulsory tasks without pay, called *munera* (burdens). Some of these required only service; others involved expenses or the threat of expenses, as in the requirement that the 10 leading councilors see to tax collection and meet any deficiencies out of their own pockets. In some fields, as in arms production and linen and wool manufacture, direct state activity became extensive.

The result was not, as it turned out, utter economic collapse; for the Empire had built up a great inherited store of physical capital and spiritual strength thanks to its unification and prosperity in the past 200 years. Even so, the unrest brought rebellions in Gaul, Egypt, and other areas and led the rulers toward freezing life lest more change ensue. Before the end of the century, for instance, peasants were made responsible for the land of any neighbor who fled. Industry and commerce suffered especially in the western provinces, where population had always been thin and large areas had really lain outside the advanced system of the Early Empire. The cities in the west thenceforth were small, walled centers of weakening economic weight. While cities in the east held up better, trade to India and across Sassanian Persia to China sloped off abruptly.

Socially, the distinction between the upper classes (*honestiores*), comprising the senatorial and equestrian orders and the decurions, and the lower classes (*humiliores*) became sharp in law, and mobility upward was almost halted. Yet here too the change of the era could not be denied. The senatorial class in particular lost much of its political influence as military circles threw up a new governing class. The decline of the Senate began to be obvious under Septimius Severus, who executed a number of senators and reserved new posts for equestrians; Gallienus (253–68) formally banned senators from serving as generals. The upper classes of Gallic and African cities found urban life less rewarding and needed to keep closer watch on their estates. In these areas rural villas accordingly grew in importance as the permanent homes of the nobles, as local centers of industry, and as focal points for protection and control even for the small landowners of the vicinity.

When the economic and social ties of the Empire weakened, local ways of life and thought emerged again from below the mask of Greco-Roman civilization. In the western provinces, interestingly enough, the Latin language gained an ever firmer hold as peasants were forced to concentrate about the villas or in the walled cities. In the east, however, such tongues as Syriac now came to be written. By 200 it appears that a Syriac translation of the Gospels was made; and Tatian's *Harmony* (*Diatessaron*) of the Gospels was either composed in Syriac or soon translated. Regional cults and art styles became more evident; even in the Church a tendency toward separatism occasionally appears in the rise of heresies. On the whole the men of the Empire still wished to be united, but the cleavages that eventually split the Mediterranean world into diverse cultural provinces can first be sensed in this era of unrest.

POLITICAL HISTORY OF THE THIRD CENTURY

Descent into Chaos (180–260). The political history of the era 180–284 falls into two unequal portions: a deterioration which was ever swifter down to 260, and then a restoration of imperial unity and reinvigoration of the government. Very soon after the death of Marcus Aurelius his son Commodus (180–92) turned to capricious autocracy, which endured 12 years. Then came his throttling by a professional athlete on the last day of 192 and a series of bloody civil wars (193–97), ending in the victory of the Balkan legions under L. Septimius Severus. Unlike Augustus and Vespasian, who rose to power on the swords of their soldiers, Septimius was ruthless to his opponents and confiscated huge quantities of property; after the defeat of his last opponent, Clodius Albinus, he permitted his troops to sack and burn the major Gallic city Lugdunum. The Severan house ruled thereafter until the murder of Severus Alexander in 235.

Apart from the brutal Caracalla (211–17), son of Septimius, the Severan dynasty was cultivated and supported the arts and letters. This was the era of some of the greatest Roman jurists, including Paul (fl. *c.* 200), Papinian (executed 212), and Ulpian (murdered 228), who served as civilian heads of the governmental machinery (Praetorian Prefects) and wrote great commentaries on the Praetor's Edict and other aspects of the law. When eventually the emperor Justinian came to codify Roman law in the sixth century, one-third of his *Digest* came from Ulpian, though Papinian had earlier (by a law of 426) been made ultimate authority if other jurists disagreed evenly.

Septimius' wife, Julia Domna, together with her sister Julia Maesa, wielded extensive influence on the government and also maintained a great literary salon. This was graced by the doctor Galen; by Philostratus, who wrote a very popular account of the Neopythagorean miracle-worker Apollonius of Tyana; and by other Greek rhetoricians and philosophers. In Rome Septimius built a huge palace, and his son erected the baths of Caracalla; at Lepcis in Africa, the home of the Severi, great public works were constructed; and the mammoth complex of temples at Baalbek in Syria was now completed.

Yet the Severan emperors could not escape the problems of internal unrest, which led to several surviving petitions by oppressed villagers and to brigandage; nor could they overlook the increasing external threats to the Empire. Septimius himself defeated the Parthians and annexed northern Mesopotamia. As he lay dying on the far distant British frontier, ablaze with Scottish raids, he is said to have advised his sons, "Enrich the soldiers"; [2] and certainly he granted the army far more privileges, as well as a raise in pay, than had Vespasian after the civil wars of 68–69. Thenceforth the army became an ever more vocal and powerful element in determining who would be ruler and what would be his policies, and men of military training had increasingly great weight even in civil administration. Military discipline sank noticeably as less-civilized elements, including barbarians, became a more important source of recruits; but enough order survived to carry the army through its great strains of the century.

Caracalla first murdered his brother Geta and then spent most of his time with the army on the German frontier. One famous event of his reign was the grant of Roman citizenship to virtually all free inhabitants by the Constitutio Antoniniana. Although practically insignificant, this decree marks the expansion of the term "Rome" to its ultimate extent, at the very time when Rome and Italy were sinking to the level virtually of the provinces. While preparing to fight the Parthians Caracalla was murdered, but after an interloper (Macrinus) the Severan house came back to the throne in the form of Elagabalus (218–22), hereditary high priest of the Sun at Emesa in Syria, who spent most of his years in Rome in extravagant worship of his patron deity. His cousin, Severus Alexander, who replaced him in 222, was governed by his mother Julia Mammaea, daughter of Julia Maesa, but sought earnestly to face the needs of his empire. In 235 he was murdered by his contemptuous generals on the Rhine and replaced by Maximinus Thrax, the first emperor to rise purely through the military chain from the ranks.

After 235 ruler succeeded ruler swiftly as the Empire sought in desperation to meet its opponents. The emperor Decius (249–51) fell in battle against the Goths, that is, the Visigoths, who repeatedly ravaged the lower Balkans by land; over the next few years some bands seized ships and roamed the Aegean, where they burned the temple of Artemis at

[2] Dio Cassius 76.15.2.

Ephesus. The Alamanni attacked the upper Danube, wrested the south-western corner of Germany from the Empire, and broke into north Italy several times. The Franks along the Rhine swept across Gaul and Spain in 253–57 in raids, the lines of which can still be traced by the buried coin hoards of frightened provincials; in consequence Gaul threw up an independent emperor, Postumus, in 259. To meet a major Sassanian threat the emperor Valerian (253–60) marched east, only to be captured by ruse, the first Roman emperor to meet such a fate. Here too a local leader, P. Septimius Odenathus of Palmyra (d. 266/7), became a virtually independent master of a large part of the Empire and halted the Sassanian attack.

Restoration of Unity (260–84). At the low point of the third century Valerian's son and co-emperor Gallienus (253–68) ruled only Italy, Africa, Illyricum, Achaea, Asia Minor, and Egypt. Gaul and much of the west formed one independent state; the Palmyrene power in the east, another. Yet the old traditions of Mediterranean unity and the power of its connective tissue, Greco-Roman culture, were still strong enough to pull back together the fragmented realm.

Gallienus himself began the task by taking the first steps to separate military and civil administration and by creating a field army with a heavy proportion of cavalry. The heaviest attack of the century was delivered in 268 by the Heruli, with the Goths. Greece was assailed by land and by sea, and even Athens fell; but Gallienus defeated the invaders on their return homewards. His operations were interrupted by a revolt in north Italy, and while he was besieging Milan his generals murdered him.

The new ruler, Claudius II Gothicus (268–70), once more expelled the Alamanni from north Italy in a battle near Lake Garda, decisively defeated the Goths, and regained Spain before he died of the plague. Claudius was the first of the "Illyrian emperors," who came from the Balkans and used especially the military strength of this area in their restoration of unity.

The stern general Aurelian (270–75), nicknamed "Hand on Hilt," came next. His first task was to throw out the renewed German invasion of north Italy, after which he ordered Rome itself to be walled lest raids reach so far. The Aurelian wall, begun in 271 by the civil population, was a plain brick defense 12 miles long; later elaborated, it still stands

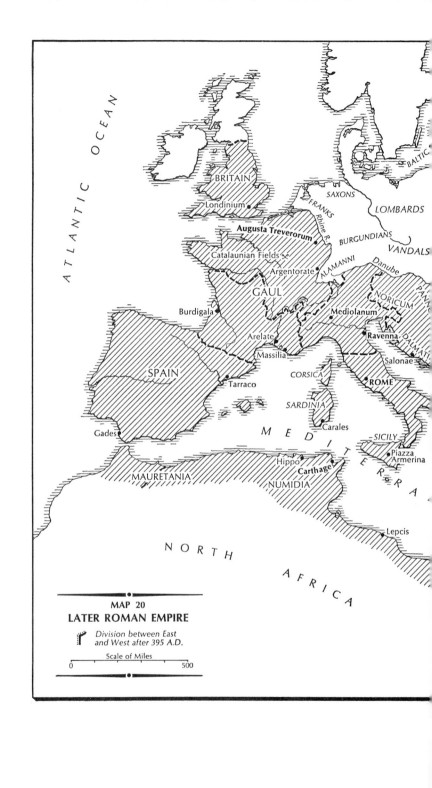

ATLANTIC OCEAN

BALTIC

BRITAIN

Londinium

SAXONS

FRANKS

LOMBARDS

Augusta Treverorum

BURGUNDIANS

Rhine R.

VANDALS

Catalaunian Fields

ALAMANNI

Danube

Argentorate

NORICUM

PANN

GAUL

Burdigala

Mediolanum

Ravenna

DALMATI

Arelate

Massilia

Salonae

SPAIN

CORSICA

ROME

Tarraco

SARDINIA

Carales

Gades

MEDITERRA

SICILY

Piazza
Armerina

Hippo

Carthage

MAURETANIA

NUMIDIA

R

Lepcis

NORTH

AFRICA

MAP 20

LATER ROMAN EMPIRE

Division between East
and West after 395 A.D.

Scale of Miles

0   500

HUNS

Dnieper R.

OSTROGOTHS

CASPIAN SEA

VISIGOTHS
DACIA

CAUCASUS MTS.

BLACK SEA

Danube R.

MOESIA

dica

Constantinople

Adrianople
THRACE
alonica
CE-
NIA

Chalcedon
Nicomedia
Nicaea

CAPPADOCIA

Nyssa

Nisibis

SASSANIAN
EMPIRE

ASIA
Ephesus

Caesarea

Nazianzus

Tigris R.

Athens

ISAURIA

Antioch

Ctesiphon

Seleucia

CRETE

CYPRUS

Emesa
Palmyra

Euphrates R.

A N   S E A

Caesarea

Cyrene

LIBYA

Alexandria

EGYPT

Nile R.

RED SEA

G·

today over most of its course. Although Rome was not actually to be attacked for over a century thereafter, its circumvallation suggests clearly men's lack of confidence in the far distant frontiers of the Empire. Similar fortification took place about this time over much of the Empire, as at Athens and Olympia, and created tiny nuclei dotted over the landscape which normally could ride out barbaric incursions.

Then Aurelian turned to deal with the swollen realm of Palmyra, now governed by Queen Zenobia for her son Waballath; for Palmyrene forces had occupied Antioch in 268/9, gained control of Egypt, and taken much of Asia Minor. In 272 Aurelian pushed the Palmyrene armies back to their oasis capital, which he took after a desperate siege; when a revolt broke out, he returned in the next year and sacked it, a blow which ended its importance. The turn of the Gallic empire came in 273 too, but its ruler Tetricus voluntarily deserted his troops. Once more the Empire was one. The southwest corner of Germany, to be sure, had been lost by 260, and Aurelian decided not to try to essay reconquest of the vulnerable outpost of Dacia from the Goths. Some Roman settlers here, however, withdrew to the Carpathian mountains and preserved their tongue over obscure centuries to serve as the root of the modern Rumanian language.

Once again a military plot led to the murder of an able emperor as Aurelian fell, while marching against the Persians. After a brief interlude in which the Senate chose a ruler (Tacitus), the third great Illyrian emperor, Probus (276–82), halted new invasions of Gaul and the Balkans before he too was murdered in 282. The era 235–84 is often called the period of the Barracks Emperors, who were made and unmade by the armies at their whim as a result of defeat, overly harsh discipline, or rival ambitions of generals. Twenty emperors, apart from pretenders and local rulers, came and went across this period before finally Dalmatian-born C. Aurelius Valerius Diocletianus gained the purple in 284 and removed his last opponent early in the following year. With Diocletian begins the era called the Later Roman Empire.

The means by which the wily, subtle Diocletian restored order and, with the reforms of his eventual successor Constantine, gave the Empire a new breath of life must be considered in the next chapter. In general they were a consolidation of the terrific alterations required by the stresses of the third century, including open autocracy, the standard use of violence and terrorism, and the loss of social and economic freedom by the subjects. Nonetheless the rulers who paved the way for these reforms had made their own changes almost unknowingly, under the sheer pressure of ineluctable need, while doing their utmost to preserve old Roman ways. Their coins, however debased, had paraded the imperial virtues of peace and justice and had proclaimed the eternity of Rome; the transitory ruler Philip had celebrated in April 248 the 1000th anniversary of the founding of Rome with great pomp. Consuls continued to be chosen each year; the Senate still existed, if only as an honorary body; and, above all, the classical structure of ideas remained outwardly dominant.

CULTURAL AND RELIGIOUS CROSSCURRENTS

Maintenance of Classical Civilization. Classical civilization continued to stand across the third century as a buttress to the Mediterranean world or, to change the metaphor, as a façade to mask ever-greater changes. Schools were still supported by state and individuals; historians, poets, and others received imperial posts and favors; rhetoricians delivered panegyrics before the rulers which stressed not only their divinity but also their devotion to the good of their subjects and their high level of culture. Possession or absence of culture, indeed, became a powerful basis for judging the quality of rulers, administrators, and other notable men. Of the emperors only Caracalla, who aped the ways of his soldiers, and the Syrian Elagabalus moved outside the conventional pattern; and the imperial bureaucracy became more of a "mandarin" class than ever before.

This process was a defensive reaction against the rise of barbarism and the loss of real power by the old leading classes, but its effect in preserving a dying outlook well into the fourth and fifth centuries was considerable. Long ago, when Rome was conquering Greece, it had been valorous but uncivilized; now its military power was tottering, but it boasted ever more of its culture. The rulers, indeed, were not ill-advised in supporting this culture, which was a powerful bond toward political unity as against the many divisive forces now at work.

Beneath the surface swirled many cross-currents, which made the third century a true era of transition culturally as well as politically. In terms of quantity there was a great drop both in arts and in letters. Scholarship and learned commentary on the works of the past decreased tremendously, and even the collection of bits of learning in anthologies disappeared after the *Sophists at Dinner (Deipnosophistae)* of Athenaeus of Naucratis (*c.* 200), the *Carpet Bags (Stromateis)* of Clement of Alexandria, and the *Chests (Kestoi)* of Julius Africanus early in the century; so too the copying of classical statues ceased. There was virtually no poetry of significance in the era, and the production of history was so scanty that the brief reigns of many emperors are quite dark.

Yet particularly in the limited artistic output of the century one can detect at work many of the forces best expressed in Christianity. On the arch of Septimus Severus at Rome, and still more on his arch at Lepcis, frontality was accepted, and the minor figures were depicted as a flat, undifferentiated mass before their lord. Elsewhere, especially in sarcophagi, there was much use of lights and shadows, in which the background often disappeared; and the figures here tended to become isolated, not so much in space as outside it.[3] Human beings, in short, were becoming symbols in art, spiritually connected with each other and charged with moral significance; and artists were turning away from the physical, material, and rational to an inward, emotional meditation which led to communion with a superhuman force. Now and then there arose flurries of opposition to the new styles, as in a revival of classic forms under Gallienus; but the drift was to become clear in the buildings and sculpture of the Constantinian age.

Religious Syncretism. Men's search for a new meaning and a guide to life, while clinging outwardly to old forms, led to interesting developments in religion and philosophy. Already in the second century thinkers like Plutarch and Lucian had tried to strip off the primitive aspects of

[3] The Philosopher Sarcophagus of Gallienus' reign (Plate XXVIII) is located on the borderline between the classic artistic spirit and that which followed (for this, see Plates XXXI and XXXII). Despite the emphasis on lights and shadows the figures have volume in the classic manner and are still linked with each other, yet the serious, monumental philosopher is faced squarely to the front. To do so the sculptor had to shorten his legs so far that they almost disappear. Such a violation of reality was impossible when sculptors had a strong sense of plastic reality, but by the third century the psychological necessity of expressing reverence had broken this sense. Although the suggestion that this was the sarcophagus of the philosopher Plotinus is fanciful, its artistic spirit fits his transcendentalizing mood.

paganism, carried along through the ages, though in doing so they could not help but kill the spirit of the Greco-Roman cults. In the unified Empire, under its one master, religious thinkers also came to speak of God ever more as One. The multiplicity of gods was not directly assailed; but a syncretistic effort was apparent, in which the followers of each deity attempted to gain the mastery for their god by equating other divinities with it.

In the third century the most successful essay in this direction revolved about the sun god as men sought to magnify the generative principle and master of human destinies, who supported and justified imperial rule. Aurelian erected a temple to Sol Invictus, as embodying Apollo, Sarapis, Mithras, and other deities with the great pagan gods as assistants, and his coins proclaimed "Sol master of the Roman Empire." With this last truly pagan religious effort the Empire had thrown up almost as exclusive a force as was Christianity, and at his death Aurelian was moving toward persecution of the Christians. Constantine, in his early years, passed through a period as Sun worshiper and found it easy to step from this cult to the reverence of Christ.

Neoplatonism. Even more remarkable was the creation of the last major philosophy of the ancient world. Stoicism, Epicureanism, and other answers of the Hellenistic world were now essentially dead; but out of these views together with those of Neopythagoreanism and Platonism began to emerge an amazing new philosophic outlook. From Plutarch onward men turned especially to Plato as a base for their merger of religious and philosophic views. Chief, but not alone in the creation of Neoplatonism, was Plotinus (205–69/70), who studied at Alexandria under Ammonius Saccas, the master of the Christian scholar Origen. Plotinus lived his most creative years, however, at Rome.

The great work of Plotinus, the *Enneads,* was a series of essays which ranged over almost all the fields of philosophy in a highly condensed, allusive style. The root was the dialogues of Plato, who had pictured the toilsome upward progress of the human mind to the concept of the perfect idea of the Good. Yet where Plato tried to fit his fellow men for life in the ideal city-state, Plotinus addressed himself to his contemporaries as individuals, and his aim was not political in any degree. Rather, men must withdraw into intellectual retirement so that they might gain individual communion with the divine force. The method of Plotinus was basically philosophical in its utilization of a rational inquiry into the nature of the world, but the result of Neoplatonism was the establishment of a universal power. Between Plato and Plotinus there yawns a gulf which measures the great changes of half a millennium in ancient civilization.

The governing power of the universe in Neoplatonism was pure intellect, yet transcendentally divine; and it could be comprehended in its full manifestation only by a mysterious, rapturous contemplation. This divine element was called One, as being the perfect absolute; below it, in turn, were first Mind (*Nous*) as the rational principle of the world and then the Soul of the Whole as the source of all action. The Neoplatonist cosmos was also equipped with a series of subsidiary beings who emanated from the divine level; man himself stood between God and the animals, endowed with divine beauty and equipped with a spiritual power which liberated him from his body. Unlike the Christians Plotinus asserted that the human soul could by itself, without divine aid, rise to ecstatic union with the perfect One. Mystical, even religious, though this scheme of thought was, fundamentally it was built upon reason.

Neoplatonism thus admirably fitted the needs of that level of the Empire which wished to remain rational in the classical tradition but could not be satisfied with the old answers. Plotinus himself had the favor of senators and the emperor Gallienus, and Neoplatonism remained powerful across the fourth century; St. Augustine came to Christianity only through a preliminary acceptance of this pagan philosophy. Yet its defects, as measured by Christianity, were many. Neoplatonism could not truly formulate a metaphysical explanation of human individuality in relation to transcendental unity, and it could not excise the defects of its pagan inheritance. On the one hand, the ordinary man was warned away from his abstruse thought-spinning, as by Plotinus' chief disciple Porphyry (232/3-c. 305); yet on the other hand, later adherents were often credulous fanatics who incorporated all of pagan mythology.

The Christian Church. The eventual victor in the competition for men's adherence made great strides forward in the third century. The chaos of the age led many to prize a promise of heavenly salvation more dearly, and the semicollapse of orderly life drew others to the tight bond of mutual unity afforded by the local churches.

Christianity, too, had developed a solid, far-flung organization and was crystallizing its practices of church services and sacraments, a process that produced a stream of manuals including Hippolytus' *Apostolic Tradition* and others. The many local variations in the formal questions posed at baptism and in the summations of Christian belief (the "rule of faith") suggest the wide diversity which still existed, but Christian theology was rising to a more developed plane in the works of the Christian Platonist, Origen. Christianity thus appealed to uneducated and educated alike.

Christianity, however, did not entirely benefit from its increased attractiveness. As the numbers of the faithful grew, so too did the dangers of secular influences. The director of the imperial purple factory at Tyre was a priest in the late third century; other men even served as officials in the cult of Rome and the emperor. A bishop of Antioch, Paul of Samosata, was accused of exacting money from the faithful; "he clothes himself with worldly honors and wishes to be called *ducenarius* rather than bishop, and struts in the marketplaces, reading and dictating letters as he walks in public, and attended by a bodyguard." [4]

While internal heresies continued to plague the orthodox, the most serious danger in this respect came from outside in the form of Persian Manicheism. Mani himself had proclaimed Jesus as one of the prophets who recalled man to his duty of fighting evil, and the explanation of life in terms of the fight of good and evil, with an independent devil, had strong attractions. Once inserted into Christianity, the concept was to reappear continually on into the Middle Ages.

Far more troublesome at the time was the sporadic outbreak of open war between the Church and the Empire. The groundwork had been laid long before in the imperial ban on Christianity, but real trouble came only in the middle of the third century. The emperor Decius felt that arms alone could not withstand the winds of dissolution and in despair turned to the gods of Rome. At the turn of the year 249/50 he accordingly issued an edict which apparently ordered all citizens to appear before a local commission and make public profession of worship of the gods of the state. Men were not thereby forbidden to worship other gods, but true Christians could not thus revere the official cult.

The result was empire-wide persecution for the first time as Decius

[4] Eusebius, *Church History* 7.30.

sought conformity. Even some bishops as well as many of the laity bent before the storm or bribed commissions to issue the *libelli* or certificates that they had sacrificed; these *lapsi* caused serious trouble to the Church afterwards when they sought to return to the fold. Others stood firm. Rome, thus, had no bishop for 15 months; the great scholar Origen was tortured, though great care was taken that he not be killed.

Although the persecution ceased when Decius was killed by the Goths, the Christians were now marked as unpatriotic. After a brief flurry under Gallus (251–53) a far more serious attack was delivered by Valerian, who was further moved by the need of money. A first edict in August 257 struck only at the Church proper by ordering its clergy to sacrifice on pain of exile and by banning Christian assembly or entrance to their cemeteries. The second, of 258, went on to order the confiscation of the property of *honestiores* who were adherents. The financial spur led to a rigorous application of the edicts. The bishop of Rome was killed; Cyprian, one of the greatest leaders of the century, was ferreted out at Carthage and executed.

While Cyprian was in prison, the faithful assembled in his cell to hold services; and at his execution Christians rushed forward to dip handkerchiefs in his blood as mementos of the saint. For the laity proper were not attacked save if they sought martyrdom — as ecstatic Christians did to a surprising extent — and the three persecutions in the decade 250–60 produced in reality a very limited number of victims. Valerian's son Gallienus was confronted by so many secular problems that he halted the attack in 260. Not only did he order the restoration of churches and cemeteries, but also he even addressed a rescript to the bishops which was virtually a *de facto* acceptance of the existence of the Christian hierarchy. For the next four decades the Church enjoyed an uneasy peace, until the closing years of the reign of Diocletian.

BIBLIOGRAPHY

Sources. For the early part of the third century we have fragments of the history of Dio Cassius to A.D. 229 (Loeb Classical Library) and the superficial account by Herodian covering 180–238 (tr. E. C. Echols; Berkeley: University of California Press, 1961). Thereafter the only continuous thread is, first, the collection of imperial lives called the *Historia*

Augusta (Loeb Classical Library), which becomes at points useless in its rhetoric and fictitious documents; and, secondly, some brief histories written in the fourth and fifth centuries by Eutropius, Aurelius Victor, and Orosius. The fifth-century Greek historian Zosimus, bitterly pagan, preserves part of the *Gothic Wars* of Dexippus the Athenian. The greatest work of the century, Plotinus' *Enneads,* can be sampled in A. H. Armstrong, *Plotinus* (New York: Colliers AS358V, 1962), and Joseph Katz, *Philosophy of Plotinus* (New York: Appleton, 1950); a complete translation is that of Stephen MacKenna, *Enneads of Plotinus* (4th ed.; London: Faber and Faber, 1970).

Christian material grows in bulk, and may usually be found in the series, *Ancient Christian Writers,* ed. Johannes Quasten and Joseph C. Plumpe (Westminster, Maryland: Newman Press, 1946 on), or *The Fathers of the Church,* founded by Ludwig Schopp (New York: Cima Press, 1947 on). Apart from theological works of Origen, letters and sermons of Cyprian, and similar work, Julius Africanus synthesized pagan and Christian history from the creation of the world in 5500 B.C to A.D. 221, a study which underlay Eusebius' canonical *Chronicon.* The *Church History* of the latter is full, and the trial records of some martyrs have survived; see E. C. E. Owen, *Some Authentic Acts of the Early Martyrs* (Oxford: Oxford University Press, 1927).

The fullest ancient treatment of the Germans is the idealized essay by Tacitus (*On Britain and Germany,* tr. H. Mattingly [Harmondsworth: Penguin, 1971]); Germanic legends were preserved in part by Jordanes, *Gothic History,* tr. C. C. Mierow (New York: Columbia University Press, 1915). For Sassanian Persia we must rely, as in Parthian times, mainly on scanty archeological evidence, boastful inscriptions, the coins, and references in Greco-Roman authors; but some dim memories lingered into Arab historiography.

Further Reading. Francis Owen, *The Germanic People* (New York: Bookman Associates, 1960), is a straightforward survey; E. A. Thompson, *The Early Germans* (Oxford: Oxford University Press, 1965), discusses their society; Tamara T. Rice, *The Scythians* (New York: Praeger, 1957), sketches the background of the steppes. For Sassanian Persia, see Richard N. Frye, *Heritage of Persia* (Cleveland: World, 1963), and R. Ghirshman, *Persian Art, 249* B.C.–A.D. *651* (New York: Golden Press, 1962).

The dim history of this period is treated by H. M. D. Parker, *History of the Roman World from* A.D. *138 to 337* (rev. ed.; London: Methuen, 1969), *Cambridge Ancient History,* Vol. XII (Cambridge: Cambridge University Press, 1939), and R. MacMullen, *Roman Government's Response to Crisis,* A.D. *235-337* (New Haven: Yale University Press, 1976). A popular survey, emphasizing the influence of the eastern provinces, is Stewart Perowne, *Caesars and Saints* (London: Hodder and Stoughton, 1962); A. Birley has written a life of Septimius Severus (New York: Doubleday, 1972). Social and economic changes are well treated in M. I. Rostovtzeff, *Social and Economic History of the Roman Empire,* 2 vols. (2d ed.; Oxford: Oxford University Press, 1957), though his emphasis on class cleavage is generally rejected; the intellectual shift is discussed in Chester G. Starr, *Civilization and the Caesars* (New York: Norton, 1965) and M. Grant, *The Climax of Rome* (New York: NAL, 1968).

On Plotinus, see J. M. Rist, *Plotinus and the Road to Reality* (Cambridge: Cambridge University Press, 1967); Emile Bréhier, *Philosophy of Plotinus* (Chicago: University of Chicago Press, 1958); and W. R. Inge, *Philosophy of Plotinus,* 2 vols. (3d ed.; London: Longmans, 1948). Recent studies of Christian leaders include for Clement those of J. Ferguson (New York: Twayne, 1974) and S. R. C. Lilla (Oxford: Oxford University Press, 1971); for Cyprian, that of M. M. Sage (Philadelphia: Philadelphia Patristic Foundation, 1975); for Tertullian, that of T. D. Barnes (Oxford: Clarendon Press, 1971). The general works on Christianity in Bibliography, Chapter 28, cover the third century also.

31

THE LATER ROMAN EMPIRE

The political and social system that was consolidated by Diocletian and Constantine is distinguished by the name of the Later Roman Empire. This system, though based ultimately on the values of classical civilization, was the product of tremendous upheavals in the third century; both logically and historically it was the end of ancient development in the Mediterranean world.

Politically, local autonomy and individual freedom were yielded to the demands of the all-powerful state. Socially and economically, the emperors sought to freeze life by assigning each person a niche or status which his children inherited. Intellectually, the ideal of ancient humanism became a sterile glory which men of culture cherished solely for itself, rather than seeking to fashion new literary and artistic creations.

The Later Empire, accordingly, was not a system which could last forever. By the fifth century the eastern provinces were moving on their own paths toward the Byzantine Empire, and the western provinces were separating from each other as Germanic kingdoms. Yet in the era 284–395, which we shall examine in this chapter, the Empire still had considerable strengths in its inherited capital resources, in the loyalty of the upper classes, and in the common veneer of Greco-Roman civilization. The survival of the imperial system throughout this century had two further important effects. First, the Germans on the frontier absorbed so much during the period that they were far less barbarous on their final entry than had been their ancestors of the third century. Secondly, the Church had time to meet some of its most serious heresies and so to settle its fundamental doctrines. From the Christian point of view, indeed, the century that produced Ambrose, Augustine, Basil, Jerome, and Prudentius must be accounted one of the greatest peaks of all history.

POLITICAL REORGANIZATION

From Diocletian to Constantine (284–337). By early 285 Diocletian had gained sole mastery over the Roman Empire, which the other Illyrian emperors of the past two decades had reunited. Nonetheless the problems of internal dissidence, born of the economic decay and oppression, and the external threats by Sassanian Persia and the Germans remained so grave and so numerous that the cool-headed new ruler felt the need of assistance. Diocletian, indeed, seems to have been more interested in the civil side of reorganization and largely turned over military activity to others. Immediately he sent a deputy, Maximian, to Gaul to repress the brigand rebellion of the Bagaudae, and in 286 accepted his elevation to the rank of co-Augustus by Maximian's troops. In 293 two crown princes or Caesars were appointed, Galerius in the east and Constantius Chlorus in the west. By this tetrarchy the succession was assured — a thorny problem in the preceding decades — and Diocletian had three assistants with major authority.

Under the deft guidance of Diocletian this system worked reasonably well. Diocletian himself concentrated mainly on determining policy, although he did put down a revolt in Egypt in 296–97; Maximian held the northern frontier. One Caesar, Constantius, suppressed the rebel Carausius and his successor Allectus (289–96), who had based their power on Britain and on naval strength in the English channel; and the other, Galerius, after initial defeats, finally threw back the Persians in 296–97. In 303 Diocletian, who was ailing, forced his co-ruler Maximian to agree on a mutual abdication, which took place in 305. The new Augusti, Galerius and Constantius, in turn chose two Caesars.

Physical testimony to the restoration of the Empire is spectacularly available in several places. Diocletian's choice of Nicomedia in Bithynia as the best spot for central direction foreshadowed the creation of Constantinople; but his most impressive building came after his retirement to Salonae, where he erected a huge palace-fortress within which the modern town of Split is ensconced. Constantius and later deputies in Gaul embellished Augusta Treverorum (Trier) in the Rhineland; Max-

TABLE 9

Roman Emperors

A.D. 284–395

Diocletian	284–305
Maximian	286–305
Constantius	305–06
Galerius	305–11
Severus	306–07
Licinius	308–24
Maximinus Daia	310–13
Constantine	306–37
Constantine II	337–40
Constans	337–50
Constantius	337–61
Magnentius	350–53
Julian	361–63
Jovian	363–64

East		West	
Valens	364–78	Valentinian I	364–75
Theodosius I	379–95	Gratian	367–83
		Valentinian II	383–92
		Eugenius	392–94
		Theodosius I	394–95

imian commonly lived at Mediolanum (Milan) in north Italy, which remained usually the western capital until Honorius moved for greater safety to the swamp-surrounded Ravenna after 395. Maximian's major architectural memento, however, is far off in Sicily at his hunting villa (Piazza Armerina), the mosaic floors of which are among the greatest artistic achievements of the Later Empire. Rome, though enriched by the mammoth baths of Diocletian, was merely the titular capital now, which Diocletian visited but once. It lay too far from the embattled frontiers to be a permanent home for emperors; and the Augustan tradition of veiled absolutism, incarnated in the Senate, accorded ill with the new political spirit.

Only the political skill of Diocletian had made cooperative rule possible; after his retirement the Empire was again torn asunder in civil wars of ambitious generals. In these wars, which went on to 324, the ultimate victor was Constantine, the son of Constantius Chlorus and a Balkan serving girl Helena. Passed over in the choice of Caesars in 305, he escaped from Galerius' control the next year, made his way to his father in Britain, and upon the death of Constantius in June seized his army. Galerius reluctantly granted Constantine the title of Caesar, only to encounter the rebellion in Italy of Maxentius (the son of Maximian), who had also been passed over in 305.

After wars and marches Galerius died in 311, and four men of the younger generation faced each other, Constantine against Maxentius in the west, Licinius (who had been made Augustus in 308) and Maximinus Daia, nephew of Galerius, in the east. Constantine invaded Italy in 312 despite great odds and defeated and killed Maxentius outside Rome at the battle of the Milvian bridge. He then held a conference in February 313 at Milan with Licinius, who went on to remove his own rival Maximinus Daia later in the year. The two rulers who were left alternated friendship and war until 324, when Constantine invaded the east. After victory by land at Adrianople and by sea at the Hellespont, he forced the abdication of Licinius, who was soon executed.

From 324 until his death in 337 Constantine was sole master. Apart from completing the reorganization of the Empire begun by Diocletian, Constantine independently took two great steps. One was his firm support of Christianity; the other was his construction of a new capital on the site of the Greek city of Byzantium. Begun in 324, Constantinople was dedicated on May 11, 330, as a Christian rival to Rome. From this point some modern historians date the Byzantine Empire, for the new city ever more clearly stood forth as the heart of the Greek-speaking eastern provinces even though it was originally founded as a Latin center.

Consolidation of Bureaucratic Autocracy. As between Diocletian and Constantine it is often difficult to determine responsibility for the major reforms which produced the Later Roman Empire. On the whole Diocletian, who was much better educated and more flexible, probably had the main hand in shaping the civil administration. It could, indeed, be argued that Diocletian, who faced far greater problems with smaller resources than had Augustus, was the greatest reformer in Roman history, though he was at the same time earnest in preserving what he took to be the old ways of Rome. Military reorganization, on the other hand, owed much to Constantine, a son of war, who was more brutal and dictatorial in his actions.

The elevation of the imperial position now received full recognition, for the emperor or Augustus henceforth was admittedly absolute and was called *dominus* or lord (whence the term Dominate occasionally used for the Later Empire). He took advice only from his chief officials, who stood with other "companions" (*comites*) in the privy council or *sacrum consistorium*. All who gained an audience with the ruler had to kneel and kiss the hem of his garment on entry and departure; both to enhance the ruler's dignity and to safeguard his life approach was made more difficult and ceremonial greater. Beneath the divinely appointed emperor was a vast, decentralized bureaucracy. This was divided into military and civil sections, though civil officials commonly wore military dress as an inheritance from the militarization of the third century. Besides the Praetorian Prefect, who ran the civil government, were the Quaestor of the Sacred Palace (laws, petitions, formal patents of office), the Master of Offices (foreign affairs, arsenals, bodyguard, police), the Count of Sacred Gifts, the Count of the Privy Purse, the Supervisor of the Sacred Bedchamber (a eunuch), and others in a well-defined order. In Rome there continued to be a Senate, which served as town council, and a similar body was created at Constantinople. Politically the powers of the Senate were virtually nil; but members of the senatorial class, with which the equestrians were merging, formed the most cultured and

wealthy element of the realm, resting their power upon vast landhold-
ings.

Stepwise below the emperor's court the government descended through
four prefectures (eventually) to 12 dioceses under vicars and on to the
many provinces, in which most of Italy was included (see Map 20).
Septimius Severus had begun the policy of dividing provinces lest any
one governor have too great powers; by the reign of Diocletian this
subdivision had produced some 96 provinces. The urban councils (*cu-
rias*) were the lowest rung in the hierarchy under the supervision of the
curators, now locally chosen; but the decurions had the vital role, without pay, of apportioning and collecting taxes, of making up deficits, of
providing recruits, and in general of serving as local auxiliaries of the
imperial autocracy. It is small wonder that the *curiales* class, whence
decurions were chosen, was not one which men voluntarily entered;
although the wealthier landlords managed to escape from it, all others of
any means were obligated by law to take their place in this closed
caste.

Superficially this mutual checking structure, fully equipped with
spies (the *agentes in rebus*), appears more complicated than that of the
Augustan world; but in reality the rich local variations and subtle adjustments of the earlier period had now been sacrificed to an essentially
simple, authoritarian policy. All else had to give way to the maintenance
of the all-important army and the majesty of the emperor. Yet, while the
simpler bureaucracy of the Early Empire had essentially carried out the
aim of its rulers, the system of the Later Empire operated all too often
for its own benefit, regardless of imperial needs. Corruption, waste of
precious funds, and inefficiency were marks of all levels of government.
In the later fourth century the direction shifted from clique to clique,
each in turn exploiting the subjects and heaping up private piles of gold
while the Empire tottered.

The New Army. On the military side equally great changes were the
product of the third-century catastrophes. The army of the Later Empire
was divided into two sections, frontier and mobile. Members of the
frontier force, descendants of the old legions and auxiliaries, had become
a militia which held farming lands to support itself; this local protection
was grouped by districts under a *dux,* independent of the governors.
Across the fourth century the emperors built a good many stone forts on
the northern frontier — in vain, as it later turned out.

The second part, under Masters of the Soldiery (*magistri militum*) and others, was the central reserve, ready to march swiftly on the somewhat restored road network of the Empire to any threatened zone. The two grades of troops in this force were the *palatini* (Household Troops) and the *comitatenses* (Guards), which fought under emblems like the *draco* (dragon) rather than the legionary eagles of old. Barbarians were used in appreciable numbers along with volunteers and drafted men, but Roman discipline and skill in organization were still living qualities which enabled the field forces to throw back the serious threats to the frontiers across most of the fourth century. Down to the disastrous battle of Adrianople in 378 the infantry remained the backbone, though cavalry units of archers and heavily-armored spearsmen had precedence; probably the over-all size of the army grew to about 400,000.

The Freezing of Life. Diocletian was able to carry through an extensive reorganization of imperial finances. A census was carried out which measured all productive forces in units called in many parts of the Empire the *iugum* (of land) and *caput* (of human beings and animals); even though these units varied in size according to their quality or crop, the subtle gradations of earlier days were no longer possible. On the basis of these assessments the taxes in kind (*annona*) could be fairly levied by a decree (*indictio*) published every 5, or later 15, years, instead of resorting to the arbitrary, spasmodic confiscations of the third century. Other taxes in coin and gold were levied on city wage-earners and senators. Diocletian also conducted in 294 a thorough reform of the coinage, issuing from 15 mints gold, silver, and bronze coins; as reformed by Constantine, the gold *solidus* was to be used for a millennium in the Mediterranean.

The immediate effect was a great rise in prices which Diocletian tried to check by his Edict of Maximum Prices in 301; but economic activity seems to have revived, though on a lower plane than in earlier centuries. Throughout the fourth century, however, trade and industry dwindled, especially in the west; the coinage was once again inflated; and the tax burden grew more and more intolerable both in its weight and in its brutal, inequitable collection as privileged elements escaped their just share.

Since change meant decay, the Empire was resolved to stop change. The Theodosian Code, which is in the main a collection of fourth-century edicts, contains provision after provision by which the state sought to lock men in their places and organize the population according to its professions into hereditary classes. Only thus could it secure from every subject his due services and due contribution to the coffers and granaries of the Empire. "No man," said one edict to the people, "shall possess any property that is tax-exempt." [1] At what date the peasants became tied to their land virtually as serfs we do not know, but by the reign of Constantine they were generally attached so firmly to the tax register of their estate or village that movement was impossible. This measure was required so that the landowners could meet their taxes and calls for recruits; but in the towns too the decurions and the members of the guilds were chained to their positions of state service. At this time the Mediterranean world came closer to a caste system than at any other time in its history.

The more the fabric of society tottered, the more evident became violence and terrorism. When emperors felt insecure, they were quick to strike down dangerous elements. Astrological predictions, magic, and poisoning were employed against the rulers or against fellow nobles on a scale unprecedented in earlier ages, and the discovery of their employment led to fearful repression by such rulers as Valens, who carried "death at the tip of his tongue." [2]

The edicts of fourth-century rulers, true, show a hitherto unprecedented concern over morality and piety. Yet these same men commonly ordained as punishments the maiming of legs or gouging out of eyes; and only crucifixion was abolished by the Christian sympathizer Constantine, as was also branding on the face. The Empire was sinking into barbarism long before the barbarians came.

If a modern reader of the Theodosian Code took at face value the legal picture of state control and brutal regimentation, he would have to conclude that the Later Empire was one of the most frightful examples in all history of the victory of the state over the individual. Some scholars of recent generations, acquainted with modern despotisms and growing bureaucracies, have so construed the period. In truth, however, the very vehemence of the edicts was itself a clear sign that the power of the state was diminishing; further evidence of this development will appear as we follow the decline of the Empire.

[1] *Theodosian Code* 13.10.8 (A.D. 383).
[2] Ammianus Marcellinus 29.1.19.

The Later Fourth Century (337–95). Down to 363 the succession to the throne lay in the house of Constantine. Before his death in 337 Constantine had killed his eldest son and his wife, but in true dynastic spirit he divided the Empire among his three remaining sons and two nephews. This situation invited new struggles, as a result of which the suspicious, unpredictable Constantius II wound up as sole master in 353. Two years later Constantius had to appoint his cousin Julian as Caesar to defend Gaul; and from a bookish lad Julian turned into a remarkably successful general, winning a great battle near Argentorate (Strassburg) against the Alamanni in 357. In 361 his troops made Julian Augustus; fortunately Constantius died before open battle could be joined, so that Julian became sole ruler (361–63).

Julian has long been famous as an apostate from Christianity, but after his childhood it is doubtful if he was ever a genuine Christian. Addicted as he was to magic and superstition, Julian was scarcely a real representative of truly rational Hellenism, though he paraded as such in his voluminous writings. After taking some steps against Christianity Julian had to concentrate his attention on a Persian campaign, which was far from successful. Although his army reached the vicinity of Ctesiphon, Julian was forced to retreat to upper Mesopotamia, where he was wounded and died in 363.

His eventual successor was the bluff warrior Valentinian I (364–75), who found, as did most other rulers of the century, that the problems of defending the Empire were too much for one man. Valentinian took over the protection of the west and placed his brother Valens in charge of the east. Each had his own full court; this division of the Empire was essentially never undone, save for a period of five months in 394–95.

Culturally and religiously as well, the split between east and west became ever more apparent. Knowledge of Greek by western men had long since become relatively rare and from this point on sank even more rapidly; although the administration of the Empire was formally in Latin, business in the east was largely conducted in Greek. At the council of Nicaea in 325, of the 250-odd bishops present, only 5 came from the west (with two presbyters representing the bishop of Rome); at the council of Serdica in 343 the eastern and western bishops met separately, and each side finally condemned the leader of the other in a brief schism.

In 376 the Visigoths on the Danube petitioned the Empire that they be allowed to enter its realm and thus secure protection against the onrushing Huns. Valens granted this request, but the Visigoths so little enjoyed the blessings of imperial peace, as represented by the exactions of the imperial officials, that they rose in revolt. Valens failed to wait for reinforcements from the west, was caught in an ill-prepared battle at Adrianople in 378, and was killed with the bulk of his army. Immediately the results were limited, for Gratian, son and successor of Valentinian I (375–83), sent one of his best generals, Theodosius, east to restore the situation. The Visigoths were allowed semiautonomy; Theodosius rebuilt the field army of the east on the basis of cavalry; and when the imperial succession in the west was troubled he conquered the western half of the Empire late in 394.

At his death early in the next year the Empire still held the same territory as in 284, but much had changed in its intellectual and religious atmosphere. Politically, too, the central government exercised ever-weaker control over the great landlords, over local bureaucrats, and over its all-important armies, which by now were heavily barbarian. In 395 the sons of Theodosius, Arcadius in the east and Honorius in the west, became emperors over a divided Empire, one-half of which was to disappear in the next century.

VICTORY OF CHRISTIANITY

Persecution and Imperial Favor. Equally as important as the political reorganization of the Later Empire were the spectacular changes in Christianity 284–395. First came persecution, then the even more dangerous and insidious temptations of imperial friendship; but churchmen had also to deal with the threats of heresies and to channel the great growth in numbers of the faithful.

At the accession of Diocletian the Church lay under an ancient ban of the state, though it enjoyed *de facto* toleration. The numbers of Christians had grown so remarkably that perhaps 10 per cent of the Empire was Christian, including members of the imperial government and the army. On the other hand, pagan opposition on the intellectual level had become much sharper. Porphyry, pupil of Plotinus, had once spoken well of Christ but later wrote a slashing attack *Against the Christians* in which he assailed Paul as incoherent and coarse and pointed out inconsistencies in the Bible. The eucharist, to Porphyry, was cannibalistic, and Christian doctrine nonrational. By 300, a considerable body of directly anti-Christian material was in circulation, ranging from the philosophic to the scurrilous.

In restoring order to the Empire Diocletian was unusually tolerant toward political foes, but he displayed no enthusiasm for intellectual deviations. The first general prohibition of astrology came in his reign. The alchemists of Egypt were banned and their writings burned. In about 297 he fulminated against the Manicheans, who also seemed connected with the revolt in Egypt; his edict sweepingly proclaimed his "great desire to punish the obstinacy of wicked mind among the most evil men." [3] Unlike Aurelian, Diocletian did not favor a syncretistic Sun worship and sought rather to reinvigorate the old state faith of Jupiter Capitolinus, "Jupitor conservator," as he was called on coins among other titles; to emphasize his divine protection Diocletian was called Jovius, and Maximian — the active protector of the realm — was termed Herculius. Nevertheless Christianity continued to exist in an uneasy toleration down to 303, when Diocletian's illness perhaps reinforced his prejudices and weakened his political sensitivity.

The Diocletianic persecution was the worst the Church ever experienced. In the opening blow, on February 23, 303, the Christian church at Nicomedia — in sight of the palace — was invaded and burned, and the Holy Scriptures within it were deliberately given to the flames. Edict followed edict to sharpen the punishments for the recalcitrant and broadened the persecution from the *honestiores* and office-holders to include the clergy and then all the laity; but at the abdication of Diocletian the persecution had not achieved its ends. Galerius, who may have had considerable responsibility for starting it in the first place, continued the assault intermittently down to 311, when he issued an anguished decree of toleration on April 30. At the close of the edict Galerius, seriously ill, asked the prayers of the Christians for his own well-being and that of the state, but in five days he was dead. In this persecution only the first decree (against Christian office-holders and the upper classes) was generally enforced over all the Empire, and the Caesar Constantius Chlorus seems to have engaged solely in token destruction

---

[3] *Fontes iuris romani anteiustiniani,* II, ed. J. Baviera (2d ed.; Florence, 1940), p. 580.

of the churches as ordered by Diocletian. Interestingly enough, the Christians in many places enjoyed protection from their pagan neighbors; the local grounds of intolerance were now waning.

The rise of Constantine brought an almost unbelievable alteration in the situation. During his earlier years Constantine had been an adherent first of Hercules, then of Sol Invictus, but he had had the Spanish bishop Hosius at his court and had otherwise shown interest in Christianity. During the campaign of 312 against Maxentius, Constantine had a dream in which, according to our best source (Lactantius), the worried general was bidden to mark a Christian emblem on the shields of his soldiers; the famous story that he saw a cross in the sky with the words "By this you shall conquer" appears later in Eusebius. At all events Constantine's victory at the Milvian bridge sealed his belief in the power of the Christian God to bring success, and his meeting with Licinius at Milan in February 313 produced a policy of universal toleration.

Constantine never wavered thereafter in his support of Christianity. In Rome the first great Christian basilicas now arose at St. John Lateran's and St. Peter's; his mother Helena built the church of the Nativity in Bethlehem and others; and the new capital of Constantinople was deliberately designed as a Christian city. Episcopal courts were granted jurisdiction, the clergy exempted from liturgies, confiscated property restored, and free bequest to the Church permitted. Yet Constantine himself was not baptized until he lay on his deathbed, partly in order that he might wipe away as many of the black sins in his ruthless life as possible, partly because the great majority of his subjects were still pagan. Throughout the reign of Constantine and those of his family, who were all Christians save Julian, the imperial cult went on; superficial edicts against sacrifice had little effect in practice.

Slowly, however, the scale sank against the old faiths. Gratian no longer accepted the title of *pontifex maximus* and in 382 again removed the pagan statue of Victory from the Roman Senate House, taken away earlier by Constantius and restored by Julian. This step brought a famous appeal from Symmachus and other pagan senators, which was countered by the impassioned arguments of Bishop Ambrose of Milan; in this test case Christianity won, and the statue was not restored. In 392 Theodosius banned all pagan sacrifices, and by his death in 395 Christianity was definitely the state religion.

Dangers of Imperial Friendship. In the first flush of joy at the end of the persecutions the Church tended to pay the deepest respect to Constantine, "the first Roman ruler to repudiate error and to acknowledge the majesty of God."[4] It happily assisted his use of the machinery of state to suppress the Donatists and accepted both his lavish grant of state funds for building and his virtual dictation of decisions at the council of Nicaea in 325. As time went on, the Church came perilously close to replacing in practice its ideal of a heavenly Redeemer by the old, well-established figure of an earthly shepherd; it even took over many terms and customs of the imperial cult into its own use. Imperial friendship was far more dangerous to the independence of Christianity than had ever been the threat of persecution.

If the absolutism of the Later Empire failed to extend itself completely over the Church, the reasons must be sought both in accidents and in the fundamental qualities of Christian thought. It was, thus, an accident that the son of Constantine, Constantius II, leaned toward Arianism; but his blandishments and his threats, while coercing the pope (after an exile of three years from Rome) and other ecclesiastics, failed to intimidate several important orthodox leaders. The chief opponent of Arianism, bishop Athanasius of Alexandria, impelled the Christian community there to address a signed, public protest to its ruler "for the salvation of his immortal soul." Even more remarkable a defiance of the autocracy of the state were the open attacks of bishop Lucifer of Cagliari (Sardinia), which abused Constantius as "the filth of all the sewers," "founder of blasphemy," and so on.[5]

The pagan revival under Julian was essentially another accident which checked the tendency of union between Church and state, but even the ever more openly Christian rulers of the late fourth century faced notable challenges by two great leaders, Ambrose of Milan (*c.* 337-97) in the west and John Chrysostom of Antioch and Constantinople (*c.* 345-407) in the east. After a bloody massacre of the unruly residents of Thessalonica in 390 Theodosius was regretfully but firmly banned by Ambrose from the rites of the Church until he made penance. As bishop of Constantinople from 398 John Chrysostom at times flattered the imperial

---

[4] Lactantius, *Divine Institutes* 1.1.
[5] Quoted by Kenneth M. Setton, *Christian Attitude towards the Emperor in the Fourth Century* (New York: Columbia University Press, 1941), p. 97.

family but more often was fluently abusive in attacking the luxury of the court and the unjust actions of the Empress Eudoxia, wife of Arcadius.

Twice banished, John Chrysostom died in exile, and the continuing political strength of the Empire in the east was to make its Church largely a subservient tool of state. The Christian leaders of the west were perhaps more fortunate in the fact that the political system about them was decaying and so allowed them ever greater opportunity to assert the separation of church and state, especially with respect to the determination of dogma. Throughout the fourth century itself, however, the effort begun by Constantine to gain the spiritual and earthly strengths of Christianity for the political support of the Empire proved a doubtfully advantageous bargain even for the state. The new view implicit in Christian doctrine was in the last analysis incompatible with a political structure based on the old order of civilization.

Heresies of the Fourth Century. If the orthodox leaders at times found the interference of the state in matters of belief a heavy burden, the followers of the great heresies of the fourth century were even more likely to be thrown into opposition to the Empire. From the time of Constantine onward heresy became a means of expressing discontent with the terrific demands of the political system as well as a vehicle of theological disagreement with the orthodox administration of the Church.

The Donatist schism in north Africa thus had strong overtones of social protest. This heresy took its name from Bishop Donatus of Numidia, who appealed in 313 to Constantine against the validity of the consecration of a new bishop of Carthage. The ground of the complaint was the presence at the consecration of a bishop who had bent during the Diocletianic persecution; that is, Donatus argued that the validity of a sacrament depended upon the moral worthiness of the celebrant or celebrants. This theory was rejected by a council which Constantine called at Arles, and two years later (316) Constantine himself ordered Donatists expelled from their churches. So much disturbance ensued in Africa that in 321 Constantine finally had to yield his effort to require religious unity by political means, a potent demonstration of the actual limits of the outwardly despotic rule of the fourth century. The Donatists continued to flourish in a position of semirebellion. At the end of the century Augustine devoted much labor to establishing the fact that any consecrated official of the Church was a valid minister of the sacraments and, finding that reasoned argument did not prevail, descended finally to countenance physical punishment against the contrary-minded Donatists.

Far more serious was the Arian heresy. Arius, trained at Antioch but a priest at Alexandria in the early fourth century, followed out the main lines of thought of the third-century Church to deny that God the Son was equal to God the Father, as being begotten by the Father and also as being susceptible to human change and emotion. The Arian creed made the divine essence One and gained wide popular support. At the outset friends and foes of Arius were divided largely on political grounds, but eventually orthodox leaders came to see in Arianism an intrusion of pagan rationalism, which subverted the basic tenets of Christianity, especially in weakening the value of Christ's redemption of mankind by His sacrifice.

Constantine, fresh from facing the Donatist heresy in the west, found himself after his victory over Licinius confronted by a Church in the east that was split wide open. In 325 he took the great step of convoking a general council of Christian leaders at Nicaea. The emperor himself appeared to inaugurate the council and listened attentively; his adviser, Bishop Hosius, worked behind the scenes to secure a rejection of the Arian doctrine, but on theological grounds which pleased few of the outwardly assenting bishops.

The end result was the Nicene creed, though this was stated in its canonical form only at a council at Constantinople in 381. For wrangling over the problem of the Trinity continued all during the fourth century, and the chief orthodox leader at Alexandria, Athanasius (who became bishop in 328), was exiled no less than four times in the reigns of Constantine, the semi-Arian Constantius, and the equally semi-Arian Valens. On the one side stood those who affirmed Christ was equal to God, if one may simplify the very involved theological debates; eventually the term *homoousios,* "of the same substance," came to be used of Christ's nature by this group. On the other stood those who placed an iota in the term to make Him "of similar substance," *homoiousios.*

This argument descended at times to the lowest of abuse and appeals to passion, but on its highest level represented an intensity of thought which had not been seen for seven centuries, since the days of Plato.

Among the great theologians who appeared in the east were Basil of Caesarea in Cappadocia (327–79), his brother Gregory of Nyssa (*c.* 331–95), and Gregory of Nazianzus (*c.* 323–89). Beside them stood in the west Ambrose of Milan and, above all, Augustine of Hippo, who produced one of the greatest treatises *On the Trinity*. To the modern world these theological debates sometimes seem meaningless, but in actuality the Church was here breaking once for all with the last serious assault of ancient idealism and rationalism. The definition of the Trinity in the Nicene creed was a mystery, based on faith; but having believed, the good Christian was led to a view of man as an individual, though dependent upon a transcendental deity. For centuries to come, contentions over the nature of Christ were to lead to persecution and even death; the monophysite churches of the east, including the Armenian, Nestorian, and Ethiopian, ultimately took their root in the controversy.

Expansion of Christianity. The very vehemence of the doctrinal disputes in the fourth century attests the power of Christianity. Within the Empire the favor of the emperors made it ever more popular, though probably most men were still pagan by the end of the century. Christians and pagans lived side by side without serious conflicts, for even the intellectual leaders in either camp, while disagreeing in their publications, maintained social relationships. Yet foreshadowings of the bitter intolerance of later centuries, when barbarism had more play, could be found in the essay of Julius Firmicus Maternus, *The Error of Pagan Cults* (*c.* 346–50), which laid down clearly the duty of the rulers to save pagans from immortal destruction; and in the verbal attacks of Ambrose, Jerome, and Augustine on Judaism.

In its internal expansion the Church drew closer and closer to the world in which it lived. Ecclesiastical organization had long followed political boundaries. Now the bishop of Rome rose ever higher in the west, partly because the emperors no longer lived in the old capital; but Constantinople, as New Rome, claimed equal place, which was granted it by the council of Chalcedon in 451. The style of life of bishops became more elegant and more politically oriented; the buildings and properties of the Church grew in magnificence and in extent, as we shall see in considering Christian arts.

In another respect as well the Church mirrored its world. As the frontiers of the Empire grew to mean less and less, Christianity expanded far afield. In southern Scotland the missionary Ninian founded a church in 397; in the next century Patrick consolidated the beginnings of Christianity in Ireland. Ulfilas, the apostle of the Goths, spread Christianity among the Germans; but unfortunately for amicable relations he propagated the Arian creed. In the east Armenia had been Christianized in the third century to the degree that Tiridates (261–316) was the first monarch to make Christianity a state church (apart from a legendary king of Edessa); and Persian Christianity was extensive enough both to be persecuted by Shapur II (309–79) and to survive to become the root of Nestorianism. Even to the south Christianity spread up the Nile in the fourth century to Ethiopia.

CULTURE OF THE LATE EMPIRE

The Pagan Side. The fourth century looms two-faced at the threshold of the Middle Ages. On its pagan side it looked mostly to the past; on the Christian, mainly to the future. In both areas there was much more intellectual and artistic activity than in the dismal third century, thanks to the breathing spell afforded by the reforms of Diocletian and Constantine. This activity was centered largely about the court and the Church, which commanded most of the scanty surplus of society; only at Rome, Antioch, Athens, and a few other cities were there still aristocratic literary circles.

During the fourth and fifth centuries the texts of classical authors and also the store of ancient wisdom were put in the shape in which the Middle Ages studied them. The use of the long-lived parchment codices, rather than the papyrus roll, became common and helped to preserve many great works besides the Bible. Important literary commentaries were written, as by Aelius Donatus (fourth century) and Macrobius (active *c.* 400); and the Middle Ages was to rely heavily on the grammars of Donatus and the survey of ancient learning by Martianus Capella (early fifth century). While classical art as such was dead, the emperor Theodosius specifically kept open the pagan temples and preserved their statues as works of art; and on the whole Christians united with pagans in copying classical authors.

Beyond preserving and commenting on the past, as a mark of the true gentleman, pagans were not often able to be truly creative. The mildly

Christian D. Magnus Ausonius (*c.* 310–95) wrote secular poetry which was competent, but little more. The orations and letters of the Greek Libanius of Antioch (314–93) and the Roman senator Q. Aurelius Symmachus (345–405) are exceedingly rhetorical, though they occasionally afford valuable historical material. Libanius, who taught Basil, Gregory of Nazianzus, and John Chrysostom, does at least show a breath of real life in his works, unlike his elder contemporary, the rhetorician Themistius of Constantinople (d. *c.* 390). In philosophy the fourth-century Syrian popularizer of Neoplatonism, Iamblichus, was a sorry figure beside the great Christian theologians. The adherents of the old order were fighting a hopeless rearguard action, and their pessimism is often evident.

Yet now and then an invigorating blast of the new wind appears outside the Christian area. In the fields of architecture and sculpture secular and Christian thought coursed virtually in the same channel. The early buildings of Constantinople are long since gone, as are also the palace of Diocletian at Nicomedia and the imperial structures at Milan; but three significant works of the early fourth century still stand in Rome. One is the great baths of Diocletian; a second is the basilica begun by Maxentius and dedicated by Constantine shortly after 312. Both are mammoth structures of vaulted nave and aisles which embody the new sense of space emerging since the days of the Pantheon. The third is the arch of Constantine, erected 313–15 to commemorate his defeat of Maxentius. Both its complicated structure and the contemporary reliefs, which jar against the second-century sculpture reused in the decoration of the arch, breathe a far different spirit than the nearby arch of Titus. Classical idealism had yielded in favor of the transcendental and symbolic, a shift which is apparent in the few, but commonly very impressive, statues of fourth-century emperors.[6]

In literature one surprising pagan author appears, the major historian Ammianus Marcellinus (*c.* 330–after 392). Sprung from the middle class of Syrian Antioch, Ammianus wrote his history of the Empire amid the Roman aristocratic circles in the last decades of the century. In honesty

[6] The bronze statue at Barletta, illustrated on Plate XXXI, perhaps represents Valentinian I (364–75), one of the last great emperors; it well suggests the majestic immobility of an absolute ruler of the Later Empire. Traditionally this statue once stood in Constantinople, was looted by the Crusaders in 1204, and was salvaged from a shipwreck. The hands and legs are Renaissance work.

and balanced judgment the surviving books on the period 353–78 justify placing him beside Livy and ahead of Tacitus. Both Tacitus and Ammianus Marcellinus had good reason to feel hopeless, the one at seeing the victory of first-century absolutism over the Senate, the other at witnessing the barbarian incursions of the fourth century, the ruthless violation of justice by despotic emperors, and the internal decay. But the spirit of the later historian rose above the gloom with an inner certainty of faith in the divine protection of Rome. Interesting also in Ammianus are his distinct sense of justice and ethics, his incisive portraiture, and his frankness in an era when open expression of political judgments could be extremely dangerous.

The Christian Side. In both arts and letters fourth-century Christianity was fertile in setting patterns for the future. Once the Church had become a tolerated faith and, moreover, enjoyed the financial support of the emperors, it could house its services in ever more magnificent fashion. A church building required large, open internal spaces within which the baptized could assemble to celebrate the eucharist; for this purpose the state and private Christian architects of the reign of Constantine adapted the secular basilica. The fourth-century Christian basilicas were fundamentally simple, barn-like buildings with nave and side aisles, pitched roof, and lighting from above via a clerestory; those not yet baptized or those excluded for reasons of penitence could hearken from the vestibule or forecourt. From this root eventually developed the medieval cathedral of the west. Baptisteries and shrines, which did not need to be so large, were at times domed, centralized structures, a source of the soaring domed churches of the east in the sixth century.

Both types were decorated with paintings and mosaics which made use of Jewish scenes of the Old Testament as well as events of the life of Christ in classical molds; Christ was still normally shown as young and unbearded. On sarcophagi, too, Christian motifs could now be explicit rather than being limited, as in earlier days, to the fish, dove, and similar symbolic hints. Apart from such reliefs and the decoration of capitals and doorframes, Christianity made little use of sculpture, especially that in the round which smacked of pagan and imperial antecedents.

In volume and in quality the Christian output of literature in the fourth century is extraordinary. Paulinus of Nola (*c.* 353–431), a pupil of Ausonius, became a monk and wrote impressive poetry; even more able was Aurelius Prudentius Clemens (*c.* 348–after 405), the last great Latin poet to write in classical meters. Although Prudentius' verse displays great knowledge of pagan poetry, it was devoted to the doctrine of the Trinity, the defense of Christian doctrine against a tract of Symmachus, and other Christian purposes in a joyous, happy belief in divine providence. Bishop Ambrose of Milan composed hymns as well as powerful letters, sermons, commentaries on books of the Bible, and a treatise *On the Duties of Priests* which was largely modeled on Cicero's *On Duties*.

Among Christian scholars the great figure was the contentious, abusive Jerome (348–420) of Dalmatia, who was trained in rhetoric under Donatus and studied Greek with the theologian Gregory of Nazianzus. While living in Rome, Jerome was directed by Pope Damasus to revise the variant Latin translations of the Bible; his version, later called the Vulgate, became the standard for the Middle Ages and for the Catholic church of modern times. In 386 Jerome moved to Bethlehem, where he poured out letters and commentaries in a pure Latin style full of reminiscences of Cicero, Virgil, and Horace.

One of Jerome's most influential works was his *Chronicle,* a parallel chronology of pagan and Christian events, which was basically a translation from Eusebius of Caesarea's *Chronicon.* Eusebius himself (*c.* 260–*c.* 340) was a leading figure in the Arian controversy, of moderate tendencies, but was also a prolific writer. Apart from his two major apologetic works, *Preparation for the Gospel* and *Proof of the Gospel,* his greatest composition was his *Church History,* in several editions from about 312 to 325. The style of this latter work, though adapted perhaps from Alexandrian literary history, marked a break with classical historiography in its sober use of documents and in its sense that history was important as a working-out of God's will. Eusebius' eulogistic *Life of Constantine* led on to the writing of saints' lives, begun by Athanasius in the *Life of St. Antony,* which was to be a main literary form of the Middle Ages.

On the Latin side the main Christian historical writer was Lactantius (*c.* 250–317), often called the Christian Cicero because of his polished literary style. Lactantius was thoroughly steeped in classical rhetoric and occupied a public chair in the subject before the Diocletianic persecution.

Shortly after 315 he wrote a bitter study *On the Death of the Persecutors;* even more important was his *Divine Institutes,* a defense of Christianity which was a forerunner of Augustine's *City of God*.

Saint Augustine. Of the many eminent theologians of the age, Augustine (354-430) may be singled out; for he, more than any other man after Paul, set the intellectual framework of Latin Christendom. Educated at Carthage and at Rome, Augustine was firmly grounded in the classical learning of the age and became professor of rhetoric at Milan, the western capital. While at Carthage he entered so fully into the ways of the world as to have an illegitimate son, but his driving search for a spiritual base led him in turn through Manicheism, skepticism, and Neoplatonism. At Milan he came under the influence of Ambrose and was converted in 386 to Christianity, the religion of his mother Monnica. Augustine abandoned his profession and his intention of marriage, and returned to Africa where he became bishop of Hippo in 395/6. Here he lived a busy, long life as shepherd of his flock and expositor of the orthodox faith.

Among his many influential works the two which are most widely known are the *Confessions* and the *City of God*. The *Confessions* are in a sense the first autobiography, for they reveal as no pagan work had ever done Augustine's quest for the meaning of life until he came to his safe mooring in the Church. The *City of God* in 22 books, which was written 413-26, was a rebuttal of the pagan charge that the abandonment of the pagan gods had produced the Gothic sack of Rome in 410. Augustine's meditation on this problem led him into a majestic treatment of the intervention of God in human history, down to the coming of Christ, and a contrast of the earthly plane or "city" with that of the eternal.

Here Augustine swept away the hopeless wavering of the classical world between Fate and Fortune; in their place he gave man a sense of predestination which has at times had no less evil an effect. Nevertheless the coming of Christ marked a real break, a new order; for from this unique event the course of human history must run toward eventual salvation — though Augustine saw no reason to assert that the actual course of events before the Last Judgment was a constant earthly amelioration. Equally significant in Augustine's thought is the place of a human being as a true individual, dependent upon the grace of God and yet an agent of independent volition, of an entirely different order from physical nature.

Yet other products of his ever active pen, such as *On the Trinity, On Christian Education,* and his letters, reveal the terrific powers of Augustine's mind and his blend of classical logic and philosophy with Christian belief. Augustine attacked pagan pride in reason and concomitant elevation of man as an end in himself. He warned that man could not penetrate beyond certain limits in conjecture "lest freedom of thought beget impiety of opinion"; and elsewhere he bluntly asserted, "God and the soul, that is what I desire to know. Nothing more? Nothing whatever!"[7] No one, however, who reads any of his work can fail to note how widely Augustine employed earlier knowledge, both pagan and Christian, and how powerfully his mind operated to couple faith with reason. "We could not even believe," he observes, "unless we possessed rational souls."[8]

If we may take Augustine as an illustration, Christianity was a spur to intellectual activity; and, as in the cases of Jerome, Prudentius, Lactantius, and others, Augustine illuminates the carry-over of classical culture into the Church. Unfortunately he also at times manifests the growing intolerance of a victorious Church, a spirit which was mingled with naïve credulity by less intellectually inclined Christians. The rash of forgeries attached to the apostles and fathers of the Church, especially Clement (pseudo-Clementine *Homilies, Recognitions, Apostolic Constitutions*), was perhaps a tribute to Christian desire to have evidence for beliefs and ritual, but it was a back-handed one.

An Ambivalent Century. Although William James could call Augustine "the first modern man," the bishop of Hippo lived in the fourth century after Christ. A new spirit looked forward, but the forms in which that spirit was expressed still derived from the past. So too in Christian churches the new purpose was clothed in an old architectural form and in classical artistic motifs; and the builders of these churches did not scruple to use columns from pagan temples. The scene of Augustine's death bed, when the Vandals were besieging his city, is a parable of the union of old and new in Christianity; before his aged eyes

---

[7] *City of God* 10.23; *Letters* 55.39.
[8] *Letters* 120.3.

Augustine had placed a copy in large letters of a Psalm, but among his last words were a quotation from the Neoplatonist Plotinus.

The unfortunate fact was that the political, social, and economic setting of this merger was one of decay. The reorganization of Diocletian and Constantine had given a new base of stability, which did carry on the Empire for another century; but in the end their measures sufficed neither to halt internal dissolution in many areas nor to protect the frontiers from outside threats. In the closing decades of the lives of Augustine and Jerome, after 395, the western part of the Empire began to collapse; and in that collapse the potentialities of Latin Christendom suffered a check which was not undone for centuries to come.

BIBLIOGRAPHY

Sources. The fourth century offers a wider array of detailed literary sources, often emanating from main characters, than any other period of ancient history. On the political side the *Theodosian Code,* assembled in 429–38 under Theodosius II (tr. Clyde Pharr et al., Princeton: Princeton University Press, 1952), contains a large volume of edicts from Constantine on. Unique is the *Notitia Dignitatum,* a list kept by the *primicerius notariorum* of all the offices in the imperial government, together with insignia of office and the military units for each general; this seems to have been incompletely revised from time to time but generally represents the situation of the late fourth century. Apart from Ammianus Marcellinus' great history for 353–78 (Loeb Classical Library), there are the open pagan survey of the period 270–410 by the fifth-century Zosimus, brief accounts by Aurelius Victor and Eutropius, the anonymous *Epitome de Caesaribus,* and the Christian tract by Orosius, *Against the Pagans,* tr. I. W. Raymond (New York: Columbia University Press, 1936). A fascinating illustration of the corruption of the Later Empire is given in the tract translated and discussed by E. A. Thompson, *A Roman Reformer and Inventor* (New York: Arno, 1980).

For such an issue as the removal of the statue of Victory we have both the pagan argument, in Symmachus, and the Christian argument, in Ambrose and Prudentius. Christian history proper is represented by the works of Lactantius and Eusebius noted in the text; mediocre accounts were written later by Sozomen, Socrates, and Theodoret. For translations of the Christian authors, see the series noted in Bibliography, Chapter 30. Samples may be found in *Satirical Letters of St. Jerome,* tr. Paul Carroll (Chicago: Gateway 6020, 1956); St. Augustine, *Confessions,* tr. Rex Warner (New York: Mentor MT490, 1963); St. Augustine, *On Christian Doctrine,* tr. D. W. Robertson, Jr. (Indianapolis: Bobbs-Merrill LLA80, 1958); St. Augustine, *City of God,* tr. M. Dods (New York: Modern Library Giant, 1950).

The emperor Julian wrote highly rhetorical speeches and letters, an attack on Antioch (which had jeered him), and an attack on Christianity, which has not survived (Loeb Classical Library). The poetry and prose of Claudian (Loeb Classical Library; A. Cameron, *Claudian* (Oxford: Oxford University Press, 1970]), Ausonius (Loeb Classical Library), Libanius (*Autobiography,* ed. A. F. Norman [Oxford: Oxford University Press, 1965]), and Symmachus forms an extensive bulk; we have also lives of fourth-century rhetoricians by Eunapius. The evidence from inscriptions and archeology, on the other hand, sloped off rapidly across the fourth century in testimony to its physical decline. Only occasionally, as at Aquileia, can a fourth-century church be found under a later edifice; but the fundamental fabric of several Roman churches goes back to this period.

Further Reading. The reorganization of the Later Empire is described by H. M. D. Parker, *History of the Roman World from* A.D. *138 to 337* (rev. ed.; London: Methuen, 1969), P. Brown, *The World of Late Antiquity* (New York: Harcourt Brace, 1971), and Joseph Vogt, *The Decline of Rome* (New York: New American Library, 1967). There is no good life of Diocletian in English; Constantine is well treated by A. Alföldi, *Conversion of Constantine and Pagan Rome* (Oxford: Oxford University Press, 1969), and A. H. M. Jones, *Constantine and the Conversion of Europe* (Toronto: University of Toronto Press, 1979). Jacob Burckhardt, *The Age of Constantine the Great* (New York: Doubleday Anchor A65, 1964), is a somewhat antiquated but stimulating classic. Constantine's relations to Christianity are also summed up briefly but in an influential essay by N. H. Baynes, *Constantine the Great and the Christian Church* (Brooklyn: Haskell, 1972).

On Christianity, beyond the general works noted in Bibliography, Chapter 28, see W. H. C. Frend, *The Donatist Church* (Oxford: Oxford University Press, 1952); F. H. Dudden, *Life and Times of St. Ambrose,* 2 vols. (Oxford: Oxford University Press, 1935); P. Brown, *Augustine of Hippo* (Berkeley: University of California Press, 1967); J. N. D. Kelly, *Jerome* (London: Duckworth, 1975); and A. Momigliano, ed., *Conflict between Paganism and Christianity in the Fourth Century* (Oxford: Oxford University Press, 1963). Chester G. Starr, *Civilization and the Caesars* (New York: Norton, 1965), and C. M. Cochrane, *Christianity and Classical Culture* (New York: Oxford Galaxy GB7, 1957), treat the intellectual changes in detail, including the significance of the Arian heresy; see also M. L. W. Laistner, *Christianity and Pagan Culture in the Later Roman Empire* (Ithaca: Cornell University Press, 1967). Early Christian art is well illustrated by W. F. Volbach, *Early Christian Art* (London: Thames and Hudson, 1961); see also the magisterial study by C. R. Morey, *Early Christian Art* (2d ed.; Princeton: Princeton University Press, 1953), and the argument of E. H. Swift, *Roman Sources of Christian Art* (Westport, Conn.: Greenwood).

Samuel Dill, *Roman Society in the Last Century of the Western Empire* (Philadelphia: R. West), is a classic; the greatest historian of the Empire is admirably studied in E. A. Thompson, *Historical Work of Ammianus Marcellinus* (Cambridge: Cambridge University Press, 1947).

32

THE END OF THE ANCIENT WORLD

The major periods of human history are conventional divisions imposed on a seamless flow of generation after generation. Men were not suddenly aware in 27 B.C. that they were passing from the Roman Republic to the Empire, nor were the residents of western Europe conscious at any point that they were then becoming "medieval." As modern scholars look back, they can conclude that by 400 Augustine stood outside the ancient frame of thought and that in the next two generations the Germanic invasions ended the Empire politically in the west. But anyone reading the literary work of the era will be surprised again and again to discover that life went on with little recognition of change.

To understand what was happening at the end of the Roman Empire in the western provinces we must first review the rise of a stable agricultural unit in place of the cities and the decline of political loyalty, as against the consolidation of the Church's structure. Only on this base is it possible to assess the effects of the Germanic invasions and to isolate the issues involved in the "decline and fall." Our focus, accordingly, will be on the western provinces of the Empire, which produced that Latin, Christian, feudal society which is properly called medieval; for the modern civilization of the western world developed through this avenue of contact with antiquity. Yet it will be helpful also to consider what was taking place across Eurasia. In the period A.D. 300–700 there occurred a great wave of change from China through the Near East to far-off Britain, after which the ancient period everywhere was ended.

DISSOLUTION OF THE ROMAN EMPIRE IN THE WEST

Rise of the Villas. Throughout the Mediterranean world a significant development in agricultural organization had long been under way. Virtually self-sufficient, large estates were an ancestral characteristic of the eastern provinces, and had appeared in Greece and Italy during the Roman Republic as a vehicle for capitalistic agriculture. During the early centuries of the Empire land appears to have become steadily more concentrated in a few hands and to have passed frequently, by confiscation or by the execution of aristocrats, into the emperors' patrimony. Meanwhile, as slaves grew more difficult to get, there was a tendency to divide estates into plots of scattered strips, farmed by free tenants called *coloni* or by slave families; these tenants paid rents in money or, very

TABLE 10
Roman Emperors
A.D. 395—476

East		West		(Patricians or equivalent)
Arcadius	395—408	Honorius	395—423	(Stilicho 395—408)
				(Constantius 410—21)
Theodosius II	408—50	Valentinian III	425—55	(Aetius 433—54)
Marcian	450—57	Maximus	455—57	
Leo I	457—74	Majorian	457—61	
		Severus	461—67	(Ricimer 456—72)
		Anthemius	467—72	
		Olybrius	472—73	
Leo II	474	Glycerius	473—74	
Zeno	474—91	Julius Nepos	474—75	
		Romulus Augustulus	475—76	Odoacer 476—93)

often, in kind. That part of the estate retained by the master or overseer was farmed by the tenants, who gave part of their time to the task.

In the third century parts of the imperial property moved into aggressive hands, which could better keep the land in cultivation. When oppressed by imperial bailiffs, peasants at times threatened to flee from the imperial estates to private protectors. In other areas, where peasants had previously owned their own lands, they turned to the patronage (*patrocinium*) of local magnates for economic support or for protection against both the imperial soldiery and the barbarian invaders. Independent small landholders did not entirely disappear in the process—they remained in scattered areas throughout the Middle Ages—but the typical form of rural organization tended ever more to be the large estate dependent socially, economically, and even politically on the *villa* or country-house of the owner. Although this process can be followed alike in Asia Minor, Africa, and Gaul, to name only three areas, its effects were most significant in the western provinces, when joined to contemporary changes in urban life.

In the east the cities continued to be strong, based as they were on enduring industry and commerce; even Rome remained through the fourth century the center of a luxurious aristocratic life. In the inland districts of the west, however, many areas had reached only a very low level of civilization, and cities were mostly new creations of the Empire. Not deeply rooted enough to withstand the political and economic stresses of the third and following centuries, they tended to decline into fortified strongpoints; in most places the tiny area which was enclosed by walls, generally 25 to 50 acres, suggests a population of not more than 5000 and demonstrates their economic insignificance. By the fifth century the old forms of city government in the west had commonly yielded to military commanders, appointed to hold one or more cities like forts. Beside the "count" (*comes*) or "duke" (*dux*) usually stood a bishop as local protector, for ecclesiastical organization had long been based on the cities.

The western villas, on the other hand, throve. Archeological exploration has turned up countless luxurious mansions, often extending into veritable industrial complexes of forges, glassworks, and the like. Especially in Britain the villas of the fourth century reached a new peak, but in Gaul too the same picture is suggested both by the remains and by the verse of Ausonius. Everywhere in the west (except Italy) the nobility withdrew more and more from the cramped, melancholy towns to the villas where they might enjoy hunting and other sports, pictured in their mosaics, and a freer social life. Although this pattern foreshadowed that of the nobles of the Middle Ages, it should be noted that as late as Sidonius Apollinaris (c. 431–79), many great landowners still affected a cultured life of visiting, elegant dinners, and exchange of poems and letters, in the very period in which Clovis the Frank was rising to power.

Theoretically the writ of the emperors still ran in estates and cities alike, and the emperors of the fourth century struggled to stem the current by repeated bans on *patrocinium*, by asserting their sacred position, and by supporting the urban machinery. Yet the great senatorial families escaped from the crushing burdens of the *curiales* class while taking only a minor part in imperial government; and one desperate decree of 383 admitted that only provincial governors, not the cities, had any power to enforce collection of taxes on their estates. In the east the struggle to keep them under control was largely successful; in the west the rural nobility rose ever higher.

Sometimes, indeed, the peasants refused to accept their lot of serfdom calmly. The countryside of Africa was harassed by bands called *agonistae* or *circumcelliones,* who adopted the cloak of the Donatist heresy; in the fifth century the peasants at times turned in relief to the invading barbarians, who might free them from the terrific social and economic pressures of the decaying imperial system. More commonly, however, the tillers of the soil relied on their masters to protect them against barbarians and bureaucrats alike. In many ways the western provinces were reverting toward the Neolithic level of simple food-production, but in doing so they were fashioning a network of stable, independent cells which could survive the withering away of the imperial machinery and the disappearance of a money economy in the early Middle Ages. These cells became the manors of medieval Europe.

Decline in Political Loyalty. Although the apparatus of government and the military system were powerful elements in holding together the Roman Empire, they could be effective only so long as the subjects were bound together by a common culture and a common loyalty. Both bonds were declining by the fourth and fifth centuries. Here again the decline was more marked in the west than in the east, where the complicated tissues of urban civilization were tougher and more persistent.

True enough, the dwindling cultivated levels in the west remained attached to the ideals of the Empire on down into the fifth century, when two poets, Claudius Claudianus (active 395–404), and Rutilius Claudius Namatianus (active 416), celebrated the eternity and power of Rome in the most glowing terms it ever received. Apart from the great aristocrats, however, who could protect themselves by holding civil posts of distinction or by owning estates, the middling elements of the west smarted under the rapacity and injustice of the imperial bureaucrats. Salvian (*c.* 400–70), fiercely assailing this misgovernment, goes far toward explaining the collapse of western imperial authority in the observation: "In the districts taken over by the barbarians, there is one desire among all the Romans, that they should never again find it necessary to pass under Roman jurisdiction." [1]

A far more powerful loyalty, that to the Christian faith, rose higher and higher during the Later Empire, but this attachment had two great defects from the point of view of the state. In the first place, Christian loyalty was not a unified sentiment that could easily be directed in one specific channel. The sole means by which the Church could achieve common agreement was through councils, which were largely held in the east and therefore had only very limited representation from the west. Bishops in the latter area tended to look toward Rome, especially for guidance in matters of orthodox doctrine; by the time of Leo I, pope from 440 to 461, the medieval position of the papacy was beginning to emerge. Yet even western bishops sometimes followed a different line from that of Rome, and the views of Roman bishops and eastern leaders frequently clashed as a presage of the later division between Roman Catholic and Greek Orthodox churches. Nor could the orthodox guides anywhere put down the schism of heresies, which continued to spring up across the fifth and following centuries.

In the second place, a devout Christian was not necessarily inclined to support the political and social framework of secular life; in some ways the reverse was true. In general, to be sure, the machinery of the Church favored the survival of the imperial political structure. From the days of Eusebius there had been open appreciation of the imperial peace, which

[1] Salvian, *On the Governance of God* 5.8.

had facilitated the growth of Christianity; Augustine himself, while condemning the secular orientation of the state, had praised Roman political virtues in his *City of God*. Christian doctrine, moreover, came to feel that the end of the Empire would immediately be followed by the reign of Antichrist. Yet the early Christian assertion of independence from the state was reinforced in the preaching of Ambrose and John Chrysostom, and the western bishops of the fifth century commonly found it possible to strike compromises with the invading Germans which preserved their ecclesiastical structure without much concern for political matters.

Even more significant was the fact that many Christians deliberately turned away from secular life. If pagan thought became ever poorer, it was in large part due to the absorption of the more able men, such as Augustine, in the dynamic growth of Christian theology or in the challenges of Christian leadership; Ambrose, for instance, had been governor of Milan before his election as bishop in 373. Men of lesser abilities who were offended by the corruptness of secular politics and society could escape via monasticism.

Both pagans and Christian rulers fulminated against the ensuing rise of hermit life; and even Christian bishops cast worried glances at the ecstatic, almost inhuman quality of the monastic search for God. Augustine, in several works, underlined the need for man to love his fellow men even in seeking his own salvation. Yet the monastic life had gained popularity with a rush in Egypt after St. Antony's example (*c.* 270), and the introduction of more organized monastic life in the fourth century by Pachomius proved even more attractive to many men and women.

Whether in the self-denying life of the monasteries or in the more secular existence of the individual churches, Christians were grouped in powerful units which, like the incipient manors, could survive the political collapse of the Empire in the west. One must, indeed, wonder what would have happened in this area had not the two forms of life already been well implanted before the chaos of the Middle Ages. One unit preserved a fundamental stock of agricultural and industrial technology, as well as affording a frame for family life; the other carried on, through ecclesiastical organization and the use of writing, some of the most important political and cultural achievements of earlier centuries. And the essential promise of heavenly salvation remained an anchor to Christian life which actually encouraged men to endure their hardships on earth.

The Entry of the Germans (395–476). Throughout the fourth century the surface of the Later Empire appeared ever more despotic and the demands of the state more ruthless, while in reality the power of the emperors to reach the peasants or to claim the affection of their subjects was dwindling. This process of decay might have gone on indefinitely had not German tribes begun to pour across the frontiers (see Map 20).

The invasions of the late fourth and early fifth centuries were facilitated by the decline of the Empire, which weakened its armies and its will to resist. A critical factor in this respect was the final division of the Mediterranean world between Honorius and Arcadius, sons of Theodosius I; for thereafter the west, which was more directly threatened, could not call on the still-considerable strength of the east. Those German groupings which lay directly on the frontiers, moreover, were more civilized and much better organized now than they had been in the Early Empire, while the Romans themselves had become more barbarous. Far to the rear lay a powerful spur to the quickening advance of the Germans; for the inhabitants of the Eurasian steppe were beginning to move, a process which had also great effects on Persia, India, and China.

One group from the steppes, the Huns, had entered south Russia by 355 and destroyed the Ostrogothic kingdom on the Dnieper about 374. As the Huns moved on to the Hungarian plain, they frightened the Visigoths, who were allowed by the Empire to cross the Danube in 376. After the resulting disaster at Adrianople two years later the Visigoths had to be permitted to remain in the Balkans as an organized body, their king serving also as a Roman general. The young emperors after 395 each had a German commander-in-chief, Rufinus under Arcadius in the east and Stilicho under Honorius in the west. Through much of the fifth century the titular rulers were sorry recluses at Constantinople and Ravenna while generals entitled "patricians," that is, adopted fathers of the rulers, sought to govern their realms.

Unfortunately the weak, suspicious Honorius had his protector, Stilicho, murdered in 408 and thereby removed the bar which had held back the restless Visigoths. When Honorius went on to refuse their King Alaric the province of Noricum (south Austria), Alaric marched on

Rome in 410 and sacked the city of its more movable wealth. Alaric was a Roman "master of the soldiers" who, like Stilicho, had served in Theodosius' army, but the event shocked the Empire. By negotiation and by threats to their food supply, the Visigoths were eventually moved on to southern Gaul, then to Spain, and back to southwest Gaul. Here they were granted lands in 418 by the patrician Constantius as vassals of the Empire, but the Romans of the area remained under imperial government.

By this time other powerful German tribes had entered the Empire without permission. First came the Vandals, Alans, and Suevi, who broke across the Rhine and, thanks to their cavalry, drove rapidly across the Pyrenees in 408. In Spain they were partially wiped out by the Visigoths on imperial directives and were pushed away from the seacoast. The Suevi remained in northwest Spain; but in 429 the able Vandalic leader Gaiseric led his people across the straits of Gibraltar to Africa, where he secured Carthage in 439 and was reluctantly recognized by the Empire as independent in 442. Gaiseric became strong enough on the sea to attack Rome in 455 and to sack it once more; the patrician Aetius, who might have halted the attack, had been murdered by the emperor in the preceding year.

The entry of the Franks into Gaul was a more gradual process which had already begun in the days of the emperor Julian. By the middle of the fifth century the Franks, still heathen, held most of north-central Gaul, and the Burgundians sat astride the Rhine; in 436 the royal family of the latter people was exterminated at Worms by mercenary Huns under Aetius, the source of the Nibelungen legend. In Britain the bulk of the Roman troops were withdrawn by a pretender to the imperial throne in 407 and never returned; mercenary bodies of Saxons had already been used for coastal defense, and more Saxons, together with Angles and Jutes, came thereafter.

Romans and Germans alike faced a serious threat in the mid-fifth century, when the truly barbarous Huns irrupted from the Hungarian plain under Attila, ruler 434–53. The remnants of the imperial armies under Aetius and the Visigoths joined to defeat Attila at the Catalaunian plains near Troyes (451), but when he turned then to Italy only the embassy of Pope Leo I and heavy payments induced the Huns to withdraw. After the death of Attila the Huns split apart, but any effective imperial control from Ravenna swiftly dissolved over the western sea-coast towns and the "Roman" troops in Italy.

In 476, a date which is often taken as marking the end of the Roman Empire in the west, the German mercenary leader Odoacer deposed the usurper Romulus Augustulus, a boy with a truly ironic name, and sent the imperial paraphernalia to Constantinople. Even thereafter most of the Germanic chieftains gave deference to the emperor in the east, so long as he did not actually try to rule them; and Odoacer himself was overthrown in 493 by Theodoric, leader of the Ostrogoths, who had been directed toward Italy by the eastern emperor.

Effects of the German Invasions. To set any great development in its proper perspective the historian must always distinguish short-range, medium-range, and long-range effects, which may not always be of the same character. With respect to the entry of the Germans, the immediate results were not revolutionary. The best estimate of the numbers of invaders puts them at 5 per cent of the imperial population; when the Vandals crossed to Africa, they numbered only 80,000. Generally the Germans settled in rural clumps, taking one-third to two-thirds of the land in the unlucky estates which they commandeered; the kings governed their Germans by German law but continued the normal Roman administration and Roman law for their other subjects. Since the Germans had no distinctive culture of their own, they accepted what they found. Nowhere except in far-removed Britain did a Germanic tongue survive; in modern French only some 300 Germanic words remain as a dim reflection of the German conquest. Nor were the new realms powerfully and enduringly rooted. By 700 further invasions by more distant German tribes and by the Arabs in Africa and Spain had ended every Germanic state of 500 save the Frankish kingdom and the Anglo-Saxon principalities.

As this instability may suggest, the medium-range effects of the entry of the Germans were a further acceleration of the decline in the west or, in other terms, the beginnings of the Middle Ages. The Germanic principle of personal loyalty, rather than adherence to abstract ideals and territorial unity, was not a solid base in an era of unrest; and each king's power depended greatly upon his own force of character. The population of western Europe continued to sink, and economic deterioration went on, with minor interruptions.

During the first years of Germanic rule in the fifth and sixth centuries there was still a good deal of intellectual and artistic vigor. At the hidden capital of Ravenna several great basilicas were constructed, which still glow with superb mosaic decoration from the time of Theodoric the Ostrogoth and Justinian.[2] Two literary figures also graced Ostrogothic Italy: Cassiodorus Senator (*c.* 490–*c.* 575), of an old Roman house, who served Theodoric as formal secretary and administrator before retiring to Vivarium, where he helped to save Latin manuscripts by copying them; and Boethius (*c.* 480–524), equally noble, who gave to the Middle Ages much of its knowledge of mathematics and Aristotelian logic ere he was executed on charges of treason. Then literary activity withered.

Eventually, however, western Europe was again able to move forward, and at least from the twelfth century progressed on a great path which has carried it without interruption down to the present. The long-range effects of the Germanic invasions, indeed, may not have been as destructive as they appear in looking at the decline of the centuries after 500; but before considering this aspect more fully we need first to examine briefly the end of the ancient world across Eurasia as a whole.

THE REST OF EURASIA

The East Roman Empire. Violent winds of change blew over Eurasia in the era A.D. 300–700. Long ago, in the early first millennium B.C., the civilized and uncivilized belts of this land mass had achieved a state of balance, which underlay the emergence of the historic civilizations of China, India, the Near East, and Greece and their subsequent expansion. Now that balance yielded, and invaders both from the northern steppes and from the Arabian peninsula were to cause repeated upsets down to the attacks of Timurlane in the fifteenth century after Christ.

In large part this turbulence was the result of the weakening of the fabric of civilization itself, which we can best see in the Roman Empire and in Han China; but it may also have been due to a greater aggressiveness of the mounted nomads of the Eurasian steppe. Their blows,

[2] In the apse of the church of San Vitale at Ravenna, built 526–47, were placed facing scenes of the emperor Justinian and his wife Theodora. Plate XXXII shows in detail the head of Theodora, a solemn, dignified, symbolic figure. Against a green background and yellow halo she is adorned with red and green jewels and chains of pearls which drop down from her diadem.

which often set other peoples in motion as well, varied greatly in intensity, depending upon geographical conditions and accidents of leadership. As it happened, the two poles of China and western Europe suffered more severely than did the center of the civilized belt.

The eastern part of the Roman Empire, thus, was shielded from the direct onslaughts of the Germans by the Balkans and by its impregnable fortress of Constantinople. Skillful diplomacy, bribery, and naval command also played a part; these rested on the wealth and shipping produced by the still-vigorous economic life of the eastern Mediterranean. By the fifth century, indeed, the rulers of the East Roman Empire were finding it possible to relinquish some of the iron controls imposed on society and economic activity in the previous 200 years. In the countryside the landlords remained highly important but never quite shook off imperial authority; the cities maintained their strength in the era in which many western towns became simple forts. Trade remained significant and was even resumed to some degree with the farther east; early in the sixth century a retired sailor, Cosmas Indicopleustes, wrote an account of his journey to the Malabar coast of India. Among other examples of the survival of scholarship, legal studies noticeably revived in the eastern law schools.

For a time in the early fifth century it nevertheless appeared that the Germans might take over the court by serving as troops and generals for the weak emperors of the Theodosian line, but this danger was largely removed by the emperor Zeno (474–96), who turned to recruit native stocks from Isauria in south Asia Minor and from Thrace. In the next century Justinian (527–65) could even essay to reconquer much of Italy and north Africa and paid out imperial funds on a great building program which produced among other works Haghia Sophia, the greatest domed church of eastern Christianity. By Justinian's death, however, the East Roman Empire lay financially exhausted, and the important provinces of Syria and Egypt were sullenly discontent. Immediately their dissatisfaction showed itself in adherence to the monophysite heresy; in the seventh century they fell away easily to the conquering Arabs.

The East Roman Empire was a fascinating blend of Hellenic culture, Christian faith, and Roman principles of administration and law. Precisely when this blend passed into the style called Byzantine is a much-argued point. The inception certainly was the building of Constantinople early in the fourth century. Yet as late as the reign of Justinian the language of the court was still officially Latin; Justinian himself directed the great compilation in Latin of the *Corpus iuris civilis,* the form in which later ages knew Roman law. Justinian, however, closed the pagan philosophical schools of Athens and abolished the consulate in 541 as a meaningless survival; from his period on, arts and letters entered ever more into the distinctive Byzantine world.

Persia and India. The center of the civilized belt in Eurasia, from Mesopotamia to the Indus-Ganges basins, also suffered severe blows, but at a later date than most other areas. The Sassanian rulers of Persia held their own in repeated wars with the East Roman Empire and even forced Justinian to pay tribute; they also maintained and at times extended their southeastern frontier toward India. Internally, however, the village landlords gained ever greater power over the peasants, and the repeated Hunnish onslaughts from the north finally brought the death of King Peroz in a battle in 484. Thereafter the Sassanian rulers were little more than vassals of the White Huns for a century until the fabulous reign of Chosroes I (531-79). But like his contemporary Justinian, Chosroes could give no real strength to his state; in 637-51 it fell before the onrush of the Arabs.

In north India the Gupta dynasty had emerged by 320 and for the next century and a half maintained a well-organized state, though local power fell into the hands of landlords and the use of money declined. In its capital of Pataliputra the Chinese Buddhist pilgrim Fa-hsien found that the great palace and halls of Asoka still stood; two great monasteries, one for each of the two major Buddhist sects, were thronged with monks who taught their doctrines to eager students; the land was peaceful, and men could come and go as they desired from one rich town to another.

The Gupta era has been called a Hindu Renaissance, for the heavy currents from the west in Mauryan and Kushan times had now been absorbed and much altered in the process. The rulers were tolerant but favored Hinduism, which blossomed in arts, letters, and sciences alike. As the Brahmans consolidated their hold on education, Sanskrit grammar was clearly defined, and the great Sanskrit epics took final form. The renowned Indian poet, Kalidasa, whose greatest play was the *Sakuntala,* lived in the early fifth century; in the same era worked some of the greatest Indian sculptors and painters in the Ajanta caves and else-where. Buddhism, on the other hand, was steadily ebbing; in becoming a religion that could spread to the rest of Asia, it had lost its basic ties with the main stream of Indian thought.

By the last decade of the fifth century this era of peace had ended, for the Huns had come. The last major Gupta king held them at bay a short while; then Sassanian Persia fell vassal to the White Huns, who soon added Afghanistan and north India to their temporary empire. The invasions of the Huns were a turning point in Indian history, for subsequent ages remembered almost nothing of what had occurred before; from that point, too, no more significant native dynasties emerged in India.

Collapse of Han China. The similarities between Han China and the Early Roman Empire were amazingly extensive, as we saw in Chapter 29. Even more remarkable and suggestive is the parallel in the decline of these advanced societies.

In both areas, thus, internal decay came first. Against a background of declining population and decreasing economic activity, the local lords became ever more important in the Chinese countryside. Han China temporarily split apart in the third century into three separate political and economic realms. In the period 280–317 a brief restoration of unity was achieved by the Chin line, which was marked by the same bureaucratic corruption, reliance on violent edicts, and taxation in kind as that which characterized the system of Diocletian and Constantine.

The ensuing disruption of China by external invasion seems to have been more abrupt and complete superficially than was the collapse of Roman rule. A branch of the Huns set up a line of local rulers in north China early in the fourth century; then Mongolian nomads as well as Tibetans poured in. The remnants of the previous governmental structure fled to south China, together with many of the literate upper classes; from this point dates the full absorption of south China into the pattern of Chinese culture.

In the north a kaleidoscopic variety of Hunnish, Mongol, and Turkish rulers tried to maintain the advanced civilization they found, and were remarkably open to the preachings of Buddhist missionaries; but their intent was outweighed by their destructive spirit. China remained divided thenceforth until the late sixth century. Art and literature suffered severely; admission to governing circles no longer depended upon knowledge of the Confucian classics. Buddhism and Taoism became popular modes of salvation, and Christianity (in its Nestorian form) even made its way overland to north China.

In China, however, the old patterns of civilization were far more deeply rooted than had been Greco-Roman culture in western Europe. In the centuries of chaos after the fall of the Han dynasty practical Chinese thinkers invented new devices like the water mill and the wheelbarrow, expanded many scientific fields, and preserved the old humanistic knowledge. From the seventh century on China revived rapidly. One obvious mark of the greater endurance of Chinese civilization is the greater degree to which it absorbed its invaders; another may be found in the fact that Buddhism (as noted in Chapter 29) had to adapt itself to the basic premises of Confucianism far more than Christianity yielded to Greco-Roman civilization.

OLD AND NEW

The End of the Ancient World. Across Eurasia the period from A.D. 300 to 700 thus brought tremendous changes. If we compare it with that earlier upheaval which occurred in the centuries centering on 1000 B.C., the dimensions of the Germanic and Hunnic invasions shrink; for they nowhere cut the inherited threads of civilization as ruthlessly as did the invaders who brought the fall of the Minoan-Mycenaean world, of the Hittite empire, and (somewhat earlier) of the Indus civilization.

Nevertheless the centuries after A.D. 300 formed a dismal era for many peoples, a great turning point which must be termed the end of the ancient world. The change did not take place everywhere at the same time or with the same intensity; the history of Eurasia cannot be compressed into facile patterns of uniformity. Yet whether one explores in detail the history of modern China, of modern India, or of modern Europe, the story after this period is distinctly different from that which lay before.

Why, then, did the change take place? And exactly what is its meaning in the long development of human history? Questions of this nature are so sweeping that they can have no pat answers; they are, indeed, upsetting questions even to pose. Yet each responsible historian is obligated to set down his own interpretation, when queried; but in doing so he must seek to provide his interrogator with food for thought and disagreement. To narrow the field for greater precision, let us turn back to the western provinces of the Roman Empire, the area from which modern European civilization has sprung and also the district which suffered most severely in the end of the ancient world.

The "Decline and Fall." Throughout the Middle Ages men in western Europe felt themselves directly linked to Rome — a significant fact in itself in suggesting the fundamental continuity between ancient and medieval. Rome, however, they visualized in terms of the Later Empire, as preserved in Justinian's code and in the organization of the church. During the Renaissance of the fourteenth and fifteenth centuries scholars, artists, and despots came to glorify the earlier Caesars, and citizens of such free cities as Florence even at times appreciated some of the qualities of the Republic. As men thus looked back, they began to realize there had been a break, and the term "medieval" was soon coined.

Once the modern world decided that there had been a "Decline and Fall of the Roman Empire," as Edward Gibbon entitled his great study, it sought to explain why this lugubrious interruption of civilization — as the modern western world egotistically measured the event — had occurred. An historian can gain both profit and amusement from surveying the bewildering diversity of explanations which have been seriously advanced.

Some scholars fix on a mechanical or external cause, independent of human foresight, for example, exhaustion of the soil, the rise of malaria, plague (as under Marcus Aurelius), changes in climate, or even the Germanic invasions themselves. Others seek an evil person or bad policy, such as the unworthy emperor Commodus (180–92), or the loss of power by the old upper classes in the third or fourth centuries. Others still slip off into truly mystical explanations by talking of the "victory of the Orient," that is, the purported conquest of Greco-Roman rationality by Oriental faith; by emphasizing an assumed foundation of the imperial economy upon slave exploitation; or even by asserting that after the fall of Athens in 404 B.C. classical civilization was doomed.

Sometimes such explanations can absolutely be disproved. There is, for instance, no solid evidence of any change in climate or of exhaustion of the soil. Other factors can be shown to be merely attendant circumstances; malaria, thus, became more widespread as cultivation of the soil declined. More generalized explanations will commonly be found to have a close link with the social, religious, or intellectual preconceptions of the modern scholars who have advanced them; for in the end all students are really trying to explain the modern world when they speak of the past. And so, as their points of view may clash on the meaning of the present and hopes or fears of the future, so too vary their reconstructions of the past.

Although this fact must at times disturb historical students who hope to find a certainty in history which they cannot establish in the present, it is not grounds for despair. The true test of historical spirit is the ability to broaden the preconceptions born of contemporary life as one investigates the complicated tissue of men's past development; for thereby one comes to understand more clearly not only the history of a past age but also the character of the world which surrounds us today. The student of the Roman Empire, thus, must always keep in mind that its history was not a simple one. On the one hand classical civilization became sterile, and the political and economic organization of the western provinces underwent a serious change which, as measured by earlier standards, must be called a decline. Yet at the same time a new scheme of thought about the most fundamental qualities of man was rising. Both developments, moreover, were long protracted in chains which extended back clearly to the second century after Christ and, less obviously, into earlier centuries.

Any explanation of the "decline and fall" must accordingly be phrased in wide terms; and it is the conviction of the present writer, which has underlain the story of the past several chapters, that the historian must always come back to the movement of human emotion and the human mind in his deepest probings of the forces moving man's history. In this area one great key may be suggested which will perhaps unlock an understanding of the basic pattern — though not of all the ramifications — of the progress of imperial civilization. Mankind, that is to say, was liberated from its ties to state and to society in the Empire to a degree never before known, for the bonds of family and other social units, as well as active participation in political life, sharply diminished. One result has already been suggested in Chapter 27, the inability of men to create new thoughts within the inherited classical pattern. Another was their turn, as noted in Chapter 28, to a new social and intellectual framework in Christianity, which bound them to each other and to a transcendental force above. To couple the old and new, however, was more than could be achieved once the political and economic structure of the western provinces had started to deteriorate, as we observed in Chapters 30 and 31; and those external pressures which have been discussed in the past two chapters accelerated the plunge. The full triumphs of the new outlook could not be achieved until western society had fashioned a new political and economic organization in the Middle Ages.

The long-range effects of the Germanic invasion and of the end of the Roman Empire in the west, to return to a remark made earlier, were perhaps not bad but rather essentially good. Politically, for instance, the result was to wipe out the despotism of the Later Empire. This despotism was really a "dead end" to ancient political development; for in it all political capacity had been concentrated in one man, aided by a corrupt, tyrannical bureaucracy which governed the subjects like cogs. The organization of the Germanic kingdoms was very simple, but it could proceed afresh on new lines; and not all that was useful in the past was lost. Regional ties in the Middle Ages could never quite wipe out the memory of the union of large areas under a single ruler. The kings of the western states became very weak, but they did not vanish; about these royal houses the modern national kingdoms were to rise. Beside the kings stood the Church, which preserved much of the administrative achievement and law of the Empire; but here too a basic principle of the ancient world, the union of Church and state, had essentially been broken.

Intellectually the view of man, of the world, and of God which underlay Christian thought was of a new order, which had broken through the limitations of ancient culture. When western Europe began to revive, its thinkers were able to drive forward on new lines, fructified but not unduly hampered by the inheritance of the past; throughout the cultural diversity of medieval and modern times there lurks a concept of the unity of western civilization, based as it is — whether in Russia or in Britain — on a common classical background.

Economically, too, as one views the technological and social basis of ancient industry and commerce, one cannot see any possibility that this structure could have continued to expand indefinitely, or that it could have endured as political conditions worsened. The agricultural units which survived, the manors, resembled in many ways the villages from which urban life had sprung millennia before; yet the practice of agriculture in the Middle Ages was far above that of prehistoric times in variety and rotation of crops, quality of implements, and other important aspects, and the life of the nobles was, despite its rudeness, a thing unknown in the prehistoric era. One must also note that slavery virtually disappeared in western Europe; once the battle for survival had been won, the economic development of this area proceeded apace, and men might eventually hope to create a society in which not the few but the many could escape grinding poverty. An important factor in this possibility was the willingness of men in the medieval period to experiment and develop technology; new ways of doing things and of using non-human power — wind and water first — are a hallmark of the economic development of western Europe from the Middle Ages down to the present.

In sum the outward decay of the west was a necessary, if immediately devastating, step in its later surge; for in that decay the limiting bonds of ancient civilization were snapped. The other civilized areas of Eurasia clung more fully to their earlier cultures, and accordingly were the centers of intellectual and political life during the medieval period of western Europe. Yet once the energies of this relatively tiny area were unleashed, its peoples were to spring forward; the history of modern times is largely of the impact of that spring on the rest of the globe.

BIBLIOGRAPHY

Sources. Throughout the era of violent change at the end of the ancient world literary and other evidence sloped off sharply everywhere; but it does not appear appropriate here to survey in detail the writers over this extended period. For the western provinces Salvian, *On the Governance of God,* tr. E. M. Sanford (New York: Octagon, 1967), gives a fearful picture of imperial corruption; but this is to be corrected by Sidonius Apollinaris (Loeb Classical Library; *Letters,* tr. O. M. Dalton, 2 vols. [Oxford: Oxford University Press, 1915]). Some of Boethius' works, including his famous *Consolation of Philoso-*

phy written during his imprisonment, are translated by H. K. Stewart and E. K. Rand (Loeb Classical Library); for Cassiodorus' *Letters,* see Thomas Hodgkin, *The Letters of Cassiodorus* (London: Frowde, 1886). Some of the fragmentary sources for the political history of the fifth century may be found in C. D. Gordon, *Age of Attila* (Ann Arbor: University of Michigan Press, 1960).

An interesting picture of the troubled state of the East Roman Empire about A.D. 400 is given by Synesius, bishop of Ptolemais, in his *Letters,* tr. A. Fitzgerald (London: Oxford University Press, 1926), and *Essays and Hymns,* tr. A. Fitzgerald (London: Oxford University Press, 1930). The later conquests and building program of Justinian are surveyed by Procopius (Loeb Classical Library), who also retailed scandal in his *Secret History* (Loeb Classical Library). An illustration of the relative tranquillity of the farther east is to be found in *The Travels of Fa-hsien (399–414 A.D.),* tr. H. A. Giles (Cambridge: Cambridge University Press, 1923).

Further Reading. The course of events in the western provinces is described briefly in Solomon Katz, *Decline of Rome and the Rise of Medieval Europe* (Ithaca: Cornell University Press, 1961); and F. W. Walbank, *The Awful Revolution* (Toronto: Toronto University Press, 1979), who presents a Marxist interpretation. Recent Russian historians, incidentally, have been much interested in the social strife of the period. Fuller studies on the transition to medieval Europe are H. St. L. B. Moss, *Birth of the Middle Ages, 395–814* (Oxford: Oxford Paperback 60, 1963); *Cambridge Economic History,* Vols. I–II (Cambridge: Cambridge University Press, 1942–52); and A. H. M. Jones, *The Later Roman Empire,* 3 vols. (Oxford: Blackwell, 1964). The invasions proper are studied by J. B. Bury, *Invasion of Europe by the Barbarians* (New York: Norton, 1967), and E. A. Thompson, *History of Attila and the Huns* (Westport, Conn.: Greenwood, 1975).

The Byzantine Empire is superficially treated by David T. Rice, *The Byzantines* (New York: Praeger, 1962); much more successfully, in N. H. Baynes and H. St. L. B. Moss, *Byzantium* (Oxford: Oxford Paperback 16, 1961). For later Sassanian times, see the general works listed in

Bibliography, Chapter 30; for Chinese and Indian history, the general studies in Bibliography, Chapter 28. The Gupta and later achievements in the Ajanta caves are pictured in M. Singh, *India: Paintings from the Ajanta Caves* (New York: New York Graphic Society, 1954).

Besides the explanations of the "decline and fall" noted above, see also the concluding section in M. I. Rostovtzeff, *Social and Economic History of the Roman Empire,* 2 vols. (2d ed.; Oxford: Oxford University Press, 1957); and in Chester G. Starr, *Civilization and the Caesars* (New York: Norton, 1965), and *The Roman Empire, 27 B.C.–A.D. 476: A Study in Survival* (New York: Oxford University Press, 1982). R. M. Haywood, *Myth of Rome's Fall* (Westport, Conn.: Greenwood, 1979), and S. Mazzarino, *The End of the Ancient World* (Westport, Conn.: Greenwood, 1976), summarize the principal theories.

The immediate survival of classical culture is noted in E. K. Rand, *Founders of the Middle Ages* (New York: Dover), and E. S. Duckett, *Latin Writers of the Fifth Century* (Hamden, Conn.: Shoe String Press, 1969), and *Gateway to the Middle Ages* (Ann Arbor: University of Michigan Press, 1961). Longer-range survival is discussed in G. Highet, *The Classical Tradition* (New York: Oxford Galaxy, 1957); two fine examples are K. Clark, *The Nude: A Study in Ideal Form* (New York: Doubleday Anchor, 1959), and J. Seznec, *Survival of the Pagan Gods* (Princeton: Princeton University Press, 1972).

GENERAL BIBLIOGRAPHY

GENERAL BIBLIOGRAPHY

In selecting the bibliographies of this volume, I have kept always in mind the needs of the beginning student of ancient history. Such a student will soon discover that not every major work is written in English, but it seems pointless here to list volumes in the western European languages, let alone Finnish, Russian, Turkish, and Japanese. The truly curious and intelligent man can easily make his way from the general studies in this bibliography both to the fundamental works in foreign languages and to specialized monographs.

Again I have included, as far as possible, only books published in the past generation, not because they are necessarily better but because they will lead students to the other, earlier studies. Works of lasting value are often reprinted; I have given the latest issue wherever possible, so that the dates of publication given herein (not all reprints bear dates) and publishers are not necessarily those of original issue in such cases. Books bearing on the subject of only one chapter have not normally been repeated below.

INTRODUCTORY

GEOGRAPHY AND CLIMATE

H. Bengtson, *Grosser historischer Weltatlas,* Vol. I (4th ed.; Munich: Bayerischer Schulbuch-Verlag, 1963).
C. E. P. Brooks, *Climate through the Ages* (New York: Dover, 1970).
Max Cary and E. H. Warmington, *The Ancient Explorers* (Harmondsworth: Pelican A420, 1963).

Max Cary, *Geographic Background of Greek and Roman History* (Oxford: Oxford University Press, 1967).

N. G. L. Pounds, *An Historical Geography of Europe 450 B.C.–A.D. 1330* (Cambridge: Cambridge University Press, 1973).

Ellen C. Semple, *Geography of the Mediterranean Region: Its Relation to Ancient History* (New York: AMS Press).

Harlow Shapley, ed., *Climatic Change* (Cambridge, Mass.: Harvard University Press, 1953).

A. A. M. van der Heyden and H. H. Scullard, *Atlas of the Classical World* (London: Nelson, 1960).

C. Vita-Finzi, *The Mediterranean Valleys* (Cambridge: Cambridge University Press, 1969).

ARCHEOLOGY

George Bass, *Archaeology beneath the Sea* (New York: Harper and Row, 1976).

Geoffrey Bibby, *Testimony of the Spade* (New York: Mentor, 1974).

R. J. Braidwood, *Archaeologists and What They Do* (New York: Franklin Watts, 1960).

Glyn Daniel, *The Idea of Prehistory* (Harmondsworth: Penguin A650, 1964).

Jack Finegan, *Archaeology of World Religions* (Princeton: Princeton University Press, 1952).

Kathleen M. Kenyon, *Beginning in Archaeology* (New York: Praeger PPS41, 1961).

Paul MacKendrick, *The Greek Stones Speak* (New York: Norton, 1979).

Paul MacKendrick, *The Mute Stones Speak: The Story of Archaeology in Italy* (New York: Norton, 1976).

Richard Stillwell et al., *The Princeton Encyclopedia of Classical Sites* (Princeton: Princeton University Press, 1976).

GENERAL HISTORIES AND DICTIONARIES

Hermann Bengtson, *Introduction to Ancient History* (Berkeley: University of California Press, 1976).

Cambridge Ancient History, 12 vols. (Cambridge: Cambridge University Press, 1923–39); new edition of Vols. I–III in publication.

Fustel de Coulanges, *Ancient City* (New York: Doubleday Anchor A76, 1980).

Mason Hammond, *The City in the Ancient World* (Cambridge, Mass.: Harvard University Press, 1972).

F. M. Heichelheim, *Ancient Economic History,* I–III (2d and 3d eds. Sijthoff, 1968–70).

Herbert J. Muller, *Freedom in the Ancient World* (New York: Harpers, 1961).

Oxford Classical Dictionary (2d ed.; Oxford: Oxford University Press, 1970).

A. E. Samuel, *Greek and Roman Chronology* (Munich: C. H. Beck, 1972).

SPECIAL TOPICS

D. and P. Bothwell, *Food in Antiquity* (New York: Praeger, 1969).

A. Burford, *Craftsman in Greek and Roman Society* (Ithaca: Cornell University Press, 1972).

Lionel Casson, *Ships and Seamanship in the Ancient World* (Princeton: Princeton University Press, 1971).

Lionel Casson, *Travel in the Ancient World* (Toronto: University of Toronto Press, 1974).

M. I. Finley, *Ancient Slavery and Modern Ideology* (New York: Viking, 1980).

Y. Garlan, *War in the Ancient World* (New York: Norton, 1975).

H. A. Harris, *Sport in Greece and Rome* (London: Thames & Hudson, 1972).

J. F. Healey, *Mining and Metallurgy in the Greek and Roman World* (London: Thames & Hudson, 1978).

J. G. Landels, *Engineering in the Ancient World* (Berkeley: University of California Press, 1978).

N. Lewis, *Papyrus in Antiquity* (Oxford: Clarendon Press, 1974).

A. C. Lovejoy, *Primitivism and Related Ideas in Antiquity* (New York: Octagon, 1965).

H. I. Marrou, *History of Education in Antiquity* (New York: Mentor, 1964).

Georg Misch, *History of Autobiography in Antiquity* (Westport, Conn.: Greenwood).

L. A. Moritz, *Grain-Mills and Flour in Classical Antiquity* (Oxford: Oxford University Press, 1958).

H. A. Ormerod, *Piracy in the Ancient World* (Totowa, N.J.: Rowman, 1978).

S. B. Pomeroy, *Goddesses, Whores, Wives and Slaves: Women in Classical Antiquity* (New York: Schocken, 1976).

D. S. Robertson, *Handbook of Greek and Roman Architecture* (2d ed.; Cambridge: Cambridge University Press, 1969).

W. L. Rodgers, *Greek and Roman Naval Warfare* (Annapolis: United States Naval Institute, 1964).

H. J. Rose, *Religion in Greece and Rome* (New York: Harper Torchbook, 1959).

J. Holland Rose, *Mediterranean in the Ancient World* (Chicago: Ares, 1980).

Giorgio de Santillana, *Origins of Scientific Thought* (New York: Mentor MQ336, 1961).

Charles Singer and others, *History of Technology,* Vols. I–II (Oxford: Oxford University Press, 1954–56).

F. M. Snowden, *Blacks in Antiquity* (Cambridge, Mass.: Harvard University Press, 1970).

B. L. van der Waerden, *Science Awakening* (2d ed.; New York: Oxford University Press, 1961).

W. L. Westermann, *Slave Systems of Greek and Roman Antiquity* (Philadelphia: American Philosophical Society, 1955).

ANCIENT NEAR EAST

Edward Chiera, *They Wrote on Clay* (Chicago: University of Chicago Phoenix P2, 1956).

R. C. Dentan, ed., *Idea of History in the Ancient Near East* (New Haven: Yale University Press, 1955).

Henri Frankfort, *Art and Architecture of the Ancient Orient* (rev. ed.; Harmondsworth: Penguin, 1971).

Henri Frankfort and others, *Intellectual Adventure of Ancient Man* (Chicago: University of Chicago Press, 1977).

Henri Frankfort, *Kingship and the Gods* (Chicago: University of Chicago Press, 1978).

Richard N. Frye, *Heritage of Persia* (Cleveland: World, 1963).

René Ghirshman, *Iran* (Harmondsworth: Penguin A239, 1978).

W. W. Hallo and W. K. Simpson, *The Ancient Near East* (New York: Harcourt Brace Jovanovich, 1971).

Jacquetta Hawkes, *The First Great Civilizations* (New York: Knopf, 1973).

S. H. Hooke, *Babylonian and Assyrian Religion* (Norman: University of Oklahoma Press, 1963).

S. N. Kramer, ed., *Mythologies of the Ancient World* (New York: Doubleday Anchor A229, 1961).

Seton Lloyd, *Art of the Ancient Near East* (New York: Praeger PPS96, 1961).

Isaac Mendelsohn, *Slavery in the Ancient Near East* (Westport, Conn.: Greenwood, 1978).

S. Moscati, *Ancient Semitic Civilizations* (New York: Putnam Capricorn 202, 1960).

S. Moscati, *Face of the Ancient Orient* (New York: Doubleday Anchor A289, 1963).

Otto Neugebauer, *Exact Sciences in Antiquity* (2d ed.; New York: Dover, 1969).

J. Oates, *Babylon* (London: Thames & Hudson, 1979).

A. Leo Oppenheim, *Ancient Mesopotamia* (Chicago: University of Chicago Press, 1977).

James B. Pritchard, ed., *Ancient Near East in Pictures* (Princeton: Princeton University Press, 1958–73).

James B. Pritchard, ed., *Ancient Near Eastern Texts Relating to the Old Testament* (Princeton: Princeton University Press, 1955; supplementary volume, 1969).

H. W. F. Saggs, *Everyday Life in Babylonia and Assyria* (New York: Putnam, 1965).

Henry E. Sigerist, *History of Medicine,* Vols. I–II (New York: Oxford University Press, 1961–67).

Yigael Yadin, *The Art of Warfare in Biblical Lands,* 2 vols. (New York: McGraw-Hill, 1963).

GREECE
(INCLUDING HELLENISTIC AGE)

SOURCES

W. H. Auden, ed., *Portable Greek Reader* (New York: Viking, 1952).

G. W. Botsford and E. G. Sihler, ed., *Hellenic Civilization* (New York: Octagon, 1965).

M. R. Cohen and I. E. Drabkin, *Source Book in Greek Science* (Cambridge, Mass.: Harvard University Press, 1959).

F. M. Cornford, *Greek Religious Thought from Homer to the Age of Alexander* (New York: AMS Press) (other volumes in this series cover medicine, ed. A. J. Brock; astronomy, ed. T. L. Heath; economics, ed. M. L. W. Laistner, etc.).

Francis R. B. Godolphin, ed., *The Greek Historians* (New York: Random House, 1942).

Moses Hadas, ed., *The Greek Poets* (New York: Modern Library 203, 1953).

Loeb Classical Library (Cambridge, Mass.: Harvard University Press), translations and texts of most major Greek authors.

POLITICAL AND ECONOMIC

F. E. Adcock, *Greek and Macedonian Art of War* (Berkeley: University of California Paperback 54, 1967).

G. W. Botsford and C. A. Robinson, Jr., *Hellenic History* (5th ed.; New York: Macmillan, 1969).

R. J. Buck, *A History of Boeotia* (Edmonton: University of Alberta Press, 1979).

J. B. Bury, *History of Greece to the Death of Alexander,* rev. by Russell Meiggs (4th ed.; New York: Macmillan, 1975).

V. Ehrenberg, *The Greek State* (2d ed.; London: Methuen, 1974).

V. Ehrenberg, *From Solon to Socrates* (New York: Barnes and Noble, 1973).

W. G. Forrest, *History of Sparta 950–152* B.C. (London: Hutchinson, 1968).

George Grote, *History of Greece,* 12 vols. (New York: Dutton reprint, 1934).

N. G. L. Hammond, *History of Greece to 322* B.C. (2d ed.; Oxford: Oxford University Press, 1977).

Johannes Hasebroek, *Trade and Politics in Ancient Greece* (London: Bell, 1979).

C. Hignett, *History of the Athenian Constitution to the End of the Fifth Century* B.C. (Oxford: Oxford University Press, 1970).

John Walter Jones, *Law and Legal Theory of the Greeks* (New York: Adler, 1980).

T. Kelly, *A History of Argos to 500* B.C. (Minneapolis: University of Minnesota Press, 1976).

R. Legon, *History of Megara* (Ithaca: Cornell University Press, 1980).

D. M. MacDowell, *Law In Classical Athens* (Ithaca: Cornell University Press, 1978).

H. Michell, *Economics of Ancient Greece* (2d ed.; Cambridge: Heffer, 1958).

J. S. Morrison and R. T. Williams, *Greek Oared Ships 900–322* B.C. (Cambridge: Cambridge University Press, 1968).

John L. Myres, *Political Ideas of the Greeks* (New York: AMS Press, 1971).

M. I. Rostovtzeff, *Social and Economic History of the Hellenistic World,* 3 vols. (Oxford: Oxford University Press, 1941).

T. A. Sinclair, *History of Greek Political Thought* (2d ed.; London: Routledge and Paul, 1967).

Chester G. Starr, *Economic and Social Growth of Early Greece* (New York: Oxford University Press, 1977).

Chester G. Starr, *Political Intelligence in Classical Greece* (Leiden: Brill, 1974).

W. W. Tarn and G. T. Griffith, *Hellenistic Civilization* (London: Methuen, 1974).

GREEK CIVILIZATION

A. W. H. Adkins, *Moral Values and Political Behaviour in Ancient Greece* (Ithaca: Cornell University Press, 1972).

A. Andrewes, *Greek Society* (Penguin, 1975).

K. J. Dover, *Greek Homosexuality* (London: Duckworth, 1978).

M. I. Finley and H. W. Pleket, *The Olympic Games* (New York: Viking, 1976).

R. Flacelière, *Daily Life in Greece at the Time of Pericles* (New York: Macmillan, 1966).

W. Jaeger, *Paideia,* 2 vols. (2d ed.; New York: Oxford University Press, 1943-45).

H. D. F. Kitto, *The Greeks* (Penguin, 1951).

B. Snell, *Discovery of the Mind* (New York: Harper Torchbook, 1960).

G. E. M. de Ste. Croix, *The Class Struggle in the Ancient Greek World* (Ithaca: Cornell University Press, 1981).

Chester G. Starr, *Origins of Greek Civilization, 1100–650 B.C.* (New York: Knopf, 1961).

ARTS

J. Boardman, *Greek Art* (rev. ed.; London: Thames & Hudson, 1973).

J. Boardman, *Greek Gems and Finger Rings* (New York: Abrams, 1971).

R. M. Cook, *Greek Painted Pottery* (rev. ed.; London: Methuen, 1972).

W. B. Dinsmoor, *Architecture of Ancient Greece* (3d ed.; New York: Norton, 1975).

I. T. Hill, *Ancient City of Athens* (Cambridge, Mass.: Harvard University Press, 1953).

C. M. Kraay, *Archaic and Classical Greek Coins* (Berkeley: University of California Press, 1976).

C. M. Kraay and M. Hirmer, *Greek Coins* (London: Thames & Hudson, 1966).

Arthur Lane, *Greek Pottery* (New York: International Publishing Service, 1971).

A. W. Lawrence, *Greek Architecture* (3d ed.; Penguin, 1973).

R. Lullies and Max Hirmer, *Greek Sculpture* (New York: Abrams, 1957).

G. M. A. Richter, *The Portraits of the Greeks,* 3 vols. (London: Phaidon, 1965).

G. M. A. Richter, *Sculpture and Sculptors of the Greeks* (4th ed.; New Haven: Yale University Press, 1970).

M. C. Robertson, *Greek Painting* (New York: Rizzoli, 1979).

M. C. Robertson, *History of Greek Art* (New York: Cambridge University Press, 1975).

T. B. L. Webster, *Greek Terracottas* (London: King Penguin, 1950).

R. E. Wycherley, *How the Greeks Built Cities* (2d ed.; New York: Norton, 1976).

LITERATURE

C. M. Bowra, *Greek Lyric Poetry from Alcman to Simonides* (2d ed.; Oxford: Oxford University Press, 1961).

J. B. Bury, *Ancient Greek Historians* (Magnolia, Mass.: Peter Smith).

Moses Hadas, *History of Greek Literature* (New York: Columbia University Press, 1950).

G. Kennedy, *The Art of Persuasion in Greece* (Princeton: Princeton University Press, 1963).

A. Lesky, *History of Greek Literature* (New York: Crowell, 1976).

L. R. Palmer, *The Greek Language* (Atlantic Highlands, N.J.: Humanities Press, 1979).

RELIGION

E. R. Dodds, *Greeks and the Irrational* (Boston: Beacon BP43, 1957).

A. J. Festugière, *Personal Religion among the Greeks* (Berkeley: University of California Press, 1960).

J. Fontenrose, *The Delphic Oracle* (Berkeley: University of California Press, 1978).

W. K. C. Guthrie, *Greeks and Their Gods* (London: Methuen, 1968).

M. P. Nilsson, *History of Greek Religion* (2d ed.; New York: Norton, 1964).

H. W. Parke, *Festivals of the Athenians* (Ithaca: Cornell University Press, 1977).

H. W. Parke and D. E. W. Wormell, *The Delphic Oracle,* 2 vols. (Oxford: Blackwell, 1956).

SCIENCE AND PHILOSOPHY

Marshall Clagett, *Greek Science in Antiquity* (New York: Collier BS156, 1963).

W. K. C. Guthrie, *History of Greek Philosophy,* Vols. I–V (Cambridge: Cambridge University Press, 1962–75).

T. L. Heath, *Manual of Greek Mathematics* (Oxford: Oxford University Press, 1931).

G. E. R. Lloyd, *Early Greek Science* (New York: Norton, 1970).

G. E. R. Lloyd, *Greek Science after Aristotle* (New York: Norton, 1973).

E. D. Phillips, *Greek Medicine* (London: Thames & Hudson, 1973).

Edward Zeller, *Outlines of the History of Greek Philosophy* (New York: Meridian M9, 1955).

ROME

SOURCES

F. R. B. Godolphin, ed., *The Latin Poets* (New York: Modern Library 217, 1949).

Naphthali Lewis and Meyer Reinhold, *Roman Civilization*, 2 vols. (New York: Harper TB 1231–32, 1966).

Loeb Classical Library (Cambridge, Mass.: Harvard University Press), translations and texts of major Latin authors.

POLITICAL AND ECONOMIC

F. E. Adcock, *Roman Political Ideas and Practice* (Ann Arbor: University of Michigan Press, 1967).

A. E. R. Boak, *History of Rome to 565 A.D.* (5th ed.; New York: Macmillan, 1969).

Diana Bowder, ed., *Who Was Who in the Roman World 753 B.C.–A.D. 476* (Ithaca: Cornell University Press, 1980).

Max Cary, *History of Rome down to the Reign of Constantine* (3d ed.; New York: Macmillan, 1975).

D. C. Earl, *The Moral and Political Tradition of Rome* (Ithaca: Cornell University Press, 1967).

Tenney Frank, ed., *Economic Survey of Ancient Rome*, 5 vols. (New York: Octagon, 1972).

Edward Gibbon, *History of the Decline and Fall of the Roman Empire*, first publ. 1776–88; best edited recently by J. B. Bury, 7 vols. (London: Methuen, 1909–14).

H. Hill, *Roman Middle Class in the Republican Period* (Oxford: Blackwell, 1979).

F. B. Marsh, *History of the Roman World from 164 to 30 B.C.* (3d ed.; London: Methuen, 1963).

F. Millar, *The Emperor in the Roman World* (London: Duckworth, 1977).

F. Millar and others, *The Roman Empire and Its Neighbours* (New York: Delacorte, 1968).

Theodor Mommsen, *History of Rome*, 5 vols. (Chicago: Free Press reprint, 1957; abridged ed. New York: Meridian MG32, 1958).

C. Nicolet, *The World of the Citizen in Republican Rome* (Berkeley: University of California Press, 1980).

H. M. D. Parker, *History of the Roman World from A.D. 138 to 337* (rev. ed.; London: Methuen, 1969).

M. I. Rostovtzeff, *Social and Economic History of the Roman Empire*, 2 vols. (2d ed.; Oxford: Oxford University Press, 1957).

E. T. Salmon, *History of the Roman World from 30 B.C. to A.D. 138* (6th ed.; London: Methuen, 1968).

H. H. Scullard, *From the Gracchi to Nero* (4th ed.; New York: Praeger, 1976).

A. N. Sherwin-White, *The Roman Citizenship* (Oxford: Oxford University Press, 1973).

Chester G. Starr, *The Roman Empire* 27 B.C.–A.D. *476: A Study in Survival* (New York: Oxford University Press, 1982).
L. R. Taylor, *Roman Voting Assemblies* (Ann Arbor: University of Michigan Press, 1966).
K. D. White, *Roman Farming* (Ithaca: Cornell University Press, 1970).

ROMAN CIVILIZATION

M. L. Clarke, *The Roman Mind* (2d ed.; Cambridge, Mass.: Harvard University Press, 1960).
C. M. Cochrane, *Christianity and Classical Culture* (New York: Oxford Galaxy GB7, 1957).
D. R. Dudley, *Civilization of Rome* (New York: Mentor MT472, 1960).
Michael Grant, *World of Rome* (London: Weidenfeld and Nicolson, 1960).
Chester G. Starr, *Civilization and the Caesars: The Intellectual Revolution in the Roman Empire* (New York: Norton, 1965).

ARTS AND SCIENCES

Thomas Ashby, *Aqueducts of Ancient Rome* (Oxford: Oxford University Press, 1935).
A. Boethius and J. B. Ward-Perkins, *Etruscan and Early Roman Architecture* (Penguin, 1979).
Frank E. Brown, *Roman Architecture* (New York: Braziller, 1961).
R. J. Charleston, *Roman Pottery* (New York: Pitman, 1955).
R. Chevallier, *Roman Roads* (Berkeley: University of California Press, 1976).
O. Davies, *Roman Mines in Europe* (New York: Arno, 1980).
W. L. MacDonald, *The Architecture of the Roman Empire,* Vol. I (New Haven: Yale University Press, 1965).
A. Maiuri, *Roman Painting* (Geneva: Skira, 1953).
I. A. Richmond, *City Wall of Imperial Rome* (Oxford: Oxford University Press, 1930).
G. E. Rickman, *The Corn Supply of Ancient Rome* (Oxford: Oxford University Press, 1980).
Jocelyn Toynbee, *Art of the Romans* (New York: Praeger, 1965).
Mortimer Wheeler, *Roman Art and Architecture* (New York: Praeger, 1964).

CHRISTIANITY

See Bibliographies, Chapters 28, 31, and 32.

LAW

W. W. Buckland, *Textbook of Roman Law from Augustus to Justinian* (3d ed.; Cambridge: Cambridge University Press, 1964).

J. A. Crook, *Law and Life of Rome* (Ithaca: Cornell University Press, 1977).

Fritz Schulz, *Classical Roman Law* (Oxford: Oxford University Press, 1951).

Fritz Schulz, *History of Roman Legal Science* (Oxford: Oxford University Press, 1967).

Fritz Schulz, *Principles of Roman Law* (Oxford: Oxford University Press, 1936).

A. Watson, *Law-making in the Later Roman Republic* (Oxford: Clarendon Press, 1974).

LITERATURE

M. L. Clarke, *Rhetoric at Rome* (London: Cohen and West, 1962).

J. W. Duff, *Literary History of Rome from the Origins to the Close of the Golden Age* (rev. ed.; London: Benn, 1959).

J. W. Duff, *Literary History of Rome in the Silver Age* (rev. ed.; Westport, Conn.: Greenwood, 1979).

Tenney Frank, *Life and Literature in the Roman Republic* (Berkeley: University of California Paperback 2, 1957).

A. O. Gwynn, *Roman Education from Cicero to Quintilian* (New York: Teachers College, 1966).

G. Kennedy, *The Art of Rhetoric in the Roman World* (Princeton: Princeton University Press, 1972).

M. L. W. Laistner, *Greater Roman Historians* (Berkeley: University of California Press, 1963).

H. J. Rose, *Handbook of Latin Literature* (3d ed.; London: Methuen, 1966).

MILITARY AND NAVAL

F. E. Adcock, *Roman Art of War under the Republic* (New York: Barnes & Noble, 1971).

P. K. B. Reynolds, *Vigiles of Imperial Rome* (London: Oxford University Press, 1926).

Chester G. Starr, *Roman Imperial Navy* (Westport, Conn.: Greenwood, 1979).

G. R. Watson, *The Roman Soldier* (Ithaca: Cornell University Press, 1969).

G. Webster, *The Roman Imperial Army* (New York: Funk and Wagnall, 1979).

PROVINCES AND DISTRICTS

F. F. Abbott and A. C. Johnson, *Municipal Administration in the Roman Empire* (New York: Russell, 1968).

G. Alföldy, *Noricum* (London: Routledge & Kegan Paul, 1979).

Olwen Brogan, *Roman Gaul* (London: Bell, 1953).

G. E. F. Chilver, *Cisalpine Gaul* (New York: Arno, 1975).

Glanville Downey, *History of Antioch in Syria* (Princeton: Princeton University Press, 1961).

S. S. Frere, *Britannia* (3d ed.; London: Routledge & Kegan Paul, 1978).

A. C. Johnson, *Egypt and the Roman Empire* (Ann Arbor: University of Michigan Press, 1951).

A. H. M. Jones, *Cities of the Eastern Roman Provinces* (2d ed.; Oxford: Oxford University Press, 1971).

David Magie, *Roman Rule in Asia Minor to the End of the Third Century after Christ,* 2 vols. (Princeton: Princeton University Press, 1975).

A. Mocsy, *Pannonia and Upper Moesia* (London: Routledge & Kegan Paul, 1974).

Theodor Mommsen, *Provinces of the Roman Empire,* 2 vols. (London: Bentley, 1886).

M. I. Rostovtzeff, *Caravan Cities* (New York: AMS Press).

G. H. Stevenson, *Roman Provincial Administration till the Age of the Antonines* (Westport, Conn.: Greenwood, 1975).

J. J. Wilkes, *Dalmatia* (London: Routledge and Kegan Paul, 1969).

J. G. Winter, *Life and Letters in the Papyri* (Ann Arbor: University of Michigan Press, 1933).

F. J. Wiseman, *Roman Spain* (London: Bell, 1956).

RELIGION AND PHILOSOPHY

Franz Altheim, *History of Roman Religion* (London: Methuen, 1928).

E. V. Arnold, *Roman Stoicism* (New York: Arno).

F. H. Cramer, *Astrology in Roman Law and Politics* (Philadelphia: American Philosophical Society, 1954).

R. MacMullen, *Paganism in the Roman Empire* (New Haven: Yale University Press, 1981).

R. M. Ogilvie, *The Romans and Their Gods in the Age of Augustus* (New York: Norton, 1979).

H. J. Rose, *Ancient Roman Religion* (New York: Harper Torchbook 55, 1959).

SOCIAL

J. P. V. D. Balsdon, *Life and Leisure in Ancient Rome* (New York: McGraw-Hill, 1969).

J. P. V. D. Balsdon, *Roman Women* (Westport, Conn.: Greenwood, 1975).

Samuel Dill, *Roman Society from Nero to Marcus Aurelius* (Norwood, Pa.: Norwood).

Samuel Dill, *Roman Society in the Last Century of the Western Empire* (Philadelphia: R. West).

A. M. Duff, *Freedmen in the Early Roman Empire* (2d ed.; New York: Barnes and Noble, 1958).

Michael Grant, *Gladiators* (New York: Delacorte, 1967).

Harold Mattingly, *Man in the Roman Street* (New York: Norton, 1966).

S. Treggiari, *Roman Freedmen during the Late Republic* (Oxford: Oxford University Press, 1969).

INDEX

Abraham, 146
Academy, 382, 426
Achaean league, 364, 404, 493
Achaemenid dynasty, *see* Persia
Achilles, 197–201
Acragas, *see* Agrigentum
Acropolis, 109–10, 208, 248, 253–5, 264, 289; Periclean, 309, 312, 333
Adadnirari II, 130
Adrianople, 672, 675, 678
Aegean Sea, 105, 186
Aegina, 221, 261, 287, 31(, 335
Aelius Aristides, 581, 593
Aeneid, 564–5
Aeolic dialect, 190, 198
Aeschylus, 285, 295, 302, 321–3, 326
Aetolian league, 364, 404, 486, 491
Afghanistan, 172, 401, 589, 627, 632–3, 651
Africa, *see* Carthage, Egypt, Numidia, Sahara
Agesilaus, 362–4
Agora, 208, 253, 315, 334
Agriculture: Near Eastern, 17–22, 30, 32; Greek, 187, 220, 314; Roman, 505, 513, 589, 695–6; European, 439–41
Agrigentum, 262, 335, 452, 479
Agrippa, 548–50, 555, 558–9
Ahab, 130, 151, 154–5
Ahura-Mazda, 277, 280, 631
Akhenaten, 91–4

Akkad, 29, 45, 77
Al Mina, 213
Alalia, 261, 452–3
Alamanni, 650, 657, 677
Alaric, 700–701
Alcaeus, 140, 224, 265
Alcibiades, 343–6, 351, 355, 381
Alcman, 237, 256
Alcmeonid clan, 253–5, 302
Alexander the Great, 172, 370–71, 382, 390, 394–403, 551
Alexandria: Hellenistic, 398, 402, 407–9, 416–18, 421, 427, 540; Roman, 582, 591, 619
Alphabet: Aramaic, 127, 169, 280; Phoenician, 87, 127; Greek, 201; Latin, 449, 461
"Alpine type," 8
Ambrose, St., 680–81, 684, 688–9, 699
Amen, 89, 91–4
Americas, 14, 17, 20, 28
Ammianus Marcellinus, 686–7
Amorites, 46, 77, 146
Amos, 153, 155, 157
Amphictyony of Delphi, 207, 261, 369
Amphipolis, 313, 342, 367–8, 402
Anacreon, 253, 261, 265
Analects, 176–7
Anath, 151, 157–8
Anaxagoras, 329–30
Anaximander, 266

Anaximenes, 266
Antioch, 407–8, 591, 610, 651, 660
Antiochus III, 488–92
Antiochus IV, 493
Antigonid dynasty, 404, 488–91
Antiphon (orator), 349; (sophist), 349
Antony, Mark, 539, 541, 543–4, 548–51
Anyang, 115
Apelles, 389
Apennines, 440
Aphrodite, 239
Apollo, 239, 242, 555, 663
Apollodorus, 334
Apollonius Rhodius, 418
Appius Claudius clan, 465, 467, 471–2, 474, 479, 512–3
Apuleius, 596, 605
Apulia, 441, 505
Arabia, 30, 55, 77, 100, 401, 654, 705
Arameans (Aramaic), 80, 125, 128, 130, 138, 280, 618, 630
Arbela, 397–400
Arcadia, 190, 363–4
Archilochus, 236–7, 241
Archimedes, 428, 430, 486
Architecture: Near Eastern, 31, 33, 37, 58, 91–2, 128, 134, 281; Greek, 107, 232–3, 263–4, 331–5, 389, 421; Etruscan, 450–51; Roman, 461–2, 497, 522, 568, 592, 596–7, 655, 686; Christian, 687
Archon, 208, 249, 256, 286, 321
Areopagus, 249, 256, 299, 323
Argos, 190, 194, 207, 211, 257, 259, 287–8, 343
Arianism, 681, 683
Aristarchus of Samos, 428
Aristides, 285–6, 290–91, 293
Aristocratic code, 205–6, 223–4, 473, 697
Aristophanes, 306, 312, 326–7, 350, 381, 385
Aristotle, 322, 363, 382–4, 387, 426–7, 522; political philosophy, 185, 206, 210, 374–5, 403, 478
Armenia, 86, 130, 146, 627, 629, 685
Army: Assyrian, 132–3; Greek, 210–11, 366, 368, 399, 406; Roman, 459, 466–7, 518–9, 559–61, 585–7, 656, 674–5

Arrian, 410, 593
Arsacid dynasty, see Parthia
Art, see Architecture, Painting, Pottery, Sculpture
Artemisium, 288–9, 298
Aryans, 81, 114, 165–7, 280
Asclepius, 391
Ashur, 86, 130, 133, 136–7, 151
Ashurbanipal, 131, 134–6, 138
Ashurnasirpal II, 130, 133–4
Asia (province), 513
Asia Minor, 86–7, 101, 186, 492, 611; see also Armenia, Hittites, Ionia, Lydia, Phrygia
Asoka, 632
Assembly: Athenian, 208, 249, 252, 255–6, 303, 343, 369; Roman, 460, 469–70, 482, 553–4
Assyria, 46, 86, 95–6, 129–38, 151
Astrology, 137, 508, 604, 679
Astronomy, 36, 46, 136, 280, 330, 428–9
Athanasius, St., 681, 683, 688
Athena, 199, 200, 208, 239–40, 253, 311
Athens: early, 106, 190–91, 193–6, 207–8, 211, 213; archaic, 217, 221, 230, 240, 243, 248–56, 261, 264; classic, 282–375, 404, 416, 421; Roman, 520, 592, 657, 660, 705
Attalid dynasty, 421; see also Pergamum
Attica, see Athens
Auctoritas, 470, 472–3, 554
Augustine, St., 682–4, 689–91, 699
Augustus, 543–4, 547–70, 575, 580
Aurelian, 655, 657, 660, 663
Aurignacian culture, 11
Australopithecines, 7

Baals, 80, 147, 153
Babylon and Babylonia, 29, 46, 48, 83, 102, 130–31, 136, 138–41, 157, 279, 400, 402
Bacchylides, 320, 327
Bactria, 400, 404, 407, 632–3
Barracks Emperors, 660
Basilica, 687
Bishops, 613–16, 665, 684
Bithynia, 404, 590

Black Sea, 218–19, 313
Boeotia, 187, 190, 208, 217, 234, 256, 260, 291, 310, 342; see also Thebes
Book of the Dead, 65, 94
Bosporus (Crimea), 313, 404, 626
Boule, see Council
Brasidas, 342, 352
Britain, see England
Bronze age, 76, 129
Brutus, 542, 548
Buddha, the, 169–71
Buddhism, 167, 171–2, 632–5, 641, 705–7
Bureaucracy: Near Eastern, 59, 65, 132, 174; Greek, 373, 406, 409; Roman, 555, 582–4, 673–4, 698; Chinese, 637, 639–40
Burgundians, 650, 701
Byblos, 64, 87, 91, 127
Byzantine Empire, 521, 673, 704–5
Byzantium, 219, 293, 370, 404, 408

Caesar, Julius, 426, 528–9, 531–44, 568
Calendar, 37, 62, 330, 539, 542
Callias, 294
Callimachus, 417–19
Callinus, 237
Cambyses, 277
Camillus, 464
Campania, 441, 448, 452, 465, 484, 505
Canaanites, 80, 87–8, 127, 147–9
Cannae, 485
Capitoline hill, 457–8
Capua, 448–9, 465, 485–6
Caracalla, 653, 655–6, 661
Carmel, Mt., 13, 15
Carneades, 496–7
Carthage, 128, 261, 316–17, 409, 447, 452–3, 465, 478–87, 493; Roman, 514–15, 591, 701
Cassius, 542, 548
Catholic Church, 616
Catiline, 528–30
Cato the Censor, 492, 495–7, 504
Cato the Younger, 530, 534–5, 537, 541
Catullus, 531
Celts, see Gauls
Censor, 469
Centuriate assembly, see Assembly

Chaeronea, 370, 592
Chalcis, 211, 217–19, 256, 311, 383
Chaldaeans, 131, 139–40, 151, 156–7
Chandragupta, 632
Ch'in, 174, 637
China, 9, 114–16, 172–8, 589, 636–41, 706–7
Chios, 186, 310
Chou dynasty, 116, 173–8
Christianity, 603, 606–22, 664–6, 678–85, 687–91, 698–700, 707; and classical culture, 618–20, 690–91
Ch'u, 174, 637
Cicero, 510, 519, 526–35, 540, 542–4
Cilicia, 87, 101, 131, 216, 518
Cimbri and Teutones, 517
Cimmerians, 137, 262
Cimon, 293–4, 299, 302–3, 307, 309–10
Cinna, 520–21
Cisalpine Gaul, 482, 522, 534–5, 542
Citizenship: Athenian, 255, 302–3; Roman, 467–8, 514, 519, 556, 560, 580–81, 656
City, defined, 32
City-state: Near Eastern, 32–4, 39; Greek, 205–13, 359, 373–5; Roman, 458–60, 519
City of God, 689–90, 699
Civil wars: Greek, 316, 346–7, 371–3, 410; Roman, 515, 539–41, 543–4, 548–51, 655–60
Civilization, defined, 27, 67–8, 116–17
Clan: Greek, 192, 210, 224, 236, 255; Roman, 460, 470
Classes: Mesopotamian, 41–4, 47; Indian, 166; Greek, 192, 209, 212, 222–5, 252, 315, 347, 407–8; Roman, 460–61, 470–73, 526–7, 553–4, 589–90, 654, 676
Claudius, 576, 581, 583, 586, 594, 617
Clement of Alexandria, 619, 662
Cleomenes, 254–5, 259, 282
Cleon, 326, 342–3
Cleopatra, 540, 550–51
Cleruchs, 256, 311
Clients, 460
Climate, 4, 14, 29, 54, 99, 218, 438
Clisthenes, 254–6
Clodius, 531, 535, 538

Cnossus, 106–9

Coinage, 134, 169, 174; Greek, 221, 226, 252, 254, 279, 315, 368, 402; Roman, 505, 556, 591, 653, 675

Collegia, 653

Coloni, 590, 695

Colonization: Phoenician, 128, 447; Greek, 213–20, 225, 403, 406–7, 447; Roman, 467, 514, 535, 542

Comedy: Greek, 325–7, 385–6, 419; Roman, 495, 497

Comitia, see Assembly

Commerce: Near Eastern, 20, 30, 42, 46, 64, 76, 86–7, 100, 113, 128, 134, 150; Greek, 109, 187, 216, 221, 263, 313–16, 372, 408–9; Roman, 467, 504, 588–9, 630

Commodus, 577, 587, 655, 708

Confucius and Confucianism, 175–8, 637–41

Constantine, 663, 672–3, 675–6, 680, 682–3, 686

Constantinople, 672–3, 680, 684, 704–5

Constantius II, 677, 681, 683

Consuls, 463, 467–8, 472, 705

Corcyra, 218, 341, 347

Corinth, 106, 190, 211, 213, 216–19, 221, 230, 259, 287, 316, 340–42, 493–4

Corsica, 261, 453, 481–2

Council of Four Hundred, 252; of Five Hundred, 256, 302–4, 372

Councils of bishops, 615, 677, 681–3, 698

Crassus, 527–9, 533–4, 538

Crete, 64, 105–10, 186, 189, 209–10, 258, 261

Critias, 350, 361

Croesus, 140, 263, 269

Croton, 262, 267

Ctesiphon, 627–30, 650, 677

Cumae, 218, 447, 453, 465

Cuneiform, 35

Cybele, 606

Cyclades, 105–6, 186

Cynics, 384, 423, 426

Cyprian, St., 616, 666

Cyprus, 109, 128, 131, 216, 282–3, 294, 316, 404, 535

Cyrenaics, 385

Cyrene, 219, 282, 404, 518

Cyrus, 140–41, 157, 277

Cyzicus, 219, 408

Dacia, 542, 586, 660

Dalmatia, 482, 486

Damascus, 87, 128, 131

Danube river, 21–2, 109, 282, 439, 559, 587

Darius I, 277–86

Darius III, 396–400

David, 149–50, 152

Decius, 656, 665–6

"Decline and Fall," 708–11

Decurions, 653, 674, 676

Deification, 45, 397, 402, 406; Roman, 541, 556–7, 594, 598, 605, 617

Delian league, 292–4, 307, 310

Delos, 186, 231, 239, 242, 263, 293, 493, 504

Delphi, 213, 217, 239, 242, 257, 260, 262–3, 287, 292, 323, 365, 520

Demes, 255, 321

Demeter, 239–40, 242

Democracy, 190, 254–8, 286, 299–307, 347, 374, 472

Democritus, 329–30, 425

Demosthenes, 369–71, 387

Diaspora, 158–9, 607, 618

Didyma, 217, 242

Diocletian, 660, 670–75, 679, 686

Diodorus Siculus, 567

Dionysius of Halicarnassus, 448, 567

Dionysius of Syracuse, 365–6, 380

Dionysus, 238, 242–3, 320–21, 326, 508

Dipylon style, 195–6, 198

Dithyramb, 238, 253, 320

Domitian, 577, 588, 596

Donatists, 681–3, 697

Dorians, 110, 189, 191, 193, 196, 211, 256

Doric dialect, 190, 386

Draco, 249, 255

Dura-Europos, 414, 631, 651

Ecbatana, 138, 279, 627

Ecclesia, see Assembly

Economics, *see* Agriculture, Coinage, Commerce, Industry, Technology
Education, 223, 258, 348, 387, 415–16, 495, 592–3
Egypt: predynastic, 19, 54–5; pharaonic, 55–69, 88–96, 125, 146; Assyrian, 131, 138–9, 216; Persian, 277, 279, 286, 294, 397–8; Hellenistic, 404–10, 427, 489, 493, 540, 551; Roman, 558, 581–2, 590, 679
El-Amarna, 90, 93
Elam, 31, 45, 131
Elbe river, 439, 444, 559
Elegiac poetry, 237
Eleusis and Eleusinian mysteries, 242–3, 249, 253, 263, 344, 361, 555
Elijah, 155
Empedocles, 329–30
England, 10, 20, 109, 408, 438, 440, 535–6, 542, 558; Roman, 586, 590–91, 656, 670, 696, 701–2
Ennius, 495
Epaminondas, 364, 367
Ephesus, 263, 279
Ephialtes, 299, 302, 309
Epic: Mesopotamian, 40–41; Greek, 197–201; Roman, 495, 564–5
Epictetus, 593, 604
Epicurus and Epicureanism, 385, 424–6, 496, 531
Epidaurus, 211, 389, 391
Equestrian order, 483, 511–12, 514–15, 521, 527, 534, 554, 583
Eratosthenes, 417, 429
Erechtheum, 314, 334
Eretria, 211, 217–19, 282–3
Esarhaddon, 131, 134, 138
Ethics: Egyptian, 65–6; Jewish, 144, 154, 159; Greek, 223–4, 234–5, 241, 252, 379–80, 424–5; Christian, 609, 621
Etruria and Etruscans, 218, 261, 441, 448–53, 459, 461–3
Euboea, 187, 288, 310, 345, 369
Euclid, 428
Euphrates river, 29–30
Euripides, 321, 324–6, 352–4
Europe, western (early), 11, 21, 100, 437–47

Eurybiades, 288
Eusebius, 680, 688
Ezekiel, 157–8

Fertile Crescent, 30, 51, 75; *see also* Near East
Flamininus, 489–92
Flaminius, 482, 484
Forum, 457–8, 505
France, *see* Gaul
Franks, 650, 657, 701–2

Galen, 594, 655
Galerius, 670–72, 679
Gallienus, 654, 657, 662, 664, 666
Gandhara, 634
Ganges river, 165, 169
Gauls and Gaul, 421, 447, 449, 464–6, 483, 486, 534–7; Roman, 590, 657–60, 670, 696, 701
Geometric pottery, 194–6
Geometry, 36, 267, 330, 428
Germans, 439, 536, 559, 586–8, 591, 648–50, 700–703
Gilgamesh, 32, 40–41, 46, 62, 104, 136, 199–200
Gnostics, 621
Good Emperors, 577
Gordium, 262, 398
Gorgias, 349
Government, *see* Assembly, Bureaucracy, Democracy, Kingship
Gracchus, Gaius, 513–16
Gracchus, Tiberius, 512–13, 515
Graphe paranomon, 305, 372
Greece and Greeks: geography, 105, 186–8; early, 105–11; dark ages, 189–202; archaic, 140, 205–70, 449–50; classic, 275–392; Hellenistic, 394–431, 488–93, 510; Roman, 520–21, 581, 588, 657; in western Mediterranean, 447, 452–3, 465
Greek language, 82, 105, 109–10, 190–91, 198, 386
Gupta dynasty, 705–6
Gymnasia, 232, 407, 415–16, 630

Hadrian, 583–6, 596–9
Hammurapi, 46–8
Han dynasty, 638–41, 706
Han Wu Ti, 638, 640
Hannibal, 483–7, 492
Hapiru, 125, 146
Harappa, 111, 113
Haruspices, 451
Hatshepsut, 90, 92
Hattusas, 86, 95, 101–2
Hebrews, 143–60; *see also* Jews
Hecataeus, 270, 283, 327
Heliaea, 252, 304
Hellanicus, 327
Hellenistic age, 394–5, 403–31, 488–98, 510, 630–31
Hellespont, 254, 282, 292, 307, 346, 370
Helots, 275–8, 309, 316, 346
Heracles, 196–7, 230
Heraclitus, 328, 423
Heresies, 620–21, 665, 682–4
Herodotus, 53, 282, 285–6, 294–6, 351, 386, 448
Hesiod, 222, 234–6, 239–40, 266, 268, 417
Hieroglyphic writing, 56
Hinduism, 165, 167–9, 172, 635–6, 705
Hipparchus, 528–9
Hippias, 253–4, 283
Hippocrates, 330–31
Hippodamus, 334, 414
Hiram, 127, 150
History, written: Near Eastern, 103, 136, 145; Greek, 270, 327–8, 351–2; Roman, 495, 509, 567, 686–7; Chinese and Indian, 180, 640
Hittites, 82, 86, 91, 95, 100–104, 109, 128–9
Homer, 195–200, 223, 236, 239–40, 253, 268, 374, 417
Homeric Hymns, 234
Hominids, 7
Homo sapiens, 7, 10–11
Hoplites, 210
Horace, 549, 561–6
Hsün Tzû, 178
Huns, 638, 700–701, 705–6
Hurrians, 82, 86–7, 130, 146
Hybris, 241, 295, 325, 344, 353

Hydaspes river, 401
Hyksos, 88–9

Ibycus, 261–2, 265
Ice ages, 4, 14
Ictinus, 333, 335
Ignatius, St., 612–13
Iliad, 41, 109, 185, 197–202, 396, 417
Imperialism: Near Eastern, 42, 44–5, 76, 89–92, 130–41; Greek, 259, 276–80, 307–13, 340, 352, 361–4; Roman, 465–8, 477–94, 516–21, 526–7, 558–9
Imperium, 460, 463, 468, 472, 552
India, 10, 111–14, 165–72, 401, 409, 588, 631–6, 705–6
Indo-Europeans, 22, 80–82, 101, 103, 105, 124–5, 445
Indus river, 111–14, 165, 277, 402
Industry, 220, 315, 587–8, 590, 652–3
Ionia, 191, 218, 248, 263, 266, 282, 292, 311, 316, 362, 372
Ionic dialect, 190
Iran, 138, 629; *see also* Persians
Irenaeus, St., 619, 621
Iron, 128, 169, 175, 193
Irrigation, 30, 32, 53, 174
Isaiah, 153, 156; the Second, 157
Ishtar, 39, 41, 88, 134, 139, 158
Isis, 61, 508, 605
Isocrates, 366, 370, 386–8, 391
Israel, 147–51, 155; *see also* Palestine
Issus, 398
Italian war, 519
Italy: geography, 440–41; early, 441–54; *see also* Romans

Jainism, 167, 170–71, 635
Jarmo, 18, 32
Jaxartes river, 140, 400
Jeremiah, 153, 156–7
Jericho, 18, 20, 87
Jerome, St., 161, 684, 688
Jerusalem, 87, 91, 150–51, 156–8, 581, 610–13
Jesus Christ, 157, 608–10, 618
Jews, 158–9, 279, 493, 508, 542, 581; *see also* Hebrews, Judaism
Jezebel, 151, 154–5

John Chrysostom, St., 681–2
Josiah, 151, 156
Judah, 150–51, 156
Judaism, 144, 152–60, 581, 607–8, 651, 684
Jugurtha, 516–17
Julian, 677, 680, 701
Jupiter, 462, 580, 679
Justinian, 655, 703–5

Kassites, 83, 95
Kerameikos, 193–4
Kingship: Near Eastern, 33, 43, 59–60, 102, 106, 132, 150, 277–9; Greek, 191, 207–9, 405–6; Roman, 459–60, 463, 576–80, 673; German, 649, 702
Koine, 387, 430, 618
Kore, 231, 254, 264
Kouros, 231, 264
Kushan dynasty, 629, 633, 651

La Tène culture, 535–6, 648
Lactantius, 680, 688–9
Latin language, 82, 445, 461, 495, 497, 654
Latium and Latins, 441, 445, 457, 459, 463–7, 505
Laurium, 248, 286, 314
Law: Near Eastern, 42, 44, 47–8, 60, 103; Greek, 209, 226, 252; Roman, 460, 472, 509–10, 584–5, 655, 704–5
Leagues, 364; of Corinth, 370–71, 396–7; see also Achaean, Aetolian, Delian leagues
Legalists, 178, 637
Legion, 459, 466, 518, 559–60, 587
Leonidas, 288–9
Lepidus, 544, 548–9
Lesbos, 186, 265, 310, 345
Libraries, 136, 417, 593
Libya, 54, 313, 553
Lilybaeum, 452, 481
Limes, 586, 626
Literature: Mesopotamian, 40–41, 136; Egyptian, 62, 65; Chinese, 175–6; Indian, 166–8, 635–6, 705; Greek, 197–201, 234–8, 265, 320–28, 385–8, 417–20, 567, 593–4, 662; Roman, 474, 509, 530–32, 561–7, 594–6, 685–7; Christian, 618–20, 687–91
Liturgies, 315
Livius Andronicus, 495
Livius Drusus (Elder), 514; (Younger), 519
Livy, 474–5, 542, 567
Lucian, 593–4, 662
Lucilius, 509
Lucretius, 425, 523, 530–31, 565
Lugal, 33, 43, 45
Lyceum, 382–3, 426–7
Lydia, 139, 221, 236, 263
Lyric poetry, 237, 265
Lysander, 346, 360–62
Lysippus, 390, 421

Maccabees, 493, 607
Macedonia, 187, 260, 282, 313, 354, 366–71, 395, 493
Macedonian wars: First, 486; Second, 489–91; Third, 493
Maecenas, 548, 561–5
Magdalenian culture, 11–12, 15
Magi, 280, 652
Magic, 12, 57, 62, 67, 240, 391, 604, 676
Maglemosian culture, 15
Mahabharata, 636
Manasseh, 151
Manicheans, 651–2, 665, 679
Marathon, 283–5
Marcus Aurelius, 576–80, 582, 587, 589, 591, 593, 596–7, 599, 617
Mardonius, 283, 291
Marduk, 46, 130, 140, 277
Marius, 516–18, 520, 533
Massilia, 219, 483, 517, 535
Mathematics, 36, 46, 62, 172, 280, 428; see also Geometry
Mauryan dynasty, 632
Maximian, 670–72, 679
Medes, 138–40
Medicine, 62, 137, 330–31, 427, 594
Mediterranean Sea, 128
"Mediterranean type," 8, 441
Megalithic monuments, 440
Megara, 211, 219, 221, 249, 259, 310, 340–41

Megaron, 232
Menander, 419–20
Mencius, 177–8
Mesolithic age, 14–17
Mesopotamia, 28–48, 53, 68, 83–7, 627
Messenia, 211, 257, 309
Metals, 20, 59, 109, 188, 444, 450
Metics, 314, 382
Middle Ages, 207, 383, 696–7, 702, 710–11
Miletus, 211, 217–19, 263, 282–3, 316
Miltiades, 254, 285–6, 303, 307
Mimes, 326, 386, 419
Mimnermus, 237
Minoan culture, 106–8, 444
Mitanni, 86–7, 90, 95, 129
Mithras, 605–6, 663
Mithridates VI, 520–21, 528
Mitylene, 341, 343
Moesia, 559
Mohenjo-daro, 111, 113
Moses, 146–7
Mousterian culture, 10, 13
Music, 238, 256, 322, 334, 386
Mycale, 291–2
Mycenaean age, 108–10, 189, 197, 444
Myron, 335
Mysteries, 606; *see also* Eleusinian mysteries
Myths, 38, 68, 88, 118, 196–7, 203, 210

Nabataeans, 404, 409, 627
Naevius, 495
Natufians, 15
Naucratis, 216, 263, 407
Naupactus, 316, 342
Naxos, 261, 283, 309
Navy: Greek, 211, 261, 287, 341; Roman, 481, 539–40, 549–51, 559
Neanderthal man, 7, 9–10, 13
Near East, 15–96, 123–60, 394–431, 627–31, 650–52; *see also* Parthians, Persians
Nebuchadrezzar, 139–40, 151
Neolithic age, 17–21, 30–32, 54–5
Neoplatonism, 663–4, 686
Nero, 576–7, 591, 594, 596, 617
New Testament, 612, 618, 622
Nicaea, council of, 677, 681, 683
Nicias, 342–4

Nicolaus of Damascus, 567
Nile river, 53–4, 60
Nineveh, 131, 134–8
Nomads, 18, 80–81, 125, 282, 629, 703–4
"Nordic type," 8
Nubia, 54, 59, 89, 216
Numidia, 516

Octavia, 549–50
Octavian, *see* Augustus
Odyssey, 109, 194, 200–201, 230, 495
Oedipus the King, 323–5
Oikoumene, 405, 581
Old Oligarch, 306, 311, 314
Old Testament, 143–5, 150, 152, 158, 160–62, 607
Olympia, 239, 263, 335, 660
Olympus, Mt., 199, 239
Olynthus, 367, 369
Optimates, 519, 522, 534
Orientalizing pottery, 229–30, 241
Origen, 161, 619–21, 666
Orphics, 243
Osiris, 60–63, 89, 95
Ostia, 459, 588–9
Ostracism, 286, 299, 312
Ostrogoths, 650, 700, 702
Ovid, 566

Paestum, 218, 262, 335
Painting: prehistoric, 12; Egyptian, 57; Greek, 107, 334, 388–9; Etruscan, 450; Roman, 568
Palatine hill, 457, 504, 529, 555
Paleolithic age, 4–17
Palestine, 15, 87, 89–90, 125, 145–52, 158, 558, 607–9
Palmyra, 626, 657–60
Pamphylia, 216
Panaetius, 497
Pannonia, 559
Pantheon, 568, 596–7, 686
Papacy, *see* Rome (church)
Parmenides, 328, 384
Parrhasius, 388
Parthenon, 185, 233, 281, 312, 333
Parthian dynasty, 538, 549, 558, 586–7, 627–31

Patricians, 460–61, 463, 470–73
Paul, St., 419, 595, 611–13, 618, 620
Peasants, *see* Agriculture
Peloponnesian league, *see* Sparta
Peloponnesian war, 312, 340–46, 353, 371
Peloponnesus, 187, 190, 197, 211, 231
Pentateuch, 145, 158, 161
Pergamum, 404, 417, 421–2, 489–93, 513
Pericles, 294, 299–306, 310–15, 319, 322, 334, 340–42, 350
Perioikoi, 257–8
Peripatetic school, *see* Aristotle
Persecutions, 508, 608, 616–18, 665–6, 678–80
Persepolis, 281, 400
Persian wars, 282–95
Persians: Achaemenid, 140–41, 172, 261, 263, 276–95, 345, 361–4, 395–400; Sassanian, 650–52, 677, 705
Peter, St., 611–12, 615–16
Petronius, 589, 595
Phalanx, 132, 210, 218, 459
Pharaoh, 59–61, 63, 92
Phidias, 333–5
Philip II, 366–71
Philip V, 486, 488–91
Philistines, 149
Philo, 607, 620
Philosophy: Chinese, 175–8; Greek, 236, 265–8, 328–30, 379–85, 422–6; Roman, 531–2, 594–5, 598, 604, 663–4
Phocis, 260, 291, 365, 368–9
Phoenicia, 59, 125–8, 213, 447, 452
Phratries, 191, 255
Phrygians, 103, 262
Pindar, 298, 320, 327, 395, 417
Piracy, 211, 312, 405, 482, 518, 528, 559, 653
Piraeus, 286, 314–16, 334
Pisistratus, 253–4, 261
Pithecanthropus, 7
Plataea, 261, 283, 291–2, 347
Plato, 206, 258, 373–5, 380–84, 391, 663
Plautus, 495
Plebeians, 460, 470–73
Pliny the Elder, 588, 590, 595
Pliny the Younger, 577–80, 583, 590, 596, 616–17

Plotinus, 663–4
Plutarch, 270, 541, 592–3, 604, 662
Po river and valley, 440, 444–5, 448–9, 488, 505; *see also* Cisalpine Gaul
Poetry, *see* Literature
Polis, see City-state
Polybius, 494, 498
Polyclitus, 335–6
Polycarp, St., 617–18
Polycrates, 261
Polygnotus, 334
Pomerium, 451, 461
Pompeii, 448, 497, 504, 589, 592, 642
Pompeius, Sextus, 548–9
Pompeius Trogus, 567
Pompey (Cn. Pompeius), 519, 521, 527–9, 534–5, 538–40
Pontus, *see* Mithridates VI
Populares, 519, 521, 527
Porphyry, 664, 678
Posidonius, 510, 528, 530
Potidaea, 219, 341
Pottery: prehistoric, 19; Greek, 107, 192–6, 202, 229–30, 264–5, 388; Etruscan, 450
Praeneste, 448, 464, 522
Praetor, 468, 482, 509, 522
Praetor's Edict, 509, 585
Praetorian Guard, 558, 561, 576
Praetorian Prefect, 582, 655, 673
Praxiteles, 389–90
Princeps, 552, 555, 580
Propertius, 566
Prophets, 153–8
Prose: Greek, 327, 386; Latin, 496, 531
Protagoras, 349–51
Protogeometric pottery, 192–4
Provinces, Roman, 482, 493–4, 511, 522, 529, 553, 556–7, 580–84, 674
Prudentius, 688
Psammetichus I, 138
Psyttalia, 290
Ptolemaic dynasty, 404–7, 409–10, 416, 427, 489, 493, 540, 550–51
Ptolemy (astronomer), 428, 594, 643
Punic wars: First, 479–82; Second, 483–7; Third, 493
Pylos, 108–10, 342

Pyramids, 58, 63
Pyrrhonism, 426, 604
Pyrrhus, 465–7
Pythagoras, 172, 267, 381

Ramayana, 635–6
Ramesses II, 95
Ramesses III, 96, 125
Ravenna, 672, 700, 702–3
Red Sea, 89
Religion: prehistoric, 12, 20; Near Eastern, 37–41, 46, 54, 60–62, 67, 80, 88, 103–4, 137, 280; Greek, 106–7, 191, 196–7, 199, 238–44, 268, 350, 430–31; Etruscan, 451; Roman, 457, 462, 466, 508, 555, 605–6, 662–3; see also Buddhism, Christianity, Hinduism, Judaism, Zoroaster
Rhetoric, 348–9, 387–8, 495, 592, 598
Rhine river, 439, 536, 559
Rhodes, 186, 189, 216, 261, 335; Hellenistic, 404–5, 408, 416, 421, 489, 492–3, 504
Rhone river, 439, 536
Roads, 279, 315; Roman, 461, 467, 482, 514, 588, 653
Romans: Kingdom, 448–52, 454, 457–63; Early Republic, 463–98; Late Republic, 503–47; Early Empire, 547–600, 647–66; Later Empire, 669–705
Rome (church), 612, 615–16, 618, 684, 698
Rome (city), 457–8, 474, 504–5, 568, 591, 657–60, 672, 701
Russia, see Bosporus, Ostrogoths, Scythians

Sacraments, 614
Sahara, 14, 21, 588
Salamis, 249, 289–90
Sallust, 532
Samaria, 150–51
Samnites, 448, 465–6
Samos, 186, 211, 221, 261, 310, 312
Sanskrit, 81, 165, 169, 705
Sappho, 265
Sarapis, 421, 431, 605, 663
Sardinia, 447, 453, 481–2, 493, 539, 548

Sardis, 263, 282–3, 286, 363
Sargon I, 45
Sargon II, 131–2, 134, 151
Sassanian dynasty, 650–52, 670, 705
Satrapies, 279
Saxons, 650, 701–2
Scandinavia, 15, 438–40, 648
Science, 330–31, 383–4, 426–30, 593–4; see also Geometry, Mathematics, Medicine
Scipio Aemilianus, 492–3, 497, 512
Scipio Africanus, 486–8, 492, 512
Scopas, 389–90
Sculpture: prehistoric, 12, 20; Near Eastern, 37, 57, 65, 93, 104, 135, 281; Greek, 107, 230–32, 264, 333–6, 389–90, 421–2; Etruscan, 450; Roman, 509, 568–9, 597–8, 604–5, 662; Christian, 687
Scythians, 220, 262, 282, 314, 612
Sea power, see Navy
Segesta, 262, 335, 343
Seleucia on the Tigris, 408, 627, 630
Seleucid dynasty, 403–4, 406–7, 488–92, 528
Semites, 22, 45, 55, 77–80, 96, 125, 146
Senate, 460, 469, 473, 511, 521–2, 538–9, 541, 543–4, 552, 554, 577–81, 654, 673
Seneca, 424, 594–5
Sennacherib, 131, 134, 138
Septimius Severus, 653–6, 674
Septuagint, 161, 607
Shang dynasty, 114–16, 175
Shapur I, 651–2
Shapur II, 651, 685
Shih Huang Ti, 178, 637
Ships, 218, 221, 315, 408, 588; see also Navy
Sicily, 109, 218–19, 316–17, 343–4, 444, 452–3, 479–82, 508, 539, 548
Sicyon, 213, 242
Sidon, 127
Silk Route, 100, 588, 630
Simonides, 253, 265, 320, 327
Sinai, 59, 64
Sinope, 219, 313
Siva, 113, 167, 635
Skepticism, see Pyrrhonism
Slavery, 43, 59, 134, 192, 209, 221, 314, 345, 430, 505–8, 527, 555, 590, 711

Smyrna, 233, 263, 491, 617
Society, *see* Aristocratic code, Classes, Slavery, Women
Socrates, 326, 350, 372–3, 379–80, 384–5
Solomon, 150
Solon, 216, 222–3, 237, 249–53, 265, 269
Sophists, 348–51, 592
Sophocles, 321, 323–5, 391
Spain, 128, 219, 440, 446, 452–3, 483–4, 486, 488, 493, 539, 558, 590, 657, 701
Sparta: early, 190, 207–12, 217, 237–8, 254, 256–60; classic, 282–5, 287–94, 309–10, 313, 340–48, 360–66, 371; Hellenistic, 404, 410, 491
Ssu-ma Ch'ien, 177, 643
Stasis, see Civil War
Stesichorus, 238, 262
Stoicism, 423–4, 497, 593, 595
Strabo, 567, 588
Snetonius, 545
Sulla, 516–23, 533, 629
Sumerians, 30–46, 69
Suppiluliumas, 102
Susa, 47, 140, 279, 282
Sybaris, 218, 262, 453
Symmachus, 680, 686
Syracuse, 219, 316–17, 326, 343–4, 365, 453, 479, 485–7, 494
Syria, 54, 87–91, 95–6, 128, 130–31, 216, 316

Tacitus, 575, 596, 600–601, 687
Talmud, 160, 581, 651
Taoism, 641
Tarentum, 217, 219, 465
Tarquinia, 448, 450
Technology, 9, 11, 136, 221, 315, 429, 587, 711
Temple, *see* Architecture: Greek; *and* Jerusalem
Ten Thousand, 362, 395
Terence, 494–5
Tertullian, 596, 615, 618–19
Thales, 266
Thasos, 236, 309
Thebes (Egypt), 64, 68, 91–3; (Greece), 106, 196, 261, 287, 323, 362–5, 370, 395
Themistocles, 286–90, 292, 303, 306, 309

Theocritus, 418
Theodosian Code, 675–6
Theodosius I, 678, 681, 685
Theognis, 224, 265
Theophrastus, 383, 427
Theopompus, 367, 376
Thermopylae, 288–9, 294, 368, 492
Theseus, 196, 309, 324
Thespis, 253, 320
Thessaly, 109, 187, 190, 209, 242, 260, 288, 291, 364, 368, 540
Thirty, 347, 361
Thrace, 260, 313, 368, 491, 558
Thucydides, 306, 328, 340, 348, 351–2, 363, 386
Thurii, 316, 335, 465
Thutmose III, 90
Tiber river, 441, 459, 461
Tiberius, 555–6, 558–9, 575–6
Tiglath-Pileser III, 131, 133
Tigris river, 29, 83
Tragedy, 253, 320–25, 385, 495, 594
Trajan, 577–8, 584, 586, 596–7, 617
Trapezus, 219
Tribal assembly, *see* Assembly
Tribes, 191, 255, 460, 470
Tribunes, 471–2, 513–14, 521–2, 527
Trinity, 683–4
Triumvirate: First, 534–5, 538; Second, 544, 552
Troy, 101, 105, 109, 197, 396
Tutankhamun, 92, 94
Twelve Tables, 472, 495, 509
Tyrants, 212–13, 223, 253–4, 262
Tyre, 127, 261, 397
Tyrtaeus, 238, 257

Ugarit, 87–8, 96, 108–9, 147
Ulfilas, 650, 685
Upanishads, 168
Ur, 32, 43, 45, 113
Urartu, 130–31, 137, 220
Uruk, 31–2, 35, 40, 55
Urukagina, 44
Utica, 128, 447

Valerian, 657, 666
Vandals, 650, 690, 701–2

Varro, 505, 532, 539
Vedas, 166
Veii, 448, 461, 464, 467, 470
Vespasian, 577, 596
Via Appia, 467; see also Roads
Villanovan culture, 445, 448–9
Villas, 588, 590, 654, 695–7
Virgil, 548–9, 561–5, 604
Vishnu, 167, 635
Visigoths, 650, 656, 677–8, 700–701

Wang Mang, 638
Wars, see Civil Wars, Imperialism, Macedonian wars, Punic wars
Women, 13, 18; Near Eastern 44, 48, 90; Greek, 192, 209, 223, 235, 258, 331, 364, 415; Etruscan, 451; Roman, 461, 584

Writing, 28, 35, 49, 55–6, 103, 106, 109, 113, 115, 117, 640; see also Alphabet

Xenophanes, 267–8, 350
Xenophon, 362, 374, 376
Xerxes, 286–92, 294

Yahweh, 147, 150, 152–8
Yangtze river, 173
Yellow river, 114–15, 173, 639
Yueh-chi, 629, 633, 638

Zeno (logician), 328; (Stoic), 423–4
Zeus, 107, 191, 198–9, 235–6, 239, 241, 323, 423
Zeuxis, 388
Ziggurat, 33
Zoroaster and Zoroastrianism, 277, 280, 608, 631, 652